# The Official Guide to the TOEFL iBT® Test
# Using the Digital Resources

Authentic TOEFL iBT test questions are used in this book. However, the screens and delivery formats are not identical to the actual test. When you take the actual TOEFL iBT test, you may ⎯⎯⎯⎯⎯⎯⎯⎯ ʰe questions are presented to you on screen.

## Installation

First, go to **www.mhprofessional.com/toefl7e**. Once on the site, you'll be prompted to enter your access code—if you are using a paperback, you will find your code inside the back cover. If you are using an eBook, your code will be in your ETS account. Please note that this code is redeemable only by you and a maximum of four times.

Once you enter your access code, a download will automatically begin. This download will contain the audio files you need as well as files that contain the practice tests in both PC and Mac® format.

## Main Menu for Practice Tests

When you launch the program, the following screen will appear:

 The Official Guide to the TOEFL® Tests, 7th Edition

Options    Main Menu

Application Overview

Practice Test 1    Test Sections

Practice Test 2    Test Sections

Practice Test 3    Test Sections

Practice Test 4    Test Sections

## Taking TOEFL iBT® Practice Tests on Your Computer

From the **Main Menu**, choose Practice Test 1, 2, 3, or 4. Then select the test section you wish to take: **Reading, Listening, Speaking**, or **Writing**. Note that you can take each section more than once.

When you open a test section, you will first be provided with instructions for that section. A timer on the screen shows how many minutes and seconds you have left for that section. You can hide the timer if you find it distracting.

If you must take a break during the test, select **Main Menu** at the top of the screen. This will take you back to the main menu. When you are ready to resume, open the test section again, and select the **Continue** button. Your work will not be lost, and you will begin exactly where you left off. The timer clock will stop while you are on your break and will restart immediately when you resume the test. Try not to take breaks too often, because on the actual test the clock keeps running even if you leave the room on a break.

## Answering Questions

To answer the questions in the Reading and Listening sections, select the best answer or follow the instructions given. For some questions, you will need to select more than one answer. Select the **Next** button to move forward to the next question. In the Listening section, the **Next** button is enabled only after you select an answer choice or choices. In the Reading section, you can select the **Next** button at any time to move forward to the next question, and you can select the **Back** button to move back to the previous question.

For the Speaking section, you should record your response to each question using a recording device after you hear the instruction telling you to begin speaking. Stop recording once the response time expires.

For the Writing section, write your response to each question in the space provided within the time allowed.

When all the questions in a section have been answered, select the **Next** button to complete the section.

## Playing Audio Tracks

In the Listening, Speaking, and Writing sections, you will listen to audio tracks. Audio controls are available at the bottom of the screen. At the end of a track, select the **Next** button to start answering questions.

## Your Performance

On the **Main Menu**, select any test you have taken. The percentage of questions answered correctly will be displayed for only the Reading and Listening sections. By selecting a test section and then selecting **Review**, you will be able to review the questions from that section. For the Reading and Listening sections, you will see the correct answer for each question and the rationale explaining why the answer is correct. For the Speaking section, you will be provided with important points for each question, sample responses, and rater comments on the responses. Use these to evaluate your performance on the Speaking section. For the Writing section, you will be given topic notes, sample essays, and rater comments on the essays. Use these to evaluate your performance on the Writing section.

## Audio Files for Working Through the Tests in the Book

You may choose to work with the tests printed in the book rather than with the tests on your computer. If so, you will still need to listen to the audio tracks. Once you copy the folder named "Audio Files" to your computer, you will be able to select the audio tracks by number as you proceed through the book. As you work through the tests in the book, a headphones symbol ⌒ will indicate each time you need to play a track. Select the number of the track as instructed in the book.

The
**Official
Guide** to the
**TOEFL iBT®**
Test

SEVENTH EDITION

# The
# **Official**
# **Guide** to the
# **TOEFL iBT®** Test

## SEVENTH EDITION

1 2 3 4 5 6 7 8 9   LON   29 28 27 26 25 24

Domestic Edition
ISBN        978-1-265-47731-8
MHID        1-265-47731-0

e-ISBN      978-1-265-47787-5
e-MHID      1-265-47787-6

ETS, the ETS logo, SpeechRater, TOEFL, TOEFL iBT, and TOEFL GO! are registered trademarks of Educational Testing Service (ETS) in the United States. TOEFL GOLEARN! and MyBest are trademarks of ETS in the United States and other countries.

McGraw Hill books are available at special quantity discounts to use as premiums and sales promotions or for use in corporate training programs. To contact a representative, please visit the Contact Us pages at www.mhprofessional.com.

McGraw Hill is committed to making our products accessible to all learners. To learn more about the available support and accommodations we offer, please contact us at accessibility@ mheducation.com. We also participate in the Access Text Network (www.accesstext.org), and ATN members may submit requests through ATN.

# Contents

# 3 Listening Section 121

Listening Passages ........................................................................................ 121
    Conversations............................................................................................ 121
    Lectures .................................................................................................... 122
Listening Questions ...................................................................................... 123
    Basic Comprehension Questions .............................................................. 124
    Pragmatic Understanding Questions......................................................... 130
    Connecting Information Questions ........................................................... 133
Strategies for Preparing for and Taking the Listening Section...................... 139
Listening Practice Sets .................................................................................. 141
    Practice Set 1............................................................................................ 141
    Practice Set 2............................................................................................ 146
    Practice Set 3............................................................................................ 151
    Practice Set 4............................................................................................ 156
    Practice Set 5............................................................................................ 162


# 4 Speaking Section 167

The Speaking Section .................................................................................... 167
Speaking Tasks.............................................................................................. 169
    The Independent Task............................................................................... 169
    The Integrated Tasks................................................................................. 171
Speaking Scoring Rubric............................................................................... 184
    Independent Task: Question 1 .................................................................. 184
    Integrated Tasks: Questions 2, 3, and 4 ................................................... 186
Strategies for Preparing for and Taking the Speaking Section ...................... 188
Frequently Asked Questions About the Speaking Section.............................. 189

# 5 Writing Section 191

# 6 Authentic TOEFL iBT Practice Test 1 217

# 7 Authentic TOEFL iBT Practice Test 2 309

Contents

The
**Official**
**Guide** to the
**TOEFL iBT®**
Test

SEVENTH EDITION

# 1 About the TOEFL iBT® Test

**Read this chapter to learn**
- ⬔ The main features of the TOEFL iBT test
- ⬔ What kind of questions are on the test
- ⬔ How you can use this book to help you prepare for the test

This Official Guide has been created to help English language learners understand the TOEFL iBT test and prepare for it. By preparing for the test, you will also be building the skills you need to succeed in an academic setting and go anywhere in your career and in life.

## Getting Started

Start your preparation for the TOEFL iBT test by reading the following important information about the test, testing requirements, and your TOEFL iBT scores.

Undergraduate, graduate, and postgraduate programs around the world require students to demonstrate their ability to communicate in English as an entrance requirement.

The TOEFL iBT test gives test takers the opportunity to prove they can communicate ideas effectively by simulating university classroom and student-life communication. The language used in the test reflects real-life English language usage in university lectures, classes, and laboratories. It is the same language professors use when they discuss coursework or concepts with students. It is the language students use in study groups and everyday university situations, such as buying books at the bookstore. The academic reading passages are based on textbooks and other academic publications.

### TOEFL iBT Scores Can Help You Go Anywhere

The TOEFL iBT test measures how well test takers *use* English, not just their knowledge of the language. Because it is a valid and reliable test with unbiased, objective scoring, the TOEFL iBT test confirms that a student has the English language skills necessary to succeed in an academic setting.

That's why it's the world's premier academic English test. TOEFL iBT scores are accepted by more than 12,000 universities and other institutions in more than 160 countries, including Australia, Canada, New Zealand, the United States, the United Kingdom, and all across Europe and Asia. The test is administered at thousands of secure, ETS-approved test centers in more than 180 countries. More than 35 million people around the world have taken the TOEFL test to help achieve their dreams.

## Who Creates the TOEFL iBT Test?

The TOEFL iBT test is developed and administered by ETS, the world's largest private educational testing and measurement organization. Our mission is to advance quality and equity in education. Providing fair, valid, and reliable assessments is central to why we exist.

## Who Is Required to Take the TOEFL iBT Test?

Most colleges and universities where English is the language of instruction require an English proficiency test. The TOEFL iBT test is the most widely accepted English-language test worldwide, so it's a great choice to meet those requirements. Be sure to check with each institution where you are applying to confirm what scores they accept.

## How Is the TOEFL iBT Test Used in the Admissions Process?

Your test scores will be considered together with other information you supply to the institution to determine if you have the appropriate academic and language background to be admitted to a regular or modified program of study. Often, your field of study and if you are applying as a graduate or undergraduate student will determine what TOEFL iBT scores you need.

## Is There a Minimum Acceptable Score?

Each institution that uses TOEFL iBT scores sets its own minimum level of acceptable performance. These minimums vary from one institution to another, depending on factors such as the applicant's field of study, the level of study (undergraduate or graduate), whether the applicant will be a teaching assistant, and whether the institution offers English as a Second Language support for its students.

# How to Use This Book

This book and its digital resources give you instruction, practice, and advice on strategies for performing well on the TOEFL iBT test.

- **Chapter 1** provides an overview of the test, information about test scores, and an introduction to the on-screen appearance of the different parts of the TOEFL iBT test, along with general test-taking suggestions.

- **Chapters 2, 3, 4, and 5** provide in-depth discussions of the kinds of questions that appear in each section of the test. Each chapter also includes practice questions and explanations of correct answers so that you will understand the language skills that are being tested in each section.

- **Chapters 6–9** provide four full-length TOEFL iBT tests that will give you an idea of how you might perform on the actual test.

- **Chapter 10** is the Writer's Handbook for English Language Learners, a guide to help you write essays in English. It covers grammar, usage, mechanics, style, and organization and development. In addition, it contains a discussion of different types of essays, tips on how to improve your writing by revising, editing, and proofreading, and a glossary.

- The **digital download** supplied with this book provides on-screen versions of the full-length tests from Chapters 6–9. It also includes numbered audio tracks for all of the listening materials that accompany the practice questions in this book. For more information about how to use the digital resources, see the instruction page in the front of the book.

You can use this book to familiarize yourself with the format and content of the test, and to understand the language skills you will need to succeed on it. For additional practice tests and other materials, visit **ets.org/toefl/shoptestprep**.

Practice tests include TOEFL Practice Online, which offers an on-screen appearance and experience similar to the actual test, so you can become familiar with the way the test is delivered and what it is like to answer the questions under timed conditions. You also will receive performance feedback and scores for all four skills within 24 hours.

Use the practice tests in this book and from TOEFL Practice Online to determine which of your skills are the weakest. Then follow the advice in each skill chapter to improve those skills. You should use other materials to supplement the practice test questions in this book.

Because the TOEFL iBT test is designed to assess the actual skills you will need to be successful in your studies, the very best way to develop the skills being measured is to study in an English program that focuses on:

- communication using all four skills, especially speaking
- integrated skills (for example, listening/reading/speaking, listening/reading/writing)

However, even students who are not enrolled in an English program should practice the underlying skills that are assessed on the TOEFL iBT test. In other words, the best way to improve performance on the test is to improve your skills. Each chapter of this book gives you explicit advice on how to connect your learning activities to the kinds of questions you will be asked on the test. Perhaps you want to improve your score on the Reading section. The best way to improve your English reading skills is to read frequently and to read many different types of texts in various subject areas (sciences, social sciences, arts, business, and others). It is best to progress to reading texts that are more academic in style, the kind that would be found in university courses.

In addition, you might try these activities:

- Scan the passages to find and highlight key facts (dates, numbers, terms) and information.
- Increase vocabulary knowledge, perhaps by using flash cards.
- Rather than carefully reading each word and each sentence, practice skimming a passage quickly to get a general impression of the main idea.
- Choose some unfamiliar words in the passage and guess the meanings from the context (surrounding sentences).
- Practice making inferences and drawing conclusions based on what is implied in the passage as a whole.

# All About the TOEFL iBT Test

The TOEFL iBT test consists of four sections: Reading, Listening, Speaking, and Writing. The estimated time to complete the test is under two hours, and all sections are taken on the same day.

## Key Features

- **The TOEFL iBT test measures all four language skills that are important for effective communication: reading, listening, speaking, and writing**, emphasizing the test taker's ability to use English effectively in academic settings.

- **It reflects how language is really used** with integrated tasks that combine more than one skill, just as in real academic settings. The integrated questions ask test takers to:
  - read, listen, and then speak in response to a question
  - listen and then speak in response to a question
  - read, listen, and then write in response to a question

- **It represents the best practices in language learning and teaching.** In the past, English instruction focused on learning *about* the language (especially grammar), and students could receive high scores on tests without being able to communicate in English. Now teachers and learners understand the importance of using English to communicate, and activities that integrate language skills are popular in many English language programs.

## Format

- The TOEFL iBT test is administered securely and conveniently around the world at test centers and at home.
- Instructions for answering questions are given with each section.

- The test is not computer-adaptive. Each test taker receives items that cover the full range of ability.
- Test takers can take notes throughout the entire test. At the end of testing, all notes are destroyed to ensure test security.
- The Listening and Speaking sections include English-speaker accents from North America, the U.K., Australia and New Zealand, to better reflect the variety of accents you might encounter while studying abroad. To hear samples, visit **www.ets.org/toefl/ibt/about/content/**.
- For the Speaking section, test takers speak into a microphone. Responses are recorded digitally and sent to ETS to be scored.
- For the Writing section, test takers type their responses. The typed responses are sent to ETS for scoring.
- For the Speaking and Writing responses, ETS uses both certified human raters and artificial intelligence (AI) scoring to provide a complete and accurate picture of a test taker's ability.
- After finishing the test, test takers will be able to view their unofficial scaled scores for the Reading and Listening sections. Scoring of the Speaking and Writing sections takes place only after the test administration and cannot be provided in real time.
- Official scores are reported both online and by mail.

The following chart shows the number of questions and the estimated timing for each section.

**Test Format**

| Test Section | Number of Questions | Estimated Timing |
|---|---|---|
| Reading | 2 passages, 10 questions per passage | 35 minutes |
| Listening | 3 lectures, 6 questions each<br>2 conversations, 5 questions each | 36 minutes |
| Speaking | 4 tasks: 1 independent and 3 integrated | 16 minutes |
| Writing | 1 integrated task | 20 minutes |
| | 1 writing for an academic discussion task | 10 minutes |

## Toolbar

The on-screen toolbar in each section allows you to navigate through the test with ease. The following are examples of testing tools from the Reading and Listening sections of the test. The section is always listed in the upper left-hand corner of the toolbar.

**The toolbar for the Reading section has some important features.**

You can view the entire passage when answering questions. For some questions, you need to select the **View Passage** to see the entire passage.

You can view all your answers by selecting **Review**. This allows you to return to any other question and change your answer. You can also see which questions you have skipped and still need to answer.

In the Reading section you can also select **Back** at any time to return to the previous question.

**This is what the toolbar looks like in the Listening section.**

- You will always know which question you are on and how much time remains for answering questions in the section. It is possible to hide the clock by selecting **Hide Time.**
- **Volume** allows you to adjust the volume as you listen.
- **Help** allows you to get relevant help. When you use the **Help** feature, the clock does not stop.
- **Next** allows you to proceed to the next question. In the Listening section, you cannot see a question again once you select **Next**.

# Reading Section

## Academic Reading Skills

The Reading section measures your ability to understand university-level academic texts and passages. In many academic settings around the world, students are expected to read and understand information from textbooks and other academic materials written in English. The following are three purposes for academic reading

*Reading to find information*
- effectively skimming text for key facts and important information
- increasing reading fluency and rate

*Basic comprehension*
- understanding the general topic or main idea, major points, important facts and details, vocabulary in context, and pronoun references[1]
- making inferences[2] about what is implied in a passage

*Reading to learn*
- recognizing the organization and purpose of a passage
- understanding relationships between ideas
- organizing information into a summary in order to recall major points and important details
- inferring how ideas throughout the passage connect

## Description

### Reading Section Format

| Length of Each Passage | Number of Passages and Questions | Estimated Timing |
|---|---|---|
| Approximately 700 words | 2 passages<br>10 questions per passage | 35 minutes |

## Reading Passages

The TOEFL iBT test uses reading passages from university-level books that introduce a discipline or topic. The excerpts are changed as little as possible so the test can measure how well test takers can read real-world academic materials.

The passages cover a variety of subjects. You should not be concerned if you are unfamiliar with a topic. The passage contains all the information needed to answer the questions.

---

1. Pronoun references: The nouns that pronouns refer to in a passage
2. Make an inference: To comprehend an argument or an idea that is strongly suggested but not explicitly stated in a passage

All passages are classified into three basic categories:

- exposition[3]
- argumentation[4]
- historical and biographical narrative

Often, passages present information about the topic from more than one perspective or point of view. This is something you should note as you read. Usually, you are asked at least one question that allows you to demonstrate that you understood the general organization of the passage. Common organization types that you should be able to recognize are:

- classification
- compare/contrast
- cause/effect
- problem/solution

You must read through or scroll to the end of each passage before receiving questions on that passage. Once the questions appear, the passage appears on the left side of the computer screen. The questions are on the right.

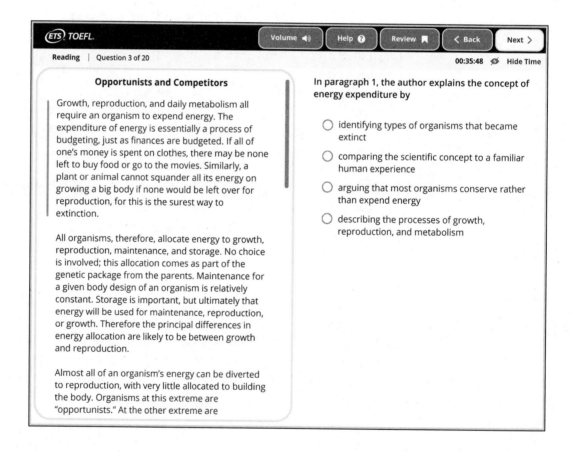

---

3. Exposition: Material that provides an explanation of a topic
4. Argumentation: Material that presents a point of view about a topic and provides evidence to support it

You do *not* need any special background knowledge to answer the questions in the Reading section correctly. The definition of special-purpose words or phrases in the passage may be provided. If you select a hyperlinked word, a definition appears in the lower right part of the screen.

The estimated time to complete the Reading section is 35 minutes, but you'll be allowed up to 36 minutes.

### Reading Question Formats

There are four question formats in the Reading section:

- questions with four choices and a single correct answer in traditional multiple-choice format
- multiple-choice questions with more than one answer (for example, two correct answers out of four choices)
- questions with four choices and a single answer that ask test takers to "insert a sentence" where it fits best in a passage
- reading-to-learn questions that have more than four choices and require more than one answer

## Features

### Reading-to-Learn Questions

These questions test your ability to recognize how the passage is organized and understand the relationships among facts and ideas in different parts of the passage.

You are asked to sort information by placing the text options provided into a **summary** (see the example on the next page). The summary questions are worth up to 2 points each. Partial credit is given for summary questions.

## Reading to Learn—Prose Summary Question Example

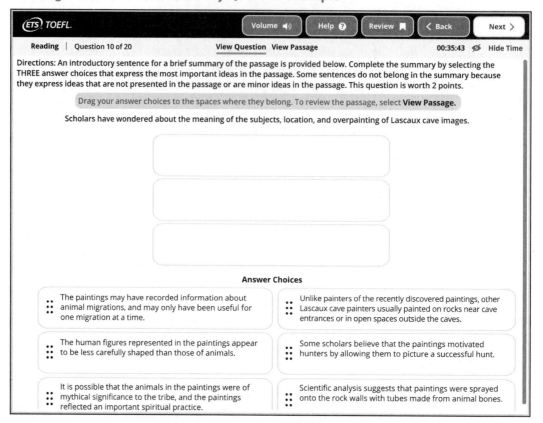

## Glossary Feature

You can select some special-purpose words and phrases in the reading passages to view a definition or explanation of the term. In the example below, test takers can select the word "shamans" to view its definition.

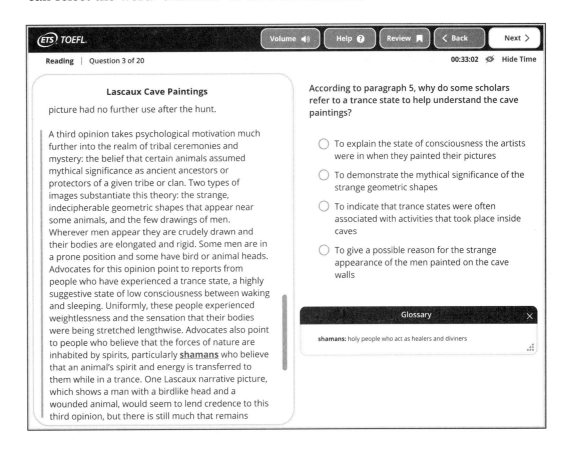

# Listening Section

## Academic Listening Skills

The Listening section measures your ability to understand spoken English. In academic settings, students must be able to listen to lectures and conversations. Three of the purposes of academic listening are:

*Listening for basic comprehension*

- comprehend the main idea, major points, and important details related to the main idea (comprehension of all details is not necessary)

*Listening for pragmatic understanding*

- recognize a speaker's attitude and degree of certainty
- recognize the function or purpose of a speaker's statement

*Connecting and synthesizing[5] information*

- recognize the organization of information presented
- understand the relationships between ideas presented (for example, compare/contrast, cause/effect, or steps in a process)
- make inferences[6] and draw conclusions based on what is implied in the material
- make connections among pieces of information in a conversation or lecture
- recognize topic changes (for example, digressions[7] and aside statements[8]) in lectures and conversations, and recognize introductions and conclusions in lectures

## Description

Listening material in the test includes academic lectures and long conversations. You can take notes on any listening material throughout the entire test, and you may use your notes to answer the questions though the estimated time for the Listening section is 36 minutes, you will have up to 41 minutes.

**Listening Section Format**

| Listening Material | Number of Questions | Estimated Timing |
|---|---|---|
| 3 lectures, each 4–5 minutes long, about 500–750 words | 6 questions per lecture | 36 minutes |
| 2 conversations, each about 3 minutes long, about 12–25 exchanges | 5 questions per conversation | |

5. Synthesize: To combine information from two or more parts of a lecture or conversation
6. Make an inference: To comprehend an argument or an idea that is strongly suggested but not explicitly stated in a passage
7. Digressions: Side comments in which the speaker briefly moves away from the main topic and then returns
8. Aside statements: Comments interrupt the flow of information or ideas (Example: "Pay attention now; this will be on the test.")

## Academic Lectures

The lectures in the TOEFL iBT test reflect the kind of listening and speaking that occurs in the classroom. In some of the lectures, the professor does all or almost all of the talking, with an occasional comment by a student. In other lectures, the professor may engage the students in discussion by asking questions that are answered by the students. Pictures on the computer screen are intended to help you identify the roles of the speakers.

### Professor Giving a Lecture

### Professor Interacting with a Student

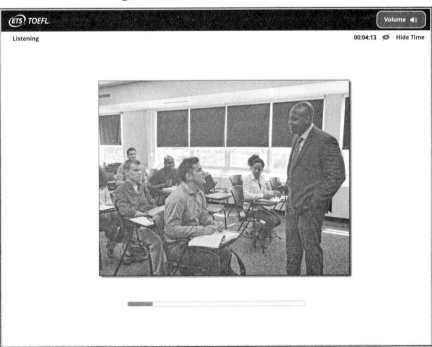

## Conversations in an Academic Setting

The conversations on the TOEFL iBT test may take place during an office meeting with a professor or teaching assistant, during a service encounter with university staff, or between two students. The contents of the office conversations are generally academic in nature or related to course requirements. Service encounters could involve conversations about nonacademic university activities such as making a housing payment, registering for a class, or requesting information at the library. Student conversations could be about a class project or an event on campus, for example.

Pictures on the computer screen help you imagine the setting and the roles of the speakers.

**Professor Meeting with a Student**

## Listening Question Formats

After the listening material is played, you will answer questions about it. Each question will be displayed on the screen and read aloud before the answer choices are displayed.

There are four question formats in the Listening section:
- traditional multiple-choice questions with four answer choices and a single correct answer
- multiple-choice questions with more than one answer (for example, two correct answers out of four choices or three answers out of five choices)
- questions that require you to order events or steps in a process
- questions that require you to match objects or text to categories in a chart or place check marks in a cell

**Chart Question Example**

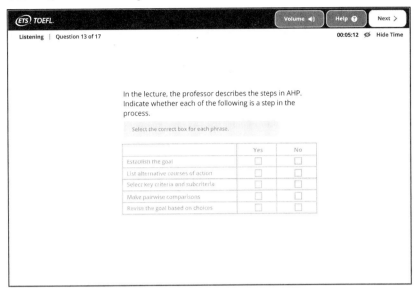

## Features

- Taking notes is allowed. After testing, all notes are destroyed to ensure test security.
- Most questions are worth one point. Some questions, however, are worth two points. Special directions will indicate which, if any, questions are worth two points. No more than one such question will appear on any test.
- In some questions, a portion of the lecture or conversation is replayed. In the replay format, you listen to part of the conversation or lecture again and then answer a question.

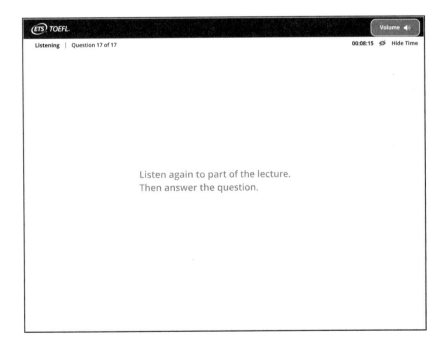

This is an example of a replay question. The headphones icon indicates that you will hear a small part of a lecture or conversation again. The question "Why does the professor say this?" is an example of a question that asks about the purpose of a speaker's statement.

# Speaking Section

## Academic Speaking Skills

Students should be able to speak English successfully in and outside the classroom. The Speaking section measures your ability to speak effectively in academic and campus settings.

In classrooms, students must:

- respond to questions
- participate in academic discussions with other students
- synthesize and summarize what they have read in their textbooks and heard in class
- express their views on topics under discussion

Outside of the classroom, students must:

- participate in casual conversations
- express their opinions
- communicate with people in such places as the bookstore, the library, and the housing office

## Description

The Speaking section is approximately 16 minutes long and includes four tasks.

- The first task is an **independent speaking task** asking you to make a choice about a topic familiar to you. It asks you to draw upon your own ideas, opinions, and experiences to support your response.

- The remaining three tasks are **integrated tasks**, so you must use more than one skill when responding. Two of the tasks require you to read, listen, and then speak in response to a question. The other task requires you to listen and then speak in response to a question. You can take notes and use those notes when responding to the speaking tasks.

Like the other sections of the test, the Speaking section is delivered via the internet. For all speaking tasks, you will deliver your response into a microphone. Responses are digitally recorded and sent to ETS, where they are scored by certified raters and the automated scoring system.

## Speaking Task Types

| Task Type | Task Description | Timing |
|---|---|---|
| **Independent Task** | | |
| 1: Paired Choice | This question asks the test taker to make and defend a personal choice between two contrasting behaviors, ideas, or courses of action. | Preparation time: 15 seconds<br>Response time: 45 seconds |
| **Integrated Tasks** | | |
| | **Read/Listen/Speak** | |
| 2: Fit and Explain Campus Situation | • A reading passage (approximately 90–115 words) presents a campus-related issue.<br>• A conversation (60–80 seconds) features two speakers commenting on the issue in the reading passage.<br>• The question asks the test taker to summarize the opinion of one of the speakers within the context of the reading passage. | Preparation time: 30 seconds<br>Response time: 60 seconds |
| 3: General/Specific Academic Course Topic | • A reading passage (approximately 90–115 words) broadly defines a term, process, or idea from an academic subject.<br>• An excerpt from a lecture (60–90 seconds) provides examples and specific information to illustrate the term, process, or idea from the reading passage.<br>• The question asks the test taker to combine and convey important information from the reading passage and the lecture excerpt. | Preparation time: 30 seconds<br>Response time: 60 seconds |
| | **Listen/Speak** | |
| 4: Summary Academic Course Topic | • An excerpt from a lecture (90–120 seconds) explains a term or concept and gives concrete examples to illustrate that term or concept.<br>• The question asks the test taker to summarize the lecture and demonstrate an understanding of the relationship between the examples and the overall topic. | Preparation time: 20 seconds<br>Response time: 60 seconds |
| **Estimated Total Time** | | **16 minutes** |

# Writing Section

## Academic Writing Skills

In all academic situations where writing in English is required, students must be able to present their ideas in a clear, well-organized manner. The Writing section measures your ability to write in English in an academic setting.

Often, students need to write a paper or an essay response about what they are learning in their classes. This requires combining information they have heard in class lectures with what they have read in textbooks or other materials. This type of writing is referred to as **integrated writing**. In this type of writing, students must:

- take notes on what they hear and read, and use them to organize information before writing
- summarize, paraphrase, and refer to information from the source material accurately
- write about the ways the information they heard relates to the information they read

For example, in an academic course, a student might be asked to compare and contrast the points of view expressed by the professor in class with those expressed by an author in the assigned reading material. The student must successfully draw information from each source to explain the contrast.

In all types of writing, it is helpful for students to:

- express information in an organized, logical, and coherent manner
- use effective linking words (transitional phrases) to connect ideas and help the reader understand the flow of ideas
- use a range of grammar and vocabulary for effective expression
- use grammar and vocabulary accurately; use idiomatic expressions appropriately
- follow the conventions of spelling, punctuation, and layout

## Description

The total response time for the Writing section is 30 minutes. Test takers write their responses to two writing tasks (see the following table). Responses are typed into the computer and sent to ETS, where they are scored by both certified raters and the automated scoring system.

### Writing Task Types

| Task Type | Task Description |
|---|---|
| **Task 1**<br>Integrated Writing:<br>Read/Listen/Write | • Test takers read a short text of about 250–300 words (reading time, 3 minutes) on an academic topic.<br>• Test takers may take notes on the reading passage.<br>• The reading passage disappears from the screen during the lecture that follows. It reappears when test takers begin writing so they can refer to it as they work.<br>• Test takers listen to a speaker discuss the same topic from a different perspective. The listening passage is about 250–320 words long (listening time, about 2 minutes).<br>• The listening passage provides additional information that relates to points made in the reading passage. Test takers may take notes on the listening passage.<br>• Test takers express information in an organized, logical, and coherent manner.<br>• Response time: 20 minutes |
| **Task 2**<br>Writing for an<br>Academic Discussion | • Test takers write a post that contributes to an online academic discussion. The discussion has been initiated by a professor's question, and two classmates have already contributed their posts. An effective response will usually contain a minimum of 100 words.<br>• Test takers may refer to or engage with their classmates' posts or introduce entirely new ideas in response to the professor's question. Test takers' posts must be relevant to the discussion and test takers must clearly contribute to the discussion in their own words.<br>• Typical discussion topics ask students whether they agree or disagree with a position or an argument, prompt them to choose between different positions or arguments, or ask them to articulate their own opinion and explain it.<br>• Response time: 10 minutes |

# About Test Scores

## Score Scales

The TOEFL iBT® test provides scores in four skill areas:

| | |
|---|---|
| Reading | 0–30 |
| Listening | 0–30 |
| Speaking | 0–30 |
| Writing | 0–30 |
| **Total Score** | **0–120** |

The total score is the sum of the four skill scores.

## *MyBest* ® Scores

MyBest® scores (or superscores) show your best overall performance by combining your highest section scores from all test dates within the last 2 years. This means you may be able to meet score requirements for your institution with fewer tests and reach your goals sooner.

## Score Reports

TOEFL iBT score reports provide valuable information about a test taker's readiness to participate and succeed in academic studies in an English-speaking environment. Score reports include

- total score
- section scores
- your proficiency level for each section
- MyBest scores

In addition, you will have access to enhanced score reporting in your TOEFL iBT account. This provides you with personalized feedback and performance insights, including

- feedback on which Reading and Listening question types you've successfully demonstrated performance consistent with advanced test-taker performance and which question types you are still developing your skills at
- a closer look at your Speaking and Writing skills, with insights into your language use, grammar, and mechanics
- more sample high-scoring Speaking and Writing responses with explanations to help you practice and improve

## Rating of Speaking and Writing Responses

### Speaking

Responses to all four Speaking tasks are digitally recorded and sent to ETS. The responses from each test taker are scored by four different certified raters and the automated scoring system. The response for each task is rated on a scale from 0 to 4 according to the rubrics on pages 184–187. The scores from the four tasks together are converted to a scaled score of 0 to 30.

Raters listen for the following features in test takers' responses:

- **Delivery:** How clear is the speech? Good responses are fluid and clear, with good pronunciation, natural pacing, and natural-sounding intonation patterns.

- **Language use:** How effectively does the test taker use grammar and vocabulary to convey ideas? Raters determine the test taker's ability to control both basic and more complex language structures and to use appropriate vocabulary.

- **Topic development:** How fully do test takers answer the question and how coherently do they present their ideas? How well did the test taker synthesize and summarize the information in the integrated tasks? Good responses generally use all or most of the time allowed, and the relationships between ideas and the progression from one idea to the next are clear and easy to follow.

It is important to note that raters do not expect test takers' responses to be perfect. Even high-scoring responses may contain occasional errors and minor problems in any of the three areas described above.

## Writing

Responses to all writing tasks also are sent to ETS. The responses are rated by two certified raters and the automated scoring system on a scale of 0 to 5 according to the rubrics on pages 199–200 and 210–211. The average of the scores on the two writing tasks is converted to a scaled score of 0 to 30.

- The response to the integrated writing task is scored on the quality of writing (organization, appropriate and precise use of grammar and vocabulary) and the completeness and accuracy of the content.

- The academic discussion task is scored on the overall quality of the writing: development, contribution to the discussion, and appropriate and precise use of grammar and vocabulary.

It is important to note that the raters recognize that the responses are first drafts. They do not expect test takers to produce a well-researched, comprehensive essay. For that reason, test takers can earn a high score with a response that contains some errors.

**Sample TOEFL iBT ® Score Report**

| | **Test Taker Score Report** |
|---|---|

# Kumar, Kaira
Last (Family/Surname) Name, First (Given) Name Middle Name
**Email:** Kaira.Kumar@123gmail.com

Kaira Kumar
33, Pantheon Rd
Chennai, Tamil Nadu
600008 INDIA

| | Institution Code | Department Code |
|---|---|---|
| | ABCD | 40 |
| | M987 | 41 |
| | P654 | 42 |
| | i321 | 43 |

**Test Date:** May 15, 2023
**Appointment #:** 1234 8052 1411 0011
**Native Language:** Tamil
**Test Center Country:** India
**Test Center:** STN20038A – ANCONS International

**Gender:** F
**Date of Birth:** October 14, 2004
**Country of Birth:** India

---

**Test Date: May 15, 2023**
**ETS® Security Guard**
See back for details

| Total Score | ▤ Reading | 🎧 Listening | 🗣 Speaking | ✎ Writing |
|---|---|---|---|---|
| **91** out of 120 | **27** out of 30 | **23** out of 30 | **21** out of 30 | **20** out of 30 |

---

***MyBest® Scores*** | Your highest section scores from all valid test dates, as of May 17, 2023.

| Sum of Highest Section Scores **94** out of 120 | Reading (0–30) | Listening (0–30) | Speaking (0–30) | Writing (0–30) |
|---|---|---|---|---|
| | **27** Test Date May 15, 2023 | **24** Test Date Apr 15, 2023 | **21** Test Date May 15, 2023 | **22** Test Date Apr 15, 2022 |

**SECURITY IDENTIFICATION**
**ID Type:** Passport
**ID No:** xxxxx...0372
**Issuing Country:** India

A total score is not reported when one or more sections have not been administered. Expired scores are not included in ***MyBest***® calculations.

80-80

Page 1 of 2

**Sample TOEFL iBT® Score Report**

 **TOEFL iBT.**

**Kumar, Kaira**
**Test Date:** May 15, 2023
**Appointment Number:** 1234 8052 1411 0011

For additional TOEFL iBT® scoring details, score ranges, and how to improve your skills, visit www.ets.org/toefl/ibt/scores.

## Score Ranges
Total Score Range: 0–120

| **Reading** | **0–30** |
|---|---|
| Advanced | 24–30 |
| High-Intermediate | 18–23 |
| Low-Intermediate | 4–17 |
| Below Low-Intermediate | 0–3 |

| **Listening** | **0–30** |
|---|---|
| Advanced | 22–30 |
| High-Intermediate | 17–21 |
| Low-Intermediate | 9–16 |
| Below Low-Intermediate | 0–8 |

| **Speaking** | **0–30** |
|---|---|
| Advanced | 25–30 |
| High-Intermediate | 20–24 |
| Low-Intermediate | 16–19 |
| Basic | 10–15 |
| Below Basic | 0–9 |

| **Writing** | **0–30** |
|---|---|
| Advanced | 24–30 |
| High-Intermediate | 17–23 |
| Low-Intermediate | 13–16 |
| Basic | 7–12 |
| Below Basic | 0–6 |

## Institution Codes

| Department | Where the Report Was Sent |
|---|---|
| 00 | Admissions office for undergraduate study |
| 01, 04–41, 43–98 | Admissions office for graduate study in a field other than management (business) or law according to the codes selected when you registered |
| 02 | Admissions office of a graduate school of management (business) |
| 03 | Admissions office of a graduate school of law |
| 42 | Admissions office of a school of medicine or nursing or licensing agency |
| 99 | Institution or agency that is not a college or university |

**IMPORTANT NOTE TO SCORE USERS:** To verify the scores on this report, please contact the TOEFL® Score Verification Service at **+1-800-257-9547** or **+1-609-771-7100**. Scores more than two years old cannot be reported or validated.

ETS® Security Guard text is printed with a special heat-sensitive ink for security. To activate this security feature, apply heat to the text, either by rubbing it or blowing on it, and the ETS Security Guard text will disappear.

150256-149717 • S722E1200 • Printed in U.S.A.
831186

Page 2 of 2

# General Skill-Building Tips

The best way for English language learners to develop the skills measured by the TOEFL® test is to enroll in an English language learning program that features:

- reading, listening, speaking, and writing skills, with an emphasis on speaking
- an integrated skills approach (for example, instruction that builds skills in listening/reading/speaking or listening/reading/writing)

In addition to the advice for improvement listed in the Appendix of this book, ETS has created the following tips for test takers, which also contain information useful to teachers.

## Reading Tips

English language learners can improve their English reading skills by reading regularly, especially university textbooks or other materials that cover a variety of subject areas (for example, sciences, social sciences, arts, business, and others) and are written in an academic style. A wide variety of academic texts can be found on the internet as well as in magazines and journals.

### Reading to Find Information

- Skim passages to find and highlight key facts (dates, numbers, terms) and information.
- Practice frequently to increase reading rate and fluency.

### Reading for Basic Comprehension

- Practice skimming a passage quickly to get a general impression of the main idea.
- After skimming a passage, read it again more carefully and write down the main idea(s), major points, and important facts.
- Choose some unfamiliar words in the passage and look them up in a dictionary to determine their meaning.

**Check Your English Reading Skills**

TOEFL Practice Online gives you an experience similar to taking a real TOEFL iBT test. It includes real past test questions, and scores and performance feedback are provided within 24 hours. Full tests, half tests, and Speaking-only tests are available. **www.ets.org/toefl/shoptestprep**

### Reading to Learn

- Identify the passage type (for example, cause/effect, compare/contrast, classification, problem/solution, description, narration) and its organization.
- Organize the information in the passage,
  - Create an outline of the passage to distinguish between major and minor points.
  - If the passage categorizes information, create a chart and place the information in appropriate categories.

## Listening Tips

English language learners can improve their listening skills by listening regularly to spoken English. Watching movies, television, and videos, and listening to podcasts and radio broadcasts provide excellent opportunities to build general listening skills. Listening to a variety of academic materials is the best way to improve academic listening skills. Video recordings and audio recordings in a variety of formats are available at libaries, at bookstores, and on web sites. Those with transcripts are particularly helpful. Some web sites that are a good source of listening material are **npr.org**, **bbc.co.uk/sounds**, **bbc.co.uk/learningenglish**, or **learningenglish.voanews.com**.

### Listening for Basic Comprehension

- Increase vocabulary.
- For an unfamiliar word, try to guess the general sense of the word's meaning based on the context in which it is used.
- Focus on the content and flow of spoken material. Do not be distracted by the speaker's style and delivery.
- Anticipate what a person is going to say as a way to stay focused.
- Stay active by asking yourself questions (for example: What main idea is the professor communicating?).
- Listen for words or phrases that indicate a change in topic or a digression.
- Listen to a portion of a lecture or talk and create an outline of important points. Do not try to write down every word that you hear. Do make a note of major points and important details. When you are finished, listen again to check, modify, or add to what you have written. Gradually increase the length of the lecture or talk you listen to and create an outline.
- Listen to an entire lecture or talk. Write a sentence that indicates the main idea of what you heard. Listen again to check what you have written and to write down key details.

## Listening for Pragmatic Understanding

- Think about what each speaker hopes to accomplish when making an assertion or asking a question. Is the speaker apologizing, complaining, or making a suggestion? For example, if a speaker says, "It's cold in this room," is the speaker doing more than making a comment about room temperature? Is that speaker suggesting that someone do something to adjust the room temperature? If a speaker makes an assertion such as, "I'm sure you must have thoughts about that," is the speaker indirectly asking people to share their thoughts?
- Notice the speaker's degree of certainty. How sure is the speaker about the information? Does the speaker's tone of voice indicate something about his or her degree of certainty?
- Listen for aside statements.
- Watch television or movie comedies. Pay careful attention to the way stress and intonation patterns are used to convey meaning.

## Listening to Connect and Synthesize Ideas

- Think about how the lecture you're hearing is organized. Listen for the signal words that indicate the introduction, major steps or ideas, examples, and the conclusion or summary.
- Identify the relationships between ideas. Possible relationships include cause/effect, compare/contrast, and steps in a process.
- Listen for words that show connections and relationships between ideas.
- Listen to recorded material and stop the recording at various points. Predict what information or idea will be expressed next.
- Create an outline of the information discussed either while listening or after listening.

---

**Check Your English Listening Skills**

TOEFL Practice Online gives you an experience similar to taking a real TOEFL iBT test. It includes real past test questions, and scores and performance feedback are provided within 24 hours. Full tests, half tests, and Speaking-only tests are available. **www.ets.org/toefl/shoptestprep**

## Speaking Tips

The best way to practice speaking is with fluent speakers of English. If you do not live in an English-speaking country, finding fluent speakers of English might be quite challenging. In some countries, there are English-speaking tutors or assistants who help students with conversation skills and overall communication skills. You may also be able to find online tutors or conversation partners with whom you can practice speaking English. Another way to practice speaking is by joining an English club whose members converse in English about movies, music, and travel. If a club does not exist in your area, start one and invite fluent speakers to help you get started.

### Independent Speaking Task

- Make a list of topics that are familiar, and practice speaking about them.
- Describe a preference and your reason for the preference.
- Express an opinion by clearly stating your point of view and providing clear and detailed reasons for your opinion.
- Make a recommendation and explain why it is the best way to proceed.
- Practice giving one-minute responses to topics.

### Integrated Speaking Tasks

- Find a textbook that includes questions about the material at the end of chapters, and practice answering the questions orally.
- Read a short article (100–200 words). Make an outline that includes only the major points of the article. Use the outline to orally summarize the information.
- Find listening and reading material on the same topic covered by the article. The material can contain similar or different views. (The internet and the library are good places to find information.) Take notes or create outlines on the listening and reading material:
  - Orally summarize the information in both the written and spoken materials. Be sure to paraphrase using different words and grammatical structures.
  - Orally synthesize the material by combining the information from the reading and listening materials and explaining how they relate.
  - State an opinion about the ideas and information presented in the reading and listening material and explain how they relate.

### All Speaking Tasks

- Try to use one new vocabulary word or phrase each day.

- Make a one-minute recording of a fluent speaker of English. (It can be someone you know or a recording from the internet, TV, radio, etc.) Replay the recording two times to get familiar with the speaker's rhythm and intonation. Then play the recording a third time, and try to speak aloud along with the speaker. Even if you don't pronounce all the words correctly, this will help you become familiar with the stress and intonation patterns of fluent speakers.

- When practicing for the TOEFL iBT test using the tips above, take 15 seconds to think about what you are going to say before you speak. Write down a few key words and ideas, but do not attempt to write down exactly what you are going to say. (Raters will be able to detect responses that are read and will give them a lower score.)

- As you listen to English speakers, try to identify words and expressions that help connect the speakers' ideas. Then try to include these expressions when you speak in order to introduce new information, to connect ideas, and to mark important words or ideas. This helps listeners more easily follow what you are saying. (For example, "on the one hand," "what that means is," "one reason is," "another difference might be.")

- Monitor your progress and ask an English teacher or tutor to evaluate your speech using the appropriate Speaking rubrics. (See pages 184–187 for the rubrics.)

**Check Your English Speaking Skills**

TOEFL Practice Online gives you an experience similar to taking a real TOEFL iBT test. It includes real past test questions, and scores and performance feedback are provided within 24 hours. Full tests, half tests, and Speaking-only tests are available. **www.ets.org/toefl/shoptestprep**

## Writing Tips

### Integrated Writing Tasks

- Find a textbook that includes questions about the material at the end of chapters, and practice writing answers to the questions.

- Read an article that is about 300–400 words long. Make an outline that includes the major points and important details of the article. Use the outline to write a summary of the information and ideas. Summaries should be brief and clearly communicate only the major points and important details. Be sure to paraphrase using different words and grammatical structures.

- Find listening and reading material on a single topic on the internet or in the library. The material can provide similar or different views. Take notes on the written and spoken portions, and do the following.
  - Summarize the information and ideas in both the written and spoken portions.
  - Synthesize the information and discuss how the reading and listening materials relate. Explain how the ideas expressed are similar, how one idea expands upon another, or how the ideas are different or contradict each other.

### Paraphrasing

Paraphrasing involves restating something from the source material in one's own words. On the TOEFL iBT test, test takers receive a score of zero if all they do is copy words from the reading passage. Practice paraphrasing words, phrases, sentences, and entire paragraphs frequently using the following tips.

- Learn to find synonyms with ease. Pick 10 to 15 words or phrases in a reading passage and quickly think of synonyms without looking them up in a dictionary or thesaurus.
- Write a paraphrase of a reading passage using only your notes. If you have not taken notes, write the paraphrase without looking at the original text. Then check the paraphrase with the original passage to make sure that it is factually accurate and that you have used different words and grammatical structures.

### Academic Discussion Writing Tasks

- Make a list of familiar topics and practice writing about them.
- For each topic, state an opinion or a preference and then support it with evidence.
- Practice writing at least one discussion post for each topic. Be sure to take 10 minutes to write and revise each post. Try to write different posts on the same topic.
- Brainstorm a couple of ideas before you start writing and pursue the idea that seems the most promising.
- Do not spend too much time planning your response. Focus instead on giving your post coherence and a good flow as you write. Connect your ideas well and elaborate on them so the reader is clear about what your opinion is and why you hold it. Be sure to leave a bit of time at the end to revise your post and fix its flaws.
- Do not use memorized, formulaic, or vague language. Give the post your own voice, and express your own ideas using your own language.

## All Writing Tasks

- Increase vocabulary and knowledge of idiomatic speech so you can use it appropriately.
- Learn grammatical structures so well that you can use them naturally when writing.
- Learn the conventions of spelling, punctuation, and formatting (for example, paragraph creation).
- Express information in an organized manner, displaying unity of thought and coherence.
- As you practice, ask yourself these questions:
  - Did I complete the task?
  - Did I write clearly?
  - Did I avoid making grammatical errors?
  - Did I use words correctly?
  - Did I organize my ideas clearly and coherently?
  - Did I use the time effectively?
- Monitor your own progress and ask an English teacher or tutor to evaluate the writing by using the appropriate Writing rubric. (See pages 199–200 and 210–211 for the rubrics.)

### Check Your English Writing Skills

Are you ready for test day? TOEFL Practice Online gives you an experience similar to taking a real TOEFL iBT test. It includes real past test questions, and scores and performance feedback are provided within 24 hours. Full tests, half tests, and Speaking-only tests are available.
**www.ets.org/toefl/shoptestprep**

### Note

**Teachers**: It is a good idea for English programs to use the TOEFL® Speaking and Writing rubrics (pages 184–187, 199–200, and 210–211) to measure students' abilities and evaluate their progress. This helps test takers build their skills for the TOEFL test.

# Test Preparation Tips from ETS

Once you have built your skills and practiced, you will be ready for the TOEFL iBT test. Here are some good test-taking strategies recommended by ETS:

- **Carefully follow the directions** in each section to avoid wasting time.

- **Select Help** to review the directions only when absolutely necessary because the test clock will not stop when the Help function is being used.

- **Do not become overwhelmed.** Concentrate on the current question only, and do not think about how you answered other questions. This is a habit that can be learned through practice.

- **Avoid spending too much time on any one question.** If you have given the question some thought and you still do not know the answer, eliminate as many answer choices as possible and then select the best remaining choice. You can review your responses in the Reading section by selecting **Review**. However, it is best to do this only after all the questions have been answered so you stay focused and save time.

- **Pace yourself** so you have enough time to answer every question. Be aware of the time limit for every section/task, and budget enough time for each question/task so you do not have to rush at the end. You can hide the test clock if you wish, but it is a good idea to check the clock periodically to monitor progress. The clock will automatically alert you when 5 minutes remain in the Listening and Reading sections, as well as in each task in the Writing section.

# Questions Frequently Asked by Test Takers

## Test Benefits

### Why should I take the TOEFL iBT test?

No matter where in the world you want to study, the TOEFL iBT test can help you get there. TOEFL scores are accepted by more than 12,000 institutions worldwide, including the top colleges and universities in the United States, Canada, the United Kingdom, Australia, and New Zealand. See the Destination Search at **www.ets.org/toefl/destinations**.

The TOEFL iBT test gives you more flexibility on when, where, and how often you take the test, and more practice tools and feedback than any other English language test in the world.

Test takers who are well prepared for the TOEFL iBT test can feel confident that they are also well prepared for academic success.

### What makes the TOEFL iBT test better than other English language tests?

The TOEFL iBT test assesses a test taker's ability to integrate English skills and to communicate about what he or she reads and hears. These are the skills you will actually use in an academic classroom.

The test also measures speaking more fairly than other tests. The responses from each test taker are scored by at least four different certified raters and the automated scoring system, which combine to provide more objective and reliable information about a test taker's speaking skills than other tests that use only one interviewer from a local test site.

### Who else benefits from the test?

Admissions officials and faculty at colleges and universities, as well as administrators of certification and licensing agencies, receive better information on an applicant's English communication skills.

## Registration

### How and when do I register for the test?

Online registration is the easiest method. You can also register by mail or by phone. See **www.ets.org/toefl** for details. Registration is available 5 to 6 months before the test date. Register early, as seats can fill up quickly.

### When and where can I take the TOEFL iBT Test?

The TOEFL iBT test is available globally, with testing available in more than 200 countries and territories. It's offered three different ways, so you can choose the best option to fit your needs and preferences. Take the test on a computer at a test center, on a computer at home, or on paper at a test center. Go to **ets.org/toefl** to find testing options that are convenient for you.

### How much does the TOEFL iBT test cost?

The price of the test varies by country. Please check the TOEFL web site at **www.ets.org/toefl** for the test fees in your country.

## Test Preparation

### Are sample questions available?

Yes. The TOEFL iBT Free Practice Test, on the TOEFL web site at **https://www.ets.org/toefl/test-takers/ibt/prepare**, provides many opportunities for repeated practice using real test questions from all four skill areas: reading, listening, speaking, and writing. You can also see sample responses with rater commentary for the Speaking and Writing questions. An opportunity to practice each section of the test is available—with free sets of TOEFL iBT questions from previous tests available on the web site.

### Can I take a practice test and get a score?

Yes. Practice tests can be purchased at **www.ets.org/toefl/shoptestprep**. This site features practice tests that include exclusive TOEFL iBT practice questions covering all four skills: reading, listening, speaking, and writing, with scoring provided by certified ETS raters.

## Scores and Score Reports

### How do I get my scores?

Your scores will be available in your ETS account. How soon they'll be available depends on how you took the test:

- Taken at a test center: 4–8 days after your test date
- TOEFL iBT Home Edition: 4–8 days after your test date
- TOEFL iBT Paper Edition: 11–13 business days after your test date

### What is included in my score report?
All score reports include:

- Total score and section scores from your selected test date
- MyBest scores, which combine your highest section scores from tests in the last two years

In your ETS account, you will also get personalized performance feedback and deeper insights into your results.

### What is included with my registration fee?

- One online score report for you and one printed score report if requested
- Up to four official score reports that ETS will send directly to the institutions or agencies that you select before you take the test

### Can I order additional score reports?

Yes. For a small fee, you can send score reports to as many institutions as you choose. See **www.ets.org/toefl** for details.

### How long are scores valid?
ETS will report scores for two years after the test date.

### Will institutions accept scores from previous tests?
Check with each institution or agency directly.

## Test Delivery

*What skills are tested on the TOEFL iBT Test?*

The test is given in English. It includes the Reading, Listening, Speaking, and Writing sections, and it takes an estimated two hours or less to complete.

| Section | Estimated Timing | Number of Questions |
|---------|------------------|---------------------|
| Reading | 35 minutes | 2 passages, 10 questions per passage |
| Listening | 36 minutes | 3 lectures, 6 questions each; 2 conversations, 5 questions each |
| Speaking | 16 minutes | 4 tasks |
| Writing | 29 minutes | 2 tasks |

*Can I take only one section of the test?*

No. The entire test must be taken to receive a score.

*Which computer keyboard is used?*

The TOEFL iBT test uses a standard QWERTY English-language keyboard, which takes its name from the first six letters in the top row of the keyboard If you haven't used this kind of keyboard before, practice on one before test day to become familiar with it. In some countries, the common keyboard used is configured to QWERTY, and a template is provided to each test taker to help with locating the few keys that are in a different location.

# 2 Reading Section

**Read this chapter to learn**

- The 9 types of TOEFL Reading questions
- How to recognize each Reading question type
- Tips for answering each Reading question type
- Strategies for preparing for the Reading section

The TOEFL iBT Reading section includes two reading passages, each approximately 700 words long. There are ten questions per passage. You will have up to 36 minutes to read both passages and answer all the questions in the section. In the Reading section, you may skip questions and come back to them later, as long as you answer all the questions before time is up.

## Reading Passages

TOEFL iBT Reading passages are excerpts from college-level textbooks and other books that would be used in introductions to an academic discipline or topic. The excerpts are changed as little as possible because the goal of the test is to assess how well test takers can read the kind of writing that is actually used in an academic environment. In the following discussion, a passage and the ten items associated with it are referred to as a set.

The passages cover a variety of subjects. Do not worry if you are unfamiliar with the topic of a passage. All the information needed to answer the questions is in the passage. All TOEFL reading passages are classified into three basic categories based on author purpose: (1) exposition, (2) argumentation, and (3) historical and biographical narrative.

Often, passages will present information about the topic from more than one perspective or point of view. This is something you should note as you read, because usually you will be asked at least one question that allows you to show that you have understood the relationships of the different perspectives to one another and to the overall passage organization. Common types of organization you should be able to recognize are:

- classification
- compare/contrast
- cause/effect
- problem/solution

TOEFL iBT reading passages are approximately 700 words long, but the passages used may vary in length. Some passages may be slightly longer than 700 words, and some may be slightly shorter.

# Reading Questions

Reading questions cover basic information skills, inferencing skills, and reading-to-learn skills. There are nine question types. The following chart summarizes the categories and types of TOEFL iBT Reading questions.

---

**TOEFL iBT Reading Question Types**

**Basic Comprehension questions**
1. Factual Information questions (2 to 5 questions per set)
2. Negative Factual Information questions (0 to 2 questions per set)
3. Vocabulary questions (1 or 2 questions per set)
4. Reference questions (0 or 1 question per set)
5. Sentence Simplification questions (0 or 1 question per set)

**Inferencing questions**
6. Inference questions (1 or 2 questions per set)
7. Rhetorical Purpose questions (1 or 2 questions per set)
8. Insert Text questions (1 question per set)

**Reading-to-Learn questions**
9. Prose Summary (1 question per set)

---

The following sections will explain each of these question types. You will find out how to recognize each type and see examples of each type with explanations. You will also find tips that can help you answer each Reading question type.

## Basic Information and Inferencing Questions

### Type 1: Factual Information Questions

These questions ask you to identify factual information that is explicitly stated in the passage. Factual Information questions can focus on facts, details, definitions, or other thematically relevant information presented by the author. They ask you to identify specific information that is typically mentioned only in part of the passage. They generally do not ask about general themes that the passage as a whole discusses. Often, the information needed to answer the question correctly is presented in a few sentences within a longer paragraph. Every set contains at least two Factual Information questions and some have as many as five.

*How to Recognize Factual Information Questions*
Factual Information questions are often phrased in one of these ways:
- According to paragraph X, which of the following is true about Y?
- According to paragraph X, which of the following is the main reason that Y declined?
- According to paragraph X, Y declined mainly because . . .
- In paragraph X, which of the following is identified as an advantage of having Y?

- In paragraph X, which of the following is presented as evidence supporting the conclusion that . . .
- According to paragraph X, Y differs from Z in which of the following ways?

*Tips for Factual Information Questions*

- Expect to refer back to the passage in order to determine what exactly is said about the subject of the question. Since the question may be about a detail, you may not recall the detail from your first reading of the passage.
- Realize that some or all of the answer choices may paraphrase the information relevant to answering correctly. Paraphrasing is common in the answer choices as well as in the wording of the questions for all question types in the Reading section.
- Do not select an answer just because it is mentioned in the passage. Your choice should answer the specific question that was asked.

**Example**

**PASSAGE EXCERPT:** ...Sculptures must, for example, be stable, which requires an understanding of the properties of mass, weight distribution, and stress. Paintings must have rigid stretchers so that the canvas will be taut, and the paint must not deteriorate, crack, or discolor. These are problems that must be overcome by the artist because they tend to intrude upon their conception of the work. For example, in the early Italian Renaissance, bronze statues of horses with a raised foreleg usually had a cannonball under that hoof. This was done because the cannonball was needed to support the weight of the leg. In other words, the demands of the laws of physics, not the sculptor's aesthetic intentions, placed the ball there. That this device was a necessary structural compromise is clear from the fact that the cannonball quickly disappeared when sculptors learned how to strengthen the internal structure of a statue with iron braces (iron being much stronger than bronze) ...

According to paragraph 2, sculptors in the Italian Renaissance stopped using cannonballs in bronze statues of horses because

(A) they began using a material that made the statues weigh less
(B) they found a way to strengthen the statues internally
(C) the aesthetic tastes of the public had changed over time
(D) the cannonballs added too much weight to the statues

*Explanation*

The question tells you to look for the answer in the excerpted paragraph, which in this case is paragraph 2. You do not need to skim the entire passage to find the relevant information.

Choice A says that sculptors stopped putting cannonballs under the raised legs of horses in statues because they learned how to make the statue weigh less and not require support for the leg. The passage does not mention making the statues weigh less; it says that sculptors learned a better way to support the weight. Choice C says that the change occurred only because people's taste changed, meaning that the cannonballs were never structurally necessary. That directly contradicts the passage. Choice D says that cannonballs added weight to the statues. This contradicts the passage, which says that the cannonball was needed to support the weight of the leg of the statue. Choice B correctly identifies the reason the passage gives for the change: sculptors developed a way to strengthen the statue from the inside, making the cannonballs physically unnecessary.

## Type 2: Negative Factual Information Questions

These questions ask you to verify what information is true and what information is NOT true or not included in the passage based on information that is explicitly stated in the passage. To answer this kind of question, first locate the relevant information in the passage. Then verify that three of the four answer choices are true and that the remaining choice is false. Remember, for this type of question, the correct answer is the one that is NOT true. Some sets have no Negative Factual Information questions but others have one or two.

### How to Recognize Negative Factual Information Questions

You can recognize Negative Factual Information questions because the word "NOT" or "EXCEPT" appears in the question in capital letters.

- According to the passage, which of the following is NOT true of X?
- In paragraph X, the author mentions all of the following characteristics of Y EXCEPT . . .

### Tips for Negative Factual Information Questions

- Usually a Negative Factual Information question requires you to check more of the passage than a Factual Information question does. This is true because the information relevant to determining the accuracy of the answer choices is often spread across multiple sentences.
- In Negative Factual Information questions, the correct answer either contradicts information in the passage or expresses information that is not presented in the passage.
- After you finish a Negative Factual Information question, check your answer to make sure you have accurately understood the task.

**Example**

**PASSAGE EXCERPT:** The United States in the 1800s was full of practical, hardworking people who did not consider the arts—from theater to painting—useful. In addition, the public's attitude that European art was better than American art both discouraged and infuriated American artists. In the early 1900s there was a strong feeling among artists that the United States was long overdue in developing art that did not reproduce European traditions. Everybody agreed that the heart and soul of the new country should be reflected in its art. But opinions differed about what this art would be like and how it would develop.

According to paragraph 1, all of the following were true of American art in the late 1800s and early 1900s EXCEPT:

(A) Most Americans thought art was unimportant.
(B) American art generally copied European styles and traditions.
(C) Most Americans considered American art inferior to European art.
(D) American art was very popular with European audiences.

*Explanation*

Sometimes in Negative Factual Information questions, it is necessary to check the entire passage in order to make sure that your choice is not mentioned. However, in this example, the question is limited to one paragraph, so your answer should be based just on the information in that paragraph. Choice A is a restatement of the first sentence in the paragraph: since most Americans did not think that the arts were useful, they considered them unimportant. Choice B makes the same point as the third sentence: ". . . the United States was long overdue in developing art that did not reproduce European traditions," which means that up to this point in history, American art did reproduce European traditions. Choice C is a restatement of the second sentence in the paragraph: American artists were frustrated because of "the public's attitude that European art was better than American art. . . ." Choice D is not mentioned anywhere in the paragraph. Because you are asked to identify the choice that is NOT mentioned in the passage or that contradicts the passage, the correct answer is choice D.

## Type 3: Vocabulary Questions

These questions ask you to identify the meanings of individual words and phrases as they are used in the reading passage (a word might have more than one meaning, but *in the reading passage*, only one of those meanings is relevant). Usually a word or phrase is chosen to be tested as a Vocabulary question because understanding that word or phrase is important to understanding texts in a wide variety of academic subjects. In other words, the terms selected for testing in Vocabulary questions are not technical or specific to a given academic field. When specialized words or phrases are used by a passage author, they are usually defined using either parentheses or a hyperlink. If you select the hyperlinked word in the passage, a definition will appear in a box. In this book, words of this type are defined at the end of the passage. Naturally, words that are tested as Vocabulary questions are not defined for you. Every test has at least one Vocabulary question and many have two.

*How to Recognize Vocabulary Questions*

Vocabulary questions are usually easy to identify. You will see one word or phrase highlighted in the passage. You are then asked a question such as any of the following:

- The word "X" in the passage is closest in meaning to . . .
- The phrase "X" in the passage is closest in meaning to . . .
- In stating X, the author means that . . .

*Tips for Vocabulary Questions*

- Remember that the question is not just asking the meaning of a word; it is asking for the meaning *as it is used in the passage*. Do not choose an answer just because it can be a correct meaning of the word; understand which meaning the author is using in the passage.
- Reread the sentence in the passage, substituting the word or phrase you have chosen. Confirm that the sentence still makes sense in the context of the whole passage.

**Examples**

**PASSAGE EXCERPT:** In the animal world the task of moving about is fulfilled in many ways. For some animals **locomotion** is accomplished by changes in body shape …

The word "**locomotion**" in the passage is closest in meaning to

- (A) evolution
- (B) movement
- (C) survival
- (D) escape

*Explanation*

*Locomotion* means "the ability to move from place to place." In this example, it is a way of restating the phrase "the task of moving" in the preceding sentence. So the correct answer is choice B.

**PASSAGE EXCERPT:** Some poisonous snake bites need to be treated immediately or the victim will **suffer paralysis** …

In stating that the victim will "**suffer paralysis,**" the author means that the victim will

- (A) lose the ability to move
- (B) become unconscious
- (C) undergo shock
- (D) feel great pain

*Explanation*

In this example, both the words tested from the passage and the possible answers are phrases. *Paralysis* means "the inability to move," so if the poison from a snake bite causes someone to "suffer paralysis," that person will "lose the ability to move." The correct answer is choice A.

## Type 4: Reference Questions

These questions ask you to identify referential relationships between the words in the passage. Often, the relationship is between a word or phrase and its antecedent (the expression or concept being referred to). Sometimes other kinds of grammatical reference are tested (like *which* or *this*). Sets may contain one Reference question but many have none.

*How to Recognize Reference Questions*

Reference questions look similar to vocabulary questions. In the passage, one word or phrase is highlighted. Usually the word is a pronoun. Then you are asked:

- The word "X" in the passage refers to …

The four answer choices are usually words or phrases from the passage but may also be ideas that are not stated in exact words in the passage.

- If the Reference question is about a pronoun, make sure your answer agrees in number (i.e., singular or plural) and is the same part of speech (e.g., noun, verb, adjective, or adverb) as the highlighted pronoun.
- Substitute your choice for the highlighted word or words in the sentence. Does it violate any grammar rules? Does it make sense?

**Examples**

**PASSAGE EXCERPT:** … The first weekly newspaper in the colonies was the *Boston Gazette*, established in 1719, the same year that marked the appearance of Philadelphia's first newspaper, the *American Mercury*, where the young Benjamin Franklin worked. By 1760 Boston had four newspapers and five other printing establishments; Philadelphia, two newspapers and three other presses; and New York, three newspapers. The distribution, if not the sale, of newspapers was assisted by the establishment of a postal service in 1710, **which** had a network of some 65 offices by 1770, serving all 13 colonies …

The word "**which**" in the passage refers to

(A) distribution
(B) sale
(C) newspaper
(D) postal service

*Explanation*

In this example, the highlighted word is a relative pronoun: the grammatical subject of the relative clause "which had a network of some 65 offices . . ." The relative clause is describing the postal service, so choice D is the correct answer.

**PASSAGE EXCERPT:** … Roots anchor the plant in one of two ways or sometimes by a combination of the two. The first is by occupying a large volume of shallow soil around the plant's base with a *fibrous root system,* one consisting of many thin, profusely branched roots. Since these kinds of roots grow relatively close to the soil surface, they effectively control soil erosion. Grass roots are especially well suited to **this purpose**. Fibrous roots capture water as it begins to percolate into the ground and so must draw their mineral supplies from the surface soil before the nutrients are leached to lower levels …

The phrase "**this purpose**" in the passage refers to

(A) combining two root systems
(B) feeding the plant
(C) preventing soil erosion
(D) leaching nutrients

*Explanation*

In the example, the highlighted words are a phrase containing a demonstrative adjective (*this*) and a noun (*purpose*). Because a fibrous root system can keep soil in place, it can be used to stop erosion, and grass roots are a type of fibrous root system. The sentence could be reworded as "Grass roots are especially well suited to preventing soil erosion," so choice C is the correct answer.

## Type 5: Sentence Simplification Questions

In this type of question, you are asked to choose a sentence that has the same essential meaning as a sentence that occurs in the passage. The correct answer choice is a simplified version of the tested sentence, but it retains the key information presented in the tested sentence and accurately expresses the main point of the tested sentence. Sentence simplification is a question type in the Reading section that measures whether test takers can distinguish between essential information and nonessential information. Not every reading set includes a Sentence Simplification question. There is never more than one in a set.

### How to Recognize Sentence Simplification Questions

Sentence Simplification questions always look the same. A single sentence in the passage is highlighted. You are then asked:

- Which of the following best expresses the essential information in the highlighted sentence in the passage? Incorrect answer choices change the meaning in important ways or leave out essential information.

### Tips for Sentence Simplification Questions

- Make sure you understand both ways a choice can be incorrect:
  - It misrepresents information in or otherwise distorts the meaning of the highlighted sentence.
  - It leaves out something important from the highlighted sentence.
- Make sure your answer does not contradict the main argument of the paragraph in which the sentence occurs or the passage as a whole.

**Example**

**PASSAGE EXCERPT:** ...Although we now tend to refer to the various crafts according to the materials used to construct them—clay, glass, wood, fiber, and metal—it was once common to think of crafts in terms of function, which led to their being known as the "applied arts." Approaching crafts from the point of view of function, we can divide them into simple categories: containers, shelters, and supports. There is no way around the fact that containers, shelters, and supports must be functional. The applied arts are thus bound by the laws of physics, which pertain to both the materials used in their making and the substances and things to be contained, supported, and sheltered. These laws are universal in their application, regardless of cultural beliefs, geography, or climate. If a pot has no bottom or has large openings in its sides, it could hardly be considered a container in any traditional sense. Since the laws of physics, not some arbitrary decision, have determined the general form of applied-art objects, they follow basic patterns, so much so that functional forms can vary only within certain limits. Buildings without roofs, for example, are unusual because they depart from the norm. However, not all functional objects are exactly alike; that is why we recognize a Shang Dynasty vase as being different from an Inca vase. What varies is not the basic form but the incidental details that do not obstruct the object's primary function...

Which of the following best expresses the essential information in the highlighted sentence in the passage? Incorrect answer choices change the meaning in important ways or leave out essential information.

Ⓐ Functional applied-art objects cannot vary much from the basic patterns determined by the laws of physics.

Ⓑ The function of applied-art objects is determined by basic patterns in the laws of physics.

Ⓒ Since functional applied-art objects vary only within certain limits, arbitrary decisions cannot have determined their general form.

Ⓓ The general form of applied-art objects is limited by some arbitrary decision that is not determined by the laws of physics.

### *Explanation*

It is important to note that the question says that *incorrect* answers change the original meaning of the sentence or leave out essential information. In this example, choice D changes the meaning of the sentence to its opposite; it says that the form of functional objects is arbitrary, when the highlighted sentence says that the forms of functional objects are *never* arbitrary. Choice B also changes the meaning. It says that the functions of applied-art objects are determined by physical laws. The highlighted sentence says that the *form of the object* is determined by physical laws but the function is determined by people. Choice C leaves out an important idea from the highlighted sentence. Like the highlighted sentence, it says that the form of functional objects is not arbitrary, but it does not say that physical laws determine basic form. Only choice A makes the same point as the highlighted sentence and includes all the essential meaning.

## Inferencing Questions

Unlike the correct answers to Basic Comprehension questions, the correct answers to Inferencing questions are not explicitly presented in the passage. However, the correct answer can be determined by examining the language and information in the passage.

### Type 6: Inference Questions

Inference questions test your ability to identify information that is implicit in the passage (not explicitly presented) and is required for understanding the text.

Skilled authors tend to write economically, and one way of achieving economy of expression is to leave some information to be understood by the reader without spelling it out. Good authors also often avoid pointing out obvious implications of their explicit comments, trusting that the competent reader will understand those implications without being explicitly told. As a result, most well-written texts contain implied information that is important for readers to include in their understanding of a text. Inference questions in the Reading section focus on information and ideas about the topic discussed that the passage author likely expected readers to pick up, even though the information or ideas are not stated. Every Reading set has at least one Inference question of this type and some have two.

### How to Recognize Inference Questions

Inference questions will usually include the word *infer, suggest,* or *imply*.

- Paragraph 1 suggests which of the following about X?
- The author of the passage implies that X . . .
- Which of the following can be inferred from paragraph 1 about X?

### Tips for Inference Questions

- Make sure your answer does not contradict the main idea of the passage.
- Do not choose an answer just because it seems important or true. The correct answer must be inferable from the language in the passage.
- You should be able to defend your choice by pointing to explicitly stated information in the passage that leads to the inference you have selected.

**Example**

**PASSAGE EXCERPT:** . . . The nineteenth century brought with it a burst of new discoveries and inventions that revolutionized the candle industry and made lighting available to all. In the early-to-mid-nineteenth century, a process was developed to refine tallow (fat from animals) with alkali and sulfuric acid. The result was a product called stearin. Stearin is harder and burns longer than unrefined tallow. This breakthrough meant that it was possible to make tallow candles that would not produce the usual smoke and rancid odor. Stearins were also derived from palm oils, so vegetable waxes as well as animal fats could be used to make candles . . .

Which of the following can be inferred from paragraph 1 about candles before the nineteenth century?

Ⓐ They did not smoke when they were burned.
Ⓑ They produced a pleasant odor as they burned.
Ⓒ They were not available to everyone.
Ⓓ They contained sulfuric acid.

### Explanation

In the first sentence from the excerpt, the author says that "new discoveries and inventions" made "lighting available to all." Candles are the only kind of lighting discussed in the passage. If the new discoveries were important because they made candles available to all, we can infer that before the discoveries, candles were not available to everyone. Therefore choice C is an inference about candles we can make from the passage. Choices A and B can be eliminated because they explicitly contradict the passage ("the usual smoke" and "rancid odor"). Choice D can be eliminated because sulfuric acid was first used to make stearin in the nineteenth century, not before the nineteenth century.

**PASSAGE EXCERPT:** Fossils—the mineralized remains of plants and animals—provide important clues to life in the past. The fossils collected by Mary Anning (1799–1847) along the southwest coast of England helped shape modern science. Some fossils found or excavated by Anning were truly spectacular. While still a girl, Anning recovered the body of a large, strange animal whose skull was discovered by her brother in 1810. Thought to be a crocodile when only its head had been found, the fossil set off years of debate, with the animal eventually identified as an Ichthyosaurus, a previously unknown reptile. In 1824, she discovered the first intact skeleton of Plesiosaurus, a four-limbed swimming creature with a small head, and in 1828, the remains of the first flying reptile located outside of Germany. Finds such as these were rare and dangerous to unearth. The cliffs rising above Lyme Regis beaches were unstable with frequent mudslides in winter and during storms, yet these were best times for collecting fossils—the crumbling and washing away of parts of the cliffs left fossils newly exposed. Unless such fossils were collected right away, they would be washed out to sea. Given these conditions, it is hardly surprising that Anning narrowly escaped severe injury several times.

Which of the following can be inferred about Mary Anning from her efforts to search for fossils on the cliffs of Lyme Regis?

(A) She was brave and was not easily discouraged.
(B) She stopped searching for fossils when conditions became stormy.
(C) She suffered serious injuries multiple times as a result of her searches.
(D) She sometimes waited for fossils to wash out to sea before collecting them.

*Explanation*

The correct inference—Mary Anning was "brave and not easily discouraged," choice A, is based on the final three sentences of the paragraph, which describe the conditions under which she had to search for fossils. Fossils were best found, the passage says, during storms because those events washed away parts of the cliffs leaving previously buried fossils newly exposed. Readers are also told that fossil hunters needed to collect the newly exposed fossils immediately because if they did not, the fossils could also be washed away and thereby lost. Clearly, anyone working under such conditions was brave and determined. So even though the author does not comment explicitly on Anning's personality, her qualities of bravery and determination are obvious from the details provided about the search. Choice (C) is flatly contradicted by the passage, which says that Anning "escaped severe injury," not that she suffered severe injuries. Choices (B) and (D) are contrary to the implications of the discussion. Anning was a remarkably successful fossil hunter, we are told. To be that, she would have had to search for fossils during storms—this was the best way to find them—not stop searching when storms arose, as choice (B) says. Similarly, Anning's success as a fossil hunter strongly implies that she did not wait for fossils to wash out to sea, because if she had, she should not have been able to recover them, as choice (D) says. To be successful, Anning had to remain on the cliffs during storms even as parts of the cliffs were being washed away.

### Type 7: Rhetorical Purpose Questions

*Rhetoric* is the art of speaking or writing effectively. In Factual Information questions, you are asked *what* information an author has presented. In Rhetorical Purpose questions, you are asked *why* the author has presented a particular piece of information in a particular place or manner. Rhetorical Purpose questions ask you to show that you understand the rhetorical function of a statement or paragraph as it relates to the rest of the passage.

Sometimes you will be asked to identify how one paragraph relates to another. For instance, the second paragraph may give examples to support a statement in the first paragraph. The answer choices may be expressed in general terms (for example, "a theory is explained and then illustrated") or in terms that are specific to the passage. ("The author explains the categories of adaptation to deserts by mammals and then gives an example.")

A Rhetorical Purpose question may also ask why the author quotes a certain person or why the author mentions a particular piece of information (*Example:* Why does the author mention "the ability to grasp a pencil"? *Correct answer:* It is an example of a motor skill developed by children at 10 to 11 months of age.)

*How to Recognize Rhetorical Purpose Questions*

Following are examples of the way Rhetorical Purpose questions are typically worded

- The author discusses X in paragraph 2 in order to . . .
- Why does the author mention X?
- Why does the author compare X to Y?

*Tips for Rhetorical Purpose Questions*
- Know the definitions of these words or phrases, which are often used to describe different kinds of rhetorical purposes: "to illustrate," "to explain," "to contrast," "to refute," "to note," "to criticize."
- Rhetorical Purpose questions usually do not ask about the overall organization of the reading passage. Instead, they typically focus on the logical links between sentences and paragraphs.

**Example**

**PASSAGE EXCERPT:** ... Sensitivity to physical laws is thus an important consideration for the maker of applied-art objects. It is often taken for granted that this is also true for the maker of fine-art objects. This assumption misses a significant difference between the two disciplines. Fine-art objects are not constrained by the laws of physics in the same way that applied-art objects are. Because their primary purpose is not functional, they are only limited in terms of the materials used to make them. Sculptures must, for example, be stable, which requires an understanding of the properties of mass, weight distribution, and stress. Paintings must have rigid stretchers so that the canvas will be taut, and the paint must not deteriorate, crack, or discolor. These are problems that must be overcome by the artist because they tend to intrude upon his or her conception of the work. For example, in the early Italian Renaissance, **bronze statues of horses** with a raised foreleg usually had a cannonball under that hoof. This was done because the cannonball was needed to support the weight of the leg ...

Why does the author discuss the "**bronze statues of horses**" created by artists in the early Italian Renaissance?

Ⓐ To provide an example of a problem related to the laws of physics that a fine artist must overcome

Ⓑ To argue that fine artists are unconcerned with the laws of physics

Ⓒ To contrast the relative sophistication of modern artists in solving problems related to the laws of physics

Ⓓ To note an exceptional piece of art constructed without the aid of technology

*Explanation*

You should note that the sentence that first mentions "bronze statues of horses" begins "For example." The author is giving an example of something that was introduced earlier in the paragraph. The paragraph overall contrasts how the constraints of physical laws affect the fine arts differently from applied arts or crafts. The fine artist is not concerned with making an object that is useful, so the fine artist is less constrained than the applied artist. However, because even a fine-arts object is made of some material, the artist must take into account the physical properties of the material. In the passage, the author uses the example of the bronze statues of horses to discuss how artists had to include some support for the raised foreleg of the horse because of the physical properties of the bronze. So the correct answer is choice A.

## Type 8: Insert Text Questions

In this type of question, you are given a new sentence and are asked where in the passage it would best fit. You need to understand the logic of the passage as well as the grammatical connections (like pronoun references) between sentences. Every set includes an Insert Text question. There is never more than one in a set.

*How to Recognize Insert Text Questions*

Insert Text questions are easy to identify when taking the TOEFL iBT test. In the passage you will see four black squares. The squares are located at the beginnings or ends of sentences. Sometimes all four squares appear in one paragraph. Sometimes they are spread across the end of one paragraph and the beginning of another. You are then asked this question:

Look at the four squares [■] that indicate where the following sentence could be added to the passage.

**[You will see a sentence in bold.]**

Where would the sentence best fit? Select the square [■] to add the sentence to the passage.

Your job is to select one of the squares and insert the sentence in the text. The following is an example of how this question displays on the TOEFL iBT test.

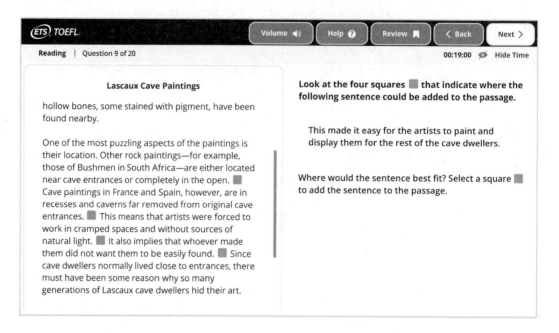

**Tips for Insert Text Questions**

- When taking the TOEFL iBT test, try the sentence in each of the places indicated by the squares. You can place and replace the sentence as many times as you want.
- Look at the structure of the sentence you are inserting. Pay special attention to connecting words; they can provide important information about where the sentence should be placed.
- Frequently used connecting words:

| | | |
|---|---|---|
| On the other hand | Further or Furthermore | Similarly |
| For example | Therefore | In contrast |
| On the contrary | In other words | Finally |
| As a result | | |

- Make sure that the inserted sentence connects logically to both the sentence before it and the sentence after it and that any pronouns agree with the nouns they refer to.

The Insert Text question is formatted differently in print versions of the test. See below for an example of what the Insert Text question will look like in the practice sets and tests of this book. Although the formatting is slightly different, the task you must complete is the same: indicate where the sentence would best fit in the passage.

**Example**

**PASSAGE EXCERPT:** One of the most puzzling aspects of the paintings is their location. Other rock paintings—for example, those of Bushmen in South Africa—are either located near cave entrances or completely in the open. **(A)** Cave paintings in France and Spain, however, are in recesses and caverns far removed from original cave entrances. **(B)** This means that artists were forced to work in cramped spaces and without sources of natural light. **(C)** It also implies that whoever made them did not want them to be easily found. **(D)** Since cave dwellers normally lived close to entrances, there must have been some reason why so many generations of Lascaux cave dwellers hid their art.

**Directions:** Look at the part of the passage that is displayed above. The letters **(A)**, **(B)**, **(C)**, and **(D)** indicate where the following sentence could be added.

> **This made it easy for the artists to paint and display them for the rest of the cave dwellers.**

Where would the sentence best fit?

(A) Choice A
(B) Choice B
(C) Choice C
(D) Choice D

*Explanation*

In this example, choice A is the correct answer. The sentence makes sense only if it occurs after sentence 2. In the paragraph, the author contrasts the location of rock art in South Africa, which tends to be placed near cave entrances or in the open, with the location of rock art in Spain and France, which tends to be deep inside a cave. The insert sentence is about a factor ("This") that would have made rock art "easy for the artists to paint and display for others." Being near a cave entrance or in the open is such a factor, so the inserted sentence must be placed after the sentence about rock art in such locations. The other three choices follow sentences that explain that cave artists would have found it difficult to paint in the locations they chose and that the sites chosen would have been difficult to access and thus not visible without effort.

## Reading-to-Learn Questions

There is one type of Reading-to-Learn question: "Prose Summary." Reading-to-Learn questions require you to do more than the Basic Information questions. As you have seen, the Basic Information questions focus on your ability to understand or locate specific points in a passage at the sentence level. The Reading-to-Learn questions also involve:

- recognizing the organization and purpose of the passage
- organizing the information in the passage into a mental framework

- distinguishing major from minor ideas and essential from nonessential information
- understanding rhetorical functions such as cause-effect relationships, compare-contrast relationships, arguments, and the like

In other words, these questions require you to demonstrate an understanding of the passage as a whole, not just specific information within it.

Reading-to-Learn questions require you to show that you are able not only to comprehend individual points, but also to place the major ideas and supporting information from the passage into the organizational framework of a prose summary. By answering correctly, you will demonstrate that you can recognize the major points of a text, how the text has been organized and why it has been organized that way, and the nature of the relationships within the text. Having an organized mental representation of a text is critical to learning because it allows you to remember important information from the text and apply it in new situations. If you have such a mental framework, you should be able to reconstruct the major ideas and supporting information from the text. By doing so, you will demonstrate an understanding of the text as a whole. On the TOEFL iBT test, each reading passage will have one Prose Summary question.

### Type 9: Prose Summary Questions

These questions measure your ability to understand and recognize the major ideas and the relative importance of information in a passage. You will be asked to select the major ideas in the passage by distinguishing them from minor ideas or ideas that are not in the passage. The correct answer choice will synthesize major ideas in the passage. Because the correct answer represents a synthesis of ideas, it will not match any particular sentence from the passage. To select the correct answer, you will need to create a mental framework to organize and remember major ideas and other important information. Understanding the relative importance of information in a passage is critical to this ability.

In a Prose Summary question, you will be given six answer choices and asked to pick the three that express the most important ideas in the passage. Unlike the Basic Information questions, each of which is worth just 1 point, a Prose Summary question is worth 2 points. You can earn 0 to 2 points depending on how many correct answers you choose. If you choose no correct answers or just one correct answer, you will earn no points. If you choose two correct answers, you will earn 1 point. If you choose all three correct answers, you will earn 2 points. The order in which you choose your answers does not matter for scoring purposes.

**Example** Because the Prose Summary question asks you to show an understanding of the different parts of the passage, it is necessary to read the entire passage. Parts of the following passage have already been used to illustrate other question types.

## APPLIED ARTS AND FINE ARTS

Although we now tend to refer to the various crafts according to the materials used to construct them—clay, glass, wood, fiber, and metal—it was once common to think of crafts in terms of function, which led to their being known as the "applied arts." Approaching crafts from the point of view of function, we can divide them into simple categories: containers, shelters, and supports. There is no way around the fact that containers, shelters, and supports must be functional. The applied arts are thus bound by the laws of physics, which pertain to both the materials used in their making and the substances and things to be contained, supported, and sheltered. These laws are universal in their application, regardless of cultural beliefs, geography, or climate. If a pot has no bottom or has large openings in its sides, it could hardly be considered a container in any traditional sense. Since the laws of physics, not some arbitrary decision, have determined the general form of applied-art objects, they follow basic patterns, so much so that functional forms can vary only within certain limits. Buildings without roofs, for example, are unusual because they depart from the norm. However, not all functional objects are exactly alike; that is why we recognize a Shang Dynasty vase as being different from an Inca vase. What varies is not the basic form but the incidental details that do not obstruct the object's primary function.

Sensitivity to physical laws is thus an important consideration for the maker of applied-art objects. It is often taken for granted that this is also true for the maker of fine-art objects. This assumption misses a significant difference between the two disciplines. Fine-art objects are not constrained by the laws of physics in the same way that applied-art objects are. Because their primary purpose is not functional, they are only limited in terms of the materials used to make them. Sculptures must, for example, be stable, which requires an understanding of the properties of mass, weight distribution, and stress. Paintings must have rigid stretchers so that the canvas will be taut, and the paint must not deteriorate, crack, or discolor. These are problems that must be overcome by the artist because they tend to intrude upon their conception of the work. For example, in the early Italian Renaissance, bronze statues of horses with a raised foreleg usually had a cannonball under that hoof. This was done because the cannonball was needed to support the weight of the leg. In other words, the demands of the laws of physics, not the sculptor's aesthetic intentions, placed the ball there. That this device was a necessary structural compromise is clear from the fact that the cannonball quickly disappeared when sculptors learned how to strengthen the internal structure of a statue with iron braces (iron being much stronger than bronze).

Even though the fine arts in the twentieth century often treat materials in new ways, the basic difference in attitude of artists in relation to their materials in the fine arts and the applied arts remains relatively constant. It would therefore not be too great an exaggeration to say that practitioners of the fine arts work to overcome the limitations of their materials, whereas those engaged in the applied arts work in concert with their materials.

An introductory sentence for a brief summary of the passage is provided below. Complete the summary by selecting the THREE answer choices that express the most important ideas in the passage. Some sentences do not belong in the summary because they express ideas that are not presented in the passage or are minor ideas in the passage. **This question is worth 2 points.**

> **This passage discusses fundamental differences between applied-art objects and fine-art objects.**

- 
- 
- 

## Answer Choices

A  Applied-art objects fulfill functions, such as containing or sheltering, and objects with the same function have similar characteristics because they are constrained by their purpose.

B  It is easy to recognize that Shang Dynasty vases are different from Inca vases.

C  Fine-art objects are not functional, so they are limited only by the properties of the materials used.

D  Renaissance sculptors learned to use iron braces to strengthen the internal structures of bronze statues.

E  In the twentieth century, fine artists and applied artists became more similar to one another in their attitudes toward their materials.

F  In all periods, fine artists tend to challenge the physical limitations of their materials, while applied artists tend to cooperate with the physical properties of their materials.

*Explanation*

*Correct Choices*

*Choice A:* Applied-art objects fulfill functions, such as containing or sheltering, and objects with the same function have similar characteristics because they are constrained by their purpose.

*Explanation:* As the introductory sentence states, the passage is mainly a contrast of applied-art objects and fine-art objects. The main point of contrast is functionality: applied-art objects are functional, whereas fine-art objects are not. The first part of the passage explains the consequences of functionality for the materials and "basic forms" of applied-art objects. The second part of the passage explains the consequences of not being functional to the materials and forms of fine-art objects. A good summary of the passage must include the definition of "applied-art objects" and the major consequence (objects with the same function will follow similar patterns), so choice A should be included.

*Choice C:* Fine-art objects are not functional, so they are limited only by the properties of the materials used.

*Explanation:* Because the passage contrasts applied-art objects and fine-art objects, a good summary should include the basic difference. Including choice C in the summary provides the basic contrast discussed in the passage: applied-art objects are functional; fine-art objects are not. Fine-art objects are not as constrained as applied-art objects because they do not have to perform a function.

*Choice F:* In all periods, fine artists tend to challenge the physical limitations of their materials, while applied artists tend to cooperate with the physical properties of their materials.

*Explanation:* The last paragraph of the passage presents a further consequence of the basic contrast between applied-art objects and fine-art objects. This is the difference between the attitude of fine artists toward their materials and the attitude of applied artists toward their materials. A good summary will include this last contrast.

*Incorrect Choices*

*Choice B:* It is easy to recognize that Shang Dynasty vases are different from Inca vases.

*Explanation:* Although this statement is true, it is not the main point of the first paragraph or of the passage. In fact, it contrasts with the main point of the paragraph: objects that have the same function are all similar. The last sentence of the first paragraph says that the Shang Dynasty vase and the Inca vase are different in "incidental details," but the "basic form" is the same. Including choice B in the summary misrepresents the passage.

*Choice D:* Renaissance sculptors learned to use iron braces to strengthen the internal structures of bronze statues.

*Explanation:* Choice D summarizes the information in sentences 9, 10, and 11 of paragraph 2. Within the context of the passage, this information helps you understand the meaning of the limitations that materials can impose on fine artists. However, remember that the directions say to choose the statements that express *the most important ideas in the passage.* The example is less important than the general statements of difference. If choice D is included, then choice A or C or F would be left out, and the summary would be missing an essential point of contrast between fine arts and applied arts.

*Choice E:* In the twentieth century, fine artists and applied artists became more similar to one another in their attitudes toward their materials.

*Explanation:* This choice should be excluded because it is not supported by the passage. It is a misreading of paragraph 3, which says that the difference in attitude between fine artists and applied artists has not changed. Obviously, a choice that contradicts the information or argument in the passage should not be part of your summary.

# Strategies for Preparing for and Taking the Reading Section

Now that you are familiar with the nine question types that are used in the TOEFL iBT Reading section, you are ready to sharpen your skills by working on whole reading sets. In the following pages, you can practice on six reading sets created by ETS for the TOEFL iBT test. The question types are not labeled, but you should be able to identify them and understand what you need to do to answer each correctly. After each passage and question set, you will find answers and explanations for each question.

In addition to practicing on these sets, following are some other suggestions for improving the skills that will help you perform well on the Reading section.

The best way to improve reading skills is to read frequently and to read many different types of texts in various subject areas (sciences, social sciences, arts, business, and others). The internet is one of the best resources for this, and of course books, magazines, and journals are very helpful as well. Make sure to regularly read texts that are academic in style, the kind that are used in university courses.

Here are some suggestions for ways to build skills for the three reading purposes covered by the TOEFL iBT test.

## 1. Reading to find information

- Scan passages to find and highlight key facts (dates, numbers, terms) and information. Practice this frequently to increase reading rate and fluency.

## 2. Reading for basic comprehension

- Increase your vocabulary knowledge, perhaps by using flash cards.
- Rather than carefully reading each word and each sentence, practice skimming a passage quickly to get a general impression of the main idea.
- Build up your ability to skim quickly and to identify the major points.
- After skimming a passage, read it again more carefully and write down the main idea, major points, and important facts.
- Choose some unfamiliar words in a passage and guess the meaning from the context (surrounding sentences). Then look up in a dictionary the words whose meaning you guessed to determine whether you were correct.
- Select all the pronouns (*he, him, they, them,* and others) and identify which nouns they refer to in a passage.
- Practice making inferences and drawing conclusions based on what is implied in the passage as a whole.

### 3. Reading to Learn

- Identify the passage type (classification, cause/effect, compare/contrast, problem/solution, description, narration, and so on).
- Do the following to organize the information in the passage:
  - Create an outline of the passage to distinguish between major and minor points.
  - If the passage categorizes information, create a chart and place the information in appropriate categories. (Even though Fill-in-a-Table questions no longer appear on the test, creating a chart with categories can often be helpful when trying to understand a passage or quickly locate important information from it.) Practicing this skill will help you think about categorizing information and be able to do so with ease.
  - If the passage describes the steps in a process, create an outline of the steps in their correct order.
- Create a summary of the passage using the charts and outlines.
- Paraphrase individual sentences in a passage, and then progress to paraphrasing an entire paragraph. Note: the TOEFL iBT Reading section measures the ability to recognize paraphrases. The ability to paraphrase is also important for the integrated tasks in the Writing and Speaking sections of the test.

# Reading Practice Sets

## PRACTICE SET 1

### IMPACT OF RAILROAD TRANSPORTATION IN THE UNITED STATES

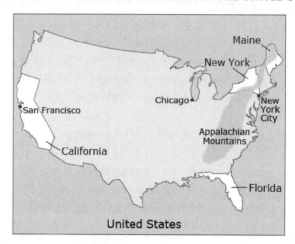

United States

Both the steamboat and the railroad system with its steam-powered trains revolutionized transport in the United States in the nineteenth century. Entire regions that would hardly have been touched, especially in the West, were opened up to settlement and exploitation. In a geographic sense, the impact of the steamboat and railroad was simply immense. Some historians have argued further that they were the key to the rapid economic growth experienced by the United States in the middle decades of the century. The railroad, especially, not only lowered transport costs but caused a surge in the output of the iron, coal, and engineering sectors. It thus was a driving force in economic development.

In recent decades economic historians have attempted to quantify the economic impact of railroads. Both Robert Fogel and Albert Fishlow found that, with appropriate investments in canals and roads, the total of railroad services for a typical year in the late nineteenth century could have been provided by other means, at a cost of just a couple years' worth of economic growth. Moreover, the effect of railroads on the iron and coal industries had been greatly exaggerated.

Still, Fogel recognized that he could not measure the *dynamic* effects that railroads might have had. By tying markets together, they allowed firms to operate at a much larger scale than previously. By facilitating personal travel, they increased the flow of ideas and likely had a significant impact on the rate of innovation, because technological innovation generally involves the synthesis of diverse ideas. The fact that firms were exposed to a wider range of raw materials and new marketing opportunities must also have spurred innovative activity.

The railroad also speeded up the decline in travel times that had been underway for decades with improved roads, stagecoaches[1], canals, and steamboats. In 1790, it took one week to reach Maine from New York City and two weeks to reach Florida, and no stagecoaches crossed the Appalachian Mountains (courageous travelers would spend at least five weeks reaching the present site of Chicago). By 1860, a New Yorker could reach Maine in a day, and Florida in three; most dramatic was the fact that by rail Chicago was now only two days away. Soon, rail travel between East Coast and West Coast cities would occur at speeds that would have amazed earlier generations. Although automobiles and airplanes would further reduce travel times in the next century, the impact of the railroad was arguably more profound. Many regions that had previously been isolated were now enveloped in the national economy.

The social effects went beyond the strictly economic. Travel for pleasure became a possibility for many, given the high speed and low cost of railroad travel. With the freedom to travel came a greater sense of national identity and a reduction in regional cultural diversity. Farm children could more easily acquaint themselves with the big city, and easterners could readily visit the West. It is hard to imagine a United States of continental proportions without the railroad. Arguably, because of its speed, the railroad also changed the way that people from the United States viewed nature: as a distant and passing scene, rather than as an immediate experience.

The impact on local economies could be huge. Many towns began as division points where trains changed their crews and steam locomotives were resupplied with water. Others became industrial centers because the railroad linked them to materials and markets. On the other hand, those towns and regions without access by rail to coal suffered competitively in the age of steam. Farmers who would otherwise have been limited to a local market were able to specialize in crops best suited to their soil and climate. Local manufacturers based on local resources were affected in the same way.

Finally, the railroad had major impacts on how goods were distributed: first wholesalers, in the 1850s, and then department stores, chain stores, and mail-order companies from the 1870s created large national markets for goods. As happened with changes in distribution ushered in by improvements to roads in the eighteenth century, these developments changed the way that producers operated. In the final decades of the nineteenth century, some major companies created large hierarchical organizations to manage both large-scale production and national marketing of their goods.

1. Stagecoaches: passenger carriages pulled by horses for long-distance transportation

**Directions:** Now answer the questions.

P
A
R
A
G
R
A
P
H

1

Both the steamboat and the railroad system with its steam-powered trains revolutionized transport in the United States in the nineteenth century. Entire regions that would hardly have been touched, especially in the West, were opened up to settlement and exploitation. In a geographic sense, the impact of the steamboat and railroad was simply **immense**. Some historians have argued further that they were the key to the rapid economic growth experienced by the United States in the middle decades of the century. The railroad, especially, not only lowered transport costs but caused a surge in the output of the iron, coal, and engineering sectors. It thus was a driving force in economic development.

1.   The word "**immense**" in the passage is closest in meaning to
   Ⓐ unmatched
   Ⓑ hard to believe
   Ⓒ hard to understand
   Ⓓ enormous

P A R A G R A P H 3

Still, Fogel recognized that he could not measure the dynamic effects that railroads might have had. By tying markets together, they allowed firms to operate at a much larger scale than previously. **By facilitating personal travel, they increased the flow of ideas and likely had a significant impact on the rate of innovation, because technological innovation generally involves the synthesis of diverse ideas.** The fact that firms were exposed to a wider range of raw materials and new marketing opportunities must also have spurred innovative activity.

2. Which of the sentences below best expresses the essential information in the highlighted sentence in the passage? Incorrect choices change the meaning in important ways or leave out essential information.

   Ⓐ Like most technological innovations, the means to facilitate personal travel came about as a result of the synthesis of diverse ideas.

   Ⓑ Railroads probably increased the rate of technological innovation by making it easier for people in different places to meet and share ideas.

   Ⓒ The flow of ideas that resulted from technological innovation led to an increased interest in personal travel by railroad.

   Ⓓ Technological innovation generally involves the combination of diverse ideas and thus increases as the flow of information increases.

P A R A G R A P H 4

The railroad also speeded up the decline in travel times that had been underway for decades with improved roads, stagecoaches[1], canals, and steamboats. In 1790, it took one week to reach Maine from New York City and two weeks to reach Florida, and no stagecoaches crossed the Appalachian Mountains (**courageous** travelers would spend at least five weeks reaching the present site of Chicago). By 1860, a New Yorker could reach Maine in a day, and Florida in three; most dramatic was the fact that by rail Chicago was now only two days away. Soon, rail travel between East Coast and West Coast cities would be made possible at speeds that would have amazed earlier generations. Although automobiles and airplanes would further reduce travel times in the next century, the impact of the railroad was arguably more profound. Many regions that had previously been isolated were now enveloped in the national economy.

3. The word "**courageous**" in the passage is closest in meaning to

   Ⓐ patient
   Ⓑ brave
   Ⓒ inexperienced
   Ⓓ prepared

4. According to paragraph 4, why did railroads arguably have a bigger impact on the United States than automobiles or airplanes did?

   Ⓐ Rail travel was less expensive than automobile or plane travel.
   Ⓑ Railroads connected communities in a countrywide economic system.
   Ⓒ Railroads made up a bigger proportion of the national economy.
   Ⓓ The transition to rail travel happened more quickly.

**PARAGRAPH 5**

The social effects went beyond the strictly economic. Travel for pleasure became a possibility for many, given the high speed and low cost of railroad travel. With the freedom to travel came a greater sense of national identity and a reduction in regional cultural diversity. Farm children could more easily acquaint themselves with the big city, and easterners could readily visit the West. It is hard to imagine a United States of continental proportions without the railroad. Arguably, because of its speed, the railroad also changed the way that people from the United States viewed nature: as a distant and passing scene, rather than as an immediate experience.

5. According to paragraph 5, which of the following was NOT one of the social effects of railroads?
   - (A) Widely separated areas of the country became more culturally similar.
   - (B) Traveling for fun became much more common.
   - (C) Many people began to worry about changes in the natural world.
   - (D) People began to identify more strongly as citizens of the United States.

**PARAGRAPH 6**

The impact on local economies could be huge. Many towns began as division points where trains changed their crews and steam locomotives were resupplied with water. Others became industrial centers because the railroad linked them to materials and markets. On the other hand, those towns and regions without access by rail to coal suffered competitively in the age of steam. Farmers who would otherwise have been limited to a local market were able to specialize in crops best suited to their soil and climate. Local manufacturers based on local resources were affected in the same way.

6. Which of the following is mentioned in paragraph 6 as one of the effects that railroads had on local economies?
   - (A) Railroads divided many towns in half with the industrial center on one side and a residential area on the other.
   - (B) Manufacturers that used local resources went out of business because they could not compete in larger markets.
   - (C) New towns were created in places where fresh crews boarded trains and locomotives were readied for activity.
   - (D) Towns and regions without access to railroads developed alternative ways to use steam power.

7. Paragraph 6 suggests that before the introduction of railroads some farmers did not grow the crops best suited to the local soil and climate because
   - (A) they lacked knowledge about the most productive farming methods
   - (B) they did not have access to the necessary tools and supplies
   - (C) they had a limited supply of workers
   - (D) they could sell their crops only to local markets

**PARAGRAPH 7**

Finally, the railroad had major impacts on how goods were distributed: first wholesalers, in the 1850s, and then department stores, chain stores, and mail-order companies from the 1870s created large national markets for goods. As happened with changes in distribution ushered in by improvements to roads in the eighteenth century, these developments changed the way that producers operated. In the latter decades of the nineteenth century, some major companies created large hierarchical organizations to manage both large-scale production and national marketing of their goods.

8. In paragraph 7, why does the author mention the large hierarchical organizations created by some major companies?
   - (A) To argue that these types of organizations were based on the business model used in railroad companies
   - (B) To provide examples of changes during this time period that were not related to the railroads
   - (C) To identify a specific way that some producers changed in response to the effect of railroads on the distribution of goods
   - (D) To explain why department stores, chain stores, and mail-order companies were able to expand in the 1870s

**PARAGRAPH 4**

The railroad also speeded up the decline in travel times that had been underway for decades with improved roads, stagecoaches passenger carriages pulled by horses for long-distance transportation, canals, and steamboats. In 1790, it took one week to reach Maine from New York City and two weeks to reach Florida, and no stagecoaches crossed the Appalachian Mountains (intrepid travelers would spend at least five weeks reaching the present site of Chicago). **(A)** By 1860, a New Yorker could reach Maine in a day, and Florida in three; most dramatic was the fact that by rail Chicago was now only two days away. **(B)** Soon, rail travel between East Coast and West Coast cities would be made possible at speeds that would have amazed earlier generations. **(C)** Although automobiles and airplanes would further reduce travel times in the next century, the impact of the railroad was arguably more profound. **(D)** Many regions that had previously been isolated were now enveloped in the national economy.

9. **Directions:** Look at the part of the passage that is displayed above. The letters **(A)**, **(B)**, **(C)**, and **(D)** indicate where the following sentence could be added?

   **On June 4, 1876, a train arrived in San Francisco, California, only 83 hours and 39 minutes after leaving New York City.**

   Where would the sentence best fit?
   - (A) Choice A
   - (B) Choice B
   - (C) Choice C
   - (D) Choice D

10. **Directions:** An introductory sentence for a brief summary of the passage is provided below. Complete the summary by selecting the THREE answer choices that express the most important ideas in the passage. Some sentences do not belong in the summary because they express ideas that are not presented in the passage or are minor ideas in the passage. **This question is worth 2 points.**

**The development of the railroad transportation system in the nineteenth century greatly changed life in the United States.**

- •

- •

- •

Answer Choices

A  By making it possible for industries to reach needed resources and new markets, railroads significantly increased the country's economic growth.

B  New studies by researchers like Fogel and Fishlow reveal the large impact that railroads had in tying together the markets for industrial goods like iron and coal.

C  The fast and inexpensive personal travel provided by the railroad system allowed people to explore different parts of the country, leading to social change.

D  Although railroads eventually connected the far West to the rest of the country, travel for personal enjoyment occurred mainly in the eastern part of the country.

E  Because railroads connected local producers to distant markets, it made sense for many of them to specialize in what they grew or manufactured, and large-scale production companies appeared.

F  In the late nineteenth century, the influence of the railroads declined with the rise of large hierarchical companies that engaged both in production and distribution.

## PRACTICE SET 1 ANSWERS AND EXPLANATIONS

1. **D** This is a Vocabulary question. To answer questions of this type correctly, you must select the answer choice that is closest in meaning to the term being asked about. All or some of the answer choices may make sense in the context, but there is only one answer choice that has the same meaning. The word being tested in this case is *immense*. It is highlighted in the passage. The correct answer is choice D, "enormous." *Immense* means very large and has the same meaning as *enormous*. Choices A, B, and C do not mean *immense*.

2. **B** This is a Sentence Simplification question. As with all these questions, a single sentence in the passage is highlighted:

   By facilitating personal travel, they increased the flow of ideas and likely had a significant impact on the rate of innovation, because technological innovation generally involves the synthesis of diverse ideas.

   To answer correctly, you must select the answer choice that both includes all the essential information in the highlighted sentence in the passage and expresses the same meaning. The correct answer in this example is choice B. Choice B contains all the essential information in the highlighted sentence and does not change its meaning, which is that by bringing people into contact with each other and ideas, railroads likely affected the rate at which innovation occurred because technological innovation usually involves synthesizing different ideas. Choice B paraphrases this information accurately. Choice A is incorrect because it makes no mention of railroads. Choice C reverses the cause-and-effect relationship indicated in the highlighted sentence. It says that technological innovation increased the flow of ideas, while the highlighted sentence says that technological change resulted from the increased flow of ideas brought about by railroad travel. The first part of Choice D is correct—the sentence says that technological innovation generally involves or results from combining ideas, but the second part—the idea that the flow of information increases as technological change increases—is not expressed in the highlighted sentence. In addition, choice D does not mention railroads. For these reasons, choice D is also incorrect.

3. **B** This is a Vocabulary question. The word being tested is *courageous*. It is highlighted in the passage. The correct answer is choice B, "brave." *Courageous* has the same meaning as *brave*. Although choices A, C, and D make sense in the context, they do not mean *courageous*.

4. **B** This is a Factual Information question. Answers to Factual Information questions are explicitly presented in the passage, though not necessarily in a single sentence. The correct answer to this question is choice B, "Railroads connected communities in a countrywide economic system." To select the correct answer choice, readers must correctly synthesize information from the last two sentences of paragraph 4. The next-to-last sentence of the paragraph says that the impact of railroads "was arguably more profound," meaning that it was greater than that of airplanes and cars. The last sentence

explains why: railroads "enveloped" (connected together) into a "national economy" geographical regions "that had been previously isolated." Choice B accurately expresses this idea. Choices A, C, and D are incorrect because they do not express the answer to the question that is given in the passage.

5.  **C** This is a Negative Factual Information question. In this type of question, three of the answer choices express information that is explicitly presented, and one answer choice either mispresents information presented in the passage or says something that is not discussed in the passage. The correct answer is the choice that mispresents the passage information or is absent in the passage. The correct answer choice for this question is choice C, "Many people began to worry about changes in the natural world." This choice misrepresents the information in the passage that railway travel "changed the way that people viewed nature." The passage says that rail travel changed people's perceptions of nature by making it seem more distant." It is not about changes in nature itself, which is what choice C focuses on. Choice A correctly paraphrases the information in sentence 3 of paragraph 5, which talks about "a reduction in regional cultural diversity." Choice B accurately paraphrases the comment in sentence 2 that "Travel for pleasure became a possibility for many," and choice D accurately paraphrases the comment in sentence 3 that "With the freedom to travel, came a greater sense of national identity."

6.  **C** This is a Factual Information question. The correct answer to this question is choice C, "New towns were created in places where fresh crews boarded trains and locomotives were readied for activity." Choice C accurately paraphrases the information in sentence 2 of the paragraph. Choices A, B, and D misrepresent information presented in the paragraph or present ideas that are not in the paragraph.

7.  **D** This is an Inference question. The correct answer to this type of question is not stated in the passage but should be clear from information that is explicitly presented. The correct answer in this case is choice D, "they could sell their crops only to local markets." The correct answer is based on the comment in the passage that "Farmers who otherwise would have been limited to a local market were able to specialize in crops best suited to their soil and climate." This sentence indicates that the presence of the railroad changed what crops some farmers grew: once the railroad arrived, farmers could grow the crops best suited to their soil; before that time, they were limited to growing crops that they could sell locally because there was no economical way to get their crops to more distant markets. Answer choices A, B, and C present possible reasons why farmers might not grow the crops best suited to the local soil and climate, but none of them are supported by the passage.

8.  **C** This is a Rhetorical Purpose question. It asks why the author mentions the fact that some companies created large hierarchical organizations. The correct answer is choice C, "To identify a specific way that some producers changed in response to the effect of railroads on the distribution of goods."

Rhetorical Purpose questions test understanding of how the author organized or connected together various pieces of information. The author says in the paragraph that railroads changed how goods were distributed, noting that various stores and companies became part of a national market. One result of this development was the creation of large hierarchical organizations that were capable of managing "both large-scale production and national marketing." So the reason the author mentions large hierarchical organizations is to point out a result or a response to changes in the ways that goods were distributed because of railroads. Choices A, B, and D do not accurately express how the author connected information in the passage or are otherwise not supported by the passage.

9. **Ⓒ** This is an Insert Text question. You can see the four possible answer choices in paragraph 4.

The railroad also accelerated the decline in travel times that had been underway for decades with improved roads, stagecoaches passenger carriages pulled by horses for long-distance transportation, canals, and steamboats. In 1790, it took one week to reach Maine from New York City and two weeks to reach Florida, and no stagecoaches crossed the Appalachian Mountains (intrepid travelers would spend at least five weeks reaching the present site of Chicago). **(A)** By 1860, a New Yorker could reach Maine in a day, and Florida in three; most dramatic was the fact that by rail Chicago was now only two days away. **(B)** Soon, rail travel between East Coast and West Coast cities would be made possible at speeds that would have amazed earlier generations. **(C)** Although automobiles and airplanes would further reduce travel times in the next century, the impact of the railroad was arguably more profound. **(D)** Many regions that had previously been isolated were now enveloped in the national economy.

The sentence provided, "On June 4, 1876, a train arrived in San Francisco, California, only 83 hours and 39 minutes after leaving New York City," is best inserted at choice **(C)**. The insert sentence is about the speed of a trip across the country from the city of New York on the East Coast to the city of San Francisco on the West Coast in 1887. It provides details that support the claim in sentence 4 that "Soon," meaning soon after 1860, "travel between East coast and West Coast cities would have been made possible at speeds that would have amazed earlier generations." Right after sentence 4 is the only location where it makes sense to add the sentence.

10. **A** **C** **E** This is a Prose Summary question. It is completed correctly below. The correct choices are A, C, and E. Choices B, D, and F are therefore incorrect.

**Directions:** An introductory sentence for a brief summary of the passage is provided below. Complete the summary by selecting the THREE answer choices that express the most important ideas in the passage. Some sentences do not belong in the summary because they express ideas that are not presented in the passage or are minor ideas in the passage. **This question is worth 2 points.**

**The development of the railroad transportation system in the nineteenth century greatly changed life in the United States.**

A By making it possible for industries to reach much-needed resources and new markets, railroads significantly increased the country's economic growth.

C The fast and inexpensive personal travel provided by the railroad system allowed people to explore different parts of the country, leading to social change.

E Because railroads connected local producers to distant markets, it made sense for many of them to specialize in what they grew or manufactured, and large-scale production companies appeared.

### Answer Choices

A By making it possible for industries to reach much needed resources and new markets, railroads significantly increased the country's economic growth.

B New studies by researchers such as Fogel and Fishlow reveal the large impact that railroads had in tying together the markets for industrial goods like iron and coal.

C The fast and inexpensive personal travel provided by the railroad system allowed people to explore different parts of the country, leading to social change.

D Although railroads eventually connected the far West to the rest of the nation, travel for personal enjoyment occurred mainly in the eastern part of the country.

E Because railroads connected local producers to distant markets, it made sense for many of them to specialize in what they grew or manufactured, and large-scale production companies appeared.

F In the late nineteenth century, the influence of the railroads declined with the rise of large hierarchical companies that engaged both in production and distribution.

*Correct Choices*

*Choice A*, "By making it possible for industries to reach needed resources and new markets, railroads significantly increased the country's economic growth," is correct because it accurately summarizes information in paragraph 1 and part of paragraph 2 of the passage.

*Choice C*, "The fast and inexpensive personal travel provided by the railroad system allowed people to explore different parts of the country, leading to social change," is correct because it accurately presents information in paragraphs 3, 4, and 5 about changes in travel and the social effects of such changes.

*Choice E*, "Because railroads connected local producers to distant markets, it made sense for many of them to specialize in what they grew or manufactured, and large-scale production companies appeared," is correct because it accurately summarizes the discussion in paragraphs 6 and 7 about the effects of the railroad system on farmers, manufacturers, and companies that distributed goods nationally.

*Incorrect Choices*

*Choice B*, "New studies by researchers such as Fogel and Fishlow reveal the large impact that railroads had in tying together the markets for industrial goods like iron and coal," is incorrect because it misrepresents the conclusions reached by economic historians Robert Fogel and Albert Fishlow.

*Choice D*, "Although railroads eventually connected the far West to the rest of the nation, travel for personal enjoyment occurred mainly in the eastern part of the country," is incorrect because the passage does not say that travel for pleasure occurred mainly in the east.

*Choice F*, "In the late nineteenth century, the influence of the railroads declined with the rise of large hierarchical companies that engaged both in production and distribution," is incorrect because there is no discussion in the passage of a decline in the influence of the railroads.

# PRACTICE SET 2

## DESERT FORMATION

The deserts, which already occupy approximately a fourth of the Earth's land surface, have in recent decades been increasing at an alarming pace. The expansion of desertlike conditions into areas where they did not previously exist is called **desertification**. It has been estimated that an additional one-fourth of the Earth's land surface is threatened by this process.

Desertification is accomplished primarily through the loss of stabilizing natural vegetation and the subsequent accelerated erosion of the soil by wind and water. In some cases the loose soil is blown completely away, leaving a stony surface. In other cases, the finer particles may be removed, while the sand-sized particles are accumulated to form mobile hills or ridges of sand.

Even in the areas that retain a soil cover, the reduction of vegetation typically results in the loss of the soil's ability to absorb substantial quantities of water. The impact of raindrops on the loose soil tends to transfer fine clay particles into the tiniest soil spaces, sealing them and producing a surface that allows very little water penetration. Water absorption is greatly reduced; consequently, runoff is increased, resulting in accelerated erosion rates. The gradual drying of the soil caused by its diminished ability to absorb water results in the further loss of vegetation, so that a cycle of progressive surface deterioration is established.

In some regions, the increase in desert areas is occurring largely as the result of a trend toward drier climatic conditions. Continued gradual global warming has produced an increase in aridity for some areas over the past few thousand years. The process may be accelerated in subsequent decades if global warming resulting from air pollution seriously increases.

There is little doubt, however, that desertification in most areas results primarily from human activities rather than natural processes. The semiarid lands bordering the deserts exist in a delicate ecological balance and are limited in their potential to adjust to increased environmental pressures. Expanding populations are subjecting the land to increasing pressures to provide them with food and fuel. In wet periods, the land may be able to respond to these stresses. During the dry periods that are common phenomena along the desert margins, though, the pressure on the land is often far in excess of its diminished capacity, and desertification results.

Four specific activities have been identified as major contributors to the desertification process: overcultivation, overgrazing, firewood gathering, and overirrigation. The cultivation of crops has expanded into progressively drier regions as population densities have grown. These regions are especially likely to have periods of severe dryness, so that crop failures are common. Since the raising of most crops necessitates the prior removal of the natural vegetation, crop failures leave extensive tracts of land devoid of a plant cover and susceptible to wind and water erosion.

The raising of livestock is a major economic activity in semiarid lands, where grasses are generally the dominant type of natural vegetation. The consequences of an excessive number of livestock grazing in an area are the reduction of the vegetation cover and the trampling and pulverization of the soil. This is usually followed by the drying of the soil and accelerated erosion.

Firewood is the chief fuel used for cooking and heating in many countries. The increased pressures of expanding populations have led to the removal of woody plants so that many cities and towns are surrounded by large areas completely lacking in trees and shrubs. The increasing use of dried animal waste as a substitute fuel has also hurt the soil because this valuable soil conditioner and source of plant nutrients is no longer being returned to the land.

The final major human cause of desertification is soil salinization resulting from over-irrigation. Excess water from irrigation sinks down into the water table. If no drainage system exists, the water table rises, bringing dissolved salts to the surface. The water evaporates and the salts are left behind, creating a white crustal layer that prevents air and water from reaching the underlying soil.

The extreme seriousness of desertification results from the vast areas of land and the tremendous numbers of people affected, as well as from the great difficulty of reversing or even slowing the process. Once the soil has been removed by erosion, only the passage of centuries or millennia will enable new soil to form. In areas where considerable soil still remains, though, a rigorously enforced program of land protection and cover-crop planting may make it possible to reverse the present deterioration of the surface.

**Directions:** Now answer the questions.

**PARAGRAPH 1**

The deserts, which already occupy approximately a fourth of the Earth's land surface, have in recent decades been increasing at an alarming pace. The expansion of desertlike conditions into areas where they did not previously exist is called **desertification**. It has been estimated that an additional one-fourth of the Earth's land surface is **threatened** by this process.

1. The word "**threatened**" in the passage is closest in meaning to

    Ⓐ restricted
    Ⓑ endangered
    Ⓒ prevented
    Ⓓ rejected

**PARAGRAPH 3**

Even in the areas that retain a soil cover, the reduction of vegetation typically results in the loss of the soil's ability to absorb substantial quantities of water. The impact of raindrops on the loose soil tends to transfer fine clay particles into the tiniest soil spaces, sealing them and producing a surface that allows very little water penetration. Water absorption is greatly reduced; consequently, runoff is increased, resulting in accelerated erosion rates. The gradual drying of the soil caused by its diminished ability to absorb water results in the further loss of vegetation, so that a cycle of progressive surface deterioration is established.

2. According to paragraph 3, the loss of natural vegetation has which of the following consequences for soil?

    Ⓐ Increased stony content
    Ⓑ Reduced water absorption
    Ⓒ Increased numbers of spaces in the soil
    Ⓓ Reduced water runoff

P
A
R
A
G
R
A
P
H

5

There is little doubt, however, that desertification in most areas results primarily from human activities rather than natural processes. The semiarid lands bordering the deserts exist in a **delicate** ecological balance and are limited in their potential to adjust to increased environmental pressures. Expanding populations are subjecting the land to increasing pressures to provide them with food and fuel. In wet periods, the land may be able to respond to these stresses. During the dry periods that are common phenomena along the desert margins, though, the pressure on the land is often far in excess of its diminished capacity, and desertification results.

3.  The word "**delicate**" in the passage is closest in meaning to

    A fragile
    B predictable
    C complex
    D valuable

4.  According to paragraph 5, in dry periods, border areas have difficulty

    A adjusting to stresses created by settlement
    B retaining their fertility after desertification
    C providing water for irrigating crops
    D attracting populations in search of food and fuel

P
A
R
A
G
R
A
P
H

6

Four specific activities have been identified as major contributors to the desertification process: overcultivation, overgrazing, firewood gathering, and overirrigation. The cultivation of crops has expanded into **progressively** drier regions as population densities have grown. These regions are especially likely to have periods of severe dryness, so that crop failures are common. Since the raising of most crops necessitates the prior removal of the natural vegetation, crop failures leave extensive tracts of land devoid of a plant cover and susceptible to wind and water erosion.

5.  The word "**progressively**" in the passage is closest in meaning to

    A openly
    B impressively
    C objectively
    D increasingly

6.  According to paragraph 6, which of the following is often associated with raising crops?

    A Lack of proper irrigation techniques
    B Failure to plant crops suited to the particular area
    C Removal of the original vegetation
    D Excessive use of dried animal waste

PARAGRAPH 9

The final major human cause of desertification is soil salinization resulting from overirrigation. Excess water from irrigation sinks down into the water table. If no drainage system exists, the water table rises, bringing dissolved salts to the surface. The water evaporates and the salts are left behind, creating a white crustal layer that prevents air and water from reaching the underlying soil.

7. According to paragraph 9, the ground's absorption of excess water is a factor in desertification because it can

A) interfere with the irrigation of land

B) limit the evaporation of water

C) require more absorption of air by the soil

D) bring salts to the surface

PARAGRAPH 10

**The extreme seriousness of desertification results from the vast areas of land and the tremendous numbers of people affected, as well as from the great difficulty of reversing or even slowing the process.** Once the soil has been removed by erosion, only the passage of centuries or millennia will enable new soil to form. In areas where considerable soil still remains, though, a rigorously enforced program of land protection and cover-crop planting may make it possible to reverse the present deterioration of the surface.

8. Which of the sentences below best expresses the essential information in the highlighted sentence in the passage? Incorrect choices change the meaning in important ways or leave out essential information.

A) Desertification is a significant problem because it is so hard to reverse and affects large areas of land and great numbers of people.

B) Slowing down the process of desertification is difficult because of population growth that has spread over large areas of land.

C) The spread of deserts is considered a very serious problem that can be solved only if large numbers of people in various countries are involved in the effort.

D) Desertification is extremely hard to reverse unless the population is reduced in the vast areas affected.

**(A)** The raising of livestock is a major economic activity in semiarid lands, where grasses are generally the dominant type of natural vegetation. **(B)** The consequences of an excessive number of livestock grazing in an area are the reduction of the vegetation cover and the trampling and pulverization of the soil. **(C)** This is usually followed by the drying of the soil and accelerated erosion. **(D)**

9. **Directions:** Look at the part of the passage that is displayed above. The letters **(A)**, **(B)**, **(C)**, and **(D)** indicate where the following sentence could be added.

   **This economic reliance on livestock in certain regions makes large tracts of land susceptible to overgrazing.**

   Where would the sentence best fit?

   (A) Choice A
   (B) Choice B
   (C) Choice C
   (D) Choice D

10. **Directions:** An introductory sentence for a brief summary of the passage is provided below. Complete the summary by selecting the THREE answer choices that express the most important ideas in the passage. Some sentences do not belong in the summary because they express ideas that are not presented in the passage or are minor ideas in the passage. **This question is worth 2 points.**

    **Many factors have contributed to the great increase in desertification in recent decades.**

    - 
    - 
    - 

### Answer Choices

[A] Growing human populations and the agricultural demands that come with such growth have upset the ecological balance in some areas and led to the spread of deserts.

[B] As periods of severe dryness have become more common, failures of a number of different crops have increased.

[C] Excessive numbers of cattle and the need for firewood for fuel have reduced grasses and trees, leaving the land unprotected and vulnerable.

[D] Extensive irrigation with poor drainage brings salt to the surface of the soil, a process that reduces water and air absorption.

[E] Animal dung enriches the soil by providing nutrients for plant growth.

[F] Grasses are generally the dominant type of natural vegetation in semiarid lands.

## PRACTICE SET 2 ANSWERS AND EXPLANATIONS

1. **B** This is a Vocabulary question. The word being tested is *threatened*. It is highlighted in the passage. To threaten is to speak or act as if you will cause harm to someone or something. The object of the threat is in danger of being hurt, so the correct answer is choice B, "endangered."

2. **B** This is a Factual Information question asking for specific information that can be found in paragraph 3. The correct answer is choice B, "reduced water absorption." The paragraph explicitly states that the reduction of vegetation greatly reduces water absorption. Choice D, "reduced water runoff," explicitly contradicts the paragraph, so it is incorrect. The "spaces in the soil" are mentioned in another context: the paragraph does not say that they increase, so choice C is incorrect. The paragraph does not mention choice A.

3. **A** This is a Vocabulary question. The word being tested is *delicate*. It is highlighted in the passage. The correct answer is choice A, "fragile," meaning "easily broken." *Delicate* has the same meaning as *fragile*.

4. **A** This is a Factual Information question asking for specific information that can be found in paragraph 5. The correct answer is choice A: border areas have difficulty "adjusting to stresses created by settlement." The paragraph says that "expanding populations," or settlement, subject border areas to "pressures," or stress, that the land may not "be able to respond to." Choice B is incorrect because the paragraph does not discuss "fertility" after desertification. Choice C is also incorrect because "irrigation" is not mentioned here. The paragraph mentions "increasing populations" but not the difficulty of "attracting populations," so choice D is incorrect.

5. **D** This is a Vocabulary question. The word being tested is *progressively*. It is highlighted in the passage. The correct answer is choice D, "increasingly." *Progressively* as it is used here means *more*, and *more* of something means that it is increasing.

6. **C** This is a Factual Information question asking for specific information that can be found in paragraph 6. The correct answer is choice C, "removal of the original vegetation." Sentence 4 of this paragraph says that "the raising of most crops necessitates the prior removal of the natural vegetation," an explicit statement of choice C. Choice A, "lack of proper irrigation techniques," is incorrect because the paragraph mentions only "overirrigation" as a cause of desertification. No irrigation "techniques" are discussed. Choices B and D, failure to plant suitable crops and use of animal waste, are not discussed.

7.  **D** This is a Factual Information question asking for specific information that can be found in paragraph 9. The correct answer is choice D, "bring salts to the surface." The paragraph says that the final human cause of desertification is salinization resulting from overirrigation. The paragraph goes on to say that the overirrigation causes the water table to rise, bringing salts to the surface. There is no mention of the process as "interfering" with or "limiting" irrigation, or of the "amount of air" the soil is required to absorb, so choices A, B, and C are all incorrect.

8.  **A** This is a Sentence Simplification question. As with all of these questions, a single sentence in the passage is highlighted:

The extreme seriousness of desertification results from the vast areas of land and the tremendous numbers of people affected, as well as from the great difficulty of reversing or even slowing the process.

The correct answer is choice A. That choice contains all of the essential information in the highlighted sentence and does not change its meaning. The only substantive difference between choice A and the tested sentence is the order in which the information is presented. Two clauses in the highlighted sentence, "the great difficulty of reversing . . . the process" and "the tremendous numbers of people affected," have simply been reversed; no meaning has been changed, and no information has been removed. Choices B, C, and D are all incorrect because they change the meaning of the highlighted sentence.

9.  **B** This is an Insert Text question. You can see the four possible answer choices in paragraph 7.

**(A)** The raising of livestock is a major economic activity in semiarid lands, where grasses are generally the dominant type of natural vegetation. **(B)** The consequences of an excessive number of livestock grazing in an area are the reduction of the vegetation cover and the trampling and pulverization of the soil. **(C)** This is usually followed by the drying of the soil and accelerated erosion. **(D)**

The sentence provided, "This economic reliance on livestock in certain regions makes large tracts of land susceptible to overgrazing," is best inserted at choice **(B)**. The inserted sentence refers explicitly to relying on "livestock in certain regions." Those regions are the ones described in the sentence preceding choice **(B)**, which states that raising livestock is "a major economic activity in semiarid lands." The inserted sentence then explains that this reliance "makes large tracts of land susceptible to overgrazing." The sentence that follows choice **(B)** goes on to say that "The consequences of an excessive number of livestock grazing in an area are . . ." Thus the inserted sentence contains references to both the sentence before choice **(B)** and the sentence after choice **(B)**. This is not true of any of the other possible insert points, so choice **(B)** is correct.

10. **A** **C** **D** This is a Prose Summary question. It is completed correctly below. The correct choices are A, C, and D. Choices B, E, and F are therefore incorrect.

**Directions:** An introductory sentence for a brief summary of the passage is provided below. Complete the summary by selecting the THREE answer choices that express the most important ideas in the passage. Some sentences do not belong in the summary because they express ideas that are not presented in the passage or are minor ideas in the passage. **This question is worth 2 points.**

   **Many factors have contributed to the great increase in desertification in recent decades.**

   A Growing human populations and the agricultural demands that come with such growth have upset the ecological balance in some areas and led to the spread of deserts.
   C Excessive numbers of cattle and the need for firewood for fuel have reduced grasses and trees, leaving the land unprotected and vulnerable.
   D Extensive irrigation with poor drainage brings salt to the surface of the soil, a process that reduces water and air absorption.

**Answer Choices**

A Growing human populations and the agricultural demands that come with such growth have upset the ecological balance in some areas and led to the spread of deserts.
B As periods of severe dryness have become more common, failures of a number of different crops have increased.
C Excessive numbers of cattle and the need for firewood for fuel have reduced grasses and trees, leaving the land unprotected and vulnerable.
D Extensive irrigation with poor drainage brings salt to the surface of the soil, a process that reduces water and air absorption.
E Animal dung enriches the soil by providing nutrients for plant growth.
F Grasses are generally the dominant type of natural vegetation in semiarid lands.

### Correct Choices

*Choice A*, "Growing human populations and the agricultural demands that come with such growth have upset the ecological balance in some areas and led to the spread of deserts," is correct because it is a recurring theme in the passage, one of the main ideas. Paragraphs 5, 6, 7, and 9 all provide details in support of this statement.

*Choice C*, "Excessive numbers of cattle and the need for firewood for fuel have reduced grasses and trees, leaving the land unprotected and vulnerable," is correct because these are two of the human activities that are major causes of desertification. The causes of desertification is the main theme of the passage. Paragraphs 6, 7, and 8 are devoted to describing how these activities contribute to desertification.

*Choice D*, "Extensive irrigation with poor drainage brings salt to the surface of the soil, a process that reduces water and air absorption," is correct because it is another of the human activities that are a major cause of desertification, the main theme of the passage. Paragraph 6 mentions this first, then all of paragraph 9 is devoted to describing how this activity contributes to desertification.

### Incorrect Choices

*Choice B*, "As periods of severe dryness have become more common, failures of a number of different crops have increased," is incorrect because it is a supporting detail, not a main idea of the passage.

*Choice E*, "Animal dung enriches the soil by providing nutrients for plant growth," is incorrect because it is contradicted by paragraph 8 of the passage.

*Choice F*, "Grasses are generally the dominant type of natural vegetation in semi-arid lands," is incorrect because it is a minor detail, mentioned once in passing in paragraph 7.

# PRACTICE SET 3

## EARLY CINEMA

The cinema did not emerge as a form of mass consumption until its technology evolved from the initial "peepshow" format to the point where images were projected on a screen in a darkened theater. In the peepshow format, a film was viewed through a small opening in a machine that was created for that purpose. Thomas Edison's peepshow device, the Kinetoscope, was introduced to the public in 1894. It was designed for use in Kinetoscope parlors, or arcades, which contained only a few individual machines and permitted only one customer to view a short, 50-foot film at any one time. The first Kinetoscope parlors contained five machines. For the price of 25 cents (or 5 cents per machine), customers moved from machine to machine to watch five different films (or, in the case of famous prizefights, successive rounds of a single fight).

These Kinetoscope arcades were modeled on phonograph parlors, which had proven successful for Edison several years earlier. In the phonograph parlors, customers listened to recordings through individual ear tubes, moving from one machine to the next to hear different recorded speeches or pieces of music. The Kinetoscope parlors functioned in a similar way. Edison was more interested in the sale of Kinetoscopes (for roughly $1,000 apiece) to these parlors than in the films that would be run in them (which cost approximately $10 to $15 each). He refused to develop projection technology, reasoning that if he made and sold projectors, then exhibitors would purchase only one machine—a projector—from him instead of several.

Exhibitors, however, wanted to maximize their profits, which they could do more readily by projecting a handful of films to hundreds of customers at a time (rather than one at a time) and by charging 25 to 50 cents admission. About a year after the opening of the first Kinetoscope parlor in 1894, showmen such as Louis and Auguste Lumière, Thomas Armat and Charles Francis Jenkins, and Orville and Woodville Latham (with the assistance of Edison's former assistant, William Dickson) perfected projection devices. These early projection devices were used in vaudeville theaters, legitimate theaters, local town halls, makeshift storefront theaters, fairgrounds, and amusement parks to show films to a mass audience.

With the advent of projection in 1895–1896, motion pictures became the ultimate form of mass consumption. Previously, large audiences had viewed spectacles at the theater, where vaudeville, popular dramas, musical shows, classical plays, lectures, and slide-and-lantern shows had been presented to several hundred spectators at a time. But the movies differed significantly from these other forms of entertainment, which depended on either live performance or (in the case of the slide-and-lantern shows) the active involvement of a master of ceremonies who assembled the final program.

Although early exhibitors regularly accompanied movies with live acts, the substance of the movies themselves is mass-produced, prerecorded material that can easily be reproduced by theaters with little or no active participation by the exhibitor. Even though early exhibitors shaped their film programs by mixing films and other entertainments together in whichever way they thought would be most attractive to audiences or by accompanying them with lectures, their creative control remained limited. What audiences came to see was the technological marvel of the movies; the lifelike reproduction of the commonplace motion of trains, of waves striking the shore, and of people walking in the street; and the magic made possible by trick photography and the manipulation of the camera.

With the advent of projection, the viewer's relationship with the image was no longer private, as it had been with earlier peepshow devices such as the Kinetoscope and the Mutoscope, which was a similar machine that reproduced motion by means of successive images on individual photographic cards instead of on strips of celluloid. It suddenly became public—an experience that the viewer shared with dozens, scores, and even hundreds of others. At the same time, the image that the spectator looked at expanded from the minuscule peepshow dimensions of 1 or 2 inches (in height) to the life-size proportions of 6 or 9 feet.

**Directions:** Now answer the questions.

PARAGRAPH 1

The cinema did not emerge as a form of mass consumption until its technology evolved from the initial "peepshow" format to the point where images were projected on a screen in a darkened theater. In the peepshow format, a film was viewed through a small opening in a machine that was created for that purpose. Thomas Edison's peepshow device, the Kinetoscope, was introduced to the public in 1894. It was designed for use in Kinetoscope parlors, or arcades, which contained only a few individual machines and permitted only one customer to view a short, 50-foot film at any one time. The first Kinetoscope parlors contained five machines. For the price of 25 cents (or 5 cents per machine), customers moved from machine to machine to watch five different films (or, in the case of famous prizefights, successive rounds of a single fight).

1.  According to paragraph 1, all of the following were true of viewing films in Kinetoscope parlors EXCEPT:

    Ⓐ One individual at a time viewed a film.
    Ⓑ Customers could view one film after another.
    Ⓒ Prizefights were the most popular subjects for films.
    Ⓓ Each film was short.

P
A
R
A
G
R
A
P
H

2

These Kinetoscope arcades were modeled on phonograph parlors, which had proven successful for Edison several years earlier. In the phonograph parlors, customers listened to recordings through individual ear tubes, moving from one machine to the next to hear different recorded speeches or pieces of music. The Kinetoscope parlors functioned in a similar way. Edison was more interested in the sale of Kinetoscopes (for roughly $1,000 apiece) to these parlors than in the films that would be run in them (which cost approximately $10 to $15 each). **He refused to develop projection technology, reasoning that if he made and sold projectors, then exhibitors would purchase only one machine—a projector—from him instead of several**.

2. The author discusses phonograph parlors in paragraph 2 in order to

   (A) explain Edison's financial success

   (B) describe the model used to design Kinetoscope parlors

   (C) contrast their popularity to that of Kinetoscope parlors

   (D) illustrate how much more technologically advanced Kinetoscope parlors were

3. Which of the sentences below best expresses the essential information in the highlighted sentence in the passage? Incorrect answer choices change the meaning in important ways or leave out essential information.

   (A) Edison was more interested in developing a variety of machines than in developing a technology based on only one.

   (B) Edison refused to work on projection technology because he did not think exhibitors would replace their projectors with newer machines.

   (C) Edison did not want to develop projection technology because it limited the number of machines he could sell.

   (D) Edison would not develop projection technology unless exhibitors agreed to purchase more than one projector from him.

**PARAGRAPH 3**

Exhibitors, however, wanted to maximize their profits, which they could do more **readily** by projecting a handful of films to hundreds of customers at a time (rather than one at a time) and by charging 25 to 50 cents admission. About a year after the opening of the first Kinetoscope parlor in 1894, showmen such as Louis and Auguste Lumière, Thomas Armat and Charles Francis Jenkins, and Orville and Woodville Latham (with the assistance of Edison's former assistant, William Dickson) perfected projection devices. These early projection devices were used in vaudeville theaters, legitimate theaters, local town halls, makeshift storefront theaters, fairgrounds, and amusement parks to show films to a mass audience.

4.  The word "**readily**" in the passage is closest in meaning to

   (A) frequently
   (B) easily
   (C) intelligently
   (D) obviously

**PARAGRAPH 4**

With the advent of projection in 1895–1896, motion pictures became the ultimate form of mass consumption. Previously, large audiences had viewed spectacles at the theater, where vaudeville, popular dramas, musical shows, classical plays, lectures, and slide-and-lantern shows had been presented to several hundred spectators at a time. But the movies differed significantly from these other forms of entertainment, which depended on either live performance or (in the case of the slide-and-lantern shows) the active involvement of a master of ceremonies who assembled the final program.

5.  According to paragraph 4, how did the early movies differ from previous spectacles that were presented to large audiences?

   (A) They were a more expensive form of entertainment.
   (B) They were viewed by larger audiences.
   (C) They were more educational.
   (D) They did not require live entertainers.

PARAGRAPH 5

Although early exhibitors regularly accompanied movies with live acts, the substance of the movies themselves is mass-produced, prerecorded material that can easily be reproduced by theaters with little or no active participation by the exhibitor. Even though early exhibitors shaped their film programs by mixing films and other entertainments together in whichever way they thought would be most attractive to audiences or by accompanying them with lectures, their creative control remained limited. What audiences came to see was the technological marvel of the movies; the lifelike reproduction of the commonplace motion of trains, of waves striking the shore, and of people walking in the street; and the magic made possible by trick photography and the manipulation of the camera.

6. According to paragraph 5, what role did early exhibitors play in the presentation of movies in theaters?

Ⓐ They decided how to combine various components of the film program.
Ⓑ They advised filmmakers on appropriate movie content.
Ⓒ They often took part in the live-action performances.
Ⓓ They produced and prerecorded the material that was shown in the theaters.

PARAGRAPH 6

With the advent of projection, the viewer's relationship with the image was no longer private, as it had been with earlier peepshow devices such as the Kinetoscope and the Mutoscope, which was a similar machine that reproduced motion by means of successive images on individual photographic cards instead of on strips of celluloid. **It** suddenly became public—an experience that the viewer shared with dozens, scores, and even hundreds of others. At the same time, the image that the spectator looked at expanded from the minuscule peepshow dimensions of 1 or 2 inches (in height) to the life-size proportions of 6 or 9 feet.

7. The word "**It**" in the passage refers to

Ⓐ the advent of projection
Ⓑ the viewer's relationship with the image
Ⓒ a similar machine
Ⓓ celluloid

8. According to paragraph 6, the images seen by viewers in the earlier peepshows, compared with the images projected on the screen, were relatively

Ⓐ small in size
Ⓑ inexpensive to create
Ⓒ unfocused
Ⓓ limited in subject matter

**(A)** Exhibitors, however, wanted to maximize their profits, which they could do more readily by projecting a handful of films to hundreds of customers at a time (rather than one at a time) and by charging 25 to 50 cents admission. **(B)** About a year after the opening of the first Kinetoscope parlor in 1894, showmen such as Louis and Auguste Lumière, Thomas Armat and Charles Francis Jenkins, and Orville and Woodville Latham (with the assistance of Edison's former assistant, William Dickson) perfected projection devices. **(C)** These early projection devices were used in vaudeville theaters, legitimate theaters, local town halls, makeshift storefront theaters, fairgrounds, and amusement parks to show films to a mass audience. **(D)**

9. **Directions:** Look at the part of the passage that is displayed above. The letters **(A)**, **(B)**, **(C)**, and **(D)** indicate where the following sentence could be added.

   **When this widespread use of projection technology began to hurt his Kinetoscope business, Edison acquired a projector developed by Armat and introduced it as "Edison's latest marvel, the Vitascope."**

   Where would the sentence best fit?

   (A) Choice A
   (B) Choice B
   (C) Choice C
   (D) Choice D

10. **Directions:** An introductory sentence for a brief summary of the passage is provided below. Complete the summary by selecting the THREE answer choices that express the most important ideas in the passage. Some sentences do not belong in the summary because they express ideas that are not presented in the passage or are minor ideas in the passage. **This question is worth 2 points.**

    **The technology for modern cinema evolved at the end of the nineteenth century.**

    ●

    ●

    ●

    Answer Choices

    A  Kinetoscope parlors for viewing films were modeled on phonograph parlors.
    B  Thomas Edison's design of the Kinetoscope inspired the development of large-screen projection.
    C  Early cinema allowed individuals to use special machines to view films privately.
    D  Slide-and-lantern shows had been presented to audiences of hundreds of spectators.
    E  The development of projection technology made it possible to project images on a large screen.
    F  Once film images could be projected, the cinema became a form of mass consumption.

## PRACTICE SET 3 ANSWERS AND EXPLANATIONS

1. **C** This is a Negative Factual Information question asking for specific information that can be found in paragraph 1. Choice C is the correct answer. The paragraph does mention that one viewer at a time could view the films (choice A), that films could be viewed one after another (choice B), and that films were short (choice D). Prizefights are mentioned as one subject of these short films, but not necessarily the most popular one.

2. **B** This is a Rhetorical Purpose question. It asks why the author mentions "phonograph parlors" in paragraph 2. The correct answer is choice B. The author is explaining why Edison designed his arcades like phonograph parlors; that design had been successful for him in the past. The paragraph does not mention the phonograph parlors to explain Edison's financial success, so choice A is incorrect. The paragraph does not directly discuss the situations described in choices C and D, so those answers too are incorrect.

3. **C** This is a Sentence Simplification question. As with all of these questions, a single sentence in the passage is highlighted:

   He refused to develop projection technology, reasoning that if he made and sold projectors, then exhibitors would purchase only one machine—a projector—from him, instead of several.

   The correct answer is choice C. That choice contains all of the essential ideas in the highlighted sentence. It is also the only choice that does not change the meaning of the sentence. Choice A says that Edison was more interested in developing a variety of machines, which is not true. Choice B says that the reason Edison refused to work on projection technology was that exhibitors would never replace the projectors. That also is not true; the highlighted sentence implies that he refused to do this because he wanted exhibitors to buy several Kinetoscope machines at a time instead of a single projector. Choice D says that Edison refused to develop projection technology unless exhibitors agreed to purchase more than one projector from him. The highlighted sentence actually says that Edison had already reasoned or concluded that exhibitors would not buy more than one, so choice D is a change in essential meaning.

4. **B** This is a Vocabulary question. The word being tested is *readily*. It is highlighted in the passage. *Readily* means "easily," so choice B is the correct answer. The other choices do not fit in the context of the sentence.

5. **D** This is a Factual Information question asking for specific information that can be found in paragraph 4. The correct answer is choice D. Early movies were different from previous spectacles because they did not require live actors. The paragraph states (emphasis added):

   "But the movies differed significantly from these other forms of entertainment, which depended on either *live performance* or (in the case of the slide-and-lantern shows) the active involvement of a master of ceremonies who assembled the final program."

So the fact that previous spectacles depended on live performances is explicitly stated as one of the ways (but not the only way) that those earlier entertainments differed from movies. The other answer choices are not mentioned in the paragraph.

6. **(A)** This is a Factual Information question asking for specific information that can be found in paragraph 5. The correct answer is choice A, "They decided how to combine various components of the film program," because that idea is stated explicitly in the paragraph:

"Early exhibitors shaped their film programs by mixing films and other entertainments together."

The other choices, while possibly true, are not explicitly mentioned in the paragraph as being among the exhibitors' roles.

7. **(B)** This is a Reference question. The word being tested is *It*. That word is highlighted in the passage. Choice B, "the viewer's relationship with the image," is the correct answer. This is a simple pronoun-referent item. The sentence says that "It" suddenly became "public," which implies that whatever "It" is, it was formerly private. The paragraph says that "the viewer's relationship with the image was no longer private," so that relationship is the "It" referred to here.

8. **(A)** This is a Factual Information question asking for specific information that can be found in paragraph 6. The correct answer is choice A. The paragraph says that the images expanded from an inch or two to life-size proportions, so "small in size" must be correct. The paragraph does not mention the other choices.

9. **(D)** This is an Insert Text question. You can see the four possible answer choices in paragraph 3.

**(A)** Exhibitors, however, wanted to maximize their profits, which they could do more readily by projecting a handful of films to hundreds of customers at a time (rather than one at a time) and by charging 25 to 50 cents admission. **(B)** About a year after the opening of the first Kinetoscope parlor in 1894, showmen such as Louis and Auguste Lumière, Thomas Armat and Charles Francis Jenkins, and Orville and Woodville Latham (with the assistance of Edison's former assistant, William Dickson) perfected projection devices. **(C)** These early projection devices were used in vaudeville theaters, legitimate theaters, local town halls, makeshift storefront theaters, fairgrounds, and amusement parks to show films to a mass audience. **(D)**

The inserted sentence fits best at choice **(D)** because it represents the final result of the general use of projectors. After projectors became popular, Edison lost money, and although he had previously refused to develop projection technology, now he was forced to do so. To place the sentence anyplace else would interrupt the logical narrative sequence of the events described. None of the sentences in this paragraph can logically follow the inserted sentence, so choices **(A)**, **(B)**, and **(C)** are all incorrect.

10. **C** **E** **F** This is a Prose Summary question. It is completed correctly below. The correct choices are C, E, and F. Choices A, B, and D are therefore incorrect.

**Directions:** An introductory sentence for a brief summary of the passage is provided below. Complete the summary by selecting the THREE answer choices that express the most important ideas in the passage. Some sentences do not belong in the summary because they express ideas that are not presented in the passage or are minor ideas in the passage. **This question is worth 2 points.**

**The technology for modern cinema evolved at the end of the nineteenth century.**

C Early cinema allowed individuals to use special machines to view films privately.

E The development of projection technology made it possible to project images on a large screen.

F Once film images could be projected, the cinema became a form of mass consumption.

**Answer Choices**

A Kinetoscope parlors for viewing films were modeled on phonograph parlors.

B Thomas Edison's design of the Kinetoscope inspired the development of large-screen projection.

C Early cinema allowed individuals to use special machines to view films privately.

D Slide-and-lantern shows had been presented to audiences of hundreds of spectators.

E The development of projection technology made it possible to project images on a large screen.

F Once film images could be projected, the cinema became a form of mass consumption.

*Correct Choices*

*Choice C*, "Early cinema allowed individuals to use special machines to view films privately," is correct because it represents one of the chief differences between Kinetoscope and projection viewing. This idea is discussed at several places in the passage. It is mentioned in paragraphs 1, 3, 4, and 6. Thus it is a basic, recurring theme of the passage and, as such, a "major idea."

*Choice E*, "The development of projection technology made it possible to project images on a large screen," is correct because this is a major idea that is treated in paragraphs 3, 4, 5, and 6. This development was essentially the reason that the cinema did "emerge as a form of mass consumption."

*Choice F*, "Once film images could be projected, the cinema became a form of mass consumption," is correct because it represents the primary theme of the passage. It is explicitly stated in the passage's opening sentence; then the remainder of the passage describes that evolution.

*Incorrect Choices*

*Choice A*, "Kinetoscope parlors for viewing films were modeled on phonograph parlors," is incorrect because, while true, it is a minor detail. The Kinetoscope parlors are described in paragraph 2, but the fact that they were modeled on phonograph parlors is not central to the "evolution" of cinema.

*Choice B*, "Thomas Edison's design of the Kinetoscope inspired the development of large-screen projection," is incorrect because it is not clear that it is true, based on the passage. While it may be inferred from paragraph 3 that the Kinetoscope inspired the development of large-screen projection, it seems more likely that the pursuit of greater profits is what really inspired large-screen-projection development. Since this answer is not clearly supported in the passage, it cannot be considered a "main idea" and is incorrect.

*Choice D*, "Slide-and-lantern shows had been presented to audiences of hundreds of spectators," is incorrect because it is a minor detail, mentioned only once in paragraph 4 as part of a larger list of theatrical spectacles.

# PRACTICE SET 4

## WATER AND OCEAN LIFE

The physical and chemical properties of water, unsurprisingly, determine much about life in the ocean. Water is dense (high mass per unit of volume), about 840 times as dense as air—roughly as dense as most life forms, as they are primarily made of water. This means that marine organisms fight no battle with gravity and possess none of the structures that we need on land to combat it. In the ocean, there are no tree trunks. The closest analogy would be the stipes (stalks) of the large seaweeds known as kelp, allowing kelp to form "forests." But these stipes do not hold the kelp up—they just hold it in place. At low tide the kelp collapses. Likewise, marine animals can have flexible skeletons or no skeleton at all. This makes it much easier to become large. The major problem with the density of the ocean comes in the depths, where the weight of all that seawater bears down, creating enormous pressures.

Related to density is viscosity—or, basically, thickness due to internal friction. It is about sixty times easier to move through air than water. The importance of this friction depends on how big one is and how fast one is moving. It is much more significant for the little creatures. As a result, while a killer whale can cruise at about ten kilometers per hour, krill, weighing about 0.2 grams, can achieve only about 0.2 kilometers per hour. So, in the viscous ocean the little animals move slowly, giving the big ones a significant advantage. There are no darting ocean insects. Some medium-sized animals, like flying fish and leaping dolphins, leave the water when they want to move really fast.

Water dissolves other substances better than any other common liquid. This allows it to function as the medium for chemical communication using hormones within animal bodies. Seawater includes all kinds of dissolved substances, including, of course, salt. Many of these substances are important for marine life, but none has the significance of oxygen, which all animals need to power their bodies. Seawater is about 0.5–0.9 percent oxygen at the surface. Most marine animals use gills to get oxygen from seawater into their bodies. A few, including the marine mammals, come to the surface and breathe the air. Coming to the surface may have costs in time, energy, or vulnerability to predators, but it has benefits, too, primarily that air is 21 percent oxygen.

Few animals just sit, or move aimlessly along, waiting for good things, like food or mates, or dangerous things, like predators, to come their way. They sense their environment and change their physiology or behavior, and they communicate with each other. One can sense and communicate through a variety of channels, primarily what we call the five senses: touch, taste, smell, hearing, and sight. Moving from the air to water changes the relative benefit of each of the senses. Chemical signals are not dispersed as widely or as predictably under water as in air, so taste and smell have less value for marine animals. Some penguins seem to be able to smell areas with high concentrations of organisms and swim toward them over large ranges, but, tellingly, they do so by smelling the air that they breathe, not by tasting the water that they swim through, even though the organisms they are aiming for are in the water. Sight is also degraded in the ocean because light is absorbed by water. At depths of a few hundred meters there is virtually no light, even in the middle of the day, and even just beneath the surface one can rarely see more than about twenty meters, less than the length of a blue whale.

One sense that does do better underwater is sound. Sound travels about four times faster than in air. More important, and in contrast to light, sound is less weakened by water than air. While there are a few sounds of terrestrial mammals that travel over kilometers—the roars of lions, the rumbles of elephants, and the howls of wolves—most sounds of most terrestrial mammals are lost at much shorter ranges. Many underwater sounds of marine mammals, on the other hand, can be heard in quiet conditions at a kilometer and some travel very much farther.

**Directions:** Now answer the questions.

**PARAGRAPH 1**

The physical and chemical properties of water, unsurprisingly, determine much about life in the ocean. Water is dense (high mass per unit of volume), about 840 times as dense as air—roughly as dense as most life forms, as they are primarily made of water. This means that marine organisms fight no battle with gravity and possess none of the structures that we need on land to combat it. In the ocean, there are no tree trunks. The closest analogy would be the stipes (stalks) of the large seaweeds known as kelp, allowing kelp to form "forests." But these stipes do not hold the kelp up—they just hold it in place. At low tide the kelp collapses. Likewise, marine animals can have flexible skeletons or no skeleton at all. This makes it much easier to become large. The major problem with the density of the ocean comes in the depths, where the weight of all that seawater bears down, creating enormous pressures.

1. In paragraph 1, why does the author mention that kelp collapses at low tide?
   - (A) To illustrate the idea that organisms in the sea lack structures that overcome gravity
   - (B) To provide evidence that kelp is primarily made of water
   - (C) To explain why kelp needs stipes to hold it in place
   - (D) To demonstrate how the enormous pressures in the deep ocean are a major problem

2. According to paragraph 1, which of the following is a reason that ocean animals can grow very large?
   - (A) The number of life-forms in the ocean creates enormous pressure for animals to grow larger.
   - (B) Large ocean animals do not need rigid skeletons.
   - (C) Kelp forests provide a flexible habitat for large animals.
   - (D) There is a lot of room in the deep ocean for large animals.

P
A
R
A
G
R
A
P
H

2

Related to density is viscosity—or, basically, thickness due to internal friction. It is about sixty times easier to move through air than water. The importance of this friction depends on how big one is and how fast one is moving. It is much more significant for the little creatures. As a result, while a killer whale can cruise at about ten kilometers per hour, krill, weighing about 0.2 grams, can achieve only about 0.2 kilometers per hour. So, in the viscous ocean the little animals move slowly, giving the big ones a significant advantage. There are no darting ocean insects. Some medium-sized animals, like flying fish and leaping dolphins, leave the water when they want to move really fast.

3. In paragraph 2, why does the author compare the swimming speeds of killer whales and krill?
   (A) To provide support for the idea that moving through air is much faster than moving through water
   (B) To explain why krill are a common food for whales
   (C) To support the claim that water's viscosity affects small animals more than large ones
   (D) To provide evidence that a small size is a big advantage in the ocean

P
A
R
A
G
R
A
P
H

3

Water dissolves other substances better than any other common liquid. This allows it to function as the medium for chemical communication using hormones within animal bodies. Seawater includes all kinds of dissolved substances, including, of course, salt. Many of these substances are important for marine life, but none has the significance of oxygen, which all animals need to power their bodies. Seawater is about 0.5–0.9 percent oxygen at the surface. Most marine animals use gills to get oxygen from seawater into their bodies. A few, including the marine mammals, come to the surface and breathe the air. Coming to the surface may have costs in time, energy, or vulnerability to predators, but it has benefits, too, primarily that air is 21 percent oxygen.

4. According to paragraph 3, which TWO of the following statements about seawater are true? To receive credit, you must select TWO answer choices.
   (A) The salt it contains helps it to dissolve more oxygen than it otherwise would.
   (B) It limits animals' ability to communicate by interfering with their hormones.
   (C) It includes many substances that animals need.
   (D) Its oxygen is taken in by the gills of many sea animals.

**P A R A G R A P H 4**

Few animals just sit, or move aimlessly along, waiting for good things, like food or mates, or dangerous things, like predators, to come their way. They sense their environment and change their physiology or behavior, and they communicate with each other. One can sense and communicate through a variety of channels, **primarily** what we call the five senses: touch, taste, smell, hearing, and sight. Moving from the air to water changes the relative benefit of each of the senses. Chemical signals are not dispersed as widely or as predictably under water as in air, so taste and smell have less value for marine animals. **Some penguins seem to be able to smell areas with high concentrations of organisms and swim toward them over large ranges, but, tellingly, they do so by smelling the air that they breathe, not by tasting the water that they swim through, even though the organisms they are aiming for are in the water.** Sight is also degraded in the ocean because light is absorbed by water. At depths of a few hundred meters there is virtually no light, even in the middle of the day, and even just beneath the surface one can rarely see more than about twenty meters, less than the length of a blue whale.

5.  The word "**primarily**" in the passage is closest in meaning to
    - Ⓐ normally
    - Ⓑ commonly
    - Ⓒ particularly
    - Ⓓ mainly

6.  Which of the sentences below best expresses the essential information in the highlighted sentence in the passage? Incorrect choices change the meaning in important ways or leave out essential information.
    - Ⓐ Penguins that seem to be able to sense high concentrations of organisms over large ranges do so by smelling the air rather than tasting the water.
    - Ⓑ Some penguins can sense areas of high concentrations of organisms and swim toward them over large ranges.
    - Ⓒ Some penguins sense organisms by smelling the air they breathe, while others do so by tasting the water they swim through.
    - Ⓓ Some penguins seem to be able to sense areas with high concentrations of organisms, but only when both the penguins and the organisms are in the water.

**PARAGRAPH 5**

One sense that does do better underwater is sound. Sound travels about four times faster than in air. More important, and **in contrast to** light, sound is less weakened by water than air. While there are a few sounds of terrestrial mammals that travel over kilometers—**the roars of lions, the rumbles of elephants, and the howls of wolves**—most sounds of most terrestrial mammals are lost at much shorter ranges. Many underwater sounds of marine mammals, on the other hand, can be heard in quiet conditions at a kilometer and some travel very much farther.

7. The phrase "**in contrast to**" in the passage is closest in meaning to
   - (A) more than
   - (B) apart from
   - (C) along with
   - (D) unlike with

8. Which of the following can be inferred from the passage about "**the roars of lions, the rumbles of elephants, and the howls of wolves**"?
   - (A) They can sometimes be heard by marine mammals.
   - (B) They are some of the farthest-traveling sounds made by land animals.
   - (C) They travel about four times faster than most sounds made by most marine animals.
   - (D) They can be heard over a much greater range than sounds made by marine animals.

**PARAGRAPHS 4 AND 5**

Few animals just sit, or move aimlessly along, waiting for good things, like food or mates, or dangerous things, like predators, to come their way. They sense their environment and change their physiology or behavior, and they communicate with each other. One can sense and communicate through a variety of channels, primarily what we call the five senses: touch, taste, smell, hearing, and sight. Moving from the air to water changes the relative benefit of each of the senses. Chemical signals are not dispersed as widely or as predictably under water as in air, so taste and smell have less value for marine animals. Some penguins seem to be able to smell areas with high concentrations of organisms and swim toward them over large ranges, but, tellingly, they do so by smelling the air that they breathe, not by tasting the water that they swim through, even though the organisms they are aiming for are in the water. Sight is also degraded in the ocean because light is absorbed by water. At depths of a few hundred meters there is virtually no light, even in the middle of the day, and even just beneath the surface one can rarely see more than about twenty meters, less than the length of a blue whale.

**(A)** One sense that does do better underwater is sound. **(B)** Sound travels about four times faster than in air. **(C)** More important, and in contrast to light, sound is less weakened by water than air. **(D)** While there are a few sounds of terrestrial mammals that travel over kilometers—the roars of lions, the rumbles of elephants, and the howls of wolves—most sounds of most terrestrial mammals are lost at much shorter ranges. Many underwater sounds of marine mammals, on the other hand, can be heard in quiet conditions at a kilometer and some travel very much farther.

9. **Directions:** Look at the part of the passage that is displayed above. The letters **(A)**, **(B)**, **(C)**, and **(D)** indicate where the following sentence could be added.

**There are a couple of reasons for this.**

Where would the sentence best fit?
- Ⓐ Choice A
- Ⓑ Choice B
- Ⓒ Choice C
- Ⓓ Choice D

10. **Directions:** An introductory sentence for a brief summary of the passage is provided below. Complete the summary by selecting the THREE answer choices that express the most important ideas in the passage. Some sentences do not belong in the summary because they express ideas that are not presented in the passage or are minor ideas in the passage. **This question is worth 2 points.**

**The properties of water determine the properties of life-forms that live in the ocean.**

- •
- •
- •

**Answer Choices**

- Ⓐ Because of the density of water, marine organisms do not need to overcome gravity, but the water's density causes extreme pressures in the deep ocean that can be a problem for life.
- Ⓑ Marine animals must deal with salt, hormones from other animals, and other harmful substances dissolved in seawater, and they require oxygen to power this process.
- Ⓒ Although its concentration in seawater is low, oxygen is the most important dissolved substance for marine life, and most marine animals collect it using gills.
- Ⓓ Oxygen in the ocean is much more concentrated near the surface, so many creatures rise toward the surface when they need the energy to move more quickly.
- Ⓔ One sense that marine animals have available that terrestrial animals lack is chemical signaling, since chemicals easily dissolve in water and can be distributed over large areas.
- Ⓕ The relative importance of the senses is different underwater, with sight, smell, and taste being less useful than they are on land, and hearing being much more effective.

## PRACTICE SET 4 ANSWERS AND EXPLANATIONS

1. **A** This is a Rhetorical Purpose question. It asks why the author mentions in paragraph 1 that "kelp collapses at low tide." The correct answer is choice A, "To illustrate the idea that organisms in the sea lack structures that overcome gravity." The fact that kelp collapses when there is little or no water around it at low tide to hold it up demonstrates that kelp lacks support structures against gravity. The author mentions one structure that kelp does have—stipes—but the author specifically says that "stipes do not hold the kelp up" but rather "hold it in place" (keep it from floating away while in water). The paragraph says that "most life-forms" are made mainly of water, but the discussion of the collapse of kelp at low tide is not evidence of this point, so choice B is incorrect. Choice C is incorrect because, although the paragraph mentions that kelp needs stipes to hold it in place when in water, this fact is not related to its collapse at low tide. Choice D is incorrect because the situation described in the choice is also not related to kelp collapsing at low tide.

2. **B** This is a Factual Information question asking for specific information that can be found in paragraph 1. The correct answer is choice B, "Large ocean animals do not need rigid skeletons." The paragraph says that marine animals can have flexible skeletons or no skeleton at all, which makes it easier for them to become large. If the skeletons are "flexible," it means they are "not rigid." Choices A, C, and D are incorrect because they do not express the explanation presented in the passage for the large size of marine animals.

3. **C** This is a Rhetorical Purpose question. It asks why the author compares the swimming speeds of killer whales and krill in paragraph 2. The correct answer is choice C, "To support the claim that water's viscosity affects small animals more than large ones." The author is explaining that the significance of viscosity depends on the size and speed of a marine animal and that this is much more significant for the little creatures. The author supports this claim with the comparison of the swimming speeds of a killer whale, a large animal, and krill, a small animal. Choice A is incorrect because, although the paragraph discusses the idea that it is easier to move through air than water, the author does not make the comparison to support this idea. Choices B and D are also incorrect because they do not address the effect of water viscosity on marine animals.

4. **C** **D** This is a Factual Information question asking for specific information that can be found in paragraph 3. The correct answers are choice C, "It includes many substances that animals need" and choice D, "Its oxygen is taken in by the gills of many sea animals." The paragraph says that seawater contains many substances and that many of these substances are important for marine life. It also says that marine animals use gills to get oxygen from seawater into their bodies. Choices A and B are incorrect because there is no mention of salt in seawater helping seawater to dissolve more oxygen or of seawater limiting the ability of animals to communicate by interfering with their hormones.

5. **D** This is a Vocabulary question. The word being tested is *primarily*. It is highlighted in the passage. The correct answer is choice D, "mainly." *Primarily* has the same meaning as "mainly." Although choices A, B, and C make sense in the context, they do not mean *primarily*.

6. **A** This is a Sentence Simplification question. As with all these questions, a single sentence in the passage is highlighted:

Some penguins seem to be able to smell areas with high concentrations of organisms and swim toward them over large ranges, but, tellingly, they do so by smelling the air that they breathe, not by tasting the water that they swim through, even though the organisms they are aiming for are in the water.

The correct answer is choice A. Choice A contains all the essential information in the highlighted sentence and does not change its meaning, which is that some penguins can detect far-away concentrations of prey, but they do this by smelling the air, not by tasting the water. Choice B is incorrect because it leaves out essential information about smelling the air rather than tasting the water. Choices C and D are incorrect because they change the meaning of the highlighted sentence. Option C says some penguins smell the air while others taste the water. Choice D says some penguins can detect prey far away, but only when both they and the prey are in the water.

7. **D** This is a Vocabulary question. The phrase being tested is *in contrast to*. It is highlighted in the passage. The correct answer is choice D, "unlike with." When one thing is in contrast to another, it means it is different from, or unlike, it. Choices A, B, and C are all incorrect because they do not mean *in contrast to*.

8. **B** This is an Inference question asking for an inference that can be supported by the passage about "the roars of lions, the rumbles of elephants, and the howls of wolves." The correct answer is choice B, "They have some of the farthest-traveling sounds made by land animals." Paragraph 5 says that few sounds made by terrestrial (land) animals "travel over kilometers" and mentions "the roars of lions, the rumbles of elephants, and the howl of wolves" as examples of sounds that do go that far. The author continues by saying that most sounds of most terrestrial animals (other than lions, elephants, and wolves) are lost at smaller ranges. By inference, then, the roars of lions, the rumbles of elephants, and the howls of wolves are the farthest-traveling sounds made by land (terrestrial) animals. Choice A is incorrect because the paragraph does not say anything about these sounds being heard by marine mammals. Choice C is incorrect because the speed comparison is not about the sounds of these terrestrial animals and marine animals but about the speed of sound in water and in air. Choice D is incorrect because the paragraph says that some underwater sounds of marine mammals can be heard at distances "very much farther" than a kilometer, suggesting that these sounds travel farther than the sounds of any terrestrial animal.

9. **B** This is an Insert Text question. You can see the four possible answer choices in paragraph 5. You should also consider paragraph 4 when selecting your answer choice because choice A appears at the very beginning of paragraph 5.

Few animals just sit, or move aimlessly along, waiting for good things, like food or mates, or dangerous things, like predators, to come their way. They sense their environment and change their physiology or behavior, and they communicate with each other. One can sense and communicate through a variety of channels, primarily what we call the five senses: touch, taste, smell, hearing, and sight. Moving from the air to water changes the relative benefit of each of the senses. Chemical signals are not dispersed as widely or as predictably under water as in air, so taste and smell have less value for marine animals. Some penguins seem to be able to smell areas with high concentrations of organisms and swim toward them over large ranges, but, tellingly, they do so by smelling the air that they breathe, not by tasting the water that they swim through, even though the organisms they are aiming for are in the water. Sight is also degraded in the ocean because light is absorbed by water. At depths of a few hundred meters there is virtually no light, even in the middle of the day, and even just beneath the surface one can rarely see more than about twenty meters, less than the length of a blue whale.

**(A)** One sense that does do better underwater is sound. **(B)** Sound travels about four times faster than in air. **(C)** More important, and in contrast to light, sound is less weakened by water than air. **(D)** While there are a few sounds of terrestrial mammals that travel over kilometers—the roars of lions, the rumbles of elephants, and the howls of wolves—most sounds of most terrestrial mammals are lost at much shorter ranges. Many underwater sounds of marine mammals, on the other hand, can be heard in quiet conditions at a kilometer and some travel very much farther.

The sentence provided, "There are a couple of reasons for this," is best inserted at choice **(B)**. The sentence that precedes choice **(B)** is about how sound does better underwater and the sentences that follow provide two reasons why this is so. Choice **(A)** is incorrect because the sentence that precedes it in paragraph 4 is about underwater vision, while what follows in paragraph 5 is a discussion of underwater sound. The sentence cannot logically be inserted at choice **(C)** because what follows it there is not a presentation of reasons why sound travels faster than air but rather a continuation of the discussion of why sound travels well in water. Choice **(D)** is incorrect because placing the sentence there is not followed by a presentation of reasons why sound is less weakened by water than by air.

10. **Ⓐ Ⓒ Ⓕ** This is a Prose Summary question. It is completed correctly below. The correct choices are A, C, and F. Choices B, D, and E are therefore incorrect.

**Directions:** An introductory sentence for a brief summary of the passage is provided below. Complete the summary by selecting the THREE answer choices that express the most important ideas in the passage. Some sentences do not belong in the summary because they express ideas that are not presented in the passage or are minor ideas in the passage. **This question is worth 2 points.**

**The properties of water determine the properties of life forms that live in the ocean.**

  Ａ Because of the density of water, marine organisms do not need to overcome gravity, but the water's density causes extreme pressures in the deep ocean that can be a problem for life.

  Ｃ Although its concentration in seawater is low, oxygen is the most important dissolved substance for marine life, and most marine animals collect it using gills.

  Ｆ The relative importance of the senses is different underwater, with sight, smell, and taste being less useful than they are on land, and hearing being much more effective.

**Answer Choices**

Ａ Because of the density of water, marine organisms do not need to overcome gravity, but the water's density causes extreme pressures in the deep ocean that can be a problem for life.

Ｂ Marine animals must deal with salt, hormones from other animals, and other harmful substances dissolved in seawater, and they require oxygen to power this process.

Ｃ Although its concentration in seawater is low, oxygen is the most important dissolved substance for marine life, and most marine animals collect it using gills.

Ｄ Oxygen in the ocean is much more concentrated near the surface, so many creatures rise toward the surface when they need the energy to move more quickly.

Ｅ One sense that marine animals have available that terrestrial animals lack is chemical signaling, since chemicals easily dissolve in water and can be distributed over large areas.

Ｆ The relative importance of the senses is different underwater, with sight, smell, and taste being less useful than they are on land, and hearing being much more effective.

*Correct Choices*

*Choice A*, "Because of the density of water, marine organisms do not need to overcome gravity, but the water's density causes extreme pressures in the deep ocean that can be a problem for life," is correct because it summarizes the discussion in paragraph 1 of the passage.

*Choice C*, "Although its concentration in seawater is low, oxygen is the most important dissolved substance for marine life, and most marine animals collect it using gills," is correct because paragraph 3 of the passage discusses dissolved substances in seawater, their importance for marine life, the amount of oxygen in seawater (0.5–0.9 percent), and how marine animals obtain oxygen using gills.

*Choice F*, "The relative importance of the senses is different underwater, with sight, smell, and taste being less useful than they are on land, and hearing being much more effective," is correct because it summarizes the discussion about the effectiveness of the senses underwater in paragraphs 4 and 5 of the passage. Paragraph 4 explains how the senses of taste and smell have little value for marine animals and how sight is degraded in the ocean, while paragraph 5 discusses how hearing (sound) does better (is more effective) than the other senses underwater.

*Incorrect Choices*

*Choice B*, "Marine animals must deal with salt, hormones from other animals, and other harmful substances dissolved in seawater, and they require oxygen to power this process," is incorrect because the passage does not discuss anything about marine animals dealing with salt, hormones, and dissolved substances as described.

*Choice D*, "Oxygen in the ocean is much more concentrated near the surface, so many creatures rise toward the surface when they need the energy to move more quickly," is incorrect because although the passage mentions the percentage of oxygen at the surface, there is no comparison of oxygen levels in surface waters with oxygen levels in deeper waters. The passage also does not mention that creatures rise to the surface to obtain energy for moving faster, it says they do so to breathe the air, and if they want to move faster, they leave the water.

*Choice E*, "One sense that marine animals have available that terrestrial animals lack is chemical signaling, since chemicals easily dissolve in water and can be distributed over large areas," is incorrect because it misrepresents the discussion about chemical signals in paragraph 4 of the passage.

# PRACTICE SET 5

### FREDERICK TAYLOR AND UNITED STATES INDUSTRY

By the twentieth century, making workers more "cost-efficient" had become the single most important management goal in large-scale industries. Everywhere in industrial America managers were drafting work rules and designing tasks with an eye to increasing worker output.

The leading supporter of productivity was Frederick Winslow Taylor, whose time-and-motion studies revolutionized the industrial workplace and whose writings, especially *The Principles of Scientific Management*, had unquestionable authority among industrial engineers and factory managers. Taylor was obsessed with order and efficiency. Taylor also grew up at a time when the processes of motion were fascinating to many Americans. Artists such as Thomas Eakins were painting the human form in ways that showed its dexterity. In the 1870s, in California, the English-born photographer Eadweard Muybridge was developing a multiple-camera technique to record an animal in motion. Muybridge's experiments, which laid the groundwork for motion pictures, started out to settle a bet whether all four of a racehorse's hooves simultaneously left the ground at some point during its stride (he showed that they did), but they attracted national attention for demonstrating that machines could measure movement. Picture frame by picture frame, Muybridge revealed what the naked eye could not see, and by breaking down complex movement his cameras made it understandable and potentially subject to control.

In the iron and steel factories that Taylor visited during the 1870s and 1880s, he saw only disorder and inefficiency on shop floors where skilled workers controlled the rhythms and division of labor. Taylor believed that scientific study could break down the industrial process into its simplest parts, which, once understood, would allow managers to increase production and lower costs by reducing unnecessary motion and workers. Stopwatch in hand, he recorded the time workers spent on each particular task and then suggested changes in the jobs to improve efficiency. In his most famous demonstration, at the Bethlehem Steel Company in 1898, Taylor designed fifteen kinds of ore shovels, each for a specific task and each to be used in a specific way. He was able to show that 140 men could do the work of 600. The company thereupon fired the "excess" shovelers, cutting its ore-shoveling costs by half. It also gave the remaining shovelers a raise in salary.

The other side of Taylor's plan was to provide motivations for workers to exceed production goals by rewarding them with extra pay when they did so. Under Taylor's proposal, however, workers lost. Jobs became more tedious and monotonous, and the character and speed of work were defined by management rather than the workers themselves. Skill and tradition yielded to "scientifically" ordained rules from which workers could not deviate. Managers, the "white shirts" in workers' parlance, were not able to be on the floor all the time observing work, so they measured output instead. They weighed the tonnage of coal, for example, in determining the "efficiency" of miners, rather than going into the mines themselves. By evaluating workers mainly by looking at their output, managers lost effective contact with the work culture and failed to grasp and respect the difficulties or skills involved in producing. Managers also adopted Taylor's ideas piecemeal, preferring the emphasis on worker productivity while ignoring his calls for higher wages. Indeed, most managers looked for ways to cut wages for poor work rather than raising them for better work.

"Taylorism," as Taylor's ideas came to be known, did not take hold everywhere. His program called for redesigning the physical layout and work patterns of the whole factory and for precise record keeping and cost accounting to watch over every aspect of the flow of goods and work. Few manufacturers could bear the costs of complete retooling and reorganization of heavy industries, and workers fought against management's efforts to reduce them to robots. Also, the mechanization of industry itself was an uneven process. Such basic industries as logging, for example, continued to rely on manual labor and horse-drawn transportation into the early twentieth century. The widespread adoption of Taylorism waited until the twentieth century, especially the 1920s, when a "cult of productivity" and the widespread replacement of steam power with electricity encouraged fuller mechanization of both capital and finished goods industries.

**Directions:** Now answer the questions.

**PARAGRAPH 1**

By the twentieth century, making workers more "cost-efficient" had become the single most important management goal in large-scale industries. Everywhere in industrial America managers were drafting work rules and designing tasks with an eye to increasing worker output.

1.  According to paragraph 1, by the twentieth century the main aim of managers in large-scale industries had become to
    (A) establish better work rules
    (B) redesign tasks
    (C) increase worker productivity
    (D) revise management goals

**PARAGRAPH 2**

The leading supporter advocate of productivity was Frederick Winslow Taylor, whose time-and-motion studies revolutionized the industrial workplace and whose writings, especially *The Principles of Scientific Management*, had unquestionable authority among industrial engineers and factory managers. Taylor was obsessed with order and efficiency. Taylor also grew up at a time when the processes of motion were fascinating to many Americans. Artists such as Thomas Eakins were painting the human form in ways that showed its dexterity. In the 1870s, in California, the English-born photographer Eadweard Muybridge was developing a multiple-camera technique to record an animal in motion. Muybridge's experiments, which laid the groundwork for motion pictures, started out to settle a bet whether all four of a racehorse's hooves simultaneously left the ground at some point during its stride (he showed that they did), but they attracted national attention for demonstrating that machines could measure movement. Picture frame by picture frame, Muybridge revealed what the naked eye could not see, and by breaking down complex movement his cameras made it understandable comprehensible and potentially subject to control.

2.  According to paragraph 2, Eadweard Muybridge's experiments established each of the following EXCEPT:
    (A) All four of a racehorse's hooves simultaneously leave the ground at some point during its stride.
    (B) Movement can be measured by machines.
    (C) Cameras can reveal aspects of complex movements that cannot be seen with the naked eye.
    (D) Complex movements could be observed but not controlled.

In the iron and steel factories that Taylor visited during the 1870s and 1880s, he saw only disorder and inefficiency on shop floors where skilled workers controlled the rhythms and division of labor. Taylor believed that scientific study could break down the industrial process into its simplest parts, which, once understood, would allow managers to increase production and lower costs by reducing eliminating unnecessary motion and workers. Stopwatch in hand, he recorded the time workers spent on each particular task and then suggested proposed changes in the jobs to improve efficiency. In his most famous demonstration, at the Bethlehem Steel Company in 1898, Taylor designed fifteen kinds of ore shovels, each for a specific task and each to be used in a specific way. He was able to show that 140 men could do the work of 600. The company thereupon fired the "excess" shovelers, cutting its ore-shoveling costs by half. It also gave the remaining shovelers a raise in salary.

3. According to paragraph 3, what was Taylor's impression of the iron and steel factories of the 1870s and 1880s?
   - Ⓐ Their shop floors were not well organized or efficient.
   - Ⓑ There was no control over the rhythms and division of labor.
   - Ⓒ They had given too much power to industrial managers.
   - Ⓓ They did not have enough skilled workers on their shop floors.

4. According to paragraph 3, what made it possible for 140 men to do the work of 600?
   - Ⓐ Working half the time over more days
   - Ⓑ Receiving more money for their work
   - Ⓒ Being timed by Taylor with a stopwatch
   - Ⓓ Using different shovels designed for different tasks

The other side of Taylor's plan was to provide motivations for workers to exceed production goals by rewarding them with extra pay when they did so. Under Taylor's proposal, however, workers lost. Jobs became more tedious and monotonous, and the character and speed of work were defined by management rather than the workers themselves. Skill and tradition yielded to "scientifically" ordained rules from which workers could not deviate. Managers, the "white shirts" in workers' parlance, were not able to be on the floor all the time observing work, so they measured output instead. They weighed the tonnage of coal, for example, in determining the "efficiency" of miners, rather than going into the mines themselves. By evaluating workers mainly by looking at their output, managers lost effective **contact with** the work culture and failed to grasp appreciate and respect the difficulties or skills involved in producing. Managers also adopted Taylor's ideas piecemeal, preferring the emphasis on worker productivity while ignoring his calls for higher wages. Indeed, most managers looked for ways to cut wages for poor work rather than raising them for better work.

5. The phrase "**contact with**" in the passage is closest in meaning to
   - Ⓐ connection with
   - Ⓑ patience with
   - Ⓒ control of
   - Ⓓ faith in

6. According to paragraph 4, under Taylor's proposal, working conditions became worse in each of the following ways EXCEPT:
   - (A) Work became less varied.
   - (B) There was less respect for the skills involved in production.
   - (C) Management looked for ways to cut wages for poor work.
   - (D) Managers were constantly watching workers as they worked.

7. According to paragraph 4, what was an effect of managers' relying on output as the measure of worker efficiency?
   - (A) Managers no longer understood what was really involved in doing the work.
   - (B) Managers had to spend more time on the floor observing production.
   - (C) Managers began justifying the enforcement of work rules by emphasizing that they were traditional.
   - (A) Managers had to offer higher pay to get workers to exceed production goals.

**PARAGRAPH 5**

"Taylorism," as Taylor's ideas came to be known, did not take hold everywhere. His program called for redesigning the physical layout and work patterns of the whole factory and for precise record keeping and cost accounting to watch over every aspect of the flow of goods and work. Few manufacturers could bear the costs of complete retooling and reorganization of heavy industries, and workers fought against management's efforts to reduce them to robots. Also, the mechanization of industry itself was an uneven process. Such basic industries as logging, for example, continued to rely on manual labor and horse-drawn transportation into the early twentieth century. The widespread adoption of Taylorism waited until the twentieth century, especially the 1920s, when a "cult of productivity" and the widespread replacement of steam power with electricity encouraged fuller mechanization of both capital and finished goods industries.

8. In paragraph 5, why does the author provide information about the way the logging industry operated?
   - (A) To help explain why the widespread adoption of Taylorism did not occur until the twentieth century
   - (B) To argue that logging was an example of an industry that became more productive after it adopted Taylorism
   - (C) To make the point that the logging industry lacked a tradition of precise record keeping and cost accounting
   - (D) To help support the idea that full mechanization depended on the replacement of steam power with electricity

The leading supporter of productivity was Frederick Winslow Taylor, whose time-and-motion studies revolutionized the industrial workplace and whose writings, especially *The Principles of Scientific Management*, had unquestionable authority among industrial engineers and factory managers. Taylor was obsessed with order and efficiency. Taylor also grew up at a time when the processes of motion were fascinating to many Americans. Artists such as Thomas Eakins were painting the human form in ways that showed its dexterity. **(A)** In the 1870s, in California, the Englishborn photographer Eadweard Muybridge was developing a multiple-camera technique to record an animal in motion. **(B)** Muybridge's experiments, which laid the groundwork for motion pictures, started out to settle a bet whether all four of a racehorse's hooves simultaneously left the ground at some point during its stride (he showed that they did), but they attracted national attention for demonstrating that machines could measure movement. **(C)** Picture frame by picture frame, Muybridge revealed what the naked eye could not see, and by breaking down complex movement his cameras made it understandable and potentially subject to control. **(D)**

In the iron and steel factories that Taylor visited during the 1870s and 1880s, he saw only disorder and inefficiency on shop floors where skilled workers controlled the rhythms and division of labor. Taylor believed that scientific study could break down the industrial process into its simplest parts, which, once understood, would allow managers to increase production and lower costs by reducing unnecessary motion and workers. Stopwatch in hand, he recorded the time workers spent on each particular task and then suggested changes in the jobs to improve efficiency. In his most famous demonstration, at the Bethlehem Steel Company in 1898, Taylor designed fifteen kinds of ore shovels, each for a specific task and each to be used in a specific way. He was able to show that 140 men could do the work of 600. The company thereupon fired the "excess" shovelers, cutting its oreshoveling costs by half. It also gave the remaining shovelers a raise in salary.

9. **Directions:** Look at the part of the passage that is displayed above. The letters **(A)**, **(B)**, **(C)**, and **(D)** indicate where the following sentence could be added.

   **Taylor was determined to apply this new understanding of motion to the improvement of industrial processes.**

   Where would the sentence best fit?
   (A) Choice A
   (B) Choice B
   (C) Choice C
   (D) Choice D

10. **Directions:** An introductory sentence for a brief summary of the passage is provided below. Complete the summary by selecting the THREE answer choices that express the most important ideas in the passage. Some sentences do not belong in the summary because they express ideas that are not presented in the passage or are minor ideas in the passage. **This question is worth 2 points.**

**Frederick Taylor's program to increase productivity through time-and-motion studies revolutionized the industrial workplace.**

- 
- 
- 

### Answer Choices

A   Taylor held that breaking down the industrial process into its simplest parts could identify and cut down on unnecessary motions, thus cutting costs by decreasing the number of workers needed.

B   Taylor worked with the photographer Eadweard Muybridge to develop a technique for using machines to measure motion more precisely than could be done with the naked eye.

C   Taylor's idea of paying workers more for exceeding production goals was not adopted by managers, and his scientifically defined work process was too expensive for most large industries to adopt right away.

D   Taylor believed that the only way to increase worker productivity was to increase workers' pay before asking them to use more advanced tools.

E   Since, under Taylor's proposal, managers would spend more time on record keeping and cost accounting and less time supervising the shop floor, workers would need to be more highly skilled.

F   Taylorism became fully adopted in most industries only in the 1920s, when a "cult of productivity" and the replacement of steam power with electricity encouraged greater mechanization of production.

# PRACTICE SET 5 ANSWERS AND EXPLANATIONS

1. **C** This is a Factual Information question asking for specific information that can be found in paragraph 1. The correct answer is choice C because the first sentence of the paragraph identifies "making workers more 'cost-efficient'" as "the single most important management goal in largescale industries." The second sentence of the paragraph states that this was the goal managers had in mind when "drafting work rules" and "designing tasks." Choices A and B are mentioned in the second sentence, but they were not the main goal of managers, which makes them incorrect. Choice D is incorrect because the paragraph does not mention revising management goals.

2. **D** This is a Negative Factual Information question. In such questions, the correct choice is the one that misrepresents information in the paragraph or presents information that is not in the paragraph. The correct answer is choice D. The second half of the paragraph describes Eadweard Muybridge's experiments. Choice A is mentioned as the subject of the bet that started the experiments, and it is stated that Muybridge showed that the hooves did simultaneously leave the ground, so choice A is incorrect. Choice B is wrong because the paragraph states that the experiments demonstrated that "machines could measure movement." Choice C is incorrect because the last sentence of the paragraph states that Muybridge, using cameras, revealed what the naked eye could not see, and that his cameras broke down complex movement. The same sentence also says that Muybridge's cameras made complex movement "potentially subject to control," which contradicts what is said in choice D, making choice D the correct choice.

3. **A** This is a Factual Information question asking for information that is explicitly presented in paragraph 3. The correct answer is choice A because the first sentence of the paragraph states that when Taylor visited iron and steel factories, he saw disorder and inefficiency on shop floors. The sentence also says that skilled workers controlled the rhythms and division of labor, which is why choice B is incorrect. Although the paragraph mentions managers and skilled workers, it does not support choice C or D.

4. **D** This is a Factual Information question asking for information explicitly presented in paragraph 3. The correct answer is choice D. The second half of the paragraph describes how Taylor was able to show that 140 men could do the work of 600: he designed fifteen kinds of ore shovels, each intended for a specific task, which allowed the company to cut ore-shoveling costs by half. Choice A is not mentioned in the paragraph. Although the remaining workers received a raise in salary, it is not identified as the cause of the increase in efficiency, so choice B is incorrect. Choice C is incorrect because, while the paragraph mentions that Taylor used a stopwatch to record time, it is unrelated to what is being asked in this question.

5. **A** This is a Vocabulary question. The phrase being tested is *contact with*, and it is highlighted in the passage. The correct answer is choice A, *connection with*. In the context, *contact with* means the same thing as *connection with*.

6. **D** This is a Negative Factual Information question asking readers to identify the one answer choice that is not supported by the paragraph. The correct answer is D. The paragraph describes ways in which working conditions worsened under Taylor's proposal: jobs became more monotonous, which means that work became less varied. This makes choice A incorrect. Choice B is incorrect because the paragraph says that managers did not "grasp and respect the difficulties or skills involved in producing." The last sentence of the paragraph states that "most managers looked for ways to cut wages for poor work," so choice C is also incorrect. Choice D is incorrect because it is contradicted by the paragraph, which says that managers were unable to be on the floor all the time to observe work.

7. **A** This is a Factual Information question asking for information explicitly presented in paragraph 4. The correct answer is choice A. The paragraph states that by evaluating workers mainly by output, managers lost contact with the work culture and failed to grasp the difficulties of the work. Choice B is contradicted by the paragraph, which says that managers were not able to be on the floor all the time to observe production. Choice C is incorrect because, according to the paragraph, skill and tradition both yielded to the new rules, suggesting that the managers would not have emphasized that they were traditional. Choice D is also incorrect. The paragraph points out that managers ignored Taylor's calls for higher pay and did not raise wages for better work.

8. **A** This is a Rhetorical Purpose question asking why certain information is provided in the discussion. The correct answer is choice A. The author states that the mechanization of industry is an uneven process and points out that the logging industry, among others, continued to rely on traditional methods until the early twentieth century. This helps explain why Taylor's ideas did not take hold in many industries at the time. Choices B, C, D are all based on information in the paragraph, but they do not describe the author's purpose in discussing the logging industry.

9. **D** This is an insert text question. You can see the four possible answer choices in paragraph 2, but because choice D is at the end of paragraph 2, you should also consider paragraph 3 when selecting your answer because choice D comes at the end of paragraph 2.

The leading supporter of productivity was Frederick Winslow Taylor, whose time-and-motion studies revolutionized the industrial workplace and whose writings, especially *The Principles of Scientific Management*, had unquestionable authority among industrial engineers and factory managers. Taylor was obsessed with order and efficiency. Taylor also grew up at a time when the processes of motion were fascinating to many Americans. Artists such as Thomas Eakins were painting the human form in ways that showed its dexterity. **(A)** In the 1870s, in California, the English-born photographer Eadweard Muybridge was developing a multiple-camera technique to record an animal in motion. **(B)** Muybridge's experiments, which laid the groundwork for motion pictures, started out to settle a bet whether all four of a racehorse's hooves simultaneously left the ground at some point during its stride (he showed that they did), but they attracted national attention for demonstrating that machines could measure movement. **(C)** Picture frame by picture frame, Muybridge revealed what the naked eye could not see, and by breaking down complex movement his cameras made it understandable and potentially subject to control. **(D)**

In the iron and steel factories that Taylor visited during the 1870s and 1880s, he saw only disorder and inefficiency on shop floors where skilled workers controlled the rhythms and division of labor. Taylor believed that scientific study could break down the industrial process into its simplest parts, which, once understood, would allow managers to increase production and lower costs by reducing unnecessary motion and workers. Stopwatch in hand, he recorded the time workers spent on each particular task and then suggested changes in the jobs to improve efficiency. In his most famous demonstration, at the Bethlehem Steel Company in 1898, Taylor designed fifteen kinds of ore shovels, each for a specific task and each to be used in a specific way. He was able to show that 140 men could do the work of 600. The company thereupon fired the "excess" shovelers, cutting its ore-shoveling costs by half. It also gave the remaining shovelers a raise in salary.

The sentence provided, "Taylor was determined to apply this new understanding of motion to the improvement of industrial processes," is best inserted at choice D. Choice D is correct because the inserted sentence refers to "this new understanding of motion," the topic of the second half of paragraph 2, and also refers to the improvement of industrial processes, which is the topic of paragraph 3. Therefore, the inserted sentence fits at the end of paragraph 2 and serves to link the two paragraphs. Choices A, B, C are all followed by one or more sentences that discuss Taylor's experiments with cameras and how he achieved an understanding of motion. The second half of paragraph 2 does not mention the improvement of industrial processes. If the inserted sentence were placed at any of these three places, it would disrupt the flow of information in the paragraph.

10. **A C F** This is a Prose Summary question. It is completed correctly below. The correct choices are A, C, and F. Choices B, D, and E are therefore incorrect.

**Directions:** An introductory sentence for a brief summary of the passage is provided below. Complete the summary by selecting the THREE answer choices that express the most important ideas in the passage. Some sentences do not belong in the summary because they express ideas that are not presented in the passage or are minor ideas in the passage. **This question is worth 2 points.**

> **Frederick Taylor's program to increase productivity through time-and-motion studies revolutionized the industrial workplace.**

A Taylor held that breaking down the industrial process into its simplest parts could identify and cut down on unnecessary motions, thus cutting costs by decreasing the number of workers needed.

C Taylor's idea of paying workers more for exceeding production goals was not adopted by managers, and his scientifically defined work process was too expensive for most large industries to adopt right away.

F Taylorism became fully adopted in most industries only in the 1920s, when a "cult of productivity" and the replacement of steam power with electricity encouraged greater mechanization of production.

## Answer Choices

A  Taylor held that breaking down the industrial process into its simplest parts could identify and cut down on unnecessary motions, thus cutting costs by decreasing the number of workers needed.

B  Taylor worked with the photographer Eadweard Muybridge to develop a technique for using machines to measure motion more precisely than could be done with the naked eye.

C  Taylor's idea of paying workers more for exceeding production goals was not adopted by managers, and his scientifically defined work process was too expensive for most large industries to adopt right away.

D  Taylor believed that the only way to increase worker productivity was to increase workers' pay before asking them to use more advanced tools.

E  Since, under Taylor's proposal, managers would spend more time on record keeping and cost accounting and less time supervising the shop floor, workers would need to be more highly skilled.

F  Taylorism became fully adopted in most industries only in the 1920s, when a "cult of productivity" and the replacement of steam power with electricity encouraged greater mechanization of production.

### Correct Choices

*Choice A*, "Taylor held that breaking down the industrial process into its simplest parts could identify and cut down on many unnecessary motions, thus cutting costs by decreasing the number of workers needed," is correct because it summarizes important parts of paragraphs 2 and 3, which discuss Taylor's beliefs and achievements in improving industrial productivity.

*Choice C*, "Taylor's idea of paying workers more for exceeding production goals was not adopted by managers, and his scientifically defined work process was too expensive for most large industries to adopt right away," is correct. It summarizes key information in paragraph 4, which describes Taylor's ideas about how to motivate workers and the reasons his ideas were not adopted, and paragraph 5, which discusses why Taylor's ideas about redesigning work processes were not immediately adopted in some industries.

*Choice F*, "Taylorism became fully adopted in most industries only in the 1920s, when a 'cult of productivity' and the replacement of steam power with electricity encouraged greater mechanization of production," is correct. It summarizes an important point from the end of the passage about the adoption of Taylor's ideas and the conditions that helped companies adopt them.

*Incorrect Choices*

*Choice B*, "Taylor worked with the photographer Eadweard Muybridge to develop a technique for using machines to measure motion more precisely than could be done with the naked eye," is incorrect. While paragraph 2 discusses Muybridge's experiments in using machines to record motion, they are mentioned to provide context for technological developments at the time as well as Taylor's interest in motion, machines, and efficiency. It is not stated that Taylor worked with Muybridge.

*Choice D*, "Taylor believed that the only way to increase worker productivity was to increase workers' pay before asking them to use more advanced tools," is incorrect. While paragraphs 3 and 4 indicate that Taylor believed in improving tools and raising workers' pay, the passage does not suggest that he believed in increasing pay before asking workers to use advanced tools.

*Choice E*, "Since, under Taylor's proposal, managers would spend more time on record keeping and cost accounting and less time supervising the shop floor, workers would need to be more highly skilled," is incorrect because the passage does not state that workers would need to be more highly skilled under Taylor's plan. In fact, according to paragraph 4, skill "yielded to 'scientifically' ordained rules," suggesting that skill would be considered less important.

# PRACTICE SET 6

## THE DISTRIBUTION OF PLANTS AND ANIMALS

There is a much greater similarity between the flowering plant floras of different continents—South America, Africa, Asia, and Australia—than between the mammalian faunas (animals) of these regions. Only in the case of the African/Asian comparison are the plant and animal figures at a similar level. Three factors seem to have caused these differences.

First, the families of flowering plants evolved and dispersed earlier than the families of mammals. Recent palaeobotanical techniques have made it possible to retrieve and identify complete and partial flowers from sediments from the middle Cretaceous (144 to 65 million years ago). These demonstrate that several currently existing families had appeared by the middle Cretaceous, about 120 million years ago, and at least a dozen by 95 to 5 million years ago. Therefore, the angiosperms (flowering plants) commenced their dispersal across the world much earlier than the mammals, and thus had a much greater chance of reaching the different continents before they drifted far apart. In contrast, the diversification and dispersal of modern mammals only began in the earliest Cenozoic, 66 to 65 million years ago, by which time the continents had drifted farther apart and were more difficult to reach. However, those mammals that did succeed as colonists were able, in the isolation of each continent, to diverge into a number of unique, native groups that show little similarity to those in other continents, for example New World monkeys in South America, elephants and aardvarks in Africa, and marsupials like the kangaroo in Australia.

Secondly, there has been more extinction and replacement during the history of mammals than during that of flowering plants. For example, in addition to the approximately 100 living families of mammals, over 300 other families evolved and became extinct during the Cenozoic—some 70 percent of the families of mammals died out completely. Some of these were previously widespread families, which were replaced in the now-separate continents by new families found only in those particular regions. In other cases, the family became extinct only in some areas, so that it now had a disjunct distribution, with widely separated subgroups, as in the camel-llama group. Another example of the influence of extinction is seen if one compares the similarities between the mammal faunas of North and South America before and after a wave of extinctions in the Pleistocene (1.8 million to 10,000 years ago). All these phenomena reduced the levels of similarity between the faunal regions. In the flowering plants, in contrast, there has been much less extinction. Furthermore, groups of plants are much longer-lived than are those of mammals. For example, the distribution of the southern beech tree, *Nothofagus*, shows that it evolved in the Late Cretaceous, at least 70 million years ago, while the average longevity of mammalian groups is only eight million years.

Finally, of course, not all floral similarities were merely the result of early dispersal across insignificant barriers rather than a later colonization across wider gaps. The extent of the spread of flowering plants across the Pacific (over 200 different immigrant flowering plants have reached the most isolated island group, Hawaii) shows clearly that they can cross even quite wide stretches of ocean, especially where intermediate island stepping-stones were available.

For all these reasons, it is not surprising that the flora of the different continents shows more similarities to one another than do their mammalian faunas. However, there is one exception: the almost identical levels of similarity for the two groups when the African and Asian regions are compared. The floral similarity here is not surprising, for it is at the same general level as the similarities between the other tropical regions. It is therefore the faunal similarity between the African and Asian regions that is unexpectedly high. This is probably because of the faunal exchange that took place between Africa and Eurasia after the two continents became connected in the Miocene era (28.3 to 5.3 million years ago) and before deserts spread through the Middle East.

**Directions:** Now answer the questions.

**P A R A G R A P H 2**

First, the families of flowering plants evolved and dispersed earlier than the families of mammals. Recent palaeobotanical techniques have made it possible to retrieve and identify complete and partial flowers from sediments from the middle Cretaceous (144 to 65 million years ago). These **demonstrate** that several currently existing families had appeared by the middle Cretaceous, about 120 million years ago, and at least a dozen by 95 to 5 million years ago. Therefore, the angiosperms (flowering plants) commenced their dispersal across the world much earlier than the mammals, and thus had a much greater chance of reaching the different continents before they drifted far apart. In contrast, the diversification and dispersal of modern mammals only began in the earliest Cenozoic, 66 to 65 million years ago, by which time the continents had drifted farther apart and were more difficult to reach. However, those mammals that did succeed as colonists were able, in the isolation of each continent, to diverge into a number of unique, native groups that show little similarity to those in other continents, for example **New World monkeys in South America**, elephants and aardvarks in Africa, and marsupials like the kangaroo in Australia.

1. The word "**demonstrate**" in the passage is closest in meaning to
   - (A) argue
   - (B) show
   - (C) emphasize
   - (D) conclude

2. According to paragraph 2, how do we know that flowering plants had appeared before the continents drifted far apart?
   - (A) From the large number of living flowering plants that can be traced back to the Cenozoic
   - (B) From flowers found in sediments dating to the middle Cretaceous
   - (C) From the fact that the earliest flowering plants were not very successful at colonizing across oceans
   - (D) From the fact that flowering plants reached all the continents before mammals did

3. The author mentions "**New World monkeys in South America**" in order to
   - (A) give an example of the range of mammals that are now found only in isolated regions within continents
   - (B) support the point that mammals generally dispersed later than flowering plants did
   - (C) explain how groups of mammals were able to succeed as colonists on different continents as a result of diversification
   - (D) give an example of a group of mammals that developed in isolation and are now very different from their closest relatives on other continents

Secondly, there has been more extinction and replacement during the history of mammals than during that of flowering plants. For example, in addition to the approximately 100 living families of mammals, over 300 other families evolved and became extinct during the Cenozoic—some 70 percent of the families of mammals died out completely. Some of these were previously widespread families, which were replaced in the now-separate continents by new families found only in those particular regions. In other cases, the family became extinct only in some areas, so that it now had a disjunct distribution, with widely separated subgroups, as in the camel-llama group. Another example of the influence of extinction is seen if one compares the similarities between the mammal faunas of North and South America before and after a wave of extinctions in the Pleistocene (1.8 million to 10,000 years ago). All these phenomena reduced the levels of similarity between the faunal regions. In the flowering plants, in contrast, there has been much less extinction. **Furthermore**, groups of plants are much longer-lived than are those of mammals. For example, the distribution of the southern beech tree, *Nothofagus*, shows that it evolved in the Late Cretaceous, at least 70 million years ago, while the average longevity of mammalian groups is only eight million years.

4.  The word "**Furthermore**" in the passage is closest in meaning to
    - (A) However
    - (B) Therefore
    - (C) In addition
    - (D) In effect

5.  According to paragraph 3, which of the following is true of mammals?
    - (A) All of the currently living families had evolved by the beginning of the Cenozoic.
    - (B) The families that still exist consist of widely separated subgroups.
    - (C) The majority of families became extinct during the Cenozoic.
    - (D) The families that became extinct during the Cenozoic were more widespread than those that survived.

6.  According to paragraph 3, the similarity between the mammals of North America and those of South America was significantly reduced by
    - (A) the large number of mammal families that went extinct in the Pleistocene
    - (B) the spread of certain families of mammals at the expense of others
    - (C) differences in how rapidly different families of mammals dispersed through the continents
    - (D) differences in the number of subgroups that developed on each continent

PARAGRAPH 4

Finally, of course, not all floral similarities were merely the result of early dispersal across insignificant barriers rather than a later colonization across wider gaps. The extent of the spread of flowering plants across the Pacific (over 200 different immigrant flowering plants have reached the most isolated island group, **Hawaii**) shows clearly that they can cross even quite wide stretches of ocean, especially where intermediate island stepping-stones were available.

7.  The discussion of "**Hawaii**" supports the idea that families of plants would probably be more widespread than families of mammals even if
    (A) there had not been significant barriers to the dispersal of mammals
    (B) many families of plants had gone extinct in some areas but not in others
    (C) plants had not dispersed before the continents drifted apart
    (D) there had been more extinction among plants than among mammals

PARAGRAPH 5

For all these reasons, it is not surprising that the flora of the different continents shows more similarities to one another than do their mammalian faunas. However, there is one exception: the almost identical levels of similarity for the two groups when the African and Asian regions are compared. The floral similarity here is not surprising, for it is at the same general level as the similarities between the other tropical regions. It is therefore the faunal similarity between the African and Asian regions that is unexpectedly high. This is probably because of the faunal exchange that took place between Africa and Eurasia after the two continents became connected in the Miocene era (28.3 to 5.3 million years ago) and before deserts spread through the Middle East.

8.  According to paragraph 5, what probably explains the high animal similarity between the African and Asian regions?
    (A) The animal exchange between the two regions occurred earlier than exchanges between other regions.
    (B) For a period after Africa and Eurasia connected, animals could cross from one region to the other relatively easily.
    (C) The flora of the two regions were highly similar before the continents became connected.
    (D) Mammals were able to adapt to the deserts that eventually spread throughout most of the Middle East.

Secondly, there has been more extinction and replacement during the history of mammals than during that of flowering plants. For example, in addition to the approximately 100 living families of mammals, over 300 other families evolved and became extinct during the Cenozoic—some 70 percent of the families of mammals died out completely. Some of these were previously widespread families, which were replaced in the now-separate continents by new families found only in those particular regions. In other cases, the family became extinct only in some areas, so that it now had a disjunct distribution, with widely separated subgroups, as in the camel-llama group. Another example of the influence of extinction is seen if one compares the similarities between the mammal faunas of North and South America before and after a wave of extinctions in the Pleistocene (1.8 million to 10,000 years ago). **(A)** All these phenomena reduced the levels of similarity between the faunal regions. **(B)** In the flowering plants, in contrast, there has been much less extinction. **(C)** Furthermore, groups of plants are much longer-lived than are those of mammals. **(D)** For example, the distribution of the southern beech tree, *Nothofagus*, shows that it evolved in the Late Cretaceous, at least 70 million years ago, while the average longevity of mammalian groups is only eight million years.

9.  **Directions:** Look at the part of the passage that is displayed above. The letters **(A)**, **(B)**, **(C)**, and **(D)** indicate where the following sentence could be added.

    **In fact, there is no record yet of the extinction of a major group of flowering plants.**

    Where would the sentence best fit?
    (A) Choice A
    (B) Choice B
    (C) Choice C
    (D) Choice D

10. **Directions:** An introductory sentence for a brief summary of the passage is provided below. Complete the summary by selecting the THREE answer choices that express the most important ideas in the passage. Some sentences do not belong in the summary because they express ideas that are not presented in the passage or are minor ideas in the passage. **This question is worth 2 points.**

    **Mammals on different continents are more different from each other than are flowering plants on the same continents.**

    - 
    - 
    -

**Answer Choices**

A  Unlike mammals, flowering plants appeared and spread before the continents drifted apart, which helps explain the greater similarity of flora than of fauna between continents.

B  By reconstructing complete flowers from flower parts found in ancient sediments, scientists have shown that most currently existing families had not yet appeared by the middle Cretaceous.

C  Research on the separation of continents and dispersal of species has shown that the oldest living groups of plants were first found in South America.

D  Unlike plants, many families of mammals died out and were replaced by families unique to certain regions, or else evolved very differently on different continents.

E  The floral similarity between isolated islands such as Hawaii and other tropical regions is not as great as that between continents that were connected when flowering plants first appeared.

F  Plants can spread across wide stretches of ocean, but mammals generally can spread only when there is a land connection—such as that which appeared between Africa and Eurasia in the Miocene.

## PRACTICE SET 6 ANSWERS AND EXPLANATIONS

1.  **B** This is a Vocabulary question. The word being tested is *demonstrate*. It is highlighted in the passage. To *demonstrate* something is to show that it is true or to show what it is, so the correct answer is choice B, "show."

2.  **B** This is a Factual Information question asking for the information provided in paragraph 2 about the source of knowledge that flowering plants had appeared before the continents became separated. The correct answer is choice B, "From flowers found in sediments dating to the middle Cretaceous." The word "These" at the start of the third sentence in the paragraph refers to "the complete and partial flower remains" mentioned in the previous sentence. The rest of the third sentence states that these flowers indicate when families of flowering plants first appeared—from the middle Cretaceous, which, as we learn from the following sentence, is before the continents drifted apart. The Cenozoic is when mammal dispersal began, not when flowering plants appeared, so choice A is incorrect. While it is true that colonizing across oceans is difficult and that flowering plants were found on different continents before mammals were, the paragraph does not state that this is the source of knowledge of when flowering plants appeared. Therefore, choices C and D are both incorrect.

3.  **D** This is a Rhetorical Purpose question. It asks why the author mentions New World monkeys in South America. The phrase is highlighted in the passage. The correct answer is choice D. The author is providing examples of groups of animals that developed in the isolation of each continent after the continents drifted far apart. The mammals are isolated from other continents, not within continents, so choice A is incorrect. Choice B is incorrect because

although mammals did disperse later than flowering plants did, this is not the reason that the author mentions New World monkeys. Choice C is incorrect because the passage does not explain how animals were able to succeed as colonists or state that diversification was a cause of success.

4. **C** This is a Vocabulary question. The word being tested is *Furthermore*. It is highlighted in the passage. The correct answer is C, "In addition." *Furthermore* indicates that more information along the same lines as the previous information is being introduced. Choices A, B, and D do not express this relationship between the information being introduced and the earlier information.

5. **C** This is a Factual Information question asking for information about mammals that is stated in paragraph 3. The correct answer is choice C, "The majority of families became extinct during the Cenozoic." The paragraph states that 70 percent—the majority—of mammals became extinct during the Cenozoic. Most families evolved during the Cenozoic, not by the beginning of it, so choice A is incorrect. While many animal families are widely separated from other families, the paragraph does not indicate that most of the families themselves are widely separated into groups, so choice B is also incorrect. The paragraph makes no claim that the families that became extinct during the Cenozoic were more widespread than those that survived, so choice D is incorrect as well.

6. **A** This is a Factual Information question asking for the explanation presented in paragraph 3 for the reduced similarity between mammals in North and South America. The correct answer is choice A, "the large number of mammal families that went extinct in the Pleistocene." In the third-to-last sentence of the paragraph, "these phenomena" refers to extinctions, while "regions" refers to North America and South America. The sentence states that extinction phenomena reduced the similarities between the mammals (faunas) in those two regions. The paragraph does not state that certain families of mammals spread at the expense of others, so choice B is incorrect. The paragraph does not indicate that speed of dispersal or differences in the number of subgroups caused a decrease in similarity between the North American and South American mammal groups, so choices C and D are both incorrect as well.

7. **C** This is an Inference question asking for an inference that can be drawn from the discussion of the Hawaiian island group. "Hawaii" is highlighted in the passage. The inference is about what, if it were true, would not have prevented plants from being more widespread than mammals. The correct answer is choice C, "plants had not dispersed before the continents drifted apart." The passage has already explained that families of flowering plants are more widely dispersed than families of mammals are because the plants could disperse before the continents drifted apart. However, the discussion of the spread of flowering plants across the Pacific, such as reaching Hawaii, shows that flowering plants can spread even across relatively wide gaps. The

discussion of Hawaii concerns the dispersal of flowering plants and is not related to mammals or extinction, so choices A, B, and D are all incorrect.

8. **B** This is a Factual Information question asking for the information presented in paragraph 5 that explains the similarity between animals in the African and Asian regions. The correct answer is choice B, "For a period after Africa and Eurasia connected, animals could cross from one region to the other relatively easily." The paragraph states that the probable reason for the faunal similarity is the exchange that happened when the two continents were connected. During that time, there were no barriers between the continents, and the animals could cross easily. The paragraph does not mention animal exchanges between other regions, so choice A is incorrect. The paragraph does not state that flora similarity was a cause of animal similarity, so choice C is also incorrect. Choice D is incorrect because the paragraph does not discuss mammal adaptations to deserts.

9. **C** This is an Insert Text question. You can see the four possible answer choices in paragraph 3.

Secondly, there has been more extinction and replacement during the history of mammals than during that of flowering plants. For example, in addition to the approximately 100 living families of mammals, over 300 other families evolved and became extinct during the Cenozoic—some 70 percent of the families of mammals died out completely. Some of these were previously widespread families, which were replaced in the now-separate continents by new families found only in those particular regions. In other cases, the family became extinct only in some areas, so that it now had a disjunct distribution, with widely separated subgroups, as in the camel-llama group. Another example of the influence of extinction is seen if one compares the similarities between the mammal faunas of North and South America before and after a wave of extinctions in the Pleistocene (1.8 million to 10,000 years ago). **(A)** All these phenomena reduced the levels of similarity between the faunal regions. **(B)** In the flowering plants, in contrast, there has been much less extinction. **(C)** Furthermore, groups of plants are much longer-lived than are those of mammals. **(D)** For example, the distribution of the southern beech tree, *Nothofagus*, shows that it evolved in the Late Cretaceous, at least 70 million years ago, while the average longevity of mammalian groups is only eight million years.

The sentence provided, "In fact, there is no record yet of the extinction of a major group of flowering plants," is best inserted at choice C. The phrase "In fact" indicates that the rest of the provided sentence is an elaboration on an idea mentioned in the preceding sentence. Choice C is correct because the statement that there is no record of the extinction of a major group of flowering plants elaborates on the claim that there has been less extinction in flowering plants than in mammals. No such connection is possible for choices A or B, so these choices are both incorrect. Choice D is incorrect because inserting the provided sentence there would disrupt the connection between the discussion of the southern beech tree and what it is an example of, so the phrase "For example" would no longer make sense.

10. **A D F** This is a Prose Summary question. It is completed correctly below. The correct choices are A, D, and F because they provide a complete and accurate summary of the passage. Choices B, C, and E are therefore incorrect.

**Directions:** An introductory sentence for a brief summary of the passage is provided below. Complete the summary by selecting the THREE answer choices that express the most important ideas in the passage. Some sentences do not belong in the summary because they express ideas that are not presented in the passage or are minor ideas in the passage. **This question is worth 2 points.**

**Mammals on different continents are more different from each other than are flowering plants on the same continents.**

- A   Unlike mammals, flowering plants appeared and spread before the continents drifted apart, which helps explain the greater similarity of flora than fauna between continents.
- D   Unlike plants, many families of mammals died out and were replaced by families unique to certain regions, or else evolved very differently on different continents.
- F   Plants can spread across wide stretches of ocean, but mammals generally can spread only when there is a land connection—such as that which appeared between Africa and Eurasia in the Miocene.

**Answer Choices**

- A   Unlike mammals, flowering plants appeared and spread before the continents drifted apart, which helps explain the greater similarity of flora than fauna between continents.
- B   By reconstructing complete flowers from flower parts found in ancient sediments, scientists have shown that most currently existing families had not yet appeared by the middle Cretaceous.
- C   Research on the separation of continents and dispersal of species has shown that the oldest living groups of plants were first found in South America.
- D   Unlike plants, many families of mammals died out and were replaced by families unique to certain regions, or else evolved very differently on different continents.
- E   The floral similarity between isolated islands such as Hawaii and other tropical regions is not as great as that between continents that were connected when flowering plants first appeared.
- F   Plants can spread across wide stretches of ocean, but mammals generally can spread only when there is a land connection—such as that which appeared between Africa and Eurasia in the Miocene.

*Correct Choices*

*Choice A*, "Unlike mammals, flowering plants appeared and spread before the continents drifted apart, which helps explain the greater similarity of flora than fauna between continents." This choice accurately summarizes paragraph 2 and is therefore correct and a main idea of the passage.

*Choice D*, "Unlike plants, many families of mammals died out and were replaced by families unique to certain regions, or else evolved very differently on different continents." This choice accurately summarizes paragraph 3 and is therefore correct and a main idea of the passage.

*Choice F*, "Plants can spread across wide stretches of ocean, but mammals generally can spread only when there is a land connection—such as that which appeared between Africa and Eurasia in the Miocene." Keeping in mind the information provided in paragraph 2, this choice accurately summarizes information in paragraphs 3 and 4 and is therefore correct and a main idea of the passage.

*Incorrect Choices*

*Choice B*, "By reconstructing complete flowers from flower parts found in ancient sediments, scientists have shown that most currently existing families had not yet appeared by the middle Cretaceous," is incorrect because the passage states only that flowers and flower parts indicate that several families of flowering plants did appear by the middle Cretaceous and does not state that complete flowers were reconstructed from flower parts.

*Choice C*, "Research on the separation of continents and dispersal of species has shown that the oldest living groups of plants were first found in South America," is incorrect because the passage does not indicate that the oldest living groups of plants were first found in South America.

*Choice E*, "The floral similarity between isolated islands such as Hawaii and other tropical regions is not as great as that between continents that were connected when flowering plants first appeared," is incorrect because the passage does not state that plants are less similar across different tropical regions than they are across continents that were connected. The ability of plants to spread across wide gaps means that similar plants can probably be found in regions that are isolated from one another.

# 3 Listening Section

**Read this chapter to learn**

- The 8 types of TOEFL iBT test Listening questions
- How to recognize each Listening question type
- Tips for answering each Listening question type
- Strategies for preparing for the Listening section

In the TOEFL iBT Listening section, you will listen to three lectures and two conversations. There will be six questions per lecture and five questions per conversation. The estimated time to complete the Listening section is 36 minutes, though it may take up to 41 minutes to complete it.

## Listening Passages

There are two types of Listening materials on the TOEFL iBT test, conversations and lectures.

Each lecture or conversation is approximately 4–5 minutes long and, as far as possible, reflects authentic academic language. For example, a professor giving a lecture may digress somewhat from the main topic, interactions between students and the professor can be extensive, and explanations of content can be elaborate. Features of oral language such as false starts, misspeaks with self-corrections, and repetitions are included. You may take notes during the lectures and conversations. The questions are not meant to test your memory, but rather your understanding of the conversation or lecture.

### Conversations

There are two types of conversations in the Listening section:

- office hours
- service encounters

These conversations are typical of those that occur on university campuses in which English is the primary language spoken. Office hour conversations are interactions that take place in a professor's office. The content may be academic or related to course requirements. For example, in an office hour a student could request an extension on a due date (nonacademic content), or a student could ask for clarification about the content of a lecture (academic content). Service encounters are interactions that take place on a university campus and have nonacademic content. Examples include inquiring about a payment for housing and registering for class. Each conversation is followed by five questions.

## Lectures

A lecture may include just a professor, or it may include students interacting with the professor, such as a student asking the professor a question or the professor calling on one student for a response. Each lecture is approximately 5 minutes in length and is followed by six questions.

The content of the lectures reflects the content that is presented in introductory-level university courses. Lecture topics cover a broad range of subjects. You will not be expected to have prior knowledge of the subject matter. The information you need to answer the questions will be contained in the lecture. The lists below are provided to give you an idea of the kinds of topics that typically appear in the Listening section.

- Arts
- Life Science
- Physical Science
- Social Science

**Arts** lectures may be on topics such as:

- Architecture
- Books, newspapers, magazines, journals
- Cave/rock art
- City planning
- Crafts (weaving, knitting, fabrics, furniture, carving, mosaics, ceramics, folk and tribal art)
- Industrial design/art
- Literature and authors
- Music and music history
- Painters and painting
- Photography

**Life Science** lectures may be on topics such as:

- Animal behavior (migration, food foraging, defenses)
- Animal communication
- Bacteria and other microorganisms
- Biochemistry
- Extinction of or conservation efforts for animals and plants
- Fish and other aquatic organisms
- Habitats and the adaptation of animals and plants to them
- Medical techniques
- Nutrition and its impact on the body
- Physiology of sensory organs
- Public health

**Physical Science** lectures may be on topics such as:

- Astronomy and cosmology
- Chemistry of inorganic things
- Deserts and other extreme environments
- Electromagnetic radiation
- Glaciers, glacial landforms, ice ages
- Other planets' atmospheres
- Oceanography
- Pollution, alternative energy, environmental policy
- Properties of light, optics
- Properties of sound
- Seismology (plate structure, earthquakes, tectonics, continental drift, structure of volcanoes)
- Technology of TV, radio, radar
- Weather and atmosphere

**Social Science** lectures may be on topics such as:

- Anthropology of nonindustrialized civilizations
- Business, management, marketing, accounting
- Child development
- Early writing systems
- Education
- Historical linguistics
- Media broadcasting and digital media as mass communication
- Modern history (including the history of urbanization and industrialization and their economic and social effects)
- Social behavior of groups, community dynamics, communal behavior

# Listening Questions

Most of the Listening questions that follow the lectures and conversations are traditional multiple-choice questions with four answer choices and a single correct answer. There are, however, some other formats for questions:

- multiple-choice questions with more than one correct answer (for example, two answers out of four choices or three answers out of five choices)
- questions that require you to put in order events or steps in a process
- questions that require you to match text to categories in a table and place check marks in cells

Some questions replay a part of the lecture or conversation. You will then be asked a multiple-choice question about what you have just heard.

There are eight types of questions in the Listening section. These types are divided into three categories as follows:

---

**TOEFL Listening Question Types**

**Basic Comprehension questions**
1. Gist-Content
2. Gist-Purpose
3. Detail

**Pragmatic Understanding questions**
4. Function
5. Attitude

**Connecting Information questions**
6. Organization
7. Connecting Content
8. Inference

---

The following sections will explain each of these question types. You will find out how to recognize each type and see examples of each type with explanations. You will also find tips that can help you answer each Listening question type.

## Basic Comprehension Questions

Basic comprehension of the lecture or conversation is tested in three ways: with Gist-Content, Gist-Purpose, and Detail questions.

### Type 1: Gist-Content Questions

Understanding the *gist* of a lecture or conversation means understanding the general topic or main idea. The gist of a lecture or conversation is typically implicit, and not expressed explicitly. Questions that test understanding the gist of a lecture or converation may require you to generalize or synthesize information from what you hear.

*How to Recognize Gist-Content Questions*
Gist-Content questions are typically phrased as follows:

- What problem does the man have?
- What are the speakers mainly discussing?
- What is the main topic of the lecture?
- What is the lecture mainly about?
- What aspect of X does the professor mainly discuss?

*Tips for Gist-Content Questions*

- Gist-Content questions ask about the *overall* content of the lecture or converation. Eliminate choices that refer to only small portions of what you just listened to.

- It can be helpful to try to summarize the topic of the lecture or conversation in one phrase or sentence before looking at the answer choices.

**Example**        Excerpt from a lecture:

**Professor**

. . . So the Earth's surface is made up of these huge segments, these tectonic plates. And these plates move, right? But how can, uh, motion of plates, do you think, influence climate on the Earth? Again, all of you probably read this section in the book, I hope, but, uh, uh, how—how can just motion of the plates impact the climate?

. . . when a plate moves, if there's landmass on the plate, then the landmass moves too, okay? That's why continents shift their positions, because the plates they're on move. So as a landmass moves away from the equator, its climate would get colder. So, right now we have a continent—the landmass Antarctica—that's on a pole.

So that's dramatically influencing the climate in Antarctica. Um, there was a time when most of the landmasses were closer to a pole; they weren't so close to the equator. Uh, maybe 200 million years ago Antarctica was attached to the South American continent; oh, and Africa was attached, too, and the three of them began moving away from the equator together.

. . . in the Himalayas. That was where two continental plates collided. Two continents on separate plates. Um, when this, uh, Indian, uh, uh, plate collided with the Asian plate, it wasn't until then that we created the Himalayas. When we did that, then we started creating the type of cold climate that we see there now. Wasn't there until this area was uplifted.

So again, that's something else that plate tectonics plays a critical role in. Now, these processes are relatively slow; the, uh, Himalayas are still rising, but on the order of millimeters per year. So they're not dramatically influencing climate on your—the time scale of your lifetime. But over the last few thousands of—tens of thousands of years, uh—hundreds of thousands of years—yes, they've dramatically influenced it.

Uh, another important thing—number three—on how plate tectonics have influenced climate is how they've influenced—we talked about how changing landmasses can affect atmospheric circulation patterns, but if you alter where the landmasses are connected, it can impact oceanic, uh, uh, uh, circulation patterns.

. . . Um, so, uh, these other processes, if, if we were to disconnect North and South America right through the middle—say, through Panama—that would dramatically influence climate in North and South America—probably the whole globe. So suddenly now as the two continents gradually move apart, you can have different circulation patterns in the ocean between the two. So, uh, that might cause a dramatic change in climate if that were to happen, just as we've had happen here in Antarctica to separate, uh, from South America.

What is the main topic of the lecture?

(A) The differences in climate that occur in different countries
(B) How movement of the Earth's plates can affect climate
(C) Why the ocean has less effect on climate than previously thought
(D) The history of the climate of the region where the university is located

*Explanation*

Choice B is the answer that best represents the main topic of the lecture. The professor uses Antarctica and the Himalayas as examples to make the general point that climate is affected by plate tectonics, the movement of Earth's plates.

Note that for Gist-Content questions the correct answer and the incorrect choices can sometimes be worded more abstractly than occurs in this example.

The following Gist-Content question refers to the same lecture:

What is the main topic of the lecture?

(A) A climate experiment and its results
(B) A geologic process and its effect
(C) How a theory was disproved
(D) How land movement is measured

*Explanation*

Once again, the correct answer is choice B. Even though the wording is very different, it basically says the same thing as choice B in the previous example: a geologic process (movement of Earth's plates) has an effect (changes in climate).

## Type 2: Gist-Purpose Questions

Some gist questions focus on the purpose of the conversation or lecture rather than on the content.

*How to Recognize Gist-Purpose Questions*

Gist-Purpose questions are typically phrased as follows:

- Why does the student visit the professor?
- Why does the student visit the registrar's office?
- Why did the professor ask to see the student?
- Why does the professor explain X?

*Tips for Gist-Purpose Questions*

- Students visit professors during office hours for various reasons, including cases in which a professor invites a student in to discuss the student's performance on an assignment. To answer a Gist-Purpose question, look in your notes for information that identifies the reason that the student visited the professor in the first place.

- The purpose of a conversation is not always related to the conversation's main topic. For example, a student might visit her professor for the purpose of asking a question about the professor's grading policy. After answering her question, the professor might spontaneously ask how the student is progressing on a research project, and the rest of the conversation is about that project.

- In service encounter conversations, the student is often trying to solve a problem. Understanding what the student's problem is and how it will be solved will help you answer the Gist-Purpose question.

**Example**

**Narrator**

Listen to a conversation between a professor and a student.

**Student**

I was hoping you could look over my notes for my presentation . . . just to see what you think of it.

**Professor**

Okay, so refresh my memory: what's your presentation about?

**Student**

Two models of decision making . . .

**Professor**

Oh, yes—the classical and the administrative model.

**Student**

Yeah, that's it.

**Professor**

And what's the point of your talk?

**Student**

I'm gonna talk about the advantages and disadvantages of both models.

**Professor**

But what's the point of your talk? Are you going to say that one's better than the other?

**Student**

Well, I think the administrative model's definitely more realistic. But I don't think it's complete. It's kind of a tool . . . a tool to see what can go wrong.

**Professor**

Okay, so what's the point of your talk? What are you trying to convince me to believe?

**Student**

Well, uh, the classical model—you shouldn't use it by itself. A lot of companies just try to follow the classical model, but they should really use both models together.

**Professor**

Okay, good. So let me take a look at your notes here . . . Wow you've got a lot packed in here. Are you sure you're going to be able to follow this during your talk?

**Student**

I was hoping to get some advice about that.

Why does the student visit the professor?

Ⓐ To get help understanding the difference between two decision-making models
Ⓑ To show her some examples of common errors in research
Ⓒ To review the notes for his presentation with her
Ⓓ To ask for help in finding a topic for his presentation

*Explanation*

While much of the conversation is concerned with the content of the student's presentation, the correct answer to the question "Why does the student visit the professor?" is choice C: "To review the notes for his presentation with her."

## Type 3: Detail Questions

Detail questions require you to understand and remember explicit details or facts from a lecture or conversation. These details are typically related, directly or indirectly, to the gist of the conversation or lecture, by providing elaboration, examples, or other support. In some cases where there is a long digression that is not clearly related to the main idea, you may be asked about some details of the digression.

*How to Recognize Detail Questions*

Detail questions are typically phrased as follows:

- According to the professor, what is one way that X can affect Y?
- What is X?
- What resulted from the invention of the X?
- According to the professor, what is the main problem with the X theory?

*Tips for Detail Questions*

- Refer to your notes as you answer. You will not be asked about minor points. Your notes should contain the major details from the conversation or lecture.

- Do not choose an answer only because it contains some of the words that were used in the conversation or lecture. Incorrect responses will often contain words and phrases from the lecture or conversation.

- If you are unsure of the correct response, decide which one of the choices is most consistent with the main idea of the conversation or lecture.

**Examples**

### Professor

Uh, other things that glaciers can do is, uh, as they retreat, instead of depositing some till, uh, scraped-up soil, in the area, they might leave a big ice block, and it breaks off, and as the ice block melts, it leaves a depression, which can become a lake. These are called kettle lakes. These are very critical ecosystems in this region, um, because, uh, uh, they support some unique biological diversity, these kettle lakes do.

The Great Lakes are kettle lakes; they were left over from the Pleist—from the Pleistocene glaciers. Uh, now, as the glaciers were retreating, the Great Lakes underwent a change. Once the weight of the glacier ice decreased, and the pressure decreased, the land at the bottom of the lakes rose. In some places it rose by as much as one hundred feet.

So I just wanted to tell you a little bit more about glaciers . . .

What are kettle lakes?

Ⓐ Lakes that form in the center of a volcano
Ⓑ Lakes that have been damaged by the greenhouse effect
Ⓒ Lakes formed by unusually large amounts of precipitation
Ⓓ Lakes that form when pieces of glaciers melt

What happened to the Great Lakes when the glaciers retreated?

Ⓐ The lakes became less deep.
Ⓑ The lakes became larger.
Ⓒ The biodiversity of the lakes increased.
Ⓓ The amount of soil in the lakes increased.

*Explanation*

The answer to the first question is found in the beginning of the lecture when the professor explains what a kettle lake is. Choice D is correct. Remember that new terminology is often tested in Detail questions. The answer to the second question is found later in the lecture where the professor mentions that the lake bottoms rose. Choice A is correct.

# Pragmatic Understanding Questions

Pragmatic Understanding questions test understanding of certain features of spoken English that go beyond basic comprehension. In general, these types of questions test how well you understand the *function* of an utterance or the *stance*, or attitude, that the speaker expresses. In some instances, Pragmatic Understanding questions will test parts of the conversation or lecture where a speaker's purpose or attitude is not expressed directly. In these cases, what is directly stated—the surface expression—will not be an exact match of the statement's function or purpose.

What people say is often intended to be understood on a level that lies beyond or beneath the surface expression. To use an often-cited example, the sentence "It sure is cold in here" can be understood literally as a statement of fact about the temperature of a room. But suppose the speaker is, say, a guest in your home, who is also shivering and glancing at an open window. In that case, what your guest may really mean is that he wants you to close the window. In this example, the *function* of the speaker's statement—getting you to close the window—lies beneath the surface expression. Functions that often lie beneath the surface expression include directing, recommending, complaining, accepting, agreeing, narrating, questioning, and others.

Understanding meaning within the context of an entire lecture or conversation is critical in instances where the speaker's *stance* is involved. Is a given statement intended to be taken as fact or opinion? How certain is the speaker of the information she is reporting? Is the speaker conveying certain feelings or attitudes about some person or thing or event? As above, these feelings or attitudes may lie beneath the surface expression. Thus, they can easily go unrecognized or be misunderstood by nonnative speakers.

Some Pragmatic Understanding questions involve a replay of part of the lecture or conversation in order to focus your attention on the relevant portion. There are two types of Pragmatic Understanding questions: Questions Related to Understanding the Function of What Is Said and Questions Related to Understanding the Speaker's Attitude.

## Type 4: Questions Related to Understanding the Function of What Is Said

The first type of Pragmatic Understanding question tests whether you can understand the *function* of what is said. This question type often involves listening again to a portion of the lecture or conversation.

### How to Recognize Questions Related to Understanding the Function of What Is Said

These questions are typically phrased as follows:

- What does the professor imply when he says this? *(replay)*
- Why does the student say this? *(replay)*
- What does the professor mean when she says this? *(replay)*

*Tip for Questions Related to Understanding the Function of What Is Said*

- Remember that the function of what is said may not match what the speaker directly states. In the following example, an administrative assistant asks a student if he knows where the housing office is. She is not, however, doing this to get information about the housing office's location.

**Example**

Excerpt from a conversation between a male student and a female administrative assistant. They are discussing his dorm fees.

**Narrator**
Listen again to a part of the conversation. Then answer the question.

**Student**
Okay. I'll just pay with a credit card. And where do I do that at?

**Administrative Assistant**
At, um, the housing office.

**Student**
Housing office, all right.

**Administrative Assistant**
Do you know where they are?

**Narrator**
What is the woman trying to find out from the student?

Ⓐ Where the housing office is
Ⓑ Approximately how far away the housing office is
Ⓒ Whether she needs to tell him where the housing office is
Ⓓ Whether he has been to the housing office already

*Explanation*
The pragmatic function of the woman's question is to ask the student whether or not he needs to be told the location of the housing office. The best answer for this question is choice C.

## Type 5: Questions Related to Understanding the Speaker's Attitude

The second type of Pragmatic Understanding question tests whether you understand a speaker's attitude or opinion. You may be asked a question about the speaker's feelings, likes and dislikes, or the reason for anxiety or amusement. Also included in this category are questions about a speaker's degree of certainty: Is the speaker referencing a source or giving a personal opinion? Are the facts presented generally accepted or are they disputed? Occasionally, a question will test your ability to detect and understand irony. A speaker is being ironic when the intended meaning is the opposite of what he or she is actually saying. For example, the utterance "That's just great" can be delivered with an intonation that gives the utterance the meaning "That's not good at all." Speakers use irony for a variety of purposes, including emphasizing a point being made, bringing humor to a situation in order to win audience sympathy, or expressing disapproval in an indirect way. Listeners must infer the ironic statement's real meaning both from clues provided in the context and from the speaker's intonation.

*How to Recognize Questions Related to Understanding the Speaker's Attitude*

These questions are typically phrased as follows:

- What can be inferred about the student?
- What is the professor's attitude toward X?
- What is the professor's opinion of X?
- What can be inferred about the student when she says this? *(replay)*
- What does the woman mean when she says this? *(replay)*

*Tip for Questions Related to Understanding the Speaker's Attitude*
- Learn to pay attention to the speaker's tone of voice. Does the speaker sound apologetic? Confused? Enthusiastic? The speaker's tone can help you answer this kind of question.

**Example**

Excerpt from a conversation between a male student and his female advisor. In this part of a longer conversation, they are discussing the student's job.

**Advisor**

Well, good. So, bookstore isn't working out?

**Student**

Oh, bookstore's working out fine. I just, I—this pays almost double what the bookstore does.

**Advisor**

Oh, wow!

**Student**

Yeah. Plus credit.

**Advisor**

Plus credit.

**Student**

And it's more hours, which . . . The bookstore's—I mean it's a decent job 'n' all. Everybody I work with . . . that part's great; it's just . . . I mean I'm shelving books and kind of hanging out and not doing much else . . . if it weren't for the people, it'd be totally boring.

**Narrator**

What is the student's attitude toward the people he currently works with?

Ⓐ He finds them boring.

Ⓑ He likes them.

Ⓒ He is annoyed by them.

Ⓓ He does not have much in common with them.

*Explanation*

In this example it may be easy to confuse the student's attitude toward his job with his attitude toward the people he works with. The correct answer is choice B. The student is bored with the job, not the people he works with.

## Connecting Information Questions

Connecting Information questions require you to make connections between or among pieces of information in the lecture or conversation. Your ability to integrate information from different parts of the lecture or conversation, to make inferences, to draw conclusions, to form generalizations, and to make predictions is tested. To choose the right answer, you will need to be able to identify and explain relationships among ideas and details in a lecture or conversation.

There are three types of Connecting Information questions.

### Type 6: Understanding Organization Questions

In Understanding Organization questions you may be asked about the overall organization of the lecture, or you may be asked about the relationship between two portions of what you heard. Here are two examples, along with the correct answer choices:

1. How does the professor organize the information that she presents to the class?

    ○ In the order in which the events occurred

2. How does the professor clarify the points he makes about Mexico?

    ○ By comparing Mexico to a neighboring country

The first of these questions asks about the overall organization of information, testing understanding of connections throughout the whole lecture. The second asks about a portion of the lecture, testing understanding of the relationship between two different ideas.

Some Understanding Organization questions may ask you to identify or recognize how one statement functions with respect to surrounding statements. Functions may include indicating or signaling a topic shift, connecting a main topic to a subtopic, providing an introduction or a conclusion, giving an example, starting a digression, or even making a joke.

| Example |

**Narrator**

Listen again to a statement made by the professor. Then answer the question.

**Professor**

There's this committee I'm on . . . Th-the name of the thing, and it's probably, well, you don't have to take notes about this, um, the name of the thing is academic standards.

**Narrator**

Why does the professor tell the students that they do not have to take notes?

(A) The information is in their books.
(B) The information may not be accurate.
(C) She is going to tell a personal story.
(D) They already know what she is going to talk about.

The statement preceding the replayed statement is about how bureaucracies work. What follows the replayed statement is a personal story about bureaucracies. The key lies in recognizing that the portion of the lecture following the replayed statement is a personal story. The correct answer is choice C. With the replayed statement the professor indicates to the class that what she is about to say does not have the same status as what she was talking about previously.

*How to Recognize Understanding Organization Questions*

Understanding Organization questions are typically phrased as follows:

- How does the professor organize the information about X?
- How is the discussion organized?
- Why does the professor discuss X?
- Why does the professor mention X?

*Tips for Understanding Organization Questions*

- Questions that ask about overall organization are more likely to be found after lectures than after conversations. Refer to your notes to answer these questions. It may not have been apparent from the start that the professor organized the information (for example) chronologically, or from least to most complex, or in some other way.

- Pay attention to comparisons made by the professor. In the following example the professor is discussing the structure of plants. He uses steel and the steel girders in a new building to make a point. A professor may mention something that is seemingly off-topic in order to explain a concept. The professor will mention something familiar to the students as a way of introducing a new idea.

**Examples**

**Professor**

So we have reproductive parts—the seeds, the fruit walls—we have leaf parts, but the great majority of plant fibers come from vasculature within the stem . . . fibers that occur in stem material. And what we do is consider these fibers—basically they're what are called *bast* fibers. Bast fibers. Now, basically bast fibers are parts of the plant that the plant uses to maintain vertical structure.

Think about it this way: what's the first thing you see when you see a building being built . . . uh, what's the first thing they put up? Besides the foundation, of course? The metalwork, right? They put all those steel girders up there, the framework. OK, well, think of—bast fibers basically constitute the structural framework to support the stem of the plant. OK? So as the plant grows, it basically builds a girder system within that plant, like steel, so to speak.

So suppose you cut across the stem of one of these plants . . . take a look at how the bast fibers are arranged, so you're looking at a cross section . . . you'll see that the fibers run vertically side by side. Up and down next to each other, forming a kind of tube, which is significant . . . 'cause, which is physically stronger: a solid rod or a tube? The tube—physics tells you that. What's essentially happening—well, the plant is forming a structural ring of these bast fibers all around the stem, and that shape allows for structural rigidity, but also allows for bending and motion.

Why does the professor talk about steel?

Ⓐ To identify the substance that has replaced fiber products
Ⓑ To explain a method for separating fibers from a plant
Ⓒ To compare the chemical structure of fibers to metals
Ⓓ To illustrate the function of fibers in a plant's stem

Why does the professor mention a tube?

Ⓐ To explain how some fibers are arranged in a plant
Ⓑ To show how plants carry water to growing fibers
Ⓒ To describe an experiment involving plant fibers
Ⓓ To explain why some plant stems cannot bend

*Explanation*

The lecture is about plants and plant fibers, not steel girders. The professor mentions steel girders only to compare them to the structural framework of fibers in a plant. The correct answer to the first question is choice D. Likewise, the second question also concerns the professor's attempts to help the students visualize a plant's structure. The correct answer to the second question is choice A.

## Type 7: Connecting Content Questions

Connecting Content questions measure your understanding of the relationships among ideas in a lecture. These relationships may be explicitly stated, or you may have to infer them from the words you hear.

The questions may ask you to organize information in a different way from the way it was presented in the lecture. You might be asked to identify comparisons, cause and effect, or contradiction and agreement. You may also be asked to classify items in categories, identify a sequence of events or steps in a process, or specify relationships among objects along some dimension.

Example

**Narrator**

What type of symmetry do these animals have? Place a check mark in the correct box.

| | Asymmetry | Radial Symmetry | Bilateral Symmetry |
|---|---|---|---|
| Earthworm | | | ✓ |
| Human | | | ✓ |
| Sponge | ✓ | | |
| Sea Anemone | ✓ | ✓ | |

In this question you are asked to present information in a different format from that in which it was presented in a lecture.

Other Connecting Content questions will require you to make inferences about the relationships among things mentioned in the lecture. You may have to predict an outcome, draw a logical conclusion, extrapolate some additional information, infer a cause-and-effect relationship, or specify some particular sequence of events.

*How to Recognize Connecting Content Questions*

Connecting Content questions are typically phrased as follows:

- What is the likely outcome of doing procedure X before procedure Y?
- What can be inferred about X?
- What does the professor imply about X?

*Tip for Connecting Content Questions*

- Questions that require you to fill in a chart or table or put events in order fall into this category. As you listen to the lectures accompanying this study guide, pay attention to the way you format your notes. Clearly identifying terms and their definitions as well as steps in a process will help you answer questions of this type.

Example

**Professor**

OK, Neptune and its moons. Neptune has several moons, but there's only ... we'll probably only worry about two of them, the two fairly interesting ones. The first one's Triton. So you have this little struggle with the word *Titan*, which is the big moon of Saturn, and the name *Triton*, which is the big moon of *Neptune*. Triton: it's, it's the only *large moon* in the solar system to go backwards, to go around its—what we call its parent planet—in this case Neptune, the wrong way. OK? Every other large moon orbits the *parent planet* in the same counterclockwise direction . . . same as most of the other bodies in the solar system. But this moon . . . the reverse direction, which is perfectly OK as far as the laws of gravity are concerned. But it indicates some sort of peculiar event in the early solar system that gave this moon a motion in contrast to the general spin of the raw material that it was formed from.

The other moon orbiting Neptune that I want to talk about is Nereid. Nereid is, Nereid has the most eccentric orbit, the most lopsided, elliptical-type orbit for a large moon in the solar system. The others tend more like circular orbits.

. . . Does it mean that Pluto and Neptune might have been related somehow in the past and then drifted slowly into their present orbits? If Pluto . . . did Pluto ever belong to the Neptune system? Do Neptune's moons represent Pluto-type bodies that have been captured by Neptune? Was some sort of . . . was Pluto the object that disrupted the Neptune system at some point in the past?

It's really hard to prove any of those things. But now we're starting to appreciate that there's quite a few junior Plutos out there: not big enough to really call a planet, but large enough that they're significant in history of the early solar system. So we'll come back to those when we talk about comets and other small bodies in the fringes of the outer solar system.

What does the professor imply about the orbits of Triton and Nereid?

Ⓐ They used to be closer together.
Ⓑ They might provide evidence of an undiscovered planet.
Ⓒ They might reverse directions in the future.
Ⓓ They might have been changed by some unusual event.

*Explanation*

In Connecting Content questions you will have to use information from more than one place in the lecture. In this example, the professor describes the orbits of Triton and Nereid. In both cases he refers to events in the early solar system that might have changed or disrupted their orbits. The correct answer for this question is choice D, "They might have been changed by some unusual event."

## Type 8: Making Inferences Questions

The final type of Connecting Information question is Making Inferences questions. In this kind of question you usually have to reach a conclusion based on facts presented in the lecture or conversation.

*How to Recognize Making Inferences Questions*
Making Inferences questions are typically phrased as follows:

- What does the professor imply about X?
- What will the student probably do next?
- What can be inferred about X?
- What does the professor imply when he says this? *(replay)*

*Tip for Making Inferences Questions*

- In some cases, answering this kind of question correctly means putting together details from the lecture or conversation to reach a conclusion. In other cases, the professor may imply something without directly stating it. In most cases the answer you choose will use vocabulary not found in the lecture or conversation.

**Example**

**Professor**

Dada is often considered under the broader category of Fantasy. It's one of the early directions in the Fantasy style. The term "Dada" itself is a nonsense word—it has no meaning . . . and where the word originated isn't known. The "philosophy" behind the "Dada" movement was to create works that conveyed the concept of *absurdity*—**the artwork was meant to shock the public by presenting the ridiculous, absurd concepts.** Dada artists rejected reason—or rational thought. They did not believe that rational thought would help solve social problems . . .

. . . When he turned to Dada, he quit painting and devoted himself to making a type of sculpture he referred to as a "ready-made" . . . probably because they were constructed of readily available objects . . . **At the time, many people reacted to Dadaism by saying that the works were not art at all . . . and in fact, that's exactly how Duchamp and others conceived of it—as a form of "non-art" . . . or anti-art.**

Duchamp also took a reproduction of da Vinci's famous painting the *Mona Lisa*, and he drew a mustache and goatee on the subject's face. Treating this masterpiece with such disrespect was another way **Duchamp was challenging the established cultural standards of his day.**

What does the professor imply about the philosophy of the Dada movement?

(A) It was not taken seriously by most artists.
(B) It varied from one country to another.
(C) It challenged people's concept of what art is.
(D) It was based on a realistic style of art.

*Explanation*

Note the highlighted portions of the lecture. You can see that Dadaism was meant to challenge the public's conception of what art was meant to be. The correct answer to the question is choice C.

# Strategies for Preparing for and Taking the Listening Section

### How to Sharpen Your Listening Skills

Listening is one of the most important skills necessary for success on the TOEFL iBT test and in academics in general. The ability to listen and understand is tested in three out of four sections of the test.

The best way to improve your listening skills is to listen frequently to many different types of material in various subject areas (sciences, social sciences, arts, business, and others). Of course, watching movies and TV and listening to the radio or podcasts are excellent ways to practice listening. Audiobooks and other recorded materials with transcripts may be especially helpful, and many useful recordings and videos can be found on the internet.

Here are some ways you can strengthen skills for the three listening purposes tested on the TOEFL iBT test.

### 1. Listening for basic comprehension

- Increase your vocabulary knowledge, perhaps by using digital flash cards.
- Focus on the content and flow of material. Do not be distracted by the speaker's style and delivery.
- Anticipate what the speaker is going to say as a way to stay focused, and adjust your predictions when you receive additional information.
- Stay active by asking yourself questions (for example, What main idea is the professor communicating?).
- Copy the words "main idea," "major points," and "important details" on different lines of paper. Listen carefully and write these things down while listening. Listen again until all important points and details are written down.
- Listen to a portion of a lecture or talk and write a brief summary of important points. Gradually increase the amount you listen to and summarize.

### 2. Listening for pragmatic understanding

- Think about what each speaker hopes to accomplish; that is, what is the purpose of the speech or conversation? Is the speaker apologizing, complaining, making suggestions?
- Notice the way each speaker talks. Is the language formal or casual? How certain does each speaker sound? Is the speaker's voice calm or emotional? What does the speaker's tone of voice tell you?

- Notice the degree of certainty of the speaker. How sure is the speaker about the information? Does the speaker's tone of voice indicate something about his or her degree of certainty?

- Watch television or movie comedies and pay attention to stress and intonation patterns used to convey meaning.

- Watch television or movies and pay attention to the way characters express disagreement or make suggestions in indirect ways in order to avoid hurting another character's feelings.

### 3. Listening to connect ideas

- Think about how the lecture is organized. Listen for the signal words that indicate the introduction, major steps or ideas, examples, and the conclusion or summary.

- Identify the relationships between ideas in the information being discussed. Possible relationships include cause/effect, compare/contrast, and steps in a process.

- Listen for words that show connections and relationships between ideas.

- When you listen to recorded material, stop the recording at various points and try to predict what information or idea will be expressed next.

- Create an outline of the information discussed while listening or after listening.

- Listen for changes in topic or side comments in which the speaker briefly moves away from the main topic and then returns (digressions).

### Tips for the Day of the Test

- Take notes while you listen. Only significant points will be tested, so do not try to write down every detail. After testing, notes are destroyed for test security purposes.

- When listening to a lecture or conversation, be aware that specialized words used by a speaker may be written on a chalkboard or notepad.

- When listening to a lecture, pay attention to the way the lecture is organized and the way the ideas in the lecture are connected.

- Choose the best answer. Once you select **Next**, you will automatically go on to the next question.

- Listening questions must be answered in order. Once you select **Next**, you cannot go back to a previous question.

# Listening Practice Sets

## PRACTICE SET 1

*Now listen to Track 1.*

### Questions

**Directions:** Mark your answer by filling in the oval next to your choice.

1. Why does the man go to see his professor?

   (A) To borrow some charts and graphs from her
   (B) To ask her to explain some statistical procedures
   (C) To talk about a report he is writing
   (D) To discuss a grade he got on a paper

2. What information will the man include in his report?
   *For each phrase below, place a check mark in the "Include" column or the "Not Include" column.*

|  | Include in Report | Not Include in Report |
|---|---|---|
| Climate charts |  |  |
| Interviews with meteorologists |  |  |
| Journal notes |  |  |
| Statistical tests |  |  |

3. Why does the professor tell the man about the appointment at the doctor's office?
   - (A) To demonstrate a way of remembering things
   - (B) To explain why she needs to leave soon
   - (C) To illustrate a point that appears in his report
   - (D) To emphasize the importance of good health

4. What does the professor offer to do for the man?
   - (A) Help him collect more data in other areas of the state
   - (B) Submit his research findings for publication
   - (C) Give him the doctor's telephone number
   - (D) Review the first version of his report

5. *Listen again to part of the conversation by playing Track 2. Then answer the question.*

   Why does the professor say this?
   - (A) To question the length of the paper
   - (B) To offer encouragement
   - (C) To dispute the data sources
   - (D) To explain a theory

## PRACTICE SET 1 SCRIPT AND ANSWERS

### Track 1 Listening Script

**Narrator**

Listen to a conversation between a student and a professor.

**Student**

Uh, excuse me, Professor Thompson. I know your office hours are tomorrow, but I was wondering if you had a few minutes free now to discuss something.

**Professor**

Sure, John. What did you wanna talk about?

**Student**

Well, I have some quick questions about how to write up the research project I did this semester—about climate variations.

**Professor**

Oh, yes. You were looking at variations in climate in the Grant City area, right? How far along have you gotten?

**Student**

I've got all my data, so I'm starting to summarize it now, preparing graphs and stuff. But I'm just . . . I'm looking at it and I'm afraid that it's not enough, but I'm not sure what else to put in the report.

**Professor**

I hear the same thing from every student. You know, you have to remember now that you're the expert on what you've done. So think about what you'd need to include if you were going to explain your research project to someone with general or casual knowledge about the subject, like . . . like your parents. That's usually my rule of thumb: would my parents understand this?

**Student**

OK. I get it.

**Professor**

I hope you can recognize by my saying that how much you do know about the subject.

**Student**

Right. I understand. I was wondering if I should also include the notes from the research journal you suggested I keep?

**Professor**

Yes, definitely. You should use them to indicate what your evolution in thought was through time. So just set up, you know, what was the purpose of what you were doing—to try to understand the climate variability of this area—and what you did, and what your approach was.

**Student**

OK. So, for example, I studied meteorological records; I looked at climate charts; I used different methods for analyzing the data, like certain statistical tests; and then I discuss the results. Is that what you mean?

**Professor**

Yes, that's right. You should include all of that. The statistical tests are especially important. And also be sure you include a good reference section where all your published and unpublished data came from, 'cause you have a lot of unpublished climate data.

**Student**

Hmm . . . something just came into my mind and went out the other side.

**Professor**

That happens to me a lot, so I've come up with a pretty good memory management tool. I carry a little pad with me all the time and jot down questions or ideas that I don't wanna forget. For example, I went to the doctor with my daughter and her baby son last week, and we knew we wouldn't remember everything we wanted to ask the doctor, so we actually made a list of five things we wanted answers to.

**Student**

A notepad is a good idea. Since I'm so busy now at the end of the semester, I'm getting pretty forgetful these days. OK. I just remembered what I was trying to say before.

**Professor**

Good. I was hoping you'd come up with it.

**Student**

Yes. It ends up that I have data on more than just the immediate Grant City area, so I also included some regional data in the report. With everything else it should be a pretty good indicator of the climate in this part of the state.

**Professor**

Sounds good. I'd be happy to look over a draft version before you hand in the final copy, if you wish.

**Student**

Great. I'll plan to get you a draft of the paper by next Friday. Thanks very much. Well, see ya.

**Professor**
OK.

## Answers and Explanations

1.  **C** This is a Gist-Purpose question. The man says, "I have some quick questions about how to write up the research project I did this semester." He is going to write a report about his project and is unsure of what to include. Choice C is the correct answer.

2.  This question is easy to recognize as a Connecting Content question. The student and the professor discuss several sources of information that the student used to investigate climate variation. They do not discuss interviewing meteorologists, even though they mention other kinds of conversations, like the professor's discussion with her child's doctor. The chart correctly filled out looks like this:

For each phrase below, place a check mark in the "Include" column or the "Not Include" column.

|  | Include in Report | Not Include in Report |
| --- | :---: | :---: |
| Climate charts | ✓ | |
| Interviews with meteorologists | | ✓ |
| Journal notes | ✓ | |
| Statistical tests | ✓ | |

3.  **Ⓐ** This is an Understanding Organization question. The correct answer is choice A. The professor's purpose in mentioning the doctor's office is to show the man how writing down questions as they occur can be useful. The man has forgotten a question he wanted to ask the professor. The professor, when she spoke to the doctor, wrote down her questions beforehand, so she would not forget. She mentions the doctor's office in order to give an example of a strategy for remembering.

4.  **Ⓓ** This is a Detail question. The discussion ends with the professor offering to "look over a draft version" of the man's paper.

5.  **Ⓑ** This question requires you to Understand the Function of What Is Said. The question asks you to listen again to this part of the conversation:

**Professor**
You know, you have to remember now that you're the expert on what you've done. So think about what you'd need to include if you were going to explain your research project to someone with general or casual knowledge about the subject, like . . . like your parents. That's usually my rule of thumb: would my parents understand this?

**Student**
OK. I get it.

**Professor**
I hope you can recognize by my saying that how much you do know about the subject.

Then you are asked specifically about this sentence:

**Narrator**
Why does the professor say this:

**Professor**
I hope you can recognize by my saying that how much you do know about the subject.

The student is unsure of how to present the information in his report. The professor is trying to give the student confidence in his own judgment. Therefore the correct answer is choice B, "To offer encouragement."

# PRACTICE SET 2

*Now listen to Track 3.*

## Philosophy
### Ethics

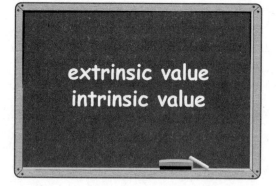

extrinsic value
intrinsic value

**Questions**

**Directions:** Mark your answer by filling in the oval next to your choice.

1.  What is the main purpose of the lecture?

    Ⓐ To illustrate the importance of extrinsic values
    Ⓑ To explain Aristotle's views about the importance of teaching
    Ⓒ To explain why people change what they value
    Ⓓ To discuss Aristotle's views about human happiness

2.  The professor gives examples of things that have value for her. Indicate for each example what type of value it has for her.
    *Place a check mark in the correct box.* **This question is worth 2 points.**

| | Only Extrinsic Value | Only Intrinsic Value | Both Extrinsic and Intrinsic Value |
|---|---|---|---|
| Teaching | | | |
| Exercise | | | |
| Health | | | |
| Playing a musical instrument | | | |

3.  Why is happiness central to Aristotle's theory?

    Ⓐ Because it is so difficult for people to attain
    Ⓑ Because it is valued for its own sake by all people
    Ⓒ Because it is a means to a productive life
    Ⓓ Because most people agree about what happiness is

4.  According to the professor, why does Aristotle think that fame cannot provide true happiness?

    Ⓐ Fame cannot be obtained without help from other people.
    Ⓑ Fame cannot be obtained by all people.
    Ⓒ Fame does not last forever.
    Ⓓ People cannot share their fame with other people.

5.  *Listen again to part of the lecture by playing Track 4.*
    *Then answer the question.*

    What does the professor mean when she says this?

    Ⓐ Teaching is not a highly valued profession in society.
    Ⓑ She may change professions in order to earn more money.
    Ⓒ The reason she is a teacher has little to do with her salary.
    Ⓓ More people would become teachers if the salary were higher.

# PRACTICE SET 2 SCRIPT AND ANSWERS

### Track 3 Listening Script

**Narrator**

Listen to part of a lecture in a philosophy class.

**Professor**

OK. Another ancient Greek philosopher we need to discuss is Aristotle—Aristotle's ethical theory. What Aristotle's ethical theory is all about is this: he's trying to show you how to be happy—what true happiness is.

Now, why is he interested in human happiness? It's not just because it's something that all people want or aim for. It's more than that. But to get there, we need to first make a very important distinction. Let me introduce a couple of technical terms: extrinsic value and intrinsic value.

To understand Aristotle's interest in happiness, you need to understand this distinction.

Some things we aim for and value, not for themselves, but for what they bring about in addition to themselves. If I value something as a means to something else, then it has what we will call "extrinsic value." Other things we desire and hold to be valuable for themselves alone. If we value something not as a means to something else, but for its own sake, let us say that it has "intrinsic value."

Exercise. There may be some people who value exercise for itself, but I don't. I value exercise because if I exercise, I tend to stay healthier than I would if I didn't. So I desire to engage in exercise, and I value exercise extrinsically . . . not for its own sake, but as a means to something beyond it. It brings me good health.

Health. Why do I value good health? Well, here it gets a little more complicated for me. Um, health is important for me because I can't . . . do other things I wanna do—play music, teach philosophy—if I'm ill. So health is important to me—has value to me—as a means to a productive life. But health is also important to me because I just kind of like to be healthy—it feels good. It's pleasant to be healthy, unpleasant not to be. So to some degree I value health both for itself and as a means to something else: productivity. It's got extrinsic and intrinsic value for me.

Then there's some things that are just valued for themselves. I'm a musician, not a professional musician; I just play a musical instrument for fun. Why do I value playing music? Well, like most amateur musicians, I only play because, well, I just enjoy it. It's something that's an end in itself.

Now, something else I value is teaching. Why? Well, it brings in a modest income, but I could make more money doing other things. I'd do it even if they didn't pay me. I just enjoy teaching. In that sense it's an end to itself.

But teaching's not something that has intrinsic value for all people—and that's true generally. Most things that are enjoyed in and of themselves vary from person to person. Some people value teaching intrinsically, but others don't.

So how does all this relate to human happiness? Well, Aristotle asks: is there something that all human beings value . . . and value only intrinsically, for its own sake and only for its own sake? If you could find such a thing, that would be the universal final good, or truly the ultimate purpose or goal for all human beings. Aristotle thought the answer was yes. What is it? Happiness. Everyone will agree, he argues, that happiness is the ultimate end to be valued for itself and really only for itself. For what other purpose is there in being happy? What does it yield? The attainment of happiness becomes the ultimate or highest good for Aristotle.

The next question that Aristotle raises is: what is happiness? We all want it; we all desire it; we all seek it. It's the goal we have in life. But what is it? How do we find it? Here he notes, with some frustration, people disagree.

But he does give us a couple of criteria, or features, to keep in mind as we look for what true human happiness is. True human happiness should be, as he puts it, complete. Complete in that it's all we require. Well, true human happiness . . . if you had that, what else do you need? Nothing.

And, second, true happiness should be something that I can obtain on my own. I shouldn't have to rely on other people for it. Many people value fame and seek fame. Fame for them becomes the goal. But, according to Aristotle, this won't work either, because fame depends altogether too much on other people. I can't get it on my own, without help from other people.

In the end, Aristotle says that true happiness is the exercise of reason—a life of intellectual contemplation . . . of thinking. So let's see how he comes to that.

## Answers and Explanations

1.  **D** This is a Gist-Purpose question. The professor discusses the difference between extrinsic and intrinsic value, but what is her purpose in doing this? "To understand Aristotle's interest in happiness, you need to understand this distinction [extrinsic and intrinsic]." The professor's purpose is choice D: "To discuss Aristotle's views about human happiness."

2.  This question is easy to recognize as a Connecting Content question. The professor gives examples of some activities and discusses whether they have intrinsic value, extrinsic value, or both. Her explanations of why she values exercise, health, and playing a musical instrument are fairly clear and explicit. For teaching, it is clear that for her it has intrinsic value, but she admits this may be different for others. The question is about "what type of value it has for her." The chart correctly filled out looks like this:

|  | Only Extrinsic Value | Only Intrinsic Value | Both Extrinsic and Intrinsic Value |
|---|---|---|---|
| Teaching |  | ✓ |  |
| Exercise | ✓ |  |  |
| Health |  |  | ✓ |
| Playing a musical instrument |  | ✓ |  |

3. **B** This is a Detail question. The question is answered by the professor when she says, "Everyone will agree, he [Aristotle] argues, that happiness is the ultimate end to be valued for itself and really only for itself." The correct answer for this question is choice B. Note that this Detail question is directly related to the main idea or gist of the passage.

4. **A** This is another Detail question. It is not as closely related to the gist as the previous question. At the end of the passage the professor compares happiness and fame. She says, "according to Aristotle, this won't work either, because fame depends altogether too much on other people. I can't get it on my own." The correct answer is choice A.

5. **C** This question requires you to Understand the Function of What Is Said. The professor discusses teaching to stress its intrinsic value for her. Therefore the correct answer is choice C. The reason she is a teacher has little to do with money. Salary would be an extrinsic value, but she does not value teaching because of the salary.

# PRACTICE SET 3

*Now listen to Track 5.*

Psychology
Behavorism

Laryngeal Habits

Questions

**Directions:** Mark your answer by filling in the oval next to your choice.

1.  What is the professor mainly discussing?

    Ⓐ The development of motor skills in children
    Ⓑ How psychologists measure muscle activity in the throat
    Ⓒ A theory about the relationship between muscle activity and thinking
    Ⓓ A study on the problem-solving techniques of people who are deaf

2.  What does the professor say about people who use sign language?

    Ⓐ It is not possible to study their thinking habits.
    Ⓑ They exhibit laryngeal habits.
    Ⓒ The muscles in their hands move when they solve problems.
    Ⓓ They do not exhibit ideomotor action.

3.  What point does the professor make when he refers to the university library?

    Ⓐ A study on problem solving took place there.
    Ⓑ Students should go there to read more about behaviorism.
    Ⓒ Students' eyes will turn toward it if they think about it.
    Ⓓ He learned about William James's concept of thinking there.

4.  The professor describes a magic trick to the class. What does the magic trick demonstrate?

    Ⓐ An action people make that they are not aware of
    Ⓑ That behaviorists are not really scientists
    Ⓒ How psychologists study children
    Ⓓ A method for remembering locations

5.  What is the professor's opinion of the motor theory of thinking?

    Ⓐ Most of the evidence he has collected contradicts it.
    Ⓑ It explains adult behavior better than it explains child behavior.
    Ⓒ It is the most valid theory of thinking at the present time.
    Ⓓ It cannot be completely proved or disproved.

6.  *Listen again to part of the lecture by playing Track 6.*
    *Then answer the question.*

    Why does the professor say this?

    Ⓐ To give an example of a laryngeal habit
    Ⓑ To explain the meaning of a term
    Ⓒ To explain why he is discussing laryngeal habits
    Ⓓ To remind students of a point he had discussed previously

# PRACTICE SET 3 SCRIPT AND ANSWERS

### Track 5 Listening Script

#### Narrator

Listen to part of a psychology lecture. The professor is discussing behaviorism.

#### Professor

Now, many people consider John Watson to be the founder of behaviorism. And like other behaviorists, he believed that psychologists should study only the behaviors they can observe and measure. They're not interested in mental processes. While a person could describe his thoughts, no one else can see or hear them to verify the accuracy of his report. But one thing you can observe is muscular habits. What Watson did was to observe muscular habits because he viewed them as a manifestation of thinking. One kind of habit that he studied are laryngeal habits.

Watson thought laryngeal habits—you know, from *larynx*; in other words, related to the voice box—he thought those habits were an expression of thinking. He argued that for very young children, thinking is really talking out loud to oneself because they talk out loud even if they're not trying to communicate with someone in particular. As the individual matures, that overt talking to oneself becomes covert talking to oneself, but thinking still shows up as a laryngeal habit. One of the bits of evidence that supports this is that when people are trying to solve a problem, they, um, typically have increased muscular activity in the throat region. That is, if you put electrodes on the throat and measure muscle potential—muscle activity—you discover that when people are thinking, like if they're diligently trying to solve a problem, that there is muscular activity in the throat region.

So Watson made the argument that problem solving, or thinking, can be defined as a set of behaviors—a set of responses—and in this case the response he observed was the throat activity. That's what he means when he calls it a laryngeal habit. Now, as I am thinking about what I am going to be saying, my muscles in my throat are responding. So thinking can be measured as muscle activity. Now, the motor theory . . . yes?

#### Student

Professor Blake, um, did he happen to look at people who sign? I mean deaf people?

#### Professor

Uh, he did indeed, um, and to jump ahead, what one finds in deaf individuals who use sign language when they're given problems of various kinds, they have muscular changes in their hands when they are trying to solve a problem . . . muscle changes in the hand, just like the muscular changes going on in the throat region for speaking individuals.

So, for Watson, thinking is identical with the activity of muscles. A related concept of thinking was developed by William James. It's called ideomotor action.

Ideomotor action is an activity that occurs without our noticing it, without our being aware of it. I'll give you one simple example. If you think of locations, there tends to be eye movement that occurs with your thinking about that location. In particular, from where we're sitting, imagine that you're asked to think of our university library. Well, if you close your eyes and think of the library, and if you're sitting directly facing me, then according to this notion, your eyeballs will move slightly to the left, to your left, 'cause the library's in that general direction.

James and others said that this is an idea leading to a motor action, and that's why it's called "ideomotor action"—an idea leads to motor activity. If you wish to impress your friends and relatives, you can change this simple process into a magic trick. Ask people to do something such as I've just described: think of something on their left; think of something on their right. You get them to think about two things on either side with their eyes closed, and you watch their eyes very carefully. And if you do that, you'll discover that you can see rather clearly the eye movement—that is, you can see the movement of the eyeballs. Now, then you say, "Think of either one and I'll tell which you're thinking of."

OK. Well, Watson makes the assumption that muscular activity is equivalent to thinking. But given everything we've been talking about here, one has to ask: are there alternatives to this motor theory—this claim that muscular activities are equivalent to thinking? Is there anything else that might account for this change in muscular activity, other than saying that it is thinking? And the answer is clearly yes. Is there any way to answer the question definitively? I think the answer is no.

**Answers and Explanations**

1.  **C** This is a Gist-Content question. The professor discusses two types of muscular activities: laryngeal habits and ideomotor activity, and how they are related to thinking. The correct answer is choice C, "A theory about the relationship between muscle activity and thinking." The other choices are mentioned by the professor, but they are not the main topic of the discussion.

2.  **C** This is a Detail question. The professor responds to a student who asks a question about people who use sign language. He says that "they have muscular changes in their hands . . . just like the muscular changes going on in the throat region for speaking individuals." The correct answer is choice C. This Detail question is related to the main idea of the passage, as both are concerned with the relationship between muscular changes and thinking.

3.  **C** This is an Understanding Organization question. The professor talks about muscular activity in the eyes that will occur if the students think about the location of the library. The question asks for the conclusion of that example. The correct answer is choice C, "Students' eyes will turn toward it if they think about it."

4.  **A** This is a Connecting Content question. Answering the question correctly requires you to understand that the magic trick the professor is describing is an "ideomotor activity" and that this type of activity "occurs without our noticing it, without our being aware of it." The correct answer to this question is choice A.

5.  **D** Questions like this one that ask for the professor's opinion require you to Understand the Speaker's Attitude. The professor's opinion can be found at the end of the lecture. He says that there may be alternative theories, but there is no way to answer the question definitively. The correct answer to this question is choice D, "It cannot be completely proved or disproved."

6.  **B** This question requires you to Understand the Function of What Is Said. The professor introduces an unusual term, "laryngeal habits." He then says, "you know, from *larynx*; in other words, related to the voice box." His brief explanation is meant to help the students understand the term "laryngeal habits." Choice B is the correct answer to this question.

# PRACTICE SET 4

*Now listen to Track 7.*

Astronomy

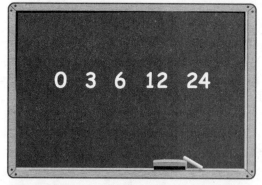

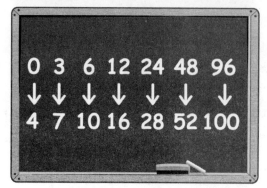

4  7  10  16  28  52  100
↓  ↓  ↓  ↓  ↓  ↓  ↓
0.4 0.7 1.0 16 2.8 5.2 10.0

.4          .7
Mercury   Venus

1.0         1.6
Earth       Mars

2.8    5.2    10.0
Jupiter  Saturn

Bode's Law

.4          .7
Mercury   Venus

1.0         1.6
Earth       Mars

2.8    5.2    10.0
Jupiter  Saturn

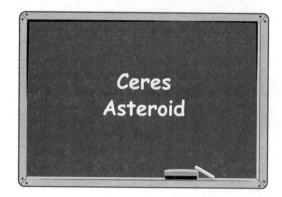

Ceres
Asteroid

**Questions**

**Directions:** Mark your answer by filling in the oval or square next to your choice.

1. What is Bode's Law?

   Ⓐ A law of gravitation
   Ⓑ An estimate of the distance between Mars and Jupiter
   Ⓒ A prediction of how many asteroids there are
   Ⓓ A pattern in the spacing of planets

2. Why does the professor explain Bode's Law to the class?

   Ⓐ To describe the size of the asteroids
   Ⓑ To explain how the asteroid belt was discovered
   Ⓒ To explain how gravitational forces influence the planets
   Ⓓ To describe the impact of telescopes on astronomy

3. How does the professor introduce Bode's Law?

   Ⓐ By demonstrating how it is derived mathematically
   Ⓑ By describing the discovery of Uranus
   Ⓒ By drawing attention to the inaccuracy of a certain pattern
   Ⓓ By telling the names of several of the asteroids

4. According to the professor, what two factors contributed to the discovery of the asteroid Ceres?
   *Select 2 answers.*

   Ａ Improved telescopes
   Ｂ Advances in mathematics
   Ｃ The discovery of a new star
   Ｄ The position of Uranus in a pattern

5. What does the professor imply about the asteroid belt?

Ⓐ It is farther from the Sun than Uranus.
Ⓑ Bode believed it was made up of small stars.
Ⓒ It is located where people expected to find a planet.
Ⓓ Ceres is the only one of the asteroids that can be seen without a telescope.

6. *Listen again to part of the lecture by playing Track 8.*
   *Then answer the question.*

   Why does the professor say this?

   Ⓐ To introduce an alternative application of Bode's Law
   Ⓑ To give an example of what Bode's Law cannot explain
   Ⓒ To describe the limitations of gravitational theory
   Ⓓ To contrast Bode's Law with a real scientific law

## PRACTICE SET 4 SCRIPT AND ANSWERS

### Track 7 Listening Script

**Narrator**

Listen to part of a lecture in an astronomy class. You will not need to remember the numbers the professor mentions.

**Professor**

OK. Let's get going. Today I'm going to talk about how the asteroid belt was discovered. And . . . I'm going to start by writing some numbers on the board. Here they are: we'll start with zero, then 3, . . . 6, . . . 12. Uh, tell me what I'm doing.

**Female Student**

Multiplying by 2?

**Professor**

Right. I'm doubling the numbers, so 2 times 12 is 24, and the next one I'm going to write after 24 would be . . .

**Female Student**

48.

**Professor**

48. Then 96. We'll stop there for now. Uh, now I'll write another row of numbers under that. Tell me what I'm doing: 4, 7, 10 . . . How am I getting this second row?

**Male Student**

Adding 4 to the numbers in the first row.

**Professor**

I'm adding 4 to each number in the first row to give you a second row. So the last two will be 52, 100, and now tell me what I'm doing.

**Female Student**

Putting in a decimal?

**Professor**

Yes, I divided all those numbers by 10 by putting in a decimal point. Now I'm going to write the names of the planets under the numbers. Mercury . . . Venus . . . Earth . . . Mars.

So, what do the numbers mean? Do you remember from the reading?

**Male Student**

Is it the distance of the planets from the Sun?

**Professor**

Right. In astronomical units—not perfect, but tantalizingly close. The value for Mars is off by . . . 6 or 7 percent or so. It's . . . but it's within 10 percent of the average distance to Mars from the Sun. But I kind of have to skip the one after Mars for now. Then Jupiter's right there at 5-point something, and then Saturn is about 10 astronomical units from the Sun. Um, well, this pattern is known as Bode's Law.

Um, it isn't really a scientific law, not in the sense of predicting gravitation mathematically or something, but it's attempting a pattern in the spacing of the planets, and it was noticed by Bode hundreds of years ago. Well, you can imagine that there was some interest in why the 2.8 spot in the pattern was skipped, and um . . . but there wasn't anything obvious there, in the early telescopes. Then what happened in the late 1700s? The discovery of . . . ?

**Female Student**

Another planet?

**Professor**

The next planet out, Uranus—after Saturn.

And look, Uranus fits in the next spot in the pattern pretty nicely, um, not perfectly, but close. And so then people got really excited about the validity of this thing and finding the missing object between Mars and Jupiter. And telescopes, remember, were getting better. So people went to work on finding objects that would be at that missing distance from the Sun, and then in 1801, the object Ceres was discovered.

And Ceres was in the right place—the missing spot. Uh, but it was way too faint to be a planet. It looked like a little star. Uh, and because of its starlike appearance, um, it was called an "asteroid." OK? *Aster* is Greek for "star," as in *astronomy*. Um, and so, Ceres was the first and is the largest of what became many objects discovered at that same distance. Not just one thing, but all the objects found at that distance form the asteroid belt. So the asteroid belt is the most famous success of this Bode's Law. That's how the asteroid belt was discovered.

**Answers and Explanations**

1.  **D** This is a Detail question. Although the entire passage is concerned with answering "What is Bode's Law?" the professor specifically answers the question when he says, "it's attempting a pattern in the spacing of the planets." The correct answer to this question is choice D.

2.  **B** This is a Gist-Purpose question. Gist questions are not usually answered very explicitly in the passage, but in this case the professor addresses the purpose of the discussion twice. At one point he says, "Today I'm going to talk about how the asteroid belt was discovered," and later he states, "That's how the asteroid belt was discovered." The correct answer to this question is choice B.

3.  **A** This is an Understanding Organization question. The professor first demonstrates the pattern of numbers before explaining Bode's Law and what the pattern means. The correct answer to this question is choice A.

4.  **A** **D** This is a Detail question. Note that for this question there are two correct answers. The professor explains that "Uranus fits in the next spot in the pattern pretty nicely" and telescopes "were getting better . . . and then in 1801, the object Ceres was discovered." Choices A and D are the correct answers. Advances in mathematics and the discovery of a new star are not mentioned by the professor.

5.  **C** This is a Making Inferences question. Starting at the point in the passage where the professor says, "there was some interest in why the 2.8 spot in the pattern was skipped . . . there wasn't anything obvious there," it's clear that what the astronomers were looking for was a planet. He later says, "Ceres was in the right place . . . but it was way too faint to be a planet." The clear implication is that astronomers were expecting to find a planet. The correct answer to the question is choice C.

6.  **D** This replay question requires you to Understand the Function of What Is Said. The pattern the professor describes is called Bode's Law. The professor is pointing out how Bode's Law differs from other scientific laws. The correct answer to this question is choice D.

# PRACTICE SET 5

*Now listen to Track 9.*

Botany

Questions

**Directions:** Mark your answer by filling in the oval or square next to your choice.

1.  What aspect of Manila hemp fibers does the professor mainly describe in the lecture?
    - Ⓐ Similarities between cotton fibers and Manila hemp fibers
    - Ⓑ Various types of Manila hemp fibers
    - Ⓒ The economic importance of Manila hemp fibers
    - Ⓓ A use of Manila hemp fibers

2.  What does the professor imply about the name "Manila hemp"?
    - Ⓐ It is a commercial brand name.
    - Ⓑ Part of the name is inappropriate.
    - Ⓒ The name has recently changed.
    - Ⓓ The name was first used in the 1940s.

3.  Why does the professor mention the Golden Gate Bridge?
    - Ⓐ To demonstrate a disadvantage of steel cables
    - Ⓑ To give an example of the creative use of color
    - Ⓒ To show that steel cables are able to resist salt water
    - Ⓓ To give an example of a use of Manila hemp

4.  According to the professor, what was the main reason that many ships used Manila hemp ropes instead of steel cables?
    - Ⓐ Manila hemp was cheaper.
    - Ⓑ Manila hemp was easier to produce.
    - Ⓒ Manila hemp is more resistant to salt water.
    - Ⓓ Manila hemp is lighter in weight.

5.  According to the lecture, what are two ways to increase the strength of rope made from Manila hemp fibers?
    *Select 2 answers.*
    - Ⓐ Coat the fibers with zinc-based paint
    - Ⓑ Combine the fibers into bundles
    - Ⓒ Soak bundles of fibers in salt water
    - Ⓓ Twist bundles of fibers

6.  *Listen again to part of the lecture by playing Track 10.*
    *Then answer the question.*

    Why does the professor mention going away for the weekend?
    - Ⓐ To tell the class a joke
    - Ⓑ To apologize for not completing some work
    - Ⓒ To introduce the topic of the lecture
    - Ⓓ To encourage students to ask about her trip

## PRACTICE SET 5 SCRIPT AND ANSWERS

### Track 9 Listening Script

**Narrator**

Listen to part of a lecture from a botany class.

**Professor**

Hi, everyone. Good to see you all today. Actually, I expected the population to be a lot lower today. It typically runs between 50 and 60 percent on the day the research paper is due. Um, I was hoping to have your exams back today, but, uh, the situation was that I went away for the weekend, and I was supposed to get in yesterday at five, and I expected to fully complete all the exams by midnight or so, which is the time that I usually go to bed, but my flight was delayed, and I ended up not getting in until one o'clock in the morning. Anyway, I'll do my best to have them finished by the next time we meet.

OK. In the last class, we started talking about useful plant fibers. In particular, we talked about cotton fibers, which we said were very useful, not only in the textile industry, but also in the chemical industry, and in the production of many products, such as plastics, paper, explosives, and so on. Today we'll continue talking about useful fibers, and we'll begin with a fiber that's commonly known as "Manila hemp."

Now, for some strange reason, many people believe that Manila hemp is a hemp plant. But Manila hemp is not really hemp. It's actually a member of the banana family—it even bears little banana-shaped fruits. The "Manila" part of the name makes sense, because Manila hemp is produced chiefly in the Philippine Islands, and, of course, the capital city of the Philippines is Manila.

Now, as fibers go, Manila hemp fibers are very long. They can easily be several feet in length, and they're also very strong, very flexible. They have one more characteristic that's very important, and that is that they are exceptionally resistant to salt water. And this combination of characteristics—long, strong, flexible, resistant to salt water—makes Manila hemp a great material for ropes, especially for ropes that are gonna be used on oceangoing ships. In fact, by the early 1940s, even though steel cables were available, most ships in the United States Navy were not moored with steel cables; they were moored with Manila hemp ropes.

Now, why was that? Well, the main reason was that steel cables degrade very, very quickly in contact with salt water. If you've ever been to San Francisco, you know that the Golden Gate Bridge is red. And it's red because of the zinc paint that goes on those stainless steel cables. That, if they start at one end of the bridge and they work to the other end, by the time they finish, it's already time to go back and start painting the beginning of the bridge again, because the bridge was built with steel cables, and steel cables can't take the salt air unless they're treated repeatedly with a zinc-based paint.

On the other hand, plant products like Manila hemp, you can drag through the ocean for weeks on end. If you wanna tie your anchor to it and drop it right into the ocean, that's no problem, because plant fibers can stand up for months, even years, in direct contact with salt water. OK. So how do you take plant fibers that individually you could break with your hands and turn them into a rope that's strong enough to moor a ship that weighs thousands of tons? Well, what you do is extract these long fibers from the Manila hemp plant, and then you take several of these fibers, and you group them into a bundle, because by grouping the fibers, you greatly increase their breaking strength—that bundle of fibers is much stronger than any of the individual fibers that compose it. And then you take that bundle of fibers and you twist it a little bit, because by twisting it, you increase its breaking strength even more. And then you take several of these little bundles, and you group and twist them into bigger bundles, which you then group and twist into even bigger bundles, and so on, until eventually, you end up with a very, very strong rope.

## Answers and Explanations

1. **D** Questions like this one that ask about what the professor mainly discusses are Gist-Content questions. This question asks what aspect of Manila hemp fibers are mainly discussed, so it has a narrower focus than other Gist-Content questions. The professor mainly discusses characteristics of Manila hemp and how these characteristics make Manila hemp useful to the shipping industry. The correct answer to this question is choice D.

2. **B** This is a Making Inferences question. The professor explains that Manila hemp is produced chiefly in the area near Manila, so the word *Manila* in the name is appropriate. However, Manila hemp is not a type of hemp plant, so the word *hemp* in the name is not appropriate. The correct answer to this question is choice B.

3. **A** This is an Understanding Organization question. The professor mentions the Golden Gate Bridge in order to make a comparison between the steel cables of the bridge and Manila hemp ropes. The fact that the steel cables must be constantly repainted is a disadvantage. The correct answer to the question is choice A.

4. **C** This is a Detail question. It is related to the professor's main point about Manila hemp. The professor says that Manila hemp is "exceptionally resistant to salt water." Much of the lecture deals with the professor's reinforcing and exemplifying this point. The correct answer to this question is choice C.

5. **B D** Near the end of the lecture, the professor describes how Manila hemp ropes are made. The answer to this Detail question can be found there. The professor talks about grouping fibers into bundles and then twisting the bundles to make them stronger. Note that this question requires two answers. The correct answers to this question are choices B and D.

6. **B** This replay question requires you to Understand the Function of What Is Said. The professor mentions that she went away for the weekend and because a flight was delayed, she was late returning. She tells this story in order to apologize for not completing marking exams. The correct answer to this question is choice B.

# 4 Speaking Section

- ➤ The format of the 4 TOEFL iBT Speaking tasks
- ➤ How your spoken responses are evaluated
- ➤ Tips for answering each Speaking task type
- ➤ Strategies for preparing for the Speaking section

## The Speaking Section

The TOEFL iBT Speaking section is designed to evaluate the English speaking proficiency of students whose native language is not English but who want to pursue undergraduate or graduate study in an English-speaking context.

In the Speaking section you will be asked to speak on a variety of topics that draw on personal experience, campus-based situations, and academic-type content material. There are four questions. The first question is called an Independent Speaking task because it requires you to draw entirely on your own ideas, opinions, and experiences when responding. The other three questions are Integrated Speaking tasks. In these tasks you will listen to a conversation or to an excerpt from a lecture, or read a passage and then listen to a brief discussion or lecture excerpt, before you are asked the question. These questions are called Integrated tasks because they require you to integrate your English-language skills—listening and speaking, or reading, listening, and speaking. In responding to these questions, you will be asked to base your spoken response on the information in the discussion or lecture, or on both the discussion or lecture and the reading passage together.

> **TIP**
>
> *For each question, you are given 45 or 60 seconds to respond. So when practicing, time your speech accordingly.*

The estimated time to complete the Speaking section is 16 minutes. Response time allowed for each question is 45 or 60 seconds. For Speaking questions that involve listening, you will hear short lectures or conversations. For Speaking questions that involve reading, you will read short written passages on your computer screen. You can take notes throughout the Speaking section and use your notes when responding to the Speaking questions. For each of the four questions, you will be given a short time to prepare a response. You will answer each of the questions by speaking into a microphone. Your responses will be recorded and sent to a scoring center, and they will be scored by a combination of AI scoring and multiple, highly trained human raters.

**TIP**

*Familiarize yourself with the scoring rubric. It will help you understand how responses are evaluated.*

Raters will score your responses holistically. This means that the rater will listen for various features in your response and assign a single score based on the overall skill you display in your answer. Although scoring criteria vary somewhat depending on the question, the raters will generally be listening for the following features in your answer:

- **Delivery:** How clear is the speech? Good responses are fluid and clear, with good pronunciation, natural pacing, and natural-sounding intonation patterns.
- **Language Use:** How effectively does the test taker use grammar and vocabulary to convey ideas? Raters determine the test taker's ability to control both basic and more complex language structures and to use appropriate vocabulary.
- **Topic Development:** How fully does the response answer the question and how coherently presented are the ideas? How well does the test taker synthesize and summarize the information in the integrated tasks? Good responses generally use all or most of the time allowed, and the relationships between ideas and the progression from one idea to the next are clear and easy to follow.

It is important to note that raters do not expect test takers' responses to be perfect. Even high-scoring responses may contain occasional errors and minor problems in any of the three areas described above.

Use the sample Independent and Integrated Speaking rubrics on pages 184 to 187 to see how responses are scored.

# Speaking Tasks

## The Independent Task

### Question 1: Paired Choice

In the Independent Speaking task, you will be presented with two possible actions, situations, or opinions. Then you will be asked to say which of the actions or situations you think is preferable or which opinion you think is more justified and then explain your choice by providing reasons and details. You will have 45 seconds to give your response.

Topics for this question include everyday issues of general interest to a student. You may be asked, for example, whether you think it is better to study at home or at the library, or whether you think students should take courses from a wide variety of fields or focus on a single subject. You could also be presented with two opposing opinions about a familiar topic—for example, about whether television has been a benefit to humanity—and you would then be asked which of the opinions you agree with. You might also be asked whether you agree or disagree with a certain statement, such as "All first-year college students should be allowed to live off campus."

This question will always ask you to state what your choice or preference or opinion is and to explain why—in other words, to support your answer with reasons, explanations, details, and/or examples. It is important that you respond to all parts of the question, and that you are clear about what your opinion is and give reasons that communicate why you have made your choice. It does not matter which of the actions, situations, or opinions you choose, because there is no "right" or "wrong" answer. Your response will be rated not on which of the alternatives you choose, but rather on how well you explain your choice by supporting it with reasons and details.

**TIP**

*One good exercise would be to state an opinion or a preference and then present supporting reasons clearly and with detail.*

This question will appear on your computer screen and be read aloud at the same time by the narrator, and you will be given 15 seconds to prepare an answer. You should use this time to think about what you want to say, organize your thoughts, and jot down some notes if you feel this will be helpful. But remember, you should not try to write out a full answer—just a few words or phrases that may help remind you of the direction you want to take in giving your response.

**TIP**

*Study and practice words and expressions commonly used to express opinions, such as:*
*In my opinion . . .*
*I believe . . .*

**Example**

A question of this type will be presented to you as follows.

*First you will hear and see these directions.*

### Narrator

You will now give your opinion about a familiar topic. After you hear the question, you will have 15 seconds to prepare and 45 seconds to speak.

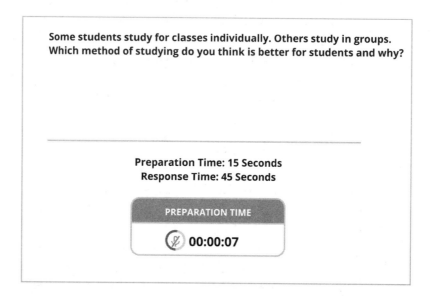

Some students study for classes individually. Others study in groups. Which method of studying do you think is better for students and why?

Preparation Time: 15 Seconds
Response Time: 45 Seconds

PREPARATION TIME

00:00:07

After you hear the question, you will be told when to begin to prepare your response and when to begin speaking. A "Preparation Time" clock will appear below the question and begin to count down from 15 seconds (00:00:15). At the end of 15 seconds you will hear a short beep. After the beep, the clock will change to read "Response Time" and will begin to count down from 45 seconds (00:00:45). When the response time has ended, recording will stop and a new screen will appear alerting you that the response time has ended.

In answering a question like this one, it is important that you begin by clearly stating what your opinion is: do you think it is better for students to study for classes individually, or do you think it is better for them to study in groups? If you do not begin by stating your opinion, it may be difficult for someone listening to your response to understand your reasons for holding that opinion.

As for the reasons you give in support of your opinion, they can vary widely and may be based on your own experience and observations. For example, if the position you take is that it is better for students to study alone, you might say that when students meet to study in groups, they often waste time discussing matters that have nothing to do with their class work. You might continue this explanation by contrasting the inefficiency of studying in a group with the kind of productivity a student can achieve when studying alone. If you have personal experiences that help illustrate your point, you might want to include them in your explanation. If so, you should be clear about how they illustrate your point.

Or perhaps you want to take the opposite position, that it is better for students to study in groups. In that case, you would explain the advantages of group study and the disadvantages of studying alone. Perhaps you think that the more capable students can help the less capable students when students study together. Or perhaps you have found that students who study in groups often share each other's lecture notes, and this way they can make sure everyone understands all the material that has been covered in a course.

There are many good reasons for either choice. In fact, it may be your opinion that in some cases it is better to study in groups and in other cases it is better to study alone. If that is the opinion you would like to express, you should explain—with reasons, examples, and/or specific details—why group study is better in some cases and individual study is better in others. Here again, there is no "right" or "wrong" answer to a question like this. The important thing is to clearly communicate to the person who will be listening to your response what your opinion is and explain the reasons you have for holding it.

> **TIP**
>
> *Do not memorize responses before the test, especially ones that you get from the internet, or from test preparation instructors who say this is a good idea. It is not a good idea, and it will lower your score. Raters will recognize a memorized response because the rhythm, intonation, and even the content of the response will be very different from a spontaneous response. Memorized responses are easy to identify.*

## The Integrated Tasks

### Question 2: Fit and Explain

This is the first of the three Integrated Tasks in the Speaking section. For this question, you will read a short passage on your computer screen about a topic of campus-related interest. You will then listen to two people discussing that topic and expressing an opinion about the topic from the reading. Then you will be asked a question based on what you have read and what you have heard. You will have 60 seconds to provide your response. The general areas from which these topics are typically drawn include university policies, rules, or procedures; university plans; campus facilities; and quality of life on campus. The topics are designed to be accessible to all test takers and will be presented to you in a way that does not require that you have prior firsthand experience of college or university life in North America.

The reading passage could take various forms. For example, it could be a bulletin from the administration of a university regarding a new parking rule, a letter to the editor of a campus newspaper suggesting ways to improve the student health services, or an article from the campus newspaper discussing a proposal to build a new football stadium. In addition to describing the proposal, the reading passage will usually present two reasons either for or against the proposal. The reading passage is brief, approximately 90 to 115 words long. You will be given sufficient time to read the passage.

In the dialogue that will be played after you have read the reading passage, you will hear two speakers discussing the same article (or letter, announcement, or e-mail) that you have just read. One of the speakers will have a strong opinion about the proposed change—either in favor of it or against it—and will give reasons to support that opinion. The discussion is brief and typically lasts between 60 and 80 seconds.

After you have read the passage and then listened to the discussion, you will be asked a question about what you have read and heard. For example, there may be a reading passage that describes plans to make a new university rule and a conversation in which two students are discussing the rule. If in the conversation one student thinks the new rule is a bad idea, you would be asked to state what the student's opinion is and to explain the reasons the student gives for holding that opinion, using information from both the reading and the discussion.

This task tests your ability to integrate information from two sources—what you read and what you heard—and to summarize some aspect of it. The reading passage provides the context that allows you to understand what the speakers are talking about. The speakers will generally refer to the reading passage only indirectly. Therefore, as you read the reading passage, you should pay attention to a number of things: the description of the proposal (*what* has been proposed, planned, or changed) and the reasons that are given for the proposal. This will help you understand what it is that the two speakers are discussing as you listen to their conversation.

In some cases, a speaker will object to the position taken in the reading and will give information that challenges the reasons offered in the reading for that position. In other cases, a speaker may agree with the position taken in the reading and will either give information that supports those reasons or will give information that supports one of the reasons but challenges the other. It is therefore important, as you listen to the discussion, to determine the speaker's opinion toward the proposal and to understand the relationship between what the speakers say and what you have learned from the reading passage.

To answer this question, it is important to understand not only what the question asks you to do, but also what the question does *not* ask you to do. This type of Integrated Speaking task does not ask for your own opinion; rather, it asks you to state the opinion of one of the speakers and to summarize the speaker's reasons for having that opinion.

You will be given 45 or 50 seconds to read the passage, depending on its length, after which you will listen to the discussion. Then you will be given 30 seconds to prepare your answer and 60 seconds to respond. As with all the other questions, you may take notes while reading, listening, and preparing your answer, and you may refer to your notes while answering the question.

**TIP**

*Remember that taking notes on the reading and listening material in the Integrated Speaking tasks on the TOEFL iBT test is allowed. But don't try to write out a full response because you won't have time, and the raters scoring your response need to hear you speaking, not reading aloud.*

**Example**
The following sample question consists of an announcement of a university's decision to increase tuition and a discussion between students about whether the increase is justified. A question of this type will be presented to you as follows.

*First you will hear and see these directions:*

**Narrator**

Now you will read a passage about a campus situation and then listen to a conversation about the same topic. You will then answer a question, using information from both the reading passage and the conversation. You will have 30 seconds to prepare and 60 seconds to speak.

**Narrator**

City University is planning to increase tuition and fees. Read the announcement about the increase from the president of City University.

You will have 45 seconds to read the announcement. Begin reading now.

*A reading passage will appear on the screen.*

---

**Announcement from the President**

The university has decided to increase tuition and fees for all students by approximately 8% next semester. For the past 5 years, the tuition and fees have remained the same, but it is necessary to increase them now for several reasons. The university has many more students than we had 5 years ago, and we must hire additional professors to teach these students. We have also made a new commitment to research and technology and will be renovating and upgrading our laboratory facilities to better meet our students' needs.

---

When the passage appears, a clock at the top of your computer screen will begin counting down the time you have to read. When reading time has ended, the passage will disappear from the screen and will be replaced by a picture of two speakers engaged in conversation.

*You will then hear:*

**Narrator**

Now listen to two students as they discuss the announcement.

*Then the dialogue will begin.*

**Man**

Oh, great, now we have to come up with more money for next semester.

**Woman**

Yeah, I know, but I can see why. When I first started here, classes were so much smaller than they are now. With this many students, it's hard to get the personal attention you need . . .

**Man**

Yeah, I guess you're right. You know, in some classes I can't even get a seat. And I couldn't take the math course I wanted to because it was already full when I signed up.

**Woman**

And the other thing is, well, I am kind of worried about not being able to get a job after I graduate.

**Man**

Why? I mean you're doing really well in your classes, aren't you?

**Woman**

I'm doing OK, but the facilities here are so limited. There are some great new experiments in microbiology that we can't even do here . . . there isn't enough equipment in the laboratories, and the equipment they have is out of date. How am I going to compete for jobs with people who have practical research experience? I think the extra tuition will be a good investment.

*When the dialogue has ended, the picture of the speakers will be replaced by the following:*

> # Now get ready to answer the question.

*The question will then appear on the computer screen and will also be read aloud by the narrator.*

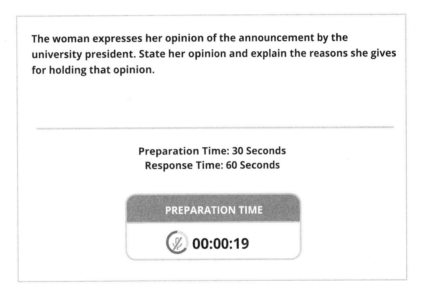

After you hear the question, you will be told when to begin to prepare your response and when to begin speaking. A "Preparation Time" clock will appear below the question and begin to count down from 30 seconds (00:00:30). At the end of 30 seconds you will hear a short beep. After the beep, the clock will change to read "Response Time" and will begin counting down from 60 seconds (00:01:00). When the response time has ended, recording will stop and a new screen will appear alerting you that the response time has ended.

**TIP**

*Try to recognize the attitude of the main speaker by listening for intonation, stress, and word choice. This helps you understand the speaker's point of view and plan an appropriate response.*

In giving your response to this question, you should state what the woman's opinion about the tuition increase is, and then explain her reasons for holding that opinion. You will probably have noticed as you listened to the conversation that the woman's reasons are essentially the same as those of the university president but are drawn from her own experience as a student. In your answer, you would want to connect information from both the conversation and the university's announcement. You could perhaps begin by saying that the woman agrees with the announcement and thinks that the university is right to increase its fees. In describing her reasons, you might say that she thinks the tuition increase is necessary because the university can then hire more teachers. She feels that classes are getting too crowded and more teachers are needed.

You might also want to mention that she has found it hard to get personal attention from her professors. You could also point out that she agrees that the money should be spent to improve laboratory facilities because they are out of date, and that this has made it hard for her to get the practical laboratory experience she feels she needs to get a good job. Your response should be complete enough that someone listening to your response who has not read the announcement or heard the conversation would understand what the new policy is, what the woman's opinion about it is, and the reasons she has for her opinion. There is a great deal of information in the reading passage and the conversation, and you are not expected to summarize all of the information in giving your response.

## Question 3: General/Specific

This is the second of the Integrated Speaking tasks. For this task you will read a short passage about an academic subject and listen to a brief excerpt of a professor's lecture on that subject. You will then be asked a question, which you will answer based on what you have read and heard. You will have 60 seconds in which to give your spoken response.

**TIP**

*Find listening and reading material on a topic that you like. The reading material and the listening material can provide similar or different views. Take notes on what you listen to and read, and create outlines. Use your notes and outlines to orally summarize the information and ideas from the listening and reading materials. Try to paraphrase what you have heard and read by using different words and grammatical structures.*

The topics for this question are drawn from a variety of fields: life science, social science, physical science, and the humanities. Although the topics are academic in nature, none of the written passages, lectures, or questions themselves requires prior knowledge of any academic field in particular. The language and concepts used are designed to be accessible to you no matter what your academic specialization may be.

The reading passage is approximately 90 to 115 words in length. It provides background or context to help you understand the lecture that will follow. The reading passage will usually treat the topic in somewhat general and abstract terms, and the lecture will treat the topic more specifically and concretely, often by providing an extended example or application of the concept presented in the reading. To answer the question that follows the lecture, you will need to draw on the reading as well as the lecture, and integrate and convey key information from both sources.

For example, some tasks will contain a reading passage that gives the definition of a general principle or process and a lecture that discusses a specific instance of the principle or process. For a pairing like this, you might be asked to explain the principle or process using the specific information from the listening. Or another pairing might include a reading passage that describes a problem and a lecture that presents the success, failure, or unintended consequences of an attempt to solve the problem, together with a question that asks you to explain the attempt to solve the problem and account for its results.

The sample General/Specific task presented below is a typical example. It begins with a reading passage discussing a general concept—the domestication of animal species—by describing two characteristics that make an animal species suitable for domestication. This passage is coupled with a lecture in which the professor talks about the behavior of two species of animals—a familiar domesticated animal that has both of the characteristics and a common, undomesticated species that lacks these characteristics. The question asks you to apply the more general information you have learned in the reading to the examples discussed in the lecture and explain how the behavior of the two species of animals is related to their suitability for domestication.

**Example**

A question of this type will be presented to you as follows. Question 3 is presented in the same way as question 2.

*First you will hear and see these directions:*

**Narrator**

Now you will read a passage about an academic subject and then listen to a lecture on the same topic. You will then answer a question, using information from both the reading passage and the lecture. You will have 30 seconds to prepare and 60 seconds to speak.

**Narrator**

Now read the passage about animal domestication. You have 45 seconds to read the passage. Begin reading now.

*A reading passage will appear on the screen.*

**Animal Domestication**

For thousands of years, humans have been able to domesticate, or tame, many large mammals that in the wild live together in herds. Once tamed, these mammals are used for agricultural work and transportation. Yet some herd mammals are not easily domesticated. A good indicator of an animal's suitability for domestication is how protective the animal is of its territory. Nonterritorial animals are more easily domesticated than territorial animals because they can live close together with animals from other herds. A second indicator is that animals with a hierarchical social structure, in which herd members follow a leader, are easy to domesticate, since a human can function as the "leader."

A clock at the top of your computer screen will count down the time you have to read. When reading time has ended, a picture of a professor in front of a class will appear on the screen:

*And you will hear this:*

**Narrator**
Now listen to a lecture on this topic in an ecology class.

*Then you will hear the lecture.*

**Professor**
So we've been discussing the suitability of animals for domestication . . . particularly animals that live together in herds. Now, if we take horses, for example . . . in the wild, horses live in herds that consist of one male and several females and their young. When a herd moves, the dominant male leads, with the dominant female and her young immediately behind him. The dominant female and her young are then followed immediately by the second most important female and her young, and so on. This is why domesticated horses can be harnessed one after the other in a row. They're "programmed" to follow the lead of another horse. On top of that, you often find different herds of horses in the wild occupying overlapping areas—they don't fight off other herds that enter the same territory.

But it's exactly the opposite with an animal like the, uh, the antelope . . . which . . . well, antelopes are herd animals too. But unlike horses, a male antelope will fight fiercely to prevent another male from entering its territory during the breeding season; OK—very different from the behavior of horses. Try keeping a couple of male antelopes together in a small space and see what happens. Also, antelopes don't have a social hierarchy—they don't instinctively follow any leader. That makes it harder for humans to control their behavior.

*When the lecture has ended, the picture of the professor will be replaced by the following:*

> # Now get ready to answer the question.

*Then the question will appear on the screen and will be read aloud by a narrator.*

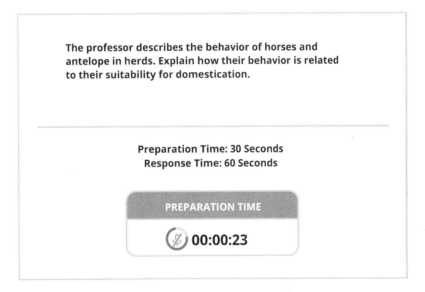

The professor describes the behavior of horses and antelope in herds. Explain how their behavior is related to their suitability for domestication.

Preparation Time: 30 Seconds
Response Time: 60 Seconds

PREPARATION TIME

00:00:23

After you hear the question, you will be told when to begin to prepare your response and when to begin speaking. A "Preparation Time" clock will appear below the question and begin to count down from 30 seconds (00:00:30). At the end of 30 seconds you will hear a short beep. After the beep, the clock will change to read "Response Time" and will begin to count down from 60 seconds (00:01:00). When the response time has ended, recording will stop and a new screen will appear alerting you that the response time has ended.

**TIP**

*Read a short article. Make an outline that includes only the major points of the article. Use the outline to orally summarize the information. Then add detail to the outline and orally summarize it again.*

To answer this question, you would use information from both the reading passage and the lecture, linking the specific information the professor provides in the lecture with the more general concepts introduced in the reading. For example, you could begin your response by saying that herd animals can be easily domesticated if they have a hierarchical social structure and are not territorial, and that this is why it is easier to domesticate horses than antelopes. You would want to provide some details about the behavior of horses, pointing out that their hierarchical social structure makes them willing to follow one another and thus allows a human being to act as their leader. You could also say that because horses are not territorial, they can be harnessed together without fighting. You would probably want to contrast horses' behavior with that of antelopes, which are territorial. You could explain that unlike horses, male antelopes fight if they are together, and that because antelopes do not have a social hierarchy, humans cannot control them by acting as their leader. Notice that you are not asked to summarize all the information in the reading and in the lecture. But you should provide enough information so that even a listener who had not read the passage or listened to the lecture would be able to understand your explanation. Here, as in all speaking questions that are based on academic content, you are provided with all the facts necessary to give your response, and no outside knowledge is required.

## Question 4: Summary

This Integrated task, the last of the four Speaking tasks, is based on academic content. For this task you will first listen to a brief excerpt from a professor's lecture on an academic subject, and then you will be asked a question about what you have heard. You will have 60 seconds in which to give your spoken response.

As with the General/Specific task (the other Speaking task that is based on academic content), the topics for this question are drawn from a variety of fields within the life sciences, social sciences, physical sciences, and humanities. Here too, no prior knowledge of any academic field in particular is required for you to understand the lecture or answer the question.

The lecture excerpt is between 60 and 90 seconds long and focuses on a single topic. Usually the professor will begin the lecture by defining a concept, by highlighting an issue, or by introducing a phenomenon, and will then go on to discuss important aspects of it or perspectives relating to it. The lecture will contain illustrative examples that help explain or clarify the main concept or issue. The question you are asked after you have heard the lecture will typically ask that you explain the main concept or issue of the lecture, using points and examples that were given in the lecture.

The lectures can be about processes, methods, theories, ideas, or phenomena of any type—natural, social, psychological, and others. If a lecture is about a process, the professor might explain the process by describing some of its functions. In a lecture about a theory, the professor might explain the theory by describing its applications. In a lecture about a phenomenon, the professor might explain it through examples that illustrate its causes or its effects.

**TIP**

*Find a textbook that includes questions about the material at the end of chapters. Practice answering the questions orally.*

In the sample Summary task given below, the lecture is about a social phenomenon—the emergence of a national culture in the United States in the early twentieth century. The professor illustrates this phenomenon by describing two of its causes—radio and the automobile—and how they contributed to it. After you hear the lecture, you are asked to use information from the lecture to explain how the causes contributed to the formation of a national culture.

**Example**

A question of this type will be presented to you as follows.

*First you will hear and see these directions:*

**Narrator**

Now you will listen to a lecture. You will then be asked to summarize the lecture. You will have 20 seconds to prepare and 60 seconds to speak.

*Then a picture of a professor will appear on the screen.*

*You will hear:*

**Narrator**

Now listen to part of a talk in a United States history class.

*The professor will then begin the lecture.*

**Professor**

Because the United States is such a large country, it took time for a common national culture to emerge. One hundred years ago there was very little communication among the different regions of the United States. One result of this lack of communication was that people around the United States had very little in common with one another. People in different parts of the country spoke differently, dressed differently, and behaved differently. But connections among Americans began to increase thanks to two technological innovations: the automobile and the radio.

Automobiles began to be mass-produced in the 1920s, which meant they became less expensive and more widely available. Americans in small towns and rural communities now had the ability to travel with ease to nearby cities. They could even take vacations to other parts of the country. The increased mobility provided by automobiles changed people's attitudes and created links that had not existed before. For example, people in small towns began to adopt behaviors, clothes, and speech that were popular in big cities or in other parts of the country.

As more Americans were purchasing cars, radio ownership was also increasing dramatically. Americans in different regions of the country began to listen to the same popular radio programs and musical artists. People repeated things they heard on the radio—some phrases and speech patterns heard in songs and radio programs began to be used by people all over the United States. People also listened to news reports on the radio. They heard the same news throughout the country, whereas in newspapers much news tended to be local. Radio brought Americans together by offering them shared experiences and information about events around the country.

*When the lecture has ended, the picture of the professor will be replaced by the following:*

> # Now get ready to answer the question.

*Then the question will appear on the screen and will be read aloud by a narrator.*

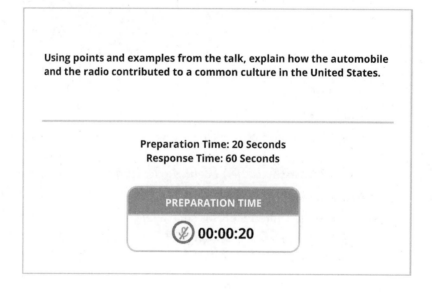

> Using points and examples from the talk, explain how the automobile and the radio contributed to a common culture in the United States.
>
> ---
>
> **Preparation Time: 20 Seconds**
> **Response Time: 60 Seconds**
>
> **PREPARATION TIME**
> 🎤 **00:00:20**

After you hear the question, you will be told when to begin preparing your response and when to begin speaking. A "Preparation Time" clock will appear below the question and begin to count down from 20 seconds (00:00:20). At the end of 20 seconds you will hear a short beep. After the beep, the clock will change to read "Response Time" and will begin to count down from 60 seconds (00:01:00). When the response time has ended, recording will stop and a new screen will appear alerting you that the response time has ended.

To answer this question, you might begin with a little background and mention that the United States did not have a common culture 100 years ago because people in different regions of the country did not communicate much with each other. Then you could say that the automobile and the radio changed this situation, and go on to summarize the information from the lecture that explains how they caused this change. For example, you could say that when automobiles became inexpensive, people from small towns could travel easily to cities or to other parts of the country, and that when they began to do this, they started acting like people from those other regions and started to dress and speak in the same way. As for the role that radio played in the emergence of a national culture, you could point out that when radio became popular, people from different parts of the country began listening to the same programs and the same news reports and began to speak alike and have similar experiences and ideas. If you have time, you could conclude by saying that these similar ways of speaking and dressing and thinking became the national culture of the United States. Remember that you do not need to repeat all of the details provided in the lecture. There is simply too much information in the lecture for you to do that. You should, however, convey enough information so that someone who has not heard the lecture would be able to form a clear idea of what the professor was explaining to the class.

Other lectures for the Summary task could include topics such as how people learn, and the central concept in that case might be that learning occurs when two events are associated in the brain. The professor would illustrate that concept by describing two different ways that events can be associated in the brain, and you would be asked to use points and examples from the lecture to explain how these ways of associating events result in learning. Or in a lecture about money, the professor might provide two different definitions of the concept and illustrate them with examples, and you would be asked in your response to explain the definitions, using the examples. The question that follows a lecture like this would typically ask you to use points and examples that you heard in the lecture to explain how people learn or what the definitions of money are.

# Speaking Scoring Rubric

## Independent Task: Question 1

| Score | General Description | Delivery | Language Use | Topic Development |
|---|---|---|---|---|
| 4 | The response fulfills the demands of the task, with at most minor lapses in completeness. It is highly intelligible and exhibits sustained, coherent discourse. A response at this level is characterized by all of the following: | Generally well-paced flow (fluid expression). Speech is clear. It may include minor lapses, or minor difficulties with pronunciation or intonation patterns, which do not affect intelligibility. | The response demonstrates effective use of grammar and vocabulary. It exhibits a fairly high degree of automaticity with good control of basic and complex structures (as appropriate). Some minor (or systematic) errors are noticeable but do not obscure meaning. | Response is sustained and sufficient to the task. It is generally well developed and coherent; relationships between ideas are clear (or there is a clear progression of ideas). |
| 3 | The response addresses the task appropriately, but may fall short of being fully developed. It is generally intelligible and coherent, with some fluidity of expression, though it exhibits some noticeable lapses in the expression of ideas. A response at this level is characterized by at least two of the following: | Speech is generally clear, with some fluidity of expression, though minor difficulties with pronunciation, intonation, or pacing are noticeable and may require listener effort at times (though overall intelligibility is not significantly affected). | The response demonstrates fairly automatic and effective use of grammar and vocabulary and fairly coherent expression of relevant ideas. Response may exhibit some imprecise or inaccurate use of vocabulary or grammatical structures. This may affect overall fluency, but it does not seriously interfere with the communication of the message. | Response is mostly coherent and sustained and conveys relevant ideas/information. Overall development is somewhat limited, usually lacking elaboration or specificity. Relationships between ideas may at times not be immediately clear. |

# Speaking Scoring Rubric

## Independent Task: Question 1

| Score | General Description | Delivery | Language Use | Topic Development |
|---|---|---|---|---|
| 2 | The response addresses the task, but development of the topic is limited. It contains intelligible speech, although problems with delivery and/or overall coherence occur; meaning may be obscured in places. A response at this level is characterized by at least two of the following: | Speech is basically intelligible, though listener effort is needed because of unclear articulation, awkward intonation, or choppy rhythm/pace; meaning may be obscured in places. | The response demonstrates limited range and control of grammar and vocabulary. These limitations often prevent full expression of ideas. For the most part, only basic sentence structures are used successfully and spoken with fluidity. Structures and vocabulary may express mainly simple (short) and/or general propositions, with simple or unclear connections made among them (serial listing, conjunction, juxtaposition). | The response is connected to the task, though the number of ideas presented or the development of ideas is limited. Mostly basic ideas are expressed, with limited elaboration (details and support). At times relevant substance may be vaguely expressed or repetitious. Connections of ideas may be unclear. |
| 1 | The response is very limited in content and/or coherence or is only minimally connected to the task, or speech is largely unintelligible. A response at this level is characterized by at least two of the following: | Consistent pronunciation, stress, and intonation difficulties cause considerable listener effort; delivery is choppy, fragmented, or telegraphic; frequent pauses and hesitations. | Range and control of grammar and vocabulary severely limit (or prevent) expression of ideas and connections among ideas. Some low-level responses may rely heavily on practiced or formulaic expressions. | Limited relevant content expressed. The response generally lacks substance beyond expression of very basic ideas. Speaker may be unable to sustain speech to complete the task and may rely heavily on repetition of the prompt. |
| 0 | Speaker makes no attempt to respond OR response is unrelated to the topic. | | | |

# Speaking Scoring Rubric

## Integrated Tasks: Questions 2, 3, and 4

| Score | General Description | Delivery | Language Use | Topic Development |
|---|---|---|---|---|
| **4** | The response fulfills the demands of the task, with at most minor lapses in completeness. It is highly intelligible and exhibits sustained, coherent discourse. A response at this level is characterized by all of the following: | Speech is generally clear, fluid, and sustained. It may include minor lapses or minor difficulties with pronunciation or intonation. Pace may vary at times as speaker attempts to recall information. Overall intelligibility remains high. | The response demonstrates good control of basic and complex grammatical structures that allow for coherent, efficient (automatic) expression of relevant ideas. Contains generally effective word choice. Though some minor (or systematic) errors or imprecise use may be noticeable, they do not require listener effort (or obscure meaning). | The response presents a clear progression of ideas and conveys the relevant information required by the task. It includes appropriate detail, though it may have minor errors or minor omissions. |
| **3** | The response addresses the task appropriately, but may fall short of being fully developed. It is generally intelligible and coherent, with some fluidity of expression, though it exhibits some noticeable lapses in the expression of ideas. A response at this level is characterized by at least two of the following: | Speech is generally clear, with some fluidity of expression, but it exhibits minor difficulties with pronunciation, intonation, or pacing and may require some listener effort at times. Overall intelligibility remains good, however. | The response demonstrates fairly automatic and effective use of grammar and vocabulary and fairly coherent expression of relevant ideas. Response may exhibit some imprecise or inaccurate use of vocabulary or grammatical structures or be somewhat limited in the range of structures used. Such limitations do not seriously interfere with the communication of the message. | The response is sustained and conveys relevant information required by the task. However, it exhibits some incompleteness, inaccuracy, lack of specificity with respect to content, or choppiness in the progression of ideas. |

# Speaking Scoring Rubric

## Integrated Tasks: Questions 2, 3, and 4

| Score | General Description | Delivery | Language Use | Topic Development |
|---|---|---|---|---|
| 2 | The response is connected to the task, though it may be missing some relevant information or contain inaccuracies. It contains some intelligible speech, but at times problems with intelligibility and/or overall coherence may obscure meaning. A response at this level is characterized by at least two of the following: | Speech is clear at times, though it exhibits problems with pronunciation, intonation, or pacing and so may require significant listener effort. Speech may not be sustained at a consistent level throughout. Problems with intelligibility may obscure meaning in places (but not throughout). | The response is limited in the range and control of vocabulary and grammar demonstrated (some complex structures may be used, but typically contain errors). This results in limited or inaccurate connections. Automaticity of expression may be evident only at the phrasal level. | The response conveys some relevant information but is clearly incomplete or inaccurate. It is incomplete if it omits key ideas, makes vague reference to key ideas, or demonstrates limited development of important information. An inaccurate response demonstrates misunderstanding of key ideas from the stimulus. Typically, ideas expressed may not be well connected or cohesive, so that familiarity with the stimulus is necessary in order to follow what is being discussed. |
| 1 | The response is very limited in content or coherence or is only minimally connected to the task. Speech may be largely unintelligible. A response at this level is characterized by at least two of the following: | Consistent pronunciation and intonation problems cause considerable listener effort and frequently obscure meaning. Delivery is choppy, fragmented, or telegraphic. Speech contains frequent pauses and hesitations. | Range and control of grammar and vocabulary severely limit (or prevent) expression of ideas and connections among ideas. Some very low-level responses may rely on isolated words or short utterances to communicate ideas. | The response fails to provide much relevant content. Ideas that are expressed are often inaccurate, or limited to vague utterances or repetitions (including repetition of prompt). |
| 0 | Speaker makes no attempt to respond OR response is unrelated to the topic. | | | |

# Strategies for Preparing for and Taking the Speaking Section

## Preparing for the Speaking Section

- When you complete the practice TOEFL iBT Speaking sections in the practice tests in this book, listen carefully to each of your recorded responses. Create a set of guiding questions to help you evaluate your performance. Here are some examples of the kind of questions you may want to include:
  - Did I complete the task?
  - Did I speak clearly?
  - Did I avoid grammatical errors?
  - Did I use words correctly?
  - Did I organize my ideas clearly and appropriately?
  - Did I provide a complete response?
  - Did I use the time effectively?

  Once you have completed your evaluation, decide what changes you want to make to your response. Then try again, making a new recording. Compare the recordings and determine if any further revisions are necessary.

- Try to periodically analyze your strengths and weaknesses. Try to understand what you are and are not able to do well and why.

- When you monitor your speaking practice, try to evaluate the pace of your speech. After each practice, ask yourself the following questions:
  - Did I speak too fast?
  - Did I speak too slowly?
  - Did I pause too often?

- You may want to monitor your own progress by keeping an audio journal, which entails keeping samples of your speaking activities or practices. You can also ask for feedback from one or more friends, tutors, or teachers.

## Tips for the Day of the Test

- Remember that taking notes on the reading and listening material in the Integrated Speaking tasks on the TOEFL iBT test is allowed.
- Listen to the item directions carefully to understand exactly what you are being asked to do.
- Use your preparation time as effectively as possible. Plan your response by thinking about the important ideas you want to convey in a simple, organized way.
- Do not begin speaking until you are told to do so.
- Answer each question as completely as possible in the time allowed.
- Make sure to adjust your microphone and volume carefully.
- Speak into the microphone at an appropriate volume. Do not put your mouth directly onto the microphone. If you touch your mouth to the microphone, raters may find it difficult to understand what you are saying.
- Avoid whispering. If you whisper, raters may find it difficult to understand what you are saying.

# Frequently Asked Questions About the Speaking Section

### 1. Why does the TOEFL iBT test include a Speaking section?

The focus of the test is on communicative competence and encompasses your ability to use English to communicate effectively in an academic setting. Speaking is a key communication skill, along with listening, reading, and writing.

### 2. Why are some of the questions in the Speaking section based on reading passages and/or dialogues or lectures?

Speaking tasks that combine reading passages and/or dialogues or lectures with speaking are called integrated tasks. They are included in the TOEFL iBT test in recognition of the fact that to succeed academically in English-speaking colleges and universities, students need to be able to combine all their English language skills—in reading, listening, and speaking, as well as writing—inside and outside the classroom.

### 3. How much reading and listening will I have to do for the Speaking section?

The reading and listening materials that are associated with the integrated tasks vary in length but are all quite brief. Reading passages range from approximately 90 to 115 words, and the dialogues or lectures are generally between 60 and 90 seconds long. In addition to being short, the reading passages, dialogues, and lectures are not intended to be difficult. They are designed to provide you with clear and accessible information to use in answering the questions.

### 4. May I take notes at all times during the Speaking section?

Yes. You may take notes at any time during the Speaking section—while reading the written passages, listening to the spoken dialogues or lectures, and preparing your responses. While you listen to the dialogues or lectures and take notes, you should *not* try to write down word for word everything you hear. If you try to do this, you will probably miss hearing important information. Similarly, while preparing your spoken response, do not try to write out an answer that you will then try to speak. You will not have enough time to write out a full response, and raters will be rating you on your ability to speak spontaneously, not on your ability to read aloud from a text that you have written. Instead, you should use your preparation time to review whatever notes you have taken and to organize your ideas.

### 5. How will my responses be rated?

Each Speaking response is scored by both human raters and ETS automated scoring engines, using the Speaking scoring rubrics (pages 184–187). The human raters evaluate your response for topic development, delivery, and language use, using the TOEFL iBT Speaking rubrics. ETS scoring engines primarily measures features described in the Speaking rubrics under Language Use and Delivery.

### 6. How will the Speaking section score be determined?

Human scores are combined with the *SpeechRater* machine scores, then optimally weighted to produce raw scores. The raw scores are then converted to scaled scores of 0 to 30, which is the Speaking section score that will be reported to the institutions that you request.

### 7. How will mistakes affect my score?

Raters will not focus on the number of errors you make. They will score the response based on the overall performance. A response that contains minor or occasional errors may still be scored at the highest level.

### 8. What happens if I do not have time to finish my answer?

You may find that for some tasks, you are not able to include in your answer all the information you would like to. The time allotted for each speaking response is considered sufficient for you to give a complete answer, and you should try to give as thorough an answer as possible. However, the raters who evaluate your responses recognize that it may not always be possible for you to anticipate precisely how much of what you want to say will fit into the amount of time provided. Keep in mind that how clearly and coherently you convey information is as important as how much information you convey. Therefore you should avoid speaking at an unnaturally rapid pace if you see that time is going to run out before you say everything you have planned to say. You may find it useful to time yourself when practicing the speaking tasks. This will help you get an idea of how much can be said in the allotted time.

### 9. What happens if I finish my response before time runs out?

If you finish your answer before time runs out, you may want to consider what additional information you could add that would make your answer more complete. If you have extra time, it may not be a good idea for you to merely repeat what you have already said. Rather, ask yourself what else you could say to clarify, elaborate on, or otherwise develop your response more fully. Timing yourself when practicing the speaking tasks should help you get accustomed to the time allowances.

### 10. May I go back and change an answer?

No. Each of your spoken responses is recorded, and it is not possible to go back and rerecord what you have said. For each question, you will be given some time to prepare your answer, and this should help you plan ahead of time what you want to say. You should also remember that your speaking responses are not expected to be perfect. If in the course of giving your spoken response, you realize that you should have said something differently, you should feel free to correct your mistake if you wish, just as you would if you had made a mistake while speaking in your native language and wanted to correct it. Otherwise you may want to simply ignore an error and continue with your response, making sure that the remainder of what you say is as intelligible, coherent, and accurate as possible.

### 11. How will my accent and pronunciation affect my score?

All TOEFL iBT test takers speak with an accent to some degree or another, and your score will not be affected by your accent, unless your accent interferes with the intelligibility of your response. Minor and/or occasional pronunciation mistakes are also expected, even among the most proficient test takers, and, here again, as long as pronunciation mistakes do not interfere with the intelligibility of your response, they will not count against your score.

# 5 Writing Section

## The Writing Section

There are two tasks in the Writing section of the TOEFL iBT test: the Integrated Writing task and the Writing for an Academic Discussion task.

The Integrated Writing task comes first because it requires some listening, and when you are taking the real TOEFL iBT test, you will be wearing headphones. When you finish the Integrated Writing task, which takes up to 20 minutes, you then work on the Writing for an Academic Discussion task. You will have up to 10 minutes to complete this task.

This chapter discusses each of the Writing tasks in detail and the scoring criteria that raters will use to evaluate your writing. It includes samples of each task, sample responses to each task, and specific advice on how to approach writing your own response.

For both Writing tasks, the raters evaluating your writing recognize that your response is a first draft. You are not expected to produce a well-researched, comprehensive essay about a highly specific, specialized topic. You can receive a high score with a response that contains some errors.

Be sure to use your own words rather than memorized sentences and examples in your response. Responses that include memorized text will receive a lower score.

# The Integrated Writing Task

You will read a passage about an academic topic for three minutes, and then you will hear a short lecture related to the topic. Then you will be asked to summarize the points in the lecture and explain how they relate to specific points in the reading passage.

This task gives you the opportunity to show that you can communicate in writing about academic information you have read and listened to.

**Example**

A reading passage like the following will appear on your computer screen. You will have three minutes to read the passage.

---

**Vitrified Forts**

A number of hill forts (fortified defensive structures) built in Scotland during the Middle Ages have an unusual feature: they are what researchers call "vitrified," which means that their stones have been exposed to extreme heat and have melted or fused together, becoming hard and glass-like. Several theories have been offered to explain how and why the forts were vitrified.

One theory holds that vitrification was part of a religious or ceremonial ritual. The ancient myths and folktales of Scotland are full of references to cities and castles made of glass, so glass must have had some special significance to the people of the area. Vitrification could have been their way of trying to create glass castles. Perhaps they believed that the vitrified forts had supernatural powers or benefits.

According to a second theory, the stones of the fort walls became vitrified accidentally by fires set by people who attacked the forts. Supporters of this theory point out that fire was used as a weapon to ignite the wood beams that were used as structural support for the fort walls. Attackers used flaming arrows and other projectiles in an attempt to start a fire. As the wood beams were being burned up by the fire, the heat from the fire could have vitrified the stone parts of the walls.

Other researchers think that it is more probable that the forts' builders purposefully vitrified the walls in order to strengthen them. When a wall becomes vitrified, the stones fuse together so that there are no gaps or openings between them. In other words, vitrification produces a solid, continuous wall surface. This makes it very hard for arrows to penetrate the walls, and so this could have been an effective defensive measure.

While the theories about vitrified forts sound convincing, unfortunately none of them adequately explain the phenomenon.

---

*Then you will hear:*

**Narrator**

Now listen to part of a lecture on the topic you just read about.

**Professor**

First, glass may have had special significance for the people of ancient Scotland. But a problem with the reading's theory is that by the time most of the forts were built, Christianity had taken hold in the area. By 900 C.E., when the last forts were being constructed, Christianity had been adopted by most people in the area, to the point that the native religious and ceremonial traditions of the area were almost completely wiped out. And the Christian religion as it was practiced at that time did not attribute any supernatural or magical powers to glass.

Second, re-creations of the vitrification process by scientists have shown that the temperatures needed for vitrification are extremely high—over one thousand degrees Celsius. A fire that was started by attackers would never reach this temperature. To reach it, a fire would have to be enclosed, blown toward the wall, and maintained, like fires in pottery ovens. There just wasn't enough wood used as structural support for the walls for this to happen. The attackers could not have maintained a fire that was hot enough to vitrify stone.

Third, it's true that the glassy substance produced by vitrification is strong, but it's also very brittle, meaning it can shatter on impact. Scottish defenders knew that the strongest forts are flexible, not brittle—that's why, when building forts, they often tended to pack the stones loosely together. Loosely packed stones would have allowed the walls to bend slightly and thus to absorb the impact of weapons beating against the walls. The brittle walls created by vitrification are actually easier to break down than non-vitrified walls are, so it hardly seems likely that vitrification was deliberately done by fort defenders wanting to strengthen their fort against attack.

**Narrator**

Summarize the points made in the lecture, being sure to explain how they challenge the specific theories proposed in the reading passage.

*The reading passage will then reappear on your computer screen, along with the following directions and writing task:*

You have **20 minutes** to plan and write your response. Your response will be judged on the basis of the quality of your writing and on how well your response presents the points in the lecture and their relationship to the reading passage. Typically, an effective response will contain a minimum of 150 words.

*The writing clock will then start a countdown for 20 minutes of writing time.*

## How the Task Is Phrased

The lecture usually contradicts or disagrees with the information presented in the reading passage. Following are some typical ways in which the writing task will be phrased.

- Summarize the points made in the lecture, being sure to explain how they challenge/cast doubt on/oppose/respond to the specific points made in the reading passage. (Opposition or contradiction)

- Summarize the points made in the lecture, being sure to explain how they challenge the specific theories presented in the reading passage. (Theories and their weaknesses)

- Summarize the points made in the lecture, being sure to explain how they present solutions to the specific problems mentioned in the reading passage. (Problems and solutions)

- Summarize the points made in the lecture, being sure to explain how they cast doubt on the specific solutions proposed in the reading passage. (Solutions and their weaknesses)

# Strategies for Taking the Integrated Writing Task

**As you read:**

- Take notes on your scratch paper.

- Look for the main idea of the reading passage. The main idea often has to do with some policy or practice or some position on an issue. Or it may have to do with proposing some overall hypothesis about the way some process or procedure works or should work or how some natural phenomenon is believed to work.

- See how this main idea is evaluated or developed. Usually it will be developed in one of the following ways:

  1. Arguments or explanations are presented that support the main position; for example, why there are good reasons to believe that some policy or practice will be beneficial or prove useful or advisable or perhaps why it has been a good thing in the past.

  2. Arguments, explanations, or problems are brought up concerning why some policy, practice, position, or hypothesis does not work or will not be useful/advisable.

- You do not need to memorize the reading passage. It will reappear on your computer screen when it is time to write.

- Note points in the passage that either support the main idea or provide reasons to doubt the main idea. Typically, the main idea will be developed with three points.

**As you listen:**

- Take notes on your scratch paper.

- Listen for information, examples, or explanations that make points in the reading passage seem wrong or less convincing or even untrue. For instance, in the example just given, the reading passage proposes a theory that vitrified forts were part of a religious or ceremonial ritual because glass held special importance in ancient Scottish tales. But the lecture says that by the time most of the vitrified forts were built, the ancient Scottish traditions had been replaced by Christianity, and Christianity does not consider glass to have special importance or special supernatural properties. According to the next theory proposed in the reading passage, the forts were vitrified accidentally as attackers of the forts set them on fire. But the lecturer points out that even if attackers set the wood supporting the walls of the forts on fire, the temperature of those fires was not high enough to vitrify the stone that the forts were built from. For fires to become that hot, they would need to be enclosed, blown toward the stone walls, and kept going for a significant amount of time. The attackers would not have been able to create and maintain such fires. The final theory presented in the reading is that the forts were vitrified on purpose by their builders because vitrified forts would be better protected against arrows or other means of attack. The lecturer, however, says that vitrified forts would not be better protected against attacks because vitrified stone is brittle, meaning that it would break easily. Loosely packed stones, instead of vitrified ones, would create more flexible walls that could better withstand the weapons of attackers. Fort builders at the time would have known the disadvantages of brittle vitrified walls.

### As you write your response:

- You may take off your headset if you wish.

- Before you start writing, briefly reread the passage, consult your notes, and make a very brief outline of the points you wish to make. You can write this outline on your scratch paper or draw lines between the notes you took on the reading passage and the notes you took on the lecture. You can even type your outline and notes right into the answer area and then replace these with sentences and paragraphs as you compose your response.

- Remember that you are *not* being asked for your opinion. You *are* being asked to explain how the points in the lecture relate to points in the reading passage.

- Write in full English sentences. The best way to organize the response is to write a short introductory paragraph that explains the main topic addressed in the two passages, and a few (usually three) body paragraphs in which each main point from the reading passage is briefly summarized and then followed by an explanation of how the corresponding lecture point responds or relates to it.

- Remember that your job is to select all the important information from the lecture and coherently and accurately present this information in relation to the relevant information from the reading passage. Your response should contain the following:

  1. The specific ideas, explanations, and arguments in the lecture that oppose or challenge points in the reading passage.

  2. Coherent and accurate presentation of each point that you make (that is, the language you use should make sense and should accurately reflect the ideas presented in the lecture and the reading passage)

  3. A clear, coherent structure that enables the reader to understand what points in the lecture relate to what points in the reading passage.

- An effective response will contain at least 150 words. That is just a bare minimum, however, and many effective responses are longer. There is no upper limit for the length of a response as long as it addresses the task presented.

- CAUTION: You will receive a score of 0 if all you do is copy words from the reading passage. You will receive a score of 1 if you write *only* about the reading passage. *To respond successfully, you must do your best to write about the ways the points in the lecture are related to specific points in the reading passage.*

# How Responses Are Scored

Raters scoring your response will focus on three main aspects: **completeness and accuracy of the content**, **organization**, and **language use**.

**Completeness and accuracy of the content** is an extremely important characteristic of a good response. Remember that for this task, you are asked to summarize the points made in the lecture and explain their relationship to the reading passage. In evaluating accurate development, raters will look for how well you can select the important information from the lecture, whether you present it **clearly and accurately**, and whether you explain its relationship to the information in the reading passage. It is important to include all the most important details from the lecture, not only the main ideas; in other words, **all** the information that supports the main lecture ideas should be included in your response. It is true that you are asked to summarize the lecture, but that does not mean that you should omit any important lecture detail from your summary. If you omit important details from the lecture, you may receive a lower score. When summarizing the lecture in your own words, you should express the ideas, even those that are complex or nuanced, as clearly as you can. The same goes for accuracy: if you convey important details or ideas from the lecture incorrectly in your response, you may receive a lower score. Finally, you should be sure to explain how the lecture information relates to (usually opposes) the information in the reading; refer to details in How the Task Is Phrased for more information about the relationship between the lecture and the reading. If you do not explain that relationship, or if you misrepresent it, you may receive a lower score.

Your response should also be **well organized**. This means that you should present information so that any reader can read it easily from beginning to end and understand the main ideas, how they are supported, and how they relate to one another. You should organize your writing in paragraphs and consider writing an introductory paragraph in which you indicate the main topic of the reading passage and then indicate the general point that the lecturer is trying to make about it. Since there are usually three main points that the reading passage expresses and the lecture responds to, a successful way to organize your response is to follow the introductory paragraph with three body paragraphs, each devoted to one of the main points. Within each body paragraph, consider devoting the first sentence or two to summarizing the idea the reading is expressing, and then explain in detail how the lecture responds to that idea. Remember that you are not required to summarize all the important ideas and details from the reading passage, so you should devote most of each paragraph to conveying important information from the **lecture**. A concluding paragraph for your response is typically not necessary. Finally, make clear transitions between ideas within paragraphs and from one paragraph to another. Note that there are various other ways to organize a response. Still, experience shows that the organization described above is usually successful and presents the information in a very clear way. If you do not organize your response well, you may receive a lower score.

A very important characteristic of responses that raters consider in scoring is your **use of language**. Your task is to write in your own words about ideas presented in the lecture and the reading. As we explained above, some of the ideas will be complex or nuanced and may require you to use a variety of grammatical structures as well as a broad range of precise vocabulary. The structure of your sentences, word choices, and vocabulary should be consistently correct, accurate, and clear. Grammar and vocabulary mistakes, especially those that interfere with the clarity of what you try to express, may also lead to a lower score. Remember that copying a lot of language from the reading passage will not help you achieve a better score. Copying phrases from the reading passage is not penalized, but raters will not reward it either. You can make notes about words, phrases, and ideas used in the lecture while listening to it and then use the notes when writing your response. However, you will have to rely on your own ability to use appropriate grammar and vocabulary, and that is what raters will be judging. Note that your writing does not have to be perfect to get a top score; however, the mistakes you make and fail to correct would have to be few and minor to receive a top score.

# Integrated Writing Scoring Rubric

Here is the official scoring guide used by raters when they read Integrated Writing Task responses.

| Score | Description |
|-------|-------------|
| 5 | A response at this level successfully selects the important information from the lecture and coherently and accurately presents this information in relation to the relevant information presented in the reading. The response is well organized, and occasional language errors that are present do not result in inaccurate or imprecise presentation of content or connections. |
| 4 | A response at this level is generally good in selecting the important information from the lecture and in coherently and accurately presenting this information in relation to the relevant information in the reading, but it may have minor omission, inaccuracy, vagueness, or imprecision of some content from the lecture or in connection to points made in the reading. A response is also scored at this level if it has more frequent or noticeable minor language errors, as long as such usage and grammatical structures do not result in anything more than an occasional lapse of clarity or in the connection of ideas. |
| 3 | A response at this level contains some important information from the lecture and conveys some relevant connection to the reading, but it is marked by one or more of the following: |

- Although the overall response is definitely oriented to the task, it conveys only vague, global, unclear, or somewhat imprecise connection of the points made in the lecture to points made in the reading.

- The response may omit one major key point made in the lecture.

- Some key points made in the lecture or the reading, or connections between the two, may be incomplete, inaccurate, or imprecise.

- Errors of usage and/or grammar may be more frequent or may result in noticeably vague expressions or obscured meanings in conveying ideas and connections.

| Score | Description |
|---|---|
| 2 | A response at this level contains some relevant information from the lecture, but is marked by significant language difficulties or by significant omission or inaccuracy of important ideas from the lecture or in the connections between the lecture and the reading; a response at this level is marked by one or more of the following: |

- The response significantly misrepresents or completely omits the overall connection between the lecture and the reading.

- The response significantly omits or significantly misrepresents important points made in the lecture.

- The response contains language errors or expressions that largely obscure connections or meaning at key junctures, or that would likely obscure understanding of key ideas for a reader not already familiar with the reading and the lecture.

| | |
|---|---|
| 1 | A response at this level is marked by one or more of the following: |

- The response provides little or no meaningful or relevant coherent content from the lecture.

- The language level of the response is so low that it is difficult to derive meaning.

| | |
|---|---|
| 0 | A response at this level merely copies sentences from the reading, rejects the topic or is otherwise not connected to the topic, is written in a foreign language, consists of keystroke characters, or is blank. |

# Sample Scored Responses for the Integrated Writing Task

The following were written in response to the task "Vitrified Forts" on pages 192 to 193.

## Score 5 Response

The lecture suggests that theories regarding the origin of the vitrification of forts in the passage are all inadequate.

The first theory in the passage, which proposes that vitrification was part of a religious ritual to create glass castles, is deemed highly improbable by the lecturer because by the time these forts were vitrified, Christianity has well-spread into Scotland. Christianity does not attribute any supernatural power over glass or glass forts, which the first theory in the passage states as the main reason for vitrification. Moreso, the lecturer also indicated that by the time the last Scottish fort was vitrified in 900 C.E., most people in the area had adopted Christianity and old religious customs have almost been entirely wiped-out.

The second theory in the passage, which states that the forts have been vitrified due to acciddental fires set by attackers, also seems impossible to the lecturer. This is due to the fact that vitrification requires an extremely high temperature. Fire produced by soldiers at the time did not even come close to the required temperature. Even if it did, the fire needed to be enclosed, blown, and maintained over the stone walls of the fort for it to be vitrified. There was not enough wood available at the fort for this to happen.

The third theory in the passage states that vitrification was done to strengthen the walls of the fort. The lecturer opposes this final theory by claiming that vitrification causes stone to be brittle. Every Scottish war expert at the time would have known that brittle forts were bad as they are easier to break down over impact. Flexible walls were preffered. In this way, the lecturer challenged the last theory used in the reading passage.

*Rater Comments*

This writer does an excellent job of presenting the lecture's points that challenge the theories presented in the reading passage. The lecture's arguments are presented clearly, and all the important supporting details are included. The writer begins each body paragraph by briefly summarizing the theory presented in the reading and then explains how the lecturer challenges that theory. This is a very effective way of organizing a response. There are a few minor errors: for example, in the first body paragraph, the writer writes, "Christianity does not attribute any supernatural power over glass," where the correct preposition should be "*to* glass." The end of the last sentence in the same paragraph should read "old religious customs *had been almost entirely wiped out.*" If your English is really good, you will find a few other minor errors and typos, but, overall, they are infrequent and typical of highly proficient nonnative speakers submitting the first draft of an essay. There is a lot of good writing in this successful response, and it earns a score of 5.

### Score 4 Response

The lecture main purpose is to cast doubt into the original theories that explained why the walls built in Scotland during the Middle Ages were vitrified.

First, the lecturer describes why vitrification could not be a ceremonial ritual as it is stated in the reading. The reason he uses is that, by the time that the last wall was constructed (around ninth century), christianity was already wiped out the rest of the religions. Christians do not attribute any magical powers to glass. Hence, there would be no reason to use vitrification as a part of a religious ritual.

After that, the lecturer explains that the temperatures needed by the rock to vitrify were really high. In order to get this temperature, a fire should be enclosed and maintained for a while. In the forts there were no enough wood to get that temperture, even if it would get close enough an open air fire can not maintain that temperature for a long time. That is why vitrification could not have been originated accidentally by fire as the reading passage states.

At last, it is not probable that defenders vitrify their walls on purpose because the material could break with impacts. Obviously, this is not intended for a wall, in fact, some walls were made in a way that they can bend to support the impacts.

*Rater Comments*

Compared to the previous response, this response conveys the lecturer's arguments a little less clearly. Some of the problems are due to poor word choice. For example, in the first body paragraph, the writer writes that "christianity was already wiped out the rest of the religions." If you are a reader who is not familiar with the lecture, you will be left guessing: did the writer mean to say that Christianity *had* wiped other religions, or that it *was* wiped out *by* other religions? In the second body paragraph the writer says in one place that for a fire to get really hot, it needed to be "enclosed," but then in the next sentence the writer writes about an "open air fire." It is unclear how those two ideas fit together. In the last paragraph, the writer points out that the "material" could break, but it is not completely clear what the material is (probably the vitrified rocks, but that would need to be expressed more clearly). In the next sentence, the writer talks about walls *supporting* impacts, but the intended word is probably *resisting*. There are other minor but noticeable grammatical errors, such as "there were no enough wood" (which should read "there *was not* enough wood"). Overall, the writer has written a strong response that directly addresses the task and conveys most of the important information well; however, due to what the Scoring Guide calls "occasional lapses of clarity," the response earns a score of 4.

## Score 3 Response

> There are three theorie of virtifications of the stones used to build some of the hill forts in scotland. The theories in the lecture were challenged in the reading passage.
>
> First theory according to the passage was that virtifying the stones to a glassy material was a part of a religious ritual, But the lecture opposed this point by mentioning that during that time all religious beleives were all wieped out and didn't exist anymore !!
>
> Second theory mentioned in the passage was that the vitrivaction of the stones happened accidentally by predatores who used to attack the forts using fires, But the professor in the lecture mentioned that the current researches don't approve this theory because the tempreture needed to vitrify the stone should be very high and the stone should be exposed to it for a long time and such thing would not be possible to happen using the traditional methods of predatores fire attacks back in those days.
>
> The third and last theory mentioned in the reading passage was that the people who built the forts did this stone vitrification to a more glassy structre on purpose !! why ?? to mak the stone more stronger so it would provide more protection, However the professor in the lecture contracted this theroy by pointing out that actually although vitrifying the stone to a glassy material will make it fuse together which might make it appear stronger, but actually it will make it more brittle, loose and easy to break down.

*Rater Comments*

This response definitely addresses the task and is mostly well organized, but the problems we see in it are more serious than those we would find a score-4 response. First of all, the writer misrepresents the relationship between the lecture and the reading passage in the opening paragraph: the lecture in fact challenges the theories introduced in the reading passage rather than the other way round. In covering the first lecture point, the writer says that "*all* religious beleives were all wieped out," which (even if we ignore the errors and typos) significantly overstates the point the lecturer is making about Christianity replacing previous religious beliefs in the area. In the second body paragraph, the writer confusingly refers to "predatores" attacking the forts. In English, "predator" usually means a predatory animal, not a human fighter, and so the writer creates the false impression that the forts were attacked by animals. There are also more frequent errors in usage and grammar: for example, in the last paragraph, the writer uses "more stronger" (should be just "stronger"); we read that the professor "contracted" a theory (should be "contradicted"); and there is a compound sentence construction that uses both "although" and "but" (where the writer should have used only "while"). This response illustrates many of the typical features that can cause a response to receive a score of 3.

### Score 2 Response

> In the lecture the professor made several points about the reasons why the stones in Scotland have been vitrified.
>
> But the lecture cast doubt on the reading.
>
> First of all the professor talks about religious ceremonies. But after some researches we know that the people didn't believe in supernatural power.
>
> On the other hand the reading argues that the vitrification was part of such an ceremonial ritual and that the people of the area believed in supernatural power.
>
> The second point in the reading is that they thougt that the stones became vitrified because of fire.
>
> But the professor in the lecture offeres that the walls were too high to fire them down. So the attacers couldn't use fire to enter the village.
>
> The last point in the reading is that they vitrified the stones to strengthen them. In contrast the professor argues that the walls were britterly. If you vitrifie the wall it is very easy to braek them down.
>
> To sum up the lecture cast doubt on the reading because all the points are different.

*Rater Comments*

Although the writer conveys some relevant information from the lecture, a lot of important information is left out or misrepresented. In conveying the lecturer's first argument, the writer says that "people didn't believe in supernatural power," which completely ignores the important details about Christianity, other religions, and the fact that the local religious beliefs had changed. The second argument, "the walls were too high to fire them down," is difficult to understand, and even if we try to fill in some meaning, it clearly does not convey what the lecturer says. In summarizing the lecturer's third argument, the writer mentions that a vitrified wall is "very easy to braek . . . down," which does convey the gist of the lecturer's point; however, the statement is not supported by any further explanation, since most readers will probably not understand that "britterly" stands for "brittle." In the terms of the Scoring Guide, this response "significantly omits or misrepresents important points" and "contains language errors that largely obscure meaning at key junctures," which are characteristics of responses that earn a score of 2.

### Score 1 Response

in the Scotland during the mild age they call " vitrified". in the past their ancient think a glass need made sothing special in their world. so they created a lot of glass and they think glass have a magic or power and vitrified could have been their way of trying to create glass castles that is the first theory.

Second they think the forrt wall become accidenttally by a fire set by a people who attacked the forts. so they support use a wepond is the wood beam because that can destroy the stucture of the forts wall because the the wood beam can be burn up by the fire. so the heat from the fire could have vitrified the stone parts of the walls.

Scotland make the vitrified very important with their life they think it can protect from everything and vitrified will give them have more powers. So that why in Scotland they have a number of hill forts build in the structure

### *Rater Comments*

In this response, the writer tries to summarize a part of the reading passage. There are many errors in grammar and usage, and the meaning is often obscured. But most importantly, this response contains no information from the lecture. Even if this reading passage summary were more complete and contained fewer errors, it could only receive the score of 1. Remember that conveying relevant and important information *from the lecture* is necessary for a response to rise above the score of 1.

# Writing for an Academic Discussion

The second task in the Writing section is the Writing for an Academic Discussion task. You will read an online discussion for which a professor has posted a question about a topic and to which some classmates have responded with their ideas. You will write a response that contributes to the discussion. You have 10 minutes to read the professor's question, to read your classmates' posts, and to write your own post.

An effective response typically contains at least 100 words. Experience has shown that responses shorter than 100 words typically do not demonstrate the development of ideas and variety of grammatical structures and vocabulary needed to earn a score of 5. There is no maximum word limit. You may write as much as you wish in the time allotted, but it is wise to set aside some time at the end to review what you have written and correct any mistakes. Also, do not write just to be writing; write to clearly and effectively contribute to the discussion. The number of ideas you express is important, but it is the quality of your ideas and the effectiveness with which you express them that will be most valued by the raters.

**Example**

Your professor is teaching a class on education. Write a post responding to the professor's question.

**In your response, you should do the following.**

- Express and support your opinion.
- Make a contribution to the discussion in your own words.

An effective response will contain at least 100 words.

**Dr. Achebe**

This week we analyzed some aspects of current educational systems. One type of school system we discussed was boarding schools, which, as the name suggests, is a type of school where students live during the school year. I would like you to discuss whether you consider boarding schools beneficial for students' education or whether you think day schools, or schools where students do not live at the schools, are better for most students. Explain why you think so.

**Claire**

I would have loved to have attended a boarding school. I feel like boarding schools would have helped me establish a strict daily routine and helped me become more disciplined. Also, being in a boarding school means that you are with friends and classmates around the clock, and I would have loved such an opportunity.

**Andrew**

I personally do not support the boarding school system as I believe it can lead to many psychological problems. In fact, I have heard about what is referred to as "boarding school syndrome," which, in simple terms, suggests that some students who attend boarding schools at a very young age can have long-term emotional or behavioral challenges. So why take that risk if most students can just go to day schools?

In this prompt, the professor asks the class whether boarding schools or day schools are better for students, and two discussion participants give their opinions. The first argues in favor of boarding schools, pointing out that they teach students discipline and provide them with companionship. The second argues against boarding schools, explaining that they create difficult psychological challenges for their students.

Test takers are expected to contribute to this discussion and provide their opinions about boarding schools and day schools, taking the existing posts as points of departure, or coming up with completely new ideas. Some test takers, for example, might write more about the ideas of discipline and companionship that were brought up by Claire; others might elaborate on the psychological challenges brought up by Andrew. Still others might focus on the economic aspects of attending boarding schools and day schools, respectively; on the quality of the education in the two types of schools; or on the age at which boarding might be appropriate.

*Tips for Writing Your Response*

- Read carefully what the professor is asking the students to write about, as well as the points made in the other posts. This should guide you in coming up with ideas to contribute to the discussion. You can spend a few seconds brainstorming what you want to write about, but do not spend too much time planning your response. Decide what you want to write about and start writing.

- In your response, clearly state your viewpoint on the professor's question. You can agree with the ideas in the other posts, disagree with them, or develop entirely new ideas that are relevant to the topic of the discussion, but always make sure to use your own words and your own voice as much as you can. Copying a lot of words and phrases from the other posts will not help you get a good score.

- Use precise words, not words that are too general. Also, do not use examples or reasons that you memorized word for word previously (at school, for example). Raters will not consider examples or reasons expressed in a completely memorized language to represent your own writing and your response will receive a lower score.

- Save a little time to proofread your work.

## How Responses Are Scored

Raters will judge the quality of your writing. They will consider whether the response is a relevant and very clearly expressed contribution to the online discussion and whether it demonstrates consistent facility in the use of language, both in terms of the variety of grammatical structure and vocabulary and of how correctly and accurately you use language.

**Contribution to the discussion** is a very important criterion used to evaluate your response. Remember that the discussion includes the professor's question as well as the posts by other students. You do not have to respond to the posts by the other students, but your response should not ignore what the other posts say. For example, if you want to use ideas that the other students have already mentioned, do not make it seem as though you are the first person in the discussion to raise them. At the same time, contributing to a discussion does not necessarily mean coming up with a lot of new ideas. One can also contribute to a discussion by agreeing with what someone else has already written. In that case, however, make sure that you don't just *repeat* what someone else has written—use your own words and your own voice, and elaborate on the ideas in your own way. Of course, other very effective ways of making your own contribution to the discussion are disagreeing with what the other posts say or introducing entirely new ideas as long as they are relevant to the topic of the discussion.

Raters are looking for ideas that are clear and well supported by reasons and examples. Since your response represents an online post, it does not need to be organized into separate paragraphs. However, your ideas need to be **well connected, coherent, and clear**. If you use a lot of words and sentences that are not well connected and do not support each other or that do not add up to a clear point of view or if you develop empty ideas, you'll receive a low score.

Another important criterion used by raters is **variety in the use of language**. The raters are looking for evidence that you can use a variety of structures and varied vocabulary. If you use very simple sentences and very basic vocabulary, you will probably not be able to express very complex or precise ideas. However, the variety of grammatical structures and vocabulary should be natural and support your ideas. If you try to use varied structures or vocabulary without a good reason, that will not help you get a high score. The final criterion is the **correct use of language**. It is important that your use of grammar is strong and consistent, that your word choices are correct and appropriate, and that your spelling, punctuation, and capitalization are correct. Your writing doesn't have to be absolutely perfect to get a top score, but the few small mistakes you may leave behind have to be typical of competent writers writing under timed conditions. If you make a lot of grammatical errors and if those errors make it hard to understand your meaning, you will get a lower score. In general, if your language is hard to follow, your sentences are overly simple, and your vocabulary is limited, you may score no higher than a 3 no matter how impressive your ideas may be.

Lastly, a few words of caution about using memorized or formulaic language or other strategies that are not helpful in composing successful responses. Do not try to add words to your response by using long memorized introductory or concluding phrases and sentences. They represent neither authentic writing nor the type of writing used in online discussions. Raters will not look favorably on wordy introductions or conclusions such as the following:

The importance of the issue raised by the posed statement, namely creating a new holiday for people, cannot be underestimated, as it concerns the very fabric of society. As it stands, the issue of creating a new holiday raises profound implications for the future. However, although the subject matter in general cannot be dismissed lightheartedly, the perspective of the issue as presented by the statement raises certain qualms regarding practical application.

In conclusion, although I have to accept that it is imperative that something be done about creating a new holiday for people and find the underlying thrust of the implied proposal utterly convincing, I cannot help but feel wary of taking such irrevocable steps and personally feel that a more measured approach would be more rewarding.

Similarly, do not use other memorized sentences and examples in your response. Extended stretches of memorized text do not represent the writer's true academic writing skills. Responses that include memorized examples, arguments, or formulaic references to sources will receive considerably lower scores than responses containing the writer's own words. Here is an example of an extensive use of memorized text:

Professor's question in brief: *Is honesty an important quality for a leader?*

By taking in mind the honesty, we can learn proper social behavior. in addition to my personal experience, there is a research that confirms my opinion. A poll, conducted by the New York times, stated an overwheming 72% who did not think the honesty lack the code of conduct in society. however, people who did regularly comtemplate the importance of not lying were better regulating themselves in the societies. the major characteristic were that they do not lie in their daily life and seve honesty is the most important value in the societies because there is a order for people's lives. therefore it helps one abiltiy to be successful either in business or in academia. it helps people to strive and achieve their goal and making them successful in life.

All the writing in this example has been memorized from a prepared text and repeated in the essay. This includes a formulaic reference to a poll in *The New York Times*. This is not genuine development and will not be credited by raters. Responses with this type of writing often receive a low score.

Likewise, raters will not look favorably on paragraphs like the following one, which uses a lot of words but fails to develop any real ideas:

At the heart of any discussion regarding an issue pertaining to creating a new holiday, it has to be borne in mind that a delicate line has to be trod when dealing with such matters. The human resources involved in such matters cannot be guaranteed regardless of all the good intentions that may be lavished. While it is true that creating a new holiday might be a viable and laudable remedy, it is transparently clear that applied wrongly such a course of action could be calamitous and compound the problem rather than provide a solution.

In your writing, make sure you develop some solid ideas about the given topic. Do not just use a lot of words saying that a certain issue exists. Your response may be 100 or even 200 words long, but if it consists largely of the sorts of empty or content-free expressions shown, you will probably earn a score of just 1 or 2.

# Writing for an Academic Discussion Rubric

Here is the official scoring guide used by raters when they read Writing for an Academic Discussion responses.

| Score | Description |
|---|---|
| **5** | **A fully successful response**<br>The response is a relevant and very clearly expressed contribution to the online discussion, and it demonstrates consistent facility in the use of language.<br><br>A typical response displays the following:<br>• Relevant and well-elaborated explanations, exemplifications, and/or details<br>• Effective use of a variety of syntactic structures and precise, idiomatic word choice<br>• Almost no lexical or grammatical errors other than those expected from a competent writer writing under timed conditions (e.g., common typos or common misspellings or substitutions like *there/their*) |
| **4** | **A generally successful response**<br>The response is a relevant contribution to the online discussion, and facility in the use of language allows the writer's ideas to be easily understood.<br><br>A typical response displays the following:<br>• Relevant and adequately elaborated explanations, exemplifications, and/or details<br>• A variety of syntactic structures and appropriate word choice<br>• Few lexical or grammatical errors |
| **3** | **A partially successful response**<br>The response is a mostly relevant and mostly understandable contribution to the online discussion, and there is some facility in the use of language.<br><br>A typical response displays the following:<br>• Elaboration in which part of an explanation, example, or detail may be missing, unclear, or irrelevant<br>• Some variety in syntactic structures and a range of vocabulary<br>• Some noticeable lexical and grammatical errors in sentence structure, word form, or use of idiomatic language |

| Score | Description |
|---|---|

**2**    **A mostly unsuccessful response**

The response reflects an attempt to contribute to the online discussion, but limitations in the use of language may make ideas hard to follow.

A typical response displays the following:

- Ideas that may be poorly elaborated or only partially relevant

- A limited range of syntactic structures and vocabulary

- An accumulation of errors in sentence structure, word forms, or use

**1**    **An unsuccessful response**

The response reflects an ineffective attempt to contribute to the online discussion, and limitations in the use of language may prevent the expression of ideas.

A typical response may display the following:

- Words and phrases that indicate an attempt to address the task but with few or no coherent ideas

- Severely limited range of syntactic structures and vocabulary

- Serious and frequent errors in the use of language

- Minimal original language; any coherent language is mostly borrowed from the stimulus

**0**    **The response is blank, rejects the topic, is not in English, is entirely copied from the prompt, is entirely unconnected to the prompt, or consists of arbitrary keystrokes.**

## Sample Scored Responses for the Writing for an Academic Discussion Task

The following were written in response to the academic discussion task on p. 206.

### Score 5 Response

I am more inclined to agree that a boarding school system is beneficial. Firstly, a boarding school is a place where you can make friends with your classmates The "roommate" relationship is somewhat strong that you may remember forever, as you wake up, eat meals, study, and go to sleep together with your roommates on every school days. Secondly, a boarding school is usually close to your school campus, which means that you do not need to commute to and from school every day. Thirdly, a boarding school is not a place merely for a disciplined life; it often conducts various activities to help you get immersed in the living environment and make your life more colorful, which cannot be experienced at home. I personally do not agree with Andrew's point that boarding school places high mental pressure on students, as boarding schools are not prisons and students are still free to leave on weekends to bond with their family and pursue their interests.

*Rater Comments*

This response earned a score of 5. The writer has composed a very clearly expressed contribution to the online discussion, demonstrating consistent facility in the use of language. The writer clearly states a preference for boarding schools and proceeds to provide several arguments explaining that preference. It praises the intense companionships with schoolmates that boarding schools offer, leaving a student with memories for a lifetime; it points out how boarding schools take commuting out of the equation and also how many varied activities the offer to their students. Finally, it takes issue with Andrew's concerns about psychological problems, explaining that boarding school students are not prisoners and can visit their families and bond with them on weekends. The writer uses an effective variety of structures and precise word choices, especially as the response moves past its opening sentences, and the few errors we can find at the beginning ("is somewhat strong that you remember" and "on every school days") can be expected from a very competent nonnative speaker writing under timed conditions that leave little time for editing and correcting all of one's slips and stumbles.

Note that high-level responses are not required to provide several arguments or reasons, as this response does. Many fully successful responses offer one extended argument or reason that is detailed and well elaborated.

## Score 4 Response

> I personally do not support the idea of boarding school. I believe that the boarding school system would cause more problems in their future. The idea of being away from your family would definitely effect of connectivity amongst them. Sending your child to a boarding school would just mean that you're leaving them with someone else, and anything can happen and the parents won't know about it, also I think that being confined into the same environment could effect the child's creativity and also social skills. making new friends, having new personalities around you and exploring new hobbies that children should experience are what makes them grow into a more mature and also diffren

*Rater Comments*

This response earned a score of 4. It is a generally successful and relevant contribution to the discussion that is generally easily understood. However, it contains a few errors that prevent some of the writer's arguments to come across as fully elaborated. The writer takes a negative stance on boarding schools, explaining how attending boarding schools compromises the connections students have with their families, how it may expose students to danger, and how the limited environment of a boarding school can negatively affect creativity and the development of a child's social skills. There are some errors that go beyond what one would expect from a competent writer working under timed conditions ("The idea . . . would definitely effect of connectivity amongst them"), and some thoughts are not elaborated as fully and clearly as we should see in a score-5 response. For example, "anything can happen" is a bit vague, the following idea ("also I think") is not clearly separated, and the final idea about making new friends is not clearly contrasted with the situation at boarding schools (where one could also make new friends). At the same time, the grammatical structures are varied, the word choices are mostly appropriate, and the errors are generally few.

## Score 3 Response

> I think boarding school is in the most interest of the students, cause they can develop some good routine, learn from each other, share their interest for commun things, discover other culture. In boarding school, the students can be more focus on the school and have better grades. Boarding school can also help the students to develop their sense of friendship, they learn they can count one on eachother and they should help each other in every situation.

*Rater Comments*

This response earned a score of 3. It is a partially successful contribution that is mostly relevant and understandable but does not display enough facility, variety, and elaboration to rise beyond 3. The writer argues in favor of boarding schools, indicating they provide routines, shared interests, and cultural exchange as well as educational focus and the sense of friendship. Some of these arguments are, however, not very well elaborated (what is "some good routine"? why are boarding schools suited to sharing things more than day schools?), and there are noticeable lexical and grammatical errors throughout the response: "is in the most interest," "cause," "interest for commun things," "discover other culture," "can be more focus," "they can count one on each other," and others. The writing shows some lexical and grammatical variety and some facility, but not enough to earn a 4.

## Score 2 Response

> For my own opinion, i would loved to have attended a boarding school too.so that you can make a lot of friends in a short time and experince a whole new things you never done before. boarding is very good learning opportunity to catch new world and also open mind to making friends.

### Rater Comments

This response earned a score of 2. It is an attempt to contribute to the discussion, but it is mostly unsuccessful because the ideas the writer provides are poorly elaborated. The writer indicates they would have loved to attend a boarding school, make friends there and experience new things, but these ideas are not developed much further, nor is it made clear why boarding schools are better places for any of these things than day schools are. The writer also makes a number of errors in sentence structure, phrasing, and word forms: "for my own opinion," "i would loved," "experince a whole new things," and others.

## Score 1 Response

> I'm partially support the boarding school system. If the term not apart from school, some students may think the boarding school is so strict and not independent. We need relea

### Rater Comments

This writer attempts to contribute to the discussion, but the attempt is unsuccessful because serious errors throughout the response make this writer's ideas incoherently expressed, especially in the second sentence. The response earned a score of 1.

# Practice Topics for Responding to the Writing for an Academic Discussion Task

The Writing for an Academic Discussion task involves responding to a professor's question in an online discussion forum.

If you wish to practice writing a response to the professor's question, you can use questions from this list; the questions are similar to those that a professor might ask as part of an online discussion post. Keep in mind that this is just a starting point for practicing how to respond to the Writing for an Academic Discussion task; in the actual test, writing a response that responds only to the professor's question is only one part of the task. In the actual test, you should read the professor and student posts carefully before planning what to write in your own post; your response should make a contribution to the discussion, which means that it should take into consideration how the student posts respond to the professor's question.

It does not matter whether you agree or disagree with the student posts in your response, which represents your own contribution to the discussion; raters of responses to the Writing for an Academic Discussion task are trained to accept many varieties of contributions to the discussion. What matters is your ability to respond to the professor's question, to make a relevant and very clearly expressed contribution to the discussion, and to write with consistent facility in the use of language. Remember that raters will not consider contributions to the discussion that are expressed in a completely memorized language to represent your own writing.

Writing for an Academic Discussion responses do not require reference to specialized knowledge. In the actual test, most topics on which the professor's questions are based are general, and the list of questions provided for accessibility follows that model: they are based on the common experiences of people in general and students in particular.

What should you do with this list of topics? To prepare for the test, choose topics from the list and practice writing responses. Make sure you time yourself, taking no more than 10 minutes to read the question, plan your response, write the response, and check it. Better yet, have a friend or teacher give you feedback on how well you have responded to the professor's question and on whether your response displays consistent facility in the use of language.

## Topic List

- The expression "Never, never give up" means to keep trying and never stop working for your goals. Do you agree or disagree with this statement? Use specific reasons and examples to support your answer.

- Why do you think some people are attracted to dangerous sports or other dangerous activities? Use specific reasons and examples to support your answer.

- Do you agree or disagree with the following statement? Grades (marks) encourage students to learn. Use specific reasons and examples to support your opinion.

- Describe a custom from your country that you would like people from other countries to adopt. Explain your choice, using specific reasons and examples.

- Do you agree or disagree with the following statement? Technology has made the world a better place. Use specific reasons and examples to support your opinion.

- Do you agree or disagree with the following statement? The content of advertisements in a particular country can tell you a lot about that country. Use specific reasons and examples to support your answer.

- A foreign visitor has only one day to spend in your country. Where should this visitor go on that day? Why? Use specific reasons and details to support your choice.

- Do you agree or disagree with the following statement? Dancing plays an important role in a culture. Use specific reasons and examples to support your answer.

- Some teachers give students large assignments that students have a month or longer to complete. What are the advantages of completing the assignment gradually by working on it a little bit each day, compared to completing the work quickly by working on it intensively for three or four days? Why?

# 6 Authentic *TOEFL iBT*® Practice Test 1

In this chapter you will find the first of four authentic TOEFL iBT practice tests. You can take the test in two different ways:

- **In the book:** You can read through the test questions in the following pages, marking your answers in the spaces provided. To hear the listening portions of the test, follow instructions to play the numbered audio tracks that accompany this book.

- **On your computer:** For a test-taking experience that more closely resembles the actual TOEFL iBT test, you can take this same test on your computer using the digital download (see code in the back of the book). Reading passages and questions will appear on-screen, and you can enter your answers by selecting the spaces provided. Follow instructions to hear the listening portions of the test.

Following this test, you will find answer keys and scoring information. You will also find scripts for the listening portions. Complete answer explanations, as well as sample test-taker spoken and written responses, are also provided.

# TOEFL iBT® Practice Test 1
# READING

In this section, you will be able to demonstrate your ability to understand academic passages in English. You will read and answer questions about **two passages**.

In the actual test, you will have 36 minutes total to read both passages and answer the questions. A clock will indicate how much time remains.

Some passages may include one or more notes explaining words or phrases. The words or phrases are marked with footnote numbers, and the notes explaining them appear at the end of the passage.

Most questions are worth 1 point, but the last question for each passage is worth 2 points.

You may review and revise your answers in this section as long as time remains.

At the end of this practice test, you will find an answer key, information to help you determine your score, and explanations of the answers.

## NINETEENTH-CENTURY POLITICS IN THE UNITED STATES

The development of the modern presidency in the United States began with Andrew Jackson, who swept to power in 1829 at the head of the Democratic Party and served until 1837. During his administration he immeasurably enlarged the power of the presidency. "The president is the direct representative of the American people," he lectured the Senate when it opposed him. "He was elected by the people, and is responsible to them." With this declaration, Jackson redefined the character of the presidential office and its relationship to the people.

During Jackson's second term, his opponents had gradually come together to form the Whig Party. Whigs and Democrats held different attitudes toward the changes brought about by the market, banks, and commerce. The Democrats tended to view society as a continuing conflict between "the people"—farmers, planters, and workers—and a set of greedy aristocrats. This "paper money aristocracy" of bankers and investors manipulated the banking system for their own profit, Democrats claimed, and sapped the nation's virtue by encouraging speculation and the desire for sudden, unearned wealth. The Democrats wanted the rewards of the market without sacrificing the features of a simple agrarian republic. They wanted the wealth that the market offered without the competitive, changing society; the complex dealing; the dominance of urban centers; and the loss of independence that came with it.

Whigs, on the other hand, were more comfortable with the market. For them, commerce and economic development were agents of civilization. Nor did the Whigs envision any conflict in society between farmers and workers on the one hand and businesspeople and bankers on the other. Economic growth would benefit everyone by raising national income and expanding opportunity. The government's responsibility was to provide a well-regulated economy that guaranteed opportunity for citizens of ability.

Whigs and Democrats differed not only in their attitudes toward the market but also about how active the central government should be in people's lives. Despite Andrew Jackson's inclination to be a strong president, Democrats as a rule believed in limited government. Government's role in the economy was to promote competition by destroying monopolies[1] and special privileges. In keeping with this philosophy of limited government, Democrats also rejected the idea that moral beliefs were the proper sphere of government action. Religion and politics, they believed, should be kept clearly separate, and they generally opposed humanitarian legislation.

The Whigs, in contrast, viewed government power positively. They believed that it should be used to protect individual rights and public liberty, and that it had a special role where individual effort was ineffective. By regulating the economy and competition, the government could ensure equal opportunity. Indeed, for Whigs the concept of government promoting the general welfare went beyond the economy. In particular, Whigs in the northern sections of the United States also believed that government power should be used to foster the moral welfare of the country. They were much more likely to favor social-reform legislation and aid to education.

In some ways the social makeup of the two parties was similar. To be competitive in winning votes, Whigs and Democrats both had to have significant support among farmers, the largest group in society, and workers. Neither party could win an election by appealing exclusively to the rich or the poor. The Whigs, however, enjoyed disproportionate strength among the business and commercial classes. Whigs appealed to planters who needed credit to finance their cotton and rice trade in the world market, to farmers who were eager to sell their surpluses, and to workers who wished to improve themselves. Democrats attracted farmers isolated from the market or uncomfortable with it, workers alienated from the emerging industrial system, and rising entrepreneurs who wanted to break monopolies and open the economy to newcomers like themselves. The Whigs were strongest in the towns, cities, and those rural areas that were fully integrated into the market economy, whereas Democrats dominated areas of semisubsistence farming that were more isolated and languishing economically.

1. **monopolies:** Companies or individuals that exclusively own or control commercial enterprises with no competitors

**Directions:** Now answer the questions.

PARAGRAPH 1

The development of the modern presidency in the United States began with Andrew Jackson, who swept to power in 1829 at the head of the Democratic Party and served until 1837. During his administration he immeasurably enlarged the power of the presidency. "The president is the direct representative of the American people," he lectured the Senate when it opposed him. "He was elected by the people, and is responsible to them." With this declaration, Jackson redefined the character of the presidential office and its relationship to the people.

1. According to paragraph 1, the presidency of Andrew Jackson was especially significant for which of the following reasons?

   Ⓐ The president granted a portion of his power to the Senate.
   Ⓑ The president began to address the Senate on a regular basis.
   Ⓒ It was the beginning of the modern presidency in the United States.
   Ⓓ It was the first time that the Senate had been known to oppose the president.

GO ON TO THE NEXT PAGE

P
A
R
A
G
R
A
P
H

2

During Jackson's second term, his opponents had gradually come together to form the Whig Party. Whigs and Democrats held different attitudes toward the changes brought about by the market, banks, and commerce. The Democrats tended to view society as a continuing conflict between "the people"—farmers, planters, and workers—and a set of greedy aristocrats. This "paper money aristocracy" of **bankers and investors** manipulated the banking system for their own profit, Democrats claimed, and sapped the nation's virtue by encouraging speculation and the desire for sudden, unearned wealth. The Democrats wanted the rewards of the market without sacrificing the features of a simple agrarian republic. They wanted the wealth that the market offered without the competitive, changing society; the complex dealing; the dominance of urban centers; and the loss of independence that came with it.

2. The author mentions "**bankers and investors**" in the passage as an example of which of the following?

   Ⓐ The Democratic Party's main source of support
   Ⓑ The people that Democrats claimed were unfairly becoming rich
   Ⓒ The people most interested in a return to a simple agrarian republic
   Ⓓ One of the groups in favor of Andrew Jackson's presidency

P
A
R
A
G
R
A
P
H

3

Whigs, on the other hand, were more comfortable with the market. For them, commerce and economic development were agents of civilization. Nor did the Whigs envision any conflict in society between farmers and workers on the one hand and businesspeople and bankers on the other. Economic growth would benefit everyone by raising national income and expanding opportunity. The government's responsibility was to provide a well-regulated economy that guaranteed opportunity for citizens of ability.

3. According to paragraph 3, Whigs believed that commerce and economic development would have which of the following effects on society?

   Ⓐ They would promote the advancement of society as a whole.
   Ⓑ They would cause disagreements between Whigs and Democrats.
   Ⓒ They would supply new positions for Whig Party members.
   Ⓓ They would prevent conflict between farmers and workers.

4. According to paragraph 3, which of the following describes the Whig Party's view of the role of government?

   Ⓐ To regulate the continuing conflict between farmers and businesspeople
   Ⓑ To restrict the changes brought about by the market
   Ⓒ To maintain an economy that allowed all capable citizens to benefit
   Ⓓ To reduce the emphasis on economic development

**P A R A G R A P H 4**

Whigs and Democrats differed not only in their attitudes toward the market but also about how active the central government should be in people's lives. Despite Andrew Jackson's inclination to be a strong president, Democrats as a rule believed in limited government. Government's role in the economy was to promote competition by destroying monopolies[1] and special privileges. In keeping with this philosophy of limited government, Democrats also rejected the idea that moral beliefs were the proper sphere of government action. Religion and politics, they believed, should be kept clearly separate, and they generally opposed humanitarian legislation.

1. **monopolies:** Companies or individuals that exclusively own or control commercial enterprises with no competitors

5. According to paragraph 4, a Democrat would be most likely to support government action in which of the following areas?

   Ⓐ Creating a state religion
   Ⓑ Supporting humanitarian legislation
   Ⓒ Destroying monopolies
   Ⓓ Recommending particular moral beliefs

**P A R A G R A P H 5**

The Whigs, in contrast, viewed government power positively. They believed that it should be used to protect individual rights and public liberty, and that it had a special role where individual effort was ineffective. By regulating the economy and competition, the government could ensure equal opportunity. Indeed, for Whigs the **concept** of government promoting the general welfare went beyond the economy. In particular, Whigs in the northern sections of the United States also believed that government power should be used to foster the moral welfare of the country. They were much more likely to favor social-reform legislation and aid to education.

6. The word "**concept**" in the passage is closest in meaning to

   Ⓐ power
   Ⓑ reality
   Ⓒ difficulty
   Ⓓ idea

7. Which of the following can be inferred from paragraph 5 about variations in political beliefs within the Whig Party?

   Ⓐ They were focused on issues of public liberty.
   Ⓑ They caused some members to leave the Whig Party.
   Ⓒ They were unimportant to most Whigs.
   Ⓓ They reflected regional interests.

GO ON TO THE NEXT PAGE ↘

In some ways the social makeup of the two parties was similar. To be competitive in winning votes, Whigs and Democrats both had to have significant support among farmers, the largest group in society, and workers. Neither party could win an election by appealing exclusively to the rich or the poor. The Whigs, however, enjoyed disproportionate strength among the business and commercial classes. Whigs appealed to planters who needed credit to finance their cotton and rice trade in the world market, to farmers who were eager to sell their surpluses, and to workers who wished to improve themselves. Democrats attracted farmers isolated from the market or uncomfortable with it, workers alienated from the emerging industrial system, and rising entrepreneurs who wanted to break monopolies and open the economy to newcomers like themselves. **The Whigs were strongest in the towns, cities, and those rural areas that were fully integrated into the market economy, whereas Democrats dominated areas of semisubsistence farming that were more isolated and languishing economically.**

8. Which of the sentences below best expresses the essential information in the highlighted sentence in the passage? Incorrect choices change the meaning in important ways or leave out essential information.

   Ⓐ Whigs were able to attract support only in the wealthiest parts of the economy because Democrats dominated in other areas.

   Ⓑ Whig and Democratic areas of influence were naturally split between urban and rural areas, respectively.

   Ⓒ The semisubsistence farming areas dominated by Democrats became increasingly isolated by the Whigs' control of the market economy.

   Ⓓ The Democrats' power was greatest in poorer areas, while the Whigs were strongest in those areas where the market was already fully operating.

During Jackson's second term, his opponents had gradually come together to form the Whig Party. **(A)** Whigs and Democrats held different attitudes toward the changes brought about by the market, banks, and commerce. **(B)** The Democrats tended to view society as a continuing conflict between "the people"—farmers, planters, and workers—and a set of greedy aristocrats. **(C)** This "paper money aristocracy" of bankers and investors manipulated the banking system for their own profit, Democrats claimed, and sapped the nation's virtue by encouraging speculation and the desire for sudden, unearned wealth. **(D)** The Democrats wanted the rewards of the market without sacrificing the features of a simple agrarian republic. They wanted the wealth that the market offered without the competitive, changing society; the complex dealing; the dominance of urban centers; and the loss of independence that came with it.

9. **Directions:** Look at the part of the passage that is displayed above. The letters **(A)**, **(B)**, **(C)**, and **(D)** indicate where the following sentence could be added.

   **This new party argued against the policies of Jackson and his party in a number of important areas, beginning with the economy.**

   Where would the sentence best fit?

   (A) Choice A
   (B) Choice B
   (C) Choice C
   (D) Choice D

GO ON TO THE NEXT PAGE ⬎

P
A
R
A
G
R
A
P
H

2

10. **Directions:** An introductory sentence for a brief summary of the passage is provided below. Complete the summary by selecting the THREE answer choices that express the most important ideas in the passage. Some sentences do not belong in the summary because they express ideas that are not presented in the passage or are minor ideas in the passage. **This question is worth 2 points.**

**The political system of the United States in the mid-nineteenth century was strongly influenced by the social and economic circumstances of the time.**

- 
- 
- 

### Answer Choices

A The Democratic and Whig Parties developed in response to the needs of competing economic and political constituencies.

B During Andrew Jackson's two terms as president, he served as leader of both the Democratic and Whig Parties.

C The Democratic Party primarily represented the interests of the market, banks, and commerce.

D In contrast to the Democrats, the Whigs favored government aid for education.

E A fundamental difference between Whigs and Democrats involved the importance of the market in society.

F The role of government in the lives of the people was an important political distinction between the two parties.

# BIRD SONGS AND CALLS

Birds use song both in courtship and to define areas of territory. Both of these are communicative purposes: the bird is passing specific messages to other members of its species. Birds communicate for other reasons as well: a blackbird, for instance, will make a sharp "pink-pink" sound when there is a cat nearby, which warns other birds in the neighborhood of the danger.

William Thorpe (1961) studied the behavior of gannets in a colony containing many thousands of birds. Thorpe found that when a bird was returning to its nest, it would drift on an updraft of air from the bottom of the cliff upwards, calling as it went. When the bird on the nest heard its mate calling, it would call in reply, showing that each bird's call could act as an identification signal. Thorpe also discovered that a bird might have as many as fifteen or sixteen different kinds of calls, each serving a different function.

J. R. Krebs (1976) realized that birds often sing more intensively in the early morning—the "dawn chorus." By investigating what the birds actually did during each day, and how much time they spent on each activity, Krebs found that the dawn chorus serves a largely territorial function. The early morning is not a particularly good time for gathering food, because it is dark, so visibility is lower, and it is also cold, so many insects are still inactive. On the other hand, at this time many birds move around looking for living space, so establishing and defending a territory is necessary. Birdsong is not just territorial, of course. A bird's song can serve a dual purpose: it can be used to defend a territory and, by indicating to a prospective mate that the singer has a territory to defend, can also attract a female bird.

P. J. B. Slater (1981) suggested that bird calls and birdsong are partly learned from other birds. He found that chaffinches which had been hand-reared and had not heard other wild birds made an entirely different kind of "chink" call from that of wild birds. In another case, Slater observed a laboratory chaffinch in a duet with a wild sparrow outside the window of the laboratory. The chaffinch imitated the sparrow's "cheep" whenever the sparrow produced it. Slater concluded that learning through copying is an important part of the way in which birds acquire their songs. Slater also found that individual chaffinches can have up to five different types of song. Some of these are personal, sung by that bird alone. Others are shared by several birds. In some cases too, Slater observed chaffinches singing songs which were almost identical to those sung by others, but with just a note or two different—possibly because the bird had made an error in copying the song from another.

Slater studied a population of 40 chaffinches on the Orkney Islands and found that among them they had seventeen different song types. So it was not a matter of each bird having its own individual songs—there was a considerable amount of sharing. Slater found that this sharing related to geographical distribution, but that the boundaries were not distinct enough for it to be accurately described as a dialect, or regional variety of a song. Instead, there was considerable overlap between the songs sung in one area and those sung in an adjoining one, but gradually the overlap would become less, until birds a long distance away from one another would be singing entirely different songs.

In 1970, Peter Marler proposed that birdsong and human speech were directly comparable in certain key respects, and that the study of birdsong might provide psychologists with some useful indicators as to the nature and development of speech in human beings. One of the parallels which Marler identified was the way that both humans and birds show

GO ON TO THE NEXT PAGE ➤

a strong genetic predisposition to pick up and imitate certain sounds rather than others. Marler showed that young birds will learn the songs of their own species if they are played to them when young, but they will ignore songs of birds from other species. Similarly, young human beings are surrounded by all kinds of sounds and noises, but it is the human voice to which they listen most closely and human speech which they imitate.

**Directions:** Now answer the questions.

**PARAGRAPH 2**

William Thorpe (1961) studied the behavior of gannets in a colony containing many thousands of birds. Thorpe found that when a bird was returning to its nest, it would drift on an updraft of air from the bottom of the cliff upwards, calling as it went. When the bird on the nest heard its mate calling, it would call in reply, showing that each bird's call could act as an identification signal. Thorpe also **discovered** that a bird might have as many as fifteen or sixteen different kinds of calls, each serving a different function.

11. The word "**discovered**" in the passage is closest in meaning to
    Ⓐ reported
    Ⓑ found
    Ⓒ estimated
    Ⓓ showed

**PARAGRAPH 3**

J. R. Krebs (1976) **realized** that birds often sing more intensively in the early morning—the "dawn chorus." By investigating what the birds actually did during each day, and how much time they spent on each activity, Krebs found that the dawn chorus serves a largely territorial function. The early morning is not a particularly good time for gathering food, because it is dark, so visibility is lower, and it is also cold, so many insects are still inactive. On the other hand, at this time many birds move around looking for living space, so establishing and defending a territory is necessary. Birdsong is not just territorial, of course. A bird's song can serve a dual purpose: it can be used to defend a territory and, by indicating to a prospective mate that the singer has a territory to defend, can also attract a female bird.

12. The word "**realized**" in the passage is closest in meaning to
    Ⓐ indicated
    Ⓑ established
    Ⓒ understood
    Ⓓ argued

13. Which of the following can be inferred from paragraph 3 about birds and food gathering?
    Ⓐ Birds become very territorial while they are gathering food.
    Ⓑ Birds are more likely to sing when gathering food is easy than when it is difficult.
    Ⓒ Most birds gather enough food for the day before they begin singing.
    Ⓓ Birds are less likely to sing intensively when they are looking for food.

14. According to paragraph 3, why are birds concerned with defending territory during the early morning?
  Ⓐ This is the time of day when male birds without mates try to take away living space and mates of other males.
  Ⓑ This is the time of day birds and other animals hunt for insects.
  Ⓒ This is the time of day birds have to defend their homes from predators who attack in darkness.
  Ⓓ This is the time of day when other birds are looking for new places to live.

**PARAGRAPH 4**

P. J. B. Slater (1981) suggested that bird calls and birdsong are partly learned from other birds. He found that chaffinches which had been hand-reared and had not heard other wild birds made an entirely different kind of "chink" call from that of wild birds. In another case, Slater observed a laboratory "**chaffinch in a duet with a wild sparrow outside the window of the laboratory**. The chaffinch imitated the sparrow's "cheep" whenever the sparrow produced it. Slater concluded that learning through copying is an important part of the way in which birds acquire their songs. Slater also found that individual chaffinches can have up to five different types of song. Some of these are personal, sung by that bird alone. Others are shared by several birds. **In some cases too, Slater observed chaffinches singing songs which were almost identical to those sung by others, but with just a note or two different—possibly because the bird had made an error in copying the song from another.**

15. Why does the author discuss the behavior of a "**chaffinch in a duet with a wild sparrow outside the window of the laboratory**"?
  Ⓐ To explain why Slater's hand-reared birds made an entirely different call than that made by wild birds
  Ⓑ To indicate how Slater arrived at the view that imitation plays an important role in how birds learn songs
  Ⓒ To explain why Slater thought that it would be advantageous for birds to sing multiple types of songs
  Ⓓ To provide evidence that there are many different ways in which birds acquire new songs and calls

16. Which of the sentences below best expresses the essential information in the highlighted sentence in the passage? Incorrect choices change the meaning in important ways or leave out essential information.
  Ⓐ Slater observed that all but one or two chaffinches were able to sing nearly identical copies of the songs of other birds.
  Ⓑ Slater observed that chaffinches sang the songs of other birds, with just a wrong note or two that may have been due to copying errors.
  Ⓒ Slater observed that chaffinches learned the songs of other birds, while sometimes adding a wrong note or two they may have learned from a different group of birds.
  Ⓓ Slater observed that chaffinches used one or two notes from their own songs when singing the songs of other birds.

GO ON TO THE NEXT PAGE ➦

**P A R A G R A P H 5**

Slater studied a population of 40 chaffinches on the Orkney Islands and found that among them they had seventeen different song types. So it was not a matter of each bird having its own individual songs—there was a considerable amount of sharing. Slater found that this sharing related to geographical distribution, but that the boundaries were not distinct enough for it to be accurately described as a dialect, or regional variety of a song. Instead, there was considerable overlap between the songs sung in one area and those sung in an adjoining one, but gradually the overlap would become less, until birds a long distance away from one another would be singing entirely different songs.

17. According to paragraph 5, the chaffinches of the Orkney Islands were not considered to sing different regional variations of songs because
   Ⓐ each bird had its own individual songs that were not shared by any other birds
   Ⓑ the birds' different songs were not based on geographical location
   Ⓒ even the birds that lived some distance apart shared many of the same songs
   Ⓓ there were no clear divisions to mark the places where differences in songs occurred

**P A R A G R A P H 6**

In 1970, Peter Marler proposed that birdsong and human speech were directly comparable in certain key respects, and that the study of birdsong might provide psychologists with some useful indicators as to the nature and development of speech in human beings. One of the parallels which Marler identified was the way that both humans and birds show a strong genetic predisposition to pick up and imitate certain sounds rather than others. Marler showed that young birds will learn the songs of their own species if they are played to them when young, but they will ignore songs of birds from other species. Similarly, young human beings are surrounded by all kinds of sounds and noises, but it is the human voice to which they listen most closely and human speech which they imitate.

18. In paragraph 6, why does the author discuss Marler's finding that young birds ignore the songs of other species and young humans listen most closely to human speech?
   Ⓐ To show that listening skills are relatively poorly developed in young birds and young humans
   Ⓑ To argue that the genetic predisposition to pick up and imitate sounds is more sophisticated in humans than in birds
   Ⓒ To explain why Marler thought that birdsong might be helpful in understanding the development of human speech
   Ⓓ To show that surrounding noises and sounds increase the difficulty that birds have learning songs and that humans have learning language

P
A
R
A
G
R
A
P
H
S

2

A
N
D

3

William Thorpe (1961) studied the behavior of gannets in a colony containing many thousands of birds. **(A)** Thorpe found that when a bird was returning to its nest, it would drift on an updraft of air from the bottom of the cliff upwards, calling as it went. **(B)** When the bird on the nest heard its mate calling, it would call in reply, showing that each bird's call could act as an identification signal. **(C)** Thorpe also calculated that a bird might have as many as fifteen or sixteen different kinds of calls, each serving a different function. **(D)**

J. R. Krebs (1976) investigated how birds seem to sing more intensively in the early morning—the "dawn chorus." By investigating what the birds actually did during each day, and how much time they spent on each activity, Krebs found that the dawn chorus serves a largely territorial function. The early morning is not a particularly good time for gathering food, because it is dark, so visibility is lower, and it is also cold, so many insects are still inactive. On the other hand, at this time many birds move around looking for living space, so establishing and defending a territory is necessary. Birdsong is not just territorial, of course. A bird's song can serve a dual purpose: it can be used to defend a territory and, by indicating to a prospective mate that the singer has a territory to defend, can also attract a female bird.

19. **Directions:** Look at the part of the passage that is displayed above. The letters **(A)**, **(B)**, **(C)**, and **(D)** indicate where the following sentence could be added.

    **These include flight calls used to coordinate the flock as well as distress calls and begging calls, which are used specifically by chicks to communicate with their parents.**

    Where would the sentence best fit?

    (A) Choice A
    (B) Choice B
    (C) Choice C
    (D) Choice D

GO ON TO THE NEXT PAGE ↘

20. **Directions:** An introductory sentence for a brief summary of the passage is provided below. Complete the summary by selecting the THREE answer choices that express the most important ideas in the passage. Some sentences do not belong in the summary because they express ideas that are not presented in the passage or are minor ideas in the passage. **This question is worth 2 points.**

**Birds sing to communicate with other birds.**

- 
- 
- 

### Answer Choices

A The number of different songs and calls a bird has varies by species, with blackbirds having some of the smallest collections of songs and calls and chaffinches having some of the largest.

B Birds that live in dense forests or other places where visibility is poor are especially dependent on songs and calls from other birds to locate sources of food and danger.

C Many birds sing to establish territory—and attract mates—during hours in which food gathering is difficult, while other birds, such as gannets, use calls to identify themselves.

D Bird songs and calls may be unique to one bird, shared among several birds, or even learned from other species.

E Although hand-reared chaffinches at first were slow to correctly copy the calls and songs of their own species in the wild, over time their copying skill improved.

F Because birds and humans have similar genetic ability to imitate certain sounds, birdsong can help explain the development of speech in humans.

# LISTENING

In this section, you will be able to demonstrate your ability to understand conversations and lectures in English.

In the actual test, the section is divided into separate timed parts. You will hear each conversation or lecture only one time. A clock will indicate how much time remains. The clock will count down only while you are answering questions, not while you are listening. You may take up to 16.5 minutes to answer the questions.

You may take notes while you listen. You may use your notes to help you answer the questions. Your notes will not be scored.

Answer the questions based on what is stated or implied by the speakers.

In some questions, you will see this icon: 🎧. This means that you will hear, but not see, part of the question.

**In the actual test, you must answer all questions in order. You cannot return to previous questions.**

At the end of this practice test, you will find an answer key, information to help you determine your score, and explanations of the answers.

*Listen to Track 11.*

**Questions**

**Directions:** Mark your answer by filling in the oval or square next to your choice.

1.  Why does the student go to see the professor?

    (A) To prepare for her graduate school interview
    (B) To get advice about her graduate school application
    (C) To give the professor her graduate school application
    (D) To find out if she was accepted into graduate school

2.  According to the professor, what information should the student include in her statement of purpose?
    *Select 2 answers.*

    [A] Her academic motivation
    [B] Her background in medicine
    [C] Some personal information
    [D] The ways her teachers have influenced her

3.  What does the professor consider unusual about the student's background?

    (A) Her work experience
    (B) Her creative writing experience
    (C) Her athletic achievements
    (D) Her music training

4. Why does the professor tell a story about his friend who went to medical school?

    Ⓐ To warn the student about how difficult graduate school can be
    Ⓑ To illustrate a point he is making
    Ⓒ To help the student relax
    Ⓓ To change the subject

5. What does the professor imply about the people who admit students to graduate school?

    Ⓐ They often lack expertise in the fields of the applicants.
    Ⓑ They do not usually read the statement of purpose.
    Ⓒ They are influenced by the appearance of an application.
    Ⓓ They remember most of the applications they receive.

GO ON TO THE NEXT PAGE

**Listen to Track 12.**

Environmental Science

**Questions**

6.  What is the talk mainly about?

    Ⓐ A common method of managing water supplies
    Ⓑ The formation of underground water systems
    Ⓒ Natural processes that renew water supplies
    Ⓓ Maintaining the purity of underground water systems

7.  What is the professor's point of view concerning the method of "safe yield"?

    Ⓐ It has helped to preserve the environment.
    Ⓑ It should be researched in states other than Arizona.
    Ⓒ It is not an effective resource policy.
    Ⓓ It ignores the different ways people use water.

8. According to the professor, what are two problems associated with removing water from an underground system?
   *Select 2 answers.*
   - [A] Pollutants can enter the water more quickly.
   - [B] The surface area can dry and crack.
   - [C] The amount of water stored in the system can drop.
   - [D] Dependent streams and springs can dry up.

9. What is a key feature of a sustainable water system?
   - (A) It is able to satisfy short-term and long-term needs.
   - (B) It is not affected by changing environmental conditions.
   - (C) It usually originates in lakes, springs, or streams.
   - (D) It is not used to supply human needs.

10. What does the professor imply about water systems managed by the "safe-yield" method?
    - (A) They recharge at a rapid rate.
    - (B) They are not sustainable.
    - (C) They must have large storage areas.
    - (D) They provide a poor quality of water.

11. *Listen to Track 13 to answer the question.*

    Why does the professor say this?
    - (A) To find out whether the students are familiar with the issue
    - (B) To introduce a new problem for discussion
    - (C) To respond to a student's question
    - (D) To encourage the students to care about the topic

GO ON TO THE NEXT PAGE ➤

*Listen to Track 14.*

transposons

**Questions**

12. What are the students mainly discussing?

　Ⓐ Drugs that are harmful to the human body
　Ⓑ Bacteria that produce antibiotics
　Ⓒ DNA that is related to athletic performance
　Ⓓ Genes that protect bacteria from antibiotics

13. According to the conversation, why are transposons sometimes called "jumping genes"?

　Ⓐ They are able to move from one bacteria cell to another.
　Ⓑ They are found in people with exceptional jumping ability.
　Ⓒ They occur in every other generation of bacteria.
　Ⓓ Their movements are rapid and unpredictable.

14. According to the conversation, what are two ways in which bacteria cells get resistance genes?
    *Select 2 answers.*

    A  The resistance genes are carried from nearby cells.
    B  The resistance genes are carried by white blood cells.
    C  The resistance genes are inherited from the parent cell.
    D  The resistance genes are carried by antibiotics.

15. What can be inferred about the resistance genes discussed in the conversation?

    Ⓐ They are found in all bacteria cells.
    Ⓑ They are not able to resist antibiotics.
    Ⓒ They make the treatment of bacterial diseases more difficult.
    Ⓓ They are essential to the body's defenses against bacteria.

16. *Listen to Track 15 to answer the question.*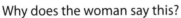
    Why does the woman say this?

    Ⓐ To find out if the man has done his assignment
    Ⓑ To ask the man to find out if the library is open
    Ⓒ To let the man know that she cannot study much longer
    Ⓓ To ask if the man has ever met her roommate

GO ON TO THE NEXT PAGE

*Listen to Track 16.*

Botany

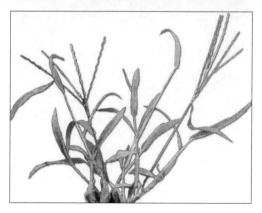

Questions

17. What is the main topic of the lecture?
   - (A) The size of root systems
   - (B) Various types of root systems
   - (C) The nutrients required by rye plants
   - (D) Improving two types of plant species

18. According to the professor, why did one scientist grow a rye plant in water?
   - (A) To expose the roots to sunlight
   - (B) To be able to fertilize it with gas
   - (C) To be able to see its entire root system
   - (D) To see how minerals penetrate its roots

19. The professor mentions houseplants that receive too much water. Why does she mention them?
   - (A) To show that many different types of plants can grow in water
   - (B) To explain why plants grown in water should have a gas bubbled through them
   - (C) To remind the students of the importance of their next experiment
   - (D) To make a point about the length of houseplants' roots

20. According to the professor, what similarity is there between crabgrass and rye plants?
   - (A) Both start growing in the month of May.
   - (B) Both have root systems that require a lot of water.
   - (C) Both have more shoot surface than root surface.
   - (D) Both produce many shoots from a single seed.

GO ON TO THE NEXT PAGE

21. *Listen again to part of the lecture by playing Track 17.*
    *Then answer the question.*

    Why did the professor say this?

    - (A) She wanted to correct the wording of a previous statement.
    - (B) She wishes she did not have to bubble gas through it.
    - (C) She realized the odor of gas could be unpleasant.
    - (D) She forgot to tell the students about a step in the experiment.

22. *Listen again to part of the lecture by playing Track 18.*
    *Then answer the question.*

    What does the professor intend to explain?

    - (A) Why a mistake made in textbooks was never corrected
    - (B) Why she does not believe that the roots of rye plants extend to 1,000 kilometers
    - (C) How the roots of rye plants develop to such a great length
    - (D) How plants grown in water make use of fertilizer

*Listen to Track 19.*

Business Management

## Questions

23. What is the lecture mainly about?

    Ⓐ Technological innovations in the automobile industry
    Ⓑ The organizational structure of companies
    Ⓒ Ways to improve efficiency in an engineering department
    Ⓓ Methods of resolving conflicts in organizations

24. Why does the professor talk about a construction company that has work in different cities?

    Ⓐ To give an example of functional organization
    Ⓑ To give an example of organization around projects
    Ⓒ To illustrate problems with functional organization
    Ⓓ To illustrate the types of conflict that can arise in companies

GO ON TO THE NEXT PAGE ◥

25. What is an example of a violation of the "unity of command" principle?

   Ⓐ More than one person supervises the same employee.
   Ⓑ A company decides not to standardize its products.
   Ⓒ Several project managers are responsible for designing a new product.
   Ⓓ An employee does not follow a supervisor's instructions.

26. According to the professor, where might there be a conflict in an organizational structure based on both projects and function?

   Ⓐ Between architects and finance experts
   Ⓑ Between the need to specialize and the need to standardize
   Ⓒ Between two engineers who work on the same project
   Ⓓ Between the needs of projects in different cities

27. Indicate whether each sentence below describes functional organization or project organization. Place a check mark in the correct box.

| | Functional Organization | Project Organization |
|---|---|---|
| A. It encourages people with similar expertise to work closely together. | | |
| B. It helps the company to adapt quickly and meet changing needs. | | |
| C. It helps to achieve uniformity in projects. | | |

28. *Listen again to part of the lecture by playing Track 20.*  *Then answer the question.*

   Why does the professor say this?

   Ⓐ He does not understand why the student is talking about engineers.
   Ⓑ He wants to know how the engineers will communicate with their coworkers.
   Ⓒ The student has not provided a complete answer to his question.
   Ⓓ He wants the student to do more research on the topic.

**STOP. This is the end of the Listening section of TOEFL iBT ® Practice Test 1.**

# SPEAKING

In this section, you will be able to demonstrate your ability to speak about a variety of topics.

In the actual test, the Speaking section will last approximately 16 minutes. You will answer four questions by speaking into the microphone. You may use your notes to help you answer the questions. Your notes will not be scored. For each question, you will have time to prepare before giving your response. You should answer the questions as completely as possible in the time allowed.

For this practice test, you may want to use a personal recording device to record and play back your responses.

For each question, play the audio track listed and follow the directions to complete the task. You may take notes while you listen.

At the end of this Practice Test, you will find scripts for the audio tracks, Important Points for each question, sample responses, and comments on those responses by official raters.

Questions

1. *You will now give your opinion about a familiar topic. After you hear the question, you will have 15 seconds to prepare and 45 seconds to speak.*

**Now play Track 21 to hear Question 1.**

Some people who unexpectedly receive a large amount of money spend it on practical things, while others spend it for pleasure only. Which do you think is better and why?

| Preparation Time: 15 Seconds |
| --- |
| Response Time: 45 Seconds |

2. *Now you will read a passage about a campus situation and then listen to a conversation about the same topic. You will then answer a question, using information from both the reading passage and the conversation. You will have 30 seconds to prepare and 60 seconds to speak.*

**Now play Track 22 to hear Question 2.**

| Reading Time: 50 Seconds |
| --- |

### Student Health Services Need Improvement

The situation at the health center is unacceptable: you sit in a crowded waiting room for hours waiting to get treatment for minor ailments. Then when it's your turn, you get about three minutes with an overworked doctor. I have two suggestions: first, the health center needs to hire more doctors so that each patient receives quality treatment. And as far as the wait time issue is concerned, the health center is currently open only Monday through Friday, which means that people who get sick over the weekend wait until the following week to get treatment. So, opening the health center on weekends should solve that problem too.

Sincerely,

Megan Finch

The man expresses his opinion about the student's suggestions that are made in the letter. State the man's opinion and explain the reasons he gives for holding that opinion.

> **Preparation Time: 30 Seconds**
> **Response Time: 60 Seconds**

*3. Now you will read a passage about an academic subject and then listen to a lecture on the same topic. You will then answer a question, using information from both the reading passage and the lecture. You will have 30 seconds to prepare and 60 seconds to speak.*

**Now play Track 23 to hear Question 3.**

> **Reading Time: 45 Seconds**

### Social Loafing

When people work in groups to perform a task, individual group members may feel less motivated to contribute, since no one person is held directly responsible for completing the task. The result is that people may not work as hard, or accomplish as much, as they would if they were working alone and their individual output were being measured. This decrease in personal effort, especially on a simple group task, is known as social loafing. While it is not a deliberate behavior, the consequence of social loafing is less personal efficiency when working in groups than when working on one's own.

Using the example from the lecture, explain what social loafing is and how it affects people's behavior.

**Preparation Time: 30 Seconds**
**Response Time: 60 Seconds**

*4. Now you will listen to a lecture. You will then be asked to summarize the lecture. You will have 20 seconds to prepare and 60 seconds to speak.*

*Now play Track 24 to hear Question 4.*

Using points and examples from the talk, explain internal and external locus of control.

**Preparation Time: 20 Seconds**
**Response Time: 60 Seconds**

**STOP. This is the end of the Speaking section of TOEFL iBT® Practice Test 1.**

# WRITING

In this section, you will be able to demonstrate your ability to use writing to communicate in an academic environment. There will be two writing tasks.

At the end of this Practice Test, you will find a script for the audio track, topic notes, sample responses, and comments on those responses by official raters.

Turn the page to see the directions for the first writing task.

## Integrated Writing

For this task, you will read a passage about an academic topic. Then you will listen to a lecture about the same topic. You may take notes while you listen.

In your response, provide a detailed summary of the lecture and explain how the lecture relates to the reading passage.

In the actual test, you will have 3 minutes to read the passage and 20 minutes to write your response. While you write, you will be able to see the reading passage. If you finish your response before time is up, you may go on to the second writing task.

Now you will see the reading passage. It will be followed by a lecture.

### Reading Time: 3 minutes

Some fuels, known as biofuels, can be extracted from plants that produce natural oils. One kind of biofuel comes from algae, the simplest plant organisms. Some people believe that fuel derived from algae could replace other kinds of fuel as our main source of energy. However, manufacturing fuel from algae creates some unique problems.

To get enough oil from algae, algae would have to be farmed on a large scale; this would require a good deal of land and water. In many parts of the world, however, there are dangerous shortages of farmable land, usable water, and agricultural food products. Since algae farming uses up land and water without producing food, building large-scale algae farming operations could make food shortages worse.

A second problem with using algae as a fuel source is that the equipment required to grow and extract oil from the algae is expensive. The cost of starting an algae farm is high. Companies would have to invest in large facilities to contain the algae and expose them to sunlight, in complicated machines to squeeze oil out of the algae, and in other equipment necessary to make the oil usable as fuel.

Third, farming algae is problematic because algae require a large quantity of carbon dioxide gas to grow. All plants need some carbon dioxide ($CO_2$), which they generally pull directly from the air. Algae, however, do not thrive without a very high concentration of this gas in their environment. To grow large amounts of algae, farmers would have to pump pure $CO_2$ into algae-growing tanks. Not all of this $CO_2$ would be absorbed by the algae; a significant amount would pass into the atmosphere. Since $CO_2$ is considered a pollutant, this would be harmful to the environment.

*Now play Track 25.*

**Question 1**

Summarize the points made in the lecture, being sure to explain how they respond to the specific concerns presented in the reading passage.

You have 20 minutes to plan and write your response.

**Response Time: 20 minutes**

_____

_____

_____

_____

_____

_____

_____

_____

_____

_____

_____

_____

GO ON TO THE NEXT PAGE

## Writing for an Academic Discussion

For this task, you will read an online discussion. A professor has posted a question about a topic, and some classmates have responded with their ideas.

In the actual test, you will have 10 minutes to write a response that contributes to the discussion.

### Question 2

Your professor is teaching a class on human resource management. Write a post responding to the professor's question.

**In your response, you should do the following.**

- Express and support your opinion.
- Make a contribution to the discussion in your own words.

An effective response will contain at least 100 words.

**Dr. Diaz**

This week, we are discussing professional development, or workplace training. Some employees prefer to develop skills that will help them do their current job better. Others prefer to focus on training that helps them prepare for a better position in the future. Which kind of professional development opportunities are more important for an employee to take advantage of? Why?

**Claire**

It is far more important to focus on expanding skills that are relevant to your current job. By strengthening skills that can be put to use immediately, employees will get themselves noticed by their managers and be able to quickly advance at the company.

**Paul**

Companies offer a variety of training programs, and employees should take whatever opportunity is given to them, even if it is not directly related to their current job. You never know when a better job opportunity will present itself. Focusing only on skills related to your current job will not necessarily make you the best candidate for a better position.

**Response Time: 10 minutes**

GO ON TO THE NEXT PAGE ⬃

**STOP. This is the end of the Writing section of TOEFL iBT ® Practice Test 1.**

# Answers, Explanations, and Listening Scripts

# Reading

## Answer Key and Self-Scoring Chart

**Directions:** Check your answers against the answer key below. Write the number 1 on the line to the right of each question if you picked the correct answer. For questions worth more than one point, follow the directions given. Total your points at the bottom of the chart.

| Question Number | Correct Answer | Your Raw Points |
|---|---|---|
| **Nineteenth-Century Politics in the United States** | | |
| 1. | C | |
| 2. | B | |
| 3. | A | |
| 4. | C | |
| 5. | C | |
| 6. | D | |
| 7. | D | |
| 8. | D | |
| 9. | A | |
| 10.* | A, E, F | |
| | **TOTAL:** | |

*For question 10, write 2 if you picked all three correct answers. Write 1 if you picked two correct answers.

| Question Number | Correct Answer | Your Raw Points |
|---|---|---|
| **Bird Songs and Calls** | | |
| 11. | B | |
| 12. | C | |
| 13. | D | |
| 14. | D | |
| 15. | B | |
| 16. | B | |
| 17. | D | |
| 18. | C | |
| 19. | D | |
| 20.* | C, D, F | |
| | **TOTAL:** | |

* For question 20, write 2 if you picked all three correct answers. Write 1 if you picked two correct answers.

On the next page is a table that converts your Reading practice section answers into a TOEFL iBT Reading scaled score. Take the total of raw points from your answer key for both sets and find that number in the left-hand column of the table. The right-hand column of the table gives a range of TOEFL iBT Reading scores for each number of raw points. For example, if the total points from your answer key is 18, the table shows a scaled score of 24 to 29.

You should use your score estimate as a general guide only. Your actual score on the TOEFL iBT test may be higher or lower than your score on the practice version.

## Reading

| Raw Point Total | Scale Score |
| --- | --- |
| 22 | 30 |
| 21 | 29–30 |
| 20 | 28–30 |
| 19 | 26–29 |
| 18 | 24–29 |
| 17 | 22–28 |
| 16 | 21–26 |
| 15 | 19–25 |
| 14 | 18–23 |
| 13 | 16–22 |
| 12 | 14–20 |
| 11 | 12–19 |
| 10 | 11–17 |
| 9 | 9–16 |
| 8 | 7–14 |
| 7 | 4–12 |
| 6 | 3–10 |
| 5 | 1–7 |
| 4 | 0–4 |
| 3 | 0–2 |
| 2 | 0 |
| 1 | 0 |
| 0 | 0 |

# Answer Explanations

## Nineteenth-Century Politics in the United States

1. **C** This is a Factual Information question asking for specific information that can be found in paragraph 1. The correct answer is choice C because the first sentence of the paragraph explicitly states that this was when the development of the modern presidency began. The remainder of the paragraph is devoted to explaining the significant changes in government that this development involved. The result, as stated in sentence 5, was that the nature of the presidency itself was redefined. Choice A is contradicted by the paragraph; Jackson did not give presidential power away, but rather he increased it. Choice B is not mentioned in the paragraph: it says Jackson addressed the Senate, but not that this was the beginning of regular addresses. Choice D, which says that this was the first time the Senate opposed the president, is not stated in the passage.

2. **B** This is a Rhetorical Purpose question. It is asking you why the author mentions "bankers and investors" in the passage. The phrase being tested is highlighted in the passage. The correct answer is choice B. The author is using bankers and investors as examples of people that the Democrats claimed "manipulated" the banking system for their own profit. That means that they were unfairly becoming rich. Choices A, C, and D are all incorrect because, based upon the passage, they seem unlikely to be true. Therefore the author would not use them as examples.

3. **A** This is a Factual Information question asking for specific information that can be found in paragraph 3. Choice A is the correct answer. The paragraph says that Whigs believed commerce and economic development "would benefit everyone." That means essentially the same thing as choice A, which says that Whigs believed economic growth "would promote the advancement of society as a whole." "Society as a whole" is another way of saying "everyone." Choices B and C are not mentioned in the paragraph. Choice D, about conflict between groups, is mentioned but in a different context, so it is not a belief held by Whigs.

4. **C** This is a Factual Information question asking for specific information that can be found in paragraph 3. The correct answer is choice C: the Whigs viewed government as responsible for maintaining an economy that allowed all capable citizens to benefit. This is a restatement of paragraph 3, sentence 5. The paragraph states that Whigs did not envision continuing conflict between farmers and businesspeople, so choice A is wrong. Whigs favored changes brought about by the market, so choice B is wrong. Whigs were in favor of increased emphasis on economic development, so choice D is incorrect.

5. **C** This is a Factual Information question asking for specific information that can be found in paragraph 4. The correct answer is choice C, which is explicitly stated in sentence 3 of the paragraph. Sentences 4 and 5 explicitly refute the other choices.

6. **D** This is a Vocabulary question. The word being tested is "concept." It is highlighted in the passage. The passage says, "for Whigs the concept of government . . ." In other words, "the way Whigs thought about government . . ." That process of thinking represents ideas, so choice D is the correct answer here.

7. **D** This is an Inference question asking for an inference that can be supported by paragraph 5. The correct answer is choice D: variations in Whigs' political beliefs reflected regional differences. This is supported by sentence 5 of the paragraph, which says that certain beliefs "In particular" reflected the views of northern Whigs. That suggests that Whigs in other regions of the country had beliefs that varied from this view and implies that such differences were regional. The other three choices are not mentioned in the passage in connection with "variations" in Whig beliefs, so there is no basis for inferring any of them.

8. **D** This is a Sentence Simplification question. As with all of these questions, a single sentence in the passage is highlighted:

The Whigs were strongest in the towns, cities, and those rural areas that were fully integrated into the market economy, whereas Democrats dominated areas of semisubsistence farming that were more isolated and languishing economically.

The correct answer is choice D. Choice D contains all of the essential information in the tested sentence, but the order in which it is presented is reversed. The highlighted sentence describes areas of Whig strength first and then the areas where Democrats were strong. The correct answer, choice D, describes Democrat strongholds first and then Whig areas. No meaning has been changed, and no information has been left out.

Choice A is incorrect because it states that Whigs were able to attract support only in the wealthiest areas. The highlighted sentence does not say that; it says their support came from places integrated into the market, which can include areas of all economic levels.

Choice B is incorrect because it says that the two parties were split between rural and urban areas. However, the highlighted sentence says that Whigs were strong in rural areas that were integrated into the market economy. In other words, the split between the parties was based on the degree to which an area was integrated into the market, not whether it was urban or rural.

Choice C is incorrect because the highlighted sentence makes no mention of how (or if) the Whigs' control of the market economy affected the areas dominated by the Democrats.

9.   **Ⓐ** This is an Insert Text question. You can see the four possible answer choices in paragraph 2.

During Jackson's second term, his opponents had gradually come together to form the Whig Party. **(A)** Whigs and Democrats held different attitudes toward the changes brought about by the market, banks, and commerce. **(B)** The Democrats tended to view society as a continuing conflict between "the people"—farmers, planters, and workers—and a set of greedy aristocrats. **(C)** This "paper money aristocracy" of bankers and investors manipulated the banking system for their own profit, Democrats claimed, and sapped the nation's virtue by encouraging speculation and the desire for sudden, unearned wealth. **(D)** The Democrats wanted the rewards of the market without sacrificing the features of a simple agrarian republic. They wanted the wealth that the market offered without the competitive, changing society; the complex dealing; the dominance of urban centers; and the loss of independence that came with it.

The sentence provided, "This new party argued against the policies of Jackson and his party in a number of important areas, beginning with the economy," is best inserted at choice **(A)**.

Choice **(A)** is correct because the phrase "This new party" refers directly and only to the Whigs, who are first mentioned (as a recently formed party) in sentence 1 of this paragraph.

Choice **(B)** is incorrect because the sentence before is not limited to the new Whig Party. It discusses both Whigs and Democrats.

Choices **(C)** and **(D)** are both incorrect because the sentences preceding them refer to the Democrats (the old party), not the Whigs.

10. **A** **E** **F** This is a Prose Summary question. It is completed correctly below. The correct choices are A, E, and F. Choices B, C, and D are therefore incorrect.

**Directions:** An introductory sentence for a brief summary of the passage is provided below. Complete the summary by selecting the THREE answer choices that express the most important ideas in the passage. Some sentences do not belong in the summary because they express ideas that are not presented in the passage or are minor ideas in the passage. **This question is worth 2 points.**

> **The political system of the United States in the mid-nineteenth century was strongly influenced by the social and economic circumstances of the time.**

A The Democratic and Whig Parties developed in response to the needs of competing economic and political constituencies.

E A fundamental difference between Whigs and Democrats involved the importance of the market in society.

F The role of government in the lives of the people was an important political distinction between the two parties.

**Answer Choices**

A The Democratic and Whig Parties developed in response to the needs of competing economic and political constituencies.

B During Andrew Jackson's two terms as president, he served as leader of both the Democratic and Whig Parties.

C The Democratic Party primarily represented the interests of the market, banks, and commerce.

D In contrast to the Democrats, the Whigs favored government aid for education.

E A fundamental difference between Whigs and Democrats involved the importance of the market in society.

F The role of government in the lives of the people was an important political distinction between the two parties.

*Correct Choices*

*Choice A,* "The Democratic and Whig Parties developed in response to the needs of competing economic and political constituencies," is correct because it is a recurring theme throughout the entire passage. It is a general statement about the development of the Whigs and Democrats. Paragraphs 2, 3, 4, 5, and 6 all provide support for this statement with examples of the nature of the competing constituencies in the United States at that time and the ways in which these two parties responded to them.

*Choice E,* "A fundamental difference between Whigs and Democrats involved the importance of the market in society," is correct because it is a general statement about the differences between the Whigs and Democrats. Paragraphs 2, 3, 4, and 6 all provide support for this statement with examples of the differences in the ways that the two parties viewed the market and society.

*Choice F,* "The role of government in the lives of the people was an important political distinction between the two parties," is correct because it is another general statement about the differences between the Whigs and Democrats. Paragraphs 2, 3, 4, and 5 all explicitly explore this distinction between Whigs and Democrats.

*Choice B,* "During Andrew Jackson's two terms as president, he served as leader of both the Democratic and Whig Parties," is incorrect because it contradicts the passage. Jackson was head of the Democratic Party.

*Choice C,* "The Democratic Party primarily represented the interests of the market, banks, and commerce," is incorrect because it is not true. The Whigs primarily represented these groups, as stated in paragraphs 3 and 6.

*Choice D,* "In contrast to the Democrats, the Whigs favored government aid for education," is incorrect because the passage states only that Whigs in the North were likely to favor aid to education. It is not clearly stated how other Whigs or Democrats felt on this issue.

## Birds Songs and Calls

11. **B** This is a Vocabulary question. The word being tested is "discovered." It is highlighted in the passage. The correct answer is choice B, "found." "Discovered" has the same meaning as "found." Although choices A, C, and D make sense in the context, they do not mean "discovered."

12. **C** This is a Vocabulary question. The word being tested is "realized." It is highlighted in the passage. The correct answer is choice C, "understood." "Realized" has the same meaning as "understood." Although choices A, B, and D make sense in the context, they do not mean "realized."

13. **D** This is an Inference question. The correct answer is choice D, "They are less likely to sing intensively when they are looking for food." To answer correctly, readers must put together the information in sentence 1 that birds often sing more intensively in the early morning with the information in sentence 3 that early morning is a bad time to look for food because it is cold and dark. This combination of facts suggests that birds look for food at times when they are <u>not</u> singing more intensively, which is what choice D says. There is no support in the paragraph for choices A, B, and C.

14. **D** This is a Factual Information question asking for specific information explicitly presented in paragraph 3. The correct answer is choice D, "This is the time of day when other birds are looking for new places to live." Sentence 4 of paragraph 3 says "at this time of day," meaning the early morning, "many birds move around looking for living space," which is what choice D says. Choice A is wrong because there is no discussion in the paragraph about some males trying to take away the mates of other males. Sentence 3 indicates that early morning is <u>not</u> a good time to hunt for insects, so choice B is

wrong. Choice D is incorrect because there is no mention in paragraph 3 of predators attacking the homes of birds.

15. **B** This is a Rhetorical Purpose question. It asks why the author includes specific information about the behavior of a chaffinch in a laboratory. The correct answer is choice B, "To indicate how Slater arrived at the view that imitation plays an important role in how birds learn songs." To answer correctly, readers must understand how information in sentences 3, 4, and 5 is connected. Sentence 4 says that the laboratory chaffinch copied the sparrow's "cheep" sound, and sentence 5 says that from his observation of this behavior, "Slater concluded that learning through copying is an important part of" song learning in birds. Choice B ties this information together correctly. Choice A is incorrect because it is not about the chaffinch and sparrow but about interactions between a different pair of birds. Choice C is wrong because the paragraph does not indicate that Slater thought it would be advantageous for birds to single multiple songs. The chaffinch-sparrow interaction observed by Slater indicates one way—copying—that birds can learn songs, but it is not evidence that there are many different ways for birds to learn a song, making choice D incorrect.

16. **B** This is a Sentence Simplification question. As with all such questions, a single sentence in the passage is highlighted:

In some cases too, Slater observed chaffinches singing songs which were almost identical to those sung by others, but with just a note or two different—possibly because the bird had made an error in copying the song from another.

The correct answer is choice B. Choice B contains all the essential information in the highlighted sentence and does not change its meaning, which is that Slater noticed chaffinches singing songs that exactly copied the songs of other birds except for a few small differences, which may have been copying errors. Choice A is incorrect because it expresses a different idea: it says that Slater observed one or two chaffinches that were unable to sing songs that were nearly identical to the songs of other birds. Choices C and D also express different ideas than the sentence highlighted in the passage does. Choice C says that Slater observed chaffinches "sometimes adding a wrong note or two," and Choice D says that Slater observed chaffinches using "one or two notes from their own songs when singing the songs of other birds."

17. **D** This is a Factual Information question asking for specific information explicitly presented in paragraph 5. The correct answer is choice D, "there were no clear divisions to mark the places where differences in songs occurred." Choice D accurately paraphrases the second part of sentence 3 of paragraph 5, which states, "the boundaries were not distinct enough for it [a song] to be accurately described as a dialect or regional variety of a song." Choice A is contradicted in sentence 1 of the paragraph, which states "So it was not a matter of each bird having its own individual song." Choice B is also contradicted. The first part of sentence 3 says, "Slater found that this sharing related to geographical distribution." It can be inferred from the dis-

cussion that birds living some distance apart share at least aspects of their songs, but this implication does not answer the question asked. The question demands that readers identify the information presented in the passage for the conclusion that chaffinches do not sing a regional variety of the same song, and that reason is the indistinctness of the geographical boundaries.

18. **C** This is a Rhetorical Purpose question. It asks why the author includes information about certain bird and human behaviors. The correct answer is choice C, "To explain why Marler thought that birdsong might be helpful in understanding the development of human speech." The behaviors described identify one of the "parallels" between humans and birds that Marler thought might help psychologists better understand human speech development. Marler was not making the point that young birds and human babies have poor listening skills, so choice A is incorrect. Nor was Marler making the point that their genetic disposition to imitate is unsophisticated or that surrounding noises make song learning and language learning difficult, so choices B and D are incorrect.

19. **C** This is an Insert Text question. You can see the four possible answer choices in paragraph 2. You should consider paragraph 3 when selecting your answer choice because choice D appears at the very end of paragraph 2.

William Thorpe (1961) studied the behavior of gannets in a colony containing many thousands of birds. **(A)** Thorpe found that when a bird was returning to its nest, it would drift on an updraft of air from the bottom of the cliff upwards, calling as it went. **(B)** When the bird on the nest heard its mate calling, it would call in reply, showing that each bird's call could act as an identification signal. **(C)** Thorpe also calculated that a bird might have as many as fifteen or sixteen different kinds of calls, each serving a different function. **(D)**

J. R. Krebs (1976) investigated how birds seem to sing more intensively in the early morning—the "dawn chorus." By investigating what the birds actually did during each day, and how much time they spent on each activity, Krebs found that the dawn chorus serves a largely territorial function. The early morning is not a particularly good time for gathering food, because it is dark, so visibility is lower, and it is also cold, so many insects are still inactive. On the other hand, at this time many birds move around looking for living space, so establishing and defending a territory is necessary. Birdsong is not just territorial, of course. A bird's song can serve a dual purpose: it can be used to defend a territory and, by indicating to a prospective mate that the singer has a territory to defend, can also attract a female bird.

The sentence provided, "**These include flight calls used to coordinate the flock as well as distress calls and begging calls, which are used specifically by chicks to communicate with their parents**," is best inserted at choice **(D)**. The sentence that precedes choice D is about the fact that gannets have many different calls and that these calls have different functions. The inserted sentence explains the function of some of these different calls. Choice D is the only location that makes sense for the inserted sentence. Placing the sentence at choice C interrupts the flow of information in the paragraph. The sentence also cannot be meaningfully added at choices A or B.

20. **C** **D** **F** This is a Prose Summary question. It is completed correctly below. The correct choices are C, D, and F. Choices A, B, and E are therefore incorrect.

**Directions:** An introductory sentence for a brief summary of the passage is provided below. Complete the summary by selecting the THREE answer choices that express the most important ideas in the passage. Some sentences do not belong in the summary because they express ideas that are not presented in the passage or are minor ideas in the passage. **This question is worth 2 points.**

### Birds sing to communicate with other birds.

C Many birds sing to establish territory—and attract mates—during hours in which food gathering is difficult, while other birds, such as gannets, use calls to identify themselves.

D Bird songs and calls may be unique to one bird, shared among several birds, or even learned from other species.

F Because birds and humans have similar genetic ability to imitate certain sounds, birdsong can help explain the development of speech in humans.

### Answer Choices

A The number of different songs and calls a bird has varies by species, with blackbirds having some of the smallest collections of songs and calls and chaffinches having some of the largest.

B Birds that live in dense forests or other places where visibility is poor are especially dependent on songs and calls from other birds to locate sources of food and danger.

C Many birds sing to establish territory—and attract mates—during hours in which food gathering is difficult, while other birds, such as gannets, use calls to identify themselves.

D Bird songs and calls may be unique to one bird, shared among several birds, or even learned from other species.

E Although hand-reared chaffinches at first were slow to correctly copy the calls and songs of their own species in the wild, over time their copying skill improved.

F Because birds and humans have similar genetic ability to imitate certain sounds, birdsong can help explain the development of speech in humans.

### Correct Choices

*Choice C*, "Many birds sing to establish territory—and attract mates—during hours in which food gathering is difficult, while other birds, such as gannets, use calls to identify themselves," is correct because it accurately summarizes important information in paragraphs 1, 2, and 3 of the passage.

*Choice D*, "Bird songs and calls may be unique to one bird, shared among several birds, or even learned from other species," is correct because it accurately summarizes Slater's findings in paragraphs 4 and 5 of the passage.

*Choice F*, "Because birds and humans have similar genetic ability to imitate certain sounds, birdsong can help explain the development of speech in humans," is correct because it summarizes the discussion in paragraph 6 of the passage.

### Incorrect Choices

*Choice A*, "The number of different songs and calls a bird has varies by species, with blackbirds having some of the smallest collections of songs and calls and chaffinches having some of the largest," is incorrect because the passage does not compare the number of songs that blackbirds sing to the number that chaffinches sing.

*Choice B*, "Birds that live in dense forests or other places where visibility is poor are especially dependent on songs and calls from other birds to locate sources of food and danger," is incorrect because the passage does not discuss the effect of low visibility on birds' dependence on songs and calls for communication.

*Choice E*, "Although hand-reared chaffinches at first were slow to correctly copy the calls and songs of their own species in the wild, over time their copying skill improved," is incorrect. Paragraph 3 compares the songs of hand-reared and wild chaffinches, but there is no discussion of the speed at which each learns songs.

# Listening

## Answer Key and Self-Scoring Chart

**Directions:** Check your answers against the answer key below. Write the number 1 on the line to the right of each question if you picked the correct answer. For questions worth more than one point, follow the directions given. Total your points at the bottom of the chart.

| Question Number | Correct Answer | Your Raw Points |
|---|---|---|
| 1. | B | |
| 2. | A, C | |
| 3. | D | |
| 4. | B | |
| 5. | C | |
| 6. | A | |
| 7. | C | |
| 8. | C, D | |
| 9. | A | |
| 10. | B | |
| 11. | D | |
| 12. | D | |
| 13. | A | |
| 14. | A, C | |
| 15. | C | |
| 16. | C | |
| 17. | A | |
| 18. | C | |
| 19. | B | |
| 20. | D | |
| 21. | A | |
| 22. | C | |
| 23. | B | |
| 24. | B | |
| 25. | A | |
| 26. | B | |
| 27.* Functional: | A, C | |
| Project: | B | |
| 28. | C | |
| | **Total:** | |

* For question 27, write 1 if you placed three answer choices correctly. Write 0 if you placed fewer than three choices correctly.

On the next page is a table that converts your Listening section answers into a TOEFL iBT scaled score. Take the total of raw points from your answer key and find that number in the left-hand column of the table. On the right-hand side of the table is a range of TOEFL iBT Listening scores for that number of raw points. Your scaled score is given as a range instead of a single number for the following reasons:

- The estimates of scores are based on the performance of students who participated in a field study for these listening comprehension questions. Those students took the test on computer. You took your practice test by listening to audio tracks and answering questions in a book. Although the two experiences are comparable, the differences make it impossible to give an exact prediction of your score.

- The students who participated in the field study were volunteers and may have differed in average ability from the actual TOEFL test-taking population.

- The conversion of scores from the field study in which these questions were administered to the current TOEFL iBT test score scale involved two scale conversions. Converting from one scale to another always involves some statistical error.

You should use your score estimate as a general guide only. Your actual score on the TOEFL iBT test may be higher or lower than your score on the practice section.

## Listening

| Raw Point Total | Scale Score |
|:---:|:---:|
| 28 | 30 |
| 27 | 29–30 |
| 26 | 27–30 |
| 25 | 25–30 |
| 24 | 24–29 |
| 23 | 23–27 |
| 22 | 22–26 |
| 21 | 21–25 |
| 20 | 19–24 |
| 19 | 18–23 |
| 18 | 17–21 |
| 17 | 16–20 |
| 16 | 14–19 |
| 15 | 13–18 |
| 14 | 12–17 |
| 13 | 10–15 |
| 12 | 9–14 |
| 11 | 7–13 |
| 10 | 6–12 |
| 9 | 5–10 |
| 8 | 3–9 |
| 7 | 2–7 |
| 6 | 1–6 |
| 5 | 1–4 |
| 4 | 0–2 |
| 3 | 0–1 |
| 2 | 0 |
| 1 | 0 |
| 0 | 0 |

# Listening Scripts and Answer Explanations

## Questions 1–5

### Track 11 Listening Script

**Narrator**

Listen to a conversation between a student and a professor.

**Professor**

Hey, Ellen. How are you doing?

**Student**

Oh, pretty good, thanks. How are you?

**Professor**

OK.

**Student**

Did you, um, have a chance to look at my grad school application . . . you know, the statement of purpose I wrote?

**Professor**

Well, yeah. In fact, here it is. I just read it.

**Student**

Oh, great! What did you think?

**Professor**

Basically, it's good. What you might actually do is take some of these different points here, and actually break them out into separate paragraphs. So, um, one: your purpose for applying for graduate study—uh, why do you want to go to graduate school—and an area of specialty; and, uh, why you want to do the area you're specifying; um, and what you want to do with your degree once you get it.

**Student**

OK.

**Professor**

So those are . . . they're pretty clear on those four points they want.

**Student**

Right.

**Professor**

So you might just break them out into, uh . . . you know, separate paragraphs and expand on each point some. But really what's critical with these is that, um, you've gotta let yourself come through. See, you gotta let them see you in these statements. Expand some more on what's happened in your own life and what shows your . . . your motivation and interest in this area—in geology. Let 'em see what really, what . . . what captures your imagination about this field.

**Student**

OK. So make it a little more . . . personal? That's OK?

**Professor**

That's fine. They look for that stuff. You don't wanna go overboard . . .

**Student**

Right.

**Professor**

. . . but it's critical that . . . that somebody sees what your passion is—your personal motivation for doing this.

**Student**

OK.

**Professor**

And that's gotta come out in here. Um, and let's see, uh, you might also give a little, uh—since this is your only chance to do it, you might give a little more explanation about your unique undergraduate background. So, you know, how you went through, you know, the music program; what you got from that; why you decided to change. I mean it's kind of unusual to go from music to geology, right?

**Student**

Yeah. I was . . . I was afraid that, you know, maybe the personal-type stuff wouldn't be what they wanted, but . . .

**Professor**

No, in fact it's . . . um, give an example: I . . . I had a friend, when I was an undergrad, um, went to medical school. And he put on his med school application—and he could actually tell if somebody actually read it 'cause, um, he had asthma and the reason that he wanted to go to med school was he said he wanted to do sports medicine because he, you know, he had this real interest. He was an athlete too, and . . . and wanted to help athletes who had this physical problem. And he could always tell if somebody actually read his letter, because they would always ask him about that.

**Student**

...Mmm...so something unique.

**Professor**

Yeah. So see, you know, that's what's good and, and, I think for you probably, you know, your music background's the most unique thing that you've got in your record.

**Student**

Right.

**Professor**

...Mmm...so you see, you gotta make yourself stand out from a coupla hundred applications. Does that help any?

**Student**

Yeah, it does. It gives me some good ideas.

**Professor**

And...what you might also do too is, you know, uh, you might get a friend to proof it or something at some point.

**Student**

Oh, sure...sure.

**Professor**

Also, think about presentation—how the application looks. In a way, you're actually showing some other skills here, like organization. A lot of stuff that's...that they're not... they're not formally asking for, they're looking at. So your presentation format, your grammar, all that stuff, they're looking at in your materials at the same time.

**Student**

Right. OK.

## Answer Explanations

1.  **B** For Listening conversations that take place during a professor's office hours, it is very likely that the first question will be a Gist-Purpose question. That is the case here. This discussion is about how the woman should write her graduate school application, not about an interview or whether she had been admitted. The professor already has her application and has reviewed it, so the purpose cannot be for her to give him the application. Thus choice B is the correct answer: she wants advice about the application.

2.  **A C** When you are taking the TOEFL iBT test on computer, whenever you see squares in front of the question choices instead of ovals, you should recognize that the question calls for you to select two or more answers from among the choices. In this case, the professor stresses the following two items that the woman needs to include in her application letter:

1. How her college career has made her interested in graduate school
2. How she stands out as an individual

Thus the correct answers are choices A and C. She does not have a background in medicine (choice B), and the professor does not mention her teachers (choice D).

3. **D** This is a Detail question. The professor mentions twice that the woman's decision to go from studying music to geology is unusual.

4. **B** This is an Understanding Organization question. Clearly the professor is illustrating his point that a good application should individualize the writer. His friend who went to medical school is an example.

5. **C** This is a Making Inferences question. The last thing the professor mentions to the student is that she should think about the format of her application and the statement of purpose. He says that the format of the application can demonstrate her organizational skills and strongly implies that avoiding any writing errors shows thoroughness. By making these points, he is implying that the readers of the application will be influenced by its appearance, even if the influence is unconscious. He says nothing about the readers' expertise (choice A); he implies that sometimes they may not read the application carefully, but he does not imply that this is what usually happens (choice B); and he says the opposite of choice D. The correct answer is choice C.

## Questions 6–11

### Track 12 Listening Script

**Narrator**
Listen to part of a talk in an environmental science class.

Environmental Science

**Professor**

So I wanted to discuss a few other terms here . . . actually, some, uh, some ideas about how we manage our resources.

Let's talk about what that . . . what that means. If we take a resource like water . . . well, maybe we should get a little bit more specific here—back up from the more general case—and talk about underground water in particular.

So hydrogeologists have tried to figure out . . . how much water can you take out from underground sources? This has been an important question. Let me ask you guys: how much water, based on what you know so far, could you take out of, say, an aquifer . . . under the city?

**Male Student**

As . . . as much as would get recharged?

**Professor**

OK. So we wouldn't want to take out any more than naturally comes into it. The implication is that, uh, well, if you only take as much out as comes in, you're not gonna deplete the amount of water that's stored in there, right?

Wrong, but that's the principle. That's the idea behind how we manage our water supplies. It's called "safe yield." Basically what this method says is that you can pump as much water out of a system as naturally recharges . . . as naturally flows back in.

So this principle of safe yield—it's based on balancing what we take out with what gets recharged. But what it does is, it ignores how much water naturally comes out of the system.

In a natural system, a certain amount of recharge comes in and a certain amount of water naturally flows out through springs, streams, and lakes. And over the long term the amount that's stored in the aquifer doesn't really change much. It's balanced. Now humans come in . . . and start taking water out of the system. How have we changed the equation?

**Female Student**

It's not balanced anymore?

**Professor**

Right. We take water out, but water also naturally flows out. And the recharge rate doesn't change, so the result is we've reduced the amount of water that's stored in the underground system.

If you keep doing that long enough—if you pump as much water out as naturally comes in—gradually the underground water levels drop. And when that happens, that can affect surface water. How? Well, in underground systems there are natural discharge points—places where the water flows out of the underground systems, out to lakes and streams. Well, a drop in the water level can mean those discharge points will eventually dry up. That means water's not getting to lakes and streams that depend on it. So we've ended up reducing the surface water supply, too.

You know, in the state of Arizona we're managing some major water supplies with this principle of safe yield, under a method that will eventually dry up the natural discharge points of those aquifer systems.

Now, why is this an issue? Well, aren't some of you going to want to live in this state for a while? Want your kids to grow up here, and your kids' kids? You might be concerned with . . . does Arizona have a water supply which is sustainable—key word here? What that means . . . the general definition of *sustainable* is will there be enough to meet the needs of the present without compromising the ability of the future to have the availability . . . to have the same resources?

Now, I hope you see that these two ideas are incompatible: sustainability and safe yield. Because what sustainability means is that it's sustainable for all systems dependent on the water—for the people that use it and for . . . uh, for supplying water to the dependent lakes and streams.

So I'm gonna repeat this: so if we're using a safe-yield method, if we're only balancing what we take out with what gets recharged, but—don't forget, water's also flowing out naturally—then the amount stored underground is gonna gradually get reduced and that's gonna lead to another problem. These discharge points—where the water flows out to the lakes and streams—they're gonna dry up. OK.

### Track 13 Listening Script (Question 11)

**Narrator**

Why does the professor say this:

**Professor**

Now, why is this an issue? Well, aren't some of you going to want to live in this state for a while? Want your kids to grow up here, and your kids' kids?

## Answer Explanations

6.  **A** The first question in this set is a Gist-Content question, as is usually the case in a lecture set. It is important to remember that you are hearing only part of the lecture.

    The beginning of this excerpt shows that the professor is talking about different ways to manage natural resources. He chooses underground water as an example of a natural resource, and then goes on to discuss one particular way of managing the underground water supply called "safe yield." His focus is on the "safe-yield" approach to managing underground water supplies. Thus the correct answer is choice A. The other choices are aspects of underground water that an environmental scientist might discuss, but they are not the focus of this excerpt.

7. **C** The lecture makes clear that the professor does not think the "safe-yield" approach is appropriate. He communicates this indirectly in several ways, particularly when he says, "we're managing some major water supplies with this principle of safe yield, under a method that will eventually dry up the natural discharge points of those aquifer systems." Although the term "safe yield" indicates that it is safe, the professor is saying that it is, in reality, not safe, because it does not take into account the other ways that water can leave the system besides pumping water out for people's use. The correct answer is choice C.

8. **C D** This is a Detail question. All four choices are possible results of removing water from an underground system, but the professor discusses only C and D.

9. **A** This is a Detail question. The professor defines *sustainability* as the ability to meet present and future needs. Since his main criticism of "safe-yield" management is that it is not sustainable, knowing the meaning of *sustainable* is key to understanding the lecture. "Short-term and long-term needs" are the same as "present and future needs," so choice A is the correct answer.

10. **B** Because the question uses the word *imply*, we expect this to be a Making Inferences question. It is, however, a very easy inference. The professor says, "these two ideas are incompatible: sustainability and safe yield." If the "safe-yield" method is incompatible with sustainability, then water supplies managed by "safe yield" are not sustainable. The correct answer is choice B.

11. **D** This question requires that you understand the function of what is said. The professor asks these questions:

Now, why is this an issue? Well, aren't some of you going to want to live in this state for a while? Want your kids to grow up here, and your kids' kids?

The purpose is to point out to the students that, over time, there will be serious consequences to depleting the underground water supply. He thinks the students should consider the future of the state of Arizona. Therefore the correct answer is choice D.

## Questions 12–16

### Track 14 Listening Script

**Narrator**
Listen to part of a conversation between two students. The woman is helping the man review for a biology examination.

**Male Student**

OK, so . . . what do you think we should go over next?

**Female Student**

How about if we go over this stuff about how bacteria become resistant to antibiotics.

**Male Student**

OK.

**Female Student**

Um, but first of all, though, how many pages do we have left? I told my roommate I'd meet her at the library at seven o'clock.

**Male Student**

Ummm . . . There's only a few pages left. We should be finished in a few minutes.

**Female Student**

OK. So, ummm . . .

**Male Student**

About how bacteria become resistant to antibiotics.

**Female Student**

Oh yeah, OK. So you know that some bacteria cells are able to resist the drugs we use against them, and that's because they have these special genes that, like, protect them from the drugs.

**Male Student**

Right. If I remember correctly, I think the genes, like . . . weaken the antibiotics, or, like . . . stop the antibiotics from getting into the bacteria cell, something like that?

**Female Student**

Exactly. So when bacteria have these genes, it's very difficult for the antibiotics to kill the bacteria.

**Male Student**

Right.

**Female Student**

So do you remember what those genes are called?

**Male Student**

Umm . . .

**Female Student**

Resistance genes.

**Male Student**

Resistance genes. Right. Resistance genes. OK.

**Female Student**

And that makes sense, right? Because they help the bacteria resist the antibiotics.

**Male Student**

Yeah, that makes sense. OK.

**Female Student**

OK. But the question is: how do bacteria get the resistance genes?

**Male Student**

How do they get the resistance genes? They just inherit them from the parent cell, right?

**Female Student**

OK, yeah, that's true. They can inherit them from the parent cell, but that's not what I'm talking about.

**Male Student**

OK.

**Female Student**

I'm talking about how they get resistance genes from other cells in their environment, you know, from the other cells around them.

**Male Student**

Oh, I see what you mean. Umm, is that that stuff about "hopping genes," or something like that?

**Female Student**

Right. Although actually they're called "jumping genes," not "hopping genes."

**Male Student**

Oh, OK. Jumping genes.

**Female Student**

Yeah, but they have another name, too, that I can't think of. Umm . . . lemme see if I can find it here in the book . . .

**Male Student**

I think it's probably on . . .

**Female Student**

Oh, OK. Here it is. Transposons. That's what they're called.

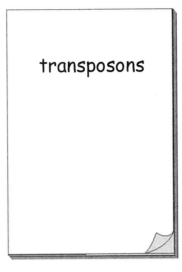

**Male Student**

Lemme see. OK. Trans . . . po . . . sons . . . trans . . . posons. So "transposon" is another name for a jumping gene?

**Female Student**

Right. And these transposons are, you know, like, little bits of DNA that are able to move from one cell to another. That's why they're called "jumping genes." They kind of, you know, "jump" from one cell to another.

**Male Student**

OK.

**Female Student**

And these transposons are how resistance genes are able to get from one bacteria cell to another bacteria cell. What happens is that a resistance gene from one cell attaches itself to a transposon and then, when the transposon jumps to another cell . . .

**Male Student**

The other cell gets the resistance gene and . . .

**Female Student**

Right.

**Male Student**

That's how it becomes resistant to antibiotics.

**Female Student**

Right.

**Male Student**

Wow. That's really cool. So that's how it happens.

**Female Student**

That's how it happens.

Track 15 Listening Script (Question 16)

**Narrator**

Why does the woman say this:

**Female Student**

Um, but first of all, though, how many pages do we have left? I told my roommate I'd meet her at the library at seven o'clock.

## Answer Explanations

12. **D** This conversation is about academic content in the area of Life Science. The man is trying to learn something for his biology test. It makes sense, then, that the first question is a Gist-Content question: "What are the students mainly discussing?" The students discuss drugs, but they are drugs that fight bacteria, so choice A is eliminated. They are not discussing how antibiotics are produced, but how they are resisted, so choice B is eliminated. If all you understood was "jumping" and "hopping," you might think they were discussing athletics, but that is not how those words are being used, so choice C is eliminated. Choice D is the correct answer: the man is learning how some bacteria acquire genes that make them resistant to antibiotics.

13. **A** This is a Detail question. When you hear a new term defined, in either a lecture or a conversation, you should note it. Here the students spend a large part of the conversation discussing why the "transposons" are called "jumping genes." The woman says twice that the reason is that the genes can migrate, or "jump," from one cell to another. The correct answer is choice A.

14. **A C** This is another Detail question. It asks you to identify two ways that bacteria acquire the resistance gene. Both students mention that the gene can be inherited from a parent cell. They then have a longer discussion about the "jumping gene" and how a "jumping gene" can carry the resistance gene to a new cell. Nothing is mentioned about "white blood cells," and resistance genes being "carried by antibiotics" is directly contradicted by the discussion. The correct answers are choices A and C.

15. **C** The question uses the verb *inferred*, so you know this is a Making Inferences question. The students say that some bacteria "resist the drugs we use against them." From this you can infer that an antibiotic is a medicine used against some bacteria. The students say the resistance genes "weaken the antibiotics" and "stop the antibiotics." From these clues you should infer that choice C, the resistance genes "make the treatment of bacterial diseases more difficult," is the correct answer.

16. **C** This replay question requires you to Understand the Function of What Is Said. You are asked why the woman says the following:

Um, but first of all, though, how many pages do we have left? I told my roommate I'd meet her at the library at seven o'clock.

Her statement about meeting her roommate is part of the context in which the main discussion takes place. The man is trying to learn about bacteria, but she is saying they have only a limited amount of time to spend on the discussion. The function of her statement is to tell the man that she must keep her appointment with her roommate and therefore they must finish soon.

## Questions 17–22

### Track 16 Listening Script

**Narrator**

Listen to part of a talk in a botany class.

**Professor**

OK. So we've talked about some different types of root systems of plants, and I've shown you some pretty cool slides, but now I want to talk about the extent of the root system—the overall size of the root system . . . the depth. I want to tell you about one particular experiment. I think you're going to find this pretty amazing. OK. So there was this scientist . . . this very meticulous scientist decided that the best place to see a whole root system—to actually see how big the entire system got—the best place would be to grow it . . . where?

**Female Student**

Um, water?

**Professor**

In water. So he took rye plants—it was rye plants—and he started growing them in water. Now, you've all heard of growing stuff in water before, right?

**Male Student**

It's done commercially, right? Uh, like to grow vegetables and flowers?

**Professor**

Right. They grow all kinds of commercial crops in water. So if you're growing things in water, you can add the fertilizer. What do you need to do to that water besides put fertilizer in it? Anyone ever actually tried to grow plants in water? You must bubble water through it. Bubble gas through it. I'm sorry, you must bubble gas through it. So, gas, you have to bubble through. Think about the soil we talked about last week, about growing plants in soil. Think about some of you who have killed your favorite houseplants, 'cause you loved them too much. If you overwater, why do your favorite houseplants die?

**Female Student**

Oh, no oxygen.

**Professor**

Not enough oxygen for the roots . . . which do what twenty-four hours a day in all seasons?

**Female Student**

Respiration?

**Professor**

Respire . . . respiration . . . they breathe. So if you just stick rye plants in water, it doesn't make a difference how much fertilizer you add, you also need to bubble gas through the water, so they have access to that oxygen. If they don't have that, they're in big trouble. OK. So this guy—this scientist—grew a rye plant in water so he could see the root system, how big it got—its surface area. I read about this and the book said one thousand kilometers of roots. I kept thinking: this has to be a mistake. It just doesn't make any sense to me that . . . that . . . that could be right. But that's what all the books have, and no one's ever corrected it. So let me explain to you about this rye plant. If you take a little seed of many grasses—and remember rye is a grass; if you take a tiny little seed and you germinate it—actually, take one of my least favorite grasses that starts growing about May. What's my least favorite grass that starts growing about May?

**Male Student**

Crabgrass.

**Professor**

Crabgrass.

Remember how I showed you in the lab, one little seed starts out producing one little shoot. Then at a week or so later you've got about six shoots, and then, three weeks later you've got about fifteen shoots coming out all directions like this—all those little shoots up there? Well, that's what they did with the rye. And the little seedling started and pretty soon there were several shoots, and then more shoots. In the end, that one single seed produced eighty shoots, with an average of fifty centimeters of height . . . from one seed. Eighty shoots coming out, average fifty centimeters high. When they looked at the shoot versus the root surface, they found that the shoot surface, with all of its leaves, had a total surface area of about five square meters. Now, here's the biggie: when they looked at the root surface area, you would expect that the root and the shoot would be in balance, right? So they should be pretty close in terms of surface area, right?

**Male Student**

Uh-un.

**Professor**

What's that? Did somebody say "no"? Well, you're absolutely correct. Instead of five square meters, the root system was found to have more than two hundred square meters of surface area. Where did all of that extra surface area come from? Who did it? Who was responsible for all those extra square meters of surface area? What did roots do to increase their surface area?

**Female Student**

Root hairs.

**Professor**

Root hairs, that's exactly it. So those root hairs were responsible for an incredible chunk of surface area. They constantly have to be spread out in the water so they can absorb minerals from the fertilizer, and of course they need oxygen access as well.

## Track 17 Listening Script (Question 21)

**Narrator**

Listen again to part of the lecture. Then answer the question.

**Professor**

What do you need to do to that water besides put fertilizer in it? Anyone ever actually tried to grow plants in water? You must bubble water through it. Bub-ble gas through it. I'm sorry, you must bubble gas through it. So, gas, you have to bubble through.

**Narrator**

Why did the professor say this:

**Professor**

I'm sorry, you must bubble gas through it.

**Track 18 Listening Script (Question 22)**

**Narrator**

Listen again to part of the lecture. Then answer the question.

**Professor**

I read about this and the book said one thousand kilometers of roots. I kept thinking: this has to be a mistake. It just doesn't make any sense to me that ... that ... that could be right. But that's what all the books have, and no one's ever corrected it. So let me explain to you about this rye plant.

**Narrator**

What does the professor intend to explain?

## Answer Explanations

17. **A** This is a Gist-Content question. This lecture is not highly organized and includes interaction from the students. However, despite the short digressions, the lecturer at the beginning and at the end repeats that the point of the talk is to explain how big root systems can be compared with the other parts of the plant. She mentions nutrients and different kinds of grasses, but they are subordinate to her main point. The correct answer is choice A.

18. **C** This is a Detail question. The professor says that the scientist in the experiment wanted "to actually see how big the entire system got." That "entire system" refers to the root system, so the correct answer is choice C.

19. **B** This is an Understanding Organization question. Although this might seem to be a digression, the professor is using an example to explain why plants that are grown in water must have gas bubbled through the water. When people give houseplants too much water, they are, in effect, "growing the plants in water" unintentionally. The plants die because the roots are deprived of oxygen. The purpose of the discussion of houseplants is to explain why, in the experiment, gas was bubbled through the water. The correct answer is choice B.

20. **D** This is a Detail question. The professor mentions crabgrass because it is more familiar to her students than rye. She is making the point that many different kinds of grasses produce many roots from a single seed. She mentions that crabgrass begins growing in May, but that is not her point (choice A). She does not say anything about how much water it requires (choice B). Choice C is the opposite of what she says. Choice D is the correct answer.

21. **A** This question requires that you Understand the Function of What Is Said. You are asked to listen to this part of the lecture again:

What do you need to do to that water besides put fertilizer in it? Anyone ever actually tried to grow plants in water? You must bubble water through it. Bubble gas through it. I'm sorry, you must bubble gas through it. So, gas, you have to bubble through.

Then you are asked specifically why the professor says, "I'm sorry, you must bubble gas through it."

In real speech, people sometimes misspeak; that is, they say a word that is different from the one they intended. This happens more often in informal speech, and this discussion is informal. As you can see from the script, in the previous sentence the professor said, "You must bubble water through it." *It* refers to water. So she has said, in effect, "You must bubble water through water," which does not make sense. The professor immediately corrects herself and repeats the correction twice, so the students know she meant to say "gas." Her purpose is to correct her previous words, so choice A is the correct answer.

22. **C** You are asked to listen again to this part of the lecture:

I read about this and the book said one thousand kilometers of roots. I kept thinking: this has to be a mistake. It just doesn't make any sense to me that . . . that . . . that could be right. But that's what all the books have, and no one's ever corrected it. So let me explain to you about this rye plant.

Like most replay questions, this question requires that you Understand the Function of What Is Said. The lecturer says that "one thousand kilometers of roots" did not make any sense to her. She seems to be expressing doubt. But her next sentence makes clear that the "one thousand kilometers" figure is accurate. She intends to explain why such a surprising, or unbelievable, statement is true. The correct answer is choice C.

## Questions 23–28

### Track 19 Listening Script

**Narrator**
Listen to part of a lecture in a business management class.

Business Management

**Professor**

OK. Uh, let's talk about organization and structure in a company. How are companies typically structured?

**Female Student**

Functionally.

**Professor**

And . . . ?

**Female Student**

By projects.

**Professor**

Right. By function . . . and by projects. Twenty years ago companies were organized in function groups, where people with a certain expertise worked together as a unit—the, uh, architects in one unit, the finance people in another unit. Well, nowadays a lot of companies are organized around projects—like a construction company could be building an office building in one city and an apartment house somewhere else, and each project has its own architects and engineers.

Now, the good thing about project organization is that it's easier to change to adapt to the needs of the project—it's a small group, a dedicated team, not the whole company.

Now, with that in mind, here's a question for you: why do we continue to organize ourselves by function, even now, when in fact we admit that projects are the lifeblood of a lot of organizations? Why do some companies maintain a functional organization instead of organizing around projects? Yes?

**Female Student**

Because, um, if you don't have that functional structure within your organization, chances are you'd have a harder time meeting the goals of the projects.

**Professor**

Why?

**Female Student**

Why?

**Professor**

Listen, let's say we got four new cars we want to design. Why do we need a functional organization? Why not just organize the company around the four projects—these people make car number one, these other people make car number two . . .

**Female Student**

Yeah, but who's gonna be responsible for what? You know, the way you tell who's . . .

**Professor**

Well . . . well, we'll appoint a manager: new car number one manager, car number two manager—they're completely responsible. Why should we have a single engineering department that has all four cars passing through it?

**Female Student**

When you design a car, you need the expertise of all the engineers in the company. Each engineer needs to be in touch with the entire engineering department.

**Professor**

Yeah, but I keep . . . I keep asking why. I wanna know why. Yes.

**Male Student**

Well, to eliminate redundancy's probably one of the biggest factors in an organization. So that, uh. . . so that there's, there's . . . standards of . . . for uniformity and efficiency in the organization.

**Professor**

OK. And . . . and that's probably the primary reason for functional organization right there— is that we want some engineering consistency. We want the same kind of technology used in all four cars. If we disperse those four engineers into four parts of the organization and they work by themselves, there's a lot less chance that the technology's gonna be the same from car to car. So instead we maintain the functional organization—that means the engineers work together in one part of the building. And their offices are next to each other because we want them to talk to each other. When an engineer works on a project, they bring the expertise of their whole functional group with them.

But there's a downside of that, though, isn't there? I mean organizing a company into functional groups is not all positive. Where's the allegiance of those engineers? It's to their coordinator, right? It's to that chief engineer. But we really want our one engineer, the engineer that's working on car number one, we want that person's loyalty to be to that project as well as to the head of the engineering group. We . . . we really want both, don't we? We want to maintain the functional organization, so we can maintain uniformity and technology transfer, and expertise. We want the cutting-edge expertise in every group. But at the same time we also want the engineer to be totally dedicated to the needs of the project. Ideally, we have a . . . a hybrid, a combination of both functional and project organization.

But there's a problem with this kind of hybrid structure. When you have both functional and project organization, well, what does that violate in terms of basic management principles?

**Female Student**

Unity of command.

**Professor**

Unity of command. That's exactly right. So this . . . this is a vicious violation of unity of command, isn't it? It says that this engineer working on a project seems to have two bosses. We . . . we got the engineering boss, and we got the project manager boss. But the project manager is responsible for the project, and is not the official manager of the engineer who works on the project. And we try to maintain peace in the organizations, and sometimes it's disrupted and we have conflicts, don't we? The project manager for car one wants a car part to fit in a particular way, for a specific situation, a specialized case. Well, the, uh, engineering director says no, we gotta have standardization. We gotta have all the cars done this way. We can't make a special mold for that particular part for that particular car. We're not gonna do that. So we got a conflict.

### Track 20 Listening Script (Question 28)

**Narrator**

Listen again to part of the lecture. Then answer the question.

**Professor**

Why should we have a single engineering department that has all four cars passing through it?

**Female Student**

When you design a car, you need the expertise of all the engineers in the company. Each engineer needs to be in touch with the entire engineering department.

**Professor**

Yeah, but I keep . . . I keep asking why. I wanna know why.

**Narrator**

Why does the professor say this:

**Professor**

Yeah, but I keep . . . I keep asking why. I wanna know why.

## Answer Explanations

23. **B** This is a Gist-Content question. Although the lecture includes exchanges between the professor and the students, it is clearly organized around a comparison of the strengths and weaknesses of two different organizational principles. It is not about the automobile industry; that is just an example (choice A). It is not even about engineering; that is a function that is used as an example (choice C). It does not offer a resolution of the conflict it describes (choice D). The correct choice is B: it is about two alternative organizational structures.

24. **B** This is an Understanding Organization question. The professor discusses the construction company as an example of the kind of company that could be organized around project teams. Choice B is correct. The other choices are about functional organization, the opposite organizing principle.

25. (A) This is a Detail question. In this lecture, the professor does not explicitly define "unity of command." But in the last part of the talk, he gives an example of the absence of unity of command: "this engineer working on a project seems to have two bosses." Choice A is the correct answer.

26. (B) To answer this question, you need to recognize the difference between the examples the professor uses in the lecture and the principle that the lecture is actually about. The question asks about a "conflict" discussed in the lecture. Choices A, C, and D are about specific conflicts that might occur in one of the organizations the professor uses as examples. Only choice B is about the general principle of a conflict between two equally important goals. Choice B is the correct answer.

27. This question is easy to recognize as a Connecting Content question. Based on information in the lecture, you must indicate whether certain statements describe functional organization or project organization. The chart correctly filled out looks like this:

| | Functional Organization | Project Organization |
|---|---|---|
| It encourages people with similar expertise to work closely together. | ✓ | |
| It helps the company to adapt quickly and meet changing needs. | | ✓ |
| It helps to achieve uniformity in projects. | ✓ | |

28. (C) In this replay question, you listen again to a question from the professor, an answer by a student, and another question by the professor. It requires that you Understand the Function of What Is Said. In order to understand the professor's second question, you must recognize that it is a repetition of the previous question. By repeating his question after the student's answer, the professor is signaling that it has not been satisfactorily answered. He is also signaling that the answer to his question is an important point. The correct answer is choice C: the student's answer does not include a point the professor wants to make.

# Speaking

## Listening Scripts, Important Points, and Sample Responses with Rater Comments

Use the Speaking rubrics on pages 184–187 to see how responses are scored. The raters who listen to your responses will analyze them in three general categories. These categories are Delivery, Language Use, and Topic Development. All three categories have equal importance.

This section includes important points that should be covered when answering each question. All of these points must be present in a response in order for it to receive the highest score in the Topic Development category. These important points are guides to the kind of information raters expect to hear in a high-level response.

This section also refers to example responses on the accompanying audio tracks. Some responses were scored at the highest level, while others were not. The responses are followed by comments by certified ETS raters.

## Question 1: Paired Choice

### Track 21 Listening Script

**Narrator**

Some people who unexpectedly receive a large amount of money spend it on practical things, while others spend it for pleasure only. Which do you think is better and why?

| Preparation Time: 15 Seconds |
| --- |
| Response Time: 45 Seconds |

### Important Points

In this question you need to choose the action you think is better and explain why. In order to give an effective response, you should provide a clear reason for your opinion. You will not be scored on which action you prefer, but rather on how effectively you are able to present and support your opinion. You may choose to speak about this topic more generally by describing what people in this situation would do, or you may choose to respond from a personal standpoint by talking about what you would do if you were given this money unexpectedly.

Whichever option you choose—spending money on practical things or spending it for pleasure—you should include specific details and examples. For example, if you choose to spend money on practical things, you could mention what type of practical objects or experiences you mean (such as a new washing machine or car to make your family's life easier or something to further your career, such as paying for college tuition). If you choose to spend the money for pleasure, be specific about what kinds of things would give you pleasure and why (taking a trip to a favorite vacation spot, donating to a charity, buying a gift for your mother, and so on). It is also acceptable to support your choice of one option by explaining what is wrong with the other option.

### Sample Responses

*Play Track 26 to hear a high-level response for Question 1.*

*Rater Comments*

In this high-level response, the speaker chooses to develop the idea of using money for practical items and explains why she thinks this is better than spending money on things for pleasure. To explain her opinion, she uses very specific detailed language with almost no errors or awkward phrasing: *"there's been a lot of cases with people who win the lottery and they spent almost all the money for their own pleasure."* She goes on further to explain that this leads to a *"luxurious lifestyle,"* which she claims is unsustainable. However, this response is not perfect. It lacks some specificity: she does not describe what she would consider "practical things" that people should spend money on, so while the listeners know what the speaker **disapproves of**, they do not know what she would **approve of** when spending money. Lastly, her pronunciation is clear throughout, and her words are easily followed. Her intonation and pausing are natural and appropriate and do not distract the listener. Overall, this is a mostly well-developed response that is easy to follow.

***Play Track 27 to hear a mid-level response for Question 1.***

*Rater Comments*

This speaker is able to express an opinion—that the money should be used for pleasure—and provides a general reason for her choice. However, she does not develop her reason at all. The content is vague and lacks details. She states that spending money on things for pleasure is better: *"First, because now the life is so stressful, if you can buy something or do something to relax is so important."* This is an interesting idea, but it would be better to include more specific information such as **what** to buy with the money and **how** or why that would give someone pleasure. While she has good, basic vocabulary and grammar, she does make some errors, such as using "so" instead of "very" or she says, "the life" instead of "life." She has mostly clear pronunciation; it is usually easy to understand her words. However, she speaks very slowly, enunciating each word separately, and as a result, her use of intonation is limited and her speech lacks fluidity.

## Question 2: Fit and Explain

### Track 22 Listening Script

#### Narrator

A student has written a letter to the editor of City University's newspaper concerning the campus health center. You have 50 seconds to read the letter. Begin reading now.

> **Reading Time: 50 Seconds**

---

#### Student Health Services Need Improvement

The situation at the health center is unacceptable: you sit in a crowded waiting room for hours waiting to get treatment for minor ailments. Then when it's your turn, you get about three minutes with an overworked doctor. I have two suggestions: first, the health center needs to hire more doctors so that each patient receives quality treatment. And as far as the wait time issue is concerned, the health center is currently open only Monday through Friday, which means that people who get sick over the weekend wait until the following week to get treatment. So, opening the health center on weekends should solve that problem too.

Sincerely,

Megan Finch

---

**Narrator**

Now listen to two students discussing the letter.

**Woman**

Did you read that letter in the paper?

**Man**

Sure. And though she's right about the problems, I don't think what she proposes will do much good.

**Woman**

Really?

**Man**

Yeah, take her first suggestion—I mean, have you seen the health center?

**Woman**

Of course. Why?

**Man**

Well, it's tiny, right? The center suffers from lack of space. So unless they build more treatment rooms or offices or something. . . .

**Woman**

I see.

**Man**

And also, her second suggestion . . .

**Woman**

Seems like that'll help things out.

**Man**

Well, not necessarily. I mean think about it. A lot of students aren't even here on the weekends.

**Woman**

That's true.

**Man**

They leave town and get away. There's not a lot of people here . . .

**Woman**

Yeah, like me . . . I go home probably at least twice a month.

**Man**

Right. And a lot of us leave campus for the weekend even more often than that. So there's just not a lot of demand for treatment then. See what I mean?

**Narrator**

The man expresses his opinion about the student's suggestions that are made in the letter. State the man's opinion and explain the reasons he gives for holding that opinion.

| Preparation Time: 30 Seconds |
| --- |
| Response Time: 60 Seconds |

## Important Points

To respond to this question, you could explain that the man does not think that the student's suggestions will improve treatment quality or wait times at the health center. To explain the reasons he gives, you should say that he does not think hiring more doctors will help, since there is not enough space at the health center for additional staff. Optionally, you could add that he mentions the health center would need more treatment rooms. You should also explain that he does not think opening the center on weekends will be helpful because many students go away for the weekend.

## Sample Responses

### *Play Track 28 to hear a high-level response for Question 2.*

*Rater Comments*

This speaker effectively combines the important points from the reading and the listening in his response, though he could have included more detail about the points made in the reading (for instance, he could have mentioned the problem with wait times at the health center). He demonstrates good control of grammar with only minor errors and uses varied vocabulary ("take into consideration," "viable") to express the ideas. While his pronunciation is obviously influenced by his native language, the response is mostly clear and is easy to follow.

### *Play Track 29 to hear a mid-level response for Question 2.*

*Rater Comments*

This speaker demonstrates a basic understanding of the information from the conversation. However, because of some limitations with language use, the response does not effectively convey the points from the listening or link them to points from the reading. Limited vocabulary and grammar are evident in the repetition of simple phrases such as "he think that" and vague expression of ideas ("The man's opinion is he think that a student's opinion is not so good"). The response also contains many grammatical errors. Despite some pronunciation difficulties, the speaker is generally clear enough to be understandable, with no major problems in pacing.

## Question 3: General/Specific

### Track 23 Listening Script

**Narrator**

Now read the passage about the nature of social interaction. You have 45 seconds to read the passage. Begin reading now.

**Reading Time: 45 Seconds**

---

**Social Loafing**

When people work in groups to perform a task, individual group members may feel less motivated to contribute, since no one person is held directly responsible for completing the task. The result is that people may not work as hard, or accomplish as much, as they would if they were working alone and their individual output were being measured. This decrease in personal effort, especially on a simple group task, is known as *social loafing*. While it is not a deliberate behavior, the consequence of social loafing is less personal efficiency when working in groups than when working on one's own.

---

**Narrator**

Listen to part of a lecture in a psychology class.

**Professor**

Now, a study was done that illustrated this phenomenon. In the study people were given an ordinary task that everyone has probably done before—they were simply asked to peel potatoes. And to peel as many potatoes as possible in a given amount of time. OK, so some people worked alone—and they were told that the number of potatoes they each peeled would be recorded. Others peeled potatoes together, as part of a group, and they were told that only the total number of potatoes peeled would be recorded. So it would be impossible to tell how many any one person had done.

Then researchers compared the results of the people who worked alone and those that worked together to see if there was any difference. That is, they took the average score of the people working alone and compared it to the average score of the people working together in a group. And they **did** discover a difference. It turns out that people working as a group peeled significantly **fewer** potatoes than people who worked alone.

**Narrator**

Using the example from the lecture, explain what social loafing is and how it affects people's behavior.

**Preparation Time: 30 Seconds**
**Response Time: 60 Seconds**

### Important Points

In this item, you need to explain the concept of social loafing and explain how the professor's example relates to this idea. Social loafing is a term that describes what happens when people work in groups. Members of a group may not be as motivated and may not do as much as they would if they were working by themselves. The reading states that this happens because one person does not feel responsible for the task. The professor's example then describes people's behavior in a study in which people were asked to peel potatoes. Some people worked alone, and others worked in groups. The people working in the group did not peel as many potatoes as the people working alone. This study is a good example of social loafing because it illustrates that people working in a group do not do as much as people working by themselves.

### Sample Responses

#### *Play Track 30 to hear a high-level response for Question 3.*

*Rater Comments*

This speaker provides a complete and clear response to the task. She first explains what social loafing is and why it might happen ("It means that people who work in a group do not feel responsible for the result"). She then describes the example of people peeling potatoes and again explains why the people in the group may not be peeling as many potatoes ("They know they're not going to be held responsible for the number of potatoes that are peeled in a group"). This effectively explains how the example relates to the reading. The speaker's pronunciation is clear, and her pace of speech is also good. She does hesitate at times and makes a few minor language errors, but these do not prevent her from communicating her ideas.

#### *Play Track 31 to hear a mid-level response for Question 3.*

*Rater Comments*

This speaker does provide important information from the reading and the lecture, but she is not able to show their relationship very clearly. She starts with a definition and struggles to find language for that but is able to communicate her idea somewhat ("Social loafing is decreasing an individual's efficiency in a work when they're working in a group"). She then describes the example but is slowed down by trying to provide information that is not really necessary ("they were not sure how to count how many potatoes they did each when they worked in a group"). The response has this lack of precise language and wording throughout, as well as language difficulties and a slower pace when the speaker is searching for language. On the positive side, she does include some important and accurate information about the study, and her pronunciation is clear for the most part. She has difficulty, however, connecting the material from the reading with the example. She gets across the idea that people work less efficiently in a group, but she leaves out the very important point about people in a group having less motivation or not feeling as responsible for their work.

## Question 4: Summary

### Track 24 Listening Script

**Narrator**

Now listen to part of a talk in a psychology class.

**Professor**

OK. Ever thought about the things that happen to you, and what's responsible for them? We psychologists have a term—*locus of control*. Locus of control refers to *[hesitates]* where people think control over their lives comes from: whether it comes from themselves, or from somewhere else. People who think that control is in *themselves* are "internals." And people who think it comes from somewhere else are "externals."

Let's say there're two people going for job interviews. One of them is an "internal"—she has an *internal* locus of control. Since she thinks that control comes from *within* herself, she'll believe that her success and her preparation are really her responsibility. So, she's likely to really work on her interview skills ahead of time. Then, if she gets the job, she'll believe that it's because she's worked so hard, and if she doesn't get it, well . . . she'll probably be disappointed with herself and try to figure out how she can improve for the next time.

OK, and another job candidate is an "external." He perceives other things—say, his *interviewers*—to have more influence. After all, it's their decision. It depends on what mood they're in, and you know . . . luck! Now, with his external locus of control, he's not as hard on himself, so he's more likely to take risks. He might interview for a job that he's not completely qualified for. If he gets it, he'll think he's really lucky and, because he believes external forces are in control, he might think it's because the interviewers were having a good day. If he doesn't get it, he'll probably *blame* the interviewers . . . or bad luck . . . rather than look at himself and try to figure out what he could've done better.

**Narrator**

Using points and examples from the talk, explain internal and external locus of control.

> **Preparation Time: 20 Seconds**
> **Response Time: 60 Seconds**

## Important Points

In your response to this prompt, you need to explain that locus of control refers to where people believe control over their lives comes from, internal (from within the person) or external (from somewhere else). You should explain the example the professor discusses about job candidates. A job candidate who has an internal locus of control sees herself as responsible for her own success. She feels that whether she gets a job is the result of the effort she puts into preparing. A job candidate who has an external locus of control perceives other forces to be in control. He feels that whether he gets a job is the result of other factors such as luck or the mood of the interviewers.

## Sample Responses

*Play Track 32 to hear a high-level response for Question 4.*

*Rater Comments*

This speaker conveys his understanding of the concept through a discussion of the example about the people interviewing for the job. He uses intonation very effectively ("it's **her** responsibility to get the job . . .") to convey the ideas, and his pronunciation is clear. Use of vocabulary and grammar is varied and precise. While there is some occasional natural hesitation while the speaker gathers his thoughts, overall the response flows and is easy to follow.

*Play Track 33 to hear a mid-level response for Question 4.*

*Rater Comments*

This speaker is able to convey the ideas from the lecture fairly well; however, issues with word choice and grammar prevent the response from being fully and clearly developed. For example, the speaker's definition of the two types of locus of control is somewhat vague ("internal locus of control means one believe that she can control her life and she will response for her . . . behaviors, and the external control means the opposite"). Inaccurate word choice causes some confusion for the listener ("if she lost it she would disappear," and "the external person will do the interview just for risk"). Some difficulties with pronunciation also cause listener effort at times.

# Writing

## Listening Script, Topic Notes, and Sample Responses with Rater Comments

Use the Integrated Writing and Writing for an Academic Discussion scoring rubrics on pages 199–200 and 210–211 to see how responses are scored.

### Integrated Writing

#### Track 25 Listening Script

**Narrator**

Now listen to part of a lecture on the topic you just read about.

**Professor**

I think algae-derived biofuel has a bright future despite the concerns you just read about. Let's see how those concerns can be addressed.

Let's talk first about the farmland issue. Your reading says algae farming uses up valuable land and water without giving us food. Actually, this doesn't have to happen with algae farming. Algae can grow pretty much anywhere, even in relatively infertile areas where we cannot grow any other crop. And algae isn't sensitive to the kind of water it grows in: seawater or water that's too dirty to use on food crops works fine. So you can use land and water for growing algae that's useless for growing food; this way nothing at all is wasted.

What you read next is that algae farms have a big start-up cost. But what you may not know is that many kinds of algae can be harvested and re-grown every single week, not just once or twice a year like other plants we use to make fuel—you know, like corn, for example. This means algae can produce something like twenty times more usable fuel each year compared to corn. The income generated by the high volume of fuel production will help algae farmers to make up for the high cost of the equipment very quickly.

Finally, using carbon dioxide gas, or $CO_2$, should be no cause for concern either. We don't have to generate new $CO_2$ to feed the algae. Instead, we can use $CO_2$ that's released by factories as a waste product. You see, $CO_2$ from factories normally goes straight into the atmosphere and adds to pollution. But if we pump this $CO_2$ into algae-growing tanks, the algae will absorb some of it, and less of it will end up as pollution. By using $CO_2$ released by factories, algae farming can actually help lower $CO_2$ pollution.

**Narrator**

Summarize the points made in the lecture, being sure to explain how they respond to the specific concerns presented in the reading passage.

**Topic Notes**

The overall point made in the reading is that while biofuel made of algae may appear like a promising source of clean energy, there are serious concerns associated with its production. The lecturer then addresses those concerns and shows why making biofuel from algae is a good idea.

A high-scoring response will include an introduction and then cover the following points made by the lecturer while explaining how they relate to the points made in the reading passage.

| Point Made in the Reading Passage | Contrasting Point from the Lecture |
|---|---|
| Farming algae on a large scale means using land and water that needs to be used for growing food. | Algae can grow well in areas too infertile to grow other crops and can use water that is too dirty for other crops; algae can even grow in seawater. |
| Equipment needed to manufacture fuel from algae is very costly. | Unlike other crops, algae can be harvested every week. The frequent harvesting generates a lot of income, which helps to pay off the start-up costs quickly. |
| $CO_2$ that algae require for growth is a dangerous pollutant, and some of it might escape into the atmosphere. | Algae farms can use $CO_2$ released by factories as a waste product. Using this source of $CO_2$ can decrease the overall $CO_2$ pollution of the atmosphere. |

Responses scoring 4 and 5 discuss and connect the points and the counterpoints in the table while adding all the important supporting details mentioned by the lecturer. The table includes the main lecture points but may not include all the important supporting details.

## Sample Responses with Rater Comments

*High-Level Response (5)*

The reading states several disadvantages in the production process of algae based fuel. In the lecture the professer refutes every single point that has been made in the article, therefore expecting a bright future for this specific kind of biofuel.

The first statement made in the passage is that algae farms would have to use up vast amounts as landmass and water and therefore occupy regions that might have been used to decrease the worldwide food scarcity. Contrary to this statement, the professor explains that algae can be grown nearly everywhere, even on land, which is considered infertile for other kind of crops. Furthermore, the needed water might be salty and dirty to still be effecient. In conclusion, no ressources would be wasted by algae farms.

The passage mentions as well the enourmous investment costs that would have to be made in starting up an algaefuel business. Refuting the article, the professor states that compared to other corps such as corn, farmers are able to harvest algae nearly once a week and are hence able to generate a sales amount up to twenty times bigger than corn would. She believes that the revenues would easily make up the initial investments.

Finally, the reading explains that environmentally harmfull $CO_2$ is needed to feed the plants and the amount that is not absorbed by algaes will be polluting the atmosphere. In the lecture, the professor agrees that $CO_2$ needs to be used but she offers the viable solution to pump it directly from factories to the farmingtanks. The usage of this technique would help to greatly decrease the pollution and help to effectively fight the global warming.

*Rater Comments*

This answer meets the criteria for a high-level response to an integrated task. The writer does a good job of selecting, framing, and connecting points from the lecture and reading. The overall piece is well organized, with each body paragraph first briefly summarizing one of the arguments made in the reading passage and then summarizing the lecturer's reply to it. All the important information presented by the lecturer is included. Language is used accurately and effectively. The few minor errors and typos are consistent with this being the first draft of a response by a highly proficient nonnative speaker.

*Mid-level Response (3)*

Despite the concerns presented in the passage, algae might have a great future in terms of fuel production. These concerns are about farm-land issue , equipments to grow and extract oil,and Carbondioxide need of algae.

It is presented in the passage that fuel derived from algae creates problems due to that algae have to be farmed on larger areas. Since they would cover fertile land, farming may cause food shortages. However, as it is proposed in the listening section that it is quite easy to grow algae in infertile areas. Furthermore, they regrown every single week. For instance; they are 20 times more usable than corn.

In the passage, it is also stated that algae pull a large quantity of Carbondioxide from the air, and not all of them's absorbed by the algae. This forms the other concern for algae extraction to produce oil, whereas as put it in the listening section, less polluted gas can pass into the atmosphere, if the Carbondioxide gas thrown from factories is used for algae. Carbondioxide gas can be pump into algae growing lands,and the amount of Carbondioxide gas pass into the atmosphere can be decreased.

Although manufacturing fuel from algae can create some problems, it is possible to reduce the harmful effects of other pullution causes by using their waste products in algae manufacturing.

*Rater Comments:*

The writer conveys important points made in the lecturer's reply to the reading passage, but some of the writing is unclear and some important information is left out. In the first body paragraph, for example, the writer writes that "it is quite easy to grow algae in infertile areas," which conveys only a part of the lecturer's response to the first point made in the reading passage leaving out the information about algae growing in dirty water or seawater. The final two sentences of the first body paragraph seem to convey some information from the lecturer's second point, but that information is both unclear and unconnected to the second point made in the reading passage. In the next two paragraphs, the writer covers the last point made in the reading and the lecturer's response to it, but the coverage is inaccurate in some places and unclear in others. The writer does not write with the proficiency and facility we saw in the high-level response (". . . the Carbondioxide gas thrown from factories is used for algae. Carbondioxide gas can be pump into algae growing lands . . .").

## Writing for an Academic Discussion

For this task, you will read an online discussion. A professor has posted a question about a topic, and some classmates have responded with their ideas.

In the actual test, you will have 10 minutes to write a response that contributes to the discussion.

*Question*

Your professor is teaching a class on human resource management. Write a post responding to the professor's question.

**In your response, you should do the following.**

- Express and support your opinion.
- Make a contribution to the discussion in your own words.

An effective response will contain at least 100 words.

**Dr. Diaz**

This week, we are discussing professional development, or workplace training. Some employees prefer to develop skills that will help them do their current job better. Others prefer to focus on training that helps them prepare for a better position in the future. Which kind of professional development opportunities are more important for an employee to take advantage of? Why?

**Claire**

It is far more important to focus on expanding skills that are relevant to your current job. By strengthening skills that can be put to use immediately, employees will get themselves noticed by their managers and be able to quickly advance at the company.

**Paul**

Companies offer a variety of training programs, and employees should take whatever opportunity is given to them, even if it is not directly related to their current job. You never know when a better job opportunity will present itself. Focusing only on skills related to your current job will not necessarily make you the best candidate for a better position.

## Topic Notes

In this prompt, the professor asks whether employees who seek workplace training should focus on improving skills they need for their current jobs, or on acquiring skills that may be useful to them in the future. One discussion participant argues that it's best to improve the skills relevant to one's current job and that doing so is also the most appealing to management; the other argues it might be good to take a training program in a different area because one might use new skills when a new job opportunity comes. Test takers might seize on the ideas already stated and develop them in greater detail or introduce entirely new ideas. Some test takers may argue, for example, that even one's own job is likely to evolve and require new skills; others will talk about acquiring the widest range of skills possible to improve one's chances when looking for a new job; still others may explain how important it is to refresh rarely used skills important for one's current job through training; etc.

## Sample Responses with Rater Comments

*High-Level Response*

> I believe it depends on the stage of employment and the year of experience the employee has at the current position. On the one hand, if an employee just joined a new team, it is definitely for the new entrant to focus on training and learning skills that would be helpful for the current position. On the other hand, if an experience employee who is already familiar enough with all current tasks is looking for advancements, it would be helpful to learn new techniques to help them do better in the future. Also, with the development of technology, it is critical to keep learning new technical skills in the fast-changing business world.

*Rater Comments*

This writer has composed a very clearly expressed contribution to the online discussion, demonstrating consistent facility in the use of language. The writer clearly explains that the strategy employees should use for training depends on how long they have stayed with a company: new employees should focus on perfecting the skills they need for the current jobs, while experienced employees should learn new skills for the future. The writer adds that technological changes force everyone to keep up. The writer uses an effective variety of structures and precise word choices, with just a few slipups that can be expected from competent writers working under timed conditions: "it is definitely for the new entrant" (missing "important" after "definitely") and "an experience employee."

*Mid-Level Response*

> Its better to get trained in different programmes irrespective of the current skills. World is getting update with technologies . So when companies offer veritie of training programmes all the employees should take oppurtunity to update with new skills. We should always be ready for better and should be bale to always prove best in our current skill along with updated and new skils.
>
> Focusing on current skills and updating will only prove and sustain in current suituation but we will not be able to achieve new skills. For professional development and to get more oppprtunities for all employees compies also should boost employees to get trained irrespective of their personal interest

*Rater Comments*

This writer provides a partially successful response to the task. It is mostly understandable and mostly relevant, but parts of it are unclear and there are noticeable lexical and grammatical errors. The writer argues that since technologies get updated, employees should participate in training to keep up with them. Focusing on only current skills is not advisable; furthermore, employers should make employees participate in training whether the employees like it or not, for their own and the company's good. There are noticeable errors throughout, however, which create lapses in clarity in the way the argument is conveyed: "companies offer veritie," "we should always be ready for better," "always prove best in our current skill," "will only prove and sustain," "compies also should boost employees."

# 7 Authentic TOEFL iBT® Practice Test 2

I n this chapter you will find the second of four authentic TOEFL iBT Practice Tests. You can take the test in two different ways:

- **In the book:** You can read through the test questions in the following pages, marking your answers in the spaces provided. To hear the listening portions of the test, follow the instructions to play the numbered audio tracks that accompanies this book.

- **On your computer:** For a test-taking experience that more closely resembles the actual TOEFL iBT test, you can take this same test on your computer using the digital download (see code in the back of the book). Reading passages and questions will appear on-screen, and you can enter your answers by selecting the spaces provided. Follow the instructions to hear the listening portions of the test.

Following this test, you will find answer keys and scoring information. You will also find scripts for the listening portions. Complete answer explanations, as well as sample test taker spoken and written responses, are also provided.

# TOEFL iBT® Practice Test 2
# READING

In this section, you will be able to demonstrate your ability to understand academic passages in English. You will read and answer questions about **two passages**.

In the actual test, you will have 36 minutes total to read both passages and answer the questions. A clock will indicate how much time remains.

Some passages may include one or more notes explaining words or phrases. The words or phrases are marked with footnote numbers and the notes explaining them appear at the end of the passage.

Most questions are worth 1 point, but the last question for each passage is worth 2 points.

You may review and revise your answers in this section as long as time remains.

At the end of this practice test, you will find an answer key, information to help you determine your score, and explanations of the answers.

## LOIE FULLER

The United States dancer Loie Fuller (1862–1928) found theatrical dance in the late nineteenth century artistically unfulfilling. She considered herself an artist rather than a mere entertainer, and she, in turn, attracted the notice of other artists.

Fuller devised a type of dance that focused on the shifting play of lights and colors on the voluminous skirts or draperies she wore, which she kept in constant motion principally through movements of her arms, sometimes extended with wands concealed under her costumes. She rejected the technical virtuosity of movement in ballet, the most prestigious form of theatrical dance at that time, perhaps because her formal dance training was minimal. Although her early theatrical career had included stints as an actress, she was not primarily interested in storytelling or expressing emotions through dance; the drama of her dancing emanated from her visual effects.

Although she discovered and introduced her art in the United States, she achieved her greatest glory in Paris, where she was engaged by the Folies Bergère in 1892 and soon became "La Loie," the darling of Parisian audiences. Many of her dances represented elements or natural objects—Fire, the Lily, the Butterfly, and so on—and thus accorded well with the fashionable Art Nouveau style, which emphasized nature imagery and fluid, sinuous lines. Her dancing also attracted the attention of French poets and painters of the period, for it appealed to their liking for mystery, their belief in art for art's sake, a nineteenth-century idea that art is valuable in itself rather than because it may have some moral or educational benefit, and their efforts to synthesize form and content.

Fuller had scientific leanings and constantly experimented with electrical lighting (which was then in its infancy), colored gels, slide projections, and other aspects of stage technology. She invented and patented special arrangements of mirrors and concocted chemical dyes for her draperies. Her interest in color and light paralleled the research of several artists of the period, notably the painter Seurat, famed for his Pointillist technique of creating a sense of shapes and light on canvas by applying extremely small dots of color rather than by painting lines. One of Fuller's major inventions was underlighting, in which she stood on a pane of frosted glass illuminated from underneath. This was particularly effective in her *Fire Dance* (1895), performed to the music of Richard Wagner's "Ride of the Valkyries." The dance caught the eye of artist Henri de Toulouse-Lautrec, who depicted it in a lithograph.

As her technological expertise grew more sophisticated, so did the other aspects of her dances. Although she gave little thought to music in her earliest dances, she later used scores by Gluck, Beethoven, Schubert, Chopin, and Wagner, eventually graduating to Stravinsky, Fauré, Debussy, and Mussorgsky, composers who were then considered progressive. She began to address more ambitious themes in her dances such as *The Sea*, in which her dancers invisibly agitated a huge expanse of silk, played upon by colored lights. Always open to scientific and technological innovations, she befriended the scientists Marie and Pierre Curie upon their discovery of radium and created a *Radium Dance*, which simulated the phosphorescence of that element. She both appeared in films—then in an early stage of development—and made them herself; the hero of her fairy-tale film *Le Lys de la Vie* (1919) was played by René Clair, later a leading French film director.

At the Paris Exposition in 1900, she had her own theater, where, in addition to her own dances, she presented pantomimes by the Japanese actress Sada Yacco. She assembled an all-female company at this time and established a school around 1908, but neither survived her. Although she is remembered today chiefly for her innovations in stage lighting, her activities also touched Isadora Duncan and Ruth St. Denis, two other United States dancers who were experimenting with new types of dance. She sponsored Duncan's first appearance in Europe. Her theater at the Paris Exposition was visited by St. Denis, who found new ideas about stagecraft in Fuller's work and fresh sources for her art in Sada Yacco's plays. In 1924 St. Denis paid tribute to Fuller with the duet *Valse à la Loie*.

**Directions:** Now answer the questions.

**PARAGRAPH 1**

The United States dancer Loie Fuller (1862–1928) found theatrical dance in the late nineteenth century artistically unfulfilling. She considered herself an artist rather than a mere entertainer, and she, in turn, attracted the notice of other artists.

1. What can be inferred from paragraph 1 about theatrical dance in the late nineteenth century?
    - Ⓐ It influenced many artists outside of the field of dance.
    - Ⓑ It was very similar to theatrical dance of the early nineteenth century.
    - Ⓒ It was more a form of entertainment than a form of serious art.
    - Ⓓ It was a relatively new art form in the United States.

**PARAGRAPH 2**

Fuller devised a type of dance that focused on the shifting play of lights and colors on the voluminous skirts or draperies she wore, which she kept in constant motion principally through movements of her arms, sometimes extended with wands concealed under her costumes. She rejected the technical virtuosity of movement in ballet, the most prestigious form of theatrical dance at that time, perhaps because her formal dance training was minimal. **Although her early theatrical career had included stints as an actress, she was not primarily interested in storytelling or expressing emotions through dance; the drama of her dancing emanated from her visual effects.**

2. According to paragraph 2, all of the following are characteristic of Fuller's type of dance EXCEPT
    - Ⓐ experimentation using color
    - Ⓑ large and full costumes
    - Ⓒ continuous movement of her costumes
    - Ⓓ technical virtuosity of movement

GO ON TO THE NEXT PAGE

3. Which of the sentences below best expresses the essential information in the high-lighted sentence in the passage? Incorrect choices change the meaning in important ways or leave out essential information.

Ⓐ Fuller was more interested in dance's visual impact than in its narrative or emotional possibilities.

Ⓑ Fuller used visual effects to dramatize the stories and emotions expressed in her work.

Ⓒ Fuller believed that the drama of her dancing sprang from her emotional style of storytelling.

Ⓓ Fuller's focus on the visual effects of dance resulted from her early theatrical training as an actress.

**PARAGRAPH 3**

Although she discovered and introduced her art in the United States, she achieved her greatest glory in Paris, where she was engaged by the Folies Bergère in 1892 and soon became "La Loie," the darling of Parisian audiences. Many of her dances represented elements or natural objects—Fire, the Lily, the Butterfly, and so on—and thus accorded well with the fashionable Art Nouveau style, which emphasized nature imagery and fluid, sinuous lines. Her dancing also attracted the attention of French poets and painters of the period, for it appealed to their liking for mystery, their belief in art for art's sake, a nineteenth-century idea that art is valuable in itself rather than because it may have some moral or educational benefit, and their efforts to **synthesize** form and content.

4. The word "**synthesize**" in the passage is closest in meaning to

Ⓐ improve
Ⓑ define
Ⓒ simplify
Ⓓ integrate

5. According to paragraph 3, why was Fuller's work well received in Paris?

Ⓐ Parisian audiences were particularly interested in artists and artistic movements from the United States.

Ⓑ Influential poets tried to interest dancers in Fuller's work when she arrived in Paris.

Ⓒ Fuller's work at this time borrowed directly from French artists working in other media.

Ⓓ Fuller's dances were in harmony with the artistic values already present in Paris.

PARAGRAPH 4

Fuller had scientific leanings and constantly experimented with electrical lighting (which was then in its infancy), colored gels, slide projections, and other aspects of stage technology. She invented and patented special arrangements of mirrors and concocted chemical dyes for her draperies. Her interest in color and light paralleled the research of several artists of the period, notably the painter Seurat, famed for his Pointillist technique of creating a sense of shapes and light on canvas by applying extremely small dots of color rather than by painting lines. One of Fuller's major inventions was underlighting, in which she stood on a pane of frosted glass illuminated from underneath. This was particularly effective in her *Fire Dance* (1895), performed to the music of Richard Wagner's "Ride of the Valkyries." The dance caught the eye of artist Henri de Toulouse-Lautrec, who depicted it in a lithograph.

6. According to paragraph 4, Fuller's *Fire Dance* was notable in part for its

   Ⓐ use of colored gels to illuminate glass
   Ⓑ use of dyes and paints to create an image of fire
   Ⓒ technique of lighting the dancer from beneath
   Ⓓ draperies with small dots resembling the Pointillist technique of Seurat

PARAGRAPH 5

As her technological expertise grew more sophisticated, so did the other aspects of her dances. Although she gave little thought to music in her earliest dances, she later used scores by Gluck, Beethoven, Schubert, Chopin, and Wagner, eventually graduating to Stravinsky, Fauré, Debussy, and Mussorgsky, composers who were then considered progressive. She began to address more ambitious themes in her dances such as *The Sea,* in which her dancers invisibly agitated a huge expanse of silk, played upon by colored lights. Always open to scientific and technological innovations, she befriended the scientists Marie and Pierre Curie upon their discovery of radium and created a *Radium Dance,* which simulated the phosphorescence of that element. She both appeared in films—then in an early stage of development—and made them herself; the hero of her fairy-tale film *Le Lys de la Vie* (1919) was played by René Clair, later a leading French film director.

7. Why does the author mention Fuller's "*The Sea*"?

   Ⓐ To point out a dance of Fuller's in which music did not play an important role
   Ⓑ To explain why Fuller sometimes used music by progressive composers
   Ⓒ To illustrate a particular way in which Fuller developed as an artist
   Ⓓ To illustrate how Fuller's interest in science was reflected in her work

GO ON TO THE NEXT PAGE

**PARAGRAPH 6**

At the Paris Exposition in 1900, she had her own theater, where, in addition to her own dances, she presented pantomimes by the Japanese actress Sada Yacco. She assembled an all-female company at this time and established a school around 1908, but neither survived her. Although she is remembered today chiefly for her innovations in stage lighting, her activities also touched Isadora Duncan and Ruth St. Denis, two other United States dancers who were experimenting with new types of dance. She sponsored Duncan's first appearance in Europe. Her theater at the Paris Exposition was visited by St. Denis, who found new ideas about stagecraft in Fuller's work and fresh sources for her art in Sada Yacco's plays. In 1924 St. Denis paid tribute to Fuller with the duet *Valse à la Loie*.

8. According to paragraph 6, what was true of Fuller's theater at the Paris Exposition?

    Ⓐ It presented some works that were not by Fuller.
    Ⓑ It featured performances by prominent male as well as female dancers.
    Ⓒ It became a famous school that is still named in honor of Fuller.
    Ⓓ It continued to operate as a theater after Fuller died.

**PARAGRAPH 5**

As her technological expertise grew more sophisticated, so did the other aspects of her dances. **(A)** Although she gave little thought to music in her earliest dances, she later used scores by Gluck, Beethoven, Schubert, Chopin, and Wagner, eventually graduating to Stravinsky, Fauré, Debussy, and Mussorgsky, composers who were then considered progressive. **(B)** She began to address more ambitious themes in her dances such as *The Sea*, in which her dancers invisibly agitated a huge expanse of silk, played upon by colored lights. **(C)** Always open to scientific and technological innovations, she befriended the scientists Marie and Pierre Curie upon their discovery of radium and created a *Radium Dance*, which simulated the phosphorescence of that element. **(D)** She both appeared in films—then in an early stage of development—and made them herself; the hero of her fairy-tale film *Le Lys de la Vie* (1919) was played by René Clair, later a leading French film director.

9. **Directions:** Look at the part of the passage that is displayed above. The letters **(A)**, **(B)**, **(C)**, and **(D)** indicate where the following sentence could be added.

    **For all her originality in dance, her interests expanded beyond it into newly emerging artistic media.**

    Where would the sentence best fit?

    Ⓐ Choice A
    Ⓑ Choice B
    Ⓒ Choice C
    Ⓓ Choice D

10. **Directions:** An introductory sentence for a brief summary of the passage is provided below. Complete the summary by selecting the THREE answer choices that express the most important ideas in the passage. Some sentences do not belong in the summary because they express ideas that are not presented in the passage or are minor ideas in the passage. **This question is worth 2 points.**

**Loie Fuller was an important and innovative dancer.**

- 
- 
- 

### Answer Choices

A Fuller believed that audiences in the late nineteenth century had lost interest in most theatrical dance.

B Fuller transformed dance in part by creating dance interpretations of works by poets and painters.

C Fuller's work influenced a number of other dancers who were interested in experimental dance.

D Fuller introduced many technical innovations to the staging of theatrical dance.

E Fuller continued to develop throughout her career, creating more complex works and exploring new artistic media.

F By the 1920s, Fuller's theater at the Paris Exposition had become the world center for innovative dance.

GO ON TO THE NEXT PAGE

# GREEN ICEBERGS

Icebergs are massive blocks of ice, irregular in shape; they float with only about 12 percent of their mass above the sea surface. They are formed by glaciers—large rivers of ice that begin inland in the snows of Greenland, Antarctica, and Alaska—and move slowly toward the sea. The forward movement, the melting at the base of the glacier where it meets the ocean, and waves and tidal action cause blocks of ice to break off and float out to sea.

Icebergs are ordinarily blue to white, although they sometimes appear dark or opaque because they carry gravel and bits of rock. They may change color with changing light conditions and cloud cover, glowing pink or gold in the morning or evening light, but this color change is generally related to the low angle of the Sun above the horizon. However, travelers to Antarctica have repeatedly reported seeing green icebergs in the Weddell Sea and, more commonly, close to the Amery Ice Shelf in East Antarctica.

One explanation for green icebergs attributes their color to an optical illusion when blue ice is illuminated by a near-horizon red Sun, but green icebergs stand out among white and blue icebergs under a great variety of light conditions. Another suggestion is that the color might be related to ice with high levels of metallic compounds, including copper and iron. Recent expeditions have taken ice samples from green icebergs and ice cores—vertical, cylindrical ice samples reaching down to great depths—from the glacial ice shelves along the Antarctic continent. Analyses of these cores and samples provide a different solution to the problem.

The ice shelf cores, with a total length of 215 meters (705 feet), were long enough to penetrate through glacial ice—which is formed from the compaction of snow and contains air bubbles—and to continue into the clear, bubble-free ice formed from seawater that freezes onto the bottom of the glacial ice. The properties of this clear sea ice were very similar to the ice from the green iceberg. The scientists concluded that green icebergs form when a two-layer block of shelf ice breaks away and capsizes (turns upside down), exposing the bubble-free shelf ice that was formed from seawater.

A green iceberg that stranded just west of the Amery Ice Shelf showed two distinct layers: bubbly blue-white ice and bubble-free green ice separated by a one-meter-long ice layer containing sediments. The green ice portion was textured by seawater erosion. Where cracks were present, the color was light green because of light scattering; where no cracks were present, the color was dark green. No air bubbles were present in the green ice, suggesting that the ice was not formed from the compression of snow but instead from the freezing of seawater. Large concentrations of single-celled organisms with green pigments (coloring substances) occur along the edges of the ice shelves in this region, and the seawater is rich in their decomposing organic material. The green iceberg did not contain large amounts of particles from these organisms, but the ice had accumulated dissolved organic matter from the seawater. It appears that unlike salt, dissolved organic substances are not excluded from the ice in the freezing process. Analysis shows that the dissolved organic material absorbs enough blue wavelengths from solar light to make the ice appear green.

Chemical evidence shows that platelets (minute flat portions) of ice form in the water and then accrete and stick to the bottom of the ice shelf to form a slush (partially melted snow). The slush is compacted by an unknown mechanism, and solid, bubble-free ice is formed from water high in soluble organic substances. When an iceberg separates from the ice shelf and capsizes, the green ice is exposed.

The Amery Ice Shelf appears to be uniquely suited to the production of green icebergs. Once detached from the ice shelf, these bergs drift in the currents and wind systems surrounding Antarctica and can be found scattered among Antarctica's less colorful icebergs.

**Directions:** Now answer the questions.

**PARAGRAPH 1**

Icebergs are massive blocks of ice, irregular in shape; they float with only about 12 percent of their mass above the sea surface. They are formed by glaciers—large rivers of ice that begin inland in the snows of Greenland, Antarctica, and Alaska—and move slowly toward the sea. The forward movement, the melting at the base of the glacier where it meets the ocean, and waves and tidal action cause blocks of ice to break off and float out to sea.

11. According to paragraph 1, all of the following are true of icebergs EXCEPT:

  Ⓐ They do not have a regular shape.
  Ⓑ They are formed where glaciers meet the ocean.
  Ⓒ Most of their mass is above the sea surface.
  Ⓓ Waves and tides cause them to break off glaciers.

**PARAGRAPH 2**

Icebergs are ordinarily blue to white, although they sometimes appear dark or opaque because they carry gravel and bits of rock. They may change color with changing light conditions and cloud cover, glowing pink or gold in the morning or evening light, but this color change is generally related to the low angle of the Sun above the horizon. However, travelers to Antarctica have repeatedly reported seeing green icebergs in the Weddell Sea and, more commonly, close to the Amery Ice Shelf in East Antarctica.

12. According to paragraph 2, what causes icebergs to sometimes appear dark or opaque?

  Ⓐ A heavy cloud cover
  Ⓑ The presence of gravel or bits of rock
  Ⓒ The low angle of the Sun above the horizon
  Ⓓ The presence of large cracks in their surface

GO ON TO THE NEXT PAGE

**P A R A G R A P H 4**

The ice shelf cores, with a total length of 215 meters (705 feet), were long enough to **penetrate** through glacial ice—which is formed from the compaction of snow and contains air bubbles—and to continue into the clear, bubble-free ice formed from seawater that freezes onto the bottom of the glacial ice. The properties of this clear sea ice were very similar to the ice from the green iceberg. The scientists concluded that green icebergs form when a two-layer block of shelf ice breaks away and capsizes (turns upside down), exposing the bubble-free shelf ice that was formed from seawater.

13. The word "**penetrate**" in the passage is closest in meaning to

    Ⓐ collect
    Ⓑ pierce
    Ⓒ melt
    Ⓓ endure

14. According to paragraph 4, how is glacial ice formed?

    Ⓐ By the compaction of snow
    Ⓑ By the freezing of seawater on the bottom of ice shelves
    Ⓒ By breaking away from the ice shelf
    Ⓓ By the capsizing of a two-layer block of shelf ice

15. According to paragraph 4, ice shelf cores helped scientists explain the formation of green icebergs by showing that

    Ⓐ the ice at the bottom of green icebergs is bubble-free ice formed from frozen seawater
    Ⓑ bubble-free ice is found at the top of the ice shelf
    Ⓒ glacial ice is lighter and floats better than sea ice
    Ⓓ the clear sea ice at the bottom of the ice shelf is similar to ice from a green iceberg

P
A
R
A
G
R
A
P
H

5

A green iceberg that stranded just west of the Amery Ice Shelf showed two distinct layers: bubbly blue-white ice and bubble-free green ice separated by a one-meter-long ice layer containing sediments. **The green ice portion was textured by seawater erosion.** Where cracks were present, the color was light green because of light scattering; where no cracks were present, the color was dark green. No air bubbles were present in the green ice, suggesting that the ice was not formed from the compression of snow but instead from the freezing of seawater. Large concentrations of single-celled organisms with green pigments (coloring substances) occur along the edges of the ice shelves in this region, and the seawater is rich in their decomposing organic material. The green iceberg did not contain large amounts of particles from these organisms, but the ice had accumulated dissolved organic matter from the seawater. It appears that unlike salt, dissolved organic substances are not **excluded** from the ice in the freezing process. Analysis shows that the dissolved organic material absorbs enough blue wavelengths from solar light to make the ice appear green.

16. Why does the author mention that "**The green ice portion was textured by seawater erosion**"?
    - (A) To explain why cracks in the iceberg appeared light green instead of dark green
    - (B) To suggest that green ice is more easily eroded by seawater than white ice is
    - (C) To support the idea that the green ice had been the bottom layer before capsizing
    - (D) To explain how the air bubbles had been removed from the green ice

17. The word "**excluded**" in the passage is closest in meaning to
    - (A) kept out
    - (B) compressed
    - (C) damaged
    - (D) gathered together

18. Paragraph 5 supports which of the following statements about the Amery Ice Shelf?
    - (A) The Amery Ice Shelf produces only green icebergs.
    - (B) The Amery Ice Shelf produces green icebergs because its ice contains high levels of metallic compounds such as copper and iron.
    - (C) The Amery Ice Shelf produces green icebergs because the seawater is rich in a particular kind of soluble organic material.
    - (D) No green icebergs are found far from the Amery Ice Shelf.

GO ON TO THE NEXT PAGE ↘

Icebergs are ordinarily blue to white, although they sometimes appear dark or opaque because they carry gravel and bits of rock. They may change color with changing light conditions and cloud cover, glowing pink or gold in the morning or evening light, but this color change is generally related to the low angle of the Sun above the horizon. **(A)** However, travelers to Antarctica have repeatedly reported seeing green icebergs in the Weddell Sea and, more commonly, close to the Amery Ice Shelf in East Antarctica.

**(B)** One explanation for green icebergs attributes their color to an optical illusion when blue ice is illuminated by a near-horizon red Sun, but green icebergs stand out among white and blue icebergs under a great variety of light conditions. **(C)** Another suggestion is that the color might be related to ice with high levels of metallic compounds, including copper and iron. **(D)** Recent expeditions have taken ice samples from green icebergs and ice cores—vertical, cylindrical ice samples reaching down to great depths—from the glacial ice shelves along the Antarctic continent. Analyses of these cores and samples provide a different solution to the problem.

19. **Directions:** Look at the part of the passage that is displayed above. The letters **(A)**, **(B)**, **(C)**, and **(D)** indicate where the following sentence could be added.

**Scientists have differed as to whether icebergs appear green as a result of light conditions or because of something in the ice itself.**

Where would the sentence best fit?

  (A) Choice A
  (B) Choice B
  (C) Choice C
  (D) Choice D

20. **Directions:** An introductory sentence for a brief summary of the passage is provided below. Complete the summary by selecting the THREE answer choices that express the most important ideas in the passage. Some sentences do not belong in the summary because they express ideas that are not presented in the passage or are minor ideas in the passage. **This question is worth 2 points.**

**Several suggestions, ranging from light conditions to the presence of metallic compounds, have been offered to explain why some icebergs appear green.**

- 
- 
- 

### Answer Choices

A  Ice cores were used to determine that green icebergs were formed from the compaction of metallic compounds, including copper and iron.

B  All ice shelves can produce green icebergs, but the Amery Ice Shelf is especially well suited to do so.

C  Green icebergs form when a two-layer block of ice breaks away from a glacier and capsizes, exposing the bottom sea ice to view.

D  Ice cores and samples revealed that both ice shelves and green icebergs contain a layer of bubbly glacial ice and a layer of bubble-free sea ice.

E  Green icebergs are white until they come into contact with seawater containing platelets and soluble organic green pigments.

F  In a green iceberg, the sea ice contains large concentrations of organic matter from the seawater.

**STOP. This is the end of the Reading section of TOEFL iBT Practice Test 2.**

GO ON TO THE NEXT PAGE

# LISTENING

In this section, you will be able to demonstrate your ability to understand conversations and lectures in English.

In the actual test, the section is divided into two separately timed parts. You will hear each conversation or lecture only one time. A clock will indicate how much time remains. The clock will count down only while you are answering questions, not while you are listening. You may take up to 16.5 minutes to answer the questions.

In this practice test, there is no time limit for answering questions.

You may take notes while you listen. You may use your notes to help you answer the questions. Your notes will not be scored.

Answer the questions based on what is stated or implied by the speakers.

In some questions, you will see this icon:  . This means that you will hear, but not see, part of the question.

**In the actual test, you must answer each question. You cannot return to previous questions.**

At the end of this practice test, you will find an answer key, information to help you determine your score, and explanations of the answers.

*Listen to Track 34.*

## Questions

**Directions:** Mark your answer by filling in the oval or square next to your choice.

1.  Why does the student go to see the professor?

    Ⓐ For suggestions on how to write interview questions
    Ⓑ For assistance in finding a person to interview
    Ⓒ To ask for advice on starting a business
    Ⓓ To schedule an interview with him

2.  Why does the student mention her high school newspaper?

    Ⓐ To inform the professor that she plans to print the interview there
    Ⓑ To explain why the assignment is difficult for her
    Ⓒ To show that she enjoys writing for school newspapers
    Ⓓ To indicate that she has experience with conducting interviews

3.  How does the professor help the student?

    Ⓐ He gives her a list of local business owners.
    Ⓑ He allows her to interview business owners in her hometown.
    Ⓒ He suggests that she read the business section of the newspaper.
    Ⓓ He gives her more time to complete the assignment.

4. What does the professor want the students to learn from the assignment?

   (A) That starting a business is risky
   (B) Why writing articles on local businesses is important
   (C) How to develop a detailed business plan
   (D) What personality traits are typical of business owners

5. *Listen again to part of the conversation by playing Track 35.*
   *Then answer the question.*

   What does the student imply?

   (A) She is surprised by the professor's reaction.
   (B) The professor has not quite identified her concern.
   (C) The professor has guessed correctly what her problem is.
   (D) She does not want to finish the assignment.

GO ON TO THE NEXT PAGE

*Listen to Track 36.*

Anthropology

## Questions

6. What does the professor mainly discuss?

   Ⓐ Various errors in early calendars
   Ⓑ Why people came to believe that Earth moves around the Sun
   Ⓒ Examples of various types of calendars used in different cultures
   Ⓓ The belief that the position of planets and stars can predict future events

7. The professor discusses various theories on how Stonehenge was used. What can be inferred about the professor's opinion?

   Ⓐ She is sure Stonehenge was used as a calendar.
   Ⓑ She believes the main use for Stonehenge was probably as a temple or a tomb.
   Ⓒ She thinks that the stones were mainly used as a record of historical events.
   Ⓓ She admits that the purpose for which Stonehenge was constructed may never be known.

8.  According to the professor, how was the Mayan calendar mainly used?

    Ⓐ To keep track of long historical cycles
    Ⓑ To keep track of the lunar months
    Ⓒ To predict the outcome of royal decisions
    Ⓓ To allow priests to compare the orbits of Earth and Venus

9.  According to the professor, what was the basis of the ancient Chinese astrological cycle?

    Ⓐ The cycle of night and day
    Ⓑ The orbit of the Moon
    Ⓒ The cycle of the seasons
    Ⓓ The orbit of the planet Jupiter

10. How did the Romans succeed in making their calendar more precise?

    Ⓐ By changing the number of weeks in a year
    Ⓑ By adding an extra day every four years
    Ⓒ By carefully observing the motion of the planet Jupiter
    Ⓓ By adopting elements of the Chinese calendar

11. How does the professor organize the lecture?

    Ⓐ By mentioning the problem of creating a calendar, then describing various attempts to deal with it
    Ⓑ By speaking of the modern calendar first, then comparing it with earlier ones
    Ⓒ By discussing how a prehistoric calendar was adapted by several different cultures
    Ⓓ By emphasizing the advantages and disadvantages of using various time cycles

GO ON TO THE NEXT PAGE ➤

*Listen to Track 37.*

## Questions

12. Why does the student go to Professor Kirk's office?

   Ⓐ To find out if he needs to take a certain class to graduate
   Ⓑ To respond to Professor Kirk's invitation
   Ⓒ To ask Professor Kirk to be his advisor
   Ⓓ To ask Professor Kirk to sign a form

13. Why is the woman surprised at the man's request?

   Ⓐ He has not tried to sign up for Introduction to Biology at the registrar's office.
   Ⓑ He has waited until his senior year to take Introduction to Biology.
   Ⓒ A journalism student should not need a biology class.
   Ⓓ Professor Kirk no longer teaches Introduction to Biology.

14. What does the man say about his advisor?

   Ⓐ She encouraged the man to take a science class.
   Ⓑ She encouraged the man to major in journalism.
   Ⓒ She is not aware of the man's problem.
   Ⓓ She thinks very highly of Professor Kirk.

15. How will the man probably try to communicate his problem to Professor Kirk?

    (A) By calling her
    (B) By sending an e-mail to her
    (C) By leaving her a note
    (D) By visiting her during office hours

16. *Listen to Track 38 to answer the question.*

    Why does the man say this to the woman?

    (A) To thank the woman for solving his problem
    (B) To politely refuse the woman's suggestion
    (C) To explain why he needs the woman's help
    (D) To show that he understands that the woman is busy

GO ON TO THE NEXT PAGE

*Listen to Track 39.*

## Questions

17. What is the lecture mainly about?

Ⓐ Various theories explaining why Mars cannot sustain life
Ⓑ Various causes of geological changes on Mars
Ⓒ The development of views about the nature of Mars
Ⓓ Why it has been difficult to obtain information about Mars

18. According to the professor, what was concluded about Mars after the first spacecraft flew by it in 1965?

Ⓐ It had few geological features of interest.
Ⓑ It was similar to Earth but colder.
Ⓒ It had at one time supported life.
Ⓓ It had water under its surface.

19. What does the professor imply about conditions on Mars billions of years ago?
    *Select 2 answers.*

    - [A] Mars was probably even drier than it is today.
    - [B] The atmospheric pressure and the temperature may have been higher than they are today.
    - [C] Mars was inhabited by organisms that have since become fossilized.
    - [D] Large floods were shaping the planet's surface.

20. What is the possible significance of the gullies found on Mars in recent years?

    - (A) They may indicate current volcanic activity on Mars.
    - (B) They may indicate that the surface of Mars is becoming increasingly drier.
    - (C) They may indicate the current existence of water on Mars.
    - (D) They may hold fossils of organisms that once existed on Mars.

21. *Listen to Track 40 to answer the question.*

    Why does the professor say this?

    - (A) To stress that Mars is no longer interesting to explore
    - (B) To describe items that the spacecraft brought back from Mars
    - (C) To share his interest in the study of fossils
    - (D) To show how much the view of Mars changed based on new evidence

22. *Listen again to part of the lecture by playing Track 41.*
    *Then answer the question.*

    Why does the student say this?

    - (A) To ask for clarification of a previous statement
    - (B) To convey his opinion
    - (C) To rephrase an earlier question
    - (D) To express his approval

GO ON TO THE NEXT PAGE ▶

*Listen to Track 42.*

Art History
Colossal Statues

Questions

23. What does the professor mainly discuss?

    Ⓐ The design and creation of the Statue of Liberty
    Ⓑ The creators of two colossal statues in the United States
    Ⓒ The purpose and symbolism of colossal statues
    Ⓓ The cost of colossal statues in ancient versus modern times

24. What evidence does the professor give that supports the idea that modern-day colossal statues are valued social and political symbols?

    Ⓐ They are very costly to build.
    Ⓑ They are studied in classrooms around the world.
    Ⓒ They are designed to last for thousands of years.
    Ⓓ They are inspired by great poetry.

25. According to the professor, what was one result of the Great Depression of the 1930s?

    Ⓐ International alliances eroded.
    Ⓑ Immigration to the United States increased.
    Ⓒ The public experienced a loss of confidence.
    Ⓓ The government could no longer provide funds for the arts.

26. According to the professor, why did the state of South Dakota originally want to create a colossal monument?

    Ⓐ To generate income from tourism
    Ⓑ To symbolize the unity of society
    Ⓒ To commemorate the Great Depression
    Ⓓ To honor United States presidents

27. Why does the professor discuss the poem by Emma Lazarus?

    Ⓐ To emphasize the close relationship between literature and sculpture
    Ⓑ To illustrate how the meaning associated with a monument can change
    Ⓒ To stress the importance of the friendship between France and the United States
    Ⓓ To point out a difference between Mount Rushmore and the Statue of Liberty

GO ON TO THE NEXT PAGE ↘

28. *Listen again to part of the lecture by playing Track 43.*
    *Then answer the question.*

    What does the professor imply about the poem by Emma Lazarus?

    Ⓐ It is one of his favorite poems.
    Ⓑ Few people have read the entire poem.
    Ⓒ He does not need to recite the full text of the poem.
    Ⓓ Lazarus was not able to complete the poem.

**STOP. This is the end of the Listening section of TOEFL iBT Practice Test 2.**

# SPEAKING

In this section, you will be able to demonstrate your ability to speak about a variety of topics.

In the actual test, the Speaking section will last approximately 16 minutes. You will answer four questions by speaking into the microphone. You may use your notes to help you answer the questions. Your notes will not be scored. For each question, you will have time to prepare before giving your response. You should answer the questions as completely as possible in the time allowed.

For this practice test, you may want to use a personal recording device to record and play back your responses.

For each question, play the audio track listed and follow the directions to complete the task. You may take notes while you listen.

At the end of this Practice Test, you will find scripts for the audio tracks, Important Points for each question, sample responses, and comments on those responses by official raters.

**Questions**

*1. You will now give your opinion about a familiar topic. After you hear the question, you will have 15 seconds to prepare and 45 seconds to speak.*

***Now play Track 44 to hear Question 1.***

---

Some students would prefer to live with roommates. Others would prefer to live alone. Which option would you prefer and why?

| **Preparation Time: 15 Seconds** |
| --- |
| **Response Time: 45 Seconds** |

---

*2. Now you will read a passage about a campus situation and then listen to a conversation about the same topic. You will then answer a question, using information from both the reading passage and the conversation. You will have 30 seconds to prepare and 60 seconds to speak.*

***Now play Track 45 to hear Question 2.***

| **Reading Time: 50 Seconds** |
| --- |

---

### University May Build New Student Apartments Off Campus

The Department of Student Housing is considering whether to build new student housing off campus in a residential area of town. Two of the major factors influencing the decision will be parking and space. Those who support building off campus argue that building new housing on campus would further increase the number of cars on and around campus and consume space that could be better used for future projects that the entire university community could benefit from. Supporters also say that students might even have a richer college experience by being connected to the local community and patronizing stores and other businesses in town.

The woman expresses her opinion of the university's plan. State her opinion and explain the reasons she gives for holding that opinion.

**Preparation Time: 30 Seconds**
**Response Time: 60 Seconds**

*3. Now you will read a passage about an academic subject and then listen to a lecture on the same topic. You will then answer a question, using information from both the reading passage and the lecture. You will have 30 seconds to prepare and 60 seconds to speak.*

**Now play Track 46 to hear Question 3.**

**Reading Time: 45 Seconds**

### Actor-Observer

People account for their own behavior differently from how they account for the behavior of others. When observing the behavior of others, we tend to attribute their actions to their character or their personality rather than to external factors. In contrast, we tend to explain our own behavior in terms of situational factors beyond our own control rather than attributing it to our own character. One explanation for this difference is that people are aware of the situational forces affecting them but not of situational forces affecting other people. Thus, when evaluating someone else's behavior, we focus on the person rather than the situation.

GO ON TO THE NEXT PAGE

Explain how the two examples discussed by the professor illustrate differences in the ways people explain behavior.

> **Preparation Time: 30 Seconds**
> **Response Time: 60 Seconds**

*4. Now you will listen to a lecture. You will then be asked to summarize the lecture. You will have 20 seconds to prepare and 60 seconds to speak.*

*Now play Track 47 to hear Question 4.*

Using points and examples from the talk, explain how learning art can impact a child's development.

| **Preparation Time: 20 Seconds** |
| **Response Time: 60 Seconds** |

**STOP. This is the end of the Speaking section of TOEFL iBT Practice Test 2.**

# WRITING

In this section, you will be able to demonstrate your ability to use writing to communicate in an academic environment. There will be two writing tasks.

At the end of this Practice Test, you will find a script for the audio track, topic notes, sample responses, and comments on those responses by official raters.

Turn the page to see the directions for the first writing task.

## Integrated Writing

For this task, you will read a passage about an academic topic. Then you will listen to a lecture about the same topic. You may take notes while you listen.

In your response, provide a detailed summary of the lecture and explain how the lecture relates to the reading passage.

In the actual test, you will have 3 minutes to read the passage and 20 minutes to write your response. While you write, you will be able to see the reading passage. If you finish your response before time is up, you may go on to the second writing task.

Now you will see the reading passage. It will be followed by a lecture.

| Reading Time: 3 minutes |
| --- |

Professors are normally found in university classrooms, offices, and libraries doing research and lecturing to their students. More and more, however, they also appear as guests on television news programs, giving expert commentary on the latest events in the world. These television appearances are of great benefit to the professors themselves as well as to their universities and the general public.

Professors benefit from appearing on television because by doing so they acquire reputations as authorities in their academic fields among a much wider audience than they have on campus. If a professor publishes views in an academic journal, only other scholars will learn about and appreciate those views. But when a professor appears on TV, thousands of people outside the narrow academic community become aware of the professor's ideas. So when professors share their ideas with a television audience, the professors' importance as scholars is enhanced.

Universities also benefit from such appearances. The universities receive positive publicity when their professors appear on TV. When people see a knowledgeable faculty member of a university on television, they think more highly of that university. That then leads to an improved reputation for the university. And that improved reputation in turn leads to more donations for the university and more applications from potential students.

Finally, the public gains from professors' appearing on television. Most television viewers normally have no contact with university professors. When professors appear on television, viewers have a chance to learn from experts and to be exposed to views they might otherwise never hear about. Television is generally a medium for commentary that tends to be superficial, not deep or thoughtful. From professors on television, by contrast, viewers get a taste of real expertise and insight.

*Now play Track 48.*

## Question 1

Summarize the points made in the lecture, being sure to explain how they respond to the specific concerns presented in the reading passage.

You have 20 minutes to plan and write your response.

**Response Time: 20 minutes**

_____

_____

_____

_____

_____

_____

_____

_____

_____

_____

_____

_____

### Writing for an Academic Discussion

For this task, you will read an online discussion. A professor has posted a question about a topic, and some classmates have responded with their ideas.

In the actual test, you will have 10 minutes to write a response that contributes to the discussion.

### Question 2

Your professor is teaching a class on ecology. Write a post responding to the professor's question.

**In your response, you should do the following.**
- Express and support your opinion.
- Make a contribution to the discussion in your own words.

An effective response will contain at least 100 words.

**Dr. Gupta**

Today, there is debate over how we should treat natural ecosystems, meaning wilderness areas that are basically untouched by human activity. These natural ecosystems were once seen purely as resources to be exploited, but many people now believe that wilderness areas should be protected from any human use or interference so that they continue developing completely naturally. To what extent do you support protecting and preserving natural ecosystems? Should some wilderness areas be totally protected from human use?

**Andrew**

People who are already struggling to feed their families are the ones most likely to be affected by, for example, a ban on mining in a wilderness area. We cannot prohibit human activities in natural ecosystems without economic consequences. I believe humans have a fundamental right to use natural resources for survival and to build wealth.

**Kelly**

There are very few truly wild places left on Earth, and once they're gone, we can never get them back. I believe we need to protect our remaining natural ecosystems from human interference. Not only will the animals and plants in those places benefit, but so will we humans because our own survival depends on the health of our planet.

**Response Time: 10 minutes**

GO ON TO THE NEXT PAGE

**STOP. This is the end of the Writing section of TOEFL iBT® Practice Test 2.**

# Answers, Explanations, and Listening Scripts

# Reading

## Answer Key and Self-Scoring Chart

**Directions:** Check your answers against the answer key below. Write the number 1 on the line to the right of each question if you picked the correct answer. For questions worth more than one point, follow the directions given. Total your points at the bottom of the chart.

| Question Number | Correct Answer | Your Raw Points |
|---|---|---|
| Loie Fuller | | |
| 1. | C | |
| 2. | D | |
| 3. | A | |
| 4. | D | |
| 5. | D | |
| 6. | C | |
| 7. | C | |
| 8. | A | |
| 9. | D | |
| 10.* | C, D, E | |
| TOTAL: | | |

\* For question 10, write 2 if you picked all three correct answers. Write 1 if you picked two correct answers.

| Question Number | Correct Answer | Your Raw Points |
|---|---|---|
| **Green Icebergs** | | |
| 11. | C | |
| 12. | B | |
| 13. | B | |
| 14. | A | |
| 15. | D | |
| 16. | C | |
| 17. | A | |
| 18. | C | |
| 19. | B | |
| 20.* | C, D, F | |
| **TOTAL:** | | |

\* For question 10, write 2 if you picked all three correct answers. Write 1 if you picked two correct answers.

Below is a table that converts your Reading section answers into a TOEFL iBT Reading scaled score. Take the total raw points for both sets from your answer key and find that number in the left-hand column of the table. The right-hand column of the table gives a TOEFL iBT Reading scaled score for each number of raw points. For example, if the total points from your answer key is 18, the table shows a scaled score of 24 to 29.

You should use your score estimate as a general guide only. Your actual score on the TOEFL iBT test may be higher or lower than your score on the practice version.

## Reading Comprehension

| Raw Point Total | Scale Score |
| --- | --- |
| 22 | 30 |
| 21 | 29–30 |
| 20 | 28–30 |
| 19 | 26–29 |
| 18 | 24–29 |
| 17 | 22–28 |
| 16 | 21–26 |
| 15 | 19–25 |
| 14 | 18–23 |
| 13 | 16–22 |
| 12 | 14–20 |
| 11 | 12–19 |
| 10 | 11–17 |
| 9 | 9–16 |
| 8 | 7–14 |
| 7 | 4–12 |
| 6 | 3–10 |
| 5 | 1–7 |
| 4 | 0–4 |
| 3 | 0–2 |
| 2 | 0 |
| 1 | 0 |
| 0 | 0 |

# Answer Explanations

## Loie Fuller

1. **C** This is an Inference question asking about an inference that can be supported by paragraph 1. The correct answer is choice C. The phrase "mere entertainer" in sentence 2 suggests that entertainment is less serious than art. Choice A is incorrect because we know only that other artists were attracted to Loie Fuller as an artist; there is no information about what fields these artists were in or if their work was actually influenced by Loie Fuller. Choice B is incorrect because there is no information about theatrical dance in the early nineteenth century. Choice D is incorrect because there is no indication in the paragraph about the length of time theatrical dance had been practiced.

2. **D** This is a Negative Factual Information question asking for specific information that can be found in paragraph 2. Choice D is the correct answer. Sentence 2 in the paragraph states that Loie Fuller rejected technical virtuosity, so it cannot be a characteristic of her type of dance. The information in choices A, B, and C is stated in sentence 1 as part of her type of dance.

3. **A** This is a Sentence Simplification question. As with all of these questions, a single sentence in the passage is highlighted:

   Although her early theatrical career had included stints as an actress, she was not primarily interested in storytelling or expressing emotions through dance; the drama of her dancing emanated from her visual effects.

   The correct answer is choice A. Choice A contains all of the essential information in the tested sentence. It omits the information in the first clause ("Although her early theatrical career had included stints as an actress") because this information is secondary to Loie Fuller's main interest in dance.

   Choices B, C, and D are all incorrect because they change the meaning of the highlighted sentence. Choices B and C are incorrect because the highlighted sentence states that Fuller was not interested in storytelling, so to say that she dramatized stories or had a particular style of storytelling is incorrect.

   Choice D is incorrect because the highlighted sentence indicates the opposite idea: it indicates that Fuller's early career had little effect on her style of dance.

4. **D** This is a Vocabulary question. The word being tested is "synthesize." It is highlighted in the passage. The correct answer is choice D, "integrate." According to the passage, French poets and painters wanted to blend, or integrate, form and content.

5.  **D** This is a Factual Information question asking for specific information that can be found in paragraph 3. The correct answer is choice D. Sentence 2 in this paragraph states that Fuller's dances were in accord, or agreed, with the Art Nouveau style that was fashionable in Paris at the time. Choice A is incorrect because the paragraph says only that Parisian audiences liked Fuller's work; artists and artistic movements from the United States, in general, are not mentioned in this paragraph. Choice B is incorrect because the paragraph states that poets themselves were interested in Fuller's work. It does not state that poets tried to make other people interested in her work. Choice C is incorrect because the paragraph states in the first sentence that Fuller discovered and introduced her ideas herself; she did not borrow or take them from other artists.

6.  **C** This is a Factual Information question asking for specific information that can be found in paragraph 4. The correct answer is choice C. Sentence 4 in the paragraph states that Fuller invented the technique of underlighting, or lighting the dancer from beneath. Choices A, B, and D are incorrect because they inaccurately describe how certain techniques were used by Fuller. Furthermore, none of these techniques is mentioned in connection with Fuller's *Fire Dance*.

7.  **C** This is a Rhetorical Purpose question asking why the author mentions Fuller's dance titled *The Sea*. The correct answer is choice C. The paragraph begins by stating that aspects of Fuller's expertise with dance grew along with her technical expertise. *The Sea* is mentioned as an example of one way that Fuller's expertise grew, or one way that she developed as an artist, which, in this case, is in the scope of her themes. Choices A and B are incorrect because *The Sea* is not mentioned in connection with the use of music. Choice D is incorrect because *The Sea* is not mentioned in connection with science. The paragraph states that science is the theme of a different dance by Fuller, the *Radium Dance*.

8.  **A** This is a Factual Information question asking for specific information that can be found in paragraph 6. The correct answer is choice A. Sentence 1 in this paragraph states that Fuller presented works by another artist, Sada Yacco. Choice B is incorrect because the paragraph states that Fuller created an all-female dance company at the time of the Paris Exposition, but we do not know if that company, or any particular company, performed in Fuller's theater. Choice C is incorrect because the paragraph states only that she established a school in 1908; we do not know that the school directly resulted from the Paris Exposition. Furthermore, we do not know from the paragraph that a school exists today that is named after Fuller. Choice D is incorrect because the paragraph does not state that Fuller's theater continued to operate after the Paris Exposition ended.

9. **D** This is an Insert Text question. You can see the four possible answer choices in paragraph 5.

As her technological expertise grew more sophisticated, so did other aspects of her dances. **(A)** Although she gave little thought to music in her earliest dances, she later used scores by Gluck, Beethoven, Schubert, Chopin, and Wagner, eventually graduating to Stravinsky, Fauré, Debussy, and Mussorgsky, composers who were then considered progressive. **(B)** She began to address more ambitious themes in her dances such as *The Sea*, in which her dancers invisibly agitated a huge expanse of silk, played upon by colored lights. **(C)** Always open to scientific and technological innovations, she befriended the scientists Marie and Pierre Curie upon their discovery of radium and created *Radium Dance*, which simulated the phosphorescence of that element. **(D)** She both appeared in films—then in an early stage of development—and made them herself; the hero of her fairy-tale film *Le Lys de la Vie* (1919) was played by René Clair, later a leading French film director.

The sentence provided, "For all her originality in dance, her interests expanded beyond it into newly emerging artistic media," is best inserted at choice **(D)**.

The "newly emerging artistic media" are elaborated on with the information about films in the sentence following choice **(D)**.

Choices **(A)**, **(B)**, and **(C)** are incorrect because the information provided in the sentences before and after each of these squares is focused on Fuller's dance work, whereas the given sentence directs the reader away from Fuller's dance work and toward other forms of art.

10. Ⓒ Ⓓ Ⓔ This is a Prose Summary question. It is completed correctly below. The correct choices are C, D, and E. Choices A, B, and F are therefore incorrect.

**Directions:** An introductory sentence for a brief summary of the passage is provided below. Complete the summary by selecting the THREE answer choices that express the most important ideas in the passage. Some sentences do not belong in the summary because they express ideas that are not presented in the passage or are minor ideas in the passage. **This question is worth 2 points.**

**Loie Fuller was an important and innovative dancer.**

- Ⓒ Fuller's work influenced a number of other dancers who were interested in experimental dance.
- Ⓓ Fuller introduced many technical innovations to the staging of theatrical dance.
- Ⓔ Fuller continued to develop throughout her career, creating more complex works and exploring new artistic media.

### Answer Choices

- Ⓐ Fuller believed that audiences in the late nineteenth century had lost interest in most theatrical dance.
- Ⓑ Fuller transformed dance in part by creating dance interpretations of works by poets and painters.
- Ⓒ Fuller's work influenced a number of other dancers who were interested in experimental dance.
- Ⓓ Fuller introduced many technical innovations to the staging of theatrical dance.
- Ⓔ Fuller continued to develop throughout her career, creating more complex works and exploring new artistic media.
- Ⓕ By the 1920s, Fuller's theater at the Paris Exposition had become the world center for innovative dance.

### Correct Choices

*Choice C*: "Fuller's work influenced a number of other dancers who were interested in experimental dance." This is a main idea, presented in paragraph 6. Fuller's influence on dancers who later became famous for their own work is discussed.

*Choice D*: "Fuller introduced many technical innovations to the staging of theatrical dance." This is a main theme of the passage that is repeated in several paragraphs. Her technical innovations are detailed at length in paragraph 4 but are also mentioned in paragraphs 5 and 6.

*Choice E*: "Fuller continued to develop throughout her career, creating more complex works and exploring new artistic media." This main idea is the focus of paragraph 5, which discusses her use of music, the more complex themes that she addressed in her dances, and also the films that she appeared in and directed.

*Choice A,* "Fuller believed that audiences in the late nineteenth century had lost interest in most theatrical dance," is incorrect because, while it could be true, the passage never makes this claim. The passage suggests only that Fuller lost interest in theatrical dance.

*Choice B,* "Fuller transformed dance in part by creating dance interpretations of works by poets and painters," is incorrect because the passage does not state that Fuller based her dances on the works of other artists. The passage states several times that Fuller's work was entirely original: she developed her own work and, in fact, invented many techniques.

*Choice F,* "By the 1920s, Fuller's theater at the Paris Exposition had become the world center for innovative dance," is incorrect because Fuller's theater existed for only one year, the year of the Paris Exposition (1900). Furthermore, the passage makes no claim about any particular place as being the "center for innovative dance."

## Green Icebergs

11. **C** This is a Negative Factual Information question testing specific information in paragraph 1. The correct answer is choice C. The information in choice C is contradicted in sentence 1, which states that icebergs "float with only about 12 percent of their mass above the sea surface." The information given in the other choices is stated in the paragraph.

12. **B** This is a Factual Information question testing specific information in paragraph 2. The correct answer is choice B. The information in choice B is taken directly from sentence 1 in the paragraph, which states that icebergs "sometimes appear dark or opaque because they carry gravel and bits of rock." Choice A is incorrect because, as sentence 2 states, cloud cover may result in "pink or gold" colors, not dark colors. Choice C is incorrect because "the low angle of the Sun above the horizon" is discussed as a possible cause of pink or gold colors. Choice D is incorrect because the issue of large cracks in icebergs is not discussed in paragraph 2.

13. **B** This is a Vocabulary question. The word being tested is "penetrate." It is highlighted in the passage. The correct answer is choice B, "pierce." In other words, ice shelf cores were long enough to pierce through glacial ice.

14. **A** This is a Factual Information question testing specific information in paragraph 4. The correct answer is choice A. Sentence 1 in the paragraph discusses "glacial ice—which is formed from the compaction of snow." Choice B is incorrect because the information given describes sea ice, a different type of ice. Choice C is incorrect because the information given describes the first step in the formation of green icebergs. Choice D is incorrect because the information given describes the second step in the formation of green icebergs.

15. **D** This is a Factual Information question testing specific information in paragraph 4. The correct answer is choice D. Sentence 2 in the paragraph states that clear sea ice is "very similar" to the ice from green icebergs. Choices A, B, and C do not answer the question asked. Choice A is also incorrect because it mistakenly identifies green icebergs as having frozen seawater at the bottom, whereas the last sentence in the paragraph says that the blocks that form green icebergs have capsized so that the bubble-free ice is on top of them. Choice B is incorrect because the information given is the opposite of what is stated in the passage, which is that bubble-free ice is formed and found on the bottom of shelf ice. Choice C is incorrect because the information given is not discussed in the passage at all.

16. **C** This is a Rhetorical Purpose question. It tests why the author mentions that "The green ice portion was textured by seawater erosion." This sentence is highlighted in the passage. The correct answer is choice C. The highlighted sentence is evidence that the green ice part of the iceberg was once under water. The fact that this green ice is no longer under water but is now exposed to air is evidence that the green icebergs are formed from pieces of the ice shelf that have broken off and turned upside down. Choice A is incorrect because the information given, while factual according to the passage, does not explain why the author includes the information that the green ice portion was textured by seawater erosion. Choice B is incorrect because there is no comparison made between the erosion of green ice and white ice in the paragraph. Choice D is incorrect because, while sentences 1 and 4 in the paragraph state that green ice has no bubbles, there is no information in the paragraph indicating that green ice initially has bubbles and that they are removed.

17. **A** This is a Vocabulary question. The word being tested is "excluded." It is highlighted in the passage. The correct answer is choice A, "kept out." In other words, dissolved organic substances are not kept out of the ice in the freezing process.

18. **C** This is an Inference question asking for an inference that can be supported by the passage. The correct answer is choice C. Sentences 5, 6, and 7 in paragraph 5 support this information by indicating that the seawater around these icebergs contains the decomposing material of green-pigmented organisms. This decomposing material dissolves in seawater, which then freezes as part of the iceberg. The information in choice A is incorrect because paragraph 7 says that the Amery Ice Shelf is well suited to the production of green icebergs. This does not mean that the Amery Ice Shelf produces *only* green icebergs. The information in choice B is incorrect because copper and iron are mentioned in paragraph 3 only as *possible* color sources in green icebergs. The last sentence in paragraph 3 states that a source other than copper and iron was found. The information in choice D is incorrect because the passage gives no indication of where all green icebergs are located. Paragraph 2 mentions the Weddell Sea in Antarctica, and paragraph 7 states that green icebergs "drift" around Antarctica. Therefore green icebergs can be found far from the Amery Ice Shelf.

19. **B** This is an Insert Text question. You can see the four possible answer choices in paragraphs 2 and 3.

Icebergs are ordinarily blue to white, although they sometimes appear dark or opaque because they carry gravel and bits of rock. They may change color with changing light conditions and cloud cover, glowing pink or gold in the morning or evening light, but this color change is generally related to the low angle of the Sun above the horizon. **(A)** However, travelers to Antarctica have repeatedly reported seeing green icebergs in the Weddell Sea and, more commonly, close to the Amery Ice Shelf in East Antarctica.

   **(B)** One explanation for green icebergs attributes their color to an optical illusion when blue ice is illuminated by a near-horizon red Sun, but green icebergs stand out among white and blue icebergs under a great variety of light conditions. **(C)** Another suggestion is that the color might be related to ice with high levels of metallic compounds, including copper and iron. **(D)** Recent expeditions have taken ice samples from green icebergs and ice cores—vertical, cylindrical ice samples reaching down to great depths—from the glacial ice shelves along the Antarctic continent. Analyses of these cores and samples provide a different solution to the problem.

The sentence provided, "Scientists have differed as to whether icebergs appear green as a result of light conditions or because of something in the ice itself," is best inserted at choice **(B)**.

Choice **(B)** is correct because the sentence provided introduces two possible explanations for the color of green icebergs. Paragraph 3 is the first place in the passage where explanations are offered for the color of green icebergs. The beginning of paragraph 3 is the only appropriate place to introduce these possible explanations.

Choice **(A)** is incorrect because green icebergs are mentioned for the first time in the last sentence in paragraph 2. It does not make sense to insert the given sentence, which introduces explanations for the color of green icebergs, before the first mention of green icebergs.

Choice **(C)** is incorrect because its position is *between* the detailed discussions of the two explanations introduced in the given sentence. The given sentence introduces the two explanations; therefore it must come *before* the discussions.

Choice **(D)** is incorrect because its position is *after* the detailed discussions of the two explanations introduced in the given sentence. The given sentence introduces the two explanations; therefore it must come *before* the discussions.

20. **C** **D** **F** This is a Prose Summary question. It is completed correctly below. The correct choices are C, D, and F. Choices A, B, and E are therefore incorrect.

**Directions:** An introductory sentence for a brief summary of the passage is provided below. Complete the summary by selecting the THREE answer choices that express the most important ideas in the passage. Some sentences do not belong in the summary because they express ideas that are not presented in the passage or are minor ideas in the passage. **This question is worth 2 points.**

**Several suggestions, ranging from light conditions to the presence of metallic compounds, have been offered to explain why some icebergs appear green.**

C   Green icebergs form when a two-layer block of ice breaks away from a glacier and capsizes, exposing the bottom sea ice to view.

D   Ice cores and samples revealed that both ice shelves and green icebergs contain a layer of bubbly glacial ice and a layer of bubble-free sea ice.

F   In a green iceberg, the sea ice contains large concentrations of organic matter from the seawater.

### Answer Choices

A   Ice cores were used to determine that green icebergs were formed from the compaction of metallic compounds, including copper and iron.

B   All ice shelves can produce green icebergs, but the Amery Ice Shelf is especially well suited to do so.

C   Green icebergs form when a two-layer block of ice breaks away from a glacier and capsizes, exposing the bottom sea ice to view.

D   Ice cores and samples revealed that both ice shelves and green icebergs contain a layer of bubbly glacial ice and a layer of bubble-free sea ice.

E   Green icebergs are white until they come into contact with seawater containing platelets and soluble organic green pigments.

F   In a green iceberg, the sea ice contains large concentrations of organic matter from the seawater.

### Correct Choices

*Choice C*, "Green icebergs form when a two-layer block of ice breaks away from a glacier and capsizes, exposing the bottom sea ice to view," is correct because it summarizes important parts of paragraphs 4 and 5. These explain that green icebergs are capsized pieces of ice that have broken off of an ice shelf.

*Choice D*, "Ice cores and samples revealed that both ice shelves and green icebergs contain a layer of bubbly glacial ice and a layer of bubble-free sea ice," is correct because it summarizes the key information in paragraphs 3 and 4 that explains how scientists were able to determine how green icebergs are formed. The scientists compared ice from green icebergs to ice from ice shelves by drilling ice core samples out of ice shelves.

*Choice F*, "In a green iceberg, the sea ice contains large concentrations of organic matter from the seawater," is correct because it summarizes the key information from paragraph 5 about the source of the green pigments in green icebergs.

*Incorrect Choices*

*Choice A*, "Ice cores were used to determine that green icebergs were formed from the compaction of metallic compounds, including copper and iron," is incorrect because it is factually incorrect according to the passage. The last sentence in paragraph 3 contradicts this idea.

*Choice B*, "All ice shelves can produce green icebergs, but the Amery Ice Shelf is especially well suited to do so," is incorrect because the passage does not state at any point that ice shelves other than the Amery Ice Shelf can produce green icebergs.

*Choice E*, "Green icebergs are white until they come into contact with seawater containing platelets and soluble organic green pigments," is incorrect because the passage never discusses whether green icebergs are originally white, or any particular color.

# Listening

## Answer Key and Self-Scoring Chart

**Directions:** Check your answers against the answer key below. Write the number 1 on the line to the right of each question if you picked the correct answer. Total your points at the bottom of the chart.

| Question Number | Correct Answer | Your Raw Points |
|:---:|:---:|:---:|
| 1. | B | |
| 2. | D | |
| 3. | C | |
| 4. | D | |
| 5. | B | |
| 6. | C | |
| 7. | A | |
| 8. | A | |
| 9. | D | |
| 10. | B | |
| 11. | A | |
| 12. | D | |
| 13. | B | |
| 14. | A | |
| 15. | C | |
| 16. | B | |
| 17. | C | |
| 18. | A | |

For question 19, write 1 if you picked both correct answers. Write 0 if you picked only one correct answer or no correct answers.

| | | |
|:---:|:---:|:---:|
| 19. | B, D | |
| 20. | C | |
| 21. | D | |
| 22. | B | |
| 23. | C | |
| 24. | A | |
| 25. | C | |
| 26. | A | |
| 27. | B | |
| 28. | C | |
| | **TOTAL:** | |

Below is a table that converts your Listening section answers into a TOEFL iBT Listening scaled score. Take the total of raw points from your answer key and find that number in the left-hand column of the table. The right-hand column of the table gives a TOEFL iBT Listening scaled score for each total of raw points. For example, if the total points from your answer key is 27, the table shows a scaled score of 29 to 30.

You should use your score estimate as a general guide only. Your actual score on the TOEFL iBT test may be higher or lower than your score on the practice version.

## Listening

| Raw Point Total | Scaled Score |
| --- | --- |
| 28 | 30 |
| 27 | 29–30 |
| 26 | 27–30 |
| 25 | 25–30 |
| 24 | 24–29 |
| 23 | 23–27 |
| 22 | 22–26 |
| 21 | 21–25 |
| 20 | 19–24 |
| 19 | 18–23 |
| 18 | 17–21 |
| 17 | 16–20 |
| 16 | 14–19 |
| 15 | 13–18 |
| 14 | 12–17 |
| 13 | 10–15 |
| 12 | 9–14 |
| 11 | 7–13 |
| 10 | 6–12 |
| 9 | 5–10 |
| 8 | 3–9 |
| 7 | 2–7 |
| 6 | 1–6 |
| 5 | 1–4 |
| 4 | 0–2 |
| 3 | 0–1 |
| 2 | 0 |
| 1 | 0 |
| 0 | 0 |

# Listening Scripts and Answer Explanations

## Questions 1–5

### Track 34 Listening Script

**Narrator**

Listen to a conversation between a student and a professor.

**Professor**

Sandy, how's class been going for you this semester?

**Female Student**

Oh, it's great. I really like your business psychology class, but I have one major concern about the last assignment: you know—the one where we have to interview a local business owner, uh, I mean entrepreneur?

**Professor**

Are you having trouble coming up with interview questions?

**Female Student**

Well, that's just it. I mean I worked on my high school newspaper for years, so I actually have great questions to ask. The thing is . . . I'm new to the area, and I don't know people off campus . . . So I was wondering if . . . well, could you possibly give me the name of someone I could interview . . . ?

**Professor**

You don't know anyone who owns a business?

**Female Student**

Well, yeah, back home . . . my next-door neighbors—they own a shoe store, and they're really successful—but they're not local.

**Professor**

Well, it wouldn't be fair to the other students if I gave you the name of a contact—but I could help you figure out a way to find someone on your own. Let's see . . . Do you read the local newspaper?

**Female Student**

Sure, whenever I have the time.

**Professor**

Well, the business section in the paper often has stories about local business people who've been successful. If you find an article, you could call the person who is profiled.

**Female Student**

You mean, just call them up . . . out of the blue . . . and ask them if they'll talk to me?

**Professor**

Sure, why not?

**Female Student**

Well, aren't people like that awfully busy? Too busy to talk to a random college student.

**Professor**

Many people enjoy telling the story of how they got started. Remember, this is a business psychology class, and for this assignment, I want you to get some real insight about business owners, their personality, what drives them to become an entrepreneur.

**Female Student**

Like, how they think?

**Professor**

And what motivates them. Why did they start their business? I'm sure they'd talk to you, especially if you tell them you might start a business someday.

**Female Student**

I'm not sure I'd have the guts to do that. Opening a business seems so risky, so scary.

**Professor**

Well, you can ask them if they felt that way too. Now you just need to find someone to interview to see if your instincts are correct.

## Track 35 Listening Script (Question 5)

**Narrator**

Listen again to part of the conversation.

**Professor**

Are you having trouble coming up with interview questions?

**Student**

Well, that's just it. I mean I worked on my high school newspaper for years, so I actually have great questions to ask.

**Narrator**

What does the student imply?

# Answer Explanations

1. **B** This is a Gist-Purpose question. This type of question is typically asked first in listening conversations that take place in a professor's office. At the beginning of the conversation, the student explains that she does not know anyone off campus to interview for her business class assignment and asks the professor if he could recommend someone. This is why she came to his office, so choice B is correct. The student mentions that she has already written her questions; therefore she does not need suggestions on how to write them (choice A). She does not ask for advice on how she might start a business (choice C). She does not say anything about scheduling an interview or any further meetings with the professor (choice D).

2. **D** This is an Understand Organization question. You need to understand why the student talks about having worked on her high school newspaper. Choice A is incorrect because the interview is for a class assignment, not for publication in a newspaper. The student suggests that working on her high school newspaper has made part of the assignment—coming up with questions—easy for her, not difficult (choice B). And while it may be true that she enjoys newspaper work (choice C), that is not why she mentions her high school paper. She mentions it to show she is an experienced interviewer; thus the correct choice is D.

3. **C** This is a Detail question. To help the student solve her problem, the professor does not offer a list of business owners (choice A), nor does he offer to change the due date of the student's assignment (choice D). The student mentions people who own a shoe store in her hometown, but she does not ask the professor to allow her to interview them (choice B) because she realizes that the assignment is to interview owners of a *local* business. The professor helps the student by referring her to the business section of the local newspaper, which often prints stories about successful businesspeople in the local area; thus choice C is correct.

4. **D** This is another Detail question. It is the student, not the professor, who says that opening a business seems risky (choice A); the assignment does not involve writing an article (choice B) or developing a detailed business plan (choice C). The professor says explicitly that he wants the class to learn about the personalities of business owners and what motivates them. Therefore choice D is the correct answer.

5. **B** This question requires that you Make an Inference. The conversation begins with the student telling the professor that she has a concern about the assignment, but she does not say at first exactly what her concern is. When the professor asks if she is having trouble coming up with interview questions, he is trying to find out what her specific concern is. When she says that she has written some great questions already, she is telling him indirectly that interview questions are not the problem. He has not quite identified her

concern, so choice B is the correct answer, and choice C, which states the opposite, is incorrect. Nothing in the student's words or tone of voice suggests that she does not want to finish the assignment (choice D) or that she is surprised by what the professor has said to her (choice A).

## Questions 6–11

### Track 36 Listening Script

**Narrator**

Listen to part of a lecture in an anthropology class.

**Professor**

OK, I, I want to begin today by talking about calendars. I know, some of you are thinking it's not all that fascinating, right? But listen, the next time you look at a calendar, I want you to keep something in mind. There are at least three natural ways of measuring the . . . the passage of time—by day, by month, and by year. And these are all pretty easy to see, right? I mean a day is based on one rotation of Earth. A month is how long the Moon takes to move around the Earth. And a year is the time it takes for Earth to move around the Sun, right? So they're all based on natural events. But the natural clocks of Earth, the Moon, and the Sun run on different times, and you can't divide any one of these time periods by another one without having some messy fraction left over. I mean one lunar month—that's the time it takes for the Moon to go around Earth—one month is about 29 and a half days . . . not really a nice round number. And one year is a little more than 365 days. So these are obviously numbers that don't divide into each other very neatly. And this makes it pretty difficult to create some sort of tidy calendar that really works.

Not that different cultures haven't tried. Have any of you ever been to Stonehenge? No . . . you know, that amazing circle of giant stones in England? Well, if you ever go, and find yourself wondering why this culture way back in prehistoric England would go to so much work to construct this monumental ring of enormous stones, . . . well, keep in mind that a lot of us think it was designed, at least partially, as a calendar—to mark when the seasons of the year begin, according to the exact day when the Sun comes up from a particular direction. I have colleagues who insist it's a temple, maybe, or a tomb . . . but they can't deny that it was also used as a calendar . . . probably to help figure out, for example, when farmers should begin their planting each year.

The Mayans, in Central America, also invented a calendar, but for a different purpose. The Mayans, especially the royalty and priests, wanted to look at long cycles of history—so the calendar they used had to be able to count far into the future as well as far into the past. And not only were the Mayans keeping track of the natural timekeepers we mentioned before—Earth, the Moon, and the Sun—but another natural timekeeper: the planet Venus.

Venus rises in the sky as the morning star every 584 days, and the Venus cycle was incorporated in the Mayan calendar. So the Mayans kept track of long periods of time, and they did it so accurately, in fact, that their calendar is considered about as complicated and sophisticated as any in the world.

Now, the ancient Chinese believed very strongly in astrology—the idea that you can predict future events based on the positions of the stars and planets like, say, Jupiter. Incidentally, the whole Chinese system of astrology was based on the fact that the planet Jupiter goes around the Sun once every 12 years, so one orbit of Jupiter lasts 12 of our Earth years. Apparently, that's why the Chinese calendar has a cycle of 12 years. You know, like, "The Year of the Dragon,""The Year of the Tiger," and so on . . . all parts of a 12-year astrological cycle, that we get from the orbit of Jupiter.

Calendars based on the orbits of other planets, though, are a lot less common than those based on the cycle of the Moon—the lunar month. I could mention any number of important cultures around the world that have depended on lunar calendars, but there really isn't time.

So let's go right to the calendar that's now used throughout most of the world—a solar calendar—based on the number of days in a year. This calendar's mainly derived from the one the ancient Romans devised a couple thousand years ago. I mean the Romans—with more than a little help from the Greeks—realized that a year actually lasts about 365 and one-quarter days. And so they decided to round off most years to 365 days but make every fourth year into a leap year. I mean, somehow, you have to account for that extra one-fourth of a day each year, so every four years, they made the calendar one day longer. By adding the leap year, the Romans were able to make a calendar that worked so well—that, with a few minor adjustments, this calendar is still widely used today.

## Answer Explanations

6. **C** This is a Gist-Content question. Choice C is correct because the professor spends almost the entire lecture discussing four types of calendars used historically in England, Central America, China, and ancient Rome, as well as the modern calendar used throughout the world today. Errors in early calendars (choice A) are not discussed; in fact, the professor emphasizes how surprisingly accurate and sophisticated these early calendars were. Choice D is incorrect because astrology—the belief that the position of stars and planets can predict events—is mentioned only in the context of the Chinese calendar. Why people came to believe that Earth moves around the Sun (choice B) is not discussed at all.

7. **A** This question requires you to Understand the Speaker's Attitude. The professor indirectly expresses her certainty that Stonehenge served as a calendar by stating, "a lot of us think it was designed, at least partially, as a calendar." Her use of the pronoun *us* indicates that she includes herself in that group. When mentioning colleagues who think Stonehenge served another purpose, she adds that "they can't deny that it was also used as a calendar." Thus the correct answer is choice A.

8. **A** This is a Detail question. Choice A is correct because the professor states that the Mayans were interested in tracking long cycles of history. There is no mention of lunar months in the discussion of the Mayan calendar (choice B). It was the ancient Chinese, not the Mayans, who wanted a calendar system to predict events (choice C). The Mayan calendar was *based on* the appearance of Venus in the morning sky and on the movements of other natural time-keepers like Earth, but comparing the orbits of Earth and Venus (choice D) was not the calendar's *purpose*.

9. **D** This is another Detail question. Choice D is correct because the professor states that the ancient Chinese calendar was based on Jupiter's 12-year-long orbit around the Sun, not on night-day cycles (choice A), the Moon (choice B), or the seasons (choice C).

10. **B** This is also a Detail question. Choice B is correct because the professor says that the ancient Romans put an extra day into the calendar every 4 years to account for the actual length of a single Earth orbit, which is 365¼ days. According to the professor, this addition, which improved the calendar's precision, is what made the calendar work so well that it is still widely used.

11. **A** This is an Understanding Organization question. Before discussing any specific calendars, the professor identifies a problem: that all calendars are based on natural astronomical cycles, which are not coordinated with one another mathematically. The professor then describes various historical calendars and the natural cycles on which they were based, ending with a description of the modern calendar and its solution to the coordination problem. Thus choice A is correct.

## Questions 12–16

### Track 37 Listening Script

**Narrator**

Listen to part of a conversation between a student and a university employee.

**Employee**

Oh, hello . . . can I help you?

**Student**

Um . . . yeah . . . I'm looking for Professor Kirk; is she here? I mean is this her office?

**Employee**

Yes, you're in the right place—Professor Kirk's office is right behind me—but no . . . she's not here right now.

**Student**

Um, do you know when she'll be back?

**Employee**

Well, she's teaching all morning. She won't be back until . . . let me check . . . hmm, she won't be back until . . . after lunch. That's when she has her office hours. Perhaps you could come back then?

**Student**

Oh, unfortunately no. I have class this afternoon. And I was really hoping to talk to her today. Hey, um, do you know if . . . she's accepting any more students into her Introduction to Biology class?

**Employee**

You wanna know if you can take the class?

**Student**

Yes, if she's letting any more students sign up, I'd like, I'd like to join the class.

**Employee**

Introduction to Biology is a very popular class, especially when she teaches it. A lot of students take it.

**Student**

Yeah, that's why the registrar said it was full. I've got the form the registrar gave me, um, to get her permission to take the class. It's all filled out except for her signature. I'm hoping she'll let me in even though the class is full. You see, I'm a senior this year, and, uh . . . this'll be my last semester, so it's my last chance . . .

**Employee**

Oh, wow, really. I mean most students fulfill their science requirement the first year.

**Student**

Well, I mean, um . . . to be honest, I kept putting it off. I'm not really a big fan of science classes in general, and with the labs and everything, I've never quite found the time.

**Employee**

Your advisor didn't say anything?

**Student**

Well, to tell you the truth, she's been after me to take a class like this for a while, but I'm double-majoring in art and journalism and so my schedule's been really tight with all the classes I gotta take, so somehow I never . . .

**Employee**

Well, perhaps you could leave the form with me and I'll see if she'll sign it for you.

**Student**

You know, I appreciate that, but maybe I should explain the problem to her in person . . . I didn't want to do it, but I guess I'll have to send her an e-mail.

**Employee**

Hmm. You know, not all professors check their e-mails regularly—I . . . I'm not sure if Professor Kirk does it or not. Here's an idea . . . why don't you stick a note explaining your situation under her door and ask her to call you if she needs more information?

**Student**

Hey, that's a good idea, and then I can leave the form with you—if you still don't mind.

## Track 38 Listening Script (Question 16)

**Narrator**

Why does the man say this to the woman:

**Student**

You know, I appreciate that, but maybe I should explain the problem to her in person . . .

## Answer Explanations

12. **D** This is a Gist-Purpose question. The student wants Professor Kirk to give him permission to enroll in a course that is already full. In order to do this, the professor must sign a form that the student has brought with him. That is why he is there; thus choice D is correct. The student already knows that he must take a science course in order to graduate (choice A). There is no indication that Professor Kirk has invited the student to her office (choice B), and the student already has an advisor (choice C).

13. **B** This is a Detail question. When the man says he will graduate soon, the woman says, "Oh, wow" and points out that most students fulfill their science requirement their first year. This indicates that she is surprised that the man has waited so long, making choice B the correct answer. None of the other choices is factually true, according to the information in the conversation.

14. **A** This is another Detail question. Choice A is correct because it paraphrases the man's statement that his advisor has "been after me to take a class like this for a while." She wants him to take the class because she is aware of the man's situation and knows he cannot graduate without the science class. Therefore choice C, which states that she is unaware of his problem, is incorrect. There is nothing in the conversation indicating that the advisor encouraged the man to major in journalism (choice B). And although Professor Kirk's popularity among students is mentioned in the conversation, no reference is made to the advisor's opinion of Professor Kirk (choice D).

15. **C** This is a Connecting Content question. After the woman suggests that the man stick a note under Professor Kirk's door, the man says, "that's a good idea," indicating that he will follow her advice. Thus choice C is correct. There is some discussion about sending an e-mail (choice B), but that idea is rejected. There is no discussion of calling Professor Kirk (choice A), and the man explains early in the conversation that his schedule conflicts with the professor's office hours (choice D).

16. **B** This question requires you to Understand the Function of What Is Said. In the replayed audio, the man rejects the woman's offer to give the form to Professor Kirk. Instead of simply saying, "No," the man says he does "appreciate" her offer but thinks it would be better for him to speak with Professor Kirk directly. Choice B captures both the man's politeness and his intention. The man's problem is not yet solved (choice A), and he has already explained what he needs (choice C). Choice D is incorrect because the woman implied earlier that it is Professor Kirk, not she, who is busy.

## Questions 17–22

### Track 39 Listening Script

#### Narrator

Listen to part of a lecture in an astronomy class.

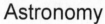

#### Professor

I'm sure y'all have been following the news about Mars. A lot of spacecraft have been visiting the planet recently—some have gone into orbit around it, while others have landed on it. And, they've sent back a . . . an abundance of data that's reshaping our knowledge . . . our vision of the planet in a lot of ways. Is there anything that you've been particularly struck by in all the news reports?

#### Female Student

Well, they seem to mention water a lot, which kinda surprised me, as I have this picture in my head that Mars is dry . . . sorta dry and dead.

#### Professor

You're not the only one. You know, for centuries, most of our knowledge of the planet came from what we saw through telescopes, so, obviously, it was pretty limited—and our views of the planet were formed as much by writers . . . as they were by serious scientists. When the first science-fiction stories came out, Mars was described as being a lot like Earth except . . .

**Male Student**

I know: the planet was red and, uh, the people were green. I've seen some of those old movies. What were they thinking? I mean really . . . they . . .

**Professor**

Well, it seems silly to us now, but those ideas were quite imaginative and, occasionally, scary in their time. Anyway, we began to rethink our image of Mars when the first space-craft flew by the planet in 1965 and sent pictures back to Earth. Those pictures showed a planet that looked a lot more like our Moon than Earth—lots of craters and not much else. It was bitterly cold, it had a very thin atmosphere, and that atmosphere was mostly carbon dioxide. So the view of Mars after this first flyby mission was that dry, dead planet that Lisa mentioned.

But, then there were more visits to the planet in the 1970s—and this time the space-craft didn't just fly by; they orbited . . . or landed. This allowed us to receive much more de-tailed images of the planet, and it turned out to be a pretty interesting place. Mars had . . . has a lot more than craters—it has giant volcanoes and deep canyons. It also showed signs of dried-up riverbeds and plains that had been formed by massive floods. So we concluded that there must have been water on the planet at one time—billions of years ago. Now, what does it take for water to exist?

**Male Student**

You need to have a warm-enough temperature so that it doesn't freeze.

**Professor**

That's one thing—and the other is that you need enough atmospheric pressure, thick-enough air so that the water doesn't instantly vaporize. The Mars we see today doesn't have either of those conditions—it is too cold and the air is too thin—but a long time ago, there may have been a thicker atmosphere that created a greenhouse effect that raised tem-peratures—and maybe that combination produced water on the surface of the planet. So maybe Mars wasn't just a dead, boring rock; maybe, it was, uh, a fascinating fossil that was once alive and dynamic—worthy of exploration. Now let's jump forward a few decades to the beginning of this century, and a new generation of orbiters and landers that have been sent to Mars. Of course, the scientific instruments now surveying Mars are far more sophis-ticated than the instruments of the '70s, so we're getting all kinds of new data for analysis. And, not surprisingly, that data is challenging our notions of what Mars is like. Lisa, you mentioned that a lot of the news reports talked about water—do you remember any of the details?

**Female Student**

Well, they were showing these pictures of these long, uh, cuts in the ground, which would be gullies here; I mean on Earth. They say that since, uh, gullies are usually formed by water, it seems like they might be evidence that water still exists on Mars, but I didn't get how that worked.

**Professor**

I'm not surprised. There're a lot of theories . . . a lot of speculation . . . and some argue the formations aren't caused by water at all. But there're some ingenious theories that assume that there's a lot of water right under the planet's surface that somehow is causing the gullies to form. If we could only get a lander there . . . but the gullies aren't in places where we can send landers yet. Anyway, if there is some kind of water activity, it may change our view of the planet once again . . . to something that's not dead, not even a fossil, but rather a planet like Earth that undergoes cycles—think of our ice ages—over long periods of time. Maybe Mars could sustain water again at some distant date.

### Track 40 Listening Script (Question 21)

**Narrator**

Why does the professor say this:

**Professor**

So maybe Mars wasn't just a dead, boring rock; maybe, it was, uh, a fascinating fossil that was once alive and dynamic—worthy of exploration.

### Track 41 Listening Script (Question 22)

**Male Student**

I know: the planet was red and, uh, the people were green. I've seen some of those old movies. What were they thinking? I mean really . . .

**Narrator**

Why does the student say this:

**Male Student**

What were they thinking?

## Answer Explanations

17. **C** This is a Gist-Content question. The professor begins by saying that an abundance of data is reshaping "our vision of the planet in a lot of ways." He goes on to discuss how Mars was imagined before it was visited by spacecraft, and then how, in recent years, successive spacecraft have sent back detailed images that are providing an increasingly realistic view of the planet. Thus choice C is correct.

18. **A** This is a Detail question. Choice A is correct because the professor says that the images obtained in 1965 made Mars appear as dry and dead as the Moon, with "lots of craters and not much else." He mentions the 1965 view that Mars was very cold, but he does not say that the images showed it to be similar to Earth (choice B)—quite the opposite. The existence of life on Mars in the distant past is presented not as a conclusion (choice C) but as a matter of theory and speculation coming after the 1970s orbits and the even more recent Mars landings. The theory that water exists under Mars's surface (choice D) is also a recent development.

19. **B** **D** This is a Making Inferences question. Note that the square boxes in front of the answer choices indicate that you must select two correct answers. In the lecture, the professor contrasts the dry conditions of Mars today with the possibility that Mars had water on its surface billions of years ago. Choice B, which says that the atmospheric pressure and the temperature may have been higher on Mars in the past than they are today, forms part of his explanation of how Mars could once have had water. Choice D is also correct because part of the evidence for the existence of water on Mars is the plains and the dried-up riverbeds currently visible on Mars's surface; according to the professor, they could have been created by flooding.

20. **C** This is a Detail question. One of the students mentions that she has seen news reports that showed gullies on Mars, and she says that they seem to be evidence of water. The professor confirms that gullies may indeed be evidence of water on Mars and says that there are theories that water under the surface caused the gullies to form. Thus choice C is correct. The professor mentions volcanoes on Mars (choice A) and Mars's dry climate (choice B), but he does not associate either with gullies. References are made to fossils but not to any actual fossils (choice D); the professor uses the word *fossil* metaphorically when he likens the entire planet to an object that may be dead but that is nevertheless worth investigating because it was once alive.

21. **D** This is an Understanding Organization question. In this replayed statement, the professor uses imagery to describe the early conception of Mars—"a dead, boring rock"—and the modern conception formed by additional evidence—"a fascinating fossil that was once alive and dynamic." By making this contrast, the professor both sums up the lecture and emphasizes that the change in our view of Mars was a very significant one. Thus the correct answer is choice D.

22. **B** This question requires you to Understand the Function of What Is Said. The student's comment is an indirect criticism of early filmmakers for their unrealistic portrayals of Mars. Thus choice B is correct. His opinion is a negative one, so he is not expressing approval (choice D). The student is not seeking clarification or rephrasing a previous question, so choices A and C do not accurately reflect the intention of his statement.

## Questions 23–28

### Track 42 Listening Script

**Narrator**

Listen to part of a lecture in an art history class. The professor has been talking about colossal statues.

**Professor**

We've been looking at colossal statues—works of exceptionally huge size—and their essentially public role, in commemorating a political or religious figure. We've seen how some of these statues date back thousands of years . . . like the statues of the pharaohs of ancient Egypt—which you can still visit today—and how others, though surviving only in legend, have fired the imagination of writers and artists right up to our own time, such as the Colossus of Rhodes, that 110-foot statue of the Greek god Helios. Remember, this same word, *colossus*—which means a giant or larger-than-life-size statue—is what today's term *colossal* derives from.

Now, it was one thing to build such statues, at an equally colossal cost, when the funds were being allocated by ancient kings and pharaohs. But if we're going to think about modern-day colossal statues, we need to reexamine more closely their role as social and political symbols, in order to understand why a society today—a society of free, taxpaying citizens—would agree to allocate so much of its resources to erecting them. A good example to start out with would be Mount Rushmore.

Now, many of you have probably seen pictures of Mount Rushmore; perhaps you've actually visited the place. Mount Rushmore, in South Dakota, is a colossal representation of the faces of four U.S. presidents: George Washington, Thomas Jefferson, Theodore Roosevelt, and Abraham Lincoln, carved directly into a mountain. Imagine: each of those faces in the rock is over 60 feet high! Now, carving their faces took over six and a half years, and cost almost a million dollars. And this was in the 1930s, during the worst economic depression in U.S. history! Does that strike any of you as odd?

Well, I personally think that the Great Depression of the 1930s actually makes this more understandable, not less so. Often it's the case that, precisely at times of hardship—when the very fabric of society seems to be unraveling and confidence is eroding—uh, that people clamor for some public expression of strength and optimism, perhaps as a way of symbolizing its endurance in the face of difficulty.

So with that in mind, let's go back to Mount Rushmore. Actually, the original motivation for a colossal monument in South Dakota had very little to do with all this symbolism . . . and everything to do with money: you see, it was first conceived of basically as a tourist attraction, and it was supposed to feature the images of legendary figures of the American West, like the explorers Lewis and Clark. The government of South Dakota thought it would bring lots of money into the state.

It was only later on that the sculptor—the artist who designed and oversaw the project, a man named Gutzon Borglum—decided the project should be a monument honoring four of the most-respected presidents in U.S. history; much more than a tourist attraction . . . its very prominence and permanence became perceived as a symbol of the endurance of U.S. ideals and the greatness of the country's early leaders. So, you see, what began as a tourist attraction became something far loftier.

Let's look at another example of this phenomenon.

The Statue of Liberty is another colossal statue—one that I assume a number of you are familiar with. But, umm, I would guess that—like many people today—you don't realize that, when it was designed, over a century ago—by a French sculptor—it was intended to symbolize the long friendship between the people of France and the people of the United States—one which dated back to France's support of the American colonies' war for independence from the British.

But the shift in the statue's meaning started soon after it was built. Back in 1883, Emma Lazarus wrote that famous poem—you know, the one that goes: "Give me your tired, your poor . . ." and so on and so forth. That poem describes the Statue of Liberty as a beacon of welcome for the entire world. Well, in the early 1900s, it was put on a plaque on the pedestal that the Statue of Liberty stands on.

From that point on, the Statue of Liberty was no longer perceived as just a gift between friendly republics. It now became a tribute to the United States' history of immigration and openness.

This association was strengthened in the imagination of the general public just a few decades after the statue's completion, with the immigration waves of the early twentieth century . . . especially since the statue happened to be the first sign of America seen by those immigrants sailing into the port of New York. So, as with Mount Rushmore, the original motivation for this colossal statue was forgotten, and the statue is now valued for more important reasons.

### Track 43 Listening Script (Question 28)

**Professor**

Back in 1883, Emma Lazarus wrote that famous poem—you know, the one that goes: "Give me your tired, your poor . . ." and so on and so forth.

**Narrator**

Why does the professor discuss the poem by Emma Lazarus?

## Answer Explanations

23. **C** This is a Gist-Content question. The lecture is part of a larger art history lecture on the general topic of colossal statues. Having completed his discussion of ancient colossal statues, the professor now focuses on modern times and begins by raising this question: why would elected officials be willing to invest enormous sums of public money to create colossal statues? To understand why, he says, one needs to "reexamine more closely their role as social and political symbols." Choice C best expresses that idea. Choices A, B, and D are mentioned but are not the main focus of this excerpt.

24. **A** This is a Making Inferences question. In examining the role of modern colossal statues as social and political symbols, the professor explains that these very expensive statues are built only when free, taxpaying citizens agree to fund their construction. If these symbols are so costly to build, then the people who agree to fund their construction must place a high value on them. Therefore choice A is correct. While it is probably true that important colossal statues are discussed in many classrooms (choice B), this fact is not mentioned by the professor. The fact that the statues last thousands of years is discussed with regard to ancient, not modern, statues (choice C). A famous poem is discussed in the lecture, but this poem was inspired by the Statue of Liberty, not the other way around (choice D).

25. **C** This is a Detail question. In his discussion of the Great Depression, the professor says that people's confidence gets eroded in times of financial hardship, making choice C correct. While the other events may have resulted from the Great Depression, they are not mentioned by the professor in this regard.

26. **A** This is a Detail question. At the opening and again at the closing of his discussion of Mount Rushmore, the professor says that the monument was originally intended as a tourist attraction to bring money to the state of South Dakota. Choice A is correct because it paraphrases these statements. The unity of society (choice B) is addressed in the lecture in connection with colossal statues, and symbolizing this ideal might have been one of the sculptor's goals. Nevertheless, the professor emphasizes that neither unifying society nor the Great Depression (choice C) was the original motivation for the state of South Dakota. Choice D is incorrect for the same reason: honoring United States presidents was not the original purpose of the statue; in fact, the monument started out as a depiction of legendary figures of the American West, not U.S. presidents.

27. **B** This is an Understanding Organization question. Choice B is correct because the professor talks about Emma Lazarus's poem as a second example of how the meaning associated with a monument can change. Before mentioning the poem, the professor points out that the Statue of Liberty was given to the United States by France as a gift symbolizing the long friendship between the two countries. But then Lazarus wrote the poem describing the

statue as a beacon of welcome for the entire world. The professor says that the poem gave a new meaning to the statue and that this meaning strengthened after the poem was placed on the statue's pedestal. The professor is not making a general observation about literature and sculpture (choice A). He mentions the friendship between the United States and France only to set up a contrast with the newer meaning of the statue (choice C). And he discusses the poem to show a similarity, not a difference, between Mount Rushmore and the Statue of Liberty, that similarity being the fact that the symbolism of both monuments has shifted over time.

28. Ⓒ You are asked to listen again to part of the lecture and to decide what the professor is implying about the poem.

Back in 1883, Emma Lazarus wrote that famous poem—you know, the one that goes: "Give me your tired, your poor . . . " and so on and so forth.

This is a Making Inferences question. To arrive at the correct answer (choice C), you must understand that the expression "so on and so forth" is typically used when a listener does not need any further information to understand what the speaker is referring to. In this case, the professor assumes that the students are very familiar with the poem, so he does not need to recite more than the first few words of it.

# Speaking

## Listening Scripts, Important Points, and Sample Responses with Rater Comments

Use the Speaking rubrics on pages 184–187 to see how responses are scored. The raters who listen to your responses will analyze them in three general categories. These categories are Delivery, Language Use, and Topic Development. All three categories have equal importance.

This section includes important points that should be covered when answering each question. All of these points must be present in a response in order for it to receive the highest score in the Topic Development category. These important points are guides to the kind of information raters expect to hear in a high-level response.

This section also refers to example responses on the accompanying audio tracks. Some responses were scored at the highest level, while others were not. The responses are followed by explanations of their scores.

### Question 1: Paired Choice

#### Track 44 Listening Script

**Narrator**

Some students would prefer to live with roommates. Others would prefer to live alone. Which option would you prefer and why?

> **Preparation Time: 15 Seconds**
> **Response Time: 45 Seconds**

#### Important Points

In this question, you need to state whether you, as a student, would prefer to live with roommates or live alone, and then you need to explain your preference. You should explain your reason or reasons fully and clearly, using details and examples where you can. For instance, you could say you prefer to live with a roommate and then explain one or two reasons, such as having someone to discuss problems with, being able to share the cooking and cleaning, or avoiding loneliness. If you want to talk about the advantages or disadvantages of *both* options and say they are equally good, that is permissible. However, it might be more difficult for you to finish discussing both options in the time allowed.

## Sample Responses

***Play Track 49 to hear a high-level response for Question 1.***

*Rater Comments*

This speaker's response presents a clear progression of ideas. He chooses to discuss an advantage of living with a roommate before he describes the disadvantages, which, to him, are stronger than the advantage. He gives an example of how a roommate might be a problem, then states his preference—living alone—and relates it to his personal experience. His pronunciation is easy to understand, and he speaks very fluently. A few of his word choices are not precise, but this would not prevent a listener from understanding his ideas.

***Play Track 50 to hear a low-level response for Question 1.***

*Rater Comments*

For the first part of his response, the speaker is only reading the question aloud and not actually answering it. His pronunciation is strongly affected by his first language, so the listener must make a great effort to try to understand what he is saying. His response is marked by long pauses as he tries to think of the next word to say, indicating that he possesses a very limited English vocabulary. The lowest level of the rubric describes the characteristics of this response.

# Question 2: Fit and Explain

## Track 45 Listening Script

### Narrator

Read the article from the university newspaper about the plan to build new student housing. You will have 50 seconds to read the article. Begin reading now.

Reading Time: 50 Seconds

---

**University May Build New Student Apartments Off Campus**

The Department of Student Housing is considering whether to build new student housing off campus in a residential area of town. Two of the major factors influencing the decision will be parking and space. Those who support building off campus argue that building new housing on campus would further increase the number of cars on and around campus and consume space that could be better used for future projects that the entire university community could benefit from. Supporters also say that students might even have a richer college experience by being connected to the local community and patronizing stores and other businesses in town.

---

**Narrator**

Now listen to two students discussing the article.

**Woman**

I can't believe these plans. It just doesn't make sense to me.

**Man**

Really? Seemed OK to me, especially the argument about the cars.

**Woman**

Yeah, I know. But the thing is, it doesn't matter where students live 'cause they still have to get to class somehow, right? At least if they built new dorms on campus, students would use campus transportation . . .

**Man**

. . . instead of their cars. I see what you're getting at. If they live off campus, they're *still* going to have to drive and park on campus. Might even create more traffic.

**Woman**

Exactly.

**Man**

OK. Still, though . . . the point about students interacting more with people in the community: that doesn't seem to be a bad thing, does it?

**Woman**

But the more time spent off campus, in town, the less time spent on campus. What about all the clubs, shows, discussions, a—all the campus happenings that just kind of . . . happen? It's important to be *on* campus to really take advantage of these things. Having a different living experience shouldn't be given up at the expense of not being as much a part of the *university* community.

**Narrator**

The woman expresses her opinion of the university's plan. State her opinion and explain the reasons she gives for holding that opinion.

> **Preparation Time: 30 Seconds**
> **Response Time: 60 Seconds**

## Important Points

The woman disagrees with the housing department's plan to build new student housing off campus. She thinks students will still have to drive to campus to get to class, so there will not be any decrease in the number of cars around campus. She also thinks students will miss opportunities to be involved in on-campus activities, which are just as important as the experience of living in town.

Sample Responses

*Play Track 51 to hear a high-level response for Question 2.*

*Rater Comments*

The speaker gives a sustained, coherent response that accurately and efficiently explains the woman's opinion of the main points of the newspaper article. He did not waste time by including unimportant details from the conversation or reading. His pacing is fluid, and he demonstrates good control of a variety of grammatical structures and vocabulary. His pronunciation is exceptionally clear.

*Play Track 52 to hear a mid-level response for Question 2.*

*Rater Comments*

This speaker covers all the important points of the woman's opinion. However, the speaker never states what the university plan is, so she does not make it entirely clear what, in general, the woman in the conversation is disagreeing with. Her response contains some minor errors in word choice, such as "assist" rather than "attend," but overall she demonstrates good control of both vocabulary and grammar. Her pacing is usually steady, though with a number of hesitations that require listener effort at times.

## Question 3: General/Specific

### Track 46 Listening Script

**Narrator**

Now read the passage about a topic in psychology. You will have 45 seconds to read the passage. Begin reading now.

**Reading Time: 45 Seconds**

---

### Actor-Observer

People account for their own behavior differently from how they account for the behavior of others. When observing the behavior of others, we tend to attribute their actions to their character or their personality rather than to external factors. In contrast, we tend to explain our own behavior in terms of situational factors beyond our own control rather than attributing it to our own character. One explanation for this difference is that people are aware of the situational forces affecting them but not of situational forces affecting other people. Thus, when evaluating someone else's behavior, we focus on the person rather than the situation.

---

**Narrator**

Now listen to part of a lecture in a psychology class.

**Professor**

So we encounter this in life all the time, but many of us are unaware that we do this . . . even psychologists who study it . . . like me. For example, the other day I was at the store and I was getting in line to buy something. But just before I was actually in line, some guy comes out of nowhere and cuts right in front of me. Well, I was really annoyed and thought, "That was rude!" I assumed he was just a selfish, inconsiderate person when, in fact, I had no idea why he cut in line in front of me or whether he even realized he was doing it. Maybe he didn't think I was actually in line yet . . . But my immediate reaction was to assume he was a selfish or rude person.

OK, so a few days after that, I was at the store again. Only this time I was in a real hurry—I was late for an important meeting—and I was frustrated that everything was taking so long. And what's worse, all the checkout lines were long, and it seemed like everyone was moving so slowly. But then I saw a slightly shorter line! But some woman with a lot of stuff to buy was walking toward it, so I basically ran to get there first, before her, and, well, I did. Now, I didn't think of myself as a bad or rude person for doing this. I had an important meeting to get to—I was in a hurry, so, you know, I had done nothing wrong.

**Narrator**

Explain how the two examples discussed by the professor illustrate differences in the ways people explain behavior.

> **Preparation Time: 30 Seconds**
> **Response Time: 60 Seconds**

## Important Points

We explain others' behavior differently from how we explain our own behavior. The professor describes how he thought that the man who cut ahead of him in line was a rude person. This example shows that we tend to explain the behavior of others by attributing it to their character or personality. Then the professor describes how he similarly cut into line but did not think of himself as rude, because he was late for a meeting. This illustrates how we explain our own behavior not in terms of our character, but by attributing it to situational factors.

## Sample Responses

### *Play Track 53 to hear a high-level response for Question 3.*

*Rater Comments*

This speaker clearly shows how the professor's examples illustrate the idea that we explain other people's behavior one way and our own behavior in a different way. He covers the main points efficiently in the time allotted. His response is sustained and fluid, and his pronunciation is easy to understand, with only occasional, minor difficulties. There are several minor grammatical errors that do not hinder understanding, and overall he demonstrates good control of grammatical structures.

***Play Track 54 to hear a mid-level response for Question 3.***

*Rater Comments*

The speaker is able to cover both of the professor's examples in a basic way, but he never clearly connects the second example to the concept from the reading (that people explain their own behavior based on situational factors, not character). His pronunciation is easy to understand, but his response is still difficult to follow at times because of his frequent hesitations.

## Question 4: Summary

### Track 47 Listening Script

**Narrator**

Now listen to part of a lecture in a child development class.

**Professor**

OK. Young children and art. Research suggests that learning art skills can benefit a young child's development. Umm . . . two of the ways it can do this is by providing a platform to express complex emotions and by encouraging persistence.

Now, what do I mean when I say "a platform to express complex emotions"? Young children have limited vocabulary. So how would they communicate the feeling of pride, for example? A drawing, though, making a drawing of feeling proud . . . this is something a young child could do. So a little girl might draw herself jumping up in the air next to her bike. In the drawing, her arms are raised up in the air and she's smiling. Children can communicate their emotions, whether positive or negative, through the drawing—mm—better than they could with words.

And encouraging persistence? Art skills can help children to develop patience and concentration to persist in an activity . . . the willingness to keep trying to reach a goal. So suppose there's a little boy who wants to mold a lump of clay into the shape of a car. The first attempt doesn't look too much like a car. He's disappointed but wants to try again. The second, third, fourth try still don't look quite right, but there's improvement with every attempt. So, after some time, he gets to the point where he's satisfied with his creation. The newly shaped clay car is an instant reminder of an accomplishment—a success resulting from his persistence. The boy may be able to transfer this lesson toward other situations and activities because, well, he's had the experience of successfully accomplishing a goal through hard work.

**Narrator**

Using points and examples from the talk, explain how learning art can impact a child's development.

**Preparation Time: 20 Seconds**
**Response Time: 60 Seconds**

## Important Points

Learning art skills can have an important impact on the emotional development of young children in two ways. One is by helping them to express complex emotions. Drawing can, for example, help children express emotions that they cannot express in words. The little girl expressed pride when she drew a picture of herself looking proud of learning to ride a bike.

The second way art can help young children is by teaching them persistence. After spending time perfecting an art piece—such as the little boy sculpting a car out of clay—they can see their success.

## Sample Responses

### *Play Track 55 to hear a high-level response for Question 4.*

*Rater Comments*

This speaker efficiently summarizes the key points from the lecture in order to explain how learning art skills can influence a child's development. His speech is highly intelligible and fluid, though there are a few minor lapses in flow. His response also demonstrates good control of both basic and more complex grammatical structures as used in spoken language.

### *Play Track 56 to hear a mid-level response for Question 4.*

*Rater Comments*

The speaker makes major errors in content as he attempts to summarize the lecture. He does not mention the second point—that learning the value of persistence is one of the ways that art can help children's emotional development. Also, his summary of the first point is inaccurate; he confuses the example for the second point with the example for the first point (helping children express emotions). His pronunciation is generally clear, but his response lacks full coherence; it is not always easy to see how one idea connects to the next.

# Writing

## Listening Script, Topic Notes, and Sample Responses with Rater Comments

Use the Integrated Writing and Writing for an Academic Discussion scoring rubrics on pages 199–200 and 210–211 to see how responses are scored.

### Integrated Writing

#### Track 48 Listening Script

**Narrator**

Now listen to part of a lecture on the topic you just read about.

**Professor**

Lately, we've been seeing some professors on television. Though it's sometimes claimed to be a good thing, we should question whether anybody really benefits from it. First of all, it's not good for the professors themselves—not from a professional standpoint. Rightly or wrongly, a professor who appears on TV tends to get the reputation among fellow professors of being someone who is not a serious scholar—someone who chooses to entertain rather than to educate. And for that reason, TV professors may not be invited to important conferences—important meetings to discuss their academic work. They may even have difficulty getting money to do research. So for professors, being a TV celebrity has important disadvantages.

A second point is that being on TV can take a lot of a professor's time—not just the time on TV but also time figuring out what to present and time spent rehearsing, travel time, even time getting made up to look good for the cameras. And all this time comes out of the time the professor can spend doing research, meeting with students, and attending to university business. So you can certainly see there are problems for the university and its students when professors are in the TV studio and not on campus.

So who does benefit? The public? Umm . . . that's not so clear either. Look, professors do have a lot of knowledge to offer, but TV networks don't want really serious, in-depth academic lectures for after-dinner viewing. What the networks want is the academic title, not the intellectual substance. The material that professors usually present on TV—such as background on current events, or some brief historical introduction to a new movie version of a great literary work—this material is not much different from what viewers would get from a TV reporter who had done a little homework.

**Narrator**

Summarize the points made in the lecture, being sure to explain how they oppose specific points made in the reading passage.

## Topic Notes

You should understand the reasons presented in the lecture for why it is not necessarily good that professors appear on television. The lecturer questions each of the benefits mentioned in the reading passage: about the professor's reputation, about the professor's time, and about educating the public.

A high-scoring response will include the following points made by the lecturer that address the points made in the reading passage:

| Point Made in the Reading Passage | Contrasting Point from the Lecture |
|---|---|
| TV appearances improve the professor's reputation. | 1. Their reputation suffers, because they are considered entertainers by their peers and not serious scholars.<br>2. As a result, they may get fewer invitations to academic conferences or lose research funding. |
| TV appearances benefit the university and lead to more student applications and more donations. | Professors spend a lot of time preparing for the TV appearances, which takes away from their true academic work, such as teaching and doing research. |
| TV appearances benefit the public because the public is exposed to more in-depth knowledge about a subject. | Professors generally do not give in-depth academic lectures on TV. |

Responses scoring 4 and 5 discuss and connect the points and the counterpoints in the table while adding all the important supporting details mentioned by the lecturer. The table above includes the main lecture points but may not include all the important supporting details.

## Sample Responses with Rater Comments

*High-Level Response*

The passage introduced three reasons why professors should appear on TV: gaining reputation for the professor, for the college, and to educate the general public. However, the lecture disagrees.

Professors who appear frequently on TV are not generally viewed as a serious scholar. As a result, those professors will receive less invitation to attend academic conferences or less likely to receive research grant. This seriously hinders the professor's opportunity to further grow as a researcher

Professors who frequently appear on TV also has negative effect on students and the university. Appearing on TV takes a lot of time to prepare, including preperation for the material, transportation time, and even time to dress up. This precious time can also be used to teach class, help students, or even do further research. As a result, professors who appear on TV waste a lot of time that they can contribute to teaching and research.

Professors appearing on TV doesn't usually help educating the general public. The TV network is not interested in having the professor explaining the intellectual substances of their researches. Rather, they are interested in having them explain some basic background information or history. This type of information can be easily presented by a serious reporter who has done his work properly.

Because of the above reasons, it is highly questionable whether professors appearing on TV has any advantage. In fact, it could bring negative consequence both to the professors themselves and the universities they teach.

### Rater Comments

This response successfully conveys all three of the main points from the lecture. The response is well organized and developed. Explicit connection between the reading passage and the lecture is explained in the first and final paragraphs. In each body paragraph, the writer opens with a topic sentence that captures how the lecture point opposes the point made in the reading passage in general, and the writer proceeds to develop the lecturer's point using relevant details and examples.

The language used by the writer is not perfect; there are minor grammatical errors in subject-verb agreement and preposition use ("Professors . . . has negative effect," "preperation for the material," "the universities they teach"). However, note that the Scoring Guide for the integrated task allows even level 5 responses to contain occasional minor errors that do not result in inaccurate or imprecise presentation of content or connections. The errors in this response do not interfere with meaning or disrupt the flow of the response.

### Mid-Level Response

The question which is asked is to know if the apparition of a professor on television is a good or a bad think? On this point, the text and the lecture completely disagree.

First, we can think that it is a good thing for the professors themselves. It seems to be something logical because today a lot of people want to be known and the television is perhaps the best thing to be known. But what the lecture say is that such a professor don't have a good reputation. People think they are not very serious when they pass on television. The effect is that they are no more invited to important conferences.

In what concerned the students and the university, the text shows the facts that some of these apparitions can bring some donation to the university, what is very good. But in the other hand according to the lecture, this professor spend a lot of time travelling and during that time, he isn't available for the students or for the researches and the university lose therefore some money.

Finally for the public himself, they could learn some interesting things and it could be a very big chance because a lot of these persons haven't had the chance going in the university. But it is true that such intervention isn't often best as something that a journalist could prepare.

*Rater Comments*

The writer organizes the response fairly well. After a brief introduction, each reading passage point is briefly summarized and then followed by ideas from the related point in the lecture. However, the response earns a mid-level score because the writer's summaries of the lecture suffer from several problems. There is imprecision (the idea that "people" rather than fellow academics think the professor appearing on television is not serious); there is omission (the idea that television networks are not interested in in-depth lectures is missing); and there is poor connection of ideas (the idea that a university loses "some money" is not connected to the idea that television appearances take away from professors' time at the university).

Most importantly, there are lapses of clarity due to the writer's poor language control. Errors in word choice ("pass on television," "intervention isn't often best as something") obscure meaning to such an extent that the lecturer's response to the first point is conveyed only vaguely, and the response to the last point is completely unclear. Although the writer of this response may have had a good grasp of the ideas, the writer failed to communicate those ideas clearly to the reader.

# Writing for an Academic Discussion

## Question

Your professor is teaching a class on ecology. Write a post responding to the professor's question.

**In your response, you should do the following.**

- Express and support your opinion.
- Make a contribution to the discussion in your own words.

An effective response will contain at least 100 words.

**Dr. Gupta**
Today, there is debate over how we should treat natural ecosystems, meaning wilderness areas that are basically untouched by human activity. These natural ecosystems were once seen purely as resources to be exploited, but many people now believe that wilderness areas should be protected from any human use or interference so that they continue developing completely naturally. To what extent do you support protecting and preserving natural ecosystems? Should some wilderness areas be totally protected from human use?

**Andrew**
People who are already struggling to feed their families are the ones most likely to be affected by, for example, a ban on mining in a wilderness area. We cannot prohibit human activities in natural ecosystems without economic consequences. I believe humans have a fundamental right to use natural resources for survival and to build wealth.

**Kelly**

There are very few truly wild places left on Earth, and once they're gone, we can never get them back. I believe we need to protect our remaining natural ecosystems from human interference. Not only will the animals and plants in those places benefit, but so will we humans because our own survival depends on the health of our planet.

## Topic Notes

In this prompt, the professor basically asks students to discuss their perspective on the extent to which wilderness areas should be preserved, and to provide a rationale for their position. Andrew's post states that he believes, for economic reasons, that humans have a right to use natural resources as needed, while Kelly supports the protection of wilderness areas as a matter of human survival. Test takers may express full or partial agreement with either of these posts or present an entirely new opinion (perhaps protecting some areas under certain, specified conditions but not others). Responses should make clear what the test taker's overall opinion is and the rationale for that opinion.

## Sample Responses with Rater Comments

*High-Level Essay*

> All living things are entitled to live on this earth. Humans are the only species that can globally affect other species and make them extinct by altering nature and affecting the lives of other species. I do agree with Kelly that we should try our best to preserve nature as much as possible. Designating areas to be preserved from human living is good. Places like national parks where people are allowed to visit but not allowed to live in, should be an adequate solution. We should still be able to enjoy the nature but not to destroy them. It is also critical to the overall survival of this world.

*Rater Comments*

The response is a relevant and very clearly expressed contribution to the online discussion, and it demonstrates consistent facility in the use of language. The writer takes the position of preserving the wilderness because "All living things are entitled to live on this earth." The writer, while agreeing with Kelly's position ("I do agree with Kelly that we should try our best to preserve nature as much as possible"), goes on to recommend a solution for the issue by suggesting that "designating areas to be preserved from human living is good. Places like national parks where people are allowed to visit but not allowed to live in, should be an adequate solution." The relevant and well-elaborated explanations, together with the presence of few lexical or grammatical errors, warrant a high score for this response.

*Mid-Level Essay*

I agree with Andrew there are some peoples who had been already suffered and struggling a lot to feed its families if there are restriction or ban on natural ecosystems then how they survive? They should get or should allowed to use natural ecosystems as its god gift and everyone has right to use it. There will be more possible chance that they get frustated with own lives because they might think they are already not getting good help from government or so and at same time even if this natural source is not available for them then they feel leftover and this effect them very badly and also for the country.

*Rater Comments*

The response is a mostly relevant and mostly understandable contribution to the online discussion, and there is some facility in the use of language. The writer agrees with Andrew that "here are some peoples who had been already suffered and struggling a lot to feed its families," so "if there are restriction or ban on natural ecosystems then how they survive?" The writer goes on to add the detail regarding the potential of people to "get frustated with own lives because they might think they are already not getting good help from government or so and at same time even if this natural source is not available for them then they feel left-over and this effect them very badly and also for the country." There are language facility issues in the response, with noticeable lexical and grammatical errors in sentence structure and word form (for one example, "there will be more possible chance that they get frustated with own lives"). Overall, the response is partially successful because it offers a mostly relevant and understandable contribution to the online discussion, but the presence of noticeable language errors affects clarity and prevents the response from receiving a high score.

# 8 Authentic TOEFL iBT® Practice Test 3

I n this chapter you will find the third of four authentic TOEFL iBT Practice Tests. You can take the test in two different ways:

- **In the book:** You can read through the test questions in the following pages, marking your answers in the spaces provided. To hear the listening portions of the test, follow the instructions to play the numbered audio tracks that accompany this book.

- **On your computer:** For a test-taking experience that more closely resembles the actual TOEFL iBT test, you can take this same test on your computer using the digital download (see code in the back of the book). Reading passages and questions will appear on-screen, and you can enter your answers by selecting the spaces provided. Follow the instructions to hear the listening portions of the test.

Following this test, you will find answer keys and scoring information. You will also find scripts for the listening portions. Complete answer explanations, as well as sample test taker spoken and written responses, are also provided.

# TOEFL iBT® Practice Test 3
# READING

In this section, you will be able to demonstrate your ability to understand academic passages in English. You will read and answer questions about **two passages**.

In the actual test, you will have 36 minutes total to read both passages and answer the questions. A clock will indicate how much time remains.

Some passages may include one or more notes explaining words or phrases. The words or phrases are marked with footnote numbers and the notes explaining them appear at the end of the passage.

Most questions are worth 1 point, but the last question for each passage is worth 2 points.

You may review and revise your answers in this section as long as time remains.

At the end of this practice test, you will find an answer key, information to help you determine your score, and explanations of the answers.

# ARCHITECTURE

Architecture is the art and science of designing structures that organize and enclose space for practical and symbolic purposes. Because architecture grows out of human needs and aspirations, it clearly communicates cultural values. Of all the visual arts, architecture affects our lives most directly for it determines the character of the human environment in major ways.

Architecture is a three-dimensional form. It utilizes space, mass, texture, line, light, and color. To be architecture, a building must achieve a working harmony with a variety of elements. Humans instinctively seek structures that will shelter and enhance their way of life. It is the work of architects to create buildings that are not simply constructions but also offer inspiration and delight. Buildings contribute to human life when they provide shelter, enrich space, complement their site, suit the climate, and are economically feasible. The client who pays for the building and defines its function is an important member of the architectural team. The mediocre design of many contemporary buildings can be traced to both clients and architects.

In order for the structure to achieve the size and strength necessary to meet its purpose, architecture employs methods of support that, because they are based on physical laws, have changed little since people first discovered them—even while building materials have changed dramatically. The world's architectural structures have also been devised in relation to the objective limitations of materials. Structures can be analyzed in terms of how they deal with downward forces created by gravity. They are designed to withstand the forces of *compression* (pushing together), *tension* (pulling apart), *bending*, or a combination of these in different parts of the structure.

Every development in architecture has been the result of major technological changes. Materials and methods of construction are integral parts of the design of architectural structures. In earlier times it was necessary to design structural systems suitable for the materials that were available, such as wood, stone, or brick. Today technology has progressed to the point where it is possible to invent new building materials to suit the type of structure desired. Enormous changes in materials and techniques of construction within the last few generations have made it possible to enclose space with much greater ease and speed and with a minimum of material. Progress in this area can be measured by the difference in weight between buildings built now and those of comparable size built one hundred years ago.

Modern architectural forms generally have three separate components comparable to elements of the human body: a supporting *skeleton* or frame, an outer *skin* enclosing the interior spaces, and *equipment*, similar to the body's vital organs and systems. The equipment includes plumbing, electrical wiring, hot water, and air-conditioning. Of course in early architecture—such as igloos and adobe structures—there was no such equipment, and the skeleton and skin were often one.

Much of the world's great architecture has been constructed of stone because of its beauty, permanence, and availability. In the past, whole cities grew from the arduous task of cutting and piling stone upon stone. Some of the world's finest stone architecture can be seen in the ruins of the ancient Inca city of Machu Picchu high in the eastern Andes Mountains of Peru. The doorways and windows are made possible by placing over the open spaces thick stone beams that support the weight from above. A structural invention had to be made before the physical limitations of stone could be overcome and new architectural forms could be created. That invention was the *arch*, a curved structure originally made of separate stone or brick segments. The arch was used by the early cultures of the Mediterranean area chiefly for underground drains, but it was the Romans who first developed and used the arch extensively in aboveground structures. Roman builders perfected the semicircular arch made of separate blocks of stone. As a method of spanning space, the arch can support greater weight than a horizontal beam. It works in compression to divert the weight above it out to the sides, where the weight is borne by the vertical elements on either side of the arch. The arch is among the many important structural breakthroughs that have characterized architecture throughout the centuries.

**Directions:** Now answer the questions.

**PARAGRAPH 1**

Architecture is the art and science of designing structures that organize and enclose space for practical and symbolic purposes. Because architecture grows out of human needs and aspirations, it clearly communicates cultural values. Of all the visual arts, architecture affects our lives most directly for it determines the character of the human environment in major ways.

1. According to paragraph 1, all of the following statements about architecture are true EXCEPT:

   (A) Architecture is a visual art.
   (B) Architecture reflects the cultural values of its creators.
   (C) Architecture has both artistic and scientific dimensions.
   (D) Architecture has an indirect effect on life.

**PARAGRAPH 2**

Architecture is a three-dimensional form. It utilizes space, mass, texture, line, light, and color. To be architecture, a building must achieve a working harmony with a variety of elements. Humans instinctively seek structures that will shelter and **enhance** their way of life. It is the work of architects to create buildings that are not simply constructions but also offer inspiration and delight. Buildings contribute to human life when they provide shelter, enrich space, complement their site, suit the climate, and are economically feasible. The client who pays for the building and defines its function is an important member of the architectural team. The mediocre design of many contemporary buildings can be traced to both clients and architects.

2. The word "**enhance**" in the passage is closest in meaning to

   (A) protect
   (B) improve
   (C) organize
   (D) match

GO ON TO THE NEXT PAGE

**PARAGRAPH 3**

**In order for the structure to achieve the size and strength necessary to meet its purpose, architecture employs methods of support that, because they are based on physical laws, have changed little since people first discovered them—even while building materials have changed dramatically**. The world's architectural structures have also been devised in relation to the objective limitations of materials. Structures can be analyzed in terms of how they deal with downward forces created by gravity. They are designed to withstand the forces of *compression* (pushing together), *tension* (pulling apart), *bending*, or a combination of these in different parts of the structure.

3. Which of the sentences below best expresses the essential information in the highlighted sentence in the passage? Incorrect choices change the meaning in important ways or leave out essential information.

Ⓐ Unchanging physical laws have limited the size and strength of buildings that can be made with materials discovered long ago.
Ⓑ Building materials have changed in order to increase architectural size and strength, but physical laws of structure have not changed.
Ⓒ When people first started to build, the structural methods used to provide strength and size were inadequate because they were not based on physical laws.
Ⓓ Unlike building materials, the methods of support used in architecture have not changed over time because they are based on physical laws.

**PARAGRAPH 4**

Every development in architecture has been the result of major technological changes. Materials and methods of construction are **integral** parts of the design of architectural structures. In earlier times it was necessary to design structural systems suitable for the materials that were available, such as wood, stone, or brick. Today technology has progressed to the point where it is possible to invent new building materials to suit the type of structure desired. Enormous changes in materials and techniques of construction within the last few generations have made it possible to enclose space with much greater ease and speed and with a minimum of material. Progress in this area can be measured by the difference in weight between buildings built now and those of comparable size built one hundred years ago.

4. The word "**integral**" is closest in meaning to

Ⓐ essential
Ⓑ variable
Ⓒ practical
Ⓓ independent

5. According to paragraph 4, which of the following is true about materials used in the construction of buildings?

  Ⓐ Because new building materials are hard to find, construction techniques have changed very little from past generations.

  Ⓑ The availability of suitable building materials no longer limits the types of structures that may be built.

  Ⓒ The primary building materials that are available today are wood, stone, and brick.

  Ⓓ Architects in earlier times did not have enough building materials to enclose large spaces.

6. In paragraph 4, what does the author imply about modern buildings?

  Ⓐ They occupy much less space than buildings constructed one hundred years ago.

  Ⓑ They are not very different from the buildings of a few generations ago.

  Ⓒ They weigh less in relation to their size than buildings constructed one hundred years ago.

  Ⓓ They take a long time to build as a result of their complex construction methods.

**P
A
R
A
G
R
A
P
H

6**

Much of the world's great architecture has been constructed of stone because of its beauty, permanence, and availability. In the past, whole cities grew from the arduous task of cutting and piling stone upon stone. Some of the world's finest stone architecture can be seen in the ruins of the ancient Inca city of Machu Picchu high in the eastern Andes Mountains of Peru. The **doorways and windows** are made possible by placing over the open spaces thick stone beams that support the weight from above. A structural invention had to be made before the physical limitations of stone could be overcome and new architectural forms could be created. That invention was the *arch*, a curved structure originally made of separate stone or brick segments. The arch was used by the early cultures of the Mediterranean area chiefly for underground drains, but it was the Romans who first developed and used the arch extensively in aboveground structures. Roman builders perfected the semicircular arch made of separate blocks of stone. As a method of spanning space, the arch can support greater weight than a horizontal beam. It works in compression to divert the weight above it out to the sides, where the weight is borne by the vertical elements on either side of the arch. The arch is among the many important structural breakthroughs that have characterized architecture throughout the centuries.

7. Why does the author include a description of how the "**doorways and windows**" of Machu Picchu were constructed?

  Ⓐ To indicate that the combined skeletons and skins of the stone buildings of Machu Picchu were similar to igloos and adobe structures

  Ⓑ To indicate the different kinds of stones that had to be cut to build Machu Picchu

  Ⓒ To provide an illustration of the kind of construction that was required before arches were invented

  Ⓓ To explain how ancient builders reduced the amount of time necessary to construct buildings from stone

GO ON TO THE NEXT PAGE ↘

8. According to paragraph 6, which of the following statements is true of the arch?

Ⓐ The Romans were the first people to use the stone arch.

Ⓑ The invention of the arch allowed new architectural forms to be developed.

Ⓒ The arch worked by distributing the structural load of a building toward the center of the arch.

Ⓓ The Romans followed earlier practices in their use of arches.

**PARAGRAPHS 4 AND 5 6**

Progress in this area can be measured by the difference in weight between buildings built now and those of comparable size built one hundred years ago.

**(A)** Modern architectural forms generally have three separate components comparable to elements of the human body: a supporting *skeleton* or frame, an outer *skin* enclosing the interior spaces, and *equipment*, similar to the body's vital organs and systems. **(B)** The equipment includes plumbing, electrical wiring, hot water, and air-conditioning. **(C)** Of course in early architecture—such as igloos and adobe structures—there was no such equipment, and the skeleton and skin were often one. **(D)**

Much of the world's great architecture has been constructed of stone because of its beauty, permanence, and availability.

9. **Directions:** Look at the part of the passage that is displayed above. The letters **(A)**, **(B)**, **(C)**, and **(D)** indicate where the following sentence could be added.

**However, some modern architectural designs, such as those using folded plates of concrete or air-inflated structures, are again unifying skeleton and skin.**

Where would the sentence best fit?

Ⓐ Choice A

Ⓑ Choice B

Ⓒ Choice C

Ⓓ Choice D

10. **Directions:** An introductory sentence for a brief summary of the passage is provided below. Complete the summary by selecting the THREE answer choices that express the most important ideas in the passage. Some sentences do not belong in the summary because they express ideas that are not presented in the passage or are minor ideas in the passage. **This question is worth 2 points.**

**Architecture uses forms and space to express cultural values.**

- 
- 
- 

### Answer Choices

A Architects seek to create buildings that are both visually appealing and well suited for human use.

B Both clients and architects are responsible for the mediocre designs of some modern buildings.

C Over the course of the history of building, innovations in materials and methods of construction have given architects ever greater freedom to express themselves.

D Modern buildings tend to lack the beauty of ancient stone buildings such as those of Machu Picchu.

E Throughout history buildings have been constructed like human bodies, needing distinct "organ" systems in order to function.

F The discovery and use of the arch typifies the way in which architecture advances by developing more efficient types of structures.

GO ON TO THE NEXT PAGE

# THE LONG-TERM STABILITY OF ECOSYSTEMS

Plant communities assemble themselves flexibly, and their particular structure depends on the specific history of the area. Ecologists use the term "succession" to refer to the changes that happen in plant communities and ecosystems over time. The first community in a succession is called a pioneer community, while the long-lived community at the end of succession is called a climax community. Pioneer and successional plant communities are said to change over periods from 1 to 500 years. These changes—in plant numbers and the mix of species—are cumulative. Climax communities themselves change but over periods of time greater than about 500 years.

An ecologist who studies a pond today may well find it relatively unchanged in a year's time. Individual fish may be replaced, but the number of fish will tend to be the same from one year to the next. We can say that the properties of an ecosystem are more stable than the individual organisms that compose the ecosystem.

At one time, ecologists believed that species diversity made ecosystems stable. They believed that the greater the diversity the more stable the ecosystem. Support for this idea came from the observation that long-lasting climax communities usually have more complex food webs and more species diversity than pioneer communities. Ecologists concluded that the apparent stability of climax ecosystems depended on their complexity. To take an extreme example, farmlands dominated by a single crop are so unstable that one year of bad weather or the invasion of a single pest can destroy the entire crop. In contrast, a complex climax community, such as a temperate forest, will tolerate considerable damage from weather or pests.

The question of ecosystem stability is complicated, however. The first problem is that ecologists do not all agree what "stability" means. Stability can be defined as simply lack of change. In that case, the climax community would be considered the most stable, since, by definition, it changes the least over time. Alternatively, stability can be defined as the speed with which an ecosystem returns to a particular form following a major disturbance, such as a fire. This kind of stability is also called *resilience*. In that case, climax communities would be the most fragile and the *least* stable, since they can require hundreds of years to return to the climax state.

Even the kind of stability defined as simple lack of change is not always associated with maximum diversity. At least in temperate zones, maximum diversity is often found in mid-successional stages, not in the climax community. Once a redwood forest matures, for example, the kinds of species and the number of individuals growing on the forest floor are reduced. In general, diversity, by itself, does not ensure stability. Mathematical models of ecosystems likewise suggest that diversity does not guarantee ecosystem stability—just the opposite, in fact. A more complicated system is, in general, more likely than a simple system to break down. (A fifteen-speed racing bicycle is more likely to break down than a child's tricycle.)

Ecologists are especially interested in knowing what factors contribute to the resilience of communities because climax communities all over the world are being severely damaged or destroyed by human activities. The destruction caused by the volcanic explosion of Mount St. Helens, in the northwestern United States, for example, pales in comparison to the destruction caused by humans. We need to know what aspects of a community are most important to the community's resistance to destruction, as well as its recovery.

Many ecologists now think that the relative long-term stability of climax communities comes not from diversity but from the "patchiness" of the environment; an environment that varies from place to place supports more kinds of organisms than an environment that is uniform. A local population that goes extinct is quickly replaced by immigrants from an adjacent community. Even if the new population is of a different species, it can approximately fill the niche vacated by the extinct population and keep the food web intact.

**Directions:** Now answer the questions.

**PARAGRAPH 1**

Plant communities assemble themselves flexibly, and their **particular** structure depends on the specific history of the area. Ecologists use the term "succession" to refer to the changes that happen in plant communities and ecosystems over time. The first community in a succession is called a pioneer community, while the long-lived community at the end of succession is called a climax community. Pioneer and successional plant communities are said to change over periods from 1 to 500 years. These changes—in plant numbers and the mix of species—are cumulative. Climax communities themselves change but over periods of time greater than about 500 years.

11. The word "**particular**" in the passage is closest in meaning to
   Ⓐ natural
   Ⓑ final
   Ⓒ specific
   Ⓓ complex

**PARAGRAPH 2**

An ecologist who studies a pond today may well find it relatively unchanged in a year's time. Individual fish may be replaced, but the number of fish will tend to be the same from one year to the next. We can say that the properties of an ecosystem are more stable than the individual organisms that compose the ecosystem.

12. According to paragraph 2, which of the following principles of ecosystems can be learned by studying a pond?
   Ⓐ Ecosystem properties change more slowly than individuals in the system.
   Ⓑ The stability of an ecosystem tends to change as individuals are replaced.
   Ⓒ Individual organisms are stable from one year to the next.
   Ⓓ A change in the numbers of an organism does not affect an ecosystem's properties.

GO ON TO THE NEXT PAGE

PARAGRAPH 4

The question of ecosystem stability is complicated, however. The first problem is that ecologists do not all agree what "stability" means. Stability can be defined as simply lack of change. In that case, the climax community would be considered the most stable, since, by definition, it changes the least over time. Alternatively, stability can be defined as the speed with which an ecosystem returns to a particular form following a major disturbance, such as a fire. This kind of stability is also called *resilience*. In that case, climax communities would be the most fragile and the *least* stable, since they can require hundreds of years to return to the climax state.

13. According to paragraph 4, why is the question of ecosystem stability complicated?

   (A) The reasons for ecosystem change are not always clear.
   (B) Ecologists often confuse the word "stability" with the word "resilience."
   (C) The exact meaning of the word "stability" is debated by ecologists.
   (D) There are many different answers to ecological questions.

14. According to paragraph 4, which of the following is true of climax communities?

   (A) They are more resilient than pioneer communities.
   (B) They can be considered both the most and the least stable communities.
   (C) They are stable because they recover quickly after major disturbances.
   (D) They are the most resilient communities because they change the least over time.

PARAGRAPH 5

Even the kind of stability defined as simple lack of change is not always associated with maximum diversity. At least in temperate zones, maximum diversity is often found in mid-successional stages, not in the climax community. Once a redwood forest matures, for example, the kinds of species and the number of individuals growing on the forest floor are reduced. In general, diversity, by itself, does not ensure stability. Mathematical models of ecosystems likewise suggest that diversity does not guarantee ecosystem stability—just the opposite, in fact. A more complicated system is, in general, more likely than a simple system to break down. (**A fifteen-speed racing bicycle is more likely to break down than a child's tricycle.**)

15. Which of the following can be inferred from paragraph 5 about redwood forests?

   (A) They become less stable as they mature.
   (B) They support many species when they reach climax.
   (C) They are found in temperate zones.
   (D) They have reduced diversity during mid-successional stages.

16. In paragraph 5, why does the author provide the information that "**A fifteen-speed racing bicycle is more likely to break down than a child's tricycle**"?

    (A) To illustrate a general principle about the stability of systems by using an everyday example

    (B) To demonstrate that an understanding of stability in ecosystems can be applied to help understand stability in other situations

    (C) To make a comparison that supports the claim that, in general, stability increases with diversity

    (D) To provide an example that contradicts mathematical models of ecosystems

**PARAGRAPH 7**

**Many ecologists now think that the relative long-term stability of climax communities comes not from diversity but from the "patchiness" of the environment; an environment that varies from place to place supports more kinds of organisms than an environment that is uniform.** A local population that goes extinct is quickly replaced by immigrants from an **adjacent** community. Even if the new population is of a different species, it can approximately fill the niche vacated by the extinct population and keep the food web intact.

17. Which of the sentences below best expresses the essential information in the highlighted sentence in the passage? Incorrect choices change the meaning in important ways or leave out essential information.

    (A) Ecologists now think that the stability of an environment is a result of diversity rather than patchiness.

    (B) Patchy environments that vary from place to place do not often have high species diversity.

    (C) Uniform environments cannot be climax communities because they do not support as many types of organisms as patchy environments.

    (D) A patchy environment is thought to increase stability because it is able to support a wide variety of organisms.

18. The word "**adjacent**" in the passage is closest in meaning to

    (A) foreign

    (B) stable

    (C) fluid

    (D) neighboring

GO ON TO THE NEXT PAGE

PARAGRAPHS 5 6 AND 7

A more complicated system is, in general, more likely than a simple system to break down. (A fifteen-speed racing bicycle is more likely to break down than a child's tricycle.)

**(A)** Ecologists are especially interested in knowing what factors contribute to the resilience of communities because climax communities all over the world are being severely damaged or destroyed by human activities. **(B)** The destruction caused by the volcanic explosion of Mount St. Helens, in the northwestern United States, for example, pales in comparison to the destruction caused by humans. **(C)** We need to know what aspects of a community are most important to the community's resistance to destruction, as well as its recovery. **(D)**

Many ecologists now think that the relative long-term stability of climax communities comes not from diversity but from the "patchiness" of the environment; an environment that varies from place to place supports more kinds of organisms than an environment that is uniform.

19. **Directions:** Look at the part of the passage that is displayed above. The letters **(A)**, **(B)**, **(C)**, and **(D)** indicate where the following sentence could be added.

**In fact, damage to the environment by humans is often much more severe than by natural events and processes.**

Where would the sentence best fit?

Ⓐ Choice A
Ⓑ Choice B
Ⓒ Choice C
Ⓓ Choice D

20. **Directions:** An introductory sentence for a brief summary of the passage is provided below. Complete the summary by selecting the THREE answer choices that express the most important ideas in the passage. Some sentences do not belong in the summary because they express ideas that are not presented in the passage or are minor ideas in the passage. **This question is worth 2 points.**

**The process of succession and the stability of a climax community can change over time.**

- 
- 
- 

Answer Choices

A  The changes that occur in an ecosystem from the pioneer to the climax community can be seen in one human generation.
B  Ecologists agree that climax communities are the most stable types of ecosystems.
C  A high degree of species diversity does not always result in a stable ecosystem.
D  Disagreements over the meaning of the term "stability" make it difficult to identify the most stable ecosystems.
E  The level of resilience in a plant community contributes to its long-term stability.
F  The resilience of climax communities makes them resistant to destruction caused by humans.

**STOP. This is the end of the Reading section of TOEFL iBT Practice Test 3.**

# LISTENING

In this section, you will be able to demonstrate your ability to understand conversations and lectures in English.

In the actual test, the section is divided into two separately timed parts. You will hear each conversation or lecture only one time. A clock will indicate how much time remains. The clock will count down only while you are answering questions, not while you are listening. You may take up to 16.5 minutes to answer the questions.

In this practice test, there is no time limit for answering questions.

You may take notes while you listen. You may use your notes to help you answer the questions. Your notes will not be scored.

Answer the questions based on what is stated or implied by the speakers.

In some questions, you will see this icon: . This means that you will hear, but not see, part of the question.

**In the actual test, you must answer each question. You cannot return to previous questions.**

At the end of this practice test, you will find an answer key, information to help you determine your score, and explanations of the answers.

*Listen to Track 57.*

## Questions

**Directions:** Mark your answer by filling in the oval or square next to your choice.

1. Why does the student go to see the man?
   - (A) To get information for a class project
   - (B) To discuss her participation in an upcoming event
   - (C) To request a letter of recommendation for a job
   - (D) To offer input on a new construction project

2. What do the speakers say about Lightstone Dormitory? *Select 2 answers.*
   - (A) It uses unconventional power sources.
   - (B) It is located next to the engineering library.
   - (C) It is equipped to harvest rainwater.
   - (D) It was built with recycled materials.

3. According to the man, why is the Green Buildings Tour taking place in winter?
   - (A) More tour guides are available in winter.
   - (B) It allows visitors to experience the effectiveness of radiant heat.
   - (C) New construction projects are usually completed before cold weather sets in.
   - (D) The university offers courses on green design during the winter months.

4.  What does the man imply about the fitness center?
    (A) He was not aware that the treadmills there use no electricity.
    (B) Only a few of the treadmills there use no electricity.
    (C) The building that houses the fitness center lacks sustainable features.
    (D) The fitness center was included in a previous tour.

5.  *Listen again to part of the conversation by playing Track 58.*
    *Then answer the question.*

    Why does the man say this?

    (A) To remind the woman that more tour guides are needed for the open house
    (B) To suggest that some information might only be interesting to engineers
    (C) To discourage the woman from gathering more information than she will have time to share
    (D) To suggest that many visitors might already be familiar with the heat-pump technology

*Listen to Track 59.*

Environmental Science

## Questions

6. What does the professor mainly discuss?

   (A) Major changes in the migratory patterns of hummingbirds
   (B) The adaptation of hummingbirds to urban environments
   (C) Concern about the reduction of hummingbird habitat
   (D) The impact of ecotourism on hummingbird populations

7. What does the professor imply might cause a decrease in the hummingbird population?

   (A) An increase in the ecotourism industry
   (B) An increase in the use of land to raise crops and cattle
   (C) A decrease in banding studies
   (D) A decrease in the distance traveled during migration

8. What does the professor say people have done to help hummingbirds survive?

   (A) They have built a series of hummingbird feeding stations.
   (B) They have supported new laws that punish polluters of wildlife habitats.
   (C) They have replanted native flowers in once-polluted areas.
   (D) They have learned to identify various hummingbird species.

9. What way of collecting information about migrating hummingbirds does the professor mention?

   (A) Receiving radio signals from electronic tracking devices
   (B) Being contacted by people who recapture banded birds
   (C) Counting the birds that return to the same region every year
   (D) Comparing old and young birds' migration routes

10. What does the professor imply researchers have learned while studying hummingbird migration?

    (A) Hummingbirds have totally disappeared from some countries due to recent habitat destruction.
    (B) Programs to replant flowers native to hummingbird habitats are not succeeding.
    (C) Some groups of hummingbirds have changed their migration patterns.
    (D) Some plant species pollinated by hummingbirds have become extinct.

11. *Listen again to part of the lecture by playing Track 60. Then answer the question.*

    What does the professor imply when she says this?

    (A) There is disagreement about the idea she has presented.
    (B) She does not plan to discuss all the details.
    (C) Her next point may seem to contradict what she has just said.
    (D) The point she will make next should be obvious to the students.

GO ON TO THE NEXT PAGE

*Listen to Track 61.*

Film History

Jean Painlevé

Jacques Cousteau

**Questions**

12. What is the main purpose of the lecture?

   (A) To discuss the style of an early filmmaker
   (B) To describe different types of filmmaking in the 1930s
   (C) To discuss the emergence of the documentary film
   (D) To describe Painlevé's influence on today's science-fiction films

13. Why are Painlevé's films typical of the films of the 1920s and 1930s?

   (A) They do not have sound.
   (B) They are filmed underwater.
   (C) They are easy to understand.
   (D) They are difficult to categorize.

14. According to the professor, how did Painlevé's films confuse the audience?

   (A) They showed animals out of their natural habitat.
   (B) They depicted animals as having both human and animal characteristics.
   (C) The narration was scientific and difficult to understand.
   (D) The audiences of the 1920s and 1930s were not used to films shot underwater.

GO ON TO THE NEXT PAGE ➘

15. Why does the professor mention sea horses?

   Ⓐ To explain that they were difficult to film in the 1930s
   Ⓑ To point out that Cousteau made documentaries about them
   Ⓒ To illustrate Painlevé's fascination with unusual animals
   Ⓓ To explain why Painlevé's underwater films were not successful

16. Why does the professor compare the film styles of Jacques Cousteau and Jean Painlevé?

   Ⓐ To explain how Painlevé influenced Cousteau
   Ⓑ To emphasize the uniqueness of Painlevé's filming style
   Ⓒ To emphasize the artistic value of Cousteau's documentary films
   Ⓓ To demonstrate the superiority of Painlevé's filmmaking equipment

17. *Listen to Track 62 to answer the question.*

   What does the student imply when he says this?

   Ⓐ He does not like Jean Painlevé's films.
   Ⓑ He thinks that the professor should spend more time discussing Jacques Cousteau's films.
   Ⓒ He believes that high-quality filmmakers are usually well known.
   Ⓓ He believes that Jean Painlevé's films have been unfairly overlooked.

*Listen to Track 63.*

Questions

18. Why does the student go to see the professor?

    Ⓐ To ask about a class assignment
    Ⓑ To find out about a mid-semester project
    Ⓒ To get information about summer jobs
    Ⓓ To discuss ways to improve his grade

19. What was originally located on the site of the lecture hall?

    Ⓐ A farmhouse
    Ⓑ A pottery factory
    Ⓒ A clothing store
    Ⓓ A bottle-manufacturing plant

20. What is mentioned as an advantage of working on this project?

    Ⓐ Off-campus travel is paid for.
    Ⓑ Students can leave class early.
    Ⓒ The location is convenient.
    Ⓓ It fulfills a graduation requirement.

GO ON TO THE NEXT PAGE ↘

21. What is the professor considering doing to get more volunteers?

    Ⓐ Offering extra class credit
    Ⓑ Paying the students for their time
    Ⓒ Asking for student volunteers from outside her class
    Ⓓ Providing flexible work schedules

22. What information does the student still need to get from the professor?

    Ⓐ The name of the senior researcher
    Ⓑ What book he needs to read before the next lecture
    Ⓒ When the training session will be scheduled
    Ⓓ Where the project is located

*Listen to Track 64.*

Art History

Rob and Nick Carter

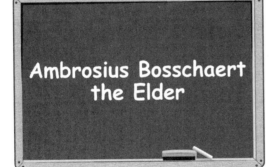

Ambrosius Bosschaert the Elder

GO ON TO THE NEXT PAGE

Questions

23. What is the lecture mainly about?
    (A) A Dutch painter's method of painting still lifes
    (B) A theory about why still lifes are scarce in contemporary art
    (C) A new discovery about an old painting
    (D) A new way of approaching a traditional art form

24. According to the professor, why could some of the bouquets in Bosschaert's paintings not have existed in real life?
    (A) The flowers grow in widely separated regions of the world.
    (B) Some of the flowers are too toxic to pick.
    (C) The flowers bloom at different times of the year.
    (D) The cost of such exotic bouquets would have been prohibitive.

25. Why does the professor mention the average length of time that people view a work of art?
    (A) To introduce one of the Carters' goals in creating their piece
    (B) To explain a technological problem with the Carters' piece
    (C) To illustrate how ideas about still lifes have changed over time
    (D) To introduce several reasons that children like the Carters' piece

26. Why does the professor mention that the Carters made video recordings of real flowers?
    (A) To emphasize a similarity between their artistic technique and that of Bosschaert
    (B) To stress that technology cannot be used as a substitute for artistic ability
    (C) To argue that the Carters' work should not be considered a still life
    (D) To show how technology can be used to improve an artistic process

27. According to the professor, why does a gust of wind blow in the animated video?
    Ⓐ To make the video seem more realistic
    Ⓑ To ensure that viewers do not lose interest toward the end of the video
    Ⓒ To allow a smoother transition from the end of the video to the beginning
    Ⓓ To symbolize the destructive power of nature

28. What is the professor's opinion about the Carters' treatment of Bosschaert's work?
    Ⓐ It damages Bosschaert's reputation as a painter.
    Ⓑ It highlights the quality of the original painting.
    Ⓒ It demonstrates a lack of familiarity with still lifes.
    Ⓓ It is superior to other attempts at animating still lifes.

**STOP. This is the end of the Listening section of TOEFL iBT Practice Test 3.**

# SPEAKING

In this section, you will be able to demonstrate your ability to speak about a variety of topics.

In the actual test, the Speaking section will last approximately 16 minutes. You will answer four questions by speaking into the microphone. You may use your notes to help you answer the questions. Your notes will not be scored. For each question, you will have time to prepare before giving your response. You should answer the questions as completely as possible in the time allowed.

For this practice test, you may want to use a personal recording device to record and play back your responses.

For each question, play the audio track listed and follow the directions to complete the task. You may take notes while you listen.

At the end of this Practice Test, you will find scripts for the audio tracks, Important Points for each question, sample responses, and comments on those responses by official raters.

## Questions

*1. You will now give your opinion about a familiar topic. After you hear the question, you will have 15 seconds to prepare and 45 seconds to speak.*

**Now play Track 65 to hear Question 1.**

Some students prefer to work on class assignments by themselves. Others believe it is better to work in a group. Which do you prefer? Explain why.

| Preparation Time: 15 Seconds |
| --- |
| Response Time: 45 Seconds |

*2. Now you will read a passage about a campus situation and then listen to a conversation about the same topic. You will then answer a question, using information from both the reading passage and the conversation. You will have 30 seconds to prepare and 60 seconds to speak.*

**Now play Track 66 to hear Question 2.**

| Reading Time: 45 Seconds |
| --- |

### Hot Breakfasts Eliminated

Beginning next month, Dining Services will no longer serve hot breakfast foods at university dining halls. Instead, students will be offered a wide assortment of cold breakfast items in the morning. These cold breakfast foods, such as breads, fruit, and yogurt, are healthier than many of the hot breakfast items that we will stop serving, so health-conscious students should welcome this change. Students will benefit in another way as well, because limiting the breakfast selection to cold food items will save money and allow us to keep our meal plans affordable.

The woman expresses her opinion of the change that has been announced. State her opinion and explain her reasons for holding that opinion.

**Preparation Time: 30 Seconds**
**Response Time: 60 Seconds**

3. *Now you will read a passage about an academic subject and then listen to a lecture on the same topic. You will then answer a question, using information from both the reading passage and the lecture. You will have 30 seconds to prepare and 60 seconds to speak.*

***Now play Track 67 to hear Question 3.***

**Reading Time: 50 Seconds**

### Cognitive Dissonance

Individuals sometimes experience a contradiction between their actions and their beliefs—between what they are doing and what they believe they should be doing. These contradictions can cause a kind of mental discomfort known as *cognitive dissonance*. People experiencing cognitive dissonance often do not want to change the way they are acting, so they resolve the contradictory situation in another way: they change their interpretation of the situation in a way that minimizes the contradiction between what they are doing and what they believe they should be doing.

GO ON TO THE NEXT PAGE

Using the example discussed by the professor, explain what cognitive dissonance is and how people often deal with it.

| Preparation Time: 30 Seconds |
| --- |
| Response Time: 60 Seconds |

*4. Now you will listen to a lecture. You will then be asked to summarize the lecture. You will have 20 seconds to prepare and 60 seconds to speak.*

**Now play Track 68 to hear Question 4.**

Using the examples from the talk, explain how persuasive strategies are used in advertising.

| Preparation Time: 20 Seconds |
| Response Time: 60 Seconds |

**STOP. This is the end of the Speaking section of TOEFL iBT ® Practice Test 3.**

# WRITING

In this section, you will be able to demonstrate your ability to use writing to communicate in an academic environment. There will be two writing tasks.

At the end of this Practice Test, you will find a script for the audio track, topic notes, sample responses, and comments on those responses by official raters.

Turn the page to see the directions for the first writing task.

**Integrated Writing**

For this task, you will read a passage about an academic topic. Then you will listen to a lecture about the same topic. You may take notes while you listen.

In your response, provide a detailed summary of the lecture and explain how the lecture relates to the reading passage.

In the actual test, you will have 3 minutes to read the passage and 20 minutes to write your response. While you write, you will be able to see the reading passage. If you finish your response before time is up, you may go on to the second writing task.

Now you will see the reading passage. It will be followed by a lecture.

**Reading Time: 3 minutes**

Rembrandt is the most famous of the seventeenth-century Dutch painters. However, there are doubts whether some paintings attributed to Rembrandt were actually painted by him. One such painting is known as *Portrait of an Elderly Woman in a White Bonnet*. The painting was attributed to Rembrandt because of its style, and indeed the representation of the woman's face is very much like that of portraits known to be by Rembrandt. But there are problems with the painting that suggest it could not be a work by Rembrandt.

First, there is something inconsistent about the way the woman in the portrait is dressed. She is wearing a white linen cap of a kind that only servants would wear—yet the coat she is wearing has a luxurious fur collar that no servant could afford. Rembrandt, who was known for his attention to the details of his subjects' clothing, would not have been guilty of such an inconsistency.

Second, Rembrandt was a master of painting light and shadow, but in this painting these elements do not fit together. The face appears to be illuminated by light reflected onto it from below. But below the face is the dark fur collar, which would absorb light rather than reflect it. So the face should appear partially in shadow—which is not how it appears. Rembrandt would never have made such an error.

Finally, examination of the back of the painting reveals that it was painted on a panel made of several pieces of wood glued together. Although Rembrandt often painted on wood panels, no painting known to be by Rembrandt uses a panel glued together in this way from several pieces of wood.

For these reasons the painting was removed from the official catalog of Rembrandt's paintings in the 1930s.

*Now play Track 69.* 🎧

### Question 1

Summarize the points made in the lecture, being sure to explain how they respond to the specific concerns presented in the reading passage.

You have 20 minutes to plan and write your response.

**Response Time: 20 minutes**

_____

_____

_____

_____

_____

_____

_____

_____

_____

_____

_____

_____

GO ON TO THE NEXT PAGE ↘

### Writing for an Academic Discussion

For this task, you will read an online discussion. A professor has posted a question about a topic, and some classmates have responded with their ideas.

In the actual test, you will have 10 minutes to write a response that contributes to the discussion.

### Question 2

Your professor is teaching a class on sociology. Write a post responding to the professor's question.

**In your response, you should do the following.**

- Express and support your opinion.
- Make a contribution to the discussion in your own words.

An effective response will contain at least 100 words.

**Dr. Diaz**

This week we will be studying trends in food shopping. One of them is meal-kit websites. On these sites, the customers first select one or more meals, and then the companies deliver to their homes the cooking instructions plus just enough grocery ingredients to prepare the selected meals. The customers then prepare their meals at home. Do you think this is a positive trend? Explain why or why not.

**Andrew**

It's especially positive if you don't have any kitchen skills. I've tried that kind of service, and even though I'm not a good cook, the meal came out tasting pretty good. I think I'm learning how to cook! It's probably especially helpful for younger people, who might not even know how to choose the best ingredients at grocery stores.

**Claire**

It might be convenient, but this is definitely not a positive trend. Think of the effect on the environment of all the trucks delivering packaged groceries for just a few meals to all those houses, week after week, all over the city! We really have to stop favoring convenience over environmental impacts.

> **Response Time: 10 minutes**

GO ON TO THE NEXT PAGE ⬿

_____

_____

_____

_____

_____

_____

_____

_____

_____

_____

_____

_____

_____

_____

_____

_____

_____

_____

_____

_____

_____

_____

_____

_____

**STOP. This is the end of the Writing section of TOEFL iBT® Practice Test 3.**

# Answers, Explanations, and Listening Scripts

# Reading

## Answer Key and Self-Scoring Chart

**Directions:** Check your answers against the answer key below. Write the number 1 on the line to the right of each question if you picked the correct answer. For questions worth more than one point, follow the directions given. Total your points at the bottom of the chart.

| Question Number | Correct Answer | Your Raw Points |
|---|---|---|
| Architecture | | |
| 1. | D | |
| 2. | B | |
| 3. | D | |
| 4. | A | |
| 5. | B | |
| 6. | C | |
| 7. | C | |
| 8. | B | |
| 9. | D | |
| 10.* | A, C, F | |
| | TOTAL: | |

* For question 10, write 2 if you picked all three correct answers. Write 1 if you picked two correct answers.

| Question Number | Correct Answer | Your Raw Points |
|---|---|---|
| The Long-Term Stability of Ecosystems | | |
| 11. | C | |
| 12. | A | |
| 13. | C | |
| 14. | B | |
| 15. | C | |
| 16. | A | |
| 17. | D | |
| 18. | D | |
| 19. | B | |
| 20.* | C, D, E | |
| | TOTAL: | |

\* For question 10, write 2 if you picked all three correct answers. Write 1 if you picked two correct answers.

Below is a table that converts your Reading section answers into a TOEFL iBT® Reading scaled score. Take the total of raw points from your answer key for both sets and find that number in the left-hand column of the table. The right-hand column of the table gives a TOEFL iBT Reading scaled score for each number of raw points. For example, if the total points from your answer key is 18, the table shows a scaled score of 24 to 29.

You should use your score estimate as a general guide only. Your actual score on the TOEFL iBT test may be higher or lower than your score on the practice version.

## Reading Comprehension

| Raw Point Total | Scale Score |
|---|---|
| 22 | 30 |
| 21 | 29–30 |
| 20 | 28–30 |
| 19 | 26–29 |
| 18 | 24–29 |
| 17 | 22–28 |
| 16 | 21–26 |
| 15 | 19–25 |
| 14 | 18–23 |
| 13 | 16–22 |
| 12 | 14–20 |
| 11 | 12–19 |
| 10 | 11–17 |
| 9 | 9–16 |
| 8 | 7–14 |
| 7 | 4–12 |
| 6 | 3–10 |
| 5 | 1–7 |
| 4 | 0–4 |
| 3 | 0–2 |
| 2 | 0 |
| 1 | 0 |
| 0 | 0 |

# Answer Explanations

## Architecture

1.  **D** This is a Negative Factual Information question asking for specific information that can be found in paragraph 1. The correct answer is choice D. Sentence 3 in the paragraph states that "architecture affects our lives most directly," which makes the information in choice D incorrect. The information in choices A to C is stated in sentences 1 and 2 in the paragraph.

2.  **B** This is a Vocabulary question. The word being tested is "enhance." It is highlighted in the passage. The correct answer is choice B, "improve." In other words, humans seek structures that will improve, or better, their lives.

3.  **D** This is a Sentence Simplification question. As with all of these questions, a single sentence in the passage is highlighted:

    In order for the structure to achieve the size and strength necessary to meet its purpose, architecture employs methods of support that, because they are based on physical laws, have changed little since people first discovered them—even while building materials have changed dramatically.

    The correct answer is choice D. Choice D contains all of the essential information in the highlighted sentence. It omits the information from the introductory phrase about the size and strength of a structure because the information is not essential to the meaning of the sentence.

    Choices A, B, and C are all incorrect because they change the meaning of the highlighted sentence. Choice A is incorrect because it inaccurately states that physical laws have limited the size and strength of buildings, whereas the highlighted sentence does not indicate this.

    Choice B is incorrect because it wrongly makes a connection between building materials and building strength and size, whereas the highlighted sentence does not make such a connection.

    Choice C is incorrect because it wrongly states that the structural methods initially used by people were not based on physical laws, whereas the highlighted sentence states that structural methods that are based on physical laws have been in use since their discovery.

4.  **A** This is a Vocabulary question. The word being tested is "integral." It is highlighted in the passage. The correct answer is choice A, "essential." In other words, materials and methods of construction are essential, or vital, parts of the design of architectural structures.

5.   **B** This is a Factual Information question asking for specific information that can be found in paragraph 4. The correct answer is choice B. Sentence 3 in the paragraph indicates that in the past, structures were built using the available materials. However, sentence 4 in the paragraph indicates that today new materials can be created as needed depending on the design of the structure. Choice A is incorrect because sentence 5 in the paragraph indicates that there have been substantial changes in materials and designs in the recent past. Choice C is incorrect because sentence 4 in the paragraph indicates that there are many types of materials available today. Choice D is incorrect because sentence 5 in the paragraph indicates that it is possible to enclose space more quickly and easily than in the past. It does not indicate that architects were not able to enclose space.

6.   **C** This is an Inference question asking for an inference that can be supported by paragraph 4. The correct answer is choice C. Sentence 5 in the paragraph states that structures are now created with a minimum of material, and sentence 6 indicates that there is a difference in weight between buildings being built now and those that were built one hundred years ago. The combined information from these two sentences suggests that modern buildings weigh less than buildings constructed one hundred years ago. Choice A is incorrect because there is no discussion of the amount of space that buildings constructed in the past or those built now occupy. Choice B is incorrect because sentence 5 in the paragraph states that substantial changes have been made to modern buildings compared with buildings constructed one hundred years ago. Choice D is incorrect because sentence 5 in the paragraph indicates that modern buildings can be built more quickly than those built one hundred years ago.

7.   **C** This is a Rhetorical Purpose question. It is asking why the author includes the description of how the "doorways and windows" of Machu Picchu were constructed. The phrase being tested is highlighted in the passage. The correct answer is choice C. The author discusses the stone structures used to support doorways and windows in order to provide an example of how the physical limitations of stone were overcome before the invention of the arch. Choice A is incorrect because there is no comparison made in the passage between the buildings of Machu Picchu and igloos and adobe structures. Choice B is incorrect because, while the passage does state that stone was used in the buildings of Machu Picchu, it never discusses the kind of stones used. Choice D is incorrect because there is no discussion of the time needed to construct buildings from stone.

8.   **B** This is a Factual Information question asking for specific information that can be found in paragraph 6. The correct answer is choice B. Sentences 5 and 6 in the paragraph indicate that the arch allowed new architectural forms to be created. The remainder of the paragraph elaborates on structures created as a result of the arch. Choice A is incorrect because sentence 7 in the paragraph indicates that early Mediterranean cultures were the first to use

the arch, not the Romans. Choice C is incorrect because sentence 10 in the paragraph indicates that the weight of a structure is distributed to the sides of the arch. Choice D is incorrect because sentence 7 indicates that the Romans created new uses for the arch, namely in aboveground structures.

9. **D** This is an Insert Text question. You can see the four possible answer choices in paragraph 5.

> Progress in this area can be measured by the difference in weight between buildings built now and those of comparable size built one hundred years ago.
> **(A)** Modern architectural forms generally have three separate components comparable to elements of the human body: a supporting *skeleton* or frame, an outer *skin* enclosing the interior spaces, and *equipment*, similar to the body's vital organs and systems. **(B)** The equipment includes plumbing, electrical wiring, hot water, and air-conditioning. **(C)** Of course in early architecture—such as igloos and adobe structures—there was no such equipment, and the skeleton and skin were often one. **(D)**
> Much of the world's great architecture has been constructed of stone because of its beauty, permanence, and availability.

The sentence provided, "However, some modern architectural designs, such as those using folded plates of concrete or air-inflated structures, are again unifying skeleton and skin," is best inserted at choice **(D)**.

Choice **(D)** is correct because it is the only place that supports both a contrasting idea and a repeated reference to the unification of skeleton and skin. The inserted sentence represents a contrast to the main idea of the paragraph. The inserted sentence also contains the phrase "again unifying skeleton and skin," indicating that there must be a previous discussion related to unifying the skeleton and skin of a structure. Choice **(D)** is the only place in this paragraph that follows such a discussion.

None of the other answer choices follow a discussion of the unifying of a structure's skeleton and skin, nor do the other answer choices provide a suitable point of contrast for the insert sentence.

10. **A** **C** **F** This is a Prose Summary question. It is completed correctly below. The correct choices are A, C, and F. Choices B, D, and E are therefore incorrect.

**Directions:** An introductory sentence for a brief summary of the passage is provided below. Complete the summary by selecting the THREE answer choices that express the most important ideas in the passage. Some sentences do not belong in the summary because they express ideas that are not presented in the passage or are minor ideas in the passage. **This question is worth 2 points.**

**Architecture uses forms and space to express cultural values.**

- A Architects seek to create buildings that are both visually appealing and well suited for human use.
- C Over the course of the history of building, innovations in materials and methods of construction have given architects ever greater freedom to express themselves.
- F The discovery and use of the arch typifies the way in which architecture advances by developing more efficient types of structures.

**Answer Choices**

- A Architects seek to create buildings that are both visually appealing and well suited for human use.
- B Both clients and architects are responsible for the mediocre designs of some modern buildings.
- C Over the course of the history of building, innovations in materials and methods of construction have given architects ever greater freedom to express themselves.
- D Modern buildings tend to lack the beauty of ancient stone buildings such as those of Machu Picchu.
- E Throughout history buildings have been constructed like human bodies, needing distinct "organ" systems in order to function.
- F The discovery and use of the arch typifies the way in which architecture advances by developing more efficient types of structures.

*Correct Choices*

*Choice A*, "Architects seek to create buildings that are both visually appealing and well suited for human use," is correct because it is a broad statement that is developed in the first two paragraphs. The first two paragraphs discuss in detail how architecture can affect and possibly improve people's lives.

*Choice C*, "Over the course of the history of building, innovations in materials and methods of construction have given architects ever greater freedom to express themselves," is correct because it is a general statement that is developed in paragraphs 3 and 4. These paragraphs discuss in detail how materials and methods have changed and improved over the history of building, continually providing architects the chance to create new designs.

*Choice F*, "The discovery and use of the arch typifies the way in which architecture advances by developing more efficient types of structures," is correct because it captures the main idea of paragraph 6, which provides a lengthy discussion of the ways that the arch has allowed new architectural forms to be created.

*Incorrect Choices*

*Choice B*, "Both clients and architects are responsible for the mediocre designs of some modern buildings," is incorrect because it is only a minor supporting detail that is mentioned in the last sentence of paragraph 2. It supports the larger idea in the paragraph that the quality of an architectural design depends on a variety of factors.

*Choice D*, "Modern buildings tend to lack the beauty of ancient stone buildings such as those of Machu Picchu," is incorrect because there is no discussion in the passage of the level of attractiveness of modern buildings.

*Choice E*, "Throughout history buildings have been constructed like human bodies, needing distinct 'organ' systems in order to function," is incorrect because paragraph 5 states that early architecture did not have equipment, such as plumbing and wiring, that is comparable to vital organs in the human body.

## The Long-Term Stability of Ecosystems

11. **C** This is a Vocabulary question. The word being tested is "particular." It is highlighted in the passage. The correct answer is choice C, "specific." In other words, the specific structure of plant communities depends on the history of the area.

12. **A** This is a Factual Information question asking for specific information that can be found in paragraph 2. The correct answer is choice A. Sentence 3 in the paragraph states that "the properties of an ecosystem are more stable," or change more slowly, than individuals within the system. Choice B is contradicted by sentences 1 and 3 in the paragraph, which indicate that ecosystems remain unchanged as individuals are replaced. Choice C is contradicted by sentence 2 in the paragraph, which indicates that individual organisms

change from year to year. Choice D is incorrect because there is no information in the paragraph about a change in the numbers of an organism and how that will affect an ecosystem. Furthermore, sentence 2 in the paragraph states that the number of fish, for example, will usually stay the same.

13. **C** This is a Factual Information question asking for specific information that can be found in paragraph 4. The correct answer is choice C. The first two sentences of the paragraph indicate that ecosystem stability is complicated because ecologists do not agree on the meaning of the word *stability*. Choice A is incorrect because it is not discussed in the paragraph. Furthermore, the idea stated in choice A is contradicted in sentence 5 of the paragraph, which states that disturbances such as fires can change an ecosystem. Choice B is incorrect because there is no discussion of confusion on the part of ecologists about the concept of resilience. Resilience is simply defined in the paragraph. Choice D is incorrect because the main idea of the paragraph is to show that the questions of different ecologists are the cause of complications. Furthermore, sentences 4 and 7 in the paragraph provide clear answers to the questions posed by ecologists.

14. **B** This is a Factual Information question asking for specific information provided in paragraph 4. The correct answer is choice B. Sentences 4 and 7 in the paragraph indicate different perspectives on climax communities: they can be viewed as the most or least stable communities. Choice A is incorrect because, according to the resilience theory of ecosystem stability, it is contradicted by sentence 7, which indicates that climax communities are the least resilient. Choice C is also contradicted by sentence 7, which indicates that climax communities take a long time to recover after a major disturbance. Choice D is incorrect because it is a misunderstanding of the concept of resilience. According to sentence 5 in the paragraph, a resilient community will revert back to a particular form after a major disturbance.

15. **C** This is an Inference question asking for an inference that can be supported by paragraph 5. The correct answer is choice C. Sentence 2 introduces the discussion of diversity in successional communities in temperate zones, and sentence 3 presents redwood forests as an example of such a community. Choice A is incorrect because we can infer the opposite, according to the paragraph. Sentence 3 indicates that the diversity in a redwood forest decreases as the forest matures, and sentence 5 indicates that increased diversity can lead to instability. Choice B is incorrect because sentences 2 and 3 indicate that the number of species declines in a redwood forest at the climax stage. Choice D is incorrect because sentences 2 and 3 indicate the opposite, namely that redwood forests have maximum diversity in successional stages.

16. Ⓐ This is a Rhetorical Purpose question. It is testing why the author provides the information that "A fifteen-speed racing bicycle is more likely to break down than a child's tricycle." The sentence being tested is highlighted in the passage. The correct answer is choice A. Sentence 6 in the paragraph asserts the general principle that a complicated system is more likely to break down than a simple one. Sentence 7, the highlighted sentence, provides an example about bicycles that the average reader can relate to. Choice B is incorrect because it emphasizes stability, whereas the highlighted information provides an example of the issues related to the complexity of a particular system. Choice C is incorrect because sentence 5 in the paragraph indicates the opposite, specifically that stability does not necessarily increase with diversity. Therefore the highlighted sentence cannot be compared to the incorrect information given in choice C. Choice D is incorrect because the example provided in the highlighted sentence actually supports the mathematical models mentioned in sentence 5.

17. Ⓓ This is a Sentence Simplification question. As with all of these questions, a single sentence in the passage is highlighted:

> Many ecologists now think that the relative long-term stability of climax communities comes not from diversity but from the "patchiness" of the environment; an environment that varies from place to place supports more kinds of organisms than an environment that is uniform.

The correct answer is choice D. That choice takes all of the essential information in the two clauses of the highlighted sentence and simplifies it into one concise sentence. It omits information from the second clause that is repetitive and therefore not essential to the meaning.

Choice A is incorrect because its meaning is the opposite of that of the highlighted sentence. Choice A states that diversity is the key to stability, whereas the highlighted sentence indicates that stability does not come from diversity but rather comes from patchiness.

Choice B incorrectly indicates a causal relationship between patchy environments and diversity.

Choice C is incorrect because there is no indication in the highlighted sentence that uniform environments cannot be climax communities.

18. Ⓓ This is a Vocabulary question. The word being tested is "adjacent." It is highlighted in the passage. The correct answer is choice D, "neighboring." In other words, a local population that goes extinct is quickly replaced by organisms from a neighboring, or nearby, community.

19. **B** This is an Insert Text question. You can see the four possible answer choices in paragraph 6.

A more complicated system is, in general, more likely than a simple system to break down. (A fifteen-speed racing bicycle is more likely to break down than a child's tricycle.)

**(A)** Ecologists are especially interested in knowing what factors contribute to the resilience of communities because climax communities all over the world are being severely damaged or destroyed by human activities. **(B)** The destruction caused by the volcanic explosion of Mount St. Helens, in the northwestern United States, for example, pales in comparison to the destruction caused by humans. **(C)** We need to know what aspects of a community are most important to the community's resistance to destruction, as well as its recovery. **(D)**

Many ecologists now think that the relative long-term stability of climax communities comes not from diversity but from the "patchiness" of the environment; an environment that varies from place to place supports more kinds of organisms than an environment that is uniform.

The sentence provided, "In fact, damage to the environment by humans is often much more severe than by natural events and processes," is best inserted at choice **(B)**.

Choice **(B)** is correct because it is the best place in the paragraph to elaborate on the idea, introduced in sentence 1, that humans contribute to damage done to the environment. The phrase "In fact" is used to indicate elaboration. Also, the phrase "natural events and processes" in the given sentence provides a logical connection to the example in sentence 2 about the volcanic explosion of Mount St. Helens.

Choice **(A)** is incorrect because it does not make sense to begin the paragraph with a sentence that elaborates on the idea of human damage to the environment before the idea has been introduced.

Choice **(C)** is incorrect because it does not make sense to follow the specific example about the damage caused by the explosion of Mount St. Helens in sentence 2 with a more general statement about damage done by "natural events and processes."

Choice **(D)** is incorrect because the sentence preceding this choice discusses a community's resistance to destruction. This is not a logical place to insert a sentence that specifically elaborates on a different idea.

20. **C** **D** **E** This is a Prose Summary question. It is completed correctly below. The correct choices are C, D, and E. Choices A, B, and F are therefore incorrect.

**Directions:** An introductory sentence for a brief summary of the passage is provided below. Complete the summary by selecting the THREE answer choices that express the most important ideas in the passage. Some sentences do not belong in the summary because they express ideas that are not presented in the passage or are minor ideas in the passage. **This question is worth 2 points.**

**The process of succession and the stability of a climax community can change over time.**

- C  A high degree of species diversity does not always result in a stable ecosystem.
- D  Disagreements over the meaning of the term "stability" make it difficult to identify the most stable ecosystems.
- E  The level of resilience in a plant community contributes to its long-term stability.

### Answer Choices

- [A]  The changes that occur in an ecosystem from the pioneer to the climax community can be seen in one human generation.
- [B]  Ecologists agree that climax communities are the most stable types of ecosystems.
- [C]  A high degree of species diversity does not always result in a stable ecosystem.
- [D]  Disagreements over the meaning of the term "stability" make it difficult to identify the most stable ecosystems.
- [E]  The level of resilience in a plant community contributes to its long-term stability.
- [F]  The resilience of climax communities makes them resistant to destruction caused by humans.

*Correct Choices*

*Choice C*, "A high degree of species diversity does not always result in a stable ecosystem," is correct because it is a main idea that is developed throughout most of the passage. The first three paragraphs introduce and develop the idea that diversity may result in a stable ecosystem. But paragraphs 4, 5, and 7 introduce arguments to support the idea that diversity does not always result in a stable ecosystem.

*Choice D*, "Disagreements over the meaning of the term 'stability' make it difficult to identify the most stable ecosystems," is correct because the key idea that ecosystem stability is difficult to quantify is introduced in paragraph 4 and developed throughout the rest of the passage.

*Choice E*, "The level of resilience in a plant community contributes to its long-term stability," is correct because it mentions one important form of stability that is introduced in paragraph 4 and further developed in paragraph 6 in the discussion of environmental damage caused by humans.

*Incorrect Choices*

*Choice A*, "The changes that occur in an ecosystem from the pioneer to the climax community can be seen in one human generation," is incorrect because paragraph 1 states that a pioneer community alone can change over a period as long as 500 years. Furthermore, a climax community typically changes over a period longer than 500 years.

*Choice B*, "Ecologists agree that climax communities are the most stable types of ecosystems," is incorrect because climax communities are described as unstable at several points in the passage, beginning in paragraph 3. The last sentence of paragraph 4 states that climax communities could be the least stable communities, while sentence 2 in paragraph 5 suggests that successional communities may be more stable than climax communities.

*Choice F*, "The resilience of climax communities makes them resistant to destruction caused by humans," is incorrect because it is a misreading of sentence 1 in paragraph 6. The sentence indicates that ecologists would like to know if resilience could make climax communities resistant to destruction. Climax communities are currently being damaged or destroyed by humans and are not therefore resistant to such destruction.

# Listening

## Answer Key and Self-Scoring Chart

**Directions:** Check your answers against the answer key below. Write the number 1 on the line to the right of each question if you picked the correct answer. Total your points at the bottom of the chart.

| Question Number | Correct Answer | Your Raw Points |
|:---:|:---:|:---:|
| 1. | B | |
| 2. | A, D | |
| 3. | B | |
| 4. | C | |
| 5. | C | |
| 6. | C | |
| 7. | B | |
| 8. | C | |
| 9. | B | |
| 10. | C | |
| 11. | D | |
| 12. | A | |
| 13. | D | |
| 14. | B | |
| 15. | C | |
| 16. | B | |
| 17. | C | |
| 18. | B | |
| 19. | A | |
| 20. | C | |
| 21. | A | |
| 22. | C | |
| 23. | D | |
| 24. | C | |
| 25. | A | |
| 26. | A | |
| 27. | C | |
| 28. | B | |
| **TOTAL:** | | |

Below is a table that converts your Listening section answers into a TOEFL iBT® Listening scaled score. Take the total of raw points from your answer key and find that number in the left-hand column of the table. The right-hand column of the table gives a TOEFL iBT Listening scaled score for each number of raw points. For example, if the total points from your answer key is 27, the table shows a scaled score of 29 to 30.

You should use your score estimate as a general guide only. Your actual score on the TOEFL iBT test may be higher or lower than your score on the practice version.

## Listening

| Raw Point Total | Scaled Score |
|:---:|:---:|
| 28 | 30 |
| 27 | 29–30 |
| 26 | 27–30 |
| 25 | 25–30 |
| 24 | 24–29 |
| 23 | 23–27 |
| 22 | 22–26 |
| 21 | 21–25 |
| 20 | 19–24 |
| 19 | 18–23 |
| 18 | 17–21 |
| 17 | 16–20 |
| 16 | 14–19 |
| 15 | 13–18 |
| 14 | 12–17 |
| 13 | 10–15 |
| 12 | 9–14 |
| 11 | 7–13 |
| 10 | 6–12 |
| 9 | 5–10 |
| 8 | 3–9 |
| 7 | 2–7 |
| 6 | 1–6 |
| 5 | 1–4 |
| 4 | 0–2 |
| 3 | 0–1 |
| 2 | 0 |
| 1 | 0 |
| 0 | 0 |

# Listening Scripts and Answer Explanations

## Questions 1–5

### Track 57 Listening Script

**Narrator**

Listen to a conversation between a student and a supervisor in the university buildings department.

**Buildings Department Supervisor**

When all of this is over, Lynne, I'll be glad to write you a letter of recommendation.

**Female Student**

Can I ask you again in a couple of years? That's probably when I'll start looking . . .

**Buildings Department Supervisor**

Why don't I write something while it's still fresh in my mind, and you can save it for later.

**Female Student**

OK. Thanks. So, which building will I be showing?

**Buildings Department Supervisor**

Buildings. Even though you'll be assigned to just one, each guide for the Green Buildings Tour will have to learn about two buildings. If a guide cancels unexpectedly, you'd first show your group around your building then around the other.

**Female Student**

How do I learn about the buildings?

**Buildings Department Supervisor**

I'll walk you through them and give you written materials. Uh, as you know from the list I e-mailed, visitors will tour all ten sustainable buildings on campus. Eight are older buildings that were retrofitted with a variety of sustainable features, like insulated windows and tanks to harvest rainwater. The other two are new construction. Both were designed to save energy costs. The engineering library was completed last year . . . and Lightstone Dormitory shortly after. Its first residents just moved in.

**Female Student**

Lightstone! Wasn't that constructed with materials salvaged from demolished city buildings?

**Buildings Department Supervisor**

Yeah. And it's totally off the electrical grid—no utility bills! Electricity is generated by solar energy, and with energy from deep under the ground; this geothermal energy provides radiant heat. In fact, the heat-pump technology we use was invented right here at the university. The pump transports and amplifies geothermal heat through a network of pipes beneath the floorboards.

**Female Student**

I learned about radiant heat when I did a project in my architecture class. I could tell visitors how the floor heats objects in the rooms, which then heats the space.

**Buildings Department Supervisor**

Right . . . unlike conventional heating systems, where warm air rises to the ceiling, radiant heat stays lower in the room. So the rooms feel warm even though the thermostat is set at a relatively low temperature. That's the reason we're having this event in winter . . . so people can "feel" how radiant heat works.

**Female Student**

Could you assign me to Lightstone Hall, then?

**Buildings Department Supervisor**

Sure, Lightstone Hall it is.

**Female Student**

Y'know, maybe I could get a bunch of details from the engineer who invented that heat-pump technology.

**Buildings Department Supervisor**

I guess. But remember, each group will walk all over campus, through **ten** buildings . . . and last year, hundreds of people attended these tours.

**Female Student**

Oh . . . right . . . so they can't take too long.

**Buildings Department Supervisor**

Right. So which building would you like to cover if someone cancels?

**Female Student**

How 'bout the fitness center, even though it's not on the list. The treadmills use zero electricity. The user's foot action recharges a battery. And the battery powers a display panel that shows information about your workout.

**Buildings Department Supervisor**

Yes, the treadmills . . . but there's nothing special about the building itself.

**Track 58 Listening Script (Question 5)**

**Narrator**

Listen again to part of the conversation. Then answer the question.

**Female Student**

Y'know, maybe I could get a bunch of details from the engineer who invented that heat-pump technology.

**Buildings Department Supervisor**

I guess. But remember, each group will walk all over campus, through ten buildings . . . and last year, hundreds of people attended these tours.

**Narrator**

Why does the man say this:

**Buildings Department Supervisor**

I guess. But remember, each group will walk all over campus, through ten buildings . . . and last year, hundreds of people attended these tours.

## Answer Explanations

1. **B** This is a Gist-Purpose question. The man asked the woman to meet with him to discuss details about a campus tour for visitors. The woman will be participating as a tour guide, so the correct answer is B. At the beginning of the conversation, the man and woman do discuss a letter of recommendation, but choice C is incorrect because the woman explains that she does not need it right away. In the middle of the conversation, the woman mentions a project she did in an architecture class, but it has been completed, so choice A is incorrect. As part of the campus tour, the visitors will see two new buildings that have just been constructed. The man does not ask the woman for any input about these buildings, however, so choice D is incorrect.

2. **A** **D** This is a Detail question. There are two correct answers, choice A and choice D. Choice A paraphrases the man's description of the unique way that energy is generated in Lightstone Dormitory. Choice D is correct because the man responds in the affirmative when the woman asks whether Lightstone Dormitory was constructed with materials from older buildings that had been demolished. Choice B is incorrect because neither speaker says anything about where Lightstone is located. Choice C is incorrect because the man says that eight older buildings were modified to harvest rainwater, but Lightstone Dormitory is not an older building.

3. **B** This is a Detail question. In the middle of the conversation, the man explains what radiant heat is and how it works. He contrasts radiant heat with conventional heating systems, and then mentions that the tour is taking place in the winter so that visitors can see firsthand how radiant heat works. So choice B is correct. Neither speaker makes a statement about the seasonal availability of tour guides (choice A), about when new construction projects are typically completed (choice C), or about university courses on green design (choice D).

4. **C** This is a Making Inferences question. At the end of the conversation, the woman suggests that the fitness center would make a good choice for a stop on the campus tour. The man does not agree, however, and he implies that the building that houses the fitness center does not have any special sustainability features. Therefore, the correct answer is choice C. The man does acknowledge that the treadmills at the fitness center are sustainable, so choice A is incorrect. There is no discussion about differences among the treadmills (choice B) or buildings visited on previous campus tours (choice D).

5. **C** You are asked to listen again to part of a conversation.

**Female Student**
Y'know, maybe I could get a bunch of details from the engineer who invented that heat-pump technology.

**Buildings Department Supervisor**

I guess. But remember, each group will walk all over campus, through **ten** buildings . . . and last year, hundreds of people attended these tours.

Then you are asked why the man says this:

But remember, each group will walk all over campus, through **ten** buildings . . . and last year, hundreds of people attended these tours.

Like most replay questions, this question requires you to understand the function of what is said. After the woman expresses her wish to collect information from an engineer about the technology used in a campus building, the man points out the number of buildings on the campus tour, as well as the large number of people attending the tours. He is implying that the woman probably won't have enough time to present all this information on her tour. This implication is acknowledged by the woman when she says "Oh . . . right . . . so they can't take too long." So the correct choice is C. The man does not comment on how many tour guides are needed (choice A). He does not say anything about which people will find the information interesting (choice B), nor does he make any sort of prediction about what people on the tour will already know about heat-pump technology (choice D).

# Questions 6–11

## Track 59 Listening Script

**Narrator**

Listen to part of a lecture in an environmental science class.

Environmental Science

## Professor

Now, we've been talking about the loss of animal habitat from housing developments, um, growing cities . . . small habitat losses. But today I want to begin talking about what happens when habitat is reduced across a large area. There are, of course, animal species that require large areas of habitat . . . and, um, some migrate over very long distances. So what's the impact of habitat loss on those animals? Animals that need large areas of habitat?

Well, I'll use the hummingbirds as an example. Now, you know a hummingbird is amazingly small. But even though it's really tiny, it migrates over very long distances . . . travels up and down the Western Hemisphere . . . the Americas . . . back and forth between where it breeds in the summer and the warmer climates where it spends the winter. So we would say that this whole area over which it migrates is its habitat, because on this long-distance journey, it needs to come down to feed and sleep every so often, right?

Well, the hummingbird beats its wings—get this—about 3,000 times per minute. So you think, wow, it must need a lot of energy, a lot of food, right? Well, it does—it drinks a lot of nectar from flowers and feeds on some insects—but it's energy-efficient, too. You can't say it isn't. I mean as it flies all the way across the Gulf of Mexico, it uses up almost none of its body fat. But that doesn't mean it doesn't need to eat! So hummingbirds have to rely on plants in their natural habitat. And it goes without saying, but . . . well, the opposite is true as well. Plants depend on hummingbirds too. There are some flowers that can only be pollinated by the hummingbird. Without it stopping to feed and spreading pollen from flower to flower, these plants would cease to exist!

But the problem, well . . . as natural habitat along these migration routes is developed by humans for housing or agriculture, or, um, cleared for raising cattle, for instance . . . there's less food available for migrating hummingbirds. Their nesting sites are affected, too . . . the same . . . by the same sorts of human activities. And all of these activities pose a real threat to the hummingbird population.

So, to help them survive, we need to preserve their habitats . . . And one of the concrete ways people have been doing this is by cleaning up polluted habitat areas . . . and then replanting flowers, uh, replanting native flowers that hummingbirds feed on. Promoting ecological tourism is another way to help save their habitat. As the number of visitors—ecotourists who come to hummingbird habitats to watch the birds—the more the number of visitors grows, the more local businesses profit. So ecological tourism can bring financial rewards. All the more reason to value these beautiful little creatures and their habitat, right?

But to understand more about how to protect and support hummingbirds the best we can, we've gotta learn more about their breeding . . . nesting . . . sites and, uh, migration routes—and also about the natural habitats we find there. That should help us determine how to prevent further decline in the population.

A good research method . . . a good way to learn more . . . is by, um, running a banding study. Banding the birds allows us to track them over their lifetime. It's a practice that's been used by researchers for years. In fact, most of what we know about hummingbirds comes from banding studies . . . where we, uh, capture a hummingbird and make sure all the information about it—like . . . its weight and, um, age and length—are all recorded . . . put into international . . . an international information database. And, then we place an extremely lightweight band around one of its legs . . . well, what looks like a leg—although, technically it's considered part of the bird's foot. Anyway, these bands are perfectly safe. And some hummingbirds have worn them for years with no evidence of any problems. The band is labeled with a tracking number . . . oh, and there's a phone number on the band for people to call, for free, to report a banded bird they've found or recaptured.

So when a banded bird is recaptured and reported, we learn about its migration route, its growth . . . and how long it's been alive . . . its life span. One recaptured bird had been banded almost 12 years earlier! She's one of the oldest hummingbirds on record.

Another interesting thing we've learned is . . . that some hummingbirds, uh, they no longer use a certain route; they travel by a different route to reach their destination. And findings like these have been of interest to biologists and environmental scientists in a number of countries, who are trying to understand the complexities of how changes in a habitat . . . affect the species in it—species like the hummingbirds.

## Track 60 Listening Script (Question 11)

**Narrator**

Listen again to part of the lecture. Then answer the question.

**Professor**

So hummingbirds have to rely on plants in their natural habitat. And it goes without saying, but . . . well, the opposite is true as well. Plants depend on hummingbirds too.

**Narrator**

What does the professor imply when she says this:

**Professor**

And it goes without saying

## Answer Explanations

6. **C** This is a Gist-Content question. After the professor establishes loss of wildlife habitat as the general topic, she turns to the hummingbird's migratory routes as an extended example of the potential impact of losing large habitats and efforts being made to reverse this trend. Thus choice C is the correct answer. Changes in the migratory patterns of hummingbirds (choice A) are discussed only briefly at the end of the lecture as an interesting finding. The adaptation of hummingbirds to urban environments (choice B) is not mentioned at all. Ecotourism (choice D) is mentioned only in passing, as one of a number of ways to preserve habitats.

7. **B** This is a Making Inferences question. Choice B is the correct answer. The professor explains how land along hummingbird migration routes is being used in farming and cattle raising, among other things. She points out that these activities reduce food availability for hummingbirds and affect their nesting sites. In saying that these human activities all "pose a real threat to the hummingbird population," she implies a potential decrease in the population if more land is used this way.

8. **C** This is a Detail question. The professor explicitly states that people have been trying to preserve hummingbird habitats by cleaning up polluted areas and then planting native flowers for the birds to feed on. Thus choice C is the correct answer. Building feeding stations (choice A), punishing polluters (choice B), and identifying various species (choice D) are also things that people could conceivably do to help hummingbirds survive, but the professor does not mention any of them.

9. **B** This is another Detail question. Choice B is correct. The professor describes a research study designed to collect information about hummingbird migration. This research involves placing lightweight bands on hummingbirds. Information is collected when people who find or recapture the hummingbirds use the phone number on the band to contact the researchers. The study does not involve radio tracking devices (choice A), counting yearly returns by birds to the same region (choice C), or comparing the migration routes of old and young birds (choice D).

10. **C** This is a Connecting Content question. A research finding mentioned at the end of the lecture is that some hummingbirds have stopped using certain routes "to reach their destination." Since the destinations the professor is referring to are migration destinations, she is implying that for some hummingbirds, a change in migration patterns has occurred. Choice C is therefore the correct answer. The other answer choices consist of specific statements concerning habitats (choice A), preservation efforts (choice B), and food sources (choice D); nothing the professor says in the lecture supports these specific statements.

11. **D** You are asked to listen again to this part of the lecture:

So hummingbirds have to rely on plants in their natural habitat. And it goes without saying, but . . . well, the opposite is true as well. Plants depend on hummingbirds too.

You are then asked what the professor implies when she says this:

And it goes without saying . . .

This question requires you to Understand the Function of What Is Said. Choice D is the correct answer. "It goes without saying" is a common phrase used by speakers to signal that they are about to say (or have just said) something that probably does not need to be said because it is very obvious. The other answer choices are all potential misunderstandings of this phrase.

# Questions 12–17

### Track 61 Listening Script

### Narrator
Listen to part of a lecture in a film history class.

Film History

### Professor
Okay, we've been discussing film in the 1920s and '30s, and, ah, how back then, film categories as we know them today had not yet been established. We, ah, said that, by today's standards, many of the films of the '20s and '30s would be considered "hybrids"; that is, a mixture of styles that wouldn't exactly fit into any of today's categories. And in that context, today we're going to talk about a, a filmmaker who began making very unique films in the late 1920s. He was French, and his name was Jean Painlevé.

Jean Painlevé

Jean Painlevé was born in 1902. He made his first film in 1928. Now, in a way, Painlevé's films conform to norms of the '20s and '30s; that is, they don't fit very neatly into the categories we use to classify films today. That said, even by the standards of the '20s and '30s, Painlevé's films were a unique hybrid of styles. He had a special way of fusing—or, or some people might say confusing—science and fiction; his films begin with facts, but then they become more and more fictional—they gradually add more and more fictional elements. In fact, Painlevé was known for saying that "science is fiction."

Painlevé was a, a pioneer in underwater filmmaking, and a lot of his short films focus on the aquatic animal world. He liked to show small underwater creatures displaying what seemed like familiar human characteristics—what we think of as unique to humans. He might take a, a clip of a mollusk going up and down in the water and set it to music—you know, to make it look as if the mollusk were dancing to the music like a human being. That sort of thing. But then he'd suddenly change the image or narration to remind us how different the animals are, how unlike humans. He confused his audience in the way he portrayed the animals he filmed, mixing up our notions of the categories "human" and "animal." The films make us a little uncomfortable at times because we're uncertain about what we're seeing. It gives his films an uncanny feature . . . the familiar made unfamiliar, the normal made suspicious. He liked twists; he liked the unusual. In fact, one of his favorite sea animals was the sea horse because with sea horses, it's the male that gets pregnant, it's the male that carries the babies. And he thought that was great. His first and most celebrated underwater film is about the sea horse.

Susan? You have a question?

**Female Student**

But underwater filmmaking wasn't that unusual, was it? I mean weren't there other people making movies underwater?

**Professor**

Well, actually it was pretty rare at that time. I mean we're talking the early 1930s here.

**Female Student**

But what about Jacques Cousteau? Wasn't he, like, an innovator, you know, with underwater photography, too?

**Professor**

Ah, Jacques Cousteau. Well, Painlevé and Cousteau did both film underwater, and they were both innovators, so you're right in that sense, but that's pretty much where the similarities end. First of all, Painlevé was about 20 years ahead of Cousteau . . . Um, and Cousteau's adventures were high-tech, with lots of fancy equipment, whereas Painlevé kind of patched equipment together as he needed it . . . Uh, Cousteau usually filmed large animals, usually in the open sea, whereas Painlevé generally filmed smaller animals, and, and he liked to film in shallow water . . . Uh, what else? Well, the main difference was that Cousteau simply investigated and presented the facts; he, he didn't mix in fiction. He was a strict documentarist; he set the standard, really, for the nature documentary. Painlevé, on the other hand, as we said before, mixed in elements of fiction, and his films are much more artistic, incorporating music as an important element.

John, you have a question?

**Male Student**

Well, maybe I shouldn't be asking this . . . Uh, but if Painlevé's films are so special, so good, why haven't we ever heard of them? I mean everyone's heard of Jacques Cousteau . . .

**Professor**

Well, that's a fair question. Uh, the short answer is that Painlevé's style just never caught on with the general public. I mean it probably goes back, at least in part, to what we mentioned earlier, that, that people didn't know what to make of his films, that they were confused by them. Whereas Cousteau's documentaries were very straightforward, uh, met people's expectations more than Painlevé's films did. But your true film-history buffs know about him, and Painlevé's still highly respected in many circles.

## Track 62 Listening Script (Question 17)

**Narrator**

What does the student imply when he says this:

**Male Student**

Well, maybe I shouldn't be asking this . . . Uh, but if Painlevé's films are so special, so good, why haven't we ever heard of them? I mean everyone's heard of Jacques Cousteau . . .

## Answer Explanations

12. **A** This is a Gist-Purpose question. The correct answer is choice A. The professor begins the lecture by briefly reviewing a previous discussion about films of the 1920s and 1930s and their hybrid style. Then he turns to a discussion of the style of one particular filmmaker, Jean Painlevé, and spends the rest of the lecture talking about him and his films.

13. **D** This is a Connecting Content question. Choice D is the correct answer. Identifying it requires integrating two important pieces of information. The first is the professor's statement at the beginning of the lecture that films from the 1920s and '30s do not fit neatly into today's film categories. The second piece of information comes right afterward, when the professor says that "Painlevé's films conform to norms of the '20s and '30s," meaning that his films, too, are difficult to categorize.

14. **B** This is a Detail question. The professor discusses the confusing aspects of Painlevé's films at considerable length and focuses, in particular, on the way Painlevé mixes up the audience's notions of human and animal characteristics. Thus the correct answer is choice B.

15. **C** This is an Understanding Organization question. The reason that the professor discusses sea horses is to illustrate the unusualness of Painlevé's subject matter. Painlevé's first film was about sea horses, which are unusual because the males carry the babies. Choice C is therefore the correct answer.

16. **B** This is another Connecting Content question. The professor compares the film styles of Jacques Cousteau and Painlevé in response to an objection raised by the female student. She questions the professor's characterization of Painlevé's films as special and points out that other filmmakers, like Cousteau, also made underwater films. The professor emphasizes the uniqueness of Painlevé's films by explaining that Cousteau's films were straightforward, fact-based documentaries that met people's expectations, unlike Painlevé's films, which mixed fact with fiction in a way that was both unique and confusing. Thus choice B is the correct answer.

17. **C** You are asked to decide what the student is implying when he says this:

> Well, maybe I shouldn't be asking this . . . Uh, but if Painlevé's films are so special, so good, why haven't we ever heard of them? I mean everyone's heard of Jacques Cousteau . . .

This question requires you to Understand the Function of What Is Said. After listening to what the professor has been saying about Painlevé's films, the student cannot understand why they are not more popular or better known. The student's replayed statement suggests that he believes that Painlevé's films deserve the same level of recognition that Cousteau's films have received. Thus choice C is the correct answer.

## Questions 18–22

Track 63 Listening Script

**Narrator**

Listen to a conversation between a student and a professor.

**Male Student**

Hi, Professor Archer. You know how in class last week you said that you were looking for students who were interested in volunteering for your archaeology project?

**Professor**

Of course. Are you volunteering?

**Male Student**

Yes, I am. It sounds really interesting. But, ummm, do I need to have any experience with these kinds of projects?

**Professor**

No, not really. I assume that most students taking the introductory-level class will have little or no experience with archaeological research, but that's OK.

**Male Student**

Oh, good—that's a relief. Actually, that's why I'm volunteering for the project—to get experience. What kind of work is it?

**Professor**

Well, as you know, we're studying the history of the campus this semester. This used to be an agricultural area, and we already know that where the main lecture hall now stands there once were a farmhouse and barn that were erected in the late 1700s. We're excavating near the lecture hall to see what types of artifacts we find—you know, things people used in the past that got buried when the campus was constructed. We've already begun to find some very interesting items like, um, old bottles, buttons, pieces of clay pottery . . .

**Male Student**

Buttons and clay pottery? Did the old owners leave in such a hurry that they left their clothes and dishes behind?

**Professor**

That's just one of the questions we hope to answer with this project.

**Male Student**

Wow—and it's all right here on campus . . .

**Professor**

That's right, no traveling involved. I wouldn't expect volunteers to travel to a site, especially in the middle of the semester. We expect to find many more things, but we do need more people to help.

**Male Student**

So . . . how many student volunteers are you looking for?

**Professor**

I'm hoping to get five or six. I've asked for volunteers in all the classes I teach, but no one's responded. You're the first person to express interest.

**Male Student**

Uh . . . sounds like it could be a lot of work. Is there . . . umm . . . is there any way I can use the experience to get some extra credit in class? I mean can I write a paper about it?

**Professor**

I think it'll depend on what type of work you do in the excavation, but I imagine we can arrange something. Well, actually, I've been considering offering extra credit for class because I've been having a tough time getting volunteers . . . Extra credit is always a good incentive for students.

**Male Student**

And . . . how often would you want the volunteers to work?

**Professor**

We're asking for three or four hours per week, depending on your schedule. A senior researcher—I think you know John Franklin, my assistant—is on-site every day.

**Male Student**

Sure, I know John. By the way, will there be some sort of training?

**Professor**

Yes, uh, I wanna wait till Friday to see how many students volunteer. And then I'll schedule a training class next week at a time that's convenient for everyone.

**Male Student**

OK, I'll wait to hear from you. Thanks a lot for accepting me!

## Answer Explanations

18. **B** This is a Gist-Purpose question. The correct answer is choice B. The student opens the conversation by asking the professor about her request for volunteers for an archaeology project. The project's timing—the middle of the semester—is mentioned later, when the professor says that she would not expect students to travel to a site in the middle of the semester. Choosing the correct answer thus requires the integration of these two pieces of information from different parts of the conversation. Choice A is incorrect because the project is voluntary, not an assignment. It takes place during the semester, not during the summer (choice C). Although the student asks about extra credit, presumably to improve his grade (choice D), he brings this up as an afterthought, when he hears how much work is involved.

19. **A** This is a Detail question. The professor states that the lecture hall was built where a farmhouse and barn from the 1700s once stood. Thus choice A is correct. Pottery (choice B), clothes (choice C), and bottles (choice D) are mentioned in the context of artifacts—items that may have belonged to the farm's owners.

20. **C** This is a Detail question. The on-campus location of the project is mentioned several times during the conversation, and both speakers cite this as an advantage: volunteers will not need to travel. Thus choice C is correct.

21. **A** This is another Detail question. Choice A is correct. When the student asks if he could earn extra credit for volunteering, the professor responds by pointing out that she is considering offering extra credit as an incentive for more students to volunteer. The other three choices could be plausible incentives as well, but the professor does not mention any of them as a way to get more volunteers.

22. **C** This is a Connecting Content question. When the student asks about training, the professor notes that she has not scheduled a specific time for it, and he responds that he will wait to hear from her. Choice C is therefore the correct answer. The professor already provided the name of the senior researcher (choice A), so this is not information the student still needs. Books (choice B) are not mentioned at all in the conversation. As for the project's location (choice D), this is information the student was given early on.

## Questions 23–28

### Track 64 Listening Script

**Narrator**

Listen to part of a lecture in an art history class.

**Professor**

We've talked a lot in this course about still lifes. And I guess if there's one thing you thought it was safe to assume about still lifes, it'd probably be that they're depictions of things that are . . . still, right? A bowl of fruit, a vase of flowers, a stack of books. But today we're gonna look at some modern-day artists who are innovating with still lifes. In fact, some of them are even taking the still—out—of still lifes!

Now, still lifes are scarce in the contemporary art scene, but some artists are looking for ways to make them new for a contemporary audience. For example, historically we think of still lifes as paintings. But more and more, artists are employing nonpaint media like photography, digital art, even animation.

Now animation doesn't sound like a likely medium for a still life, but one pair of contemporary artists is using it. What they've done is make an exact replica of a painting by the still life painter Ambrosius Bosschaert the Elder.

Bosschaert was a seventeenth-century Dutch painter known for his still lifes of rare, exotic flowers. Here, take a look at this piece.

At the time this was originally painted, there was a national obsession in the Netherlands with flowers—especially tulips, which had only recently begun to be imported from Turkey and were still considered exotic. But Bosschaert mainly specialized in painting lots of rare and expensive flowers together in a single, dazzling bouquet. It was irrelevant to him whether these flowers could be assembled together in real life—often they couldn't, because they bloomed at different times of the year. But, who cares, right? The imaginary bouquets made a great picture.

OK, so a pair of contemporary artists—Rob and Nick Carter—recently decided to reproduce this particular painting.

Rob and Nick Carter

The Carters worked with a crew of animators to make a three-hour digitalized film that brings the painting to life. When you see their piece in an art gallery, you actually watch it on a computer screen that's been placed in a wooden frame like a painting would be. And if you watch closely, you'll realize that ever so slowly, elements of the composition change. Clouds pass by. Caterpillars eat the leaves of the flowers. The light changes from dawn to daylight, to evening to nighttime. During the dark of night, the video loops and starts back over.

It's interesting; we know that a viewer at an art gallery will look at an artwork for an average of about six seconds. One of the things the artists said about creating this piece was that they really wanted people to . . . slow down and look. And it seems to have worked. When you're at a gallery with one of these animated paintings, you'll see people watching it for a long time. They want to catch something changing in the picture. Kids, even, will watch for a long time.

A moving still life may seem nontraditional, but the artists have created quite a lot of continuity with the original painting. Bosschaert—because of the flowers he wanted in his compositions—employed hundreds of people in his studio to observe and draw flowers at all different times of year. They drew them at different times of day, from different angles . . . And then Bosschaert would work from their sketches to produce his paintings. He was meticulous about realism. Same with the Carters. They took lots of video of real flowers—in different lighting, opening and closing—and then they employed 25 animators to watch these videos and digitally paint each flower in a way that's true to life. Their animated video took several years to produce, but it really preserves Bosschaert's emphasis on realism.

Now, of course, there are some . . . issues introduced into the work because it's ani-mated. I mentioned caterpillars eating the leaves, but . . . like I said, the video loops. So . . . what do you do about these chewed-up leaves? The artists had to be kind of clever about it. At the end of the video, during the nighttime period, the wind begins to blow. The leaves turn horizontal in the wind, so you're looking at them from the side and can't see the holes. When the wind stops and the leaves return to their original positions, the caterpillars' holes have been refilled.

Now, all of this might offend purists who would argue that the Carters have ruined Bosschaert's work by animating it. But for me the artists' thorough, careful treatment of Bosschaert's painting ultimately draws attention to the mastery of the original.

## Answer Explanations

23. **D** This is a Gist-Content question. For the majority of the lecture, the pro-fessor describes one way that a traditional art form, the still life, has been updated for a modern-day audience. Therefore, the correct choice is D. There is some discussion of a painting by Dutch artist Ambrosius Bosschaert, but it does not make up the majority of the lecture and his method isn't thoroughly discussed, so choice A is incorrect. The professor does mention that still lifes are not common in modern day art, but he does not elaborate on why this is the case, so choice B is incorrect. Lastly, there is no discussion of a new dis-covery related to Bosschaert's painting, so choice C is incorrect.

24. **C** This is a Detail question. Near the beginning of the lecture, the professor mentions that it was not important to Bosschaert if a certain collection of flowers could actually exist in real life. The professor provides an example of this when he mentions that often the flowers in Bosschaert's paintings were not in season at the same time, so the correct answer is choice C. There is no mention of the toxicity of flowers (choice B) or the price of certain collections of flowers (choice D). Also, the professor does not discuss where the flowers in Bosschaert's painting grow, so choice A is incorrect.

25. **A** This is an Understanding Organization question. The professor empha-sizes the fact that the Carters' animation is best experienced by people who spend a considerable amount of time watching it. He then mentions that most people only spend about six seconds looking at any given work of art. This illustrates the motivation behind the Carters' piece of art, so choice A is the correct answer. The professor does discuss one hurdle involved with the animation project related to the video loop, but this is in a different part of the lecture, so choice B is incorrect. There is no discussion of the evolution of still lifes over time (choice C) or children's assessments of the Carters' piece (choice D).

26. **A** This is an Understanding Organization question. The professor describes how, in order to make his paintings realistic, Bosschaert worked with hun-dreds of artists who produced artworks that captured flowers from different seasons, times of day, and angles. He then points out that the Carters were

also concerned with realism and they took lots of video of real flowers, so the correct answer is choice A. The professor does not state that technology can take the place of artistic ability, so choice B is incorrect. There is no mention of whether the Carters' work could be categorized as a still life, so choice C is incorrect. The Carters' use of technology (video) is elaborated on, but the extent to which technology can improve an artistic process is not mentioned, so choice D is incorrect.

27. **C** This is a Detail question. Near the end of the lecture, the professor describes some issues involved in producing the animated video. He mentions that the video loops and starts over again, and this forced the artists to consider the continuity of the video. In particular, leaves that appeared damaged at the end of the video needed to appear undamaged when the video began again. The artists used wind to make that transition seem natural, so choice C is the correct answer. In this section of the lecture, there is no discussion of realism in the video, so choice A is incorrect. The professor does not mention the viewers' level of interest or the destructive power of nature, so choice B and choice D are incorrect.

28. **B** This question requires you to Understand the Speaker's attitude. You are asked to identify an opinion that is expressed by the professor. At the end of the lecture, the professor expresses his opinion that the Carters' animated video illustrates the quality of Bosschaert's bouquet painting, so the correct answer is choice B. There is no mention of Bosschaert's reputation being hurt, so choice A is incorrect. The professor also does not discuss the idea that the Carters' work lacks familiarity with still lifes, nor is there any sort of judgment made between their work and other animation videos of still lifes, so choice C and choice D are incorrect.

# Speaking

## Listening Scripts, Important Points, and Sample Responses with Rater Comments

Use the Speaking rubrics on pages 184–187 to see how responses are scored. The raters who listen to your responses will analyze them in three general categories. These categories are Delivery, Language Use, and Topic Development. All three categories have equal importance.

This section includes important points that should be covered when answering each question. All of these points must be present in a response in order for it to receive the highest score in the Topic Development category. These important points are guides to the kind of information raters expect to hear in a high-level response.

This section also refers to example responses on the accompanying audio tracks. Some responses were scored at the highest level, while others were not. The responses are followed by explanations of their scores.

### Question 1: Paired Choice

#### Track 65 Listening Script

**Narrator**

Some students prefer to work on class assignments by themselves. Others believe it is better to work in a group. Which do you prefer? Explain why.

> **Preparation Time: 15 Seconds**
> **Response Time: 45 Seconds**

#### Important Points

In this question, you need to say whether you prefer to work alone or in groups to complete class assignments and then explain the reason for your preference. You should not simply give a list of reasons, such as *"I prefer to work in groups because it is more interesting plus many people help and also you can learn from other people . . ."* It is better if you develop one or two reasons fully. For example, if you prefer to work in groups, you could say, *"I prefer working in groups because usually in group work, different people know different things about the topic, and because of that, you get a deeper understanding of the assignment. For example, there was a student from Venezuela in a group assignment I had, and we were supposed to describe how crude oil prices are set. She helped us understand problems in oil production in a much deeper way because her parents worked in oil production."*

### Sample Responses

***Play Track 70 to hear a high-level response for Question 1.***

*Rater Comments*

This is a fully developed response to the question. She gives two reasons for preferring to work by herself—having strong opinions and managing time well—and gives a clear explanation of why each is more suitable for working alone. Her speech is fluent, and she uses appropriate intonation and stress on certain words (such as "I" in "the way I see them") to convey meaning. She uses advanced-level vocabulary, such as "a structured approach," and high-level grammatical constructions with ease.

***Play Track 71 to hear a low-level response for Question 1.***

*Rater Comments*

While her pronunciation is clear, this speaker struggles and often fails to come up with words to express her meaning, such as using "good things" rather than the more appropriate and specific "advantages" or "benefits." Since she spends time trying to describe benefits of both group work and working alone, she runs out of time before she can support her true preference for working alone, other than saying it allows more independence. Her answer is very choppy and vague. She does not demonstrate that she has command of grammar beyond a very basic level.

## Question 2: Fit and Explain

### Track 66 Listening Script

**Narrator**

The university's Dining Services Department has announced a change. Read an announcement about this change. You will have 45 seconds to read the announcement. Begin reading now.

**Reading Time: 45 Seconds**

---

**Hot Breakfasts Eliminated**

Beginning next month, Dining Services will no longer serve hot breakfast foods at university dining halls. Instead, students will be offered a wide assortment of cold breakfast items in the morning. These cold breakfast foods, such as breads, fruit, and yogurt, are healthier than many of the hot breakfast items that we will stop serving, so health-conscious students should welcome this change. Students will benefit in another way as well, because limiting the breakfast selection to cold food items will save money and allow us to keep our meal plans affordable.

---

**Narrator**

Now listen to two students discussing the announcement.

**Woman**

Do you believe any of this? It's ridiculous.

**Man**

What do you mean? It is important to eat healthy foods . . .

**Woman**

Sure it is, but they're saying yogurt's better for you than an omelet . . . or than hot cereal? I mean whether something's hot or cold, that shouldn't be the issue. Except maybe on a really cold morning, but in that case, which is going to be better for you—a bowl of cold cereal or a nice warm omelet? It's obvious; there's no question.

**Man**

I'm not going to argue with you there.

**Woman**

And this whole thing about saving money . . .

**Man**

What about it?

**Woman**

Well, they're actually going to make things worse for us, not better. 'Cause if they start cutting back and we can't get what we want right here, on campus, well, we're going to be going off campus and pay off-campus prices, and you know what? That will be expensive. Even if it's only two or three mornings a week, it can add up.

**Narrator**

The woman expresses her opinion of the change that has been announced. State her opinion and explain her reasons for holding that opinion.

| Preparation Time: 30 Seconds |
| Response Time: 60 Seconds |

## Important Points

The woman does not think that Dining Services should stop providing hot breakfast foods. She says that for health, the temperature of the food is not the issue (except on cold days, when warm food is better). She also says that the change will not make breakfasts more affordable, but rather will make them more expensive, since students will have to go off campus (where the prices are higher) to buy the food they want.

## Sample Responses

### Play Track 72 to hear a high-level response for Question 2.

*Rater Comments*

This response covers all the key points of the article and conversation with great clarity and supporting details. The speaker's pronunciation is very clear, and he uses good rhythm and intonation. He uses a good variety of vocabulary and idiomatic expressions that help him express his meaning clearly.

### Play Track 73 to hear a mid-level response for Question 2.

*Rater Comments*

This speaker does a fairly good job of explaining the woman's disagreement with the proposal in the article, but her speech is very choppy (not fluent). She has to pause often to think of the correct word or phrase to say. Sometimes her limited vocabulary prevents her from clearly expressing what she means (for example, the meaning of "the offer is their last offer for choosing" is unclear). Her pronunciation is generally easy to understand but occasionally requires listener effort.

# Question 3: General/Specific

## Track 67 Listening Script

### Narrator

Read the passage from a sociology textbook. You have 50 seconds to read the passage. Begin reading now.

| Reading Time: 50 Seconds |
| :---: |

---

**Cognitive Dissonance**

Individuals sometimes experience a contradiction between their actions and their beliefs—between what they are doing and what they believe they should be doing. These contradictions can cause a kind of mental discomfort known as *cognitive dissonance*. People experiencing cognitive dissonance often do not want to change the way they are acting, so they resolve the contradictory situation in another way: they change their interpretation of the situation in a way that minimizes the contradiction between what they are doing and what they believe they should be doing.

---

**Narrator**

Now listen to part of a lecture about this topic in a sociology class.

**Professor**

This is a true story—from my own life. In my first year in high school, I was addicted to video games. I played them all the time, and I wasn't studying enough—I was failing chemistry; that was my hardest class. So this was a conflict for me because I wanted a good job when I grew up, and I believed—I knew—that if you want a good career, you gotta do well in school. But . . . I just couldn't give up video games.

I was completely torn. And my solution was to . . . to change my perspective. See, the only class I was doing really badly in was chemistry. In the others I was, I was okay. So I asked myself if I wanted to be a chemist when I grew up, and the fact is I didn't. I was pretty sure I wanted to be a sociologist. So . . . I told myself my chemistry class didn't matter because sociologists don't really need to know chemistry. In other words, I changed my understanding of what it meant to do well in school. I reinterpreted my situation: I used to think that doing well in school meant doing well in all my classes, but now I decided that succeeding in school meant only doing well in the classes that related directly to my future career.

I eliminated the conflict, at least in my mind.

**Narrator**

Using the example discussed by the professor, explain what cognitive dissonance is and how people often deal with it.

| Preparation Time: 30 Seconds |
| Response Time: 60 Seconds |

## Important Points

Cognitive dissonance occurs when people's beliefs and actions are in conflict with each other. People deal with cognitive dissonance by changing their interpretation of the situation. For example, the professor could not stop playing video games even though he believed it was causing him to fail chemistry. He then told himself that since he wanted to be a sociologist, he did not need to do well in chemistry.

## Sample Responses

***Play Track 74 to hear a high-level response for Question 3.***

*Rater Comments*

This speaker efficiently and accurately explains the concept of cognitive dissonance and how people deal with it, as in the professor's example. Her speech is fluid, and she uses intonation and stress effectively to convey emphasis and meaning—for example, by stressing the words "actions" and "interpretation" as a contrast to demonstrate how people deal with cognitive dissonance (by changing their interpretation of a situation rather than their actions). She uses advanced-level vocabulary with accuracy and ease.

*Play Track 75 to hear a mid-level response for Question 3.*

*Rater Comments*

In this response, the speaker conveys the relevant information in the task, but not always with precision. For instance, when describing the professor's example, instead of saying the professor changed his "interpretation" of the situation, she says he began to "make up his own opinion." Her pronunciation is clear, but her speech is marked by many pauses and hesitations.

## Question 4: Summary

### Track 68 Listening Script

**Narrator**

Now listen to part of a lecture in a psychology class. The professor is discussing advertising strategies.

**Professor**

In advertising, various strategies are used to persuade people to buy products. In order to sell more products, advertisers will often try to make us believe that a product will meet our needs or desires perfectly . . . even if it's not true. The strategies they use can be subtle, uh, "friendly" forms of persuasion that are sometimes hard to recognize.

In a lot of ads, repetition is a key strategy. Research shows that repeated exposure to a message, even something meaningless or untrue, is enough to make people accept it or see it in a positive light. You've all seen the car commercials on TV . . . like . . . uh, the one that refers to its "roomy" cars . . . over and over again. You know which one I mean . . . this guy is driving around and he keeps stopping to pick up different people—he picks up 3 or 4 people. And each time, the narrator says, "Plenty of room for friends, plenty of room for family, plenty of room for everybody." The same message is repeated several times in the course of the commercial. Now, the car, uh, the car actually looks kind of small . . . it's not a very big car at all, but you get the sense that it's pretty spacious. You'd think that the viewer would reach the logical conclusion that the slogan, uh, misrepresents the product. Instead, what usually happens is that when the statement "plenty of room" is repeated often enough, people are actually convinced it's true.

Um, another strategy they use is to get a celebrity to advertise a product. It turns out that we're more likely to accept an advertising claim made by somebody famous—a person we admire and find appealing. We tend to think they're trustworthy. So . . . um, you might have a car commercial that features a well-known race car driver. Now, it may not be a very fast car—uh, it could even be an inexpensive vehicle with a low performance rating. But if a popular race car driver is shown driving it, and saying, "I like my cars fast!" then people will believe the car is impressive for its speed.

**Narrator**

Using the examples from the talk, explain how persuasive strategies are used in advertising.

| Preparation Time: 20 Seconds |
| --- |
| Response Time: 60 Seconds |

## Important Points

Advertisers persuade people to buy their products by using persuasive strategies. One strategy is repetition of information (which may not be true information), such as when an advertisement for a small car keeps repeating that it has plenty of room. Another strategy is to use celebrities, because people trust them. For example, a famous race car driver might be used in an advertisement for a car (to give the impression the car is fast, even if it is not).

## Sample Responses

### Play Track 76 to hear a high-level response for Question 4.

*Rater Comments*

The speaker conveys all of the main and supporting points from the lecture. His speech is clear and fluid, and although he does not pronounce "subtle" correctly, this is a minor error that does not interfere with overall understanding of his speech. His pacing slows down at times as he attempts to recall information, but it is still easy to follow what he is saying. He also uses a variety of advanced-level vocabulary and grammatical constructions with good control.

### Play Track 77 to hear a mid-level response for Question 4.

*Rater Comments*

This speaker discusses both advertising strategies described in the lecture, but in a vague way that is sometimes difficult to understand. For instance, he never mentions that the first example refers to a car advertisement, so it is unclear what he means when he says the message that "lots of your friends have space in it" is repeated. His pronunciation is easy to understand, but he pauses frequently throughout his response and demonstrates only a limited vocabulary range and control of grammar.

# Writing

## Listening Script, Topic Notes, and Sample Responses with Rater Comments

Use the Writing rubrics on pages 199–200 and 210–211 to see how responses are scored.

### Integrated Writing

#### Track 69 Listening Script

**Narrator**

Now listen to part of a lecture on the topic you just read about.

**Professor**

Everything you just read about *Portrait of an Elderly Woman in a White Bonnet* is true, and yet, after a thorough reexamination of the painting, a panel of experts has recently concluded that it's indeed a work by Rembrandt. And here's why.

First, the fur collar. X-rays and analysis of the pigments in the paint have shown that the fur collar wasn't part of the original painting. The fur collar was painted over the top of the original painting about a hundred years after the painting was made. Why? Someone probably wanted to increase the value of the painting by making it look like a formal portrait of an aristocratic lady.

Second, the supposed error with light and shadow. Once the paint of the added fur collar was removed, the original painting could be seen. In the original painting the woman is wearing a simple collar of light-colored cloth. The light-colored cloth of this collar reflects light that illuminates part of the woman's face. That's why the face is not in partial shadow. So in the original painting, light and shadow are very realistic and just what we would expect from Rembrandt.

Finally, the wood panel. It turns out that when the fur collar was added, the wood panel was also enlarged with extra wood pieces glued to the sides and the top to make the painting more grand—and more valuable. So the original painting is actually painted on a single piece of wood—as would be expected from a Rembrandt painting. And in fact, researchers have found that the piece of wood in the original form of *Portrait of an Elderly Woman in a White Bonnet* is from the very same tree as the wood panel used for another painting by Rembrandt, his *Self-Portrait with a Hat*.

**Narrator**

Summarize the points made in the lecture, being sure to explain how they answer the specific problems presented in the reading passage.

## Topic Notes

You should understand the reasons presented in the lecture that address the concerns in the reading passage. While the reading passage explains why people do not think the painting *Portrait of an Elderly Woman in a White Bonnet* was created by Rembrandt, the lecture presents new evidence showing that the painting was indeed created by Rembrandt.

A high-scoring essay will include the following points made by the lecturer and will explain how they address the points made in the reading passage:

| Point Made in the Reading Passage | Contrasting Point from the Lecture |
|---|---|
| The fur collar in the painting does not match clothing typical of a servant, a detail that Rembrandt would not have overlooked. | The fur collar was added later in an attempt to increase the painting's value. |
| The light and shadow appear incorrectly in the painting, but Rembrandt was a master of painting light and shadow. | The light and shadow appeared incorrectly because of the fur collar that was added later. Once the fur collar was removed, revealing the original white collar, the light and shadow appeared correctly. |
| The portrait was painted on multiple wood panels, which was not typical of Rembrandt's works. | The original was painted on a single wood panel. Additional wood panels were added to the painting later in an attempt to increase its value. |

Responses scoring 4 and 5 discuss and connect the points and the counterpoints in the table while adding all the important supporting details mentioned by the lecturer. The table above includes the main lecture points but may not include all the important supporting details.

## Sample Responses with Rater Comments

*High-Level Response*

Both texts deal with the question wheather or not the painting "Portrait of an Elderly Woman in a White Bonnet" was painted by the most famous Dutch painter Rembrandt. The text clearly states, that many facts prove that it wasn't painted by Rembrandt himself, but just attributed to him because of its style. In the lecture however the professor gives proof why it is in fact a work of the famous Dutch painter.

The first contradicting fact are the clothes of the woman in the portrait. She is wearing a white linen cap which gives her the appearance of a simple servant, whereas the luxurious fur collar she also wears doesn't fit. In the lecture is said, that after a thorough research people found out that the fur collar was added to the painting about 100 years later in order to increase the value of the workpiece, because now it illustrated an aristocratic lady instead of a servant.

Another problem with the painting was the display of light and shadow. Rembandt was known as a master of painting light and shadow, yet contradictionally the elements in the work don't fit together. But this problem could also be explained by now. By removing the additional fur collar one could see that the lady is wearing a simple light colored cloth, which reflects light into her face.

The third aspect which let people wonder about the origins of the painting was the fact, that the panel was made of several pieces of wood glued together instead of just one panel which was usual for works of Rembrandt. But the additional panels were also added later to enlarge the paiting. by doing this the painting seemed to be more valuable.

Another interesting fact is, that the main panel is made from the same tree like another painting of Rembrandt, 'Selfportrait with a hat'.

In the end it is clear that this painting is indeed a work of the Dutch painter and it should be reintegrated in the catalog of Rembrandt's paintings.

*Rater Comments*

This essay earns a high score because it successfully explains the opposing relationship between the reading and the lecture and goes on to identify all the important points and details. The response is appropriately organized, with the topic stated in the first and final paragraphs and each main point discussed in separate body paragraphs. Each main point is discussed clearly and with a good amount of detail. The writer, for example, correctly represents in the second paragraph the idea that the fur collar was added to the painting at a later date to make it appear more valuable. In the third paragraph, the light-and-shadow inconsistency is not described in concrete terms, but the writer does indicate it in general terms and explains its cause. Connectors and connecting phrases ("Another problem," "By removing the additional fur collar," "In the end") help make the writing cohesive and easy to read. The language is generally accurate, and minor errors ("In the lecture is said," "after a thorough research," "contradictionally") do not interfere with meaning.

*Mid-Level Response*

There are doubts whether Rembramdt painted Portrait of an Elderly Woman in a White Bonnet. The reading says that the painting wasn't paint by Rembrandt because of the leck of consistency observed. On the other hand the lecture says that Rembrandt is the real painter. The opinion expressed in the lecture is based on a third examination of the painting when the experts decided that Rembrandt is the real painter because of the examination of the fur colar, the light and shadow that were realistic and finally the elements of the wood panel.

Examining the fur colar from the painting, the experts noticed that the actual colar was painted over the top of the original painting over 100 years later. The reason of doing this was to increase the value of the painting.

Further on the light and color were very realistic, says the lecture. This opinion is formulated in opossition to the one from the reading that says that in this painting this elements do not fit together.

Finally the last reason why the lecture affirms that the painting belongs to Rebmrandt is based on the examination of the wood panel. Even though the wood panel was enlarged it was used the same tree that Rembrandt used in Self Portrait with a Hat.

In conclusion it seems that the argument given by the lecture overpower the reading part.

*Rater Comments*

Although this response clearly describes the relationship between the reading and the lecture in the first paragraph, it earns a mid-level score because it lacks some important details related to the three main points that follow. In the second paragraph, the writer does explain that the fur collar was added to the painting 100 years after it was created to increase its value, but the writer does not explain the initial problem mentioned in the reading (that the fur collar was not consistent with a servant's apparel). This makes it difficult for a reader who is not familiar with the passage and the lecture to see how the information about the collar is relevant to the topic. The third paragraph, in contrast, does indicate that the information from the reading and the information from the lecture regarding light and shadow differ, but this section lacks most of the important details. The third point, in paragraph 4, is not expressed precisely. The writer indicates that the fact that the wood came from the same tree as the wood for another Rembrandt painting is proof of its authenticity, yet it is not clear whether the writer is referring to the original panel or to the added panels. The writer also does not explain why the original panel was enlarged. Overall, the essay responds to the task and touches on all three main ideas, but these ideas are either vaguely or imprecisely conveyed. The language is generally clear, with only a few minor errors ("the painting wasn't paint by Rembrandt," "this elements do not fit together") that do not interfere with meaning.

## Writing for an Academic Discussion

### Question

Your professor is teaching a class on sociology. Write a post responding to the professor's question.

**In your response, you should do the following.**

- Express and support your opinion.
- Make a contribution to the discussion in your own words.

An effective response will contain at least 100 words.

**Dr. Diaz**

This week we will be studying trends in food shopping. One of them is meal-kit websites. On these sites, the customers first select one or more meals, and then the companies deliver to their homes the cooking instructions plus just enough grocery ingredients to prepare the selected meals. The customers then prepare their meals at home. Do you think this is a positive trend? Explain why or why not.

**Andrew**

It's especially positive if you don't have any kitchen skills. I've tried that kind of service, and even though I'm not a good cook, the meal came out tasting pretty good. I think I'm learning how to cook! It's probably especially helpful for younger people, who might not even know how to choose the best ingredients at grocery stores.

**Claire**

It might be convenient, but this is definitely not a positive trend. Think of the effect on the environment of all the trucks delivering packaged groceries for just a few meals to all those houses, week after week, all over the city! We really have to stop favoring convenience over environmental impacts.

## Topic Notes

In this prompt, the professor asks for student opinions about whether meal-kit delivery is a positive trend, and to explain their view. The first student, Andrew, thinks it is positive, because it can help young people learn how to cook, which has in fact helped him. Claire agrees that it is convenient but worries about the environmental impact of the package delivery to multiple households, so she thinks it is a negative trend. Test takers are expected to contribute their own opinion on the topic, either by coming up with completely new ideas, by engaging with or expanding on Claire's or Andrew's opinions, or by giving a mixed opinion. They could say, for example, that, overall, it is a positive trend and explain why, then note some comparatively negative minor drawbacks.

## Sample Responses with Rater Comments

*High-Level Essay*

Meal-kit websites have started an interesting trend—on the one hand, they try to ensure a healthy home-cooked meal and on the other hand there is a concern of additional truck traffic on the roadways hurting the environment. The important part is to stike the right balance, which is always hard to achieve. The advantages of this trend, however, might outweigh the negatives. It enables families that are busy to relax and enjoy a home-cooked meal—it can also bring families together since cooking together at home can be fun. One needs to understand that the alternative would be for individuals to potentially still get in their vehicles and drive to the grocery stores and purchase ingredients themselves, or to order delivery or pick-up food, or eat out. All of these actions also result in additional vehicle trips that affect the environment. Ultimately, it is important for individuals to ensure the right balance but overall, meal-kit websites seem to present a positive trend.

*Rater Comments*

This high-level response makes a fully successful, relevant and clearly expressed contribution to the discussion board. The response notes the opposing view-points represented by Andrew and Claire (". . . try to ensure a healthy home-cooked meal" versus "additional truck traffic on the roadways") and then goes on to say that the advantages of the meal-kit trend outweigh the disadvantages, followed by plenty of elaboration supporting this view. The response uses a variety of grammatical structures and precise, effective word choices, with few errors in either vocabulary or grammar.

*Mid-Level Essay*

> I would support Andrew.
>
> Getting the grocery for each week will reduce the amount of people going to grocery shopping, it saves the time of each individual also. It helps in not buying extra grocery items. Its in favor of customers. It may not impact enviromental impacts as too many people driving to get the grocery will reducing to one truck delivering all the grocery. The other reason why i suppor tthis it helps each invidual to cook and since they also give the recipe it would be favaourable for customer, in one shot they get the recipe , grocery and try out home food, which would be more healtier and cheaper comparing to ordering restaurant food.

*Rater Comments*

This is a mid-level response that does contribute to the discussion but is not fully successful, mainly because of the frequency of language errors. The writer agrees with Andrew that meal kits are a positive trend and outlines a couple of reasons why. The response then goes on to argue against meal-kit delivery being much more impactful on the environment than driving to the grocery store (in opposition to Claire's view), then provides additional reasons for meal kit delivery being a positive trend. However, many of the ideas are slightly obscured by the errors in language use, such as "It may not impact enviromental impacts"; "will reducing to one truck delivering all the grocery"; and "The other reason why I suppor tthis it helps . . .". The meaning of the sentence "Its in favor of customers" is also unclear.

# 9 Authentic TOEFL iBT® Practice Test 4

In this chapter you will find the fourth of four authentic TOEFL iBT Practice Tests. You can take the test in two different ways:

- **In the book:** You can read through the test questions in the following pages, marking your answers in the spaces provided. To hear the listening portions of the test, follow the instructions to play the numbered audio tracks that accompany this book.

- **On your computer:** For a test-taking experience that more closely resembles the actual TOEFL iBT test, you can take this same test on your computer using the digital download (see code in the back of the book). Reading passages and questions will appear on-screen, and you can enter your answers by selecting the spaces provided. Follow the instructions to hear the listening portions of the test.

Following this test, you will find answer keys and scoring information. You will also find scripts for the listening portions. Complete answer explanations, as well as sample test taker spoken and written responses, are also provided.

# TOEFL iBT® Practice Test 4
# READING

In this section, you will be able to demonstrate your ability to understand academic passages in English. You will read and answer questions about **two passages**.

In the actual test, you will have 36 minutes total to read both passages and answer the questions. A clock will indicate how much time remains.

Some passages may include one or more notes explaining words or phrases. The words or phrases are marked with footnote numbers and the notes explaining them appear at the end of the passage.

Most questions are worth 1 point, but the last question for each passage is worth 2 points.

You may review and revise your answers in this section as long as time remains.

At the end of this practice test, you will find an answer key, information to help you determine your score, and explanations of the answers.

## INDUSTRIALIZATION IN THE NETHERLANDS AND SCANDINAVIA

While some European countries, such as England and Germany, began to industrialize in the eighteenth century, the Netherlands and the Scandinavian countries of Denmark, Norway, and Sweden developed later. All four of these countries lagged considerably behind in the early nineteenth century. However, they industrialized rapidly in the second half of the century, especially in the last two or three decades. In view of their later start and their lack of coal—undoubtedly the main reason they were not among the early industrializers—it is important to understand the sources of their success.

All had small populations. At the beginning of the nineteenth century, Denmark and Norway had fewer than 1 million people, while Sweden and the Netherlands had fewer than 2.5 million inhabitants. All exhibited moderate growth rates in the course of the century (Denmark the highest and Sweden the lowest), but all more than doubled in population by 1900. Density varied greatly. The Netherlands had one of the highest population densities in Europe, whereas Norway and Sweden had the lowest. Denmark was in between but closer to the Netherlands.

Considering human capital as a characteristic of the population, however, all four countries were advantaged by the large percentages of their populations who could read and write. In both 1850 and 1914, the Scandinavian countries had the highest literacy rates in Europe, or in the world, and the Netherlands was well above the European average. This fact was of enormous value in helping the national economies find their niches in the evolving currents of the international economy.

Location was an important factor for all four countries. All had immediate access to the sea, and this had important implications for a significant international resource, fish, as well as for cheap transport, merchant marines, and the shipbuilding industry. Each took advantage of these opportunities in its own way. The people of the Netherlands, with a long tradition of fisheries and mercantile shipping, had difficulty in developing good harbors suitable for steamships; eventually they did so at Rotterdam and Amsterdam, with exceptional results for transit trade with Germany and central Europe and for the processing of overseas foodstuffs and raw materials (sugar, tobacco, chocolate, grain, and eventually oil). Denmark also had an admirable commercial history, particularly with respect to traffic through the Sound (the strait separating Denmark and Sweden). In 1857, in return for a payment of 63 million kronor from other commercial nations, Denmark abolished the Sound toll dues, the fees it had collected since 1497 for the use of the Sound. This, along with other policy shifts toward free trade, resulted in a significant increase in traffic through the Sound and in the port of Copenhagen.

The political institutions of the four countries posed no significant barriers to industrialization or economic growth. The nineteenth century passed relatively peacefully for these countries, with progressive democratization taking place in all of them. They were reasonably well governed, without notable corruption or grandiose state projects, although in all of them the government gave some aid to railways, and in Sweden the state built the main lines. As small countries dependent on foreign markets, they had few or low barriers to foreign trade in the main, though a protectionist movement developed in Sweden. In Denmark and Sweden agricultural reforms took place gradually from the late eighteenth century through the first half of the nineteenth, resulting in a new class of peasant landowners with a definite market orientation.

The key factor in the success of these countries (along with high literacy, which contributed to it) was their ability to adapt to the international division of labor determined by the early industrializers and to stake out areas of specialization in international markets for which they were especially well suited. This meant a great dependence on international commerce, which had notorious fluctuations; however, it also meant high returns to those aspects of production that were fortunate enough to be well placed in times of prosperity. In Sweden exports accounted for 18 percent of the national income in 1870, and in 1913, 22 percent of a much larger national income. In the early twentieth century, Denmark exported 63 percent of its agricultural production: butter, pork products, and eggs. It exported 80 percent of its butter, almost all to Great Britain, where it accounted for 40 percent of British butter imports.

**Directions:** Now answer the questions.

**PARAGRAPH 1**

While some European countries, such as England and Germany, began to industrialize in the eighteenth century, the Netherlands and the Scandinavian countries of Denmark, Norway, and Sweden developed later. All four of these countries lagged considerably behind in the early nineteenth century. However, they industrialized rapidly in the second half of the century, especially in the last two or three decades. In view of their later start and their lack of coal—undoubtedly the main reason they were not among the early industrializers—it is important to understand the sources of their success.

1.  Paragraph 1 supports which of the following ideas about England and Germany?

    Ⓐ They were completely industrialized by the start of the nineteenth century.
    Ⓑ They possessed plentiful supplies of coal.
    Ⓒ They were overtaken economically by the Netherlands and Scandinavia during the early nineteenth century.
    Ⓓ They succeeded for the same reasons that the Netherlands and Scandinavia did.

GO ON TO THE NEXT PAGE

P
A
R
A
G
R
A
P
H
S

2

A
N
D

3

All had small populations. At the beginning of the nineteenth century, Denmark and Norway had fewer than 1 million people, while Sweden and the Netherlands had fewer than 2.5 million inhabitants. All exhibited moderate growth rates in the course of the century (Denmark the highest and Sweden the lowest), but all more than doubled in population by 1900. Density varied greatly. The Netherlands had one of the highest population densities in Europe, whereas Norway and Sweden had the lowest. Denmark was in between but closer to the Netherlands.

Considering human capital as a characteristic of the population, however, all four countries were advantaged by the large percentages of their populations who could read and write. In both 1850 and 1914, the Scandinavian countries had the highest literacy rates in Europe, or in the world, and the Netherlands was well above the European average. This fact was of enormous value in helping the national economies find their niches in the evolving currents of the international economy.

2.  According to paragraphs 2 and 3, which of the following contributed significantly to the successful economic development of the Netherlands and of Scandinavia?

Ⓐ The relatively small size of their populations
Ⓑ The rapid rate at which their populations were growing
Ⓒ The large amount of capital they had available for investment
Ⓓ The high proportion of their citizens who were educated

P
A
R
A
G
R
A
P
H

4

Location was an important factor for all four countries. All had immediate access to the sea, and this had important implications for a significant international resource, fish, as well as for cheap transport, merchant marines, and the shipbuilding industry. Each took advantage of these opportunities in its own way. The people of the Netherlands, with a long tradition of fisheries and mercantile shipping, had difficulty in developing good harbors suitable for steamships; eventually they did so at Rotterdam and Amsterdam, with exceptional results for transit trade with Germany and central Europe and for the processing of overseas foodstuffs and raw materials (sugar, tobacco, chocolate, grain, and eventually oil). Denmark also had an admirable commercial history, particularly with respect to traffic through the Sound (the strait separating Denmark and Sweden). In 1857, in return for a payment of 63 million kronor from other commercial nations, Denmark **abolished** the Sound toll dues, the fees it had collected since 1497 for the use of the Sound. This, along with other policy shifts toward free trade, resulted in a significant increase in traffic through the Sound and in the port of Copenhagen.

3.  The word "**abolished**" in the passage is closest in meaning to

Ⓐ ended
Ⓑ raised
Ⓒ returned
Ⓓ lowered

4. According to paragraph 4, because of their location, the Netherlands and the Scandinavian countries had all of the following advantages when they began to industrialize EXCEPT

- (A) low-cost transportation of goods
- (B) access to fish
- (C) shipbuilding industries
- (D) military control of the seas

**PARAGRAPH 5**

The political institutions of the four countries posed no significant barriers to industrialization or economic growth. The nineteenth century passed relatively peacefully for these countries, with progressive democratization taking place in all of them. They were reasonably well governed, without notable corruption or grandiose state projects, although in all of them the government gave some aid to railways, and in Sweden the state built the main lines. As small countries dependent on foreign markets, they had few or low barriers to foreign trade in the main, though **a protectionist movement developed in Sweden**. In Denmark and Sweden agricultural reforms took place gradually from the late eighteenth century through the first half of the nineteenth, resulting in a new class of peasant land-owners with a definite market orientation.

5. The author includes the information that "**a protectionist movement developed in Sweden**" in order to

- (A) support the claim that the political institutions of the four countries posed no significant barriers to industrialization or economic growth
- (B) identify an exception to the general trend favoring few or low barriers to trade
- (C) explain why Sweden industrialized less quickly than the other Scandinavian countries and the Netherlands
- (D) provide evidence that agriculture reforms take place more quickly in countries that have few or low barriers to trade than in those that do not

6. According to paragraph 5, each of the following contributed positively to the industrialization of the Netherlands and Scandinavia EXCEPT

- (A) a lack of obstacles to foreign trade
- (B) huge projects undertaken by the state
- (C) relatively uncorrupt government
- (D) relatively little social or political disruption

GO ON TO THE NEXT PAGE

**PARAGRAPH 6**

**The key factor in the success of these countries (along with high literacy, which contributed to it) was their ability to adapt to the international division of labor determined by the early industrializers and to stake out areas of specialization in international markets for which they were especially well suited.** This meant a great dependence on international commerce, which had notorious fluctuations; however it also meant high returns to those aspects of production that were fortunate enough to be well placed in times of prosperity. In Sweden exports accounted for 18 percent of the national income in 1870, and in 1913, 22 percent of a much larger national income. In the early twentieth century, Denmark exported 63 percent of its agricultural production: butter, pork products, and eggs. It exported 80 percent of its butter, almost all to Great Britain, where it accounted for 40 percent of British butter imports.

7. Which of the sentences below best expresses the essential information in the highlighted sentence in the passage? Incorrect choices change the meaning in important ways or leave out essential information.

    Ⓐ The early industrializers controlled most of the international economy, leaving these countries to stake out new areas of specialization along the margins.

    Ⓑ Aided by their high literacy rates, these countries were able to claim areas of specialization within established international markets.

    Ⓒ High literacy rates enabled these countries to take over international markets and adapt the international division of labor to suit their strengths.

    Ⓓ The international division of labor established by the early industrializers was well suited to these countries, a key factor in their success.

8. According to paragraph 6, a major problem with depending heavily on international markets was that they

    Ⓐ lacked stability

    Ⓑ were not well suited to agricultural products

    Ⓒ were largely controlled by the early industrializers

    Ⓓ led to slower growth of local industries

PARAGRAPHS 1 AND 2

While some European countries, such as England and Germany, began to industrialize in the eighteenth century, the Netherlands and the Scandinavian countries of Denmark, Norway, and Sweden developed later. **(A)** All four of these countries lagged considerably behind in the early nineteenth century. **(B)** However, they industrialized rapidly in the second half of the century, especially in the last two or three decades. **(C)** In view of their later start and their lack of coal—undoubtedly the main reason they were not among the early industrializers—it is important to understand the sources of their success. **(D)**

All had small populations.

9.  **Directions:** Look at the part of the passage that is displayed above. The letters **(A)**, **(B)**, **(C)**, and **(D)** indicate where the following sentence could be added.

    **During this period, Sweden had the highest rate of growth of output per capita of any country in Europe, and Denmark was second.**

    Where would the sentence best fit?

    (A) Choice A
    (B) Choice B
    (C) Choice C
    (D) Choice D

GO ON TO THE NEXT PAGE

10. **Directions:** An introductory sentence for a brief summary of the passage is provided below. Complete the summary by selecting the THREE answer choices that express the most important ideas in the passage. Some sentences do not belong in the summary because they express ideas that are not presented in the passage or are minor ideas in the passage. **This question is worth 2 points.**

**Although the Netherlands and Scandinavia began to industrialize relatively late, they did so very successfully.**

- 
- 
- 

### Answer Choices

A   Although these countries all started with small, uneducated populations, industrialization led to significant population growth and higher literacy rates.

B   Thanks to their ready access to the sea, these countries enjoyed advantages in mercantile shipping, fishing, and shipbuilding.

C   Because they all had good harbors for steamships, these countries started with an important advantage in the competition for transit trade.

D   These countries were helped by the fact that their governments were relatively stable and honest and had policies that generally encouraged rather than blocked trade.

E   These countries were successful primarily because their high literacy rates helped them fill specialized market niches.

F   Because they were never fully dependent on international commerce, these countries were able to survive notorious fluctuations in international markets.

## THE MYSTERY OF YAWNING

According to conventional theory, yawning takes place when people are bored or sleepy and serves the function of increasing alertness by reversing, through deeper breathing, the drop in blood oxygen levels that are caused by the shallow breathing that accompanies lack of sleep or boredom. Unfortunately, the few scientific investigations of yawning have failed to find any connection between how often someone yawns and how much sleep they have had or how tired they are. About the closest any research has come to supporting the tiredness theory is to confirm that adults yawn more often on weekdays than at weekends, and that school children yawn more frequently in their first year at primary school than they do in kindergarten.

Another flaw of the tiredness theory is that yawning does not raise alertness or physiological activity, as the theory would predict. When researchers measured the heart rate, muscle tension, and skin conductance of people before, during, and after yawning, they did detect some changes in skin conductance following yawning, indicating a slight increase in physiological activity. However, similar changes occurred when the subjects were asked simply to open their mouths or to breathe deeply. Yawning did nothing special to their state of physiological activity. Experiments have also cast serious doubt on the belief that yawning is triggered by a drop in blood oxygen or a rise in blood carbon dioxide. Volunteers were told to think about yawning while they breathed either normal air, pure oxygen, or an air mixture with an above-normal level of carbon dioxide. If the theory was correct, breathing air with extra carbon dioxide should have triggered yawning, while breathing pure oxygen should have suppressed yawning. In fact, neither condition made any difference to the frequency of yawning, which remained constant at about 24 yawns per hour. Another experiment demonstrated that physical exercise, which was sufficiently vigorous to double the rate of breathing, had no effect on the frequency of yawning. Again, the implication is that yawning has little or nothing to do with oxygen.

A completely different theory holds that yawning assists in the physical development of the lungs early in life, but has no remaining biological function in adults. It has been suggested that yawning and hiccupping might serve to clear out the fetus's airways. The lungs of a fetus secrete a liquid that then mixes with its mother's amniotic fluid. Babies with congenital blockages that prevent this fluid from escaping from their lungs are sometimes born with deformed lungs. It might be that yawning helps to clear out the lungs by periodically lowering the pressure in them. According to this theory, yawning in adults is just a developmental fossil with no biological function. But, while accepting that not everything in life can be explained by Darwinian evolution, there are sound reasons for being skeptical of theories like this one, which avoid the issue of what yawning does for adults. Yawning is distracting, consumes energy, and takes time. It is almost certainly doing something significant in adults as well as in fetuses. What could it be?

The empirical evidence, such as it is, suggests an altogether different function for yawning—namely, that yawning prepares us for a change in activity level. Support for this theory came from a study of yawning behavior in everyday life. Volunteers wore wrist-mounted devices that automatically recorded their physical activity for up to two weeks; the volunteers also recorded their yawns by pressing a button on the device each time they yawned. The data showed that yawning tended to occur about 15 minutes before a period

GO ON TO THE NEXT PAGE

of increased behavioral activity. Yawning bore no relationship to sleep patterns, however. This accords with anecdotal evidence that people often yawn in situations where they are neither tired nor bored, but are preparing for impending mental and physical activity. Such yawning is often referred to as "incongruous" because it seems out of place, at least in the tiredness view: soldiers yawning before combat, musicians yawning before performing, and athletes yawning before competing. Their yawning seems to have nothing to do with sleepiness or boredom—quite the reverse—but it does precede a change in activity level.

**Directions:** Now answer the questions.

P
A
R
A
G
R
A
P
H

1

**According to conventional theory, yawning takes place when people are bored or sleepy and serves the function of increasing alertness by reversing, through deeper breathing, the drop in blood oxygen levels that are caused by the shallow breathing that accompanies lack of sleep or boredom**. Unfortunately, the few scientific investigations of yawning have failed to find any connection between how often someone yawns and how much sleep they have had or how tired they are. About the closest any research has come to supporting the tiredness theory is to confirm that adults yawn more often on weekdays than at weekends, and that school children yawn more frequently in their first year at primary school than they do in kindergarten.

11. Which of the sentences below best expresses the essential information in the high-lighted sentence in the passage? Incorrect choices change the meaning in important ways or leave out essential information.

　Ⓐ It is the conventional theory that when people are bored or sleepy, they often experience a drop in blood oxygen levels due to their shallow breathing.
　Ⓑ The conventional theory is that people yawn when bored or sleepy because yawning raises blood oxygen levels, which in turn raises alertness.
　Ⓒ According to conventional theory, yawning is more likely to occur when people are bored or sleepy than when they are alert and breathing deeply.
　Ⓓ Yawning, according to the conventional theory, is caused by boredom or lack of sleep and can be avoided through deeper breathing.

12. In paragraph 1, what point does the author make about the evidence for the tiredness theory of yawning?

　Ⓐ There is no scientific evidence linking yawning with tiredness.
　Ⓑ The evidence is wide-ranging because it covers multiple age-groups.
　Ⓒ The evidence is reliable because it was collected over a long period of time.
　Ⓓ The evidence is questionable because the yawning patterns of children and adults should be different.

Another **flaw** of the tiredness theory is that yawning does not raise alertness or physiological activity, as the theory would predict. When researchers measured the heart rate, muscle tension and skin conductance of people before, during and after yawning, they did detect some changes in skin conductance following yawning, indicating a slight increase in physiological activity. However, similar changes occurred when the subjects were asked simply to open their mouths or to breathe deeply. Yawning did nothing special to their state of physiological activity. Experiments have also cast serious doubt on the belief that yawning is triggered by a drop in blood oxygen or a rise in blood carbon dioxide. Volunteers were told to think about yawning while they breathed either normal air, pure oxygen, or an air mixture with an above-normal level of carbon dioxide. If the theory was correct, breathing air with extra carbon dioxide should have triggered yawning, while breathing pure oxygen should have suppressed yawning. In fact, neither condition made any difference to the frequency of yawning, which remained constant at about 24 yawns per hour. Another experiment demonstrated that physical exercise, which was sufficiently vigorous to double the rate of breathing, had no effect on the frequency of yawning. Again, the implication is that yawning has little or nothing to do with oxygen.

13. The word "**flaw**" in the passage is closest in meaning to

   (A) fault
   (B) aspect
   (C) confusion
   (D) mystery

14. In paragraph 2, why does the author compare the physiological changes that occur when subjects simply opened their mouths or breathed deeply with those that occur when people yawned?

   (A) To present an argument in support of the tiredness theory
   (B) To cast doubt on the reliability of the tests that measured heart rate, muscle tension, and skin conductance
   (C) To argue against the hypothesis that yawning provides a special way to improve alertness or raise physiological activity
   (D) To support the idea that opening the mouth or breathing deeply can affect blood oxygen levels

15. Paragraph 2 answers all of the following questions about yawning EXCEPT:

   (A) Does yawning increase alertness or physiological activity?
   (B) Does thinking about yawning increase yawning over not thinking about yawning?
   (C) Does the amount of carbon dioxide and oxygen in the air affect the rate at which people yawn?
   (D) Does the rate of breathing affect the rate at which people yawn?

GO ON TO THE NEXT PAGE

**PARAGRAPH 3**

A completely different theory holds that yawning assists in the physical development of the lungs early in life, but has no remaining biological function in adults. It has been suggested that yawning and hiccupping might serve to clear out the fetus's airways. The lungs of a fetus secrete a liquid that then mixes with its mother's amniotic fluid. Babies with congenital blockages that prevent this fluid from escaping from their lungs are sometimes born with deformed lungs. It might be that yawning helps to clear out the lungs by periodically lowering the pressure in them. According to this theory, yawning in adults is just a developmental fossil with no biological function. But, while accepting that not everything in life can be explained by Darwinian evolution, there are sound reasons for being skeptical of theories like this one, which avoid the issue of what yawning does for adults. Yawning is distracting, consumes energy and takes time. It is almost certainly doing something significant in adults as well as in fetuses.

16. According to the development theory of yawning presented in paragraph 3, what is the role of yawning?

   Ⓐ It causes hiccups, which aid in the development of the lungs.
   Ⓑ It controls the amount of pressure the lungs place on other developing organs.
   Ⓒ It prevents amniotic fluid from entering the lungs.
   Ⓓ It removes a potentially harmful fluid from the lungs.

**PARAGRAPH 4**

The **empirical** evidence, such as it is, suggests an altogether different function for yawning—namely, that yawning prepares us for a change in activity level. Support for this theory came from a study of yawning behavior in everyday life. Volunteers wore wrist-mounted devices that automatically recorded their physical activity for up to two weeks; the volunteers also recorded their yawns by pressing a button on the device each time they yawned. The data showed that yawning tended to occur about 15 minutes before a period of increased behavioral activity. Yawning bore no relationship to sleep patterns, however. This accords with anecdotal evidence that people often yawn in situations where they are neither tired nor bored, but are preparing for impending mental and physical activity. Such yawning is often referred to as "incongruous" because it seems out of place, at least on the tiredness view: soldiers yawning before combat, musicians yawning before performing, and athletes yawning before competing. Their yawning seems to have nothing to do with sleepiness or boredom—quite the reverse—but it does precede a change in activity level.

17. The word "**empirical**" in the passage is closest in meaning to

   Ⓐ reliable
   Ⓑ based on common sense
   Ⓒ relevant
   Ⓓ based on observation

18. The study of yawning behavior discussed in paragraph 4 supports which of the following conclusions?
    - (A) Yawning is associated with an expectation of increased physical activity.
    - (B) Yawning occurs more frequently when people are asked to record their yawning.
    - (C) People tend to yawn about fifteen minutes before they become tired or bored.
    - (D) Mental or physical stress tends to make people yawn.

Another flaw of the tiredness theory is that yawning does not raise alertness or physiological activity, as the theory would predict. When researchers measured the heart rate, muscle tension and skin conductance of people before, during and after yawning, they did detect some changes in skin conductance following yawning, indicating a slight increase in physiological activity. However, similar changes occurred when the subjects were asked simply to open their mouths or to breathe deeply. Yawning did nothing special to their state of physiological activity. Experiments have also cast serious doubt on the belief that yawning is triggered by a drop in blood oxygen or a rise in blood carbon dioxide. **(A)** Volunteers were told to think about yawning while they breathed either normal air, pure oxygen, or an air mixture with an above-normal level of carbon dioxide. **(B)** If the theory was correct, breathing air with extra carbon dioxide should have triggered yawning, while breathing pure oxygen should have suppressed yawning. **(C)** In fact, neither condition made any difference to the frequency of yawning, which remained constant at about 24 yawns per hour. **(D)** Another experiment demonstrated that physical exercise, which was sufficiently vigorous to double the rate of breathing, had no effect on the frequency of yawning. Again, the implication is that yawning has little or nothing to do with oxygen.

*(PARAGRAPH 2 — sidebar label)*

19. **Directions:** Look at the part of the passage that is displayed above. The letters **(A)**, **(B)**, **(C)**, and **(D)** indicate where the following sentence could be added.

    **This, however, was not the case.**

    Where would the sentence best fit?
    - (A) Choice A
    - (B) Choice B
    - (C) Choice C
    - (D) Choice D

GO ON TO THE NEXT PAGE

20. **Directions:** An introductory sentence for a brief summary of the passage is provided below. Complete the summary by selecting the THREE answer choices that express the most important ideas in the passage. Some sentences do not belong in the summary because they express ideas that are not presented in the passage or are minor ideas in the passage. **This question is worth 2 points.**

**The tiredness theory of yawning does not seem to explain why yawning occurs.**

- 
- 
- 

### Answer Choices

A  Although earlier scientific studies strongly supported the tiredness theory, new evidence has cast doubt on these findings.

B  Evidence has shown that yawning is almost completely unrelated to the amount of oxygen in the blood and is unrelated to sleep behavior.

C  Some have proposed that yawning plays a role in the development of the lungs before birth, but it seems unlikely that yawning serves no purpose in adults.

D  Fluids in the lungs of the fetus prevent yawning from occurring, which disproves the development theory of yawning.

E  New studies, along with anecdotal evidence, have shown that the frequency of yawning increases during extended periods of inactivity.

F  There is some evidence that suggests that yawning prepares the body and mind for a change in activity level.

# LISTENING

In this section, you will be able to demonstrate your ability to understand conversations and lectures in English.

In the actual test, the section is divided into two separately timed parts. You will hear each conversation or lecture only one time. A clock will indicate how much time remains. The clock will count down only while you are answering questions, not while you are listening. You may take up to 16.5 minutes to answer the questions.

In this practice test, there is no time limit for answering questions.

You may take notes while you listen. You may use your notes to help you answer the questions. Your notes will not be scored.

Answer the questions based on what is stated or implied by the speakers.

In some questions, you will see this icon: . This means that you will hear, but not see, part of the question.

**In the actual test, you must answer each question. You cannot return to previous questions.**

At the end of this practice test, you will find an answer key, information to help you determine your score, and explanations of the answers.

**Listen to Track 78.**

## Questions

1. Why does the student go to the university office?

   (A) To apply for a position at the university library
   (B) To get information about hosting an exchange student
   (C) To find out if there are any jobs available on campus
   (D) To find out the hours of the computer lab

2. Why did the student transfer to Central University?

   (A) To take advantage of an academic program
   (B) To participate in a student exchange program
   (C) To attend a smaller university than the one he was at before
   (D) To benefit from Central University's international reputation

3. Why does the student mention hosting foreign-exchange students?

   (A) To explain his interest in a particular field of study
   (B) To explain why he is looking for a job so late in the semester
   (C) To explain why he would like to be an exchange student the following year
   (D) To explain how he learned his computer skills

4. What can be inferred about students who apply for the open position at the technology-support help desk?

    Ⓐ They must be enrolled in a computer course.
    Ⓑ They will only be able to work on weekends.
    Ⓒ They are willing to work many hours each day they work.
    Ⓓ They are willing to work irregular hours.

5. *Listen again to part of the conversation by playing Track 79.*
*Then answer the question.*

    Why does the woman say this?

    Ⓐ To dissuade the student from starting a job right away
    Ⓑ To suggest looking for an off-campus job
    Ⓒ To imply that the student might not like the job that is available
    Ⓓ To encourage the student to apply to a work-study program

GO ON TO THE NEXT PAGE

*Listen to Track 80.*

Art History

Elaine Gazda

**Questions**

6.  What is the lecture mainly about?

    Ⓐ Different views of a type of sculpture popular in ancient Roman times
    Ⓑ Evidence that Romans had outstanding artistic ability
    Ⓒ The differences between Greek sculpture and Roman sculpture
    Ⓓ The relationship between art and politics in ancient Roman times

7.  According to traditional art historians, why did the Romans copy Greek sculpture?

    Ⓐ The Roman public was not interested in original works of art.
    Ⓑ The Roman government did not support other forms of art.
    Ⓒ Roman artists did not have sufficient skill to create original sculpture.
    Ⓓ Romans wanted to imitate the art they admired.

8.  What is Gazda's view of the Roman copies of Greek statues?

    Ⓐ The copies represented the idea that Roman society was similar to Greek society.
    Ⓑ The copies introduced the citizens of the Roman Empire to Greek history.
    Ⓒ The copies were inferior to the original statues.
    Ⓓ The copies had both artistic and political functions.

9.  Why does the professor mention Roman coins?

    Ⓐ To show the similarity between the likenesses of the emperor in statues and on coins
    Ⓑ To illustrate the Roman policy of distributing the emperor's image throughout the empire
    Ⓒ To imply that the citizens of the Roman Empire became quite wealthy
    Ⓓ To suggest that the Romans also copied Greek art on their coins

GO ON TO THE NEXT PAGE

10. According to the professor, why did the Romans sometimes remove the emperor's head from a statue?

    *Select 2 answers.*

    A  The head made the statue too heavy to transport.
    B  The head was placed on the body of a different statue.
    C  The emperor was no longer in power.
    D  The emperor was not satisfied with the quality of the statue.

11. *Listen again to part of the lecture by playing Track 81.*
    *Then answer the question.*

    What does the professor imply when he says this?

    Ⓐ Art historians frequently change their views.
    Ⓑ The contemporary view is not easy to understand.
    Ⓒ It is not difficult to determine why the Romans copied Greek sculptures.
    Ⓓ The view of traditional art historians is probably incorrect.

*Listen to Track 82.*

**Questions**

12. What is the conversation mainly about?

    (A) The topic of the man's research paper
    (B) Some current research projects in sociology
    (C) Effective ways of conducting sociology research
    (D) The man's possible participation in a research project

13. What does the professor imply about the man's outline?

    (A) It has revealed that he should limit the focus of his paper.
    (B) It does not provide enough information for him to write the paper.
    (C) It will help him write clearly about a complex topic.
    (D) It overstates the connection between sociology and marketing.

14. What is the main goal of the study that the professor's colleague is conducting?

    (A) To find out if some television shows will be popular with people in a certain age range
    (B) To collect information about food products that college students like
    (C) To generate ideas for new television shows
    (D) To determine sociological factors that are related to people's television-viewing preferences

GO ON TO THE NEXT PAGE

15. What does the professor imply about the owners of Fox's Diner?

    Ⓐ They would probably do a favor for her.
    Ⓑ They are unlikely to grant the man's request.
    Ⓒ They would enjoy participating in the research study.
    Ⓓ They often advertise on television.

16. *Listen again to part of the conversation by playing Track 83. Then answer the question.*

    What does the professor mean when she says this?

    Ⓐ The student could probably find a marketing professor who has an interest in sociology.
    Ⓑ The student's marketing professor might not be aware of the television study.
    Ⓒ No more students are needed to participate in the television study.
    Ⓓ The marketing department needs students for several research studies.

*Listen to Track 84.*

European History

## Questions

17. What is the main purpose of the lecture?

    Ⓐ To explore the use of spices in cooking in the Middle Ages
    Ⓑ To explain the significance of spices for medieval society
    Ⓒ To describe how the spice trade evolved in medieval Europe
    Ⓓ To examine changes in the role that spices played in the Middle Ages

18. Based on the lecture, indicate whether each of the following is true about spices in medieval Europe.

*Mark your answers with an "X" below.*

| | YES | NO |
|---|---|---|
| A. They had to be imported. | | |
| B. They were unaffordable for many people. | | |
| C. They were used to preserve meat during the winter. | | |
| D. They were believed to have medicinal properties. | | |
| E. Their sale in public markets was closely regulated. | | |

GO ON TO THE NEXT PAGE

19. What two factors explain why medieval Europeans did not use spices to cover the taste of spoiled meat?

    *Choose two answers.*

    A   Fresh meat was less expensive than spices were.
    B   Spices were mainly used in incense and perfume.
    C   The sale of spoiled food was prohibited.
    D   Salt was cheaper than most spices were.

20. Why does the professor mention the collapse of the Roman Empire?

    Ⓐ To indicate that the spice trade became more direct
    Ⓑ To explain why the price of pepper suddenly increased
    Ⓒ To indicate that spices were not available in Europe for centuries
    Ⓓ To explain why the origins of spices became more mysterious

21. What does the professor say about European explorers during the age of discovery?

    Ⓐ Their discoveries caused the price of certain spices to increase.
    Ⓑ They were responding to the demand for spices.
    Ⓒ They did not expect to find spices during their explorations.
    Ⓓ Their main goal was to discover unknown lands.

22. *Listen again to part of the lecture by playing Track 85.*
    *Then answer the question.*

    Why does the professor say this?

    Ⓐ To indicate that pepper was commonly used as payment
    Ⓑ To indicate where pepper could be found at the time
    Ⓒ To emphasize the high value of pepper at the time
    Ⓓ To suggest that pepper was nearly as plentiful as gold

*Listen to Track 86.*

Biology

GO ON TO THE NEXT PAGE

**Questions**

23. What is the main purpose of the lecture?

    Ⓐ To explain the biological advantages of a physical change that occurs in North American wood frogs

    Ⓑ To explain why the North American wood frog's habitat range has expanded

    Ⓒ To describe the functioning of the circulatory system of the North American wood frog

    Ⓓ To introduce students to an unusual phenomenon affecting North American wood frogs

24. Why does the professor first mention the arrival of spring?

    Ⓐ To encourage students to look for thawing wood frogs

    Ⓑ To point out the time period when frogs begin mating

    Ⓒ To explain why the class will soon be doing experiments with wood frogs

    Ⓓ To emphasize the speed of the thawing process

25. What happens to a wood frog as it begins to freeze?

    Ⓐ Blood is concentrated in the center of its body.

    Ⓑ Blood stops producing sugar.

    Ⓒ Water moves out of its internal organs.

    Ⓓ Water from just beneath the skin begins to evaporate.

26. What are two points the professor makes about the thawing process of the wood frog?

    *Select 2 answers.*

    Ⓐ The thawing process is not fully understood.

    Ⓑ The thawing process takes longer than the freezing process.

    Ⓒ The frog's internal organs thaw before its outer skin thaws.

    Ⓓ Thawing occurs when the frog's heart begins pumping glucose through its body.

27. What impact does freezing have on some thawed wood frogs?

   (A) It increases their reproductive success.
   (B) It decreases their life span.
   (C) It causes them to be more vocal and active.
   (D) It reduces their ability to recognize potential mates.

28. *Listen again to part of the lecture by playing Track 87.*
   *Then answer the question.*

   What does the professor imply when she says this?

   (A) She wants the student to clarify his question.
   (B) She wants the student to draw his own conclusions.
   (C) She thinks the student does not understand how car antifreeze works.
   (D) She thinks the student has misunderstood her point.

**STOP. This is the end of the Listening section of TOEFL iBT ® Practice Test 4.**

GO ON TO THE NEXT PAGE

# SPEAKING

In this section, you will be able to demonstrate your ability to speak about a variety of topics.

In the actual test, the Speaking section will last approximately 16 minutes. You will answer four questions by speaking into the microphone. You may use your notes to help you answer the questions. Your notes will not be scored. For each question, you will have time to prepare before giving your response. You should answer the questions as completely as possible in the time allowed.

For this practice test, you may want to use a personal recording device to record and play back your responses.

For each question, play the audio track listed and follow the directions to complete the task. You may take notes while you listen.

At the end of this Practice Test, you will find scripts for the audio tracks, Important Points for each question, sample responses, and comments on those responses by official raters.

## Questions

*1. You will now give your opinion about a familiar topic. After you hear the question, you will have 15 seconds to prepare and 45 seconds to speak.*

*Now play Track 88 to hear Question 1.*

---

Do you agree or disagree with the following statement?

**It is important to learn about other cultures.**

Use details and examples to explain your opinion.

| | |
|---|---|
| **Preparation Time: 15 Seconds** | |
| **Response Time: 45 Seconds** | |

---

*2. Now you will read a passage about a campus situation and then listen to a conversation about the same topic. You will then answer a question, using information from both the reading passage and the conversation. You will have 30 seconds to prepare and 60 seconds to speak.*

*Now play Track 89 to hear Question 2.*

**Reading Time: 50 Seconds**

---

### University Choir to Enter Off-Campus Singing Competitions

Currently, the university choir gives singing concerts only on campus. Next year, however, the choir will add competitive events at other locations to its schedule. The choir's new director feels that entering singing competitions will make the quality of the choir's performance even better than it is now. "Competitions will motivate students in the choir to pursue a higher standard of excellence in singing," he said. In addition, it is hoped that getting the choir off campus and out in the public will strengthen the reputation of the university's music program. This in turn will help the program grow.

The man expresses his opinion about the change described in the article. Briefly summarize the change. Then state his opinion about the change and explain the reasons he gives for holding that opinion.

> **Preparation Time: 30 Seconds**
> **Response Time: 60 Seconds**

*3. Now you will read a passage about an academic subject and then listen to a lecture on the same topic. You will then answer a question, using information from both the reading passage and the lecture. You will have 30 seconds to prepare and 60 seconds to speak.*

**Now play Track 90 to hear Question 3.**

> **Reading Time: 50 Seconds**

### Relict Behaviors

In general, animals act in ways that help them to survive within their specific habitats. However, sometimes an animal species may display a behavior that no longer serves a clear purpose. The original purpose for the behavior may have disappeared long ago, even thousands of years before. These behaviors, known as *relict behaviors*, were useful to the animal when the species' habitat was different; but now, because of changed conditions, the behavior no longer serves its original purpose. Left over from an earlier time, the behavior remains as a relict, or remnant, long after the environmental circumstance that influenced its evolution has vanished.

GO ON TO THE NEXT PAGE

Using the example of the pronghorn and lion, explain the concept of a relict behavior.

**Preparation Time: 30 Seconds**
**Response Time: 60 Seconds**

*4. Now you will listen to a lecture. You will then be asked to summarize the lecture. You will have 20 seconds to prepare and 60 seconds to speak.*

**Now play Track 91 to hear Question 4.**

Using points and examples from the lecture, explain how the characteristics of target customers influence marketing strategy for products.

**Preparation Time: 20 Seconds**
**Response Time: 60 Seconds**

**STOP. This is the end of the Speaking section of TOEFL iBT ® Practice Test 4.**

# WRITING

In this section, you will be able to demonstrate your ability to use writing to communicate in an academic environment. There will be two writing tasks.

At the end of this Practice Test, you will find a script for the audio track, topic notes, sample responses, and comments on those responses by official raters.

Turn the page to see the directions for the first writing task.

## Integrated Writing

For this task, you will read a passage about an academic topic. Then you will listen to a lecture about the same topic. You may take notes while you listen.

In your response, provide a detailed summary of the lecture and explain how the lecture relates to the reading passage.

In the actual test, you will have 3 minutes to read the passage and 20 minutes to write your response. While you write, you will be able to see the reading passage. If you finish your response before time is up, you may go on to the second writing task.

Now you will see the reading passage. It will be followed by a lecture.

| Reading Time: 3 minutes |
| --- |

In the 1950s *Torreya taxifolia*, a type of evergreen tree once very common in the state of Florida, started to die out. No one is sure exactly what caused the decline, but chances are good that if nothing is done, *Torreya* will soon become extinct. Experts are considering three ways to address the decline of *Torreya*.

The first option is to reestablish *Torreya* in the same location in which it thrived for thousands of years. *Torreya* used to be found in abundance in the northern part of Florida, which has a specific microclimate. A microclimate exists when weather conditions inside a relatively small area differ from the region of which that area is a part. Northern Florida's microclimate is very favorable to *Torreya*'s growth. This microclimate is wetter and cooler than the surrounding region's relatively dry, warm climate. Scientists have been working to plant *Torreya* seeds in the coolest, dampest areas of the microclimate.

The second option is to move *Torreya* to an entirely different location, far from its Florida microclimate. *Torreya* seeds and saplings have been successfully planted and grown in forests further north, where the temperature is significantly cooler. Some scientists believe that *Torreya* probably thrived in areas much further north in the distant past, so by relocating it now, in a process known as assisted migration, humans would simply be helping *Torreya* return to an environment that is more suited to its survival.

The third option is to preserve *Torreya* in research centers. Seeds and saplings can be moved from the wild and preserved in a closely monitored environment where it will be easier for scientists both to protect the species and to conduct research on *Torreya*. This research can then be used to ensure the continued survival of the species.

*Now play Track 92.*

## Question 1

Summarize the points made in the lecture, being sure to explain how they respond to the specific concerns presented in the reading passage.

You have 20 minutes to plan and write your response.

**Response Time: 20 minutes**

_____

_____

_____

_____

GO ON TO THE NEXT PAGE

## Writing for an Academic Discussion

For this task, you will read an online discussion. A professor has posted a question about a topic, and some classmates have responded with their ideas.

In the actual test, you will have 10 minutes to write a response that contributes to the discussion.

### Question 2

Your professor is teaching a class on psychology. Write a post responding to the professor's question.

**In your response, you should do the following.**

- Express and support your opinion.
- Make a contribution to the discussion in your own words.

An effective response will contain at least 100 words.

**Dr. Diaz**

This week we've been looking at research on human happiness. One expert has two pieces of advice that may seem contradictory: "To make yourself happier, focus on making other people happy. One of the best ways to make other people happy is to focus more on your own happiness." To increase your own happiness, do you think it is more effective to focus on both of these things or on only one? Why?

**Andrew**

I believe both of these ideas are true. It seems obvious to me that there is joy in helping others. At the same time, if a person doesn't focus on making himself or herself happy, that person will never be able to contribute much to society, because they will lack the energy and enthusiasm needed to do so.

**Claire**

I would argue that it is better to focus only on making others happy. To me, that advice about focusing more on your own happiness is a step toward selfishness and to seeing one's own interests as separate from and maybe even conflicting with the interests of everyone around you, and that is not something I'd recommend for anybody trying to reduce unhappiness.

**Response Time: 10 minutes**

GO ON TO THE NEXT PAGE ↘

_____

_____

_____

_____

_____

_____

_____

_____

_____

_____

_____

_____

_____

_____

_____

_____

_____

_____

_____

_____

_____

_____

**STOP. This is the end of the Writing section of TOEFL iBT Practice Test 4.**

# Answers, Explanations, and Listening Scripts

# Reading

## Answer Key and Self-Scoring Chart

**Directions:** Check your answers against the answer key below. Write the number 1 on the line to the right of each question if you picked the correct answer. For questions worth more than one point, follow the directions given. Total your points at the bottom of the chart.

| Question Number | Correct Answer | Your Raw Points |
|:---:|:---:|:---:|
| **Industrialization in the Netherlands and Scandinavia** | | |
| 1. | B | |
| 2. | D | |
| 3. | A | |
| 4. | D | |
| 5. | B | |
| 6. | B | |
| 7. | B | |
| 8. | A | |
| 9. | C | |
| 10.* | B, D, E | |
| **TOTAL:** | | |

* For question 10, write 2 if you picked all three correct answers. Write 1 if you picked two correct answers.

| Question Number | Correct Answer | Your Raw Points |
|---|---|---|
| **The Mystery of Yawning** | | |
| 11. | B | |
| 12. | A | |
| 13. | A | |
| 14. | C | |
| 15. | B | |
| 16. | D | |
| 17. | D | |
| 18. | A | |
| 19. | C | |
| 20.* | B, C, F | |
| **TOTAL:** | | |

\* For question 10, write 2 if you picked all three correct answers. Write 1 if you picked two correct answers.

Below is a table that converts your Reading section answers into a TOEFL iBT Reading scaled score. Take the total of raw points from your answer key for both sets and find that number in the left-hand column of the table. The right-hand column of the table gives a TOEFL iBT Reading scaled score for each number of raw points. For example, if the total points from your answer key is 18, the table shows a scaled score of 24 to 29.

You should use your score estimate as a general guide only. Your actual score on the TOEFL iBT test may be higher or lower than your score on the practice version.

## Reading Comprehension

| Raw Point Total | Scale Score |
| --- | --- |
| 22 | 30 |
| 21 | 29–30 |
| 20 | 28–30 |
| 19 | 26–29 |
| 18 | 24–29 |
| 17 | 22–28 |
| 16 | 21–26 |
| 15 | 19–25 |
| 14 | 18–23 |
| 13 | 16–22 |
| 12 | 14–20 |
| 11 | 12–19 |
| 10 | 11–17 |
| 9 | 9–16 |
| 8 | 7–14 |
| 7 | 4–12 |
| 6 | 3–10 |
| 5 | 1–7 |
| 4 | 0–4 |
| 3 | 0–2 |
| 2 | 0 |
| 1 | 0 |
| 0 | 0 |

# Answer Explanations

## Industrialization in the Netherlands and Scandinavia

1. **B** This is an Inference question asking for information that can be inferred from paragraph 1. The correct answer is choice B. Sentence 1 of the paragraph says that England and Germany industrialized early, while sentence 4 says that the main reason that the Netherlands and the Scandinavian countries did not industrialize early is that they lacked coal. From these two pieces of information, readers can infer that coal was essential for early industrialization and that England and Germany therefore had coal.

   While the paragraph says that England and Germany "began to industrialize in the eighteenth century," there is no support for thinking that the industrial process was complete by the "start of the nineteenth century," so choice A is incorrect. Choice C is contradicted in the paragraph by the statement "All four of these countries lagged considerably behind in the early nineteenth century." Although the paragraph indicates that the Netherlands and Scandinavia eventually succeeded in industrializing, it is clear that the reasons for their success were different from those that led to industrialization in England and Germany—England and Germany industrialized because they had coal—making choice D incorrect. The reasons for the success of the Netherlands and the Scandinavian countries are explored in the rest of the passage.

2. **D** This is a Factual Information question asking for specific information that can be found in paragraphs 2 and 3. The correct answer is choice D. Sentence 1 of paragraph 3 explains that the Netherlands and the Scandinavian countries were "advantaged" by having "large percentages of their populations who could read and write," making choice D the correct answer.

   Sentence 1 of paragraph 2 indicates that the Netherlands and the Scandinavian countries had small populations, but there is no indication that having a small population contributed to the economic success of these countries, so choice A is incorrect. It does not answer the specific question asked. Choice B is factually incorrect: sentence 3 of paragraph 2 indicates that the Netherlands and the Scandinavian countries experienced "moderate" population growth, not "rapid" growth. Sentence 1 of paragraph 3 mentions "human capital," meaning the human population of the Netherlands and Scandinavian countries, but this population was small and, as previously explained, there is no indication that having a small population encouraged economic success. "Capital" in the sense of money available for economic investment is not mentioned in either of the paragraphs. For all of these reasons, choice C is incorrect.

3. **A** This is a Vocabulary question. The word being tested is "abolished." It is highlighted in the passage. The correct answer is choice A, "ended." To abolish a practice is to stop it, making choice A the best answer.

4.  **Ⓓ** This is a Negative Factual Information question asking for specific information that can be found in paragraph 4. The correct answer is choice D. Paragraph 4 discusses various trade and commercial advantages that the Netherlands and the Scandinavian countries had because of their location. There is no mention of the military or of military activity, making choice D correct.

    Sentence 2 of paragraph 4 says that "transport" was "cheap," making choice A true. The same sentence indicates that the Netherlands and the Scandinavian countries had "immediate access to the sea" and thus to "fish," making choice B true, and that all these countries had a "shipbuilding industry," making choice C true. Thus, the only unsupported answer is choice D.

5.  **Ⓑ** This is a Rhetorical Purpose question. It asks readers why the author included the information that "a protectionist movement developed in Sweden." The correct answer is choice B. Sentence 4 of the paragraph says that the Netherlands and the Scandinavian countries generally had policies that encouraged trade. However, the rise of a "protectionist movement" is not favorable to trade, a fact signaled by the word "though." Thus choice B is the best answer.

    Choice A is contradicted by the paragraph: the rise of a "protectionist movement" was a barrier to trade, not support for the claim that there were no significant barriers. Choice C is factually incorrect: there is no information indicating that Sweden was slower to industrialize than the other countries discussed. Choice D is wrong for a similar reason: agricultural reforms are mentioned, but there is no discussion of what makes such reforms occur quickly.

6.  **Ⓑ** This is a Negative Factual Information question asking for specific information that can be found in paragraph 5. The correct answer is choice B. Choice B is contradicted in the paragraph. Sentence 3 of the paragraph says that the governments of the Netherlands and the Scandinavian countries did *not* undertake "grandiose state projects," making choice B incorrect.

    Sentence 4 says that the Netherlands and the Scandinavian countries "had few or low barriers" to trade, indicating that choice A is true; sentence 3 says that these countries lacked "notable corruption," indicating that choice C is true; and sentence 2 says that the "nineteenth century passed relatively peacefully for these countries," indicating that choice D is true.

7.  **Ⓑ** This is a Sentence Simplification question. As with all questions of this type, a single sentence is highlighted.

    The key factor in the success of these countries (along with high literacy, which contributed to it) was their ability to adapt to the international division of labor determined by the early industrializers and to stake out areas of specialization in international markets for which they were especially well suited.

The correct answer is choice B. Choice B accurately summarizes the essential information in the highlighted sentence. The highlighted sentence explains that the success of the Netherlands and the Scandinavian countries was due to their ability to specialize ("stake out areas of specialization") in the international market that had already been established ("the international division of labor determined by the early industrializers"), an adaptation made possible by the "high literacy" rates of these countries.

Choice A changes the meaning of the highlighted sentence by saying that early industrializers, not the Netherlands and Scandinavian countries, staked out new areas of specialization.

Choice C changes the meaning of the highlighted sentence by saying that the Netherlands and the Scandinavian countries controlled international markets and changed the division of labor. They did neither.

Choice D changes the meaning of the highlighted sentence by making the overly broad claim that the division of labor established by early industrializers was well suited to the Netherlands and Scandinavian countries. The tested sentence leaves out the information that these countries succeeded by developing specializations and that these specializations were in the parts of the established market that were well suited for the Netherlands and Scandinavian countries, implying that some parts were not well suited.

8. **(A)** This is a Factual Information question asking for specific information that can be found in paragraph 6. The correct answer is choice A. Choice A means the same as the information in sentence 2 that international commerce "had notorious fluctuations." Choice B, the idea that agricultural products were poorly suited for international markets, is contradicted by the information that Denmark exported 80 percent of its butter. Choice C is incorrect because there is no indication that control of international markets by early industrializers was a "major problem," so the choice does not answer the question asked. Choice D is incorrect because the idea that heavy dependence on international markets led to slower growth is not expressed in the passage.

9. **(C)** This is an Insert Text question. You can see the four possible answer choices in paragraph 1.

While some European countries, such as England and Germany, began to industrialize in the eighteenth century, the Netherlands and the Scandinavian countries of Denmark, Norway, and Sweden developed later. **(A)** All four of these countries lagged considerably behind in the early nineteenth century. **(B)** However, they industrialized rapidly in the second half of the century, especially in the last two or three decades. **(C)** In view of their later start and their lack of coal—undoubtedly the main reason they were not among the early industrializers—it is important to understand the sources of their success. **(D)**

All had small populations.

The sentence provided, "During this period, Sweden had the highest rate of growth of output per capita of any country in Europe, and Denmark was second," is best inserted at choice **(C)**. Choice **(C)** is correct because when the sentence is placed at **(C)**, the phrase "During this period" has a clear and logical grammatical referent ("the last two or three decades") and because the information about the impressive growth rates of Sweden and Denmark is a logical elaboration of the comment in the previous sentence that the Netherlands and the Scandinavian countries "industrialized rapidly in the second half of the century."

Choice **(A)** is incorrect because when placed at **(A)**, the phrase "During this period" would refer to "the eighteenth century," which makes no sense. The first sentence says that the Netherlands and the Scandinavian countries developed *after* the eighteenth century. Choice **(B)** is incorrect for a similar reason: placed at **(B)**, the phrase "During this period" would refer to "the early nineteenth century." Sentence 2 says that the economies of the Netherlands and the Scandinavian countries "lagged considerably behind in the early nineteenth century," which contradicts the insert sentence about the impressive growth of the Swedish and Danish economies. The insert sentence is illogical at choice **(D)** because the sentence that follows **(D)** introduces a new topic—the sources (causes) of the success of the economies of the Netherlands and the Scandinavian countries—and the insert sentence contains no information about sources of success.

10. **B** **D** **E** This is a Prose Summary question. It is completed correctly below. The correct choices are B, D, and E. Choices A, C, and F are therefore incorrect.

**Although the Netherlands and Scandinavia began to industrialize relatively late, they did so very successfully.**

- B  Thanks to their ready access to the sea, these countries enjoyed advantages in mercantile shipping, fishing, and shipbuilding.
- D  These countries were helped by the fact that their governments were relatively stable and honest and had policies that generally encouraged rather than blocked trade.
- E  These countries were successful primarily because their high literacy rates helped them fill specialized market niches.

### Answer Choices

- A  Although these countries all started with small, uneducated populations, industrialization led to significant population growth and higher literacy rates.
- B  Thanks to their ready access to the sea, these countries enjoyed advantages in mercantile shipping, fishing, and shipbuilding.
- C  Because they all had good harbors for steamships, these countries started with an important advantage in the competition for transit trade.
- D  These countries were helped by the fact that their governments were relatively stable and honest and had policies that generally encouraged rather than blocked trade.
- E  These countries were successful primarily because their high literacy rates helped them fill specialized market niches.
- F  Because they were never fully dependent on international commerce, these countries were able to survive notorious fluctuations in international markets.

*Correct Choices*

*Choice B:* "Thanks to their ready access to the sea, these countries enjoyed advantages in mercantile shipping, fishing, and shipbuilding." This statement summarizes information in paragraph 4 explaining that the locations of these countries created economic opportunities for fishing, trade, and shipbuilding. It is the first of the three "sources" discussed in the passage for success in industrialization.

*Choice D:* "These countries were helped by the fact that their governments were relatively stable and had policies that generally encouraged rather than blocked trade." This choice summarizes information in paragraph 5 asserting that having peaceful and relatively uncorrupt governments with policies friendly to trade was helpful for industrialization.

*Choice E:* "These countries were successful primarily because their high literacy rates helped them fill specialized market niches." This choice summarizes information in paragraph 6 explaining that the countries succeeded economically because they were able to specialize in areas of the established international market in part because of their high literary rates.

*Incorrect Choices*

*Choice A:* "Although these countries all started with small, uneducated populations, industrialization led to significant population growth and higher literacy rates." It is untrue that the countries started out with "uneducated" populations and that "literacy rates" grew significantly, making this choice incorrect.

*Choice C:* "Because they all had good harbors for steamships, these countries started with an important advantage in the competition for transit trade." The Netherlands did not initially have good harbors for steamships (paragraph 4, sentence 4), so it is incorrect to say that "all" the countries "started with" this particular advantage. Another reason that this choice is incorrect is that it is too narrowly focused. The passage discusses shipping, but it does so in the context of the larger issue of the advantageous location of the countries. This larger point is a main idea, not shipping by itself.

*Choice F:* "Because they were never fully dependent on international commerce, these countries were able to survive notorious fluctuations in international markets." It is not clear from the passage that this statement is true because there is no discussion in the passage of the reasons why the economies of the countries survived market fluctuations. Therefore, this statement cannot be a main idea.

## The Mystery of Yawning

11. **B** This is a Sentence Simplification question. As with all questions of this type, a single sentence is highlighted in the passage:

According to conventional theory, yawning takes place when people are bored or sleepy and serves the function of increasing alertness by reversing, through deeper breathing, the drop in blood oxygen levels that are caused by the shallow breathing that accompanies lack of sleep or boredom.

The correct answer choice is B. Choice B contains all the essential information in the highlighted sentence and correctly expresses the relationships among the various essential pieces of information: the conventional view is being expressed, the conventional view is that people yawn when they are bored or sleepy, the conventional understanding for why yawning occurs is that it increases alertness, and the conventional understanding of why yawning increases alertness is that it increases blood oxygen levels.

Choice A changes the meaning of the highlighted sentence by incorrectly stating that yawning is followed by a decrease in blood oxygen levels and includes the correct but unnecessary information that low blood oxygen levels are caused by shallow breathing.

Choice C is incorrect because it leaves out the conventional theory's explanations about why people yawn and how yawning increases their alertness.

Choice D also leaves out essential information about why people yawn and instead talks about avoiding yawning, a topic not raised in the highlighted sentence.

12. **A** This is a Factual Information question asking for specific information that can be found in paragraph 1. The correct answer choice is A, "There is no scientific evidence linking yawning with tiredness." Choice A is supported by sentence 2, which indicates that researchers have "failed to find any connection" between yawning and tiredness. Choices B, C, and D are wrong for the same reason. Since there is no evidence linking yawning and tiredness, it makes no sense to talk about evidence for the theory being "wide-ranging" (choice B), "reliable" (choice C), or even "questionable" (choice D). Choice D may seem attractive because it is negative, but it is wrong in two respects. The theory that yawning is caused by tiredness is questionable, not the non-existent evidence for the theory. Moreover, there is no reason to expect the behavior of adults to differ from that of children if yawning in both is caused by the same thing—namely, tiredness.

13. **A** This is a Vocabulary question. The word being tested is *flaw*. It is highlighted in the passage. The correct answer choice is A, "fault." A flaw is an imperfection or weakness, making "fault" the best choice.

14. **C** This is a Rhetorical Purpose question. It asks you why the author compared the physiological changes that occur when people yawn, simply open their mouths, and breathe deeply. The correct answer choice is C, "To argue against the hypothesis that yawning provides a special way to improve alertness or raise physiological activity." The paragraph indicates that three actions—yawning, simply opening the mouth, and breathing deeply—all cause the same physiological changes. This outcome contradicts the expectations of the theory that yawning is caused by tiredness. If that theory were true, yawning should cause different or more intense physiological changes than the other actions do. Thus the comparison of yawning to the other actions has been included to show that the tiredness theory is wrong.

Choice A says that the comparison supports the tiredness theory, which is incorrect. Choice B is also incorrect. In the argument against the tiredness theory being presented in the paragraph, the reliability of the various measurements taken is assumed. There is no claim in the paragraph that opening the mouth or breathing deeply affects blood oxygen levels, so choice D cannot explain why the author included the comparison in the discussion.

15. **B** This is a Negative Factual Information question asking for specific information that can be found in paragraph 2. The correct answer choice is B, "Does thinking about yawning increase yawning over not thinking about yawning?" In one experiment described in the paragraph, people were told to think about yawning while they breathed different kinds of air ("normal air, pure oxygen, or air with above-normal levels of carbon dioxide"), but this experiment measured whether the different types of air had any effect of the rate of yawning—it did not measure whether just thinking about yawning changes the rate of yawning, so there is no answer to choice B in the paragraph. Choice A is answered in sentence 2: yawning results in a slight increase in physiological activity. Choice C is answered in sentences 7 and 8: the amount of carbon dioxide and oxygen in air breathed have no effect on the rate of yawning. Choice D is answered in sentence 9: "doubling" the rate of breathing had no effect on yawning.

16. **D** This is a Factual Information question asking for specific information that can be found in paragraph 3. The correct answer choice is D, "It removes a potentially harmful fluid from the lungs." Sentences 3 and 4 explain that fetuses have a liquid in their lungs that needs to be secreted (released) and that lung deformities can occur if this liquid is prevented from being released. The development theory is that fetuses yawn and hiccup to remove this harmful liquid from their lungs. Choice A is incorrect because the development theory holds that yawning and hiccupping have the same purpose—removing harmful liquid from the lungs. Although sentence 5 indicates that removing liquid from the lungs is thought to decrease pressure in the lungs, there is no discussion of the lungs placing pressure on other organs, so choice B is wrong. Sentence 4 talks about fluid being prevented from leaving a fetus's lungs because

of "blockages," but there is no discussion of amniotic fluid entering the lungs. Sentence 3 indicates that fluid from a fetus's lungs mixes with its mother's amniotic fluid, but this mixing occurs after the fetus has secreted (released) its lung fluid, not inside the lungs of the fetus. Thus, choice C is incorrect.

17. **(D)** This is a Vocabulary question. The word being tested is *empirical*. It is highlighted in the passage. The correct answer choice is D, "based on observation." Something is *empirical* when it is based on experimentation or observation rather than on some other foundation, such as theory.

18. **(A)** This is an Inference question asking for information that can be inferred from paragraph 4. The correct answer choice is A, "Yawning is associated with an expectation of increased physical activity." This answer is supported by sentence 4: "The data showed that yawning tended to occur about 15 minutes before a period of increased behavioral activity." In the experiment that produced this data, volunteers were asked to record when they yawned, but the experiment did not indicate that people yawned more often when they recorded their yawns than when they did not, making choice B wrong. Choice C also misrepresents information in the paragraph. According to sentence 4, people yawned 15 minutes before their activity level increased, not 15 minutes before becoming "tired or bored." Participating in the activities mentioned in sentence 7 may seem physically or mentally stressful—military combat, musical performances, athletic competitions—but there is no suggestion that these activities cause yawning. According to sentence 6, people are known to yawn while they are "preparing" to participate in such activities, meaning that they yawn before beginning such activities. If yawning were caused by participation in such activities, people would yawn during or after them, not before. Thus, choice D is incorrect.

19. **(C)** This is an Insert Text question. You can see the four possible answer choices in paragraph 2.

Another flaw of the tiredness theory is that yawning does not raise alertness or physiological activity, as the theory would predict. When researchers measured the heart rate, muscle tension and skin conductance of people before, during and after yawning, they did detect some changes in skin conductance following yawning, indicating a slight increase in physiological activity. However, similar changes occurred when the subjects were asked simply to open their mouths or to breathe deeply. Yawning did nothing special to their state of physiological activity. Experiments have also cast serious doubt on the belief that yawning is triggered by a drop in blood oxygen or a rise in blood carbon dioxide. **(A)** Volunteers were told to think about yawning while they breathed either normal air, pure oxygen, or an air mixture with an above-normal level of carbon dioxide. **(B)** If the theory was correct, breathing air with extra carbon dioxide should have triggered yawning, while breathing pure oxygen should have suppressed yawning. **(C)** In fact, neither condition made any difference to the frequency of yawning, which remained constant at about 24 yawns per hour. **(D)** Another experiment demonstrated that physical exercise, which was sufficiently vigorous to double the rate of breathing, had no effect on the frequency of yawning. Again, the implication is that yawning has little or nothing to do with oxygen.

The sentence provided, "This, however, was not the case," is best inserted at choice **(C)**. Choice **(C)** is best because the insert sentence says that something did not occur or was not true. The only thing mentioned in the search area that did not occur was an increase in yawning when extra carbon dioxide was breathed and a suppression of yawning when pure oxygen was breathed. Therefore, only choice **(C)** makes sense.

20. **B** **C** **F** This is a Prose Summary question. It is completed correctly below. The correct answer choices are B, C, and F. Choices A, D, and E are therefore incorrect.

**Directions:** An introductory sentence for a brief summary of the passage is provided below. Complete the summary by selecting the THREE answer choices that express the most important ideas in the passage. Some sentences do not belong in the summary because they express ideas that are not presented in the passage or are minor ideas in the passage. **This question is worth 2 points.**

**The tiredness theory of yawning does not seem to explain why yawning occurs.**

B   Evidence has shown that yawning is almost completely unrelated to the amount of oxygen in the blood and is unrelated to sleep behavior.

C   Some have proposed that yawning plays a role in the development of the lungs before birth, but it seems unlikely that yawning serves no purpose in adults.

F   There is some evidence that suggests that yawning prepares the body and mind for a change in activity level.

**Answer Choices**

A   Although earlier scientific studies strongly supported the tiredness theory, new evidence has cast doubt on these findings.

B   Evidence has shown that yawning is almost completely unrelated to the amount of oxygen in the blood and is unrelated to sleep behavior.

C   Some have proposed that yawning plays a role in the development of the lungs before birth, but it seems unlikely that yawning serves no purpose in adults.

D   Fluids in the lungs of the fetus prevent yawning from occurring, which disproves the development theory of yawning.

E   New studies, along with anecdotal evidence, have shown that the frequency of yawning increases during extended periods of inactivity.

F   There is some evidence that suggests that yawning prepares the body and mind for a change in activity level.

*Correct Choices*

*Choice B*, "Evidence has shown that yawning is almost completely unrelated to the amount of oxygen in the blood and is unrelated to sleep behavior," correctly summarizes the reasons presented in paragraphs 1 and 2 for rejecting the tiredness theory. Thus, it is a main idea of the passage and must be included in any summary of it.

*Choice C*, "Some have proposed that yawning plays a role in the development of the lungs before birth, but it seems unlikely that yawning serves no purpose in adults," correctly summarizes the discussion in paragraph 3 of the development theory of yawning and why it is likely incorrect: it fails to explain why a behavior that takes time and energy continues into adulthood if it serves no purpose in adulthood.

*Choice F*, "There is some evidence that suggests that yawning prepares the body and mind for a change in activity level," correctly summarizes the last paragraph, which presents experimental and anecdotal evidence that yawning precedes increases in activity levels.

*Incorrect Choices*

*Choice A*, "Although earlier scientific studies strongly supported the tiredness theory, new evidence has cast doubt on these findings." This choice is factually incorrect. It can be inferred from the information in paragraph 1 that "the few scientific investigations of yawning have failed to find any connection" between yawning and tiredness that there have never been any scientific studies supporting the tiredness theory. Paragraph 2 discusses in detail evidence against the tiredness theory. This evidence against the tiredness theory is not challenged in the passage. For these reasons, choice A is incorrect.

*Choice D*, "Fluids in the lungs of the fetus prevent yawning from occurring, which disproves the development theory of yawning." This choice is also factually incorrect. Paragraph 3 explains that fetuses do have fluid in their lungs, but the development theory is that yawning is performed to remove this harmful liquid from the lungs, not that yawning is prevented from occurring by fluids in the lungs.

*Choice E*, "New studies, along with anecdotal evidence, have shown that the frequency of yawning increases during extended periods of inactivity." This choice is also factually incorrect. Paragraph 4 explains that yawning has been observed to occur *before* an increase in activity as a way of preparing for increased activity. It does not support the idea that yawning increases *during* extended periods of inactivity.

# Listening

## Answer Key and Self-Scoring Chart

**Directions:** Check your answers against the answer key below. Write the number 1 on the line to the right of each question if you picked the correct answer. Total your points at the bottom of the chart.

| Question Number | Correct Answer | Your Raw Points |
|---|---|---|
| 1. | C | |
| 2. | A | |
| 3. | A | |
| 4. | D | |
| 5. | C | |
| 6. | A | |
| 7. | C | |
| 8. | D | |
| 9. | B | |

For question 10, write 1 if you picked both correct answers. Write 0 if you picked only one correct answer or no correct answers.

| | | |
|---|---|---|
| 10. | B, C | |
| 11. | D | |
| 12. | D | |
| 13. | C | |
| 14. | A | |
| 15. | A | |
| 16. | B | |
| 17. | B | |

For question 18, write 1 if you placed five answer choices correctly. Write 0 if you placed 4 or fewer choices correctly.

| | | |
|---|---|---|
| 18. | Yes: A, B, D | |

For question 19, write 1 if you picked both correct answers. Write 0 if you picked only one correct answer or no correct answers.

| Question Number | Correct Answer | Your Raw Points |
|---|---|---|
| 19. | A, C | |
| 20. | D | |
| 21. | B | |
| 22. | C | |
| 23. | D | |
| 24. | A | |
| 25. | C | |

For question 26, write 1 if you picked both correct answers. Write 0 if you picked only one correct answer or no correct answers.

| 26. | A, C | |
|---|---|---|
| 27. | D | |
| 28. | B | |
| **TOTAL:** | | |

Below is a table that converts your Listening section answers into a TOEFL iBT Listening scaled score. Take the total of raw points from your answer key and find that number in the left-hand column of the table. The right-hand column of the table gives a TOEFL iBT Listening scaled score for each number of raw points. For example, if the total points from your answer key is 27, the table shows a scaled score of 29 to 30.

You should use your score estimate as a general guide only. Your actual score on the TOEFL iBT test may be higher or lower than your score on the practice version.

## Listening

| Raw Point Total | Scaled Score |
| --- | --- |
| 28 | 30 |
| 27 | 29–30 |
| 26 | 27–30 |
| 25 | 25–30 |
| 24 | 24–29 |
| 23 | 23–27 |
| 22 | 22–26 |
| 21 | 21–25 |
| 20 | 19–24 |
| 19 | 18–23 |
| 18 | 17–21 |
| 17 | 16–20 |
| 16 | 14–19 |
| 15 | 13–18 |
| 14 | 12–17 |
| 13 | 10–15 |
| 12 | 9–14 |
| 11 | 7–13 |
| 10 | 6–12 |
| 9 | 5–10 |
| 8 | 3–9 |
| 7 | 2–7 |
| 6 | 1–6 |
| 5 | 1–4 |
| 4 | 0–2 |
| 3 | 0–1 |
| 2 | 0 |
| 1 | 0 |
| 0 | 0 |

# Listening Scripts and Answer Explanations

## Questions 1–5

### Track 78 Listening Script

**Narrator**

Listen to a conversation between a student and an administrator in the university employment office.

**Male Student**

Hi, I hope you can help me. I just transferred from Northeastern State University, near Chicago...

**Administrator**

Well, welcome to Central University. But Chicago's such a great city, why did you leave?

**Male Student**

Everyone asks that... it's my hometown, and it was sure convenient to go to a school nearby. But Northeastern is still fairly small, and it doesn't have the program I'm interested in... I want to major in international studies and the only program in the state is here.

**Administrator**

We do have a great program. How did you get interested in international studies?

**Male Student**

My family hosted a few foreign-exchange students while I was growing up... then I took part in an international summer program after I graduated from high school. I found I really like meeting people from all over, getting to know them...

**Administrator**

Oh, OK. And that led you to our program. Right now, though, I assume you're looking for a job.

**Male Student**

Yeah, a part-time job on campus . . . I thought I'd save money, being away from the big city . . . but it doesn't seem to be working that way. Anyway, I'm not having much luck.

**Administrator**

I'm not surprised. Most of our campus jobs are taken in the first week or two of the semester. What work experience have you had?

**Male Student**

Well, I worked in the university library last year. But I already checked at the library here . . . they said their remaining positions were for work-study students getting financial aid. I've never run into that before.

**Administrator**

Well, I guess each school has its own policies. We really don't have much right now. You might be better off waiting until next semester . . . if you **really** want something . . . How are your computer skills?

**Male Student**

About average, I'd say. I helped teach some of the basic computer classes Northeastern offers for new users, if that helps any.

**Administrator**

OK . . . Uh, the technology support department needs people to work at its helpdesk. It's basically a customer-service job . . . answering questions, helping people solve their computer problems . . . give you a chance to develop your people skills.

**Male Student**

Something every diplomat needs. But, is there some problem? I mean, why's the job still open?

**Administrator**

Well, they have extended hours . . . from 6 A.M. to 2 A.M. every day, so they need a large staff. But right now they only need people early mornings, late nights, and weekends. You'd probably end up with a bit of everything rather than a regular spot. On the bright side, you'd probably be able to get some studying done between calls. At least it'd be a start and then you can try for better hours next semester.

**Male Student**

Hmm, I see where the hours might be a problem. But . . . I guess I can't afford to be too picky if I want a job. Still, maybe we can work something out.

**Track 79 Listening Script (Question 5)**

**Narrator**

Listen again to part of the conversation. Then answer the question.

**Administrator**

We really don't have much right now. You might be better off waiting until next semester . . . if you **really** want something . . .

**Narrator**

Why does the woman say this:

**Administrator**

if you really want something . . .

## Answer Explanations

1. **C** This is a Gist-Purpose question. After the student and the administrator talk about the student's reasons for transferring to another institution, the administrator says that she assumes the student has come to the employment office in the hope of finding a job. The student confirms that he is indeed looking for a part-time job; therefore, the correct answer is choice C. Since the student indicates that he already found out that he is not eligible for the library jobs, choice A is incorrect. He does not say anything that would indicate an interest in hosting an exchange student (choice B) and he does not ask the administrator to tell him the computer lab's hours (choice D).

2. **A** This is a Detail question. At the beginning of the conversation, the student explains that he has transferred from Northeastern State University to Central University because Central University offers a program in international studies. Thus, choice A is the correct response. The student says that he took part in an international summer program, but he makes no mention of participating in an exchange program at the university (choice B). He also says that the problem with his previous university is that it is too small to offer the program he wants, so choice C is incorrect. And though Central University has an international studies *program*, it is not described as having an international *reputation* (choice D).

3. **A** This is an Understanding Organization question. When the student talks about the fact that his family hosted foreign-exchange students, he is replying to the administrator's question about how he became interested in international studies, so choice A is the correct answer. There is no connection between his family's hosting experience and his search for a job (choice B). The student does not mention any plans to become an exchange student while at the university (choice C) and he does not say that he learned his computer skills from an exchange student (choice D).

4. **D** To answer this Making Inferences question, you need to recognize that the regular daytime and evening shifts at the helpdesk have already been filled. You can draw this conclusion because the administrator says that workers are needed only during early mornings, late nights, and weekends. She also says that the student's schedule would probably include a bit of each of these unusual work hours. Working irregular hours would have to be acceptable to students applying for the available helpdesk positions, so the correct answer is choice D.

5. **C** In this replay question, you are asked to listen again to a statement made by the administrator (Track 79). You are then asked to listen once more to a particular phrase that is part of the statement and to identify the reason why the administrator uses that particular phrase. This question requires you to Understand the Function of What Is Said. To answer it correctly (choice C), you need to understand that the administrator is trying to warn the student that the only job currently available is one that most students would rather not have. The tone of her voice when she speaks the phrase helps convey her intention. Choice A would make sense if the administrator's statement stopped with the suggestion that it might be better for the student to wait until next semester to look for a job, but the inclusion of the warning phrase makes choice A incorrect. Choices B and D might initially appear to make sense, but your understanding of the entire conversation tells you that the administrator is preparing to talk about the job at the computer lab, not about an off-campus job or a work-study program.

## Questions 6–11

### Track 80 Listening Script

**Narrator**

Listen to part of a lecture in an art history class.

Art History

### Professor

Today, we'll continue our examination of ancient Roman sculpture. We've already looked at **portrait** sculpture—which are busts created to commemorate people who had died—and we've looked at **relief** sculpture, or sculpting on walls. And today we look at yet another category of sculpture—copies. Roman sculptors **often** made copies of famous Greek sculptures.

### Female Student

Why did they do that?

### Professor

Well, no one knows for sure. You see, in the late fourth century B.C., the Romans began a campaign to expand the Roman Empire . . . and in 300 years they had conquered most of the Mediterranean area and parts of Europe. You know the saying, "To the victor belong the spoils?" Well, the Roman army returned to Rome with many works of Greek art. It's probably fair to say that the Romans were impressed by Greek art and culture—and they began making copies of the Greek statues. Now, the dominant view in traditional art history is that Roman artists lacked creativity and skill, especially compared to the Greek artists who came before them. Essentially, the traditional view—a view that's been prevalent for over 250 years—is that the Romans copied Greek sculptures because they couldn't create sculpture of their own.

But, finally, **some** contemporary art historians have challenged this view. One is Elaine Gazda.

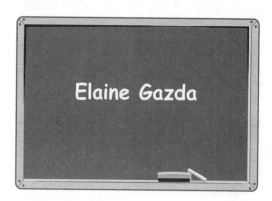

Elaine Gazda

Gazda says that there might be other reasons that Romans made copies. She wasn't convinced that it was because of a lack of creativity. Can anyone think of another possible reason?

**Male Student**

Well . . . maybe they just admired the sculptures, you know, they liked the way they looked.

**Professor**

Yes! That's one of Gazda's points. Another is that while nowadays reproduction is easy, it was not so easy in Roman times. Copying statues required a lot of skill, time, and effort. So, Gazda hypothesizes that copying didn't indicate a lack of artistic imagination—or skill—on the part of Roman artists, but rather, the Romans made copies because they admired Greek sculpture. Classical Greek statues represented an idealization of the human body and were considered quite beautiful at the time.

Gazda also believes that it's been a mistake to dismiss the Roman copies as, well, copies for copies' sake, and not to consider the **Roman** function and meaning of the statues.

**Female Student**

What do you mean . . . the Roman function? Weren't they just for decoration?

**Professor**

Well, not necessarily. Under the emperor Augustus, at the height of the Roman Empire, portrait statues were sent throughout the empire . . . they were supposed to communicate specific ideas about the emperor and the imperial family, and to help inhabitants of the conquered areas become familiar with the Roman way of life. You know, Roman coins were also distributed throughout the empire. Anybody care to guess what was on them?

**Male Student**

The emperor's face?

**Professor**

That's right. The coins were easy to distribute, and they allowed people to see the emperor, or at least his likeness, and served as an additional reminder to let them know, well, who was in charge. And the images helped people become familiar with the emperor—**statues** of him in different roles were sent all over the empire. Now, actually **some** Roman sculptures were original, but others were exact copies of Greek statues. And some Roman sculptures were combinations of some sort; some combined more than one Greek statue, and others combined a Greek god or an athlete with a Roman's head. At the time of Julius Caesar, it wasn't uncommon to create statues that had the body of a god and the head of an emperor.

And the Romans were clever . . . what they did was, they made plaster casts from molds of the sculptures. Then, they shipped these plaster casts to workshops all over the empire, where they were replicated in marble or bronze. And on some statues the heads were removable—they could put an emperor's head on different bodies showing him doing different things. And then later, when the time came, they could even use the head of the **next** emperor on the same body!

## Track 81 Listening Script (Question 11)

**Narrator**

Listen again to part of the lecture. Then answer the question.

**Professor**

Essentially, the traditional view—a view that's been prevalent for over 250 years—is that the Romans copied Greek sculptures because they couldn't create sculpture of their own. But, finally, some contemporary art historians have challenged this view.

**Narrator**

What does the professor imply when he says this:

**Professor**

But, finally, some contemporary art historians have challenged this view.

## Answer Explanations

6. **A** This is a Gist-Content item. The class has been studying ancient Roman sculpture. The professor states that it was a common practice among Roman sculptors to make copies of Greek sculptures. He discusses an opinion about this practice that was held by most art historians in the past. Then he discusses a different opinion that has been proposed by a contemporary art historian. This contrast of ideas makes choice A the correct response. The other choices present topics that are *mentioned* in the lecture but are not the *main subject* of the lecture.

7. **C** This is a Detail question. Early in the lecture, the professor describes how the Romans encountered Greek art during their conquest of the Mediterranean region. The traditional view of art historians, cited by the professor, is that the Romans copied Greek art because they were not as creative as the Greeks, so the correct answer is choice C. Choices A and B are not mentioned in the lecture. Choice D is wrong because it expresses the view of Elaine Gazda, the contemporary art historian, not the view of traditional art historians.

8. **D** This is a Connecting Content question. The professor discusses several points made by Gazda. One point is that making copies of statues requires artistic skill. Another point is that the Romans needed to circulate portrait statues of their emperor to all parts of their empire in order to foster a sense of loyalty among the inhabitants. Thus, the statues had a dual artistic and political function, making choice D the correct answer.

9. **B** This is an Understanding Organization question. The professor has just discussed the Romans' need to distribute portraits of the emperor throughout their empire. He mentions coins because they are stamped with the emperor's portrait and are easy to distribute, being small and lightweight. Thus, choice B is the correct answer. Choice A may appear to be the right response, but it is not, because it is not the professor's intention to show the similarity between the portraits on coins and the portraits on statues.

10. **B C** In this Detail question, you are asked to choose two correct answers. At the end of the lecture, the professor explains two reasons why the Romans found it useful to make portrait statues with removable heads. First, each head could be attached to a variety of statues, so choice B is correct. Second, the removable head could eventually be replaced with a different emperor's likeness, so choice C is the second correct answer. Neither the weight of the head (choice A) nor the quality of the statue (choice D) is mentioned by the professor.

11. **D** In this replay question, you are asked to listen again to a small part of the lecture in which the professor describes a belief about Roman art that most art historians have held (Track 81). You are then asked to listen once more to the last sentence of the replay and to draw a conclusion about what it means. Like many replay questions, this one requires you to Understand the Function of What Is Said. In that last sentence, the professor indicates that the belief he has just described has been challenged by some members of the current generation of art historians. Choice D is the only choice that relates to the professor's statement as a whole, and you can tell from the way the professor stresses the word "finally" that the professor agrees with this challenge to the traditional belief, so choice D is correct.

## Questions 12–16

### Track 82 Listening Script

**Narrator**

Listen to a conversation between a student and his sociology professor.

**Professor**

Well, I'm glad you redid your outline. Um, I've made a few comments, but nothing you have to act on. It's in good enough shape for you to start writing your paper.

**Male Student**

Thanks. At first I was afraid all that prep work would be a waste of time.

**Professor**

Well, especially with a challenging topic like yours—factors leading to the emergence of sociology as an academic discipline. There's just so much history to consider, you could get lost without a solid outline. Uh, so, did you have a question?

**Male Student**

Yeah, it's about. . . . You mentioned needing volunteers for a research study?

**Professor**

Yep. It's not my study, it's my colleague's in the marketing department. She needs people to watch various new TV programs that haven't been broadcast yet. Then indicate on a survey whether they liked it, why, if they'd watch another episode. . . . It'd be kinda fun, plus participants get a $50 gift certificate.

**Male Student**

Oh, well, I like the sound of that! But—so they're trying to predict if these shows are gonna succeed or fail, right? Based on students' opinions? Why would they care what we think?

**Professor**

Hey, don't sell yourself short—people your age are a very attractive market for advertisers who promote their products on television. The study's sponsored by a TV network. If enough students don't like a show, the network may actually reconsider putting it on the air.

**Male Student**

OK, well, how do I sign up?

**Professor**

You just add your name and phone number to this list and check a time slot. Although it looks like the only times left are next Monday morning and Thursday evening.

**Male Student**

Oh, well. . . . I have marketing and economics Monday mornings, and Thursday.

**Professor**

Oh, you're taking a marketing class? Who's teaching it?

**Male Student**

It's, uh, Professor Larkin, intro to marketing. He hasn't mentioned the study, though.

**Professor**

Oh. Well . . . the marketing department's pretty big. I happen to be friends with the woman who's doing the TV study. OK, well, we don't want you missing class . . . how's Thursday?

**Male Student**

Oh, I work from five till nine that night.

**Professor**

Hmm. No flexibility with your schedule? Where do you work?

**Male Student**

At Fox's Diner. I'm a server.

**Professor**

Oh, I love Fox's. I eat there every week. Maybe you could switch shifts with someone.

**Male Student**

I'm still in training, and the only night my trainer works is Thursday.

**Professor**

Look, I know the owners there really well. Why don't you let me give them a call and explain the situation?

**Male Student**

OK. It'd be cool to be part of a real research study. And the gift certificate wouldn't hurt, either!

**Track 83 Listening Script (Question 16)**

**Narrator**

Listen again to part of the conversation. Then answer the question.

**Professor**

Oh, you're taking a marketing class? Who's teaching it?

**Male Student**

It's, uh, Professor Larkin, intro to marketing. He hasn't mentioned the study, though.

**Professor**

Oh. Well . . . the marketing department's pretty big. I happen to be friends with the woman who's doing the TV study.

**Narrator**

What does the professor mean when she says this:

**Professor**

Oh. Well . . . the marketing department's pretty big.

## Answer Explanations

12. **D** This is a Gist-Content question. The professor and the student begin by briefly discussing an outline the student has written for an assignment, but the conversation shifts when the professor says, "Uh, so, did you have a question?" The rest of the conversation mainly focuses on a research project in which the student would like to participate, so the correct answer is choice D.

13. **C** This question involves Making Inferences. The professor acknowledges that the topic of the student's paper is "challenging" and there's "just so much history to consider," but she does not tell the student to narrow the focus of his paper. Therefore, choice A can be eliminated as the answer. It's clear that the professor has a favorable opinion of the outline when she says, "It's (the outline) in good enough shape for you to start writing your paper." She goes on to say that the student needs a solid outline for such a complex topic, and it's implied that he has produced an outline that is sufficient to help him write about a difficult topic. Therefore, the correct answer is choice C.

14. **A** This is a Detail question. After the student expresses interest in the research study, the professor briefly explains what is expected of the participants. The study is fairly straightforward, with participants watching several new TV shows and giving their opinions about the quality of the shows. The professor does not mention anything about sociological factors that influence participants' opinions of the shows, so choice D can be eliminated. She does mention that TV networks are interested in the opinions of university students because they are an important market, so the correct answer is choice A.

15. **A** This question requires Making an Inference. After the student explains why it will be difficult to change his work schedule at Fox's Diner, the professor says, "Look, I know the owners there really well. Why don't you let me give them a call and explain the situation?" The clear implication is that the owners of the restaurant would want to help the professor, so the correct answer is choice A.

16. **B** This question involves Understanding the Function of What Is Said. You are asked to listen again to part of the conversation (Track 83). The student comments that his marketing professor, Professor Larkin, has not said anything about the research study. The professor responds that the marketing department is big, so the correct answer is choice B. Choice D could be the meaning of this utterance in a different context, but not in this conversation because only one research study is discussed. Likewise, even though choice A could be correct in a different context, the student does not express a desire to find a marketing professor who is interested in sociology. By pointing out the size of the marketing department, the professor is suggesting that Professor Larkin probably does not know about all of the research projects that are being conducted by professors in the department.

# Questions 17–22

## Track 84 Listening Script

### Narrator
Listen to part of a lecture in a European history class.

European History

**Professor**

In order to really study the social history of the Middle Ages, you have to understand the role of spices. Now, this might sound a little surprising, even a little strange, but what seem like little things now were, back then, actually rather big things. So, first let's define what a spice is. Technically speaking, a spice is part of an aromatic plant that is not a leaf, or herb. Spices can come from tree bark, like, ah, cinnamon, plant roots like ginger, flower buds like cloves. And in the Middle Ages, Europeans were familiar with lots of different spices, the most important being pepper, cloves, ginger, cinnamon, mace, and nutmeg. These spices literally dominated the way Europeans lived for centuries—how they traded and, uh, even how they used their imaginations.

So why this medieval fascination with spices? We can boil it down to three general ideas, briefly. One was cost and rarity, ah, two was exotic taste and fragrance, and third, mysterious origins and a kind of mythical status.

Now, for cost and rarity: Spices aren't native to Europe, and they had to be imported. Spices only grew in the East Indies, and of course transportation costs were astronomical. So spices were incredibly valuable, even from the very beginning. Here's an example, um, in 408 A.D., the Gothic general who'd captured Rome demanded payment. He wanted 5,000 pounds of gold, among other things, but he also wanted 3,000 pounds of pepper. Maybe that'll give you an idea of exactly where pepper stood at the time. By the Middle Ages, spices were regarded as so important and expensive, they were used in diplomacy—as gifts by heads of state and ambassadors.

Now, for the taste, the diet then was relatively bland compared to today's. There wasn't much variety. Uh, especially the aristocracy, who tended to eat a lot of meat, um, they were always looking for new ways to prepare it—new sauces, new tastes, and this is where spices came in. Now this is a good point to mention one of the biggest myths about spices: It's commonly said that medieval Europeans wanted spices to cover up the taste of spoiled meat, but this isn't really true. Anyone who had to worry about spoiled meat couldn't afford spices in the first place. If you could afford spices, you could definitely afford fresh meat. We also have evidence that various medieval markets employed a kind of police, to make sure that people didn't sell spoiled food. And if you were caught doing it, you were subject to various fines, humiliating public punishments. So, what actually was true was this: In order to have meat for the winter, people would preserve it in salt—not a spice. Spices, actually, aren't very effective as preservatives. And, uh, throughout winter they would eat salted meat, but the taste of the stuff could grow really boring and, and depressing after a while. So the cooks started looking for new ways to improve the taste, and spices were the answer.

Which brings us to mysterious origins and mythical status. Now the ancient Romans had a thriving spice trade, and they sent their ships to the east and back. But when Rome collapsed in the fifth century and the Middle Ages began, um, direct trade stopped, and, uh, so did that kind of hands-on knowledge of travel and geography. Spices now came by way of the trade routes, with lots of intermediaries between the producer and the consumer. So these spices took on an air of mystery. Their origins were shrouded in exotic travels; they had the allure of the unknown, of wild places. Myths grew up of fantasy lands, magical faraway places made entirely of food and spices. Add to that, spices themselves had always been considered special, or magical—not just for eating—and this was already true in the ancient world where legends about spices were abundant. Spices inspired the medieval imagination, they were used as medicines to ward off diseases, and mixed into perfumes, incense. They were used in religious rituals for thousands of years. They took on a life of their own, and they inspired the medieval imagination, spurred on the age of discovery in the fifteenth and sixteenth centuries. When famous explorers like Columbus and da Gama and Magellan left Europe in their ships, they weren't looking for a new world; they were looking for spices. And we know what important historical repercussions some of those voyages had.

### Track 85 Listening Script (Question 22)

**Narrator**

Listen again to part of the lecture. Then answer the question.

**Professor**

Here's an example, um, in 408 A.D., the Gothic general who'd captured Rome demanded payment. He wanted 5,000 pounds of gold, among other things, but he also wanted 3,000 pounds of pepper. Maybe that'll give you an idea of exactly where pepper stood at the time.

**Narrator**

Why does the professor say this:

**Professor**

Maybe that'll give you an idea of exactly where pepper stood at the time.

## Answer Explanations

17. **B** This is a Gist-Purpose question. The professor introduces her purpose in the first sentence when she says, "In order to really study the social history of the Middle Ages, you have to understand the role of spices." For the rest of the lecture, the professor describes three main reasons why spices were important for medieval society. The correct answer is B.

18. **A** **B** **D** This is a Connecting Information question. It involves connecting content from different parts of the lecture. The professor discusses many aspects of spices, one of which is that spices "aren't native to Europe." The fact that spices had to be imported is mentioned throughout the lecture. Also, the professor points out the extremely high cost of spices, which made them inaccessible for many people. When the professor describes the mysterious quality that spices held for medieval Europeans, she points out that they were used for medicinal purposes. The chart correctly filled out looks like this:

|  | YES | NO |
| --- | --- | --- |
| A. They had to be imported. | ✓ | |
| B. They were unaffordable for many people. | ✓ | |
| C. They were used to preserve meat during the winter. | | ✓ |
| D. They were believed to have medicinal properties. | ✓ | |
| E. Their sale in public markets was closely regulated. | | ✓ |

The two statements marked as "No" are not true about spices in medieval Europe for the following reasons:

The professor mentions that "In order to have meat for the winter, people would preserve it in salt—**not** a spice." She goes on to say that spices are not useful as preservatives.

The professor does discuss regulations in public markets, but she's referring to rules concerning the sale of meat, not spices.

19. **A** **C** This is a Detail question. While discussing the exotic taste of spices, the professor argues against the idea that medieval Europeans used spices to cover up the taste of spoiled meat. She points out that anyone who could afford spices would be able to buy fresh meat. Also, she describes how "medieval markets employed a kind of police, to make sure that people didn't sell spoiled food." The correct answers are A and C.

20. **D** This question involves Understanding Organization. The professor mentions the collapse of the Roman Empire and how this led to an interruption in the trade route between Rome and the East. Specifically, she mentions that, "direct trade stopped," so choice A can be eliminated. Even though a direct route was no longer available, Romans were still able to acquire spices ". . . by way of the trade routes, with lots of intermediaries between the producer and the consumer." For this reason, choice C can be eliminated. The lack of a direct trade route and intimate knowledge with "travel and geography" allowed spices to be viewed as mysterious and exotic by the Romans. Therefore, the correct answer is D.

21. **B** This is a Detail question. Near the end of the lecture, the professor explains the growing importance of spices, mentioning how they came to be viewed as special or magical. She says, "When famous explorers like Columbus and da Gama and Magellan left Europe in their ships, they weren't looking for a new world; they were looking for spices." It's clear that European explorers were not motivated to discover new lands, but to find spices, so the correct answer is B.

22. **C** This question involves Understanding the Function of What Is Said. You are asked to listen again to part of the lecture (Track 85). To emphasize the value of spices in the Middle Ages, the professor provides an example of a general who captured Rome. This general demanded payment in the form of gold and pepper. When she says, "Maybe that'll give you an idea of exactly where pepper stood at the time," the professor is illustrating how valuable spices like pepper were in the Middle Ages, so the correct answer is C.

## Questions 23–28

### Track 86 Listening Script

**Narrator**
Listen to part of a lecture in a biology class.

Biology

**Professor**

Well, it's finally looking like spring is arriving—the last of the winter snow will be melting away in a few days. So before we close today, I thought I'd mention, uh, a biological event that's part of the transition from winter to spring . . . something you can go outside and watch, if you have some patience. There's a small creature that lives in this area—you've probably seen it: it's the North American wood frog.

Now the wood frog's not that easy to spot, since it stays pretty close to the ground, under leaves and things, and it blends in really well with its background, as you can see. But they're worth the effort, because they do something very unusual—something you might not have even thought possible.

OK, North American wood frogs live over a very broad territory, or range—they're found all over the northeastern United States, and all through Canada and Alaska—even inside the Arctic Circle. No other frog is able to live that far north. But wherever they live, once the weather starts to turn cold, and the temperatures start to drop below freezing—as soon as the frog even touches an ice crystal or a bit of frozen ground . . . well, it begins to freeze. Yes, Jimmy? You look a bit taken aback.

**Male Student**

Wait. You mean, it's still alive, but it freezes? Solid?

**Professor**

Well, almost. Ice forms in all the spaces outside cells, but never within a cell.

**Male Student**

But . . . then, how does its heart beat?

**Professor**

It doesn't.

**Male Student**

But—how can it do. . . .

**Professor**

How can it do such a thing? Well, that first touch of ice apparently triggers a biological response inside the frog, that first of all starts drawing water away from the center of its body. So the middle part of the frog, its internal organs—its heart, lungs, liver—these start getting drier and drier, while the water that's being pulled away is forming a puddle around the organs, just underneath the skin. And then that puddle of water starts to freeze.

OK, up to now the frog's heart is still beating, right? Slower and slower, but. . . . And in those last few hours before it freezes, it distributes glucose—a blood sugar—throughout its body, its circulatory system. Sort of acts like an antifreeze. . . .

**Male Student**

A solution of antifreeze, like you put in your car in the winter?

**Professor**

Well, you tell me. In frogs, the extra glucose makes it harder for the water inside the cells to freeze, so the cells stay just slightly wet—enough so that they can survive the winter. Then after that, the heart stops beating altogether. So, is that the same?

**Male Student**

I don't really know, but uh . . . how long does it stay that way?

**Professor**

Well, it could be days or even months—all winter, in fact. But, um, see, the heart really doesn't need to do any pumping now, because the blood is frozen too.

**Male Student**

I just . . . I guess I just don't see how it isn't—y'know, clinically dead.

**Professor**

Well, that's the amazing thing. And how it revives is pretty amazing too. After months without a heartbeat, springtime comes around again, the Earth starts to warm up, and suddenly one day—ping! A pulse—followed by another one, then another, until—maybe ten, twelve hours later, the animal is fully recovered.

**Male Student**

And—does the, uh, thawing process have some kind of trigger as well?

**Professor**

Well, we're not sure, actually. The peculiar thing is, even though the sun is warming the frog up on the outside, its insides thaw out first—the heart and brain and everything. But somehow, it all just happens that way every spring.

**Male Student**

And after they thaw? Does it affect them? Like their life span?

**Professor**

Well, hmm . . . we really don't know a lot about how long a wood frog normally lives—probably just a few years. But there's no evidence that the freezing process affects its longevity. It does have some other impacts, though. In studies we've found that, when it comes to reproduction, freezing diminishes the mating performance of males: after they've been frozen, and thawed of course, they don't seem quite as vocal, they move slower—and they seem to have a harder time recognizing a potential mate. So if a male frog could manage not to go through this freezing cycle, he'd probably have more success at mating.

**Track 87 Listening Script (Question 28)**

**Narrator**

Listen again to part of the lecture. Then answer the question.

**Male Student**

A solution of antifreeze, like you put in your car in the winter?

**Professor**

Well, you tell me. In frogs, the extra glucose makes it harder for the water inside the cells to freeze, so the cells stay just slightly wet—enough so that they can survive the winter. Then after that, the heart stops beating altogether. So, is that the same?

**Narrator**

What does the professor imply when she says this:

**Professor**

Well, you tell me.

## Answer Explanations

23. **Ⓓ** This is a Gist-Purpose question. The professor begins by telling her students about an unusual biological process involving North American wood frogs. The majority of the lecture describes this unusual occurrence, explaining in detail the steps involved. During the lecture, the professor does not discuss any biological advantages the wood frog gains from freezing and then thawing. In fact, she points out one negative consequence for some frogs that undergo this process, so choice A can be eliminated. Information about the wood frog's circulatory system is discussed, but this information only serves to describe the larger freezing process. Therefore, choice C can be eliminated. The main purpose of the lecture is to make students aware of an unusual biological process that they can observe in their area, so the correct answer is D.

24. **A** This question involves Understanding Organization. The professor mentions the arrival of spring because this is the time when wood frogs begin to thaw. She says this event is "something you can go outside and watch," and that even though it is not easy to spot the frogs, the effort is worth it. She is encouraging her students to go out and observe these thawing frogs, so the correct answer is A.

25. **C** This is a Detail question. The professor states that after a wood frog first touches ice, there is a response ". . . that first of all starts drawing water away from the center of its body." She goes on to mention that the center of a frog's body contains its internal organs, and that these organs ". . . start getting drier and drier . . ." Therefore, the correct answer is C.

26. **A C** This is a Connecting Information question. It requires connecting content from different parts of the lecture. In response to the student's question about whether there is a trigger for the thawing process, the professor states, "Well, we're not sure, actually. The peculiar thing is, even though the sun is warming the frog up on the outside, its insides thaw out first. . . ." The skin is not mentioned in this part of the explanation of the process, but the listener can infer that "first" means before the rest of the frog's body. Therefore, the correct answers are A and C.

27. **D** This is a Detail question. At the end of the lecture, the professor discusses the effects freezing has on these frogs. She says that while it doesn't seem that the freezing process has an impact on how long a frog lives, it does seem to negatively affect the frog's success at reproduction. Specifically, once a frog has thawed, it has trouble identifying potential mates. Therefore, the correct answer is D. Choice A can be eliminated since it is the opposite of the point the professor makes about the effect of freezing on reproduction.

28. **B** This question involves Understanding the Function of What Is Said. You are asked to listen again to part of the lecture (Track 87). After the professor mentions that glucose, a blood sugar, is distributed throughout the frog's body to slow down the freezing process, the student uses a familiar example of antifreeze in a car to see if he has understood the concept. The professor doesn't directly answer his question, but she continues her explanation of how glucose helps reduce the freezing effect. She then asks the student to reconsider his original question, so the correct answer is B.

# Speaking

## Listening Scripts, Important Points, and Sample Responses with Rater Comments

Use the Speaking rubrics on pages 184–187 to see how responses are scored. The raters who listen to your responses will analyze them in three general categories. These categories are Delivery, Language Use, and Topic Development. All three categories have equal importance.

This section includes important points that should be covered when answering each question. All of these points must be present in a response in order for it to receive the highest score in the Topic Development category. These important points are guides to the kind of information raters expect to hear in a high-level response.

This section also refers to example responses on the accompanying audio tracks. Some responses were scored at the highest level, while others were not. The responses are followed by explanations of their scores.

### Question 1: Paired Choice

#### Track 88 Listening Script

**Narrator**

Do you agree or disagree with the following statement?

**It is important to learn about other cultures.**

Use details and examples to explain your opinion.

> **Preparation Time: 15 Seconds**
> **Response Time: 45 Seconds**

## Important Points

When you answer this question, you should first state whether you believe, or do not believe, it is important to learn about other cultures. You may choose either point of view and will not be evaluated on your choice. The content of your response will be evaluated on how completely and clearly you explain your ideas and support your opinion. If you agree with the statement, you may choose to describe some areas in which it is important (international business, travel and tourism, and so on) and then provide details and specific examples to further explain. If you disagree, you should also provide at least one reason followed by specific details and examples to further explain your idea and to support your opinion.

## Sample Responses

### *Play Track 93 to hear a high-level response for Question 1.*

*Rater Comments*

The speaker is generally very clear and easy to understand. She uses pauses effectively (to separate phrases) and stresses important words within the phrases, which makes it easy for the listener to understand her message. ("**First** of **all**, it uh **gives** you the **opportunity** to **understand** your culture **better**.") Although she makes some minor grammatical errors sometimes, she has a strong ability to create long, accurate phrases and sentences. ("Then it helps you to understand other people from other countries better [pause] because if you know the back ground of their behavior [pause] then it is easier to understand it and not judge it.") Her response is full and includes both general reasons for her opinion ("it helps you understand other people . . .") and supports the idea with specific examples and details (since she explains that if you understand others better, then you won't judge them and you won't offend them).

### *Play Track 94 to hear a mid-level response for Question 1.*

*Rater Comments*

The speaker is mostly clear and easy to understand. However, the message is at times not easily comprehensible because of limitations in grammar and vocabulary. For example, he attempts to express a rather sophisticated idea but the meaning is not clear because of errors in word choice, word form, and agreement in particular. For example, he says "I'm gonna really expand my **verizon (?) of thoughts (?)** and **philosopher philosophical** uh ideas because I'm gonna inter . . . interact with other back grounds(?) and **that's really give me** the chance to acquire good values from other nations." A simpler and more effective paraphrase might be, "Interacting with other cultures could help me to expand my horizons/open me up to new experiences and ideas."

## Question 2: Fit and Explain

### Track 89 Listening Script

**Narrator**

City University's choir is changing its performance schedule next year. Read an article about it in the student newspaper. You will have 50 seconds to read the article. Begin reading now.

| Reading Time: 50 Seconds |
|---|

---

**University Choir to Enter Off-Campus Singing Competitions**

Currently, the university choir gives singing concerts only on campus. Next year, however, the choir will add competitive events at other locations to its schedule. The choir's new director feels that entering singing competitions will make the quality of the choir's performance even better than it is now. "Competitions will motivate students in the choir to pursue a higher standard of excellence in singing," he said. In addition, it is hoped that getting the choir off campus and out in the public will strengthen the reputation of the university's music program. This in turn will help the program grow.

---

**Narrator**

Now listen to two students discussing the article.

**Female Student**

Jim, you're in the choir, right? Whaddaya think about what they're doing next year . . . this article?

**Male Student**

I really like it.

**Female Student**

Yeah?

**Male Student**

Yeah. The new director's right that it will motivate us.

**Female Student**

How's that?

**Male Student**

Well, some of the other schools are really good . . . so we'll really have to work hard to go up against them.

**Female Student**

Yeah . . .

**Male Student**

I mean, right now we don't rehearse more than once a week, but if we know we'd be competing with other schools, we'd probably rehearse more often and improve our singing a lot.

**Female Student**

That's true. The more you practice, the better you get. So, um . . . What about what the article said about how this will help the program?

**Male Student**

I hope it works! Right now, our program is pretty small, but we have some really talented people. And it would be great to attract even more people.

**Female Student**

So how will this plan help?

**Male Student**

Well, if we go to these off campus events and other people hear us and think we're really good, we might be able to get some new students interested in coming to this university . . . to be a part of our music program and perform in our choir concerts.

**Female Student**

You're right. I hadn't really thought about that.

**Narrator**

The man expresses his opinion about the change described in the article. Briefly summarize the change. Then state his opinion about the change and explain the reasons he gives for holding that opinion.

> **Preparation Time: 30 Seconds**
> **Response Time: 60 Seconds**

## Important Points

For this item, you should be sure to address the information from both the reading and the listening. You could begin by briefly explaining the change described in the article—that the university choir will now be participating in off-campus competitions with other universities (rather than singing only on campus as they do now). You should then explain that the man in the listening agrees with the change. First, he agrees with the director that performing in these competitions would motivate the choir to improve, since they would have to practice or rehearse more often. You should then explain that the man also agrees with the director's idea that the competitions will help the music program grow. He says that if people hear them singing well in the competitions, they may become interested in attending the university (and joining the choir).

### Sample Responses

*Play Track 95 to hear a high-level response for Question 2.*

*Rater Comments*

This is a full and clear response. Although the speaker stops and starts occasionally while gathering his thoughts, his overall speech is quite fluid, and the response is easy to follow. His vocabulary is accurate and varied. Transition words like "furthermore" help the listener follow his response. Some minor grammatical errors, such as "the director think," do not cause problems for the listener. The speaker probably goes into more detail than needed in summarizing the reading; an even more efficient response might have integrated that information into a discussion of the student's reasons for agreeing with the plan. However, the speaker covers all the key information in his response.

*Play Track 96 to hear a mid-level response for Question 2.*

*Rater Comments*

While the speaker uses high-level vocabulary ("pretty happy with the change undertook," "level up their singing proficiency"), his response is not always easy to follow. Several pronunciation errors and slow pacing require the listener to make some effort in order to understand what he is saying. The content of the response is also occasionally unclear. The speaker never fully explains what the director's plan is for the choir, and he does not cover the final point about how the choir competing off-campus will get new students interested in coming to the university. By improving the fluency and pacing of his speech, this speaker would be able to more efficiently communicate the main ideas asked for in a 60-second response.

## Question 3: General/Specific

### Track 90 Listening Script

#### Narrator

Read a passage about relict behaviors from a biology textbook. You will have 50 seconds to read the passage. Begin reading now.

**Reading Time: 50 Seconds**

#### Relict Behaviors

In general, animals act in ways that help them to survive within their specific habitats. However, sometimes an animal species may display a behavior that no longer serves a clear purpose. The original purpose for the behavior may have disappeared long ago, even thousands of years before. These behaviors, known as relict behaviors, were useful to the animal when the species' habitat was different; but now, because of changed conditions, the behavior no longer serves its original purpose. Left over from an earlier time, the behavior remains as a relict, or remnant, long after the environmental circumstance that influenced its evolution has vanished.

**Narrator**

Now listen to part of a lecture in a biology class.

**Professor**

OK, so a good example of this—found right here in North America—is something an animal called the American **pronghorn** does. Pronghorns, as you may know, are a kinda deer-like animal . . . they live out on the open, grassy plains . . . somewhat in the middle of North America. . . .

And they are super fast. Pronghorns are, in fact, noted for being the **fastest** animal in the Western Hemisphere. Once a pronghorn starts running—zoom!—none of its present-day predators, like the . . . bobcat . . . or coyote, can even **hope** to catch up with it . . . it's off in a flash!

OK, so why then do pronghorns run **so** fast? That's the question.

Well, it turns out that quite a long time ago . . . I'm talking tens of thousands of years . . . things on the grassy plains used to be very different for the pronghorns.

Because back then **lions** used to live on the plains . . . chasing and preying upon the pronghorns. And lions, of course, are a very swift-moving mammal . . . **much** faster than the bobcat or coyote, or other predators that you find on the plains today. . . .

But, **now**, however, lions are all **extinct** in North America. They're no longer a predator of the pronghorn. Tens of thousands of years ago, though, the lions were there, chasing the pronghorns. So, back then, the pronghorn's speed was critical to its survival.

**Narrator**

Using the example of the pronghorn and lion, explain the concept of a relict behavior.

> **Preparation Time: 30 Seconds**
> **Response Time: 60 Seconds**

## Important Points

For this task, the prompt asks you to use the examples from the lecture to explain the concept described in the reading. You should summarize important information from the example presented in the lecture *and* explain how it illustrates the concept, which is generally defined in the reading. The concept here is relict behavior, and one way to begin your response is by *briefly* describing what that is: a relict behavior is a behavior that an animal displays that used to serve a purpose but does not serve the same purpose any more. You should then discuss the example of the pronghorn, connecting this specific example to the general concept. The pronghorn can run very fast, and the great speed of the pronghorn is a relict behavior because the pronghorn no longer needs to run fast. In the past, the pronghorn needed to run fast because the lion was its predator, and lions were also very fast. Now that the lion is extinct in North America, the pronghorn does not need to run as fast because its current predators—the bobcat and the coyote—are not as fast as the lion. Your response should contain information from both the reading and the lecture so that the listener will understand how the pronghorn's speed is a good example of relict behavior.

## Sample Responses

***Play Track 97 to hear a high-level response for Question 3.***

*Rater Comments*

This is a strong response. Speech is clear overall, and the pace of the response is appropriate, creating no difficulties for the listener. Effective intonation and word stress contributes to meaning, such as when the speaker emphasizes "need" in the last sentence ("pronghorns don't **need** to run that fast any more"). She uses a wide range of grammatical structures effectively (". . . the reasons for having developed that behavior or quality has long disappeared," ". . . the pronghorns had to flee from lions who were preying upon them"), and her word choice is effective and precise. She also develops her ideas very effectively, starting with a clear definition of relict behavior and providing a clear summary of the example and how it relates to the concept. Her final sentence clearly connects the two, though it might have been more explicit if she had used the term "relict behavior" again.

***Play Track 98 to hear a mid-level response for Question 3.***

*Rater Comments*

This speaker provides some accurate content and attempts to connect the concept of relict behavior to the example, but the response is overall incomplete and unclear, primarily because she has difficulty developing her ideas. She does mention relict behavior at the beginning of her response but does not provide a clear description of it, only saying that it "can be genetically inherit." The remainder of the response summarizes the lecture, and she does provide key details and demonstrate some understanding of it, but the description is not entirely clear, and the listener is forced to fill in gaps that the speaker does not mention; for example, the pronghorn's speed, the most important point, is not mentioned until the second half of the response, creating confusion. Unclear references create more confusion, such as in "**This** proves **that** was inherited . . ." The response also would have been stronger if the speaker specifically said that the pronghorn's speed is a relict behavior, instead of, "it is not survival for them, they just have it." Though there are a few awkward pauses, her speech is generally clear and the pace is good in the response. A larger problem is grammar and vocabulary use. There are enough inaccuracies in the response to hinder communication at times, and the ideas do not always progress clearly. Overall, the speaker does not have a wide enough range of vocabulary and grammatical structures to express her ideas clearly.

# Question 4: Summary

## Track 91 Listening Script

### Narrator

Listen to part of a lecture in a business class.

### Professor

People who are likely to buy a company's product are called target customers. And these target customers influence a company's marketing strategy. In order to develop a marketing strategy, a company will look at certain characteristics of the target customers to decide when and where to advertise . . . so that they'll reach the target customers most effectively. I'd like to talk to you today about two characteristics of target customers that can influence marketing strategy, specifically age and geographic location of the target customers.

Say a company makes toy cars. Who are its target customers? Kids, right? So, if the company wants to make sure its television advertising reaches its target customers, it'd want to advertise during times when kids are actually watching television, like during children's television shows. That way it can make sure that kids see the advertisements. And that way the company'd get people in that age group to go buy toy cars, or to ask their parents to buy 'em at least.

Now, another important characteristic to consider is geographic location . . . places where the company's target customers live. Think about a company that makes boats. Its target customers are people who own homes near oceans or lakes, places where they can use boats. After all, people who don't live near water don't have much use for boats. So, by placing advertisements on signs along the road or on television in cities and towns that are near oceans or lakes, the company'd be more likely to reach the target customers for its boats . . . and sell more of 'em as a result.

### Narrator

Using points and examples from the lecture, explain how the characteristics of target customers influence marketing strategy for products.

| Preparation Time: 20 Seconds |
| --- |
| Response Time: 60 Seconds |

## Important Points

This item requires you to listen to a lecture and summarize key points that explain the concept of target customers. In particular, you will concentrate on the characteristics of target customers that the professor discusses—age and geographic location—and how those characteristics influence marketing strategy for products. For age, you should summarize that a company that has children as its target customers should advertise at times when children are watching TV. For the characteristic of geographic location, you should summarize that the target customers for a company that makes boats are people living near water, so the company should advertise in towns near water. You should include both general information from the lecture (in this case, the concept of target customers and the general characteristics of age and location) and the specific examples in your response.

## Sample Responses

***Play Track 99 to hear a high-level response for Question 4.***

*Rater Comments*

Although the speaker's first sentence is slightly confusing, the response as a whole is clear and complete. The speaker covers all of the important points of the lecture and her response progresses clearly because of her good use of connecting language ("for example," "so," "also," "in this way"). Pronunciation and delivery are also good overall, and are a strong point; the few small problems (such as when she is discussing children and TV) do not affect overall intelligibility, and her pauses are mainly to recall information, not due to lack of language. Language use is also strong, and she uses a variety of grammatical structures effectively (for example, "and this will be the proper time to advertise your toy cars, for example"). There is some imprecise language (such as, "how you reach it is . . ."), but this does not prevent her from getting her point across. Overall, this is an excellent summary of the lecture.

***Play Track 100 to hear a mid-level response for Question 4.***

*Rater Comments*

This response does provide much of the key content of the lecture, but it is not as accurate or complete as a high-level response. The pace of the speech is satisfactory and pronunciation in general is acceptable and does not interfere with overall meaning, but there are continual pauses throughout that make the response difficult to follow. The response starts slowly because the speaker uses *"it"* instead of "target customers," which would be clearer. He also has difficulty with the general explanation; his description is not clear because of imprecise grammar and vocabulary (for example, when he says, "so companies usually seek to put their promotions and advertisement as much as it might be exposed for the targeted customer" instead of something like, "so companies want to make sure target customers will see their advertisements"). He does better with the specific examples, though he says, "they are aiming to buy for kids," when he means, "sell to kids." Overall, the response should be developed more and should include more details. This speaker did not demonstrate that he has enough language resources to give a full and coherent response.

# Writing

## Listening Script, Topic Notes, and Sample Responses with Rater Comments

Use the Writing rubrics on pages 199–200 and 210–211 to see how responses are scored.

### Integrated Writing

#### Track 92 Listening Script

**Narrator**

Now listen to part of a lecture on the topic you just read about.

**Professor**

You've just read about three ways to save *Torreya taxifolia*. Unfortunately, none of these three options provides a satisfactory solution.

About the first solution, reestablishing Torreya in the same location. That's unlikely to be successful because of what's happening to the coolest, dampest areas within Torreya's microclimate. These areas are being strongly affected by changes in the climate of the larger region. This could be because global warming has contributed to an increase in overall temperatures in the region or because wetlands throughout Florida have been drained. Either way, many areas across the region are becoming drier. So it's unlikely that Torreya would have the conditions it needs to survive anywhere within its original Florida microclimate.

Now, about the second solution, relocating Torreya far from where it currently grows. Well, let's look at what happened when humans helped **another** tree, the black locust tree, move north to a new environment.

When they did this, the black locust tree spread so quickly that it killed off many plants and trees in the new environment—and some of these plants and trees were themselves already in danger of becoming extinct. So assisted migration can have unpredicted outcomes for the new environment.

Third, research centers are probably not a solution either. That's because the population of Torreya trees that can be kept in the centers will probably not be able to resist diseases. For a population of trees to survive a disease, it needs to be relatively large and it needs to be genetically diverse. Tree populations in the wild usually satisfy those criteria. But research centers would simply not have enough capacity to keep a large and diverse population of Torreya trees, so trees in such centers will not be capable of surviving diseases in the long term.

**Narrator**

Summarize the points made in the lecture, being sure to explain how they cast doubt on the specific solutions presented in the reading passage.

## Topic Notes

You should understand the reasons presented in the lecture for why the different methods to save the *Torreya* tree might not work. The lecturer questions each of the solutions proposed in the passage: planting *Torreya* in areas where it used to grow, planting it in new areas, and preserving it in research centers.

A high-scoring response will include the following points made by the lecturer that address the points made in the reading passage.

| Point Made in the Reading Passage | Contrasting Point from the Lecture |
|---|---|
| *Torreya* trees could be planted in areas where they used to grow because those areas have a favorable cool and wet microclimate. | Unfortunately, global warming and human activities have made the locations where *Torreya* used to grow warmer and drier. |
| *Torreya* trees could be introduced in other areas whose environmental conditions are suitable for *Torreya* growth. | Introducing a tree in a new area can endanger other plants that already grow there. This has happened previously when the black locust tree was introduced in a new area. |
| If *Torreya* trees are grown in research centers, they can be both preserved and studied there. | Since research centers are small, the population of *Torreya* trees grown there would not be large and diverse enough to resist diseases. |

Responses scoring 4 and 5 discuss and connect the points and the counterpoints in the table while adding all the important supporting details mentioned by the lecturer. The table above includes the main lecture points but may not include all the important supporting details.

## Sample Responses with Rater Comments

*High-Level Response*

Torreya taxifolia is an evergreen tree that was once common in Florida region. From 1950's it is in danger of becoming extinct and scientists are considering different ways to save it.

Plans to reestablish Torreya in Florida has been ruled out by the professor in the lecture because global warming has resulted in a worse climate in that area for the tree to grow and flourish. Wetlands in Florida area have also dried up so these changes in the climate has caused the decreased growth of the tree and it is very hard to reestablish in the same area.

The second option could be very dangerous for the native species of that area. The professor explains by citing another example of black locust tree. When it was taken to a new environment, it grew to such an extent that it killed a large number of local plants and trees and hence they became endangered. So, it's not wise to grow one species by eliminating others. So it is at risk to experi

The third solution is again not appropriate because for a population to be successfull it should be relatively large and genetically diverse so that it is able to resist diseases. Research centres cannot provide a large space for the population to be reestablished.

*Rater Comments*

This response earns a high score because it successfully conveys most of the important information from the lecture and the reading passage. The subject— saving a tree that is in danger of extinction—is introduced in the first paragraph, and the writer goes on to discuss the weaknesses of each solution that has been proposed. While the writer focuses mainly on discussing what the lecturer said about the weaknesses, it remains quite clear what the solutions described in the reading passage were. The response is generally well organized. The incomplete sentence at the end of the third paragraph does not really take away from the quality of the response. Since we consider responses to be first drafts, minor problems of this kind are not evaluated harshly. There are some minor errors ("plans . . . has been ruled out") and some ideas are not expressed as well as they could be ("it's not wise to grow one species by eliminating others" would be better put as "it's not wise to grow one species at the expense of others"), but the Scoring Guide allows for some minor problems in high-level responses.

*Mid-Level Essay*

Giving that Torreya started to die out in its naturel location, three solutions were be proposed, but none of them worked.

The first solution is to reestablish the tree in Florida, its naturel home, because historicaly this kind of tree lives thanks to the microclimat of this state. But the plan fall because of the changing of the climat in this area. Benefits of the microclimat, which is specific climat of an area, do not exist yet. So Torreya loose its natural environnement.

The second solution is to establish the tree in a completely different climat, meanning in the north. But as the professor explains, this solution fall in the past with the black locust tree. This historical exemple explains how it is difficult to change the ecosystem, because it is very dangerous to provoc a migration.

Eventuelly, the last solution is to preserve Torreya in reserch centres. One more time this proposition is not good, because all experiences of capted population show that every preserve population lost its capacity to resist to deseas and external atacs. Then even if humans try to recreat a reel diversity, it is not possible, because the recreat area can not be enought to be large and diverse as the nature is.

*Rater Comments*

This response earns a mid-level score. The writer may have understood most of the passage's points and the lecturer's arguments, but errors of usage and grammar are more than minor and are more frequent throughout the response ("were be"; "fall" for "fail"; incorrect use of tense; "capted"). The errors result in vagueness as well as obscured meanings in conveying ideas and connections. Some important information is also missing. The writer conveys that the microclimate has changed (though no mention is made, specifically, that it is drier or warmer). The sentence "Benefits of the microclimate . . . do not exist yet" is unclear, probably because the writer mistakenly wrote "yet" instead of "anymore." While the black locust is cited as a historical example, the writer is vague and unclear in explaining the rest of the argument: the lecturer did not say that "it is difficult to change the ecosystem," and it is unclear what "provoc a migration" means. If a reader correctly interprets some erroneous expressions ("capted population"), important parts of the third argument become clear; however, it is not the "area" that cannot be large and diverse enough, but the captive tree population.

## Writing for an Academic Discussion

### Question

Your professor is teaching a class on psychology. Write a post responding to the professor's question.

**In your response, you should do the following.**
- Express and support your opinion.
- Make a contribution to the discussion in your own words.

An effective response will contain at least 100 words.


**Dr. Diaz**

This week we've been looking at research on human happiness. One expert has two pieces of advice that may seem contradictory: "To make yourself happier, focus on making other people happy. One of the best ways to make other people happy is to focus more on your own happiness." To increase your own happiness, do you think it is more effective to focus on both of these things or on only one? Why?


**Andrew**

I believe both of these ideas are true. It seems obvious to me that there is joy in helping others. At the same time, if a person doesn't focus on making himself or herself happy, that person will never be able to contribute much to society, because they will lack the energy and enthusiasm needed to do so.


**Claire**

I would argue that it is better to focus only on making others happy. To me, that advice about focusing more on your own happiness is a step towards selfishness and to seeing one's own interests as separate from and maybe even conflicting with the interests of everyone around you, and that is not something I'd recommend for anybody trying to reduce unhappiness.

## Topic Notes

The question and the discussion should come across clearly to the test takers. The setup is engaging and relevant to test takers, so it should elicit clear and ample opinions and contributions on both sides of the issue. The professor's central question is whether it is better to focus both on your own happiness as well as on making others happy, or whether you should focus on just one of them. Andrew argues that the focus should be on both, while Claire thinks it is better to focus only on making others happy.

Test takers can contribute to the discussion in a number of ways. They can expand on Andrew's ideas that both are important, they can agree with Claire that one should focus only on making others happy, or they could take an entirely different view—that people should only worry about making themselves happy, for instance (perhaps even adding that this does not conflict with making others happy). Regardless of their viewpoint, test takers should provide a clear explanation for their opinion.

## Sample Responses with Rater Comments

### High-Level Response

> I agree with Andrew's point that we need to focus on making ourselves happy. Happy persons are more able to help people around them. But I think Claire is right too, when she suggests that selfishness may be a risk in looking too close for your own happiness. In avoiding this danger, a good strategie could be helping others not in the way we would like to be helped, but in the way they would like to be helped. Then your happiness would not only be the condition for the happiness of people around you, but also something you owe to them (and in the measure your happiness helps them).

### Rater Comments

This high-level response makes a fully successful, relevant and clearly-expressed contribution to the discussion board. The writer takes a mid-position by agreeing with both Andrew ("I agree with Andrew's point that we need to focus on making ourselves happy") and Claire ("But I think Claire is right too, when she suggests that selfishness may be a risk in looking too close for your own happiness"). The writer then goes on to add their own contribution to the discussion by stating that the best way to help people is "helping others not in the way we would like to be helped, but in the way they would like to be helped." The writer ends their response by stating how one's happiness "would not only be the condition for the happiness of people around you, but also something you owe to them." Given the consistent language facility and very clearly expressed contribution to the online discussion, this illustrates a high-level response

*Mid-Level Response*

> I disagree, Claire. Why do you think that focusing on your own happines is selfish? From my point of view, there nothing more important than own happines and doing your best to increase your happines is must. Also, it very hard to make someone happy while you completely not satisfied with own life. I agree with Andrew regarding this. I can tell from own experience that people start to like me more and enjoy spend time with me once I got happier myself. I able to help people with confidence when I got more confident myself.

*Rater Comments*

This is a mid-level response that does contribute to the discussion but is not fully successful, mainly because of language facility and the frequency of language errors.

The writer disagrees with Claire and questions her position: "Why do you think that focusing on your own happines is selfish?" because "it very hard to make someone happy while you completely not satisfied with own life." The response includes language facility issues in the form of noticeable lexical and grammatical errors in word choice and sentence structure. Examples of language-facility errors include "it very hard to make someone happy while you completely not satisfied with own life" and "able to help people with confidence when I got more confident myself." With a mostly relevant and mostly understandable contribution to the online discussion, and the presence of some facility in the use of language, this response is only partially successful.

# 10 Writer's Handbook for English Language Learners

Use this Writer's Handbook as a guide to help you write better essays in English. It covers the following topics:

- **Grammar:** explains key grammar rules and gives examples.
- **Usage:** explains important usage rules and gives examples.
- **Mechanics:** describes the basic mechanics rules and gives examples. Mechanics includes spelling and punctuation.
- **Style:** discusses key aspects of effective style.
- **Organization and Development:** gives advice about the writing process and the development of all parts of an essay.
- **Advice to Writers:** discusses different types of essays.
- **Revising, Editing, and Proofreading:** explains what to do in each stage of improving your essay.
- **Glossary:** presents definitions for terms.

## Grammar

This section provides information on the following grammatical errors:

- Sentence Errors
- Word Errors
- Other Errors

### Sentence Errors

#### Fragments

A fragment is an incomplete sentence. It does not express a complete thought, even though it starts with a capital letter and ends with a punctuation mark. It is missing either a subject or a verb or both.

Here are three examples of fragments:

Fragment: *Where the neighbors were too noisy.*

Fragment: *A movie that inspires deep emotions.*

Fragment: *Analyzing the characters' motives.*

These three groups of words cannot stand alone as complete sentences. They can be corrected in two ways. One way is to attach the fragment to a complete sentence.

Corrected sentence: *Peter left the apartment where the neighbors were too noisy.*

Corrected sentence: *I went to see "The Silver Star," a movie that inspires deep emotions.*

Another way to correct fragments is to add a complete subject, a complete verb, or other words that express a complete thought.

Corrected sentence: *This is where the neighbors were too noisy.*

Corrected sentence: *A movie that inspires deep emotions is rare.*

Corrected sentence: *Analyzing the characters' motives is important.*

**Summary:** Sentence fragments are incomplete sentences. Sometimes readers can figure out the meaning of a fragment by rereading the sentences that come before and after it. However, turning fragments into complete sentences will improve the connections between ideas.

## Run-On Sentences

Run-on sentences happen when we join sentences together without a conjunction or the correct punctuation. Run-on sentences can be very confusing to read. Here is an example: *My sister loves to dance she is very good at it.*

There are several ways to correct run-on sentences:

1. Divide the run-on sentence into two separate sentences.

   Run-on sentence: *My sister loves to dance she is very good at it.*

   Corrected sentence: *My sister loves to dance. She is very good at it.*

   Run-on sentence: *Jim showed us his ticket someone gave it to him.*

   Corrected sentence: *Jim showed us his ticket. Someone gave it to him.*

2. Connect the parts of the run-on sentence with a coordinating conjunction and a comma. These are the most common coordinating conjunctions: *for, and, nor, but, or, yet, so.* (The acronym FANBOYS may help you remember them.)

   Run-on sentence: *My sister loves to dance she is very good at it.*

   Corrected sentence: *My sister loves to dance, and she is very good at it.*

   Run-on sentence: *She agreed to chair the meeting she didn't come.*

   Corrected sentence: *She agreed to chair the meeting, but she didn't come.*

3. Connect the parts of the run-on sentence with a subordinating conjunction. These are the most common subordinating conjunctions: *after, although, as, because, before, if, since, unless, until, when, whereas, while.*

> Run-on sentence: *My sister loves to dance she is very good at it.*
>
> Corrected sentence: *My sister loves to dance <u>because</u> she is very good at it.*

> Run-on sentence: *Maria and John like skiing Karen does not.*
>
> Corrected sentence: *<u>Although</u> Maria and John like skiing<u>,</u> Karen does not.*

4. Separate the parts of the run-on sentence with a semicolon.

> Run-on sentence: *Gordon laughed at Sandy's joke it was funny.*
>
> Corrected sentence: *Gordon laughed at Sandy's joke<u>;</u> it was funny.*

> Run-on sentence: *I thought he was here I was wrong.*
>
> Corrected sentence: *I thought he was here<u>;</u> I was wrong.*

**Summary:** Run-on sentences are two or more sentences that have been joined together without a conjunction or the correct punctuation. You can usually correct them by using punctuation, a conjunction, or both.

## Word Errors

### Noun Forms

A noun is usually defined as a *person, place,* or *thing.*

> Person: *man, woman, waiter, John*
>
> Place: *home, office, town, station, Hong Kong*
>
> Thing: *table, car, apple, money, music, love, dog, monkey*

Learning a few basic rules will help you to use nouns effectively:

1. In English, some nouns are countable. That is, they are things that we can count. For example: *house.* We can count *houses.* We can visit one, two, three, or more *houses.* Here are more examples of countable nouns:

> *dog, cat, animal, man, person, bottle, box, pound, coin, dollar, bowl, plate, fork, table, chair, suitcase, bag*

Countable nouns can be singular or plural.

> Singular: *I have <u>a friend</u>.*
>
> Plural: *I have <u>two friends</u>.*

2.  Usually, to make nouns plural, add -*s*, as in the preceding examples (*friend, friends*). However, there are special cases where you do not add -*s*.

    *   When a word ends in -*ch*, -*s*, -*sh*, -*ss*, or –*x*, the plural is formed by adding -*es*. (*benches, gases, dishes, dresses, taxes*)
    *   When a word ends in -*y preceded by a consonant*, the plural form is -*ies*. (*parties, bodies, policies*)
    *   When a word ends in -*y preceded by a vowel*, the plural is formed by adding -*s*. (*trays, joys, keys*)
    *   When a word ends in -*o*, the more common plural ending is -*es* (*tomatoes, potatoes, heroes*)
    *   When the final -*o* is preceded by a vowel, the plural ending is -*s*. (*videos, studios*)
    *   When a word ends in -*f*, the plural is formed in one of two ways:
        *   either by adding -*s* (*beliefs, puffs*)
        *   or by changing the -*f* to -*v* and adding -*es* (*wife, wives; leaf, leaves; loaf, loaves*).
    *   When a word ends in -*ex* or -*ix*, the plural ending is usually -*es*. (*appendixes, indexes*)
    *   In certain cases, the plural form of a word is the same as the singular. (*deer, sheep, fish, series*)

3.  Some nouns are uncountable. They represent things that cannot be counted. For example, we cannot count *coffee*. We can count "cups of *coffee*" or "pounds of *coffee*," but we cannot count *coffee* itself. Here are more examples of uncountable nouns:

    *music, art, love, happiness, advice, information, news, furniture, luggage, rice, sugar, butter, water, electricity, gas, money*

    We usually treat uncountable nouns as singular.

    Incorrect: *These furnitures are beautiful.*

    Correct: *This furniture is beautiful.*

4.  Some uncountable nouns refer to abstract ideas or emotions. Abstract ideas may refer to qualities that we cannot physically touch. For example: *health, justice.*

    We cannot count abstract nouns, so they are always singular.

    Incorrect: *Healths are more important than wealths.*

    Correct: *Health is more important than wealth.*

    Incorrect: *Have funs at the reunion.*

    Correct: *Have fun at the reunion.*

5.  Some nouns can be countable *and* uncountable, for example: *paper, room, hair, noise, time*. With these nouns, the singular and plural forms often have different meanings.

    Countable: *The Diwali lights make the mall very pretty.*

    Uncountable: *This room does not get enough light.*

    Countable: Othello *is one of Shakespeare's most famous works.*

    Uncountable: *I have a lot of work to do tonight.*

6.  Singular nouns that are countable usually come after an article or other determiner (*a, an, the, this, my, such*).

    Incorrect: *His mother is doctor.*

    Incorrect: *Boy standing over there is brother.*

    Incorrect: *We saw child in playground.*

    Correct: *His mother is a doctor.*

    Correct: *The boy standing over there is my brother.*

    Correct: *We saw a child in the playground.*

***Summary:*** Nouns are important words in a sentence because they form the subjects or objects. Some nouns can be counted and some cannot. Learning a few rules will help you to use nouns effectively.

## Verb Forms

Verbs are parts of speech that express action (*jump, show*) or a state of being (*are, was*). Here are a few tips that may help you to use verbs effectively:

1.  Helping verbs (also called *auxiliary verbs*) precede the main verb. All of the following verbs may be helping verbs:

    *be, am, is, are, was, were, being, been, has, have, had, do, does, did, can, will, shall, should, could, would, may, might, must*

    Here are examples of sentences with helping verbs:

    *Many people don't know what they are going to do after college.*

    *I am going to give you step-by-step instructions.*

2.  Words such as *might, must, can, would*, and *should* are also called modals. They express a wide range of meanings (ability, permission, possibility, necessity, etc.).

    The following examples show one use of modals:

    *Tom might have gone to the party if he had been invited.*

    *If I had a million dollars, I would buy a house for my parents.*

This use of modals is called the conditional use. One event relies on another or it cannot take place. In the first example, Tom cannot go to the party without being invited. In the second example, I would buy a house for my parents only if I had a million dollars.

3. The infinitive form of the verb is formed by using the word *to* plus the simple form of the verb.

> *He is too tired to go to the barbecue.*
>
> *The manager wants to hire a new secretary.*

The infinitive can also be used as the subject or object of a sentence.

> *To invest now seems risky.*
>
> *The teacher told him to leave.*

In the first example, *To invest* is the subject of the sentence, while in the second example, *to leave* is the object.

We can use the infinitive to show an action that is occurring at the same time as, or later than, the action of the main verb.

> *We like to play video games.*
>
> *My best friend wants to shop at that mall.*

In the first example, the *liking* is happening at the same time as the *playing*. In the second example, the *shopping* is going to happen at a later time than the *wanting*.

4. Do not use *of* after a helping verb. In some verb phrases, there are two or more verbs being used (*should have happened, might be eaten, could have decided*). Here are examples in which the word *of* is used incorrectly:

> Incorrect: *They would of stayed one more month if possible.*
>
> Incorrect: *In that time, he could of finished the project.*

*Of* is a preposition, not a verb, and in each of these sentences, *of* should be replaced with the helping verb *have*.

> Correct: *They would have stayed one more month if possible.*
>
> Correct: *In that time, he could have finished the project.*

**Summary:** Verbs are very important parts of a sentence. There are a few rules that you can learn to make your use of verbs more effective.

## Subject-Verb Agreement

In English, the subject and verb must always agree in number. Here are a few rules that will help you:

1. A singular subject takes a singular verb.

> *The teacher was happy with my answer.*
>
> *My cell phone is not working.*

In the first example, the singular subject *teacher* agrees with the singular verb *was*. In the second example, the singular subject *cell phone* agrees with the singular verb *is*.

2.  A plural subject takes a plural verb.

> *My parents were happy with my grades.*
>
> *Many television stations have reported that story.*

In the first example, the plural subject *parents* matches the plural verb *were*, and in the second example, the plural subject *television stations* matches the plural verb *have*.
    You should never have a plural subject with a singular verb.

> Incorrect: *Many students thinks tomorrow is a holiday.*

This sentence can be edited to make the subject and verb agree.

> Correct: *Many students think tomorrow is a holiday.*

Similarly, you should never have a singular subject with a plural verb.

> Incorrect: *The student think tomorrow is a holiday.*

This sentence can be edited to make the subject and verb agree.

> Correct: *The student thinks tomorrow is a holiday.*

3.  Sometimes subjects and verbs are separated by a word or a phrase. When that happens, students sometimes forget to make them agree in number.

> Incorrect: *Your suggestions about the show was excellent.*
>
> Incorrect: *The use of cell phones during concerts are not allowed.*
>
> Correct: *Your suggestions about the show were excellent.*
>
> Correct: *The use of cell phones during concerts is not allowed.*

In the first example, since the subject of the sentence is *suggestions*, which is plural, the plural verb *were* is used. In the second example, the singular subject *use* needs the singular verb *is*.

4.  A compound subject needs a plural verb.
    When you proofread your work, correctly identify the subject in your sentences. For example, the following sentences have more than one subject:

> *The camcorder and the tripod were returned yesterday.*
>
> *Both Chantel and Rochelle are nice names.*

In the first example, the complete subject is a compound (*camcorder* and *tripod*), and so the verb must be plural (*were*). In the second example, the compound subject is *Chantel and Rochelle* and needs the plural verb *are*.

*Summary:* A verb should always agree with its subject. A singular subject takes a singular verb, and a plural subject takes a plural verb. Sometimes a phrase separates the subject and the verb, making it hard to find the real subject.

## Pronouns

A pronoun is a word that takes the place of one or more nouns. Pronouns are words such as *he, his, she, her, hers, it, they, their, them, these, that, this, those, who, whom, which, what,* and *whose.*

If we did not have pronouns, we would have to repeat a lot of nouns. We would have to say things like:

> *Do you like the new manager? I don't like the new manager. The new manager is too unfriendly.*

With pronouns, we can say the following:

> *Do you like the new manager? I don't like him. He is too unfriendly.*

Learning a few rules will help you to use pronouns correctly and effectively:

1. In general, pronouns must agree with the nouns they refer to. If your pronoun refers to a girl or a woman, you use a feminine pronoun (*she, her, hers*). If your pronoun refers to a boy or a man, you use a masculine pronoun (*he, his, him*). However, sometimes you may not know the gender of the person or the person may not identify with any gender. Since the English language does not have a gender-neutral singular pronoun that can refer to a person, it is acceptable to use a plural pronoun (*they, their*), as long as the meaning is clear.

   A pronoun should generally agree in number with the noun it refers to. If you are using a pronoun to refer to a singular noun, you use a singular pronoun; if you are using a pronoun to replace a plural noun, you use a plural pronoun. When you do not know a person's gender or the person does not identify with any gender, you can use a plural pronoun, as long as the object of the pronoun is clear.

   > *Julia reminded us that she would not stay late.*

   > *Bob bought two computers and had them delivered to his office.*

   > *The person who answered the phone said they would leave a message for Miguel.*

   In the first example, the singular pronoun *she* is used to stand for *Julia,* a female person. In the second example, the plural pronoun *them* is used to refer to the plural noun *computers.* In the third example, the plural pronoun *they* is used to refer to the person who answered the phone.

2. Some indefinite pronouns are singular in most contexts. Indefinite pronouns such as neither and no one are usually singular, so other pronouns that refer to them should also be singular

   > *Neither of the boys sent in his report.*

However, sometimes an exception can be made for inclusiveness.

*Everyone must buy their own ticket.*

Since the gender of every ticket buyer is unknown, the neutral pronoun *their* is acceptable in today's usage, even though it is plural. Some other ways of expressing this idea include *Everyone must buy his or her ticket*, or simply, *Everyone must buy a ticket*.

3.  Some indefinite pronouns are always plural. These include *both* and *many*. Other pronouns that refer to them must also be plural.

    *Both of them are here tonight.*

    *Many of the managers have moved into their new offices.*

In the first example, *both* is plural, and so the plural pronoun *them* is used. In the second example, the plural pronoun *their* is used because *many* is plural.

4.  Some indefinite pronouns can be singular or plural. Indefinite pronouns such as *all, any, more, most, none,* and *some* can be singular or plural, depending on their meaning in a context.

    *Most of my time is spent reviewing for the test.*

    *Most of the students have turned in their reports.*

In the first example, *most* refers to *time,* a singular noun. It thus takes the singular verb *is*. In the second example, *most* refers to the plural noun *students*. This is why it takes the plural verb *have* and is referred to by the plural pronoun *their*.

5.  Overusing pronouns can cause confusion.

    Confusing: *The president informed the vice president that all of his supporters should be meeting with him.*

Whose supporters, the president's or the vice president's? With whom are they meeting? This sentence needs to be revised to fix the confusion caused by the use of *him* and *his*. This can be accomplished by replacing the pronouns with the appropriate nouns.

    Clear: *The president informed the vice president that all of the president's supporters should be meeting with the president.*

Excessive use of *it* weakens writing, especially when *it* is used to introduce a sentence, as in this example:

    Confusing: *We were visiting the museum. I saw it. It was interesting and unusual. I was amazed by it.*

You can improve the sentence by explaining what the first *it* refers to.

    Clear: *We were visiting the museum. I saw the space exhibit. It was interesting and unusual. I was amazed by it.*

In this example, can you figure out what *it* stands for?

*Although the car hit the tree, it was not damaged.*

Does *it* refer to the car or the tree? You can make the sentence clear by rewriting it.

*The car was not damaged, although it hit the tree.*

6. When you have nouns joined by a conjunction (*and, or,* or *nor*), do not forget to make a pronoun that refers to them agree in number, as in these examples:

   *If Bob and Rick want to go, they will need to take the bus because I don't have room in my car.*

   *Whether I buy a dishwasher or dryer, it will have to go in the kitchen.*

   In the first example, there is a compound noun, as *Bob* and *Rick* are joined by the conjunction *and*. So the plural pronoun *they* must be used. In the second example, the noun is singular (*dishwasher* or *dryer*). Thus the singular pronoun *it* is used.

7. You should know when to use *who, whom, which,* or *that. Who* and *whom* refer to people. *Which* refers to things, and *that* can refer to either people or things.

   *The committee interviewed all the candidates who applied.*

   *Do you still have the magazine that I lent you last week?*

   *Which courses should I take in the fall?*

   In the first example, *who* refers to a group of people (*candidates*). In the second example, *that* refers to a thing (*magazine*). In the third example, *which* refers to things (*courses*).

**Summary:** A pronoun is a word used to take the place of one or more nouns. Singular pronouns must be used to refer to singular nouns, and plural pronouns must be used to refer to plural nouns. Some indefinite pronouns can be singular or plural, according to their meaning in the sentence.

## Possessive Pronouns

Possessive pronouns are used to show possession or ownership. Here are a few rules that will help you to use possessive pronouns effectively:

1. When you are using possessive pronouns such as *his, hers, mine, theirs, yours,* or *ours,* make sure that the possessive pronoun agrees in number with the noun to which it refers.

   Incorrect: *I have my ticket, and my husband has theirs.*

   Incorrect: *This is the children's room. All those toys are hers.*

Correct: *I have my ticket, and my husband has <u>his</u>.*

Correct: *This is the children's room. All those toys are <u>theirs</u>.*

In the first sentence, the singular pronoun *his* should be used to show that the ticket belongs to the singular noun *husband*. In the second sentence, *theirs* should be used to show that the toys belong to the plural noun *children*.

2. Possessive pronouns do not take an apostrophe. *His, hers, its, ours, yours, theirs,* and *whose* are pronouns that already convey possession, so do not add an apostrophe to them.

Incorrect: *Each art room has <u>it's</u> own sink.*

Incorrect: *<u>His'</u> office is on the third floor.*

Correct: *Each art room has <u>its</u> own sink.*

Correct: *<u>His</u> office is on the third floor.*

In the first sentence, a possessive pronoun (*its*) is needed, not *it's*, which means "it is." In the second sentence, the possessive pronoun *his* is needed; *his'* is never used.

## Other Ways to Show Possession

Besides possessive pronouns, there are other ways to show possession, such as using an apostrophe and an *-s* (*-'s*).

*My <u>neighbor's</u> house is bigger than mine.*

*<u>Henry's</u> cat likes to play with our baby.*

Below are some rules for indicating possession:

1. When a noun ends in *-s* and the addition of *-'s* makes the word sound odd, some writers add only an apostrophe, as in these examples:

*I like <u>Charles'</u> company.*

*This is <u>Harris'</u> wife, Anna.*

2. Make sure you put the apostrophe in the right place. Put the apostrophe *before* the *-s* if the word is singular.

*The <u>teacher's</u> desk is right in front. (one teacher)*

*My <u>sister's</u> haircut cost $70. (one sister)*

You will put the apostrophe *after* the *-s* only if it is a plural word.

*We borrowed our <u>parents'</u> car. (more than one parent)*

*I went to a party at my <u>friends'</u> house. (more than one friend)*

3. When two or more people share ownership, you use an apostrophe and *-s* on the last noun. When each person has separate ownership, you need to indicate that by using an apostrophe on both nouns, as in these examples:

   *John and Jack's room is very messy.* (John and Jack share one room.)

   *Ian's and George's dreams are very different, even though the two boys come from the same family.* (Ian and George have different dreams.)

4. Do not use an apostrophe when you want to make a noun plural. An apostrophe shows possession, not the plural of a noun. These sentences are wrong because they should not have apostrophes:

   Incorrect: *The new student's look confused.*

   Incorrect: *There are too many car's on our street's.*

**Summary:** Possessive pronouns are used to show possession, or ownership. There are a few rules that can help you to use them correctly.

## Prepositions

A preposition is a word that is used before a noun (or noun phrase) to give more information in a sentence. Prepositions are usually used to show where something is located or when something happened. Examples of prepositions include *in, among, between, across, at, with, beside, behind, in, into, from, during, before,* and *after*.

Prepositions are used to show place, time, and action or movement.

- Place:

   *The main office is in New York.*

   *I'm meeting my colleagues at the coffee shop.*

- Time:

   *Let's try to get there by 3:30.*

   *Please do not talk during the show.*

- Action or movement:

   *He jumped into the river.*

   *We flew from Los Angeles to Toronto.*

Some verbs and adjectives are usually followed by certain prepositions.

   *They always argue about money.*

   *I borrowed a book from the library.*

Here are more examples of words and prepositions that usually go together:

*familiar with, afraid of, far from, close to, believe in, borrow from, lend to, absent from, nice to, argue with, made of, take off, turn on, happy with, sad about, famous for*

The following sentences contain *incorrect* uses of prepositions. The first sentence can be corrected by changing *at* to *of*. In the second sentence, the preposition that should go with *argued* is *with*.

Incorrect: *I am afraid at losing my textbooks.*

Incorrect: *The student argued at the teacher.*

Correct: *I am afraid of losing my textbooks.*

Correct: *The student argued with the teacher.*

***Summary:*** Prepositions are used to show relationships between a noun and other parts of a sentence. There are a few rules that can help you to use prepositions correctly.

## Other Errors

### Wrong or Missing Word

When writing or typing quickly, people often use the wrong word or omit words. When you begin to revise, edit, and proofread, read carefully for wrong words or words that you have left out.

One of the most frequent problems is the use of *the* instead of *they*.

Incorrect: *The went to the store each Monday.*

The writer most likely intended the following:

Correct: *They went to the store each Monday.*

Another common error is a missing noun after the word *the*.

Incorrect: *The go to the store each Monday.*

Correct: *The brothers go to the store each Monday.*

***Summary:*** Wrong or missing words commonly occur but are easy to correct. Proofread your sentences carefully.

### Keyboard Errors or Typos

Sometimes while writing the first drafts of an essay, you might leave out letters or make keyboard errors. They might be grammatical, usage, or mechanics errors, or they could be omitted letters or typos. Proofread carefully to correct these errors when you edit and revise your writing.

# Usage

This section provides information on the following usage errors:

- Article or Determiner Errors
- Confused Words
- Wrong Form of Word
- Faulty Comparison
- Nonstandard Verb or Word Form

## Article or Determiner Errors

This section features rules and explanations for using articles and includes examples of how articles are used correctly when you are writing in English.

### What Are Articles?

*A, an,* and *the* are called *articles.* These are words that come before a noun or its modifier. (A *modifier* is a word that makes a noun clearer or more specific. Modifiers tell how many or which one.)

| | | |
|---|---|---|
| *a* thinker | *an* apple | *the* house |
| *a* car | *an* old house | *the* newspapers |

There are two types of articles in English. *A* and *an* are called indefinite articles. *The* is called a definite article.

### When to Use *A* or *An*

*A* or *an* is used before a *singular* noun when the noun refers to *any* member of a group.

James must write *an essay* for his writing class today.

*A newspaper* is a good source of information on current events.

If the noun or the modifier that follows the article begins with a consonant sound, you should use the article *a.*

*a* basketball      *a* new automobile

On the other hand, if the noun or its modifier begins with a vowel sound—a, e, i, o, u—you should use the article *an.*

*an* elephant      *an* old truck

*A/an* is used before a noun if the noun can be counted. For example:

> I received *a letter* from my sister.

> Sending *an e-mail* is a fast way to communicate with classmates.

Sometimes a noun or a modifier can begin with a vowel *letter* but not a vowel *sound*. For example, here the vowel *o* in the word *one* sounds like the consonant *w* in *won*:

> This will be *a* one-time charge to your account.

## When to Use *The*

*The* is used before singular and plural nouns when the noun is a particular or specific noun. Use the article *the* if you can answer the question "Which one?" or "What?"

> *The art class* that I want to take is taught by a famous painter.

> *The students* in Ms. Jones's class do not want to participate in *the debate*.

In addition, *the* is used in the following ways:

- To refer to things known to everyone (*the* sky, *the* stars)
- To refer to things that are unique (*the* White House)
- To refer to time (*the* past, *the* present, *the* future)

## When Not to Use an Article

*A/an* is not used before a noun if the noun cannot be counted.

> I like to drink milk. (*Milk* is not counted.)

If a quantity of milk is specified, then the article would be used.

> I like to drink *a glass of milk* before I go to bed.

Sometimes nouns used to represent abstract general concepts (such as anger, beauty, love, or employment) do not take *a* or *an* before them.

> *Love* is a difficult emotion to describe in words.

> *Money* alone cannot buy happiness.

*The* is not used when a plural noun is used in a general sense.

> *Cameras* are an important component of many security systems. (*Cameras* refers to the general concept of cameras, not to specific cameras.)

> *The cameras* near the entrance provide images of all vehicles arriving and departing. (*The cameras* refers to a specific set of cameras.)

### Other Determiner Errors

The adjectives *this, that, these,* and *those* modify nouns that follow them by telling "which one." These adjectives must agree in number with the nouns they modify. *This* and *that* are used to describe a singular noun. *These* and *those* are used to describe plural nouns.

Incorrect: *I would buy these house for those reason.*

Incorrect: *This kinds of technologies will affect people's behavior.*

Correct: *I would buy this house for that reason.*

Correct: *These kinds of technologies will affect people's behavior.*

## Confused Words

This section explains how to avoid errors involving confused words such as homonyms and words with similar sounds and spellings.

### Homonyms

Certain words are known as *homonyms*. These are words that sound the same but differ in meaning, spelling, or usage. Homonyms can be of two types: words that are spelled alike and words that sound alike. Words that are spelled alike but differ in meaning are called *homographs*. An example of a homograph is the word *bear*, which can mean a type of animal or the verb *bear*, which means "to carry." Words that sound alike but differ in meaning and spelling are called *homophones*. The words *whole* and *hole* are homophones. *Whole* is an adjective meaning "complete," and *hole* is a noun meaning "an empty place." What follows are examples of some common homonyms. Always check your writing to make sure you are using the appropriate words.

**here** *adverb* meaning "in this place"

*We have been waiting* **here** *for an hour.*

**hear** *verb* meaning "to listen"

*Do you* **hear** *the birds singing?*

**hole** *noun* meaning "an empty place"

*The children dug a big* **hole** *in their sandbox.*

**whole** *adjective* meaning "with no part removed or left out; complete"

*Our* **whole** *project will involve cooperation from everyone.*

**its** *pronoun* possessive form of *it*

*The kitten hurt* **its** *paw.*

**it's** contraction of *it is*

**It's** *not fair to leave her behind.*

**know** *verb* meaning "to feel certain or to recognize"

> Do you **know** how to get to the subway?

**no** *adverb* used as a denial or refusal

> The employee said **no** to the job offer.

**knew** *verb* past tense of the verb *know*

> The boy **knew** how to count to ten.

**new** *adjective* meaning "not old"

> At the start of the school year, the students bought **new** books.

**desert** *noun* meaning "a dry and sandy place"

> It rarely rains in the **desert**.

**desert** *verb* meaning "to abandon"

> The officer commanded the troops to not **desert** their posts.

**dessert** *noun* meaning "the final course of a meal"

> After a big meal, I enjoy a simple **dessert** of vanilla ice cream.

**to** *preposition* meaning "toward"

> The man pointed **to** the sky.

**two** *adjective* or *pronoun* meaning "the number 2"

> Five is **two** more than three.

**too** *adverb* meaning "also"

> Tom and Eleanor wanted to go with them **too**.

**they're** *contraction* meaning "they are"

> **They're** both coming to the party.

**their** *possessive pronoun* meaning "belonging to them"

> That is **their** blue house on the corner.

**there** *adverb* meaning "at that place"

> Did you see anyone you knew **there**?

**through** *adverb* meaning "completed, or finished"

> When she was **through** eating, she put her plate in the sink.

**threw** *past tense* of the verb *throw*, meaning "tossed"

> The boy **threw** the ball to his sister.

## Other Confused Words

Besides homonyms, other words are confused in English because they are similar in spelling, sound, or meaning. Examples of some commonly confused words include *accept/except, advice/advise, affect/effect,* and *loose/lose.* Computer spell-checkers will not catch these words if you have misused them. When you review your work, proofread to see whether you have used the correct word. Even native speakers of English often make mistakes with confused words when they are writing, especially when they are in a hurry. Review the meanings of some commonly confused words.

**accept** *verb* meaning "to receive; to agree, or to take what is offered"

*I **accept** your kind invitation.*

**except** *preposition* meaning "other than, or leaving out; excluding"

*Everyone **except** Phil can attend the conference.*

**advice** *noun* meaning "an opinion given about what to do or how to behave"

*He has always given me valuable **advice** regarding my future plans.*

**advise** *verb* meaning "to recommend or counsel"

*I **advise** you to stay in school and study hard.*

**affect** *verb* meaning "to influence, or to produce an effect on"

*The weather can **affect** a person's mood.*

**effect** *noun* meaning "result"

*When students study for tests, they see a positive **effect** on their test results.*

**effect** *verb* meaning "to bring about"

*The governor can **effect** change in state education policies.*

**loose** *adjective* meaning "detached, not rigidly fixed; not tight"

*She lost her bracelet because it was too **loose** on her wrist.*

**lose** *verb* meaning "to be deprived, or to no longer have; to not win"

*If you don't pay attention to the signs, you might **lose** your way.*

**quiet** *adjective* meaning "not loud or noisy"

*Please be **quiet** when other people are speaking.*

**quit** *verb* meaning "to give up or abandon; to stop"

*The boys will **quit** their jobs the week before school starts.*

**quite** *adverb* meaning "to some extent"

*Moving to a new city will be **quite** a change for my family.*

**sense** *noun* meaning "consciousness, awareness, or rationality; the faculty of perceiving by means of sense organs"

*My brother had the good **sense** to keep out of trouble.*

*The doctor explained that my **sense** of smell is not functioning well.*

**since** *adverb* meaning "from a definite past time until now"; *conjunction* meaning "later than"

*Ginny has lived in the same house ever **since** she moved to town.*

*Karl has worked as an accountant **since** graduating from college.*

**than** *conjunction* used when comparing two elements

*Her puppy is smaller **than** mine.*

**then** *adverb* meaning "at that time, or next"

*First I will stop at the store, and **then** I will go home.*

These are just a few examples of words that are often confused in English. When you are unsure of the proper usage of a word, consult an English dictionary.

## Wrong Form of Word

When you write quickly, sometimes you use a word form that is different from the one that you intended to use. One reason why this error occurs is that a word can be used in different ways in a sentence depending on its purpose.

When you revise, read your writing very carefully to find these errors. You can also get someone else to read your work and to help you see where you are not clear. Here are examples of wrong word forms that can occur:

Incorrect: *But certain types of businesses will continue to grow to <u>an extend</u>, he thinks.*

*Extend* is a verb, and this writer meant to use the noun *extent*.

Correct: *But certain types of businesses will continue to grow to <u>an extent</u>, he thinks.*

Here is another example of a wrong word form in a sentence:

Incorrect: *Traffic has stopped because a truck is <u>disable</u> in the middle of the road.*

This writer should revise *disable* to *disabled*.

Correct: *Traffic has stopped because a truck is <u>disabled</u> in the middle of the road.*

Learning the parts of speech can teach you how each functions in a sentence. Proofreading your own work can help you correct these errors as well.

## Faulty Comparison

A faulty comparison error occurs when the word *more* is used within a comparison with a word that ends in *-er* or when the word *most* is used within a comparison with a word that ends in *-est*.

> Incorrect: *The boy with the red hair is <u>more taller than</u> the girl with the black hair.*

> Incorrect: *Yesterday was the <u>most hottest</u> day of the week.*

To avoid making these kinds of errors in your writing, you should review the following rules:

When comparing one thing with another, add the ending *-er* to short words (usually of one syllable).

> Correct: *The boy with the red hair is <u>taller</u> than the girl with the black hair.*

> Correct: *Today it is hot, but yesterday it was even <u>hotter</u>.*

When comparing three or more things, add the ending *-est* to short words (usually of one syllable).

> Correct: *The girl in the back of the room is the <u>tallest</u> girl in her entire class.*

> Correct: *Yesterday was the <u>hottest</u> day ever recorded by the National Weather Service.*

In many cases, with words of two or more syllables, you do not add *-er* or *-est* to the word; instead, use the word *more* before the word when comparing two things and use the word *most* when comparing three or more things.

> Correct: *The judges must decide which of the two remaining singers is <u>more talented</u>.*

> Correct: *Of the three new students, Amancia is the <u>most accomplished</u>.*

Comparisons that are negative use *less* for comparisons of two things and *least* for comparisons of three or more things.

> Correct: *The third-floor apartment is <u>less costly</u> than the first-floor apartment.*

> Correct: *Of the three colleges that I've visited, this one is the <u>least expensive</u>.*

## Nonstandard Verb or Word Form

The words you use in everyday conversation are often different from the words you use in standard written English. While a reader might understand these informal words—*gotta, gonna, wanna, kinda*—you should not write them in an essay. Here are two examples of nonstandard words used in sentences:

> Nonstandard: *I told her I <u>gotta</u> go to school now.*

> Correct: *I told her I <u>have got</u> to go to school now.*

> Nonstandard: *Do you <u>wanna</u> go to college?*

> Correct: *Do you <u>want to</u> go to college?*

Even though you can understand what the writer means, the words *gotta* and *wanna* do not exist in standard written English.

# Mechanics

This section provides information on the following types of mechanics errors:

- Capitalization
- Spelling
- Punctuation
- Other Errors

## Capitalization

To *capitalize* means to use capital letters. Below are some guidelines for capitalization:

1. Capitalize the first word of every sentence.

   *She is the most famous director. There is no doubt about it.*

   *Give it to me. It looks like mine.*

2. Capitalize all proper nouns; for example, names of individuals, titles, and places.

   *Francis Lloyd Mantel lives on Moore Street.*

   *The class is reading Adventures of Huckleberry Finn.*

   In the first example, "Francis Lloyd Mantel" is the name of an individual, so it is capitalized. "Moore Street" is the name of a place, so it is also a proper noun. The second example contains the title of a book, so it is capitalized.

   All names are proper nouns and must be capitalized. Other examples:

   - Names of institutions, places, and geographical areas

     *She is a new faculty member at Webler University.*

     *Their main office is in New Delhi, India.*

   - Names of historical events, days, months, and holidays

     *Independence Day is a school holiday.*

     *Classes don't meet until October.*

   - Names of languages and proper adjectives

     *He speaks Spanish and Italian fluently.*

     *They teach Korean dances at the academy.*

3. The first-person pronoun *I* is always capitalized, even when it is in the middle of a sentence.

   *It is I who sent you that letter.*

   *They told me that I should call for an appointment.*

4. Capitalize words such as *father, mother, aunt*, and *uncle* when used with proper names or when addressing a particular person.

> *Uncle Ruofan and Aunt Shanshan just moved into their new apartment.*
>
> *Yes, Mom, I'm going after dinner.*

However, when these words are used with possessive pronouns, they are not proper names and therefore are not capitalized.

> *My father is not at home.*
>
> *Their mother is my aunt.*

In the above examples, *father, mother*, and *aunt* are not capitalized because they are used with the possessive pronouns *my* and *their*.

**Summary:** In English, the first letter of the first word in a sentence is always capitalized. You must also capitalize all proper nouns. Proper nouns include all names and titles. The first-person pronoun *I* is always capitalized too.

## Spelling

English spelling rules are complex. Here are a few rules that may help you:

1. Write *i* before *e* (*fiery, friend, dried*), except

   - after *c* (*receive*)
   - with syllables sounding like *a* as in *neighbor* (*weigh, heir*)

   Note these examples:

   > *All applicants will receive a response within three weeks.*
   >
   > *The breakfast special is fried eggs and sausage.*

### Adding Endings to Words

2. If a word ends with a silent *-e*, drop the *-e* when adding a suffix that begins with a vowel (for example, the *-ing* suffix). However, do *not* drop the *-e* when the suffix begins with a consonant (for example, the *-ful* suffix).

   > *I like to skate. I enjoy skating.*
   >
   > *I could use a dictionary. A dictionary is very useful.*

   In the first example (*skate–skating*), the *-e* is dropped because the *-ing* suffix begins with the vowel *i*. In the second example, the *-e* is not dropped, because the *-ful* suffix begins with the consonant *f*.

3. When *-y* is the last letter in a word and the letter before *-y* is a consonant, drop *-y* and add *-i* before adding a suffix.

   > *The beaches in Thailand are extremely beautiful.*
   >
   > *They hurried to the gate because they were so late.*

In both examples, the -*y* is replaced with -*i* (*beauty–beautiful*; *hurry–hurried*).

4.   When forming the plural of a word that ends with a -*y* preceded by a vowel, just add -*s*. But if the letter before -*y* is a consonant, drop -*y* and add -*ie* before adding the -*s*.

> *Funkidz is a popular <u>toy</u> store. It sells all kinds of toys.*
>
> *The <u>babies</u> started to crawl.*

In the first example, the letter *o* (a vowel) comes before -*y*. So you need to add only -*s* to form the plural noun. But in the second example, in the word *baby*, the letter *b* (a consonant) comes before -*y*. You have to drop -*y* and add -*ies* to make the word plural.

5.   When a word ends in a consonant preceded by one vowel, double the final consonant before adding a suffix that begins with a vowel.

> *The children swi<u>m</u> at the community pool. They love swi<u>mm</u>ing.*
>
> *You should begi<u>n</u> at the begi<u>nn</u>ing. Start by writing the title.*

In the first example, the word *swim* ends with the letter *m*. In the second example, the word *begin* ends with the letter *n*. Both *m* and *n* are consonants. When adding -*ing*, a suffix starting with a vowel, you just need to double the final consonant.

Remember: when the ending begins with a vowel and the word ends in an -*e*, do not double the consonant. Instead, drop the -*e* and add the ending.

> Incorrect: *The children go <u>skatting</u> in the winter.*
>
> Correct: *The children go <u>skating</u> in the winter.*

The following examples contain *incorrect* spelling:

> Incorrect: *We visited the monkey house at the zoo. There were <u>monkies</u> from all over the world.*
>
> Incorrect: *My <u>neice</u> is a student in your class.*

In the first sentence, the plural form of *monkey* is *monkeys*. This is because when forming the plural of a word that ends with a -*y* preceded by a vowel, you should just add -*s*. In the second sentence, *niece* is the correct spelling. Remember, "*i* before *e* except **after** *c*" is a very useful rule!

> Correct: *We visited the monkey house at the zoo. There were <u>monkeys</u> from all over the world.*
>
> Correct: *My <u>niece</u> is a student in your class.*

These are all useful rules for learning English spelling. However, there are also some exceptions that are not covered by these rules, so it is a good idea to learn a few strategies for spelling as well.

For example, there are times when we make mistakes because we type too fast. It is easy to make the following errors on the computer:

> Incorrect: *A letter <u>frrom</u> her former neighbor came in the mail today.*

> Incorrect: *<u>Becuase</u> I lost my homework, I had to do it again.*

Both sentences contain typos, or mistakes we make when we type. One strategy for dealing with typos is to use the spell-check function on the computer.

However, there are mistakes that will not be caught by the spell-checker. For example:

> Incorrect: *Would you know <u>weather</u> he is at work today?*

> Incorrect: *Are <u>their</u> any good Indian restaurants in this area?*

In these examples, although the underlined word is a correct spelling (of a homophone), it is not the correct spelling of the word intended in the sentence. The spell-checker will not be able to find such errors, so after spell-checking, you should check for these errors as you read each sentence for meaning.

Another strategy is to keep a list of words that you often misspell. Memorize as many as you can. Check your writing specifically for these words.

You could also use a dictionary while you write to check the spelling of words that you are unsure of.

*Summary:* English spelling is complex and may sometimes seem strange. There are rules that can be memorized and learned, and there are strategies that can help you to spell better. For example, use a dictionary and the spell-check function on your computer.

## Punctuation

Punctuation refers to the use of punctuation marks. Some punctuation marks, such as the *apostrophe,* are used with individual words. Some, such as *commas,* are used either to separate parts of sentences or to separate digits in numbers. Others, such as *periods, question marks,* and *exclamation points,* are used to separate sentences. They help us to make the meaning of our sentences clear.

### Apostrophe

Use an apostrophe when you write a contraction. A contraction is the joining of two words by eliminating some letters and adding an apostrophe. It is a kind of short form. For example, *can't* is the contraction of *cannot, shouldn't* is the contraction of *should not,* and *let's* is the contraction of *let us.* Other contractions are *won't, it's, wouldn't,* and *couldn't.*

> *They <u>won't</u> be able to enter without their tickets.*

> *We could hear them, but we <u>couldn't</u> see them.*

In the first example, *won't* is the contraction of *will not,* and in the second sentence, *couldn't* is the contraction of *could not.*

Some people write contractions without the apostrophe. They are incorrect. The following sentence shows an incorrect use of a contraction:

Incorrect: *Lets go to the park tomorrow.*

Correct: *Let's go to the park tomorrow.*

*Let's* is the contraction of *let us*. Without the apostrophe, the word means "allows," as in this sentence:

Correct: *She lets us use the computer when she's not using it.*

In order to be used correctly, the apostrophe must be in the proper position. Below are examples of misplaced apostrophes:

Incorrect: *We could'nt understand the lecture.*

Incorrect: *Students were'nt in school in the summer.*

Correct: *We couldn't understand the lecture.*

Correct: *Students weren't in school in the summer.*

Note that the apostrophe should replace the vowel that is being deleted.

**Summary:** The apostrophe is used to show contraction and possession. For other uses of the apostrophe, refer to the section "Possessive Pronouns."

## Comma

The comma is the most common form of punctuation within a sentence. It is a signal for the reader to pause. In fact, if you read the examples below carefully, you will notice a natural pause where the commas are situated.

Learning a few basic rules will help you to use the comma effectively:

1.  Use a comma and conjunction (such as *and* or *but*) to join two clauses in a compound sentence.

    *The causes of the Civil War were many, and the effects of the war were numerous.*

    *The experiment was incomplete, but the lessons learned were important.*

    In the above examples, because the two clauses are independent clauses (or complete sentences) joined together by a conjunction, they need a comma between them.

2.  Use a comma to connect words to the beginning or end of your sentence. We often add information to our sentences by attaching one or more words to the beginning or end. When you do that, you can use a comma to help your reader find your main message.

    *Last night, my friend and I celebrated his 58th birthday.*

    *Many years ago, I studied French and German.*

    Each of these sentences begins with a phrase that indicates time. This information is separated from the main sentence by a comma.

3.  Use a comma between each item of a list when you are listing three or more items in a sentence.

    *The flag was red, white, and blue.*

    *I bought milk, bread, cheese, and butter.*

    The commas in the above examples clearly mark where one item on the list ends and the next one begins.

4.  Use a comma between adjectives. If you have two adjectives together before the noun they describe, they must be separated by a comma.

    *The <u>cold, wintry</u> wind chilled me to my bones.*

    *The <u>complex, diverse</u> cultures in the city add to its excitement.*

    In the above examples, the adjectives describing *wind* and *cultures* are placed before the noun, separated by commas.

5.  Use commas to set off additional information in the middle of a sentence. Some information, often telling details about the subject of the sentence, needs to be distinguished from the rest of the sentence (the verb and object). We place commas before and after these groups of words.

    *Ms. Johnson, <u>the company president</u>, will announce the winner.*

    *My brother Tom, <u>who loves to read</u>, uses the library every day.*

    In the above examples, if you take away the parts that are set off by commas, you still have a complete sentence.

6.  Use commas to separate quoted matter from the rest of the sentence.

    *"Take a break," said the instructor.*

    *Yeonsuk announces, "I am going to a job interview tomorrow."*

    In each example, the quotation is set apart from the rest of the sentence by a comma.

7.  Use commas to set off the name of a state or country when it follows a city, county, or equivalent.

    *The newspaper is based in Chicago, Illinois.*

    *Her flight to Beijing, China, took twelve hours.*

    In the above examples, the comma is used to set off the name of a state or country from a city within it.

8.  In written American English, commas are used in numbers of four or more digits and in a date to separate the year from the month and day.

    *He won $1,000,000 in the lottery.*

    *The date is March 15, 2022.*

In the first example, commas are used because of the numbers (of four or more digits). In the second example, it is used in a date.

The following sentences are missing commas:

Incorrect: *Conrad Soto the father of the bride cried at the wedding.*

Incorrect: *In conclusion I believe that technology will be the main factor affecting life in the twenty-first century.*

In the first sentence, "the father of the bride" should be set off by a pair of commas. In the second sentence, there should be a comma after "In conclusion."

Correct: *Conrad Soto, the father of the bride, cried at the wedding.*

Correct: *In conclusion, I believe that technology will be the main factor affecting life in the twenty-first century.*

*Summary:* Commas are used to separate parts of sentences and make meaning clearer. There are rules that can help you to use commas more effectively.

## Hyphen

The hyphen is the punctuation mark used to join two words together to form a compound word. The most common uses of hyphens are as part of an adjective phrase, in numbers that are spelled out, and with prefixes.

1. Hyphens with compound adjectives. Use a hyphen to join two or more words serving as a single adjective *before* a noun. For example:

   *His uncle is a well-known author.*

   However, when compound adjectives come *after* a noun, they are not hyphenated. For example:

   *The author is well-known for his mystery stories.*

2. Hyphens with compound numbers. A hyphen should be used in fractions and in the numbers twenty-one and above.

   *The cup is three-quarters full.*

   *Our teacher is sixty-three years old.*

   In the above examples, the compound numbers are joined with hyphens.

3. Hyphens with prefixes. A *prefix* is a syllable or word added to the beginning of another word to change its meaning. The prefixes *self-*, *ex-*, and *great-* always require a hyphen when they are added to words.

   *The instructions are self-explanatory.*

   *The children are with their great-grandparents.*

However, for prefixes such as *dis-*, *pre-*, *re-*, and *un-*, a hyphen is normally not used.

*My aunt dislikes loud music.*

*The answer to that question is unknown.*

**Summary:** We use hyphens to link some compound words, but not all compound words are hyphenated. In fact, American English is tending toward using fewer and fewer hyphens. Always check a recent dictionary to be sure you are hyphenating correctly.

# Final Punctuation

There are a few punctuation marks that help us to end our sentences. These are the question mark, the period, and the exclamation point.

## Question Mark

Use a question mark at the end of a direct question.

*When did the Second World War begin?*

*What were the key stages in the Romantic art movement?*

## Period

Periods are used to mark the end of a sentence that is a not a question. A period is also used at the end of an indirect question.

*I just completed the project.*

*Cindy asked me who would be taking notes at the meeting.*

## Exclamation Point

Use an exclamation point after a sentence that expresses strong feeling or requires emphasis. An exclamation point also serves to make a sentence stand out.

Correct: *That was utter nonsense!*

Correct: *What absolutely gorgeous flowers! Thank you!*

The following examples contain *incorrect* use of final punctuation:

Incorrect: *Have you called Ms. Han yet.*

Incorrect: *Oh, that's an amazing story?*

The first example is a question and needs a question mark. The second example should have either an exclamation point or a period, not a question mark.

Correct: *Have you called Ms. Han yet?*

Correct: *Oh, that's an amazing story!*

*Summary:* Question marks, periods, and exclamation points are used to end sentences. Use question marks to end direct questions, periods to end other sentences, and exclamation points when you want to express strong emotions or emphasis. Do not use too many exclamation points in your writing, or you may sound as if you are shouting!

## Other Errors

### Compound Words

A *compound word* is a word that has two or more parts. For example, the word *everywhere* is made up of two distinct words: *every* and *where*. But as a compound word, *everywhere* has a new meaning that is different from the meanings of *every* and *where*. Although there are times when experts cannot agree if a word should be a compound, in most cases there are clear rules. In the following sentences, you can see where student writers make mistakes when using compound words:

> Incorrect: *I work to support my self and my family.*

> Incorrect: *You can learn from every thing happening today.*

In each of these sentences, compound words have been written incorrectly as two separate words. The underlined words in each sentence should be written as one compound word.

> Correct: *I work to support myself and my family.*

> Correct: *You can learn from everything happening today.*

*Summary:* In English, words, especially adjectives and nouns, are sometimes combined into compound words in a variety of ways. Compound words have a meaning that is different from the meanings of the two words that form them. Not all words can be joined this way. When you are not sure whether a word is a compound, check your dictionary.

### Fused Words

Sometimes writers fuse two words together to form an incorrect compound word. The sentences below show examples of fused words:

> Incorrect: *Some people say that highschool is the best time of your life.*

> Incorrect: *I like to play soccer alot.*

Each of the underlined fused words should be two separate words.

> Correct: *Some people say that high school is the best time of your life.*

> Correct: *I like to play soccer a lot.*

*Summary:* When you join words together incorrectly, you get fused words. When you are not sure whether two words should be compounded, check your dictionary.

### Duplicate Words

When writing a first draft, you might make errors simply because you are thinking faster than you can write or type. As a result, you might write the same word twice. Sometimes you might write two words in a row that, though different, function in the same way. It is very common for writers to type two verbs, pronouns, or articles in a row in early drafts.

> Incorrect: *Sally's older sister can may help her pay for college.*
>
> Incorrect: *He was as silly as a the clown.*

In each sentence, one of the underlined words should be deleted.

> Correct: *Sally's older sister can help her pay for college.* (meaning that the sister is able to help Sally)
>
> Correct: *Sally's older sister may help her pay for college.* (meaning that the sister might decide to help Sally)
>
> Correct: *He was as silly as a clown.* (meaning that he generally acted clownish)
>
> Correct: *He was as silly as the clown.* (meaning that he acted like a specific clown)

*Summary:* You "duplicate" when you write the same word twice or when you use two different words that serve the same function. A real duplicate is easy to correct, as the spell-checker will usually identify it. But if you have typed two words that serve the same function and are not sure which to keep, check a dictionary to help you choose the word with the most appropriate meaning.

# Style

This section provides information on how you can address the following kinds of problems in writing:

- Word Repetition
- Inappropriate Words or Phrases
- Too Many Passive Sentences
- Too Many Long Sentences
- Too Many Short Sentences
- Sentences Beginning with Coordinating Conjunctions

## Word Repetition

Repeating some words to emphasize your key points is a good writing technique. However, repeating the same words or sets of words too often gives your writing an immature style. It can also make your essay seem boring.

To write more effectively, try using a variety of vocabulary. Here are a few ideas that can help you:

1.  Use synonyms (words that have similar meanings) to replace repeated words. For example, instead of repeating a common verb such as *make*, where appropriate, use synonyms like these:

    > *create, produce, perform, do, execute, bring about, cause, form, manufacture, construct, build, put up, set up, put together, compose*

    You can find synonyms in a thesaurus.

    In the following paragraph, the noun *student* is repeated too many times:

    > *Think about this situation. A student interviewed many students about what it is like to be an only child. If the teachers in charge of the school paper did not edit names of students from the paper or facts that would give that particular student away to other students, then serious problems could be caused for the students who gave their information.*

    We can improve this paragraph by using a variety of other words to refer to *student*. For example:

    > *Think about this situation. A reporter interviewed many students about what it is like to be an only child. If the teachers in charge of the school paper did not edit the individuals' names from the paper or facts that would give each person away to the readers, then serious problems could be caused for the students who gave their information.*

2.  Use phrases such as *the former, the latter, the first one*, and *the other* to avoid repeating the same nouns. In the following paragraph, the same names are repeated several times:

    > *Of the two sisters, Grace is confident and at ease with everyone. Lily is shy and cautious. Grace always gets what she wants. Lily waits patiently for whatever comes her way. Grace never misses a chance to show off her many talents. Lily never says a word unless someone asks her a question.*

    This paragraph can be improved by using a variety of phrases:

    > *Of the two sisters, Grace is confident and at ease with everyone. Lily is shy and cautious. The former always gets what she wants. The latter waits patiently for whatever comes her way. Grace never misses a chance to show off her many talents. Her sister never says a word unless someone asks her a question.*

**Summary:** When you look over your writing, think about how you can replace over-used words and phrases. You can use a thesaurus to help you add variety to your writing.

## Inappropriate Words or Phrases

Language that is too informal, such as slang, is not appropriate for academic writing. It is not always easy to tell when an expression is too informal. Some expressions are used so often in spoken English that we may think it is all right to use them in academic writing too.

> Too informal: *No way would she ever say a thing like that.*
>
> Much better: *She would never say that.*

> Too informal: *People need to get it all together and step up for the picnic.*
>
> Much better: *We need people to get organized and set up the picnic.*

*Summary:* Written language is usually more formal than spoken language. Try to avoid expressions that are too informal when writing academic essays.

## Too Many Passive Sentences

A sentence is active when the subject is the *doer* of the action. It is passive when the subject is the *receiver* of the action.

> Active sentence: <u>Only a few hundred people</u> saw the movie.
>
> Passive sentence: <u>The movie was seen</u> by only a few hundred people.

In the above examples, the action is *seeing*. In the active sentence, the subject (*two hundred million people*) is the doer of the action. In the passive sentence, the subject (*the movie*) is the receiver of the action.

Because passive sentences are usually longer and harder to read, using too many passive sentences can make your writing slow and uninteresting. Many experts think that passive sentences should make up only about 5 percent of your writing.

Active sentences, on the other hand, generally are clearer, are more direct, and seem stronger. However, this does not mean that you should stop using passive sentences. Appropriate use of passive sentences can make your writing more powerful.

Here are a few suggestions about when to use passive sentences:

1.  When the *action* is more important than the doer

    > <u>The theater was opened</u> last month.
    >
    > <u>New students are invited</u> to meet the dean in room 226.

In these sentences, the theater being opened and the new students being invited are more important than the "doers" (the people who opened the theater or invited the new students). In fact, the "doers" are not important enough to mention.

2. When the *receiver* of the action is more important than the doer

   *Everyone was given a key to the gym.*

   *The letters were sent this morning.*

   In the first sentence, we care more about the people who were given a key than the people who were doing the giving. In the second sentence, the letters that were sent are more important than the person who did the sending.

3. When the *result* of the action is more important than the doer

   *Our advice was followed by our clients.*

   *The new computers were installed by the systems staff.*

   In the first sentence, the advice being followed is more important than the people giving the advice. In the second sentence, the installation of the computers is more important than the people who installed them.

4. When you do not know who did an action, do not care, or do not want your reader to know

   Passive: *A mistake was made, and all the scholarship application files were lost.*

   Passive: *This report was written at the last minute.*

   The active forms of these examples would be as follows:

   Active: *I made a mistake and lost all the scholarship application files.*

   Active: *I wrote this report at the last minute.*

   If you were the person who made the mistake in the first sentence or the person who wrote the report in the second, would you choose the active or passive voice?

5. When you want to sound objective

   Using passive sentences is a common practice in scientific and technical writing. When you are reporting the results of an experiment or describing a study, it helps to sound objective and fair. Thus reports are filled with sentences like these:

   *The pigeons were observed over a period of three weeks.*

   *The subjects were divided into three groups.*

   The use of the passive voice in lab reports also keeps the reader focused on the experiment itself, rather than on the researchers.

*Summary:* When you look over your writing, think about whether you have used too many passive sentences. Passive sentences are longer and more difficult to read and understand, so use them only when they help you to emphasize something important.

## Too Many Long Sentences

Experts believe that the average sentence length should be between 15 and 20 words. This length allows your reader to absorb your ideas more easily. For example, the following sentence may be confusing to read because of its length:

> *My favorite place to visit is my grandparents' house near the lake where we love to fish and swim, and we often take the boat out on the lake.*

Breaking the sentence into two (or more) sentences can make your writing clearer and more interesting.

> *My favorite place to visit is my grandparents' house near the lake. We love to fish and swim there, and we often take the boat out on the lake.*

Good writers usually mix longer sentences with shorter ones to make their writing more effective. You may even want to try a short sentence (or a single-word sentence) after a few long ones to help you to emphasize what you are saying.

> *Benjamin Franklin, who was one of the Founding Fathers of the United States, helped write the Declaration of Independence. He also invented many things, such as bifocals and the Franklin stove, and he discovered electricity. Think about that discovery. Where would we be without electricity?*

In the example above, the paragraph starts with long sentences and ends with short ones. This combination makes the paragraph more lively and effective. Compare it with the paragraph below, which is made up of only long sentences:

> *Benjamin Franklin, who was one of the Founding Fathers of the United States, helped write the Declaration of Independence. He also invented many things, such as bifocals and the Franklin stove, and he discovered electricity, which became very important to modern life.*

Which paragraph do you prefer?

***Summary:*** It is a good idea to mix long sentences with short ones. A good combination of long and short sentences makes writing lively.

## Too Many Short Sentences

You may have too many short sentences in your writing. Good writing usually contains a variety of sentence lengths to make the writing more interesting. Too many short sentences often make the writing sound choppy. You should combine some of your short sentences to make the writing smoother. Here is an example of a paragraph with too many short sentences:

> *I knew my friends would throw me a party. It was for my birthday. There was something in the air. I felt it for a whole week before that. I was nervous. I was also very excited. I got home that night. My friends didn't disappoint me. I walked in my house. All my friends yelled, "Surprise!"*

The paragraph can be improved by joining some of the short sentences using sentence connectors:

*Because it was my birthday, I knew my friends would throw me a party. There was something in the air for a whole week before that. I was nervous but excited when I got home that night. I wasn't disappointed. When I walked in my house, all my friends yelled, "Surprise!"*

**Summary:** Good writing usually contains a variety of long and short sentences. A good mix of sentence lengths makes the writing more interesting. Too many short sentences often make the writing sound choppy.

## Sentences Beginning with Coordinating Conjunctions

Coordinating conjunctions are words such as *and, but, as, or, yet, for,* and *nor.* They link or join thoughts together in the middle of a sentence. For example:

*I love pizza, so I eat it for breakfast.*

*Mother drove to town to buy groceries, but she came home with a present for me.*

Coordinating conjunctions can also be used to begin sentences, as in these examples:

*And I didn't like parties.*

*So I did not do well on that test.*

When you have too many sentences beginning with coordinating conjunctions, your writing becomes choppy. To make your writing smoother, use coordinating conjunctions only when joining ideas within sentences.

In the paragraph below, the writer uses a lot of coordinating conjunctions to begin sentences:

*Baseball is the great American sport. And it is thought of as a summer pastime. So as soon as the weather turns warm, all the neighborhood kids find a field to toss a ball around. And soon they form teams and play each other. But all summer, they always find time to watch professional games on TV. Or they go see them at a ballpark.*

The paragraph can be improved by getting rid of beginning coordinating conjunctions:

*Baseball, the great American sport, is thought of as a summer pastime. As soon as the weather turns warm, the neighborhood kids find a field to toss a ball around. Soon, they form teams to play each other, but all summer, they always find time to watch professional games on TV or go see them at a ballpark.*

**Summary:** Coordinating conjunctions are very useful for joining thoughts together in the middle of a sentence. However, try to avoid using them to begin sentences in academic writing.

# Organization and Development

The purpose of this section is to explain how a strong essay is typically organized and how to develop your ideas in an essay. It will provide answers to the following questions:

**Introduction**

- What is an introduction?
- How do I write an introduction?

**Thesis**

- What is a thesis?
- How do I make sure that my reader understands my thesis?
- Do I have enough main ideas to support my thesis?

**Main Ideas**

- Does each of my main ideas begin with a topic sentence?
- Have I discussed each main idea completely?
- Have I arranged my ideas in an orderly manner?

**Supporting Ideas**

- What are some ways to develop supporting ideas?
- Have I done my best to support and develop my ideas?
- Does each of my paragraphs support and develop/explain the main idea/topic sentence?

**Transitional Words and Phrases**

- Do I use transitional words and phrases to take the reader from one idea to the next?

**Conclusion**

- What is a conclusion?
- How do I write a conclusion?

***Note:*** This section will give you advice about writing academic essays **in general**—essays for which you have plenty of time and which may be many pages long.

# Introduction

## What Is an Introduction?

An introduction is the first paragraph or two of an essay. It tells the reader what the essay is about and provides background for the thesis (main idea).

A good introductory paragraph does several things:

- It makes the reader want to read the essay.
- It tells the reader the overall topic of the essay.
- It tells the reader the main idea (thesis) of the essay.

## How Do I Write an Introduction?

Introductions can be written in many different ways. Here are some ideas you can use to write a good introduction:

- Background about the topic
- Narrative
- Quotation
- Dramatic statistics/facts
- Controversial statement
- Questions that lead to the thesis

The following are examples of these ideas. The essay's thesis sentence is highlighted in bold.

### Background About the Topic

*Since the beginning of time, there have been teachers. The "classroom" teacher has many important tasks to do. A teacher has to teach information while keeping things interesting. She also sometimes has to be a referee, a coach, and a secretary. At times, a teacher has to be a nurse or just a good listener.* ***This career demands a lot, but it's the career I most want to have.***

### Narrative

*My fourth-grade teacher, Mr. Sanchez, was not an imposing person. He was quiet-spoken and always calm. Even though he never raised his voice, he had no trouble controlling his students. He could quiet us down with just a glance. We always wanted to please him because we knew how much he wanted us to succeed. He expected us to do the best we could . . .* ***Mr. Sanchez was the kind of teacher I want to be.***

### Quotation

*"Teaching is better than tossing a pebble into a pond of water and watching those ripples move out from the middle. With teaching, you never know where those ripples will end." I remember those words of my fourth-grade teacher. Ms. Vela once told me that years after they left her class, her students would come back to tell her how much she had helped them. Ms. Vela's students said that it was because of her that they learned to work hard and to feel proud of what they did.* ***I would like to teach because I would like to make that kind of difference.***

### Dramatic Statistics/Facts

*Three out of four people said that they thought it didn't matter how many students were taught in one class. However, our class researched this and found that the opposite is true. Studies completed at a university show that having small class sizes, especially in the primary grades, makes a big difference in how much students learn.* ***Before we decide how many students to assign to a primary school teacher, we need to think more carefully about how important smaller class size is.***

### Controversial

*Some people believe that good teaching is more of an art than a science and something of a mystery when it comes to trying to explain how it comes about.* ***However, research has shown that a particular set of strategies is common to all effective teachers and can be successfully adopted by struggling teachers who practice them regularly.***

### Questions That Lead to the Thesis

*What exactly is "voice"? Is it a speaking voice or a singing voice? When people say that they have a voice in their head but no way to get it out, what does that mean?* ***"Voice" has less to do with throats and mouths than it has to do with being human, being alive.***

**TIP**

*Responses to the TOEFL iBT Writing tasks may benefit from an introduction, but typically one that is briefer than the examples above.*

## Thesis

### What Is a Thesis?

The thesis statement tells the main idea—or most important idea—of the essay. It emphasizes the writer's idea of the topic and often answers the question "What important or interesting things do I have to say?" Thinking about the thesis statement can help you decide what other information needs to be presented or omitted in the rest of the essay.

A good thesis statement

- gives the reader some hint about what you will say about the topic
- presents your opinion about the topic and is not just a fact or an observation
- is written as a complete statement
- does not formally announce your opinion about the topic

A good thesis statement gives the reader some hint about what you will say about the topic.

Weak thesis: *Abraham Lincoln was an interesting man.*

Good thesis: *Abraham Lincoln was a person of contradictions.*

Weak thesis: *Television is a total waste of time.*

Good thesis: *Parents should carefully choose appropriate, educational television shows for their children to watch.*

A good thesis statement presents your opinion about the topic and is not just a fact or an observation.

Weak thesis: *London is the capital of England.*

Good thesis: *For tourists interested in British history, London is an ideal travel destination.*

Weak thesis: *Many movies today are violent.*

Good thesis: *The violence in movies today makes children less sensitive to other people's suffering.*

A good thesis statement is written as a complete statement.

Weak thesis: *Should something be done about bad drivers?*

Good thesis: *Bad drivers should have to take a driving course before being allowed to drive again.*

Weak thesis: *There is a problem with the information on the internet.*

Good thesis: *To make sure information found on the internet is valid, internet users must make sure the sources of the information are credible.*

A good thesis statement does not formally announce your opinion about the topic.

Weak thesis: *In my paper, I will write about whether schools should require uniforms.*

Good thesis: *Public schools should not require uniforms.*

Weak thesis: *The subject of this essay is drug testing.*

Good thesis: *Drug testing is needed for all professional athletes.*

## How Do I Make Sure That My Reader Understands My Thesis?

Sometimes you might use a word in your introduction or thesis that you should define or explain. For example, if you are writing about "Who is a hero?" you should first explain what you think the word *hero* means. Is a hero a person who risks their life to save others? Is a hero a person you admire for any reason? People might have their own ways of thinking about a certain word. When you define the word, you help your reader better understand what you mean.

### Do I Have Enough Main Ideas to Support My Thesis?

A main idea is a point that you feel strongly about. It is important to you, and you want the reader to understand this idea. Some writers like to give the reader three main ideas. However, the number of main ideas will vary among good essays. The important thing to remember is that your main ideas need to support your thesis adequately.

If you do not have enough main ideas, you may want to do some rethinking. do some rethinking. Think of questions that ask who, what, when, where, why, how, and what if about your subject.

For example, a student writing an essay about becoming a teacher could ask the following questions.

- **Who?**

  *Who in my life has influenced me to consider becoming a teacher?*

- **What?**

  *What do teachers do?*

- **When?**

  *When did I start thinking about becoming a teacher?*

- **Where?**

  *Where are teachers needed the most?*

- **Why?**

  *Why would a person want to become a teacher? Why do I want to become a teacher?*

- **How? How much?**

  *How does a teacher learn how to teach?*

  *How has my idea of becoming a teacher changed over the years?*

  *How much does a teacher influence their students?*

  *How much time does a teacher have to work outside of school?*

- **What if? Why not?**

  *What if teachers do not have all of the materials they need?*

  *Why teach in the classroom and not just over the internet?*

*Talk to others about your topic.*

Lots of people are happy to share what they know. Take good notes, because you may want to quote them in your essay.

- Other students in your school probably have opinions.
- A teacher who knows about the issue or subject could give you some opinions.

- Other people who are experts may have valuable information or opinions.
- Research your subject on the internet or in a library.
- Send an e-mail to someone who may be an expert.

*Think about the kind of writing you are doing.*

Consider the questions below to help you figure out which ideas you need to add or how you should arrange those ideas.

- Are you explaining how things are alike (comparison) and different (contrast)? You can use this purpose when you are describing something *(such as how to teach primary school students compared with how to teach high school students)* or when you are analyzing different viewpoints *(such as whether children should go to school year-round).*

- Are you putting your ideas in categories? You might be able to describe something in general and then describe its particular qualities. *For example, in an essay about good teachers, you might want to talk about what it takes to be a good teacher and then talk about the unique qualities of a particular teacher you have had.*

- Are you giving reasons to show how a problem developed and what the effects of the problem are? *For example, if you were discussing how students' attitudes are affected by their environment, you might want to first describe what has caused a particular attitude to develop. Then you might want to discuss the effects of that attitude.*

- Are you trying to persuade someone to think like you or to do something that will improve a situation in the way that you want it to be improved? *For example, if you are trying to persuade a friend to think about an issue the way you think about it, you might want to start by saying what the issue is and why your ideas are the best.*

*Start all over and see where you go this time with your writing.*

Do not be afraid to start over. Lots of writers get new and better ideas when they write about something more than once.

*Reread your draft.*

Look at your previous draft and start where the writing is the most interesting or at the point that you think is your best sentence.

- Try to write three more sentences to explain your best sentence.
- Review the three new sentences, pick the best one, and write three more sentences that explain the most important idea in that best sentence.

## Main Ideas

### Does Each of My Main Ideas Begin with a Topic Sentence?

Each main idea needs to be discussed fully. The main idea is part of a sentence that explains the idea. This sentence is called the topic sentence, and its goal is to help the reader think of questions about the topic.

Pretend that you are the reader of this topic sentence:

*Not passing a test in fourth grade in Ms. Vela's class made me think about what a teacher is.*

What questions do you have?

Do you want to know more about what happened to this writer in fourth grade?

Do you think that you will learn what the writer thought or meant by the words "what a teacher is"?

*Use your topic sentence to prepare the reader for understanding what is written in the essay.*

You can review your sentences to see which words are the influential words. They are the words that seem more important in your sentence.

In this topic sentence, which words or phrases are important?

*Teachers don't get paid for every hour that they work.*

Would you say that "every hour that they work" are the important words?

Here are the other sentences in the paragraph with the topic sentence above.

*Teachers sometimes do work even when they are not in the classroom. Sometimes my mother grades papers and projects all day on Sunday. Even though she does not get paid, she says the weekend is the only time she can grade all of her students' work. My neighbor spends three weeks of his summer vacation on a ship that does scientific experiments. He doesn't get paid for any of that work, but he says the things that he learns help him be a better teacher.*

*Use topic sentences to connect two paragraphs or two main ideas.*

Here is a sample paragraph that begins with a topic sentence:

*Teachers get many benefits in their careers. My neighbor has children and likes having the summer off when his children are home. Some teachers say their work is very enjoyable. At least that's what my mom says when she mixes up her magic bubble formula for science class. My mom also says that one of the benefits of teaching is that she is using her college education every day. She also gets paid to take refresher courses. But she works hard.*

Can you see how the next topic sentence connects to another thought?

*In fact, teachers don't get paid for every hour that they work, but the teachers that I know say that they love their work.*

What do you expect the writer to tell you about in the paragraph that follows the topic sentence above?

## Have I Discussed Each Main Idea Completely?

In good writing, you (the writer) and the reader feel as if all of your questions or concerns have been discussed. Remember that your reader needs to understand what you are writing, so discuss each idea completely.

*Give each main idea its own paragraph.*

Each main idea should be treated as a unit. However, if a main idea is very broad, it will need more than one paragraph, because it is too complicated to be discussed in a single paragraph.

## Have I Arranged My Ideas in an Orderly Manner?

You can arrange your ideas in many different ways. Here are two common organizational methods.

### Chronological Order

You can organize your ideas in chronological order, which means the order in time in which they occurred. You can begin with the oldest point first and then use paragraphs to discuss what happened next or later.

Here are two main ideas that will be developed into paragraphs:

#### Idea 1

*I have wanted to be a teacher ever since I failed a test in Ms. Vela's class in fourth grade.*

#### Idea 2

*Then in eighth grade I had an assignment to teach a science lesson to a class in my former primary school, and that experience showed me how good I felt when the students didn't want the class to be over.*

### Order of Importance

You can organize your ideas by importance, either most important to least important or the other way around.

Here are two main ideas a writer wants to present:

#### Idea 1

*The most important reason I want to be a science teacher is to help the next generation learn about Earth.*

#### Idea 2

*Getting to do fun activities is another reason why I want to be a science teacher.*

The writer has chosen to introduce the most important main idea first.

**TIP**

*If your writing assignment has to be completed in a short time, as in an essay test, you probably want to begin with the most important parts or reasons first.*

## Supporting Ideas

### What Are Some Ways to Develop Supporting Ideas?

Supporting ideas help to convince your reader that your main idea is a good one. Here are some things that professional writers do:

- Tell a story that clarifies the main idea.

- Give examples of the main idea to explain what the paragraph is about.

- Give reasons that support the thesis. These can be facts, logical arguments, or the opinions of experts.

- Use details that are very specific so the reader can understand how this idea is different from others.

- Tell what can be seen, heard, smelled, touched, felt, or experienced.

- Try to see the idea from many different angles.

- Tell how other events, people, or things might have an influence on the main idea.

- Use metaphors or analogies to help the reader understand an idea by comparing it to something else.

### Have I Done My Best to Support and Develop My Ideas?

Think of your reader as a curious person. Assume that your reader wants to know everything that you can say about this subject.

Here are some specific questions that are appropriate for certain types of writing:

- **If you are describing a problem or issue, you might want to consider the following:**

  What type of problem or issue is it?

  What are the signs that a problem or issue exists?

  Who or what is affected by the problem or issue?

  What is the history of the problem or issue—what or who caused it or contributed to it, and what is the state of the problem now?

  Why is the issue or problem significant? What makes this issue or problem important or less important?

- **If you are arguing or trying to persuade your reader to agree with your opinion, consider the following:**

  What facts or statistics could you mention as support?

  What ideas could you discuss to prove your points?

  What comparison could you make that would help the reader understand the issue?

  What expert opinion would make your opinion more valid?

  Could you support your point with some examples?

  Could you describe the views of someone holding a different opinion?

TIP

*Strong arguments are often made by discussing what is good in the opponent's view. You can use expressions such as "although that is a point well taken," "granted, while it is true that," or "I agree that" to discuss an opposite view.*

- **If you are analyzing literature or writing a review of a story or movie, consider these questions:**

  Can you summarize the story so that your reader knows what happens?

  Can you give the details about the place or time so that your reader has a context for understanding the story?

  What can you say about the main characters so that the reader can understand what makes them special or interesting?

  Can you describe the point where the main characters are in a crisis and must make an interesting choice?

  Can you quote what characters say about each other or about what they are experiencing?

  Does the story have a deeper theme that you could discuss?

  Can you describe the style in which the story is told or the camera angles of the movie?

  Are there interesting images or symbols?

- **If you are describing something or providing a definition, consider the following:**

  Can you tell what the thing looks like or what its parts are?

  Can you say what it does or means?

  If what it does or means has changed over time, can you describe what it used to mean or used to do and what it now means or does?

  If what you are describing has a different name or meaning, can you tell the reader the different name or meaning?

- **If you are telling how to do or make something, consider these points:**

  Have you started at the right place—the first step—and proceeded logically?

  Have you defined any terms that might be unfamiliar to your reader?

  Have you given an example that might help your reader understand what you mean?

  Have you tried to explain your instructions clearly? Have you numbered these instructions so that the reader knows the order in which it is best to do them?

TIP

*You may want to think of a way to arrange your material so that your reader can understand it better. For example, in a recipe the ingredients are listed at the top and the instructions are in short paragraphs or are numbered as steps.*

### Does Each of My Paragraphs Support and Develop/Explain the Main Idea/Topic Sentence?

Paragraphs are a group of sentences about a thought or discussion. Each paragraph is about a main topic.

Some paragraphs are long and some are short. Some paragraphs are just one sentence, which can be a very interesting way to present information.

Some contain an interesting story that can take several sentences to tell.

Some paragraphs answer all of the topic issues. Others are more like transitions between two main ideas.

Here are some questions to help you evaluate your paragraphs:

- **Have you said enough so that each paragraph is complete?**

**TIP**

*Try giving each paragraph a title and see if, read by itself, the paragraph could be something meaningful. If the reader asked you a specific question, would this paragraph be the answer? If some of the sentences do not fit as an answer, then you should probably delete them or move them to a different paragraph.*

- **Have you used words that need to be explained or defined?** If you use unfamiliar terms and do not explain what they mean, your reader might feel frustrated. Try using more than one sentence to define or explain something. Three sentences might really explain your idea!

- **Have you provided evidence (proof)? Would an example show what you mean?** Use a good example to show that what you say is true. This is important.

- **Is there a personal experience or quotation from another source that would validate what you are trying to say?**

**TIP**

*Personal experiences are appropriate in some essays but not in others. Make sure you understand the type of information that is expected in each essay you write.*

**TIP**

*If you are quoting from another source, make certain that you are quoting (reproducing the words) accurately. Also be sure that you are using quotation marks correctly.*

# Transitional Words and Phrases

## Do I Use Transitional Words and Phrases to Take the Reader from One Idea to the Next?

Transitional words and phrases connect what a reader has already read to what the reader is going to read. They give the reader an idea of the relationships between the various ideas and supporting points. They also help to show the relationship between sentences.

You might think of your paragraph as a train: the topic sentence is the engine and the other sentences are the boxcars. Do all the parts of the paragraph link or fit together? You can guide the readers as they read an essay by using transitional words or phrases in paragraphs and sentences.

**These words can help you talk about time and the relationship between events:**

*today, tomorrow, next week, yesterday, meanwhile, about, before, during, at, after, soon, immediately, afterward, later, finally, then, when, next, simultaneously, as a result*

**These words can help you show the order of ideas:**

*first, second, third, finally, lastly, most important, of least importance*

**These words can help you show location:**

*above, over, below, beneath, behind, in front of, in back of, on top of, inside, outside, near, between, beside, among, around, against, throughout, off, onto, into, beyond*

**These words can help you compare or demonstrate similarity:**

*also, as, similarly, in the same way, likewise, like*

**These words can help you contrast or demonstrate difference:**

*in contrast, however, although, still, even though, on the other hand, but*

**These words can help you add information:**

*in addition, for instance, for example, moreover, next, likewise, besides, another, additionally, again, also, in fact*

**These words can help you clarify a point:**

*in other words, for instance, that is, in summary*

**These words can help you add emphasis to a point that you are making:**

*truly, in fact, for this reason, again, to reiterate*

**These words can help you conclude or summarize:**

*all in all, lastly, as a result, in summary, therefore, finally*

# Conclusion

## What Is a Conclusion?

The concluding paragraph is separate from the other paragraphs and brings closure to the essay.

- It discusses the importance of your ideas.
- It restates the thesis with fresh wording.
- It sums up the main ideas of the essay.
- It can also include an anecdote, a quotation, statistics, or a suggestion.

## How Do I Write a Conclusion?

You might consider some of the following approaches to writing concluding paragraphs:

- Summarize main points.
- Provide a summarizing story.
- Include a provocative or memorable quotation.
- Make a prediction or suggestion.
- Leave the reader with something to think about.

Here are two different concluding paragraphs:

*Good teaching requires flexibility, compassion, organization, knowledge, energy, and enthusiasm. A good teacher must decide when a student needs to be prodded and when that student needs mercy. Good teaching requires knowing when to listen and reflect and when to advise or correct. It requires a delicate balance of many skills and often a different mix of approaches for different students and different situations. Is this profession demanding? Yes! Boring? Never! Exciting? Absolutely!*

*When I become a teacher, I want fourth graders like Ms. Vela's. We adored her and wanted to please her. But more important, I want to be a Ms. Vela for my students. I want to challenge my students to become good citizens. When the river in our town flooded its banks and some classmates had to be evacuated, Ms. Vela asked us to think about what we could do. We came up with three decisions. We packed lunches for our classmates, we shared our books and pencils in class, and we gave them clothing. Later when we studied civics, we realized that we were taking care of our classmates the way the local or federal government does in a disaster. Ms. Vela was helping her fourth graders become more civic minded. I'm hoping to help my students think like that when I'm a teacher.*

# Advice to Writers

This section provides information about the different kinds of essays you may be asked to write.

- Persuasion
- Informative Writing
- Comparison/Contrast
- Description
- Narration
- Cause and Effect
- Problem and Solution
- Description of a Process ("How-to")
- Writing as Part of an Assessment
- Response to Literature
- Writing in the Workplace

## Persuasion

When you write a persuasive essay, you are trying to make the reader agree with you. You thus have to offer good reasons to support your opinion, deal with opposing views, and perhaps offer a solution.

**Here is how to start:**

- List specific arguments for and against your opinion (the pros and cons).
- Decide whether you need to find more information (for example, *statistics* that support your argument, *direct quotes* from experts, *examples* that make your ideas concrete, *personal experience*, *facts*).
- Think of good arguments from someone who holds the opposite view. How could you respond to that person?

*In this kind of writing, you might want to keep your best argument for last.*

*Summary:* When you write a persuasive essay, you have to be clear and convincing. Any kind of writing improves with practice. Try to practice writing and revising, and expose yourself to as many good models of persuasive essays as you can.

## Informative Writing

This kind of writing presents information that helps your reader understand a subject (for example, climate change, jazz music, pollution). Informative writing can be based on formal research (reading, interviews, internet browsing). Sometimes you may also be asked to write about a personal experience or observation.

**Here is how to start:**

- Find a specific focus (for example, not *recycling in general* but *the recycling of paper*).

- Choose several important points to discuss (*how paper is recycled, what recycled paper is used for*).

- Think about the supporting details for each point. These details can be facts, observations, descriptions, and/or examples (*items that use recycled paper are paper towels, greeting cards*).

## Comparison/Contrast

Writing a comparison/contrast paper involves comparing and contrasting two subjects. A comparison shows how two things are alike. A contrast shows how two things are different.

You can use comparison and contrast to describe, define, analyze, or make an argument—for, in fact, almost any kind of writing.

**Here is how to start:**

- Select two subjects that have some basic similarities or differences.

- Look for how these subjects are similar and different.

- Decide how you want to present your information. Choose one way and stick with it throughout your essay.
  - Do you want to discuss a point for one subject and then the same point for the second subject?
  - Do you want to show all the important points of one subject and then all the important points of the second subject?
  - Do you want to discuss how your two subjects are the same and then how they are different from each other?

- Remember to make clear to your reader when you are switching from one point of comparison or contrast to another. Use clear transitions. Some transition words that you may find useful are as follows:

  For similarities: *similarly, likewise, furthermore, besides*

  For differences: *in contrast, in comparison, on the other hand, although, however, nevertheless, whereas, yet*

# Description

In descriptive writing, you write about people, places, things, moments, and theories with enough detail to help the reader create a mental picture of what is being described. You can do this by using a wide range of vocabulary, imaginative language, interesting comparisons, and images that appeal to the senses.

**Here is how to start:**

- Let the reader see, smell, hear, taste, and feel what you are writing about. Use your five senses in the description. (For example, *The ancient driver nervously steered the old car down the red mud road, with me bouncing along on the back seat.*)

- Be specific (not *this dessert is good* but *the fudge brownie is moist, chewy, and very tasty*).

- Show the reader where things are located from your perspective. (For example, *As I passed through the wooden gates, I heard a cough. A tiny woman came out from behind the trees.*)

- Decide whether you want to give a personal view (subjective) or a neutral viewpoint (objective).

**TIP**

*What seems unusual or contradictory can make your subject more interesting. (For example,* "Martin Luther King, Jr., probably contributed more than anyone else to changes in civil rights, but he hardly earned any money for his speeches and work.")

# Narration

This kind of essay offers you a chance to think and write a story about yourself, an incident, memories, or experiences. Narratives or stories usually include a plot, a setting (where something happened), characters, a climax, and an ending. Narratives are generally written in the first person, using *I*. However, as the storyteller, you can choose to "speak" like different people to make the story more interesting.

**Here is how to start:**

- If you are writing about a quarrel with a friend:
  - Think of what caused the quarrel.
  - Think of who is involved and how.
  - Think of how the quarrel developed, how it was settled, or whether you and your friend are talking now.

- Remember the details that make the event real to you (for example, what your friend said to you and the tone of voice your friend used).

- Try to answer the question "What did this event mean to me?"

- Choose a way to begin; for example:
  - Build your story in scenes (the way you see in movies).
  - Summarize what happened and describe only the most important scene.
  - Begin at the ending and tell why this was such an important event.

## Cause and Effect

Cause-and-effect essays are concerned with why things happen (causes) and what happens as a result (effects). In the cause-and-effect essay, it is very important that your tone be reasonable and that your presentation look factual and believable.

**Here is how to start:**

- Think about the event or issue you want to write about.

- Brainstorm ideas.

- Introduce your main idea.

- Find relevant and appropriate supporting details to back up your main idea. You can organize these details in the following ways:
  - *Chronological*, the order in which things/events happen
  - *Order of importance*, from least to most important or vice versa
  - *Categorical*, by dividing the topic into parts or categories

- Use appropriate transition words and phrases, such as the following:

  *because, thus, therefore, due to, one cause is, another is, since, for, first, second, consequently, as a result, resulted in, one result is, another is*

## Problem and Solution

A problem-solution essay starts by identifying a problem (or problems) and then proposes one or more solutions. It is usually based on topics that both the writer and the reader care about (such as the quality of cafeteria food).

**Here is how to start:**

- Think of all the reasons that the problem exists.
  - Why did it happen?
  - How did it begin?
  - Why does it exist now?

- List possible solutions to the problem.

- Evaluate your solutions—which ones will most likely work?

- Write the pros and cons of one or more good solutions, but give the most space in your essay to the best solution.

- Explain why the best solution is the one to choose.

## Description of a Process ("How-to")

This kind of essay explains how to do something (for example, *how to bake your favorite cake*) or how something occurs (for example, *how movies are made*).

**For how to do something, here is how to start, along with the pertinent questions:**

- Think about all the equipment, skills, or materials needed.
- How many steps are there in the process? Put the steps in the right order. Why is each step important?
- What difficulties are involved in each step?
- How long does the process take?

**TIP**

*Give any advice that can help the reader accomplish the step with success.*

**For how something occurs, here is how to start:**

- Give any background that can help your reader understand the process.
- Tell what happens in the order that it happens.

**TIP**

*Be sure to explain any terms that your reader might not understand.*

Process essays are usually organized according to time: they begin with the first step in the process and continue until the last step. To indicate that one step has been completed and a new one will begin, we use transitions. Some common transition words and phrases used in process essays are as follows:

*first of all, first, second, third, next, soon after, after a few hours, afterward, initially, at the same time, in the meantime, before, before this, immediately before, in the meanwhile, currently, during, meanwhile, later, then, previously, at last, eventually, finally, last, last but not least, lastly*

## Writing as Part of an Assessment

This kind of writing may be more difficult because you are trying to write your best in a certain place and a limited amount of time. There are a few strategies, however.

**Here is how to start:**

- Take a few moments to understand the question and to note down some ideas that come to mind.
- Before beginning to write, take a few moments to plan. How are you going to organize your main ideas and supporting details? Some students find making an outline to be a helpful strategy.

- During your writing, if other ideas come to mind and they feel right, use them.

- Keep track of your time, but do not panic.

- Revise. Look at the paper from the reader's point of view; reorganize and add explanations if necessary.

- Save some time to proofread

**TIPS**

*As with any other kind of writing, writing on a test improves with practice.*

*On the TOEFL Writing test, you will have 20 minutes to complete the Integrated Writing Task and 10 minutes to complete the Writing for an Academic Discussion Task. Practice writing and revising responses to these tasks while working within a set time limit.*

## Response to Literature

When you write about literature, you are telling why that work of literature (story, movie, poem, or play) is interesting and what makes it effective (for example, why it makes you laugh, why you care about the characters).

You can write about why the literary work seems true, you can analyze the characters or actions, or you can analyze how the literary work accomplishes its effect.

**There are many ways to respond to literature, but here are a few ways to start, along with pertinent questions:**

- Write for a while about your personal feelings about the literature. Are you most interested in the setting, the situation, the characters, or the atmosphere that the work creates? These are clues to what you can write about.

- What is the situation or the mood?

- What clues does the author give you about the true meaning of this story, poem, or movie? (For example, the many "Cinderella" stories in the world have the same meaning: kindness is rewarded no matter how poor you are.)

- Organize your thoughts and support them with examples from the literary work. Do not assume that your reader knows the story or movie that you are writing about!

## Writing in the Workplace

Letters, memos, and reports are the kinds of writing that are most often done when we do business with each other. In this kind of writing, you want to make your points as quickly and clearly as possible. So try to be brief and direct.

**Here is how to start:**

- Organize your thoughts. Most business letters should take one page.

- Think about whether there is a special format you should follow.

- Decide if you want the reader to take action (persuasive), to understand a problem (informative), or to fix something (problem-solution). (*Refer to the relevant sections under the "Advice to Writers" heading.*)

- Write clearly and courteously.

- Include relevant quotations.

- Leave the reader with something to think about (for example, make a prediction or suggestion).

# Revising, Editing, and Proofreading

## The Writing Process

The writing process has several stages: planning, drafting, writing, revising, editing, and proofreading. Many writers and instructors maintain that improving your essay has three distinct stages: revising, editing, and proofreading. Review each column of the following chart to understand each stage completely.

As you write, you may wish to revise and edit your essay several times as you clarify and develop your ideas. Revising and editing are distinct activities. When you revise, you make major content and organizational changes. When you edit, you make word- and sentence-level changes for style and correctness. The Writer's Handbook sections on Style, Organization and Development, and Advice to Writers can be very helpful as you revise and edit your essay. When you have a final version of your essay, be sure to proofread it carefully.

| | Revising | Editing | Proofreading |
|---|---|---|---|
| **Purpose** | See the complete concept. Decide if your essay says what you want it to say. Add ideas. | Correct grammar and usage. Make changes in word choice, style, and the way you explain your ideas. | Correct typos as well as spelling, punctuation, and formatting errors. |
| **When** | Begin revising after you have a finished first draft. | Begin after you have made major content and organization changes. | Make this the final stage before you submit your essay. |
| **What** | Read your entire essay from beginning to end. | As you read each sentence, revise that sentence before you do the next sentence. | Read word by word and line by line to make corrections. |
| **Strategies** | Identify each part of the essay: introduction, thesis, main ideas, supporting ideas, and conclusion. Review carefully how the ideas are connected and the order of paragraphs. Do not be afraid to cut and paste, delete, or add new ideas. Ask a peer reviewer to say what is good and what could be better in your essay. | Ask your teacher, a peer editor, or a friend to give you ideas and advice. List the kinds of grammar and usage errors you make and look for those errors first. If a sentence seems right, do not revise it. Think about just the parts that seem to have problems. Use a handbook to help you correct errors and rewrite sentences. | Print a copy of your essay and make the changes on the paper copy. Have a peer reviewer who is more proficient in English read your essay and circle errors you might have missed. Use a dictionary, handbook, and spell-checker to help you correct errors. |

## Step 1: Organization and Development

Think about your topic and, if necessary, change the way your essay is organized and developed (revising).

## Step 2: Style

Read each sentence to see if your ideas are easy to understand (editing).

## Step 3: Grammar, Usage, Mechanics

Check each word and sentence for errors (editing).

## Step 4: Proofreading

Check for spelling and typing mistakes as you read your final draft (proofreading).

**TIP**

*In the TOEFL iBT test, you will write your responses in a window that offers much of the same functionality as a computer. You will be able to cut and paste text, undo and redo writing choices, and keep track of your word count. However, there is no spelling function in the response window. If you are unsure how to spell a word, see whether the displayed reading passage contains the word or a version of it, and use that as a spelling guide.*

# Glossary

**active voice**—English sentences can be written in either the active or passive voice. In the active voice, the subject is the doer of an action. For example, in *Sam kicked the ball*, the action is *kicked*, and the doer is *Sam*. An active sentence emphasizes the doer of an action.

**adjective**—Adjectives give more information about nouns. In English, they usually come before nouns. For example: *a red umbrella, a rainy day, A dull party.*

**adverb**—Adverbs are words such as *quickly, happily,* or *carefully*. They can tell more about an adjective (for example, *very big*), another adverb (for example, *very quietly*), or a verb (for example, *walk slowly*).

**antecedent**—A noun to which a pronoun refers is the antecedent. In the following sentence, *John* is the antecedent of the pronoun *he*: *John was late for school because he missed the bus.*

**apostrophe**—This punctuation mark (') shows the omission of letters in contractions (*cannot–can't*), or possession (The *girl's* saxophone, the *parents'* input).

**article**—Articles are *a, an,* and *the,* the little words in English that come before nouns. English has two types of articles. The definite article (*the*) is used to refer to one or more specific things, animals, or people (for example, *the house on the hill*). The indefinite articles (*a, an*) are used to refer to a thing, animal, or person in a nonspecific or general way (for example, *a house, an elephant*).

**clause**—A clause is a group of related words that contains a subject and a verb. There are two kinds of clauses: independent and dependent. An independent clause expresses a complete thought and can be seen as a sentence (for example, *She heard the music.*) A dependent clause is a part of a sentence and cannot stand on its own. (*When she heard the music* is a dependent clause.) To make a complete sentence, you need to add an independent clause (for example, *When she heard the music, she laughed.*)

**collective noun**—A collective noun refers to a *group* of people or animals: *population, family, troop, committee.*

**comma**—This punctuation mark (,) is used to separate words (*She bought apples, oranges, and grapes*) or parts of a sentence (*He was here, but he left.*)

**compound subject**—This is a plural subject, a subject that consists of more than one part: *Lions, tigers, and bears are top predators.*

**compound verb**—This type of verb consists of more than one part: *The baby started crying.*

**compound words**—These are words that are made up of two words: *Everywhere, keyboard, himself, weekend.*

**conclusion**—This is the closing paragraph of an essay. In a conclusion, you can restate the thesis or sum up the main ideas of the essay.

**conjunction**—A conjunction is a word that connects words, phrases, or sentences. It also shows relationships between words or clauses. There are two kinds of conjunctions: coordinating and subordinating. Coordinating conjunctions such as *and, but, or, nor,* and *for* connect parts that are equal: In the sentence *She bought a desk and a chair,* both *desk* and *chair* are equal nouns connected by *and.* Subordinating conjunctions such as *although, because, if, since,* and *when* connect parts that are not equal: In the sentence *Because he missed the train, he was late for work,* the conjunction *Because* shows the relationship between the dependent clause (*Because he missed the train*) and the independent clause (*he was late for work*).

**contraction**—Contractions are short forms. You make a contraction when you combine two words, shorten one of them, and add an apostrophe: *cannot–can't; does not–doesn't; should not–shouldn't; it is–it's.*

**dependent clause**—A dependent clause is a part of a sentence and cannot stand on its own. For example, *When he swept the floor* is a dependent clause. To make a complete sentence, you need to add an independent clause: *When he swept the floor, he whistled.*

**exclamation point**—This mark of punctuation (!) at the end of a sentence is used to show surprise or strong emotion.

**fragment**—A fragment is a group of words that is not a complete sentence, even though it sometimes starts with a capital letter or ends with a punctuation mark and often contains a subject and verb.

**helping verb**—This type of verb is also called an auxiliary verb. Helping verbs are used with main verbs in a verb phrase: *is going; were singing; can talk; may leave; must tell; will see.*

**hyphen**—This mark (-) is used to separate the different parts of a compound word: *mother-in-law, self-motivated student.*

**independent clause**—An independent clause has a subject and a verb, expresses a complete thought, and can be seen as a sentence. (*She saw him.*) It can also be combined with another independent clause to make a compound sentence. (*She saw him, so she called him over.*) It can also take a dependent clause to make a complex sentence. (*She saw him, even though it was dark.*)

**infinitive verb**—An infinitive consists of the word *to* plus a *verb* (for example, *to go, to swim, to wish*). It can function as a noun, adjective, or adverb. For example: *To swim the English Channel is my friend's strongest dream.* Here, the infinitive *to swim* acts as a noun. It is the subject of the sentence.

**intransitive verb**—This type of verb does not need an object to complete its meaning. For example: *John ran. Bob left. Jane slept.*

**introduction**—An introduction is the first paragraph of an essay. Effective introductions do two basic things: grab the reader's interest and let the reader know what the whole essay is about. This is why most introductions include a thesis statement that clearly states the writer's topic and main argument.

**main idea**—Main ideas are the important points of an essay. They state what will be discussed in each paragraph (or set of paragraphs for longer essays). Main ideas develop the thesis statement of an essay and are in turn developed by supporting details.

**modal verb**—A modal verb is a kind of helping verb. Modal verbs help to express meanings such as permission (*may*), obligation (*must*), prediction (*will, shall*), or ability (*can*).

**noun phrase**—This type of phrase consists of several words that together function as the noun of a sentence. For example: *Talking to my mother made me feel better*. Here, *Talking to my mother* is a noun phrase that is acting as the subject of this sentence.

**paragraph**—An essay is made up of smaller sections called paragraphs. Each paragraph should focus on one main idea; you tell your reader what this idea is by using a topic sentence. A good paragraph is one in which every sentence supports the topic sentence.

**passive voice**—English sentences can be written in either the active or passive voice. In a passive sentence, the verb *to be* is combined with the past participle form of a verb (for example, *John was introduced*.). A passive sentence emphasizes the receiver or the results of an action.

**period**—In English grammar, this punctuation mark (.) is used to signal the end of a declarative sentence. (A declarative sentence is one that is not a question or an exclamation.) It is also used to indicate abbreviations (for example, *Mr., St., Ave.*).

**phrase**—A phrase is a group of related words with a single grammatical function (for example, a noun phrase or a verb phrase). The noun phrase acts as a noun or subject in this sentence: *The girl in the corner is Mary*.

**plural**—*Plural* means "more than one." In English grammar, nouns, pronouns, and verbs can take plural forms. For example, *cars* is a plural noun, *they* is a plural pronoun, and *climb* is a plural verb.

**possessive pronoun**—These are pronouns that show possession or ownership (for example, *my, our, his, her, their, whose*). Some possessive pronouns can function as nouns: *Is this yours? That book is mine*.

**prefix**—A prefix is a word part, such as *co-* in *costar*, attached to the front of a word to make a new word. For another example, the prefix *re-* can be added to the word *sell* to make the word *resell*, which means "to sell again."

**preposition**—Prepositions are words such as *in, of, by*, and *from*. They describe the relationship between words in a sentence. In the sentence *The professor sat on the desk*, the preposition *on* shows the location of the professor in relation to the desk.

**pronoun**—A pronoun can replace a noun or another pronoun. You can use pronouns such as *she, it, which*, and *they* to make your writing less repetitive.

**question mark**—This is the punctuation mark (?) used at the end of a direct question. For example: *Is David coming to the party?*

**sentence combining**—Sometimes writers combine two or more short sentences to make a longer one. The reason for doing this is that too many short sentences often make the writing sound choppy. Using sentence-combining techniques in the revising process can improve the style of your essay.

**singular**—*Singular* means "single," or "one." In English grammar, nouns, pronouns, and verbs can take singular forms. For example, *car* is a singular noun, *he* or *she* is a singular pronoun, and *climbs* is a singular verb in the present tense.

**subject**—The subject of a sentence tells who or what a sentence is about. For example, in the sentence *Stephen ran into the parking lot*, *Stephen* is the subject of the sentence.

**supporting idea**—Supporting ideas are the details that develop the main idea of a paragraph. They can be definitions, explanations, illustrations, opinions, evidence, and examples. They usually come after the topic sentence and make up the body of a paragraph.

**tense**—Tenses indicate time. Sometimes tenses are formed by changes in the verb, as in *He sings* (present tense) and *He sang* (past tense). At other times, tenses are formed by adding modals, or helping verbs. For example: *He will give me fifty dollars* (future tense); *He has given me fifty dollars* (perfect tense).

**thesis**—The thesis or thesis statement of an essay states what will be discussed in the whole essay. It offers your reader a quick and easy summary of the essay. A thesis statement usually consists of two parts: your topic and what you are going to say about the topic. Thesis statements are supported by main ideas.

**topic sentence**—The topic sentence states the main idea of a paragraph. It tells your reader what the paragraph is about. An easy way to make sure your reader understands the topic of a paragraph is to put your topic sentence near the beginning of the paragraph. (This is a good general rule for less experienced writers, although it is not the only way to do it.)

**transition word or phrase**—Transition words and phrases are used to connect ideas and signal relationships between them. For example, *first* can be used to signal the first of several points; *thus* can be used to show a result.

**transitive verb**—Transitive verbs require an object. For example, in the sentence *He mailed the letter*, *mailed* is a transitive verb, and *letter* is its object.

**verb**—A verb is an "action" word (for example, *climb, jump, run, eat*). English verbs also express time. (For example, past tense verbs such as *climbed, jumped, ran*, and *ate* show that the action happened in the past.) Verbs also show states of being (for example, *am, are, is, to be*).

**verb phrase**—A verb phrase is a phrase (or a group of words) that consists of a main verb (for example, *climb, jump, run, eat*) plus one or more helping verbs (for example, *may, can, has, is, are*). Examples of verb phrases are *She may go*, and *The students will receive certificates*.

# Performance Feedback for Test Takers

The scores you receive on the TOEFL iBT test indicate your performance level in each of the four skill areas: reading, listening, speaking, and writing. This appendix provides descriptions of what test takers can typically do at each score level, as well as advice about how test takers at each level can improve their skills.

## TOEFL iBT Reading Section Performance Descriptors

### Advanced

(Score range 24–30, CEFR Level C1)

Test takers who receive a Reading section score at the **ADVANCED** level typically understand academic passages in English at the introductory university level. These passages are dense with propositions and information and can include difficult vocabulary, lengthy, complex sentences and paragraphs, and abstract or nuanced ideas that may be presented in complex ways.

**Test takers who score at the Advanced level typically can**

- Understand a range of academic and low-frequency vocabulary as well as less common meanings of words.
- Understand explicit connections among pieces of information and make appropriate inferences, even when the passage is conceptually dense and the language is complex.
- Recognize the expository organization of a passage and the purpose that specific information serves within the larger context, even when the purpose of the information is not marked and the passage is conceptually dense.
- Follow a paragraph-length argument involving speculation, qualifications, counterevidence, and subtle rhetorical shifts.
- Synthesize information in passages that contain complex language and are conceptually dense.

Read as much and as often as possible. Make sure to include academic texts on a variety of topics written in different genres and with different degrees of conceptual density as part of your reading.

- Read major newspapers, such as the *New York Times* or *Science Times*, and websites (National Public Radio [NPR] or the BBC).
- Write summaries of texts, making sure they incorporate the organizational pattern of the originals. Continually expand your vocabulary.

Practice using new words you encounter in your reading. This will help you remember both the meaning and correct usage of the new words.

## High-Intermediate

(Score range 18–23, CEFR Level B2)

Test takers who receive a Reading section score at the **HIGH-INTERMEDIATE** level typically understand the main ideas and important details of academic passages in English at the introductory university level, but they may have an incomplete or incorrect understanding of parts of passages that are especially dense with propositions and information or are complex in their presentation of ideas and information.

### Test takers who score at the High-Intermediate level typically can

- Understand common academic vocabulary, but sometimes have difficulty with low-frequency words or less common meanings of words.
- Understand explicit connections among pieces of information and make appropriate inferences, but may have difficulty in parts of a passage that contain low-frequency vocabulary or that are conceptually dense, rhetorically complex, or abstract.
- Distinguish important ideas from less important ones.
- Often recognize the expository organization of a passage and the purpose of specific information within a passage, even when such information is not explicitly marked.
- Synthesize information in a passage, but may have difficulty doing so when the passage is conceptually dense, rhetorically complex, or abstract.

Read as much and as often as possible. Study the organization of academic texts and overall structure of reading passages. Read entire passages from beginning to end before attempting to answer questions.

- Pay attention to the relationship between the **main ideas** and the **supporting details**.
- Outline the text to test your understanding of the structure of the reading passage.

- Write a summary of the entire passage.
- If the text is a comparison, be sure that your summary reflects that. If the text argues two points of view, be sure both points of view are reflected in your summary. Continually expand your vocabulary by developing a system for recording unfamiliar words. Group words according to topic or meaning and study the words as a list of related words.
- Study **roots**, **prefixes**, and **suffixes**; study word families.
- Use available vocabulary resources, such as a good thesaurus or a dictionary of collocations (words commonly used together).

# Low-Intermediate

(Score range 4–17, CEFR Level B1)

Test takers who receive a Reading section score at the **LOW-INTERMEDIATE** level typically understand some main ideas and important information presented in academic passages in English, but their overall understanding is limited. They are able to understand connections across two or more sentences when the relationships are clear and simple, such as a claim followed by a supporting example. However, they have difficulty following denser or more complex parts of a passage.

### Test takers who score at the Low-Intermediate level typically can

- Understand texts with basic grammar, but have inconsistent understanding of texts with complex grammatical structures.
- Understand high-frequency academic vocabulary, but often have difficulty with lower-frequency words.
- Locate information in a passage by matching words or relying on high-frequency vocabulary, but their limited ability to recognize paraphrases results in incomplete understanding of the connections among ideas and information.
- Identify an author's purpose when that purpose is explicitly stated or easy to infer from the context.
- Recognize major ideas in a passage when the information is clearly presented, memorable, or illustrated by examples but have difficulty doing so when the passage is more demanding.

### ADVICE FOR IMPROVEMENT

Read as much and as often as possible. Develop a system for recording unfamiliar words.

- Group words into lists according to topic or meaning and review and study the words on a regular basis so that you remember them.
- Increase your vocabulary by analyzing word parts; study **roots**, **prefixes**, and **suffixes**; study **word families**.
- Study the organization of academic texts and the overall structure of reading passages. Read entire passages from beginning to end before attempting to answer questions.

- Look at connections between sentences; look at how the end of one sentence relates to the beginning of the next sentence.
- Look for the **main ideas** and **supporting details** and pay attention to the relationship between them.
- Outline texts to test your understanding of the structure of reading passages. Begin your outline by grouping paragraphs that address the same concept. Continue your outline by writing one sentence for each of the groups of paragraphs that discuss the same idea.
- Write a summary of the entire passage.

## Below Low-Intermediate

(Score range 0–3)

Test takers with a Reading section score below 4 have not yet demonstrated proficiency at the Low-Intermediate level.

# TOEFL iBT Listening Section Performance Descriptors

## Advanced

(Score range 22–30, CEFR Level C1)

Test takers who receive a Listening section score at the **ADVANCED** level typically understand conversations and lectures that take place in academic settings. The conversations and lectures may include difficult vocabulary, abstract or complex ideas, complex sentence structures, various uses of intonation, and a large amount of information, possibly organized in complex ways.

**Test takers who score at the Advanced level typically can**

- Understand main ideas and explicitly stated important details, even if not reinforced.
- Distinguish important ideas from less important points.
- Keep track of conceptually complex (and sometimes conflicting) information over extended portions of a lecture.
- Understand how information or examples are being used (for example, to provide evidence for or against a claim, to make comparisons or draw contrasts, or to express an opinion or a value judgment) and how pieces of information are connected (for example, in a cause-effect relationship).
- Understand different ways that speakers use language for purposes other than to give information (for example, to express an emotion, to emphasize a point, to convey agreement or disagreement, or to communicate an intention).
- Synthesize information, even when it is not presented in sequence, and make appropriate inferences on the basis of that information.

### ADVICE FOR IMPROVEMENT

Further develop your listening ability with daily practice in listening in English and by challenging yourself with increasingly lengthy listening selections and more complex listening material.

- Listen to different kinds of materials on a variety of topics:
  - Focus on topics that are new to you.
  - Listen to academic lectures and public talks.
  - Listen to audio and video material on TV, radio, and the Internet.
  - Listen to programs with academic content, such as NOVA, BBC, and NPR broadcasts.
  - Listen to conversations, phone calls, and phone recordings.
  - Take live and audio-recorded tours (for example, tours of museums).
- Listen actively:
  - Take notes as you listen for main ideas and important details.
  - Make predictions about what you will hear next.
  - Summarize.
  - Write down new words and expressions.

For the more difficult material you have chosen to listen to, listen several times:

1. First listen for the main ideas and key details;
2. Then listen again to fill in gaps in your understanding; to understand the connections between ideas, the structure of the talk, and the speaker's attitude; and to distinguish fact from opinion.

## High-Intermediate

(Score range 17–21, CEFR Level B2)

Test takers who receive a Listening section score at the **HIGH-INTERMEDIATE** level typically understand the main ideas and important details of conversations and lectures that take place in academic settings. The conversations and lectures may include difficult vocabulary, abstract or complex ideas, complex sentence structures, various uses of intonation, and information that must be tracked across sequences of utterances. However, lectures and conversations that are dense with information may present difficulty if the information is not reinforced.

**Test takers who score at the High-Intermediate level typically can**

- Understand main ideas and explicitly stated important details that are reinforced (by repetition, paraphrase, or indirect reference).
- Distinguish main ideas from other information.
- Keep track of information over an extended portion of an information-rich lecture or conversation, and recognize multiple, possibly conflicting, points of view.
- Understand how information or examples are being used (for example, to provide support for a claim) and how pieces of information are connected (for example, in a narrative explanation, a compare-and-contrast relationship, or a cause-effect chain).
- Understand, though perhaps not consistently, ways that speakers use language for purposes other than to give information (for example, to emphasize a point, express agreement or disagreement, express opinions, or convey intentions indirectly), especially when the purpose is supported by intonation.
- Synthesize information from adjacent parts of a lecture or conversation and make appropriate inferences on the basis of that information, but may have difficulty synthesizing information from separate parts of a lecture or conversation.

*ADVICE FOR IMPROVEMENT*

Practice listening in English daily. Gradually increase the amount of time that you spend listening, the length of the listening selections, and the difficulty of the material.

- Listen to different kinds of materials on a variety of topics:
  - Start with familiar topics; then move to topics that are new to you.
  - Listen to audio and video material that you can pause and replay, such as podcasts, streamed radio and TV programs, and internet videos.
  - Listen to programs with academic content, such as NOVA, BBC, and NPR broadcasts.
  - Listen to conversations and phone recordings.
- Listen actively:
  - Take notes as you listen for main ideas and important details.
  - Ask yourself about basic information. (Who? What? When? Where? Why? How?)
  - Make predictions about what you will hear next.
  - Summarize.
  - Write down new words and expressions.

For more difficult material, listen several times:

1. First listen with English subtitles, if they are available;
2. Then, without subtitles, listen for the main ideas and key details;
3. Then listen again to fill in gaps in your basic understanding and to understand the connections between ideas.


## Low-Intermediate

(Score range 9–16, CEFR Level B1)

Test takers who receive a Listening section score at the **LOW-INTERMEDIATE** level typically understand the main idea and some important details of conversations and lectures that take place in academic settings. These conversations and lectures can include basic academic language, abstract or complex ideas that are significantly reinforced, complex sentence structures, certain uses of intonation, and a large amount of information that is repeated or significantly reinforced.

**Test takers at the Low-Intermediate level typically can**

- Understand main ideas, even in complex discussions, when the ideas are repeatedly referred to, extensively elaborated on, or illustrated with multiple examples.
- Understand explicitly stated important details but may have difficulty understanding details if they are not reinforced (such as through repetition or with an example) or marked as important, or if they are conveyed over several exchanges among different speakers.
- Understand some ways that speakers use language to express an opinion or attitude (for example, agreement, disagreement, surprise), especially when the opinion or attitude is related to a central theme, clearly marked as important, or supported by intonation.
- Understand connections between important ideas, particularly if the ideas are related to a central theme or are repeated, and can make appropriate inferences from information expressed in one or two sentences, especially when that information is reinforced.

Practice listening in English daily. Gradually increase the amount of time that you spend listening, as well as the length of the individual listening selections.

- Listen to different kinds of materials on a variety of topics:
  - recordings on topics that are familiar to you
  - recordings of English lessons
  - audio and video material that you can pause and replay, such as podcasts, streamed radio and TV programs, and internet videos
  - short programs with some academic content conversations
- Listen actively:
  - Take notes as you listen for main ideas and important details.
  - Ask yourself about basic information. (Who? What? When? Where? Why? How?)
  - Make predictions about what you will hear next.
  - Summarize.
  - Write down new words and expressions.

Listen several times to each recording:

1. First listen with English subtitles, if they are available.
2. Then, without subtitles, listen for the main ideas and key details.
3. Then listen again to fill in gaps in your basic understanding and to understand the connections between ideas.

## Below Low-Intermediate

(Score range 0–8)

Test takers with a Listening section score below 9 have not yet demonstrated proficiency at the Low-Intermediate level.

# TOEFL iBT Speaking Section Performance Descriptors

## Advanced
(Score range 25–30, CEFR Level C1)

Test takers who receive a Speaking section score at the **ADVANCED** level are typically able to communicate fluently and effectively on a wide range of topics with little difficulty.

**Test takers who score at the Advanced level typically can**

- Speak clearly and use intonation to support meaning so that speech is generally easy to understand and follow; any minor lapses do not obscure meaning.
- Speak with relative ease on a range of general and academic topics, demonstrating control of an appropriate range of grammatical structures and vocabulary; any minor errors may be noticeable, but do not obscure meaning.
- Convey mostly well-supported summaries, explanations, and opinions, including both concrete and abstract information, with generally well-controlled organization and cohesion; lapses may occur, but they rarely impact overall comprehensibility.

### ADVICE FOR IMPROVEMENT

Look for opportunities to build your fluency in English.

- Take risks and engage others in conversation in English whenever possible.
- Join an English club whose members converse in English about everyday topics, such as movies, music, and travel. If a club does not exist in your area, start one and invite fluent speakers to help you get started.

Record yourself and then listen and transcribe what you said.

- Read a short article from a newspaper or textbook. Record yourself summarizing the article.
- Transcribe the recording and review the transcription. Think about other ways to say the same thing.

## High-Intermediate
(Score range 20–24, CEFR Level B2)

Test takers who receive a Speaking section score at the **HIGH-INTERMEDIATE** level are typically able to communicate effectively on most general or familiar topics, and to make themselves understood when discussing more complex or academic topics.

### Test takers who score at the High-Intermediate level typically can

- Speak clearly and without hesitancy on general or familiar topics, with overall good intelligibility; pauses and hesitations (to recall or plan information) are sometimes noticeable when more demanding content is produced, and any mispronunciations or intonation errors only occasionally cause problems for the listener.
- Produce stretches of speech that demonstrate control of some complex structures and a range of vocabulary, although occasional lapses in precision and accuracy may obscure meaning at times.
- Convey sufficient information to produce mostly complete summaries, explanations, and opinions, but some ideas may not be fully developed or may lack elaboration; any lapses in completeness and cohesion may at times affect the otherwise clear progression of ideas.

#### *ADVICE FOR IMPROVEMENT*

Practice speaking in English about everyday topics that are important to students' lives. This will develop your fluency and confidence.

- Find a speaking partner. Set aside time each week to practice speaking with your partner in English.
- If you cannot find a fluent English speaker, find a friend who wants to practice speaking English and promise to speak only English for a certain period.
- Read articles from campus newspapers that can be found on the internet.

Practice speaking for a limited time on different academic topics.

- Read a short article from a newspaper or a textbook. Write down key content words from the article.
- Write down two or three questions about the article that include the content words
- Practice answering the questions aloud. Try to include the content words in your response
- After practicing, record your answers to the questions.

## Low-Intermediate

(Score range 16–19, CEFR Level B1)

Test takers who receive a Speaking section score at the **LOW-INTERMEDIATE** level are typically able to talk about general or familiar topics with relative ease.

### Test takers who score at the Low-Intermediate level typically can

- Speak clearly with minor hesitancies about general or familiar topics; longer pauses are noticeable when speaking about more complex or academic topics, and mispronunciations may obscure meaning at times.

- Produce short stretches of speech consisting of basic grammatical structures connected with "and," "because," and "so;" attempts at longer utterances requiring more complex grammatical structures may be marked by errors and pauses for grammatical planning or repair.
- Use vocabulary that is sufficient to discuss general or familiar topics, but limitations in range of vocabulary sometimes result in vague or unclear expression of ideas.
- Convey some main points and other relevant information, but summaries, explanations, and opinions are sometimes incomplete, inaccurate, and/or lack detail; long or complex explanations may lack coherence.

### ADVICE FOR IMPROVEMENT

Develop friendships with people who want to speak English with you. Interaction with others will improve your speaking ability. If you cannot find a fluent speaker, find a friend who wants to practice speaking English and promise to speak only English for a certain period.

- Read a short article from a newspaper or a textbook. Write down key content words from the article.
- Write down two or three questions about the article that include the content words.
- Practice answering the questions aloud. Try to include the content words in your response.
- After practicing, record your answers to the questions.

Practice speaking about current events.

- Read newspaper articles, editorials, and information about cultural events in English. Share the information that you read with a friend in English.
- Visit a university class and take notes in the class. Then use your notes to tell a friend about some of the information you heard in English.
- Develop your academic vocabulary. Write down important new words that you come across while reading or listening and practice pronouncing them.
- Listen to a weather report and take notes on what you heard. Then give the weather report to a friend in English.

## Basic

(Score range 10–15 CEFR Level A2)

Test takers who receive a Speaking section score at the **BASIC** level are typically able to communicate limited information about familiar, everyday topics. Test takers who score at the Basic level typically can

- Speak slowly and carefully so that they make themselves understood, but pronunciation may be strongly influenced by the speaker's first language and at times be unintelligible; speech may be marked by frequent pauses, reformulations, and false starts.

- Produce mostly short utterances, connecting phrases with simple linking words (such as "and") to make themselves understood; grammar and vocabulary are limited, and frequent pauses may occur while searching for words.
- Convey some limited information about familiar topics; supporting points and/or details are generally missing, and main ideas may be absent, unclear, or not well connected.

### *ADVICE FOR IMPROVEMENT*

Take a conversation class. This will help improve your fluency and pronunciation in English. Increase your vocabulary and improve your grammar in your speech.

- Study basic grammar rules so that your speech is grammatically correct.
- As you learn new words and expressions, practice pronouncing them clearly. Record yourself as you practice.

## Below Basic
(Score range 0–9)

Test takers with a Speaking section score below 10 have not yet demonstrated proficiency at the Basic level.

# TOEFL iBT Writing Section Performance Descriptors

## Advanced

(Score range 24–30, CEFR Level C1)

Test takers who receive a Writing section score at the **ADVANCED** level are typically able to write in English on a wide range of academic and nonacademic topics with confidence and clarity.

**Test takers who score at the Advanced level typically can**

- Produce clear, well-developed, and well-organized text; ungrammatical, unclear, or unidiomatic use of English is rare.
- Express an opinion on a controversial issue and support that opinion with appropriate details and explanations in writing, demonstrating variety and range of vocabulary and grammatical structures.
- Select important information from multiple sources, integrate it, and present it coherently and clearly in writing, with only occasional minor imprecision in the summary of the source information.

### ADVICE FOR IMPROVEMENT

Continue to improve your ability to relate and convey information from two or more sources. For example, practice analyzing reading passages in English.

- Read two articles or chapters on the same topic or issue, write a summary of each, and then explain the ways they are similar and the ways they are different.
- Practice combining listening and reading by searching for readings related to talks and lectures with a teacher or a friend.

Continue to improve your ability to express opinions by studying the ways that published writers express their opinions.

- Read articles and essays written by professional writers that express opinions about an issue (for example, a social, environmental, or educational issue).
- Identify the writer's opinion or opinions.
- Notice how the writer addresses possible objections to the opinions, if the writer discusses these.

## High-Intermediate

(Score range 17–23, CEFR Level B2)

Test takers who receive a Writing section score at the **HIGH-INTERMEDIATE** level are typically able to write in English well on general or familiar topics. When writing about complex ideas or ideas on academic topics, they can convey most of the main ideas.

**Test takers who score at the High-Intermediate level typically can**

- Produce summaries of multiple sources that include most of the main ideas; some important ideas from the sources may be missing, unclear, or inaccurate.
- Express an opinion on an issue clearly; some ideas and explanations may not be fully developed and lapses in cohesion may at times affect a clear progression of ideas.
- Write with some degree of facility; grammatical mistakes or vague/incorrect uses of words may make the writing difficult to follow in some places.

### *ADVICE FOR IMPROVEMENT*

Practice finding main points.

- Record news and informational programs in English from the television or radio or download talks or lectures from the internet.
- Listen and take notes. Stop the recording about every 30 seconds to write out a short summary of what you heard.
- Replay the recording to check your summary. Mark places where you are not sure if you have understood what was said or where you are not sure if you have expressed yourself well.

Write a response to an article or essay in English, taking the opposite viewpoint.

- Outline your response.
- Note the methods you use to support your ideas. Reread what you have written.
- Make sure your supporting ideas are clearly related to your main point.
- Note what method you use to develop each of your supporting points.
- Make sure you have developed each of your points in detail. Is there anything more you could have said to strengthen your points?

## Low-Intermediate

(Score range 13–16, CEFR Level B1)

Test takers who receive a Writing section score at the **LOW-INTERMEDIATE** level are typically able to produce simple written texts in English on general or familiar topics.

**Test takers who score at the Low-Intermediate level typically can**

- Produce a simple text that expresses some ideas on an issue, but the development of ideas is limited because of insufficient or inappropriate details and explanations.
- Summarize some relevant information from multiple sources, but important ideas from the sources are omitted or significantly misrepresented, especially ideas that require unfamiliar vocabulary or are complex.
- Write with limited facility, with language errors obscuring connections or meaning at key junctures between ideas in the text.

Read and listen to academic articles and other material in your own language. Take notes about what you read and hear.

- Begin by taking notes in your own language and then take notes in English.
- Summarize the points in complete English sentences.
- Ask your teacher to review your writing and help you correct your errors.
- Gradually decrease the time it takes you to read the material and write the summaries.
- Practice typing on a standard English (QWERTY) keyboard.

Study the organization of good paragraphs and essays. A good paragraph discusses one main idea. This idea is usually written in the first sentence, which is called the topic sentence. In essay writing, each paragraph should discuss one aspect of the main idea of an essay.

- Write paragraphs in English that focus on one main idea and contain several complete sentences that explain or support that idea.
- Ask your teacher to review your paragraphs for correctness.

# Basic

(Score range 7–12, CEFR Level A2)

Test takers who receive a Writing section score at the **BASIC** level are typically able to communicate very basic information in written English.

### Test takers who score at the Basic level typically can

- Produce some text that is related to the topic, but with little detail and/or lack of organization.
- Convey some information from the sources or some ideas on an issue, but grammatical errors, unclear expressions, and/or poor sentence structure make their writing difficult to comprehend.

*ADVICE FOR IMPROVEMENT*

- Practice English language comprehension and writing skills, increasing your vocabulary and improving your grammar.
- As your comprehension and writing skills improve, follow the suggestions for the Low-Intermediate level above.

# Below Basic

(Score range 0–6)

Test takers with a Writing section score below 7 have not yet demonstrated proficiency at the Basic level.

# Notes

# Notes

# Notes